Unwelcome Harvest

Agriculture and Pollution

Gordon R. Conway and Jules N. Pretty

Earthscan Publications Ltd, London

First published 1991 by
Earthscan Publications Ltd
3 Endsleigh Street, London WC1H ODD

British Library Cataloguing in Publication Data
Conway, Gordon R.
   Unwelcome Harvest: Agriculture and Pollution
   1. Crops. Effects of pollutants of atmosphere
   2. Pesticides. Toxic effects
   I. Title   II. Pretty, Jules
   632'.19

Production by Bob Towell
Typeset by Bookman Ltd, Bristol
Printed and bound by Billing & Sons Ltd, Worcester

Earthscan Publications Ltd is an editorially independent subsidiary of
the International Institute for Environment and Development (IIED)

Dedicated to

Simon, Zoe and Katherine

and to

Gill, Freya and

Theodore

Gordon R. Conway was formerly Professor of Environmental Technology at the Imperial College of Science and Technology, London, and a member of the Royal Commission on Environmental Pollution. He was also Director of the Sustainable Agriculture Programme at the International Institute for Environment and Development (IIED). He is currently Representative for the Ford Foundation for India, Nepal and Sri Lanka.

Jules N. Pretty is Director of the Sustainable Agriculture Programme at the International Institute for Environment and Development, London.

We are grateful to the following publishers for granting permission to include material for figures and tables:

Academic Press; American Association for the Advancement of Science; American Association for Cancer Research; American Geophysical Union; American Ornithological Union; American Public Health Association; Blackwell Scientific Publications Ltd; Cambridge University Press; Controller of Her Majesty's Stationery Office; Ecological Society of America; Elsevier Science Publishers; Graham & Trotman; Institute of Water and Environmental Management; IRRI; Institute of Terrestial Ecology; John Wiley and Sons; Kluwer Academic Publishers; *The Lancet*; Macmillan Magazines Ltd; National Academy Press; Oxford University Press; The Peregrine Fund; Prentice-Hall Inc.; The Royal Society; SCOPE; Taylor and Francis Ltd; UNEP; World Bank; World Resources Institute.

CONTENTS

Glossary for Units of Measurement

Length

km	kilometre	(= 1000 m)
m	metre	(= 100 cm)
cm	centimetre	(= 10 mm)
mm	millimetre	(= 1000 μm)
μm	micrometre	(= 1000 nm)
nm	nanometre	

Area

km^2	square kilometre	(= 100 ha)
ha	hectare	(100 m × 100 m)

Weight

t	tonne	(= 1000 kg)
kg	kilogram	(= 1000 g)
g	gramme	(= 1000 mg)
mg	milligram	(= 1000 μg)
μg	microgram	

Volume

l	litre

Concentration

ppm	parts per million	
ppb	parts per billion	(ppmv, ppbv – by volume)

Radiation

See Box 8.3 (page 425)

List of tables, boxes and figures

Tables

Boxes

Figures

Preface

This book was written partly at the Centre for Environmental Technology at Imperial College in London and partly at the International Institute for Environment and Development (IIED), also in London. Initial funding came from the Rockefeller Brothers Fund and the book was completed under a grant from the Ford Foundation. We also wish to thank our colleagues at Imperial College, in particular Nigel Bell, Richard Macrory and David Gilbert, and at IIED, notably Richard Sandbrook, for their advice and encouragement.

We are grateful to the following people who reviewed sections of the book and gave critical comment: Mike Ashmore, David Baldock, Ed Barbier, Nigel Bell, John Chilton, Norman Crossland, Kelley J. Donham, David Forman, Stephen Foster, Nigel Haigh, Martin Johnson, John Lukens, Richard Macrory, Graham Matthews, D J McWeeney, Brian Moss, John Mumford, Ian Newton and Dick Potts.

We acknowledge, however, that any errors and omissions remain the responsibility of the authors.

The views and opinions expressed in the book should not be construed as representing those of the Ford Foundation and the Rockefeller Brothers Fund.

1 Introduction to Agriculture and Pollution

Industrial activity has always resulted in pollution. But agriculture, for most of its history, has been environmentally benign. Even when industrial technology began to have an impact in the eighteenth and nineteenth centuries, agriculture continued to rely on natural ecological processes. Crop residues were incorporated into the soil or fed to livestock, and the manure returned to the land in amounts that could be absorbed and utilized. The traditional mixed farm was a closed, stable and sustainable ecological system, generating few external impacts.

Since the Second World War this system has disintegrated. Farms in the industrialized countries have become larger and fewer in number, highly mechanized and reliant on synthetic fertilizers and pesticides. They are now more specialized, so that crop and livestock enterprises are separated geographically. Crop residues and livestock excreta, which were once recycled, have become wastes whose disposal presents a continuing problem for the farmer. Straw is burnt since this is the cheapest and quickest method of disposal. Livestock are mostly reared indoors on grain and silage on farms whose arable land is insufficient to take up the waste.

Coincident with these changes, growing urbanization and population densities, coupled with increased affluence, have intensified the conflicts over land use. Urban populations have become reliant on agricultural catchments for their drinking water, are demanding uncontaminated food, and are increasingly valuing the countryside for attributes other than food and fibre production. Amenity, recreation and nature conservation are now important products of the countryside in their own right. Hiking, horse-riding, angling and camping are pursuits followed by millions. Thus, not only has the potential for contamination increased, so have the consequences, because of the greater value we now place on our environment.

Similar changes are beginning to occur in many parts of the Third World. The advent of new high-yielding cereal varieties as part of the

Green Revolution, together with intensification of export crop agriculture, have resulted in a dramatic growth of pesticide and fertilizer
use. Pollution problems are already apparent and are likely to grow in
importance in the next few years. Although the use of the countryside
for leisure is confined, at present, to a very few urban dwellers, many
Third World countries are developing strong conservation movements
among whose concerns are the effects of agriculture on wildlife.

The nature of pollution

At its most inclusive, the term pollution encompasses all unwanted
effects of human or natural activities. According to this definition an
unsightly farm building would be classified as "aesthetic pollution".
However, in this book we use the term as more commonly and narrowly
defined whereby a pollutant is a substance (e.g. a chemical compound
or waste material) or an energy (e.g. noise) which produces unwanted
effects. It is usual to restrict the term pollutant to substances or
energies created by human beings while recognizing that, under certain
conditions, natural processes generate "pollutants", for example the
sulphur dioxide given off during a volcanic eruption. It is also useful
to make a distinction between a contaminant, which is any substance
or energy introduced by human beings into the environment, and a
pollutant, which is a contaminant that is causing, or liable to cause,
damage or harm.[1]

The primary environmental contaminants produced by agriculture
are agrochemicals, in particular pesticides and fertilizers. These are
deliberately introduced into the environment by farmers to protect
crops and livestock and improve yields. Contamination is also caused,
though, by the various wastes produced by agricultural processes, in
much the same way as occurs in industry. The wastes comprise straw,
silage effluent and livestock slurry, and, in the Third World, the wastes
from on-farm processing of agricultural products such as oil palm and
sugar. From the immediate environment of the farm contamination
spreads to food and drinking water, to the soil, to surface and
groundwaters and to the atmosphere, in some instances reaching as
high as the stratosphere (Table 1.1).

The assessment of pollution

Pollution assessment is a complicated process. Ideally it requires an

Table 1.1 The principal pollution problems caused by agriculture

Contaminant or Pollutant	Consequences
Contamination of water	
Pesticides	Contamination of rainfall, surface and groundwater, causing harm to wildlife and exceeding standards for drinking water
Nitrates	Methaemoglobinaemia in infants; possible cause of cancers
Nitrates, phosphates	Algal growth and eutrophication, causing taste problems, surface water obstruction, fish kills, coral reef destruction; and illness due to algal toxins
Organic livestock wastes	Algal growth, plus deoxygenation of water and fish kills
Silage effluents	Deoxygenation of water and fish kills; nuisance
Processing wastes from plantation crops (rubber, oil palm)	Deoxygenation of water and fish kills; nuisance
Contamination of food and fodder	
Pesticides	Pesticide residues in foods
Nitrates	Increased nitrates in food; methaemoglobinaemia in livestock
Contamination of farm and natural environment	
Pesticides	Harm to humans; harm to humans; nuisance
Nitrates	Harm to plant communities
Ammonia from livestock and paddy fields	Disruption of plant communities; possible role in tree deaths
Metals from livestock wastes	Raised metal content in soils
Pathogens from livestock wastes	Harm to human and livestock health
Contamination of atmosphere	
Ammonia from livestock manures and paddy fields	Odour nuisance; plays role in acid rain production
Nitrous oxide from fertilizers	Plays role in ozone layer depletion and global climatic warming
Methane from livestock and paddy rice	Plays role in global climatic warming
Products of biomass burning (cereal straw, forests, savannas)	Enhances localized ozone pollution of troposphere; plays role in acid rain production, ozone layer depletion and global climatic warming; nuisance
Indoor contamination	
Ammonia, hydrogen sulphide from livestock wastes	Harm to farm worker and animal health Odour nuisance
Nitrogen dioxide from silage in silos	Harm to farm worker health

understanding of the components and linkages of a chain that stretches from underlying causes, through effects, to perceptions and costs (Figure 1.1). Once this is fully understood, it is then possible to seek out and implement appropriate preventative or control measures. But following this ordered, logical sequence of events is rarely practicable.

Figure 1.1   The components of the chain of environmental assessment

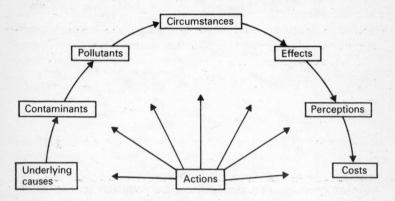

Source: Conway, G.R. (ed.) *The Assessment of Environmental Problems* (London: Imperial College Centre for Environmental Technology, 1986).

Each component and relationship generates its own set of assessment problems and what seems, at first sight, to be a simple investigation becomes a lengthy and exhaustive process. Only in one case – the effect of pesticides on predatory birds – has the complete chain been investigated. But this took over fifteen years, and measures to control the problem had to be taken long before the full assessment was completed. Pollution assessment and control is an interactive process, with new knowledge – whether acquired from long-term research or from the impact of pollution incidents – resulting in piecemeal improvements.

Underlying causes

The underlying causes of pollution are usually multifactorial. Technological and economic change, social and political policies, all play a role. Agricultural pollution in the industrialized countries, for instance, is primarily the product of a high level of subsidy which has encouraged agricultural intensification and the introduction of new technologies. In the developing countries, by contrast, the level of pollution is partly a function of inadequate education and ignorance of the potential hazards involved.

These are generic causes. Yet each particular pollution problem also has its own peculiar causative factors. Pesticide pollution, for example, is partly a consequence of pesticide "overuse". Farmers tend to spray in anticipation of a pest or disease attack that may have a very low likelihood of occurrence or little potential for harm. This is especially true of high value crops, such as fruit and salad vegetables, because of public demand for unblemished products. Pesticides and fertilizers are often subsidized, but even when farmers are paying the full market price the actual or perceived benefits are usually well in excess of the costs and this encourages profligate use.

Contaminants, pollutants and circumstances

The important contaminants, that is the materials or energies we introduce to the environment, are often easy to identify and in some cases, for example the black smoke produced by straw burning or the effluents from silage, the contaminants and pollutants are one and the same. But frequently there may exist a complex chain of intermediates between the contaminants and the final compounds that are the culprit pollutants. This is certainly the case with nitrate contamination. What farmers add to the environment, by way of nitrogen fertilizer, is readily identifiable, but the connection between this activity and the carcinogenic compounds implicated in human gastric cancer is obscure.

Circumstances are also frequently critical in determining whether there will be any effect. For example, high nitrate levels in water are a cause of the condition in infants known as methaemoglobinaemia, but probably only when accompanied by bacterial contamination. Timing and placing of pesticides is important in determining whether they will cause harm. Thus, honeybees are readily killed by many pesticides but only if these are applied during flowering when the bees are actively foraging.

The assessment of effects

In many respects, the assessment of effects presents the greatest challenge. The problem is that effects are often expressed differently at the "micro" and "macro" level. A compound may be strongly carcinogenic in tests with laboratory animals, yet show few serious long-term effects in humans. This is true of dioxin (2,3,7,8-TCDD). Alternatively, the epidemiology of human illnesses, such as gastric cancer, may suggest a strong correlation with pollution, yet this breaks down when details of the relationship are examined. The difficulty is compounded because micro and macro levels are subject to different kinds of investigation, involving different disciplines and different tools and standards for assessment. Inevitably there are problems of communication and interpretation.

The task, in essence, is to relate information gathered at three levels of investigation.[2] At the first level are pharmacokinetic, cellular and molecular studies of the effects of pollutant compounds. Such studies tend to give very precise results in terms of potential toxicity or mutagenicity. But this does not tell us whether, in practice, such effects will occur in whole organisms in their environment, or how many kinds of organisms will be affected.

At the second level are laboratory experiments involving small populations of organisms. The organisms are chosen because they are

Figure 1.2   Typical relationship between mortality and toxicant concentration, or dose, following continuous exposure of a laboratory population of organisms for a short time, usually 48 or 96 hours

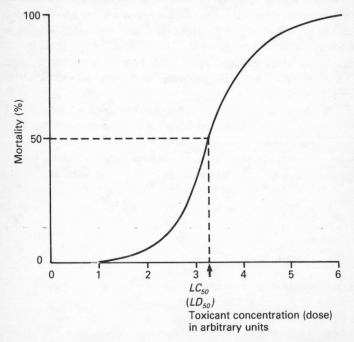

Source: Duffus, J.H. *Environmental Toxicology* (London: Edward Arnold, 1980).

genetically uniform, or particularly sensitive to pollutants, or are easily manipulated, or because they are representative of a class of organisms that are common or we value highly – or because of some combination of these criteria. The most widely used test is the measurement of the Lethal Dose$_{50}$ (LD$_{50}$) – the amount of active ingredient of the compound required to kill (or affect in the case of the Effective Dose$_{50}$ (ED$_{50}$) 50 per cent of the exposed population of organisms (Figure 1.2). The lower the LD$_{50}$ the more toxic the compound.

But there are a variety of serious drawbacks inherent in this test.[3] Quite apart from the difficulties in attaining controlled and known conditions, the test presents problems of interpretation. The 50% effect concentration, while statistically respectable, may provide a poor basis for extrapolating to the dose at which there is no or very little response. Direct determination of the dose that kills, say, only 1–2 per cent of a population would require a large number of test organisms. It is also common for compounds showing one order of relative toxicities at the LD$_{50}$ to show a different order at either extremes of the dose response curve. Most important, though, species differ greatly in their response. A case in point is dioxin (2,3,7,8-TCDD), not itself a pesticide but a contaminant of the herbicides 2,4,5-T and 2,4-D and possibly the cause of the effects in humans attributed to these herbicides. As can be seen from Table 1.2 the guinea pig is extremely sensitive to dioxin, while the hamster is several thousand times more resistant.[4]

Finally, even assuming that an extrapolation is valid, there is the problem of determining the multiplication factor to be used when going

Table 1.2   The variability of the lethal dose for dioxin (2,3,7,8-TCDD) in various animal species

	Lethal Dose LD$_{50}$ (μg/kg body weight)
Guinea pig	1
Rat (male)	22
Rat (female)	45
Monkey	<70
Rabbit	115
Mouse	114
Dog	>300
Bullfrog	>500
Hamster	5000

Source: Rawls, R.L., "Dioxins human toxicity is most difficult problem", *Chem. & Engineering News* **61** (1983) pp. 37–48.

from a laboratory animal to a wild animal or a human. The classic case of determining the effective dose of the hallucinatory drug LSD for an elephant illustrates the general problem, *reductio ad absurdum*[5] (Table 1.3). Using body weight as the multiplier, an amount which will excite a cat has been shown to be rapidly fatal to an elephant. Brain weight may be more appropriate, but it is largely a matter of guesswork.

Table 1.3 Possible calculations of a "suitable" dose of the hallucinatory drug LSD to give to an elephant

Based on body weight of elephant and dose effective in cats	297.0 mg
Based on metabolic rates of elephant and cat	80.0 mg
Based on body weight of elephant and dose effective in man	8.0 mg
Based on metabolic rates of elephant and man	3.0 mg
Based on brain sizes of elephant and man	0.4 mg

Source: Filov, V.A. et al., *Quantitative Toxicology* (New York: John Wiley and Sons, 1973).

Sometimes extrapolations produce a safe level that effectively constitutes a ban. The Canadian government calculating the possible hazard from eating fish contaminated with dioxin in Lake Ontario, have extrapolated, on a body weight basis, from the level that produces no reproductive effect in rats and then taken the "virtually safe dose" for humans to be a thousand times lower.[6] But, in practice, this is below the level of analytical detection.

The third level of investigation is epidemiology. Attempts are made to establish correlations between observable effects upon human or wildlife populations and ambient levels of contaminants in water, air, soil or food. Here the problem is that it is often easy to establish relatively high correlations but they may be misleading or, at the very least, incomplete as explanations unless other confounding factors are evaluated. The literature abounds with correlations that subsequently have been found to be incorrect as an indication of cause and effect. Two cases in point are the correlations between spontaneous abortion rates and the spraying of the herbicide 2,4,5-T in Oregon, and between nitrate levels in water and the incidence of gastric cancer in the town of Worksop (see Chapters 3 and 5 respectively).

Ideally, the results from the investigations at all three levels should be consistent, and reinforce one another, as explanations. Sometimes, as in the case of organochlorine insecticides and birds of prey, this ideal is achieved; often, though, as in the relationship between phenoxy herbicides or nitrates and human illness, the picture is inconsistent and confusing. As a consequence the setting of safe thresholds is bound, in many cases, to be a hit and miss affair.

Perceptions and costs

Even if the chain of cause and effect can be unravelled, there remains the notoriously difficult task of evaluating the social or economic impact of pollution. Since neither toxicology nor epidemiology can provide unequivocal measurements of risk from pollutants there is room for widely divergent perceptions of risk. Particularly where the effects are subtle or long term, the general public may greatly exaggerate the risk while farmers, aware of the costs of adopting alternative agricultural practices, may play it down.

Differences in perception are well illustrated by the public's attitudes towards contaminants of food products. The common assumption is that synthetic pesticides are more hazardous contaminants than those of natural origin, such as compounds derived from plants. Yet, in practice, we are ingesting 1000–10,000 times more by weight of natural products in food than of, say, synthetic pesticides.[7] Moreover, nature is not benign: an increasing number of "natural" products are being identified as carcinogens.[8] Examples include estragole from basil, safrole in root beer, phytine in comfrey, allyl isothiocyanate from brown mustard and psoralens in celery. Because attention is focused on synthetic compounds only a limited number of natural products have been tested so far, but it is likely that very many are just as hazardous.

Differences in public perception leads to different standards of control, as the contrasting cases of aflatoxin and dioxin illustrate. Aflatoxin is a widespread, natural product of moulds growing on cereals and nuts, particularly in the tropics. Although natural, it is the most significant carcinogenic pollutant of food in developing countries: intake is correlated with liver cancer rates.[9] But while, in terms of toxicity and carcinogenic potency, aflatoxin is similar to dioxin, it is subject to much weaker standards (Table 1.4). The reason seems to be that dioxin is an artificial chemical and thus perceived to be more "unwholesome" in the public, and even "official", mind.[10]

Many, if not most, people in the industrialized countries perceive a growing risk associated with the increasing use of synthetic chemicals. Some 1000 new chemical substances are marketed every year, and more than 500 tonnes of synthetic chemicals are sold annually.[11] It is commonly believed that we face more risk today than in the past and that future risks will be even greater.[12] Yet expert opinion is to the contrary: estimates based on mortality statistics indicate the risks are declining. To quote McLean, "we see a population living in a chemical era healthier than ever before. There is no evidence of

Table 1.4   Comparison of two toxic chemicals: aflatoxin B1 and dioxin

	Aflatoxin B1	Dioxin
Acute toxicity	High	High
Carcinogenic potency to rats	High	High
Mutagenic	Yes	No
Certainty of information on human carcinogenicity	High	Low
Carcinogenicity activity	Initiator	Possible promoter
Source	Natural	Synthetic
Public knowledge of chemical	Little known	"Agent Orange"
Food and Drug Administration level of concern in peanuts	20 ppb	–
Centers for Disease Control level of concern in soil	–	1 ppb

Source: Wilson, R. and Crouch, E.A.C., "Risk assessment and comparisons: an introduction". *Science* **236** (1987) pp. 267–70.

more harm to the population from new chemicals".[13] Nevertheless, public perception fuels a demand for increasingly tight restrictions, for example as embodied in the Delaney Clause in section 409 of the US Federal Food, Drug and Cosmetic Act, which prohibits the approval of any food additive, including pesticides, that has been found to induce either benign or malignant tumours in humans or animals (see Chapter 10).

The public also tends to perceive agrochemicals as posing a greater risk than other hazards that are common in everyday life. There is a persistent and highly vocal demand for higher control over the use of pesticides on the farm, yet they cause far fewer deaths than do bulls and other livestock. There is no demand for comparable control over dangerous livestock. Such perceptions are not necessarily irrational – they may be taking account of consequences that are often difficult to quantify or even express, such as harm to wildlife, and loss of amenity or the affront to moral beliefs. Research in the US has shown that perceived risk and the acceptance of risk are complex phenomena, determined by such factors as familiarity with the hazard, catastrophic potential, who is affected relative to those non-affected, how voluntary is the risk and what are its potential benefits.[14] For instance, the public are more likely to accept risk from a voluntary hazardous activity, such as skiing, than from an involuntary hazard, such as the presence of synthetic compounds in food.

A *hazard* is defined as "a situation that in particular circumstances could lead to harm", while a *risk* is "the probability that a particular adverse event occurs during a stated period of time, or results from a particular challenge".[15] Hazards give rise to risk and may be plotted along two co-ordinates, running from high to low "dread" risk and from low to high "unknown" risk as shown in Figure 1.3. A high

Figure 1.3   Comparison of risk perception of different hazards in the USA. The original graph includes 81 hazards

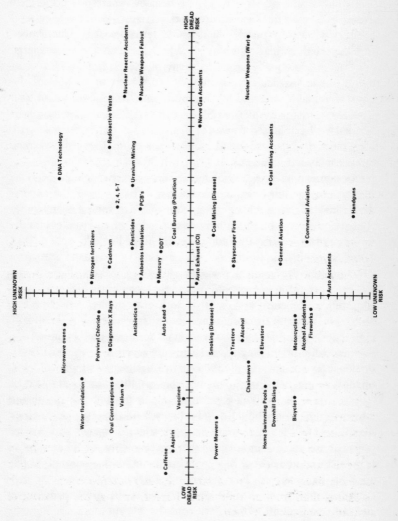

Source: Slovic, P. "Perception of risk", in: *Science* (1987), **236** pp. 280–285.

dread risk is characterized by hazards that have a perceived lack of control, a high level of "dread", and the potential for catastrophic and fatal consequences, as well as an inequitable distribution of risks and benefits. An unknown risk is posed by hazards that are unobservable, unknown, new, and delayed in their manifestation of harm.[16] The public perceives the hazards in the top right quadrant of Figure 1.3 as giving rise to a combination of high dread and high unknown risk. It is these risks that people desire to regulate most strictly.

In contrast, the perceptions of risk held by experts are not closely related to any of the various dread–risk characteristics – they tend to see riskiness in purely quantitative terms and as synonymous with expected annual mortality (Table 1.5). Nonetheless, experts' judgements are equally prone to many of the same biases as those of the public, particularly when they are forced to go beyond the limits of available data and rely on intuition.[17] In general, we all tend to overestimate the frequency and seriousness of dramatic, sensational, dreaded well-publicized causes of death, and underestimate the risk from more familiar, accepted causes that claim lives one by one. Familiarity breeds contempt.

Our perceptions of risk also change with time. Experts' perceptions tend to change slowly as knowledge improves, whereas the general public may suddenly change their attitude in response to major or dramatic events. It often happens that as soon as an issue enters the public domain, regulatory authorities are forced to take action, even though the evidence is still incomplete (Box 1.1). Situations such as these present the greatest challenge to policy makers. Experts and the public tend to agree on issues that combine high risk with high public concern or low risk with low public concern. The disagreements arise from the other combinations of risk and concern. In practice, governments try to avoid such confrontations by protecting confidentiality or keeping research results secret and, in some cases, by deliberate misinformation.[18] But the basic issue is one of costs versus potential benefits: should available resources and technology be focused where they will have greatest tangible impact upon health and the environment, or should they be focused on those problems about which the public is most upset? To those affected, anxiety and fear are very real and the question is whether governments should attempt to remove the source of such anxiety, whether or not it is rational. At this point the issue can only be resolved in political terms.

But even if the issue is more clearcut – costs of control *versus* known and tangible benefits – there are considerable difficulties in arriving

Table 1.5 Ranking of perceived risk from 30 activities and technologies according to four different groups of Americans

	Experts	League of Women Voters	College students	Active club members
Motor vehicles	1	2	5	3
Smoking	2	4	3	4
Alcoholic drinks	3	6	7	5
Handguns	4	3	2	1
Surgery	5	10	11	9
Motor cycles	6	5	6	2
X-rays	7	22	17	24
Pesticides	8	9	4	15
Electric power (non-nuclear)	9	18	19	19
Swimming	10	19	30	17
Contraceptives	11	20	9	22
Aviation (private)	12	7	15	11
Construction	13	12	14	13
Food preservatives	14	25	12	28
Bicycles	15	16	24	14
Aviation (commercial)	16	17	16	18
Police work	17	8	8	7
Fire fighting	18	11	10	6
Railroads	19	24	23	29
Nuclear power	20	1	1	8
Food colouring	21	26	20	30
Home appliances	22	29	17	27
Hunting	23	13	18	10
Antibiotics	24	28	21	26
Vaccinations	25	30	29	29
Spray cans	26	14	13	23
High school and college football	27	23	26	21
Power mowers	28	27	28	25
Mountain climbing	29	15	22	12
Skiing	30	21	25	16

Source: Slovic, P., "Perception of risk", *Science* **236** (1987) pp. 280–85.

at a satisfactory equation. Precise and accurate figures can usually be placed on control costs, for example the costs of removing nitrates from drinking water, but quantifying the monetary benefits in terms of fewer gastric cancers is, in practice, highly problematic. It is possible to place values on lives, or on workdays lost through ill health, or even on birds of prey living in the wild, but the figures are subject to considerable imprecision, far greater than that associated with the costs of control

Box 1.1　Chronology of measures taken to control the soil, grain and fruit fumigant ethylene dibromide (EDB) in the USA

1　Between 1977 and 1983 the Environmental Protection Agency, EPA, accumulates substantial evidence that EDB is a potent carcinogen in mice and rats.

2　Dietary exposure to EDB via fruits and uncooked grains is found to be extensive.

3　Model of risk criticized and risk re-evaluated downwards in 1983, nevertheless EDB a known animal carcinogen remains widely distributed in national food supply.

4　EDB is detected in drinking water drawn from aquifers.

5　EPA issues emergency suspension of use as soil fumigant in late 1983.

6　Process begun to suspend other uses; but no immediate suspension because insufficient is known of risks from residues in food.

7　Research studies are initiated.

8　Shortly after, EDB becomes a matter of intense public interest and discussion.

9　State governments begin to demand federal action.

10　States begin to adopt "safety" standards, set typically at or near level of detection.

11　Problem of differing standards in different areas thought likely to disrupt the national food distribution system.

12　All uses of EDB suspended; provision for the public of a guide to which foods present acceptable risks.

13　EPA conducts major public information effort to show that while fungicide should be suspended from use, the risks do not warrant indiscriminate destruction of food contaminated at very low levels.

Source: Russell, M. and Gruber, M., "Risk assessment in environmental policy making", *Science* **236** (1987) pp. 286–90.

(see Chapter 10). In practice, the only workable approach, at present, is to decide on clear control objectives through the political process, broadly defined, and then assess the most cost-effective means of attaining these objectives.[19] Necessarily, this involves judgements about which components and relationships in the assessment chain are the best targets for action. Much of this book is devoted to presenting and examining the information that can inform these judgements.

Outline of the book

The next six chapters of the book deal with the pollution caused by agriculture. We begin with pesticides, then fertilizers, livestock wastes and silage and end with a discussion of the role of agriculture as a global air polluter. The next two chapters take a reverse look, at the effects of pollution on agriculture. In the final chapters we discuss the economic, legal and institutional aspects of pollution control and briefly describe some of the technological approaches which can reduce agricultural pollution. In all the chapters we look at the situation worldwide, contrasting, in particular, the UK, the USA and the countries of the Third World.

References

1 RCEP, *Managing Waste: The Duty of Care*, 11th Report, Royal Commission on Environmental Pollution (London: HMSO, 1985).
2 Conway, G.R., "Agricultural pollution" in: Conway, G.R. (ed.), *The Assessment of Environmental Problems*, Contributions to a conference at Imperial College of Science and Technology (London: Imperial College, 1986).
3 Duffus, J.H., *Environmental Toxicology* (London: Edward Arnold, 1980); Filov, V.A., Golubev, A.A., Liublina, E.I. and Tolokontsev, N.A., *Quantitative Toxicology* (New York: John Wiley and Sons, 1973). Loomis, T.A., "Acute and prolonged toxicity tests", *Journal of the AOAC* 58 (1975) pp. 645–9; Morrison, J.K. and Reinert, H., "The value of LD_{50} determinations", *Industrial Medicine and Surgery* 35 (1966) pp. 617; Sharratt, M., "Uncertainties associated with the evaluation of health hazards of environmental chemicals from toxicological data", in: Hunter, W.S. and Smeets, J.G.P.M. (eds), *The Evaluation of Toxicity Data for the Protection of Public Health* (Oxford: Pergamon Press, 1977); Sperling, F. and McLaughlin, J.L., "Biological parameters and the acute LD_{50} test", *Journal of the AOAC* 59 (1976) pp. 734–6.
4 Tshirley, F., "Dioxin", *Scientific American* February 254 (1986) pp. 21–27.
5 Filov et al., 1973, *op. cit.*; Harwood, P.D., "Therapeutic dosage in small and large mammals" (letter to editor), *Science* 139 (1963) pp. 684–5.
6 National Research Council of Canada, *Polychlorinated dibenzo dioxins. Criteria for their effects on man and his environment*, (NRCC 18574: Associate Committee on Scientific Criteria for Environmental Quality, 1984).
7 Ames, B.N., Magaw, R. and Gold, L.S., "Ranking possible carcinogenic hazards", *Science* 236 (1987) pp. 271–80; Epstein, S.S. and Swartz, "Carcinogenic risk estimation", *Science* 240 (1988) pp. 1043–5; Ames,

B.N. and Gold, L.S., "Response to Epstein and Swartz", *Science* **240** (1988) pp. 1045–7.

8   Ames et al., 1987, *op. cit.*; Ames, B.N., "Dietary carcinogens and anticarcinogens", *Science* **221** (1983) pp. 1256–64.

9   Van Rensberg, S.J., Cook-Mozzaffari, P., Van Schalkwyk, D.J., Van Der Walt, J.J., Vincent, T.J. and Purchase, I.F., "Heptacellular carcinoma and dietary aflatoxin in Mozambique and in Transkei", *Br. J. Cancer* **51** (1985) pp. 713–26.

10   Wilson, R. and Crouch, E.A.C., "Risk assessment and comparisons: an introduction", *Science* **236** (1987) pp. 267–70.

11   McLean, A.E.M., "Assessment and evaluation of risks to health from chemicals", *Proc. Roy Soc. Lond. A* **376** (1981) pp. 51–64.

12   Slovic, P., "Perception of risk", *Science* **236** (1987) pp. 280–85.

13   McLean, 1981, *op. cit.*

14   Slovic, 1987, *op. cit.*; Slovic, P., Fischhoff, B. and Lichtenstein, S., "Behavioural decision theory perspectives in risk and safety", *Acta Psychologica* **5** (1984) pp. 183–203.

15   The Royal Society, *Risk Assessment. A study group report* (London: Royal Society, 1983).

16   Slovic, 1987, *op. cit.*

17   Slovic, 1987, *op. cit.*

18   Allen, F.W., "The situation: what the public believes, how the experts see it", *EPA Journal* **13** (1987) pp. 9–12.

19   Chadwick, M.J., "Co-ordinating economic and ecological goals", in: Conway, G.R. (ed.), *The Assessment of Environmental Problems*, (London: Imperial College, 1986); Holdgate, M.W., "The co-ordination of assessment", in: Conway, G.R. (ed.), 1986, *op. cit.*

2 Pesticides and the Environment

Pesticides, by design, are biocides; their value lies in their ability to kill noxious or unwanted organisms. But they are rarely selective. Most act by interfering with fundamental biochemical and physiological processes that are common to a wide range of organisms – not only pests, but ourselves as well. The safest assumption is that every pesticide is harmful to all organisms until the contrary is proved. But establishing such proof is, inevitably, an impossible task. There are too many organisms to test and too many possibilities to explore, given reasonable constraints on time and cost. Pesticide development would become prohibitively expensive and farmers would be denied many potentially useful compounds. Thus in practice, assessing the hazards of pesticide use relies on a balance of evidence accumulated through several different lines of enquiry. Thresholds are set and codes of safe practice established on the basis of biochemical studies, tests on a limited number of organisms and monitoring of wildlife in field experiments. Inevitably, though, it is only after widespread use that many problems become apparent.

The potential hazards of pesticides are ubiquitous. They confront workers engaged in their manufacture, transport and disposal; farmers and operators who apply them in the field; the general public; and wildlife in the environment. In the first case, the hazard is common to all industries dealing with toxic chemicals and is manageable by following relatively well tried procedures and practices. Of greater concern is the hazard to the field operator because of the high degree of variability in field conditions and his or her frequent lack of knowledge and skill. But at most risk are the general public and the wider environment. They are difficult to protect directly, in part because not enough is known, still, of the pathways of pesticide dispersion into the environment and of the final effects.

In this chapter we first briefly summarize the history and present-day pattern of pesticide use. We then examine the underlying causes of pesticide pollution – poor selectivity, "overuse" and unsafe methods of application. The major portion of the chapter discusses the evidence for adverse effects on wildlife.

Classes of pesticide

Chemical substances have long been used to control pests and diseases. In 2500 BC, the Sumerians were using sulphur compounds for insect control. Later, in China, seeds were treated with various natural organic substances to protect against insects, mice and birds, while inorganic mercury and arsenic compounds were applied for the control of body lice and other pests.[1] And the Greek and Roman writers, Aristotle and Cato, describe a variety of fumigants, oil sprays and sulphur ointments. Nevertheless, the widespread use of natural pesticides did not begin until the late-seventeenth and eighteenth centuries in Europe. Pyrethrum was extracted from various species of chrysanthemum, nicotine from tobacco and derris from the root of the same name. Then, in the late-nineteenth century the Bordeaux mixture – lime plus copper sulphate – was discovered, by accident, to be effective against various diseases of fruit trees. Another common mixture was Paris Green, consisting of copper and arsenic, which killed slugs and soil insects. Iron sulphate was found to have selective herbicidal properties and lead arsenate was widely adopted as a broad spectrum insecticide.

By the first half of this century the common pesticides were fungicides such as sulphur, and inorganic compounds of copper, lead and mercury, together with general poisons – nicotine, pyrethrum and derris, compounds of arsenic and cyanide and various coal tar derivatives – for the control of insect pests. Most were broad-acting in their effect on pests and diseases. Some were safe for people, such as pyrethrum, but many of the others, in particular nicotine, the arsenicals and cyanide, were extremely toxic. However, as they were mostly applied to high value products – fruits, hops, market garden and glasshouse crops – it was primarily the spray operators and farm workers who were at risk. The general public were rarely exposed and there was little effect on the wider environment. The only significant exception was the widespread use of lead and calcium arsenate on cotton in the USA.

The discovery of the insecticidal properties of the synthetic organic compounds, at about the time of the Second World War, brought about a dramatic change in the pattern and in the consequences of pesticide use. In a remarkably short time, they were being used on almost every crop and in most countries of the world. The immediate benefits were obvious, but it gradually became apparent that these new compounds had severe drawbacks. They were affecting wildlife and people in ways which had not been anticipated.

In the immediate, post-war years the most common compounds were the organochlorine insecticides, such as DDT, lindane (γ-HCH) and dieldrin, and the phenoxy herbicides, 2,4-D, 2,4,5-T and MCPA. Subsequently, these have been replaced by organophosphate, carbamate and pyrethroid insecticides and a variety of synthetic herbicides and fungicides.

Pesticide use

The value of the global, end-user, market for pesticides is around US$20.5 billion.[2] As a measure of consumption, kg of pesticide active ingredient will not be used as this can be misleading. In recent years, formulations of pesticides have been becoming increasingly concentrated, and thus active ingredient use may have declined. Although some 500 million kg are said to be consumed annually in the USA, this figure does not make clear the varying strengths of product.[3] The largest individual consumer is the USA, followed by countries of western Europe (Figure 2.1). Japan is the most intensive user of pesticides per area of cultivated land. Taken together, developing countries consume only a small proportion of the world total.

There is also considerable variation from country to country in the kind of pesticide used. Herbicides dominate the North American and European domestic markets, but insecticides are more commonly used elsewhere in the world (Figure 2.1). For instance, insecticides constitute 76 per cent of the market in the Asia-Pacific region, and this pattern is true of most developing countries, although there are exceptions: in Malaysia there is heavy herbicide use on plantation crops (Table 2.1).[4] The global use of all pesticide products is highly concentrated on a few major crops – more than 50 per cent is applied to wheat, maize, cotton, rice and soybean (Table 2.2). In developing countries the heaviest applications are to plantation crops – sugar cane, coffee, cocoa, pineapple and oil palm.

Although the growth in new products on the market has been slowing (Figure 2.2), total consumption continues to grow. The highest growth rates occurred in the 1960s, reaching 12 per cent per annum, but are now down to 3–4 per cent.[5] It is in the developing countries today that growth rates are very high: between 1980 and 1985

20 Unwelcome Harvest

Figure 2.1 Use of pesticides by world areas and proportional use of insecticides, herbicides and fungicides for World (1988), USA (1981), UK (1981) and Japan (1981)

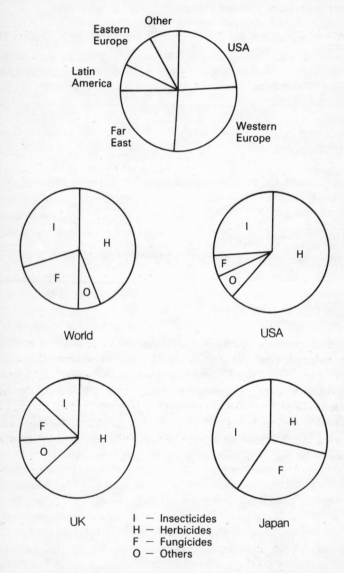

Sources: British Agrochemicals Association, *Annual Report and Handbook* (Peterborough, 1989); Patton, S., Craig, I. and Conway, G.R. "The pesticide industry" in: Conway, G.R. (ed.), *Pesticide Resistance and World Food Production* (London: Imperial College, 1982).

consumption grew by 30 per cent in Indonesia, 20 per cent in Pakistan, 14 per cent in Sri Lanka and 10 per cent in Western Samoa, albeit from low starting points.[6] Future world growth is predicted to be about 4 per cent per annum, with the greatest increases in herbicides.

Table 2.1   Consumption of different types of pesticides for some developing countries

	Proportion of each type of pesticide (%)		
	Insecticides	Herbicides	Fungicides
Burma	90	0–5	0–5
Indonesia	55–75	5–15	10–20
Malaysia	15	70–85*	5
Philippines	60–70	20–30	5–10
Thailand	50–65	20–25	10
Vietnam	70	20	10
Ivory Coast	90	10	–
Sierra Leone	90	10	–

* Heavy applications of herbicides to rubber and oil palm

Source: Balk, I.F. and Koeman, J.H., *Future Hazards for Pesticide Use* (Geneva: IUCN, 1984).

Benefits

Without question, pesticides play a major role in world agriculture. By reducing pest and disease attack, and weed competition, they have contributed significantly to improved crop yields and livestock production. In the industrialized nations, the benefits have also been in terms of reduced variable costs. One hectare of cotton crop in 1933 took 200 human-hours per year to grow and harvest using manual hoeing and picking, but by 1985 chemical weeding, defoliation and

Table 2.2   Worldwide consumption of pesticides by crop

Maize	11%
Cotton	11%
Rice	12%
Soybean	9%
Wheat	10%
Fruit, vegetables and vines	26%
Sugar beet	4%
Others	17%

Source: BAA, Annual Report and Handbook 1988–89, (Peterborough: British Agrochemicals Association, 1989).

mechanical picking reduced the demand to only 50 human-hours.[7] Over the same period, the number of human-hours required for a one hectare maize crop has declined from 135 to 22 and for peanuts from 190 to 40.

On individual crops the direct gains from pesticide use are often very obvious. But arriving at estimates of national or global benefit is more difficult. Temperate crops in the USA have been estimated to suffer losses of some 30–35 per cent, roughly equally shared among insects, diseases and weeds, despite pesticide use (Table 2.3). Most losses in tropical crops are in the range of 10–30 per cent, although losses in

Figure 2.2   Cumulative number of pesticide products introduced to markets between 1940 and 1980

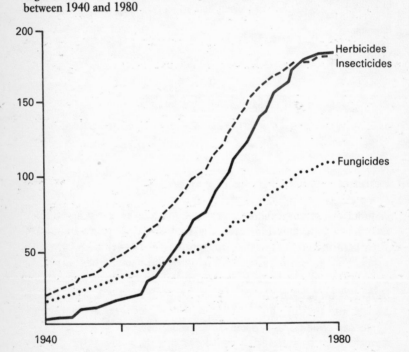

Source: Patton, S., Craig, I. and Conway, G.R., 1982, *op. cit.*

storage, where there is less pesticide usage, and in the post-harvest distribution system may remove a further 10–30 per cent (Table 2.4). But the basis for these estimates is open to question: they may well be overestimates. Often the figures are used to justify increased investment in pesticide development and greater pesticide use. Significantly, though, the proportionate loss has not declined over the past five decades. Some argue that this represents a poor achievement for the synthetic pesticide era. Others point out that the introduction of new high yielding varieties has led to a much increased potential for loss. But this implies, at best, that pesticides have kept the proportionate loss constant despite rapidly rising yields. They clearly do not represent a means of eliminating pest problems.

Table 2.3 Agricultural losses to pests in the United States

| Year | Percentage of annual crop lost to | | | |
	Insects	Diseases	Weeds	Total
1942–1950 (average)	7	11	14	32
1951–1960 (average)	13	12	9	34
1974	13	12	8	33
1984	13	12	12	37

Source: May, R.M., "Food lost to pests", *Nature* **267** (1977) pp. 669–70.

The causes of pesticide pollution

Ideally, a pesticide should be applied to, and only affect, the target – the insect, fungus, bacterium, weed or other unwanted organism – and, after killing or damaging it, should then immediately break down into benign constituents that have no harmful effect on any part of the environment. In their nature or in the manner in which they are applied, all pesticides should thus be selective and non-persistent. Not surprisingly, this ideal is far from being achieved and, hence, pollution occurs.

The problem of selectivity

In the first place, few pesticides are intrinsically selective. They commonly act by interfering with basic biological processes that are common to a wide range of organisms. It is theoretically possible to design pesticides which attack critical, but unique, biological processes in the target organism and some such pesticides have been designed. But this is difficult and costly to do. A pesticide company may spend over US$35 million before a marketable compound is introduced (this excludes the cost of constructing a production plant but includes the costs of safety and environment testing) and it may take 8 to 10 years before a compound is ready for full-scale marketing.[8]

These costs are rising and the task of finding a new pesticide is becoming increasingly more complex because of the growing requirements for safety and environmental testing. While in 1956 the synthesis of 1,800 chemicals led to one commercial pesticide, in 1976 the ratio had risen to 10,000 to 1, and now some 23,000 new compounds are screened for each new pesticide discovered.[9] One consequence is that the introduction of new pesticides is slowing down. Another is that pesticide manufacturers are being forced to seek compounds that can provide a reasonable return on these heavy research and development costs. Such a return cannot be realized by designing a pesticide which controls only one pest or disease, or protects only one crop since, except in a very few cases, the market will be insufficient. Thus most new pesticides, despite legislative pressures to the contrary, will tend to be broad spectrum compounds acting on a range of different pest organisms and, inevitably, affecting a wide range of non-target organisms, including ourselves.

Table 2.4 Estimates for yield losses on tropical crops due to insect pests

Cassava (mealybug)	38%	Mungbean	40%
Cassava (green mite)	30%	Okra	40%
Chickpea	25%	Pigeon pea	19%
Coconut	12%	Rice	20%
Coffee	8%	Sorghum	26%
Cotton	38%	Sugar cane	15%
Cowpea (Nigeria)	35%	Sweet potato	27%
Groundnut (India)	22%	Wheat	10%
Maize	25%		

Source: Walker, P.T., "Losses in yield due to pests in tropical crops and the value in policy decision-making", *Insect Sci. Applic.* 8 (1987) pp. 665–71.

It is true that selectivity can be obtained, even for broad spectrum compounds, by using formulations and techniques of application that are highly targeted, but these are often either time consuming or expensive. Persistence, too, may be desired by farmers since it may obviate the need for repeated applications. Where the compound is highly selective and eventually breaks down into harmless constituents, such persistence may not be a problem. But, because so many compounds have a broad-ranging action, persistence serves to multiply the potential for pollution.

The "overuse" of pesticides

Lack of selectivity, though, is only one factor contributing to pollution.

Perhaps equally important has been the rapid growth in use of pesticides. This has occurred for several reasons. First, the benefits relative to costs have been substantial, particularly where there have been heavy subsidies either of pesticide use or in the form of crop support prices. Second there has been a rapid intensification of agriculture through the expansion of irrigation, greater mechanization, and the introduction of new high-yielding varieties with related packages of inputs. Third, farmers have tended to apply pesticides according to their perception of the worst possible losses. And finally, changes in consumer demand have increased pesticide use as a way of improving cosmetic quality.

Relative costs and subsidies

Since the Second World War, much of the growth in pesticide use has been a reflection of high returns and low costs relative to those of other inputs, such as fertilizers and seeds. Doubling or tripling rates of application has cost little compared to the likely benefits. This is changing, to some extent, in Western Europe since pesticide prices are rising fairly rapidly. In the UK, in 1974, pesticides constituted only 8 per cent of variable costs for winter wheat, but by the mid-1980s this had increased to 36 per cent.[10] Nevertheless in the USA, where farming is more extensive, the rate of increase of agricultural chemical prices has been substantially behind all other production input prices (Table 2.5). Since there are large acreages of heavy pesticide-using crops, such as cotton, maize and soybean, current growth rates in pesticide use are likely to continue.

Low relative costs have also been a factor in many developing countries because of policies favouring heavy subsidies for both the

Table 2.5 Indices of prices paid by farmers in the USA

Year	Pesticides	Indices (1977 = 100) Fuel	Fertilizer	Tractors	Labour
1968	64	50	52	44	48
1972	65	54	52	54	63
1976	111	93	102	91	93
1980	102	188	134	136	126
1981	111	213	144	152	137
1982	119	210	144	165	143
1983	125	202	137	174	147

Source: Miranowski, J.A. and Carlson, G.A., "Economic issues in public and private approaches to preserving pest susceptibility", in: National Research Council, *Pesticide Resistance, Strategies and Tactics for Management* (Washington: National Academy Press, 1986).

production and sales of pesticides. These are aimed at increased production, particularly of cereals and export crops. They have been key components of the Green Revolution and of strategies to attain food grain self-sufficiency. In Java, for instance, annual pesticide use has grown from 1,080 to 14,200 tonnes between 1970 and 1984.[11] Subsidy mechanisms have included access to foreign exchange on favourable terms, reduced rates of tax or exemptions, easy credit and sales below cost by government-run distributors.[12] A recent study of nine developing countries puts total subsidies as high as 89 per cent of full retail cost; the costs to governments can run into hundreds of millions of dollars (Table 2.6).

Table 2.6   Pesticide subsidies in developing countries in the early 1980s

Country	Subsidy (% of full cost paid by Government)	Total cost (million US $)
China	19	285
Colombia	44	69
Ecuador	41	14
Egypt	83	207
Ghana	67	20
Honduras	29	12
Indonesia[†]	82	128
Pakistan	0	0
Senegal	89	4

[†] Indonesia has recently cut their rate of subsidy to 40 per cent

Source: Repetto, R., *Paying the Price, Pesticide Subsidies in Developing Countries* (Washington: World Resources Institute, 1985).

In addition to the incentive to use more pesticides, subsidies also discourage traditional methods of pest control, which are usually more labour and time consuming, and they work against the uptake of alternative, and perhaps less polluting, approaches (see Chapter 11). For example, the benefits of deferring spraying until pest damage reaches a given economic threshold, which is a component of Integrated Pest Management, are undermined by subsidies which significantly reduce the threshold level. Often subsidies encourage farmers to ignore thresholds altogether and engage in preventative spraying. This may result in heavy pesticide use even on relatively pest-resistant varieties. Pests may develop resistance or their natural enemies may be destroyed so producing a vicious cycle of further damage and yet more pesticide use.

In Indonesia, heavy insecticide spraying of rice appears to have induced severe outbreaks of brown planthoppers.[13] Because the insecticides were broad acting they killed off the planthopper's natural enemies. The numbers of pests rose with the number of insecticide applications, but farmers responded with more spraying until they were treating fields between 6 and 20 times over only 4–8 weeks. The latest planthopper outbreak, in 1986, caused an estimated loss of one million tonnes.[14] Recently, however, a ban on the use of nearly 60 pesticide active ingredients on rice has been imposed and farmers are learning how to assess pest and natural enemy populations before spraying.

Agricultural intensification

Linked to the financial incentives for pesticide use has been the rapid intensification of agriculture throughout the world. The introduction of high-yielding varieties, expanded irrigation, greater mechanization and widespread use of synthetic fertilizers have favoured greater pesticide applications. Actual and potential yields have greatly increased as have actual or potential economic returns.

In some parts of the world, pest problems first became serious with the expansion of irrigation and the increased use of chemical fertilizers. Year round irrigation makes double cropping possible and if the same crop is grown continuously, explosive pest outbreaks can occur. In general, the new cereal varieties tend to be more susceptible to pests and diseases and the loss of crop heterogeneity has favoured high pest and disease populations.[15]

New practices, such as the direct sowing of rice, have led to increased populations of grass weeds, requiring more herbicides, while greater use of nitrogen has heightened susceptibility to diseases such as rice sheath blight. Often the new practices come as packages of closely interlinked components. Direct seeding, for example, requires support from intensive herbicide use. In this way farmers can become locked in to an intensive system of agriculture where pesticides appear to be indispensable.

Mechanization can also trigger pest problems. In the vegetable growing region of the Thames Valley, in the UK, mechanization has produced economies of scale leading to large farms that concentrate on growing only three types of vegetable.[16] There are, now, fewer crop rotations and the farms are essentially monocropped with higher-yielding varieties that are susceptible to pests and diseases yet have a high market demand. As a direct result pesticide use has increased dramatically.

Farmer perceptions

In many situations the growth in pesticide use has been greater than might seem rational because farmers often incorrectly perceive both the pest problem and the means of control available. In part this is inevitable where information is lacking, but it may still occur when good forecasts are available. As a result pesticides are often employed as an insurance measure, spraying in anticipation of a pest outbreak, however low its likelihood. In some cases farmers will engage in calendar spraying, that is, spraying at pre-set times without regard to the level or likelihood of pest attack.

Perceptions may vary widely among farmers; perceptions of a single pest may differ more between farmers than perceptions of a variety of pests held by a single farmer.[17] As a survey of sugar beet farmers in eastern England showed, they also tend to overestimate both the worst possible losses to pest damage and the effectiveness of pesticide application in reducing those losses (Table 2.7). Farmers tend to be risk averse and hence these perceptions lead to more applications than are needed. Over 50 per cent of a sample of farmers believed it more important to consider the worst possible loss than the normal loss when deciding to use pesticides.[18] Perceptions, however, change with experience. In North Carolina farmers with little experience and training both overestimated pest damage to apples and used more pesticides compared with growers having better management skills.[19] But the sugar beet growers in England when surveyed three years later had greatly reduced their estimate of worst loss having experienced almost pest-free attack in the intervening period.[20]

Table 2.7 Comparison of measured and farmers' estimates of aphid pest damage and of the efficacy of pesticides on sugar beet in England

	Measured*	Farmers' estimates
Typical loss	4–12%	0–20%
Worst possible loss	9–29%	21–30%
Maximum efficacy of pesticides used	50%	75–100%

* Field losses calculated from field count surveys and efficacy calculated from experimental trials.

Source: Mumford, J.D., "Farmer attitudes towards the control of aphids on sugar beet", *Proc. Br. Crop Prot. Conf. – Pests and Diseases* (1977).

Farmers, particularly in developing countries, identify pesticides with modern productive agriculture. In the Philippines almost all rice farmers apply synthetic pesticides: they believe that powerful chemicals are progressive and modern, and are an effective way of controlling one element of a hazardous environment that includes floods, typhoons, and occasional droughts, as well as pests.[21] They believe that higher frequencies of pesticide application are associated with higher yields and, if they could afford it, would apply according to a calendar schedule. But these beliefs do not accord with surveys conducted on farmers' fields. Apparently at least half the farmers do not benefit in terms of increased yields. Their perceptions seem to have their beginnings in the extension activities during the early part of the Green Revolution: technical extension workers made repeated and aggressive demonstrations to persuade farmers to use insecticides. As a result, heavy pesticide use has become part of the culture of Philippine farmers.

In some instances, the decision to use a pesticide appears unrelated to the actual pest threat on the particular crop.[22] Thus the situation on a key crop in a region has been found to affect perceptions of likely problems on other crops. A serious problem requiring heavy pesticide use on one crop may encourage similar usage on other crops, even if the problems are less severe. Positive associations also commonly exist between estimates of losses due to weeds, insects and diseases. High fungicide or herbicide use may follow increasing insecticide applications. In developing countries farmers may also not distinguish between different pests and may use pesticides in the mistaken belief that they act as fertilizers or growth promoters. In the Punjab of Pakistan, farmers could name only three pest categories, with the exception of rats and termites, and, although more than 80 per cent of farmers believed that pesticides increased crop production, only 44 per cent believed they did this by controlling pests.[23]

Farmers too try to minimise the time and costs of decision making, especially in the gathering and interpreting of information.[24] It is easier to treat all decisions according to a standard operating procedure, and thus to schedule or calendar spray. Such dependence on prophylactic control is particularly common in Japan, where more than 85 per cent of rice farmers are part-time, only cultivating at the weekends.[25] Similarly in developing countries, standardized recommendations are easy to follow and make for straightforward communication by extension workers. "Spray at weekly intervals" is a powerful extension "message". One of the consequences is that farmers may observe a single fixed harvest interval, irrespective of the pesticide. In Mauritius all vegetable growers stick to a seven day harvest interval – the period between the final spray and date of harvest.[26] It is a practice that suits the weekly pattern of harvesting and spraying, but results in the majority of farmers leaving substantially less time than recommended (Table 2.8). The problem is compounded because 30 per cent of farmers also apply substantially greater dosages than recommended and over 80 per cent mix cocktails of different products.

Table 2.8   Variation in harvest intervals observed by vegetable farmers in Mauritius

Active ingredient (local name)	Number of farmers observing harvest intervals		
	Less than recommended	More than recommended	Recommended
Recommended Harvest interval of 2–4 days			
Deltamethrin (Decis)	0	31	0
Methomyl (Lannate)	0	14	0
Harvest interval of 1 week			
Trichlorfon (Dipterex)	9	2	18
Recommended Harvest interval of 2 weeks			
Monocrotophos (Azodrin)	18	1	7
Fenitrothion (Folithion)	4	0	2
Binapacryl (Morocide)	4	0	1
Dimethoate (Perfekthion)	5	0	15
Endosulfan (Thiodan)	8	0	0
Recommended Harvest interval of 3 weeks			
Parathion	18	0	0
Methamidaphos (Tamaron)	27	0	0

Source: Fagoonee, I., "Pertinent aspects of pesticide usage in Mauritius", *Insect Sci. Applic.* 5 (1984) pp. 203–12.

Cosmetic control

The final factor is the tendency of farmers to try and achieve full protection of high value crops, such as fruit and vegetables, where the appearance to the consumer or processor greatly affects the price. Such "cosmetic control" is particularly prevalent in industrialized countries. It is reinforced by the growth of supermarket shopping and the high premiums paid for blemish-free produce. Supermarkets permit shoppers to select fruit and vegetables on the basis of appearance and any produce marked by the scars of insects or disease will be rejected – "horticultural produce must sell itself or be left on the shelf".[27]

An increasing proportion of produce is being classified in higher quality grades and the premium to the grower can be considerable.

Extra pesticide applications are thus justified, even where the risk of down-grading the product is very small (Table 2.9). Recent wholesale prices in the UK for top grade Cox's apples were some 43 per cent higher than those for grade 2.[28] The premium is a powerful incentive. A survey of farmers growing brassicas in Lincolnshire showed that many make the final application of the pesticide demeton-S-methyl on the last possible day before the beginning of the three week harvest interval to try and ensure there are absolutely no signs of pests or pest damage at the time of harvest.[29] The survey also revealed that they continued to apply DDT, despite claims by processors that no DDT was used on their crops.

Table 2.9   Costs of pesticide application in relation to apple crop quality in the UK, based on 1971 prices (£ per tonne)

Wholesale price	
class I	165
class II	57
Loss of income by downgrading from class I to class II	108
Cost of an extra pesticide application	1.40

Source: Royal Commission on Environmental Pollution, *Agriculture and Pollution* 7th Report, (London: HMSO, 1979).

In the USA cosmetic control is especially prevalent on citrus. Blemishes on the skins of the fruits reduce the returns to farmers, although there is no evidence that they reduce yields or affect nutrient content, storage or flavour.[30] The citrus rust mite, for example, causes russetting or bronzing on oranges and in the early 1970s most of the Florida oranges were being sprayed for rust mites, at a total cost of some $40–50 million. Oranges from treated orchards sold at a premium, even though yields were the same as in untreated orchards. Sometimes the requirement of a cosmetically perfect product is taken to an absurd extreme. In the USA more than half of the insecticides applied to tomatoes are for control of the tomato fruitworm which, like the rust mite on citrus, affects appearance only.[31] Processors will not accept batches from farmers with more than 1 per cent damaged, yet 90 per cent of the tomatoes are used for paste, soup and juice, products in which consumers could not possibly detect cosmetic damage.

Sometimes price incentives are reinforced by legislation. In the UK, food processors face prosecution under the Food and Drugs Act 1955 if a product is contaminated by pest remains. A landmark case in the early 1970s (Smedleys Ltd v. Breed) held that a caterpillar in a tin of peas was "avoidable extraneous material". Inevitably this resulted in pressure for produce to be presented in an absolutely pest-free state.[32]

"Overuse"

To what extent these various factors cause excessive use or overuse is a matter for debate. If a farmer is receiving more in benefits than the costs incurred then he or she is behaving in an economically rational manner. Insurance spraying, too, may be rational even if the long-term average benefits do not outweigh the long-term average costs. The farmer may be protecting himself or herself against a rare but potentially disastrous situation. On the other hand, such spraying may be increasing the likelihood of pest resistance or resurgences and hence may be increasing the possibility of a disaster. Nevertheless whether overuse is involved or not, these pressures for greater pesticide use will increase the hazards to the spray operators and the environment and also the likelihood of pesticide residues in food products (see Chapter 3).

The application of pesticides

Pollution is also caused by the manner in which pesticides are applied. A great variety of formulations – sprays, granules, dusts and fogs – and of methods of application are available. Spraying, for instance, may be carried out on a large scale from the air or by tractor-mounted machinery, or by an individual worker using a knapsack sprayer. Aerial spraying is particularly useful when pests are only vulnerable for a brief period. For instance, meteorological conditions may favour a synchronous emergence of caterpillars from their eggs or may trigger a large-scale migration of flying insects. Often the window of opportunity is very small – emerging caterpillars may quickly become inaccessible in the tissues of their host plants.[33] One advantage of aerial spraying is that there is usually less damage to crops and less soil compaction than from tractor mounted sprayers. There is also a reduced chance of pests being spread by the movement of equipment and personnel in the crop. But aerial spraying greatly increases the likelihood of spray drift often less than half of the applied spray falls inside the target field.[34] For smaller fields the losses are likely to be greater.

Environmental contamination is less if crops are sprayed from tractor mounted booms or by individual workers carrying knapsack sprayers. Spraying is slower but more accurate. However the risk to operators is usually higher. They are much more intimately involved with the spraying operation, being physically closer to the equipment and to the spray itself. Appropriate protective clothing can minimize the risk. Gloves will prevent contact with the hands during mixing and application, although particularly toxic compounds may require the use of face masks to prevent inhalation. In some cases, complete coverage of the body with special protective clothing is needed. In tropical conditions, these precautions are often ignored because of the heat and humidity, or the cost of purchasing the special clothing.[35] Wearing rubber gloves or boots for any length of time is highly uncomfortable. In greenhouses, too, the climate can make workers reluctant to wear protective clothing.[36] Sometimes even the clothing is not sufficient; gloves may only slow down penetration of the pesticide. Workers in a packaging factory in the UK recently suffered poisoning from organophosphates that eventually penetrated the gloves they were wearing.[37]

The skin, especially of the hands, is usually the most important route for absorption of pesticides, but not all the pesticide is necessarily absorbed. Much can be washed off the skin.[38] The amount absorbed depends, too, on the active ingredient and the formulation. Emulsions more readily pass through gloves and skins and are more hazardous than suspensions or particulate formulations. Damaged skin, such as grazes or cuts, increases absorption as does high humidity or temperature. Because the commonest uptake is through the hands, the hazard principally arises during mixing and loading.[39] Containers have to be opened, and the pesticides poured, measured, diluted and then poured again into the equipment. Splashing and spillage are common. Once spraying begins the extent of contamination depends on the nature of the equipment (Figure 2.3). In developing countries, although operators often take some precautionary measures, they are usually under the misconception that the danger lies in inhalation, and leave the skin, and hands in particular, poorly protected.[40]

Finally, there are hazards when farmers come to clean the spraying equipment and dispose of containers. In Mauritius only 14 per cent of a sample of farmers took adequate precautions when washing equipment, the remainder doing so under taps, in rivers and in some cases in drinking wells and water tanks.[41] Poor disposal of empty containers is also common; often they are simply left by the field edge. And in developing countries resale of bottles and tins for other uses is widespread.[42] There is, now, more regulation in

Figure 2.3 Sites of absorption of pesticides on the bodies of pesticide spraying operators according to operation

Tank filling of tractor
sprayer

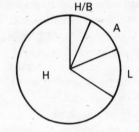

H/B – Head and body
A – Arms
L – Legs
H – Hands

Tractor spraying using booms
with hydraulic nozzles

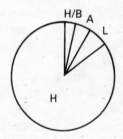

Tractor spraying using booms
with spinning disc controlled
droplet applicator

Knapsack spraying using adjustable
single nozzle lance

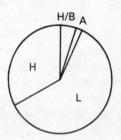

Source: Bonsalt. J.L., "Measurement of occupational exposure to pesticides" in: Turnbull, G.S. (ed.), *Occupational Hazards of Pesticide Use* (London: Taylor and Francis, 1985)

industrialized countries of disposal of containers and of the washings following cleansing. Farmers are required to wash all containers and then bury or burn them, while disposing of the washings on crops. But these precautions are labour intensive and time consuming. In particular, the proper cleaning equipment produces large volumes of liquid which are difficult to dispose of safely.

Pesticides in the environment

When a pesticide is applied to crops, most is either taken up by plants and animals or is degraded by microbial and chemical pathways (Figure 2.4). But a proportion is widely dispersed: some is vaporized to be eventually deposited in rainfall, some remains in the soil, while some reaches surface waters and groundwater, via run-off or leaching.

Figure 2.4   Fate of pesticides following application to agricultural crops

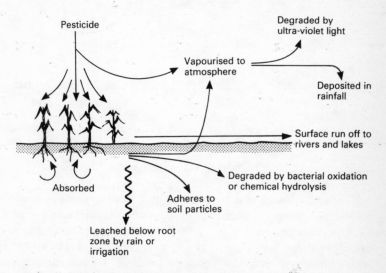

The presence of pesticides in rainfall has been detected in the USA and in Japan. Since most pesticides are usually applied in the spring of temperate countries, that is when they enter the atmosphere. The retention, though, is short and they are soon washed out in rain. Measurements in the USA show maximum concentrations of herbicides occurring in May rainfall, but levels declining by July to almost zero (Figure 2.5). Heavy rain results in rapid removal from the atmosphere – approximately 25 mm of rain falling in two days

Figure 2.5 Concentration of alachlor in rain water, April to August 1985. Asterisks represent samples from Indiana; triangles samples from Ohio

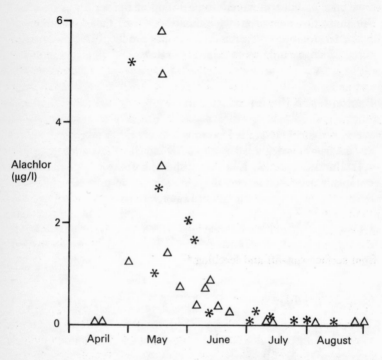

Source: Richards, R.P., Kramer, J.W., Baker, D.B., and Krieger, V.A., "Pesticide in rainwater in northeastern United States" *Nature* **327** (1987), pp. 129–131.

in May was enough to halve the concentration of herbicides in the atmosphere.[43]

Most of the pesticides deposited in rainfall are of local origin. Recent measurements suggest there is little long distance movement, perhaps because pesticides used today in the industrialized countries are not highly persistent. States on the east coast of the USA, where spraying is less intensive, have low pesticide levels in the rainfall despite being downwind of the agricultural Mid-west. There are also strong correlations between the within-state use of various products and their presence in rainfall, in terms of mean and maximum concentrations, total deposition and number of samples above detection limits. Nevertheless, there are instances of apparent long distance transport. An isolated lake in Japan, Lake Mashu, which has no inflows of streams and receives water only from rainfall or groundwater, was found to be contaminated by lindane (γ-HCH) at 0.03 μg/l. Concentrations in the rainfall reached 0.13 μg/l.[44] As this product has not officially been used in Japan since 1971, the only plausible sources are agricultural activities in China and Korea, some 1500 km distant.

Fog may also contain pesticides, in some cases the concentrations in the fog droplets being several orders of magnitude greater than in rain droplets.[45] Organophosphates have been found in fogs in California and Maryland, frequently exceeding 10 μg/l of water vapour, with a maximum of 50 μg/l of parathion at one site. The concentration of paraoxon, a highly toxic product of the reaction between parathion and ozone, was found to be as high as 184 μg/l. Herbicide concentrations were lower, in the range 0.1–3.6 μg/l.

From the rain and fog, contamination reaches surface and groundwaters. In the late 1970s, DDT in rainfall at 0.005 μg/l, and in snow at 0.001 μg/l, produced a direct annual loading of 80 kg to Lake Ontario, in Canada, by precipitation alone.[46] In some instances surface and groundwaters are directly contaminated by pesticides to control pests in fish farming or remove weeds in waterways. Nevertheless most contamination comes neither from this source nor precipitation but from surface run-off and leaching.[47]

Pesticides in surface waters

The proportion of pesticide lost to run-off is normally very low – rarely exceeding 0.5 per cent of total amount applied.[48] Compounds such as the organochlorines, arsenicals and paraquat are strongly adsorbed to soil particles and will only be lost when the soil itself is eroded. But others are more readily dissolved in water. The highest losses, up to 5 per cent, occur following the use of wettable powder herbicides. As in other environments, residues in surface waters reflect the changing use of products: in Iowa, for instance, herbicides have become more common during the 1980s while DDT has declined (Figure 2.6). Herbicide contamination is particularly high in states such as Iowa, Minnesota and Ohio with intensive corn and soybean cropping.[49] It also appears that many of the herbicides involved are not effectively removed from drinking water that is derived from surface sources, either by conventional treatment or more sophisticated carbon filtration systems.[50] Atrazine, for example, has been found in Ohio drinking water at concentrations of 30 μg/l.[51]

In the UK, a recent survey suggests there are no serious problems of general run-off.[52] The only agricultural products found consistently were the triazine herbicides, atrazine and simazine, though not exceeding 1.1 μg/l, and some synthetic pyrethroids, up to a

Figure 2.6 Pesticide residues at 12 surface water sites in Iowa

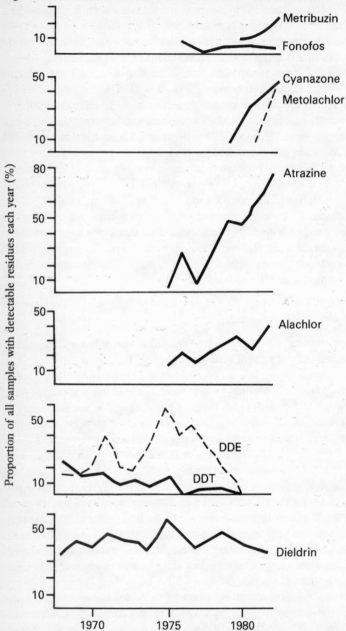

Source: Hallberg, G.R. "From hoes to herbicides. Agriculture and groundwater quality", *J. Soil Wat. Conserv.*, November–December 1986, pp. 357–364.

maximum of 60 $\mu g/l$. The major incidents of water pollution arise from point sources. The causes are poor methods of storage and disposal, but as press reports indicate there are also many cases of accidental and illegal discharges by manufacturing industry of such products as trichloroethylene, moth proofing chemicals and dieldrin contained in imported cotton or imported sheep fleeces (Table 2.10).[53] Another common point source is the deliberate release of sheep dip liquor.[54] Dipping of sheep to control sheep scab is compulsory, and produces large amounts of chemical fluids that require disposal. Until its withdrawal in 1984 dips consisted mainly of lindane (γ-HCH) and dieldrin, but have been replaced now by various organophosphate products.

Table 2.10 Incidents of damage caused by discharges of pesticides to watercourses in the UK, 1984–87

1984:	60 litres of herbicide were caused to enter a stream in Yorkshire killing a large number of fish.
1985:	Tributyl tin and dieldrin leaked from a storage vessel into the River Rother killing birds and thousands of fish.
1986:	Dieldrin, aldrin and lindane were discharged into the Severn Estuary.
1986:	A timber preservative was discharged into a river in Dorset killing numerous fish.
1987:	An aerial spraying firm discharged the washings from a pesticide spray tank into a soakaway in chalk only 2 km from a public supply borehole in Yorkshire.
1987:	Spent sheep dip solutions were discharged directly into a chalk aquifer in Yorkshire.

Source: Gilbert, D.G.R., *Pesticide safety policy and control arrangements in Britain*, PhD Thesis (London: Imperial College, 1987); ENDS, "Surveys of pesticides, chlorinated compounds in surface waters" ENDS **150** (1987) pp. 6–7.

Contamination from pesticides used in fish farming is particularly common in Scotland. The number of salmon farms increased sixfold in the early 1980s and the industry currently produces 13,000 tonnes of salmon per year. Fish lice are a problem and are treated with the organophosphate dichlorvos, which is known to be hazardous to marine organisms. However, as yet, there is no evidence of damage to marine life or to ourselves.

Pesticides in soils

Pesticide that is not lost by volatilization or in run-off enters the soil and there it is eventually degraded or it is lost down the soil profile to groundwater. The time required for degradation varies greatly according to the type of pesticide. Some products break down readily in the soil; others, particularly the organochlorines, can resist degradation for decades (Table 2.11). The intermediate products of the degradation process may also be as toxic or more toxic than the original pesticide. One such is DDE, the principal metabolite of DDT. It is so stable that, in a controlled 11 year study, the investigators were unable to calculate a half-life; it remained at about 0.4 ppm in the soil, and 7 ppm in earthworms, over the whole period.[55] In other studies, half-lives have been variously calculated at between 12 years in cultivated soils and 57 years in some uncultivated soils.[56] One authority considers that even though the use of DDT has stopped, soil organisms will remain a source of residue to predators for decades to come.[57]

Table 2.11   Pesticide persistence in soils

Low persistence (half-life less than 30 days)
  Methyl parathion
  Sulphur
  2,4-D

Moderate persistence (half-life 30–100 days)
  Maneb
  Mancozeb
  Carbaryl
  Diazinon
  Dinoseb
  Glyphosphate
  Simazine

Persistent (half-life 100 days–1 year)
  Benomyl
  Endosulfan
  Diuron

Very persistent (half-life more than 1 year)
  Paraquat
  Dieldrin
  DDT

Source: Warner, M.E., *An Environmental Risk Index to Evaluate Pesticide Programs in Crop Budgets* (Ithaca, NY: Dept of Agric. Econ., Cornell University, 1985).

How long pesticides remain in the soil also depends upon the type of soil and mode of application. In general, the absorptive capacity is highest in organic-rich soils, and is least in sandy soils. Although all soils strongly absorb DDT, one study showed that the ratio of absorption between a sandy loam soil, a clay and an organic-rich soil was 1:10:80.[58] The residence time of DDT is also very greatly extended if the pesticide is mixed with the soil: the time needed for 90 per cent to disappear grew from 1–2 years for surface application to as long as 25–40 years when well mixed.[59]

Leaching to groundwater

Finally, a proportion of the pesticide that is not degraded will leach below the root zone and eventually end up in groundwater. It used to be thought that this proportion was extremely small and insignificant. Most pesticide was assumed to be volatilized or degraded, leaving groundwater uncontaminated. But this assumption was shattered when evidence of widespread groundwater contamination began to come to light in the USA in the 1970s and in the UK in the 1980s.

What mostly determines the extent of pesticide leaching is the type of soil and rock overlying and comprising the aquifer. In permeable soils about 1 per cent of the original pesticide application may be leached. In the USA the most susceptible sites have sandy soils, shallow water tables and high rates of infiltration, together with low soil organic carbon content.[60] If there is little organic carbon present, the populations of bacteria are small and, hence, pesticides degrade much more slowly. In the UK the main aquifers are all at risk since they are low in organic matter and fed through fissured rock.[61] Pesticides may be rapidly transported thousands of metres through fissures and, once in the saturated aquifer, persist. In the soil there is considerable break-down of pesticides, and this continues in the unsaturated zone beneath, but it is much slower once the aquifers are reached. Irrigation will also increase leaching because of the greater flows of water, but sometimes irrigation practices themselves can have a direct effect. In California, the discharge of irrigation wastewater directly into abandoned dry wells contributes very rapidly to groundwater contamination.[62]

How much a pesticide is leached also depends on its persistence, solubility and mobility. The compounds most likely to leach include the water soluble herbicides, such as TCA, mecoprop (MCPP), MCPA, 2,4-D and dinoseb, and insecticides such as dimethoate.[63] The most widespread problems in the USA are from the nematocides aldicarb, dibromochloropropane (DBCP) and ethylene dibromide (EDB). In California, DBCP has been detected in some 2000 wells over an area of 18,000 km^2, even though its registration for all uses was cancelled in 1977. Severe nematode infestations tend to occur on sandy, porous soil with a low water holding capacity, conditions ideal for leaching. The herbicides atrazine, alachlor and simazine are also important contaminants.[64] The most commonly detected compounds in California groundwater are listed in Table 2.12.

Table 2.12 Most commonly detected pesticides in Californian groundwater

Pesticide	No. of wells containing pesticide	Maximum concentration detected ($\mu g/l$)
DBCP	2000	1.240
1,2-Dichloropropane	68	1.200
PCP	38	44000*
EDB	35	0.140
Lindane	32	0.046
Dimethoate	24	0.190
Aldrin	21	0.018
Aldicarb	17	0.047
Endosulfan	17	0.100
DDE	15	0.005
Dinoseb	14	0.740
Diazinon	13	0.009
2,4-D	11	0.004

* Presumed from industrial point source.
DBCP = Dibromochloropropane
PCP = Pentachlorophenol
EDP = Ethylene dibromide

Source: Holden, P.K., *Pesticides and Groundwater Quality*, National Research Council (Washington DC: National Academy Press, 1986).

Although in the UK, as in the USA, pesticides were not expected to cause contamination of groundwater, the introduction of highly water soluble herbicides in the 1970s stimulated the government to embark on a programme of monitoring.[65] The herbicides atrazine, simazine, mecoprop and 2,4-D are now commonly found, in the range of 0.02–0.4 $\mu g/l$ in chalk aquifers, particularly under the intensive agricultural regions of East Anglia.[66] These concentrations were considered by the government in the late 1980s to be lower, in almost all cases by several orders of magnitude, than those likely to cause adverse health effects.[67] But numerous groundwater supplies, particularly in East Anglian chalk, exceed the European Commission Maximum Admissible Concentrations of 0.1 $\mu g/l$ for any individual pesticide and 0.5 $\mu g/l$ for total pesticides.[68] The general hazard lies in these soluble herbicides, but localized contaminations also occur from the intensive use of carbamate insecticides on potatoes and sugar beet grown in permeable soils overlying aquifers.[69]

Aldicarb in Long Island

In 1979 the nematocide aldicarb was unexpectedly detected in water beneath Suffolk County on Long Island, New York.[70] Some 27 per cent of wells on the island were found to contain aldicarb, half exceeding the County Department of Health Service's health guideline of 7 μg/l (Table 2.13). But how serious this was to consumers of drinking water was unknown and the manufacturers and various government agencies responded by setting new but widely differing guidelines. Alongside the County Department of Health Services "no adverse effect" level of 7 μg/l, the Office of Pesticide Programs in the Environmental Protection Agency (EPA) recommended 30 μg/l as the Health Advisory Level (HAL); the Office of Drinking Water in EPA recommended 10 μg/l; the manufacturers of aldicarb, Union Carbide Corporation, suggested 21–100 μg/l; and in Wisconsin and Florida HALs were set at 10 μg/l. (See Chapter 10.)

Table 2.13   Groundwater contamination by aldicarb in Suffolk County, Long Island, New York, 1980

| | Concentration (μg/l) | | | |
	Zero	1–7	8–75	>75
Number of wells	6164	1119	941	180
Proportion (%)	73.3%	13.3%	11.2%	2.2%

Source: Zaki, M.H., Moran, D. and Harris, D., "Pesticides in groundwater: the aldicarb story in Suffolk County, New York", *Amer J. Publ. Health* **72** (1982) pp. 1391–95.

Almost all the wells containing aldicarb were found to occur within 750 metres of potato fields which had received intensive applications of aldicarb against nematodes (Table 2.14). Contributing factors were the presence of a shallow aquifer, about 20 metres deep, acidic soils low in organic carbon, together with high spring rainfall closely following the pre-emergence spraying of the pesticide. The groundwater had a pH of 5–6 and the half-life of aldicarb at pH 6 is 23 years, although at pH 8 it is only 82 days.[72] Application rates to potatoes were reduced from 8 to 3.5–4.5 kg/ha, but when this did not reduce contamination, the manufacturer's request for complete withdrawal of the product was granted by EPA in early 1980. Aldicarb was replaced by oxamyl, but it, too, was detected in wells and eventually withdrawn in 1984.[73]

Aldicarb has now been detected in the groundwater of 15 states.[74] In Florida, aldicarb has reached some aquifers below potato fields and citrus orchards, but in the northeast of the state, despite shallow groundwater and a long history of aldicarb use, no residues have been found. Here degradation is promoted by a soil high in organic carbon and the alkalinity of the groundwater.[75]

Table 2.14 Concentration of aldicarb in wells of Suffolk County according to distance from a potato farm

Aldicarb Concentration (µg/l)	Number of wells within stated distances from a potato farm				
	0–150 m	150–300 m	300–450 m	450–600 m	600–750 m
1–7	640	284	50	32	8
8–75	651	187	15	6	0
>75	144	27	1	1	0

Source: Zaki et al., 1982, *op. cit.*

Pesticides and wildlife

Environmental contamination by pesticides, both of the older and newer types, is now widespread, with serious implications for the health of wildlife and ourselves. In the rest of the chapter we will concentrate on what is known of the hazards posed by pesticides to wild animals and plants. Harm can arise in many different ways. Pesticides may directly come in contact with wildlife causing death or injury; or in the case of wild animals they may contaminate their sources of food. Finally, pesticides harm wildlife by altering the environment on which animals and plants depend.

Direct effects

Where wild animals or plants are similar to the target pest organisms and occur in the same area, then they are particularly vulnerable to direct harm from pesticides. Butterflies and wild flowers in the hedgerows may be killed by broad spectrum insecticides and herbicides applied to nearby crops.

Honeybees

One particularly beneficial group at risk are pollinating insects. Honeybees (not always wild since in many parts of the world they are domesticated) are frequently killed in large numbers when spraying occurs near or on flowers where they feed. An early published account of such a loss was in 1881, following the application of Paris Green to a pear tree in blossom.[76] The first modern insecticides, the organochlorines, were relatively non-toxic to honeybees, but many newer organophosphates and carbamates are very hazardous. During the 1970s pesticides annually destroyed 40–70,000 bee colonies in California, some 10–15 per cent of the total, while the annual national loss of colonies was estimated at half a million.[77] At lower doses, pesticides may increase the aggressiveness of bees and produce abnormalities in the dances they use to communicate information on sources of food.[78]

Alfalfa is a crop particularly attractive to both wild and domesticated honeybees. In one incident in Washington, large numbers of bees were killed by diazinon and two years later had only regained a quarter of their previous population level.[79] The problem has also become serious in the UK because of the dramatic increase in the acreage of oil seed rape, by 1983 the third most widespread arable crop. An important pest of rape, the blossom beetle, begins to attack the crop about flowering time when bees are also present. It can be controlled by the organophosphorus insecticide, triazophos, which is also harmful to bees. However it is still effective against the beetle if applied after flowering, when the bees have gone elsewhere. Triazophos was given provisional clearance in 1977 but poisoning incidents steadily increased, largely because recommendations suggested spraying "at the end of flowering", which was open to various interpretations. Spraying occurred while some plants were still flowering and bees were active. Each year some 50 to 200 incidents of bees confirmed as poisoned by pesticides are reported.[80]

In general, the poisoning of bees and other pollinators can be avoided by using selective poisons or by careful timing of spraying – by using short-life chemicals very early or late in the day when the bees are not foraging.[81] Certain pyrethroid insecticides may also be appropriate since, although they are highly toxic to bees in the laboratory, they have little effect in the field, possibly because they are repellent to bees.[82] Fungicides can also be harmful to other non-target organisms.[83]

Via the soil

Pesticides may also directly harm wildlife through contamination of soil or water. As might be expected, they are especially harmful to soil invertebrates that occur near the soil surface. Dramatic effects can occur when there is differential mortality between invertebrate predators and their prey (Figure 2.7). If the predators, say predatory mites, are more susceptible to the insecticide than the prey (springtails), then massive increases in the prey may result.[84] Sometimes it takes several years before the effect on populations is no longer detectable.

Figure 2.7 The effect of a single treatment of DDT on numbers of predatory mites and their principal prey, springtails, in the soil

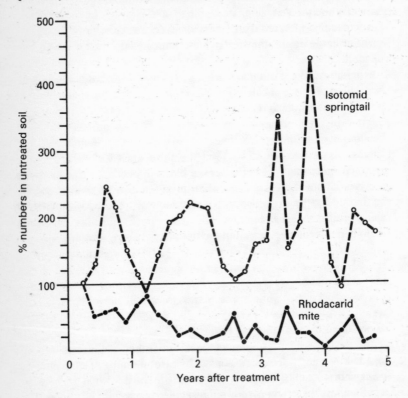

Source: Edwards, C.A. "Changes in agricultural practice and their impact on soil organisms" in: Jenkins, D. (ed.), *Agriculture and the Environment* (Swindon: NERC, 1984).

The effect varies greatly with the type of compound. Carbamates, for instance, tend to have a more drastic effect on soil invertebrates than other insecticides and are very toxic to earthworms. DDT, on the other hand, does not kill earthworms, in either temperate or tropical conditions, at normal levels of application.[85] Nematocides are particularly toxic to a range of invertebrates. A single treatment of the fumigant metham sodium will kill almost all animals in the soil and it may take as long as two years for some populations to recover. Few modern fungicides cause problems, although the compounds used in the past, such as copper fungicides, were highly toxic to soil invertebrates. An exception among the modern compounds is the class of carbendazim fungicides, including benomyl, which is particularly toxic to earthworms. Most modern herbicides are not very toxic to wildlife, but exceptions are monuron, TCA, DNOC and the triazine herbicides such as simazine.[86]

In general, soil fauna are either unaffected or recover quickly from herbicide applications.[87] But, in contrast, herbicides can have a significant impact on soil microflora, though it is difficult to distinguish pesticide-induced effects, unless they are very large, from the background of high variability in natural conditions.[88] Some herbicides, such as mecoprop, ioxynil and diuron, have been shown to reduce populations of nitrogen-mineralizing bacteria, but usually only at very high dosages.[89] Others will affect the activity of nitrogen-fixing bacteria associated with the roots of legumes, though the range of sensitivity to herbicides between species and even between strains is high.[90] Much also depends on the pattern of persistence of the herbicide. For example, paraquat, a common herbicide, becomes rapidly and strongly bound to clay minerals. It then only degrades at 5–10 per cent per year, but in this form has no adverse impact on soil organisms. Detailed studies have shown no effects, at either normal or high doses, on fungi, bacteria, endomycorrhiza or other micro-organisms or on earthworms.[91]

Via the Water

Direct effects of pesticides on organisms in fresh or sea water similarly depend on the nature of the compound. Some insecticides are particularly harmful – killing water-dwelling insects, crustacea and fish. DDT is particularly toxic, and concentrations of only a few mg/l are sufficient to kill large proportions of aquatic populations.[92] The early stages of organisms tend to be more sensitive than the adults: for example, DDT was commonly used to control crustacean pests on oyster beds, yet it was soon found that it readily kills the larvae of the oysters themselves. Fish are also very susceptible to DDT poisoning: the 96 hour LC_{50}s range from 1.5 to 56 mg/l.

At the low residue levels of DDT that are commonly found in the environment, feeding and other behaviour patterns can also be impaired, but in ways that are often subtle. When exposed to sublethal

DDT concentrations, salmon and trout change their behavioural and physiological responses to cold. The lower lethal temperature is raised and the fish exhibit avoidance when encountering water of 5°C or colder.[93] In addition, the lateral line nerves in trout become hypersensitive to mechanical stimuli and the metabolic rate is affected in complex ways.[94] In young salmon the rate decreases by as much as 25 per cent at DDT concentrations of 0.01 ppm, yet at 0.08 ppm it increases to 60 per cent above normal. The consequence is dramatic abnormalities in behaviour. After mass fish mortality in a stream in Prince Edward Island, Canada, following discharge of a mixture of nabam (a fungicide) and endrin, the surviving salmon and trout began to swim downstream contrary to the seasonal pattern.[95]

Herbicides can also be damaging. Those that are quickly leached are less likely to damage soil microflora, but may then be a hazard to aquatic flora and fauna. Two compounds, atrazine and alachlor, are present as residues in the sediment of Chesapeake Bay and are claimed to be killing bottom vegetation.[96] Herbicides may also be lethal to coral in tropical waters and may be partly responsible for the massive destruction of coral reefs that has occurred in the Gulf of Chirigui, Panama.[97] Land closest to the shore is fairly intensively cultivated; 42,000 hectares are sprayed annually with herbicides from the air. Surprisingly coral tissue was found to contain between 2 and 40 μg/kg of both 2,4-D and 2,4,5-T, despite the fact that the warm sea temperatures and high solar activity should have hastened their breakdown. Tissues also contained residues of dieldrin, dimethoate, DDT, endrin, ethion and lindane. Laboratory testing with concentrations of the phenoxy herbicides that are typically found in the corals produced tissue loss and death. Nevertheless, it seems unlikely that all the recent coral loss can be attributed to herbicides alone. The loss was widespread and changes in water temperature during the strong El Nino of 1982–3 are suspected as the principal cause of mortality.

Contamination of food sources

That pesticides may contaminate the food sources of wildlife has been long recognized. As early as 1804 in England, wheat seed dressed with arsenic to control smut was causing deaths of pheasants and partridges.[98] And it was poisoning of this kind in the 1950s that first alerted the public and the scientific community to the hazards posed by pesticides to wildlife.

Figure 2.8   Mortalities of pigeons, pheasants and house sparrows on estates in the UK in relation to dates of cereal sowing, 1961

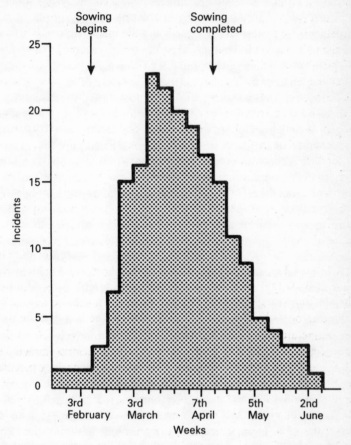

Source: Sheail, J., *Pesticides and Nature Conservation* (Oxford: Clarendon Press, 1985).

Cereal seed

From about 1956 there was widespread treatment of cereal seed in the UK with cyclodiene organochlorine insecticides, in particular aldrin and dieldrin, as a protection against such pests as wheat bulb fly and wireworms that attack the young emerging seedlings. The seed was then sown at a shallow depth so that the young seedlings would be best protected by the insecticide on the seed coat. A proportion of seed was spilled in the process and eaten by various species of grain-eating birds. In consequence, large numbers of deaths of wood pigeons, stockdoves, pheasants, partridges and other birds occurred. The mortality was most dramatic in the season 1960–1961. Sowing was delayed by a very wet autumn, and only resumed in mid-February.[99] Under pressure to complete the sowing, much of the seed remained on the surface, available to birds. Dry weather meant germination was further delayed, and mortalities continued until May (Figure 2.8).

A similar situation arose in the USA following the treatment of rice seed with another cyclodiene, aldrin. Large mortalities were recorded in Texas of fulvous whistling ducks and other birds.[100]

Following the withdrawal of organochlorine seed dressings it was hoped that such incidents would cease. But in the early 1970s there were numerous incidents of deaths of greylag and pink-footed geese in the UK feeding on wheat seed treated with the organophosphorus insecticide, carbophenothion.[101] Most of the world population of these two birds overwinter in Britain and hundreds of deaths have occurred on several occasions. The brain cholinesterase levels of the dead birds were greatly reduced, indicating organophosphate poisoning.[102] In some instances the seed had not been properly drilled, but there was also evidence of birds digging up treated seed and seedlings.

Carbophenothion had been introduced for seed dressings because of the known hazards of the organochlorines. It had been extensively tested before release and was thought to be safe. But further laboratory testing on a greater range of organisms showed it to have a great variability (by some orders of magnitude) in its acute toxicity to birds and mammals.[103] This is reminiscent of the situation for dioxin, but contrasts with dieldrin which is much more consistent in its effect (Table 2.15). In the reported incidents, pigeons and game birds feeding in the same fields as the geese were not affected. Why geese, and, in particular, the genus *Anser*, which includes the greylag and pink-footed geese, should be highly susceptible is not yet fully understood. In 1975 carbophenothion was voluntarily withdrawn from use in Scotland, but poisoning of geese and swans has continued in England, although on a minor scale.[104] In general, however, seed dressings no longer present the hazard they did in the 1960s and 1970s.[105]

Prey animals

Other early examples of wildlife poisoning occurred because of the direct pesticide contamination, at sublethal levels, of prey animals that are food for predatory birds and mammals. The phenomenon first became apparent in the USA in the late 1940s and early 1950s, when DDT was applied to elm trees to control insect vectors of Dutch elm disease.[106] The insecticide was picked up by earthworms which then were eaten by American robins with lethal results. The dead robins were found to contain an average of 100 mg/kg of DDT in the brain tissue. Most deaths occurred during spring and after heavy rains; conditions when earthworms come to the soil surface and are most available to robins. Earthworms contained an average 120 mg/kg of total DDT, and consumption of about 100 would constitute a dose equivalent to the median levels found in the dead birds. However, not all of these deaths were linked to contamination of food sources – some of the dead birds had little or no residue.

Table 2.15 Contrasting LD_{50} values (mg/kg) for dieldrin and carbophenothion

	Dieldrin	*Carbophenothion*
Rat	38–87	7–91
Mouse	38–74	106–218
Rabbit	45–50	1250
Dog	56–120	40
Chicken	48	316
Pigeon	27	35
Quail	70	57
Canada goose	50–150	29–35

Source: Stanley, P.I. and Bunyan, P.J., "Hazards to wintering geese and other wildlife from the use of dieldrin, chlorfenvinphos and carbophenothion on wheat seed treatments", *Proc. Roy. Soc. Lond. B* **205** (1979) pp. 31–45.

An even more dramatic incident in the 1950s followed the spraying of 7000 hectares of Illinois farmland around Sheldon with dieldrin against Japanese beetle, a serious pest of maize and soybeans. Fields, farms, houses, streams and roads were blanketed with spray.[107] Within the following week there were considerable wildlife deaths, particularly among vertebrates that typically spend a large amount of time on the ground, and especially those feeding on insects and earthworms. The populations of pheasants, robins, ground squirrels, rabbits and muskrats were virtually eliminated; in total, mortalities occurred in 19 species of birds and 12 of mammals. By contrast, seed feeders such as mourning doves experienced no mortality. Farm animals also suffered, again due to consumption of contaminated food: some 90 per cent of the cats died on treated farms. Some sheep and cows also died, ewes and lambs after grazing on pastures adjacent to ploughed fields sprayed from the air. One ewe was found to contain about 100 mg/kg of dieldrin in adipose tissue. There were no effects, though, on pigs and poultry that were largely given food brought into the farms.

Another, often cited, example of food contamination arose from the practice in Britain, in the mid 1960s, of dipping sheep with dieldrin to control various parasites, such as blowflies, sheep scab and ticks. This was followed by a reduction in breeding success of golden eagles, particularly in western Scotland where dead sheep constitute an important proportion of the eagle's diet.[108] The link was further suggested following the withdrawal of dieldrin sheep dips in 1966, when breeding success improved and dieldrin concentrations in both mutton and eagle eggs declined. Where eagles consumed little sheep meat, such as in eastern Scotland, they bred successfully throughout the period, and little or no dieldrin was detected in their eggs.[109]

Organophosphates can also cause wildlife deaths in a similar fashion. In Texas, parathion has killed both adult and chick laughing gulls which feed on insects. The stomach contents of the dead birds contained insects contaminated with parathion which had been sprayed on local cotton fields for control of bollworms, budworms and cabbage loopers, at twice the recommended rate.[110]

Vertebrate poisons

A similar effect on predators can result from the use of poison baits to control vertebrate pests, such as predatory birds, corvids, foxes, badgers and rodents. In the UK, the illegal use or misuse of compounds such as mevinphos, strychnine and the narcotic alpha-chloralose has caused the deaths of a great variety of animals – gulls, lapwings, pigeons, gamebirds, garden birds, domestic dogs and cats – in addition to the presumed targets. The Ministry of Agriculture records some 600 incidents of poisoning of mammals and birds a year, of which pesticides are implicated in about one third.[111] In a number of cases the deaths are due to banned poisons: in 1988 a rare red kite was killed after consuming bait laced with endrin, long since banned in the UK.

In Israel monocrotophos, an organophosphorus pesticide, was sprayed on alfalfa fields in the Huleh Valley to control voles, even though this product is only recommended for use on cotton and orchard crops.[112] Over a three month period some 115 raptors and 29 owls were found dead, and a further 69 sublethally poisoned, though population counts suggest twice as many may have died. Thallium sulphate, also used as a rodenticide in Israel, has killed many birds too.[113] These incidents arose, at least partly, because the recommendations on the original label, warning of the toxicity to birds, were not written in Hebrew. This has been a common failing of the packaging of pesticides, largely offset now by the use of pictograms to illustrate safety messages.

There is also a growing hazard from the new rodenticides adopted in response to spreading resistance of rats and mice to the traditional rodenticide, warfarin. Products such as difenacoum, bromadiolone and brodifacoum are considerably more effective than warfarin though, like warfarin, they are slow acting and several days elapse between intake and death. The predators most at risk are owls. In laboratory trials captive barn owls fed contaminated rats and mice died some 8–14 days later.[114] One owl may require as few as 1–5 contaminated rats to cause fatal internal haemorrhages.[115] Field poisoning has occurred in the USA, although the evidence tends to be circumstantial. Dead screech owls, with signs of haemorrhaging, were found in and around an apple orchard in Virginia following baiting for voles with brodifacoum.[116]

The clearest evidence of poisoning comes from the oil palm plantations of Malaysia. Until 1981 a combination of warfarin baiting and provision of nest boxes to encourage the breeding of barn owls was highly effective in controlling rats. Then, second generation products were introduced, partly because of resistance problems and partly because they were believed to be more effective. This change coincided with dramatic declines in barn owl populations. On one estate in Johore the number of birds fell from 20 breeding pairs to only 2 individuals over a 30 month period following the introduction of, first, coumachlor and, then, brodifacoum.[117] Several carcasses were found with external signs of haemorrhaging.

Owls are at most risk when rodents are the principal prey. In the UK, where commensal rodents, that is rats and mice, make up about 12 per cent of an average barn owl diet, the level of poisoning appears to be low – only 3 per cent of known causes of death between 1982 and 1986.[118] But in Ireland where commensal rodents are typically 30–70 per cent of the diet because most voles are absent, some 20 per cent of known causes of barn owl death were poisoning over the same period.[119] In temperate countries, owls are particularly at risk because farmers and gamekeepers commonly set bait to control rats in winter months, just when rats increase in importance in the owl diet.[120] But the risk is probably greater in many tropical conditions because prey populations are highly stable. As a result owls in Malaysia can raise two broods per year, so increasing their relative susceptibility to poisoning. Also brodifacoum is widely available in tropical countries, although it has yet to receive full clearance by regulatory authorities in the UK.[121]

Food chain contamination

Often the pathway of contamination may be more complicated, involving two or more stages in a food chain. Organochlorine insecticides are particularly hazardous in this respect, because of their high solubility in body fat and their considerable persistence. They are readily taken up by organisms at the bottom of a food chain and then passed on as one species feeds on another, often becoming present in large concentrations in organisms, such as predatory birds, that are at the top of the chain (Figure 2.9). However, this general pattern does not always hold true: one investigation of the passage of dieldrin from soil to earthworms to song thrushes found that concentrations decreased at each step of the chain.[122]

Figure 2.9   Food chain accumulation of *pp*-DDE in an orchard in the UK sprayed each April. Total residues are in ppm

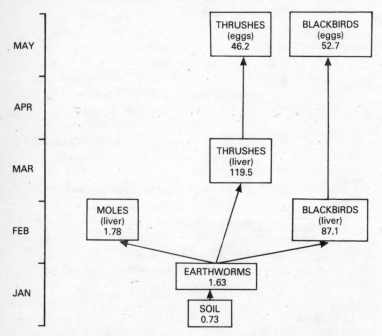

Source: Bailey, S., Bunyan, P., Jennings, D.M., Norris, J.D., Stanley, P.I. and Williams, J.H., "Hazards to wildlife from the use of DDT in orchards: a further study" in *Agro-Ecosystems* 1 (1974) pp. 323–338.

Although the phenomenon is mostly associated with organochlorines, it is also known for organophosphates. Red-tailed hawks in the western USA died after preying on magpies contaminated with the organophosphate famphur. Devouring only one such magpie was sufficient to cause death. The insecticide is applied directly to cattle for control of warble fly, and the magpie's habit of ingesting cattle hair led to the accumulation of very high levels in the gizzard. Many magpies died from acute poisoning, but those that survived, in turn, constituted a hazard to predators.[123]

Deaths of foxes, otters and bats

The deaths of predatory mammals first became apparent in the UK at the time grain eating birds were dying from feeding on dieldrin-dressed seed. Associated with this mortality were increasing numbers of deaths of owls, sparrowhawks, badgers and foxes.[124] The evidence for a linkage was only circumstantial at first, but then autopsies and laboratory feeding experiments indicated that dieldrin ingested by grain feeding birds and small mammals was being passed on to their predators with lethal effects.[125] By the spring of 1960, the effect on foxes were so great that traditional fox-hunting in some parts of the country had to be cancelled.[126]

Significant deaths of otters also occurred in the late 1950s, and populations began to decline.[127] This was attributed to the increasing use of organochlorines, particularly dieldrin, but following the bans on these compounds in the 1970s there have been no signs of recovery. Recently, dieldrin has been found in otter carcases collected from around Britain, in some cases exceeding concentrations at which reproductive failure may occur.[128] The contamination may be the result of recent agricultural activity or industrial discharges but, given the long residence time of organochlorines in sediments, it is more probably a relic of the widespread agricultural and industrial use before the bans of the 1970s. The lack of recovery of the other populations, though, is more likely due to human disturbance and the destruction of riparian habitats.[129]

Bats, too, may have been affected. They are known to be particularly sensitive to DDE, far more so than most other mammals, probably because they have marked seasonal cycles in fat content.[130] As body weight falls, during hibernation or migration, so DDT or its products in the fat are mobilized. In one case, residues of DDT in bats in East Anglia rose to just under the lethal dose after hibernation, that is about 45 mg/kg, although the levels were only a third of the lethal dose for the rest of the year. Insects in the locality had DDT residues of about 4 ppm, and this could well lead to an uptake by bats of about 3 mg/kg/day. But the recent decline in the numbers of bats in the UK has been attributed to several further causes. There has been widespread treatment of roof timbers with products such as lindane (γ-HCH), dieldrin and pentachlorophenol (PCP) to prevent infestation by wood-boring insects or wood-rotting fungi, and agricultural intensification has greatly altered bat habitats, reducing roosting sites and the amount of insect prey available.[131]

Aquatic food chains

Pesticides may also become concentrated in aquatic food chains. Unusually large amounts of pesticide residue can be accumulated in the fauna and flora of surface waters, as has happened in the Lower Rio Grande Valley of Texas. This is an intensively farmed region that also serves as an important breeding area for fish-eating birds. Large quantities of pesticides are applied to the farms and are accumulated by mosquito fish living in the drainage ditches. The fish are now resistant to high concentrations of at least one pesticide, campheclor (toxaphene), some fish having accumulated as much as 2,660 mg/kg in their body tissues.[132] Ingestion of only a few fish by birds can be lethal. A similar accumulation has occurred in rivers in Mississippi, in this case endrin from heavily sprayed cotton fields. Feeding on just one pesticide-resistant fish is enough to kill adult predatory fish, bullfrogs, turtles or snakes.[133]

Pesticide concentration in aquatic food chains is also common in the tropics. In Surinam, in South America, spraying of PCP and endrin on an 8000 hectare intensive rice-growing region near the coast caused

Table 2.16 Residues of PCP and endrin in rice fields, snails, fish and birds in Surinam

	(mg/kg)	
	PCP	Endrin
Concentration applied to rice fields (ppm)	4	0.1
Residues in snails	37	0.01
Residues in birds (snail-eating)	11–46	0.01
Residues in fish	31–59	2.0–5.0
Residues in birds (fish-eating)	3–5	0.3–2.7

Source: Vermeer, K. et al., "Pesticide effects on fishes and birds in rice fields of Surinam, South America", Environ. Pollut. 7 (1974) pp. 217–36.

extensive bird and fish kills.[134] Kites foraging in the rice fields on snails accumulated concentrations of PCP approximately 100 times greater than those from nearby fresh water marshes (Table 2.16). Approximately 25 per cent of birds roosting by the fields died. When endrin was applied, fish-eating egrets, herons and jacanas were found sick and dying, with residues sufficiently high to be the cause. In a similar situation in Chad, in Africa, egrets that were found dead or dying in cotton fields after endrin application contained residues in the range 0.08–2.6 mg/kg.[135]

Predatory birds in decline

Not long after the persistent organochlorines came into widespread use, populations of several species of predatory birds, also known as raptors, declined dramatically in both North America and Europe. A clear pattern of reduced numbers was shared by sparrowhawks, ospreys, bald eagles, barn owls and brown pelicans. The most notorious fall though, and perhaps the best documented, was that of the peregrine falcon.

Peregrine falcons

From a pre-war high of five to nine thousand nesting pairs in North America, the population began to decline in the late 1940s. The decline was persistent and widespread. By 1975 only 324 nesting pairs could be confirmed on the whole continent.[136] In Britain the decline began in the 1950s in southern England and then spread in a wave-like manner northwards.[137] By 1961 the once flourishing population in southern England had all but disappeared, and the inland populations of the Scottish Highlands were the only ones in Britain unaffected (Figure 2.10).

The more remote peregrine populations of Alaska and arctic Canada escaped at first, but by 1970 their numbers also began to fall. The birds migrate each year to the agricultural regions of Central and northern South America and by the 1970s these areas were heavily contaminated. Significantly, the gyrfalcon, which is a non-migratory arctic bird, feeding largely on non-migratory prey, has not been exposed to high levels of organochlorines and its populations have remained stable. Declines in the peregrine were also reported from most of Europe, the Middle East, Asia and Japan, wherever organochlorines were being widely used.

Figure 2.10 Decline and recovery of peregrine falcon populations in different regions of Britain. Occupation of territories is expressed as a percentage of 1930–39 population level

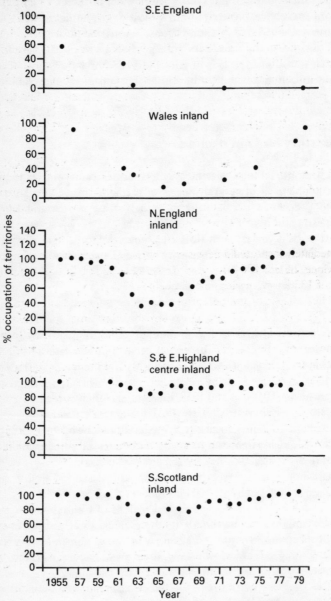

Source: Ratcliffe, D.A., *The Peregrine Falcon* (Berkhamsted: Poyser, 1980).

During these declines, ornithologists had begun to notice that breeding of the peregrine was becoming less successful. Indeed, at some locations failure was complete: the Hudson River Valley population of peregrines, formerly one of the healthiest, produced no young in the early 1950s. This fact was reported by two ornithologists, Herbert and Skelton, to the American Ornithologists Union conference in Los Angeles in 1953, yet as Kiff later put it: "their report elicited not a single question or comment from the assembled ornithologists."[138] By the early 1960s rumour had it that not a single peregrine had fledged in the northeastern United States. Reflecting recently, Hickey said he assumed that falconers had been "very, very busy".[139] Egg collectors, too, were suspected of playing a significant role.

But in 1963, the focus shifted significantly when Ratcliffe published the first article linking wholesale eyrie desertion to the failure in reproductive success, probably brought about in some unknown fashion by organochlorine pesticides. Hickey, who had conducted the survey in the 1930s of peregrine numbers in North America which was to provide a key baseline measure throughout this period, immediately instituted a new survey of the 14 states and one Canadian province. In late 1964 the team drove some 23,000 km and found not one of 133 known eyries to be inhabited.[140]

The collapse of the peregrine was on an unprecedented scale, but the declines in other predatory birds at this time could have had other causes. One complication is the hunting of predatory birds by gamekeepers. In the case of herons, a series of records of occupied nests in the UK going back to 1928 shows that numbers are drastically reduced in severe winters, but then rapidly recover to an average population of about 4,500 nests (Figure 2.11). Following the severe winters of 1962 and 1963, however, the recovery was much slower and it is claimed this may have been due to organochlorine poisoning.[141] Nevertheless, by 1973 the numbers had increased to over 5000, the highest on record, and they subsequently stabilized.

Causes of decline

By the early 1950s the deaths of adult predatory birds and the declines in their breeding success were clearly apparent. Nevertheless, it still remains unclear today which of these two factors was the most important contributor to the population collapses.

The declines coincided with the widespread use of aldrin and dieldrin and the finding of lethal levels of their residues in the bodies of wild peregrines and other raptors.[143] For sparrowhawks,

Figure 2.11   Grey heron population levels in England and Wales, 1928–77

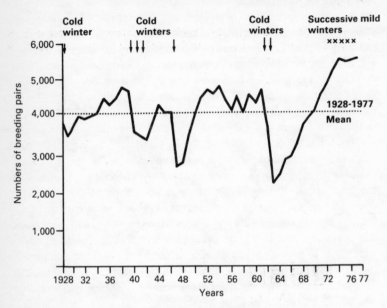

Source: Reynolds, G.M. "The heronries census: 1972–1977 population changes and a review", *Bird Study* 26 (1979), pp. 7–12.

lethal doses appear to have been acquired from wood pigeons and other grain-eating birds while for kestrels and owls, the main sources were mice. Herons were taking up heavy doses from fish and in particular oily fish, such as eels.

Woodpigeons can accumulate an LD_{50} dose of dieldrin from dressed grain in less than 5 hours of feeding and, similarly, wood mice can accumulate over 24 ppm of dieldrin in their livers within nine days after the sowing of dressed winter wheat seed.[144] At these rates of uptake it only requires a few meals for a predatory bird to acquire a lethal dose – two highly contaminated birds are sufficient to kill a predatory falcon, and 7 bank voles, given access for 24 hours to dressed wheat, have been enough to kill a kestrel.[145] The likelihood of feeding on poisoned small mammals is increased by their abnormal behaviour; they tend to run around sluggishly in the open so attracting predators.[146]

From 1963 a regular program of monitoring pesticide residues in bird carcases was instituted in the UK. Figure 2.12 shows one set of records – the monthly levels of HEOD, the active ingredient of dieldrin, in the livers of barn owl carcases. The pattern of high residues in spring and early summer was found to be also true of DDE (the metabolite of DDT).

Figure 2.12 Residues of HEOD in barn owl livers (graph) and proportion of carcasses containing more than 10 mg/kg of HEOD (histogram). HEOD is the active ingredient of dieldrin

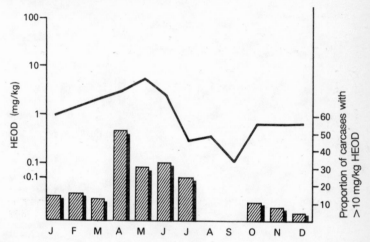

Source: Cooke, A.S., Bell, A.A., Haas, M.B., *Predatory Birds, Pesticides and Pollution* (Monks Wood: Institute of Terrestrial Ecology, 1982).

Eggshell thinning

The many deaths of adult predatory birds were thus clearly associated with uptakes of lethal doses of pesticides, aldrin and dieldrin in particular. But it was also apparent that other processes were at work. In the 1950s Ratcliffe noticed large numbers of broken peregrine eggs in Britain: between 1951 and 1956 he recorded broken or absent eggs in 13 out of 59 eyries.[147] He then surveyed egg collections in Britain going back to 1900, and demonstrated that eggshells after 1947 were significantly thinner (Figure 2.13). Similar effects were later shown for sparrowhawks, this time using collections going back to 1870 (Figure 2.14).

Both sets of data show clearly the first year of marked decline in shell thickness to be 1947. This correlates with the introduction of DDT, which began to be used in 1946 in both Britain and USA. One use in Britain was for dusting racing pigeons to control ectoparasites. A homing pigeon ring removed from a peregrine eyrie in 1947 subsequently revealed minute amounts of DDT and DDE, while

Figure 2.13 Shell thinning of peregrine falcons in Britain, 1900–67. The eggshell index measures the weight divided by the length times the breadth. The higher the index the thicker the shell.

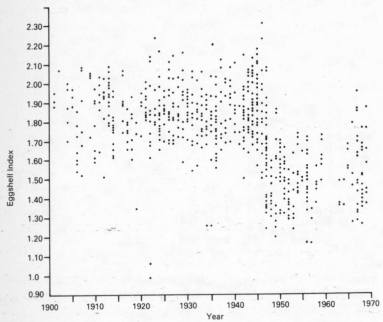

Source: Ratcliffe, D.A. "Changes attributable to pesticides in egg breakage frequency and eggshell thickness in some British birds", *J. Appl. Ecol.* 7 (1970), pp. 67–115.

solvent rinsing of eggs showed traces of DDE from 1947 onwards.[148] Publication of the thin eggshell findings in 1967 stimulated similar analyses in the USA. Hickey and Anderson were able to persuade private collectors to subject their eggs for analysis, a considerable achievement since the collections were highly illegal.[149] The analyses showed that eggs of the peregrines had similarly declined in thickness by 20 per cent and that eggshell thinning was present in 13 other North American raptors and nine other birds.

In general, shell thinning was more marked (>15 per cent) in bird- and fish-eating raptors, such as peregrines, merlins, ospreys and bald and white-tailed eagles, than in mammal-eaters (<10 per cent), such as golden eagles and various hawks, harriers and kestrels.[150] Population decline was also greater in the most intensive agricultural areas where DDT was being commonly used. In remote areas populations were less affected, except where predators seasonally

Figure 2.14 Shell thinning of sparrowhawks in Britain, 1870–1975

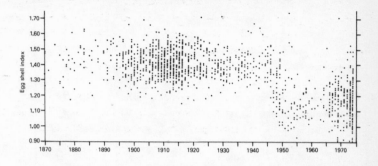

Source: Newton, I., *Population Ecology of Raptors* (Berkhamsted: Poyser, 1979).

migrated to intensive agricultural regions, as in the case of the peregrine. Populations of peregrine throughout the world produced thinned eggs compared with pre–1947 values (Figure 2.15).

Residues in eggs

During the early 1960s investigators began to search for the link between DDT, its breakdown products and eggshell thinning. The evidence establishing cause and effect came from two types of studies. The first were field analyses, in which the quantities of contaminants in eggs were measured against the degree of shell thinning. Hickey and Anderson showed that eggshell thickness in herring gull colonies in North America was statistically correlated with DDE content, the stable breakdown product of DDT.[151] A similar correlation was also obtained for the peregrine (Figure 2.16) and many other species.

The second type of study was laboratory based. Investigators dosed captive birds with DDT and/or DDE and then measured the impact on the shell thickness of subsequently produced eggs. Unfortunately, birds of prey are difficult to rear in captive conditions and hence most of these experiments were conducted on birds that are easy to raise, such as quails, ducks and doves, but are relatively insensitive to the effects of DDT.[152] The best evidence came from experiments by Lincer on captive American kestrels. The birds were fed with day-old chicks injected with DDE and, as Figure 2.17 shows, there was a very close relationship between thinning and the level of DDE residues in the eggs subsequently laid. Field data from nearby in New York State showed the same trend.

The mechanism of shell thinning is still not fully understood.[153]

Figure 2.15   Global distribution of eggshell thinning in the peregrine falcon. Figures are percentage reductions in eggshell thickness index, years of most extreme thinning in brackets

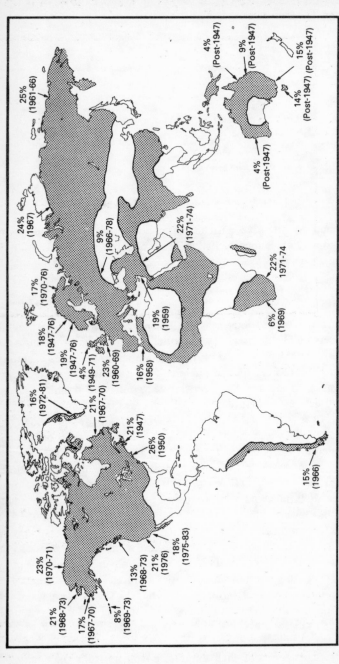

Source: Deakall, D.B. and Kiff, L.F. "DDE contamination in peregrines and American kestrels and its effect on reproduction" in: Cade et al. (eds), *Peregrine Falcon Populations. Their Management and Recovery* (Boise, Idaho: The Peregrine Fund, Inc., 1988).

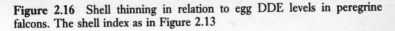

Figure 2.16 Shell thinning in relation to egg DDE levels in peregrine falcons. The shell index as in Figure 2.13

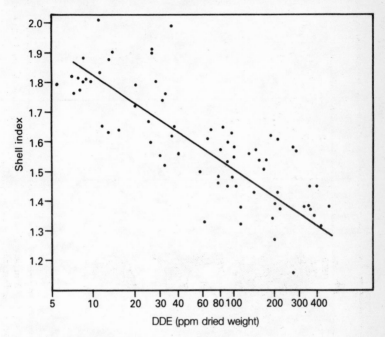

Source: Newton, I., 1979, *op. cit.*

Unfortunately many of the biochemical studies have been conducted on chickens, a species relatively resistant to eggshell thinning. Organochlorines affect many biochemical processes known to be essential for shell formation, but the two most important mechanisms are believed to be interference with the transport of calcium and of carbonate to the shell.[154]

One consequence of eggshell thinning is a tendency for eggs to crack during laying and as they are being incubated. The eggs are then eaten by the parents, often leaving the nest empty.[155] However, even eggs that do not break may not hatch, in some cases because of excessive water loss through the thinned shell.

Other effects of organochlorines

It also appeared that eggshell thinning was not the only cause of poor reproductive success in predatory birds. Breeding of affected populations was observed to be abnormally late; either no eggs were

Figure 2.17   Relationship between shell thickness and DDE residues of kestrel eggs collected in Ithaca, New York, during 1970 (dots) and same relationship experimentally induced with DDE (crosses). The shell thickness is measured on the shell index as a percentage of the index prior to DDT exposure

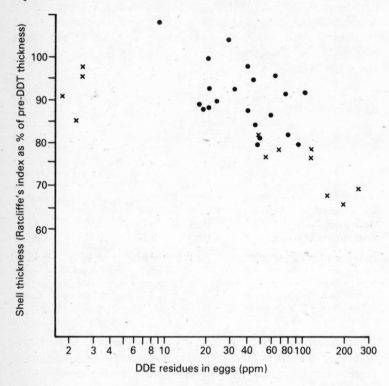

Source: Lincer, J.L., "DDE–inducced eggshell thinning in the American kestrel: a comparison of the field situation and laboratory results", in: *J. Appl. Ecol.* **12** (1975), pp. 781–793.

laid or the size of the clutch was reduced. There were increased embryo deaths and a failure by birds to lay again after loss of a clutch.[156] In some cases, embryos died as a result of direct toxicity following mobilization of pesticide residues; in others, embryos and chicks were destroyed or eaten because of the aberrant behaviour of adults.[157] Again, significant correlations were found between these effects and organochlorine pesticide content of the eggs.[158]

Most of these effects were also demonstrated in laboratory tests.[159] Experiments with raptors are difficult because of their size, but ring doves are similar in that they have altricial young (i.e. the young are hatched at an immature stage of development) and are more amenable to experimentation. Table 2.17 shows the variety of reproductive effects that can occur in doves fed a diet containing 40 ppm DDE. Hatchability does not decrease, probably because eggshell thinning is not very great. Nevertheless, the combination of reproductive effects is considerable, resulting in reproduction falling below replacement level. For comparison is a similar experiment on screech owls fed with endrin at 0.75 ppm. In this case shell thinning did not occur, but hatchability was greatly reduced.

Table 2.17   Reproductive success of ring doves and screech owls fed a diet with or without pesticide (40 ppm DDE or 0.75 ppm endrin)

| | *Doves* | | *Owls* | |
	Control	DDE-treated	Control	Endrin-treated
No. times nested/no. pairs	49/12	33/12	12/15	9/15
Mean no. eggs per clutch	2.0	1.7	4.4	4.6
Mean hatchability	0.58	0.49	0.72	0.49
Mean survival of young	0.69	0.36	0.97	1.00
Surviving offspring per pair	3.27	0.82	2.46	1.35

Source: Haegle, M.A. and Hudson, R.H., "DDE effects on reproduction of ring doves", *Environ. Pollut.* 4 (1973) pp. 53–57; Fleming, W.J., McLane, M.A.R. and Cromartie, E., "Endrin decreases screech owl productivity", *J. Wildl. Manage.* 46 (1982) pp. 462–8.

Subsequent work has now revealed a great range of sublethal effects in birds, fish and mammals.[160] They include delays in the onset of migration in white-throated sparrows, reduction in nest building activity in feral pigeons, and reduced defence of nests by herring gulls.[161] It is possible that these phenomena arise indirectly from the effects of organochlorines on the thyroid gland.

The impact on raptor populations

The effects on predator populations, in both the United States and Europe, have been very dramatic. The greatest declines occurred in bird-eating species, such as the sparrowhawk and peregrine falcon, and fish-eating species, such as the white-tailed and bald eagles. They were less marked, though, in mammal-eating species, such as the kestrel, golden eagle and buzzard.[162] Also, not all predators were affected. There were no obvious declines in numbers of small predatory mammals such as stoats and weasels, nor was there any evidence of significant effects on toads.[163] Similarly, populations of some fish-eating birds in the UK, such as the great crested grebe, were unaffected: grebe numbers actually rose in the 1950s and 1960s as a result of an increase in suitable habitats.[164] Herons in the UK had high levels of DDE and suffered eggshell thinning and breakage, but populations appear now to have recovered, perhaps because of the heron's ability to lay repeat clutches.[165]

There is still considerable controversy over the relative roles of DDE and the cyclodienes in the declines. The cyclodienes were certainly associated with large-scale incidents involving seed-eating birds and their predators, particularly in the 1950s, and DDE clearly caused shell thinning and impaired reproductive success. In general, investigators from the UK, including Ratcliffe and Newton, have concluded that adult mortality caused by dieldrin poisoning was the most important mechanism; by contrast, most North American workers have regarded DDE as the exclusive cause of the declines.[166] It could be that the situation was different in North America and Britain, but Nisbett, reviewing the timing and geographical location of peregrine population declines, together with the use of dieldrin and DDT, concluded there was no evidence of different exposure patterns. Predators in both regions were subjected to substantial amounts of DDT from 1947 and of dieldrin, in the USA from 1949 and in Britain from 1956: Nisbett argues that "the declines in some regional populations of peregrine falcons in North America were too rapid to have been caused by reproductive failure alone."[167]

It may prove impossible to clear up the controversy. Whatever the relative weights of the effects, it is clear that first, DDE had an impact upon shell thickness in the late 1940s to early 1950s, which reduced population levels by varying degrees, and secondly, that dieldrin killed adult birds, causing steep declines in numbers. One or other, or both, processes eliminated many local populations of predatory birds and greatly reduced some populations over large areas.

Patterns of recovery

DDT and the cyclodienes are now banned from agricultural use in Europe and North America; yet predatory birds still contain their residues albeit at much reduced levels (Figure 2.18). Despite the ban on spring dressings there was no sign of a significant drop in residues of HEOD, the derivate of dieldrin, in the kestrel and sparrowhawk until 1977. This was not surprising in the former case since it feeds on small mammals and thus can be affected by contaminated autumn

Figure 2.18 Changes in residues of DDE and HEOD in the livers of sparrowhawks and kestrels and proportion of total samples exceeding 100 ppm of DDE and 10 ppm of HEOD

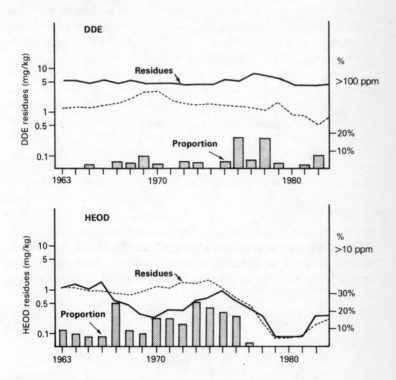

Source: Newton, I. "Uses and effects on bird population of organochlorine pesticides", in: Jenkins, D. (ed.), *Agriculture and the Environment* (Swindon: NERC, 1984).

sown seeds.[168] Some further uses of dieldrin were phased out in 1972 but it was not until 1974 that autumn seed dressing was stopped. DDT residues in the environment have been even more persistent than dieldrin, and have been slow to decline in birds of prey. In the kestrel the decline did not begin until the 1980s, while in the sparrowhawk it had barely begun by the mid-1980s.[169] Analyses of more than 1000 sparrowhawk eggs from 17 areas of Britain during 1971–80 showed that DDE residues were still present, declining to some extent in the mid-1970s but then increasing at the end of the decade.[170] Mean shell indices remained 11–20 per cent below the pre-1947 mean, and were still associated with a reduced production of young. This may have been due to the high persistence of DDT or to continued use of DDT despite it being banned.

The differences in decline of residues in predators probably reflect where they feed.[171] Pesticide levels in water will closely follow changes in pesticide use, while soil residues are likely to show a longer time lag. This may account for the rapid reduction in residues in the heron in the UK. The difference between residue declines in kestrels and sparrowhawks is probably due to the latter being a bird eater, while the former preys on mammals. In general, mammal-eating raptors tend to be less contaminated, partly because mammals are better able to metabolize organochlorines than birds but, also, because mammal prey are mostly herbivores. Many of the birds on which sparrowhawks feed will be insectivores, and this increases the number of links in the trophic chain.[172]

Figure 2.19 Bald eagle reproduction compared with DDE residues in addled eggs in northwestern Ontario, 1966–81. Dashed lines indicate weighted mean concentrations of DDE residues in clutches before (94 ppm) and after (29 ppm) the ban of DDT

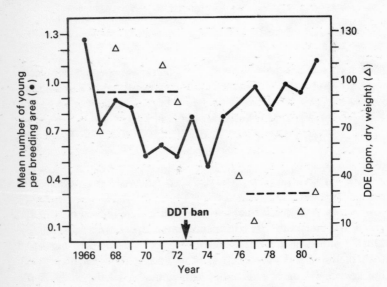

Source: Grier, J.W. "Ban of DDT and subsequent recovery of reproduction in Bald Eagles", in: *Science* **218** (1982), pp. 1232–1235.

Reductions in residue levels have also occurred in the USA. When DDT spraying to control mosquitos on the New Jersey salt-marshes was stopped in 1966, residues rapidly declined in most of the components of the food chain – aquatic snails, mussels, crabs, fish and wading birds – by as much as 84–99 per cent in 1973.[173] DDT and dieldrin in brown pelican eggs fell in South Carolina in the early 1970s from 7.8 to 1.8 μg/kg and 11.16 to 0.4 μg/kg respectively. They have also fallen, although less dramatically, in Florida, but in neither instance has there been any trend toward significantly thicker eggshells.[174] By contrast, a fall in DDT residues, from 44 to 8.1 μg/kg in the 1970s, in red-breasted merganser eggs from Lake Michigan coincided with an increase in shell thickness, up to 97 per cent of pre-1946 values.[175]

In some cases the reduction in residues correlated with increased reproductive success, but in at least one instance more rapidly than might be expected. In Canada reproductive success of the bald eagle, which migrates to the USA in winter, changed dramatically following the DDT ban (Figure 2.19). The speed of recovery was rather surprising. The persistence of DDE in the environment, and indeed in the breeding birds themselves, should have produced an effect that lasted longer after the ban had been imposed.

Figure 2.20   Present status of North American peregrine populations
A   =   areas where no significant post-DDT decline occurred
B   =   areas where complete recovery has probably occurred
C   =   areas where some degree of recovery is underway
D   =   areas where peregrines are essentially extirpated

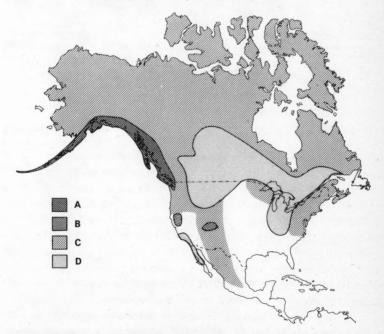

Source: Kiff, L.F. "Changes in the status of the peregrine in North America: an overview" in: Cade, T.J. et al. (eds) (1988), *op. cit.*

The sparrowhawk in the UK has also shown a rapid recovery but in this case without a reduction in DDT residues. The increase coincided with the decline in use of aldrin and dieldrin, suggesting that a reduction in mortality from HEOD was the critical factor rather than increasing breeding performance.

Numbers of the peregrine in Britain have also increased, with populations back to 1930s levels in the north and west of the country by 1981.[176] By the mid-1980s there were between 786 and 816 pairs in Britain, which compares favourably with the 1930–39 total of 820.[177] Recovery of the peregrine has occurred or has been under way in most parts of North America since the late 1970s, though in some areas the species is still not present (Figure 2.20). The most recent, post-1985, surveys suggest at least 1150 breeding pairs on the continent, a significant recovery from the low reached in 1975, but still nowhere near the pre-war levels. This pattern of improvement is closely correlated with declining residues of both HEOD and DDT, but probably it is the former factor that is critical, as in the case of the sparrowhawk.[178]

Destruction of habitat and resources

Pesticides may also directly damage the habitats and resources on which wildlife rely, for example by destroying their food or shelter. One of the most dramatic such effects has been on game birds in the UK.

Game birds

The effects on game birds were noticed relatively quickly since many farmers have an interest in them either for sport or profit. From 1952 populations began to decline, in particular of the grey partridge, a species predominantly of lowland arable landscapes.[179] Eventually the grey partridge fell to less than 20 per cent of its pre-1952 densities. One early factor was the death of adult birds through DNOC and dieldrin poisoning. But after these were withdrawn, the population continued to decline rapidly.

The cause of decline, however, has not been poisoning of the adult birds but the adverse effects of various pesticides on the partridge's food chain. Potts and his colleagues at the Game Conservancy first observed that the population decline was closely correlated with a reduction in survivability of the partridge chicks. They then showed that this was caused by decreasing densities of insects in cereal fields, such as aphids and sawfly larvae, that are the essential food of the chicks.[180] Part of this, in turn, was due to the direct effects of insecticides but also implicated was the increasing use of herbicides and fungicides in cereal fields. Weeds and fungi that constitute the food of some of the prey insects were being destroyed, and as the weeds disappeared from cereal fields, so did many of the insects crucial to partridge chick survival.[181]

The role of pesticides has recently been elegantly demonstrated in experiments carried out by the Game Conservancy. Six metre bands at the headlands of cereal fields were selectively sprayed and this resulted in sufficient insect populations remaining to increase partridge chick survival and thus brood size (Table 2.18). There was a significant increase in density of breeding birds on the experimental farms, from 3.7 pairs per km^2 in 1979 to 11.7 in 1986, increases which were not mirrored on adjacent farms where pesticide use was unchanged.[182]

Table 2.18 Grey partridge brood sizes on cereal fields with sprayed and selectively sprayed headlands, UK

| | | Average brood size | | |
| | | Sprayed | Selectively sprayed | Significance |
Study area	Year	headlands	headlands*	of difference
Hampshire	1983	4.7	8.4	$p < 0.01$
	1984	7.4	10.0	$p < 0.01$
	1985	3.3	6.2	$p < 0.05$
	1986	5.9	6.2	n.s.
	1987	5.6	6.2	n.s.
Eastern England	1984	4.7	7.8	$p < 0.001$
	1985	2.7	4.0	$p < 0.05$
	1986	4.8	8.7	$p < 0.001$
	1987	4.0	7.1	$p < 0.01$

* Selectively sprayed headlands are sprayed with herbicides that eliminate grasses and some unwelcome broad-leaf weeds such as cleavers. Remaining broad-leaf species are not killed

Source: Sotherton, N.W., "The cereals and gamebirds research project: overcoming the indirect effects of pesticides", in: Harding, D.L.J. (ed.) Britain Since 'Silent Spring' (London: Inst. of Biology, 1988).

Herbicide effects

Because herbicides are likely to destroy a wide variety of plant species over large areas they will directly, and indirectly, have a major effect on wildlife. One such example is the local destruction of birds-foot trefoil in the UK, which has resulted in the elimination of populations of the common blue butterfly whose larvae feed on the trefoil.[183] Butterflies are also encouraged by selective spraying of conservation headlands around cereal fields. In one survey, fields treated in this way had three times the number of butterflies and of the 17 species present, 13 were significantly more abundant than on fields fully sprayed.[184] The weeds are fed on by the caterpillars of butterflies and the flowers provide nectar for the adults.

Another example of the effects of herbicides is the impact, in eastern England, of the reduction in weed seeds on skylarks. The larks normally feed on weed seeds in late winter and in consequence have now turned to winter wheat.[185] Some populations of linnets deprived of weed seeds are now damaging strawberries.[186] Populations of both species have declined in recent years.

Micro-organisms, too, may be affected indirectly by herbicides. The elimination of weed cover, loss of organic matter input, and changes to the uptake of nutrients by surviving weeds, may alter the composition of soil micro-flora. There have been significant effects on nitrogen transformation in herbicide treated soils probably as a result of changes in micro-flora. On occasions there have also been falls in mineral nitrogen, but these are probably due to reductions in the populations of weeds rather than to direct effects on the micro-flora.[187]

Community effects

There have been relatively few published studies of the overall effects of pesticides on whole communities, yet their effects must be commonplace.

Grassland and forest communities

One of the earliest and most revealing accounts arose from a study of the consequences of applying carbaryl (as the trade product Sevin), a non-persistent carbamate insecticide, to one of two adjacent, one-acre blocks of semi-enclosed grassland.[188] The carbaryl only remained toxic for a few days but several long-term effects were demonstrated. The plants in the community, primarily the brown top millet, were unaffected, but the biomass and numbers of arthropods declined dramatically. After seven weeks the arthropod biomass recovered, but not the numbers (Figure 2.21). One consequence was a small but significant decrease in litter decomposition. The diversity

Figure 2.21 Effects of carbaryl (Sevin) on arthropod biomass and numbers

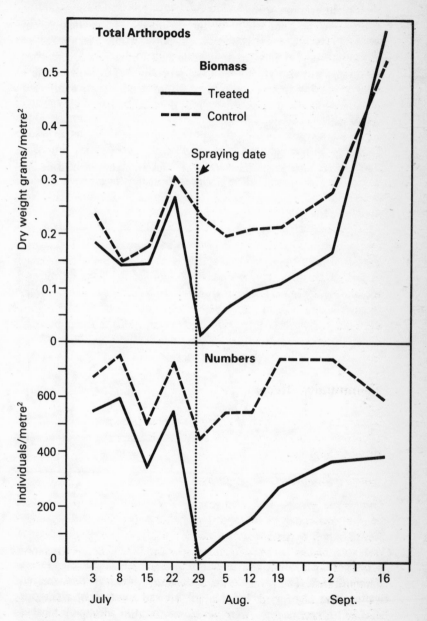

Source: Barrett, G.W. "The effects of an acute insecticide stress on a semi-enclosed grassland ecosystem" in: *Ecology* **49** (1968), pp. 1019–1035.

of arthropods also suffered but recovered quickly, at least in the case of the plant feeding species (Figure 2.22). The slower recovery of the predators was unlikely to be due to uptake of insecticide from their prey, since carbaryl is short lived, but probably was a result of a lack of prey and reduced reproduction and re-invasion. Numbers of cotton rats were also greatly reduced, probably due to a direct effect on the developing embryos. However, the house mouse was unaffected and indeed rapidly increased its population, effectively replacing the cotton rats.

Figure 2.22   Effects of carbaryl (Sevin) on community diversity. The plant feeding insects include grazing herbivores, sucking herbivores and nectar feeders. The predaceous group includes predatory bugs, beetles, flies and spiders.

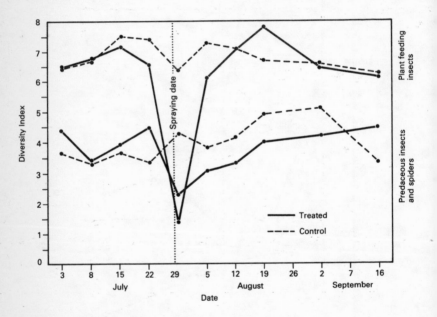

Source: Barrett, G.W. (1968), *op.cit.*

A larger scale study of the effects of the same insecticide on a forest community in New Jersey showed a decline in bird numbers, species richness and diversity which was still apparent a year later (Figure 2.23). The causes here were unknown, but the decline probably resulted from a lack of insects as food, causing poor survival of the young, and movement of the birds to new sites.

Figure 2.23   Effect of application of carbaryl (Sevin) on bird abundance, species richness, and species diversity (Shannon–Weiner index)

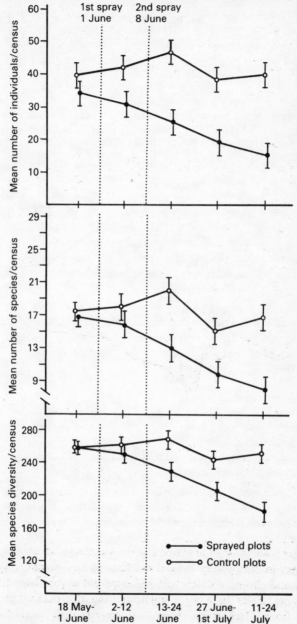

Source: Moulding, J.D., "Effects of a low-persistence insecticide on forest bird populations", *The Ark* 93 (1976), pp. 692–708.

Aquatic communities

Recently a number of studies have been conducted on model fresh-water ecosystems, using the new synthetic pyrethroids, which appear to be safe to mammals and birds but in the laboratory are toxic to fish and freshwater invertebrates.[189]

As part of an environmental assessment process[190] Crossland at Shell Research Ltd constructed a series of 50 m^3 artificial ponds which were allowed to develop to mature ecosystems, with aquatic plants, algae, amphibia and fish (rudd and tench), and a considerable variety of invertebrates. The ponds were then treated with pyrethroid insecticide at a high rate.[191] No effects were observed on the fish and amphibia, probably because the insecticide becomes quickly bound onto suspended solids in the water. However the invertebrates were affected, although they had largely recovered 15 weeks later (Figure 2.24). Slowest to recover were the zooplankton, which then exploded to levels above those in the treated ponds. The biggest effect on the community was the reduction in grazing on the algae, because of the deaths of algal feeding invertebrates such as mayfly larvae. As a consequence algae built up to a dense mat, inhibiting the penetration of light and causing oxygen depletion.

But further studies in the field showed no effects on aquatic life at levels of contamination that result from spray drift under normal operating conditions.[192] This seems to be confirmed by a study of the effects of aerial application of the pyrethroid permethrin to a forest stream.[193]

Summary

That pesticides cause harm to wildlife is hardly surprising since they are, by design, biocides. Their benefits, in terms of controlling pests, diseases and weeds and the ensuing increases in crop yields, are considerable; but their costs, in terms of wildlife damage, are also high, and indeed higher than might be expected. This is for a number of reasons.

Firstly, most pesticides have been, and still are, poorly selective. Although selectivity is in theory and practice achievable, economic incentives favour the production of broad spectrum compounds.

Secondly, there has been a dramatic increase in pesticide use in recent years. Costs have been low in relation to the perceived or actual benefits. Potential yields have increased because of the introduction of

Figure 2.24 Effect of cypermethrin on aquatic invertebrates in an artificial pond

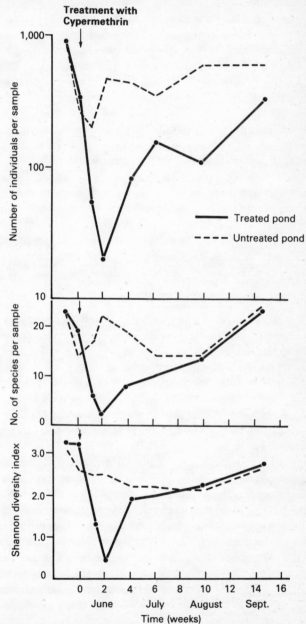

Source: Crossland, N.O., "Aquatic toxicology of cypermethrin II", in: *Aquatic Toxicology* 2 (1982), pp. 205-222.

high yielding crop varieties, the expansion of irrigation and increasing mechanization. The "insurance" use of pesticides has also grown, reflecting the risk-averse nature of most farmers who try and avert the worst possible loss from pests by scheduled spraying. On high-value market crops, such as fruits and vegetables, heavy spraying is common to meet the consumer demands for perfect quality. Finally, pesticide contamination is increased by such practices as aerial spraying and the failure among operators to wear protective clothing or take appropriate precautions.

In the environment, pesticide that is not microbially or chemically degraded either remains in the soil, is vaporized to be deposited as rainfall, or is dispersed via surface and groundwaters. Many of the older organochlorines are particularly persistent. DDT and its metabolites can have half-lives in the soil of more than 50 years. But the problem is not confined to the organochlorines. Recently, groundwater in the industrialized countries has been found to be widely contaminated with modern herbicides and nematocides. One of the latter, aldicarb, has become a common contaminant of aquifers below potato fields and citrus orchards. It has a very long half-life when the pH is low.

The evidence for serious damage to wildlife by pesticides in both the developed and developing countries is well documented. Pesticides may directly kill honeybees foraging in sprayed crops, or earthworms living in the soil, or fish and other aquatic fauna and flora. However, some of the most dramatic effects have come, indirectly, from the contamination of the food sources of wild animals. In the 1950s and 1960s there were widespread deaths of grain-eating birds that were eating cereal seed dressed with organochlorines, and of predatory birds and mammals through feeding on contaminated prey. In some cases the prey have been directly poisoned, for example in Malaysia, rats treated with rodenticides that have in turn caused deaths of owls.

Beginning in the 1950s populations of many predatory birds – eagles, ospreys, sparrowhawks and others – began to fall. The most dramatic decline was in the peregrine falcon that was virtually eliminated in many parts of North America and Europe. Part of the cause was the deaths of adult birds due to uptake of dieldrin but another factor was the presence of high residues of organochlorines, and particularly DDT in eggs that resulted directly in eggshell thinning and hence a high incidence of breakage. Organochlorines have also had more subtle effects on behaviour and physiology that have contributed to lower reproductive success.

Fortunately most of the affected predatory bird populations have recovered in recent years, following the bans on use of organochlorines. Residues in adult tissues and in eggs have declined, although not in all cases. Dieldrin, DDT and its metabolites have proven particularly persistent. While peregrine falcons have returned to 1930 levels in the UK they have not recovered to the same extent in the USA.

With the phasing out of organochlorines it was thought that pesticide effects on wildlife would greatly diminish or even disappear. But despite significant improvements damage is still occurring and is attributable to modern compounds. Examples include: the deaths of geese from eating cereal seed treated with the organophosphate, carbophenothion; the deaths of red-tailed hawks after feeding on magpies contaminated with the organophosphate, famphur; and large population declines in game birds because of reductions in the insect food of the young birds caused by modern herbicides and fungicides as well as insecticides. Experiments have also shown very far-ranging effects in grassland and forest communities of treatments with the carbamate insecticide, carbaryl. The new pyrethroids can produce similar effects in aquatic communities when applied at high dosages, but apparently not at normal field application rates.

References

1 Bray, F., "Part II. Agriculture", in: Needham, J., *Science and Civilisation in China*, vol. 6, *Biology and Biological Technology* (Cambridge: Cambridge University Press, 1984); Flint, M.L. and van den Bosch, R., *Introduction to Integrated Pest Management* (New York and London: Plenum Press, 1981).

2 BAA, *Annual Report and Handbook 1988–89*, (Peterborough: British Agrochemicals Association, 1989).

3 Patton, S., Craig, I. and Conway, G.R., "The pesticide industry", in: Conway, G.R. (ed.), *Pesticide Resistance and World Food Production* (London: Imperial College, 1982).

4 ADB, *Handbook in the Use of Pesticides in the Asia-Pacific Region*, (Manila: Asian Development Bank, 1987); Balk, I.F. and Koeman, J.H., *Future Hazards for Pesticide Use*, Commission of Ecology Papers (Geneva: IUCN, 1984).

5 BAA, 1989, *op. cit.*; Patton et al., 1982, *op. cit.*

6 ADB, 1987, *op. cit.*

7 Green, M.B., Hartley, G.S. and West, T.F., *Chemicals for Crop Improvement and Pest Management* (Oxford: Pergamon Press, 3rd edn, 1987).

8 Gilbert, D.G.R., "Pesticide Safety Policy and Control Arrangements in Britain", PhD Thesis (University of London: Centre for Environmental

Technology, Imperial College, 1987); Royal Commission on Environmental Pollution (RCEP), *Agriculture and Pollution* (London: HMSO, 1979); 7th Report, Conway, G. (ed.), *Pesticide Resistance and World Food Production* (London: Imperial College, 1982).

9   NRC, *Regulating Pesticides in Food. The Delaney Paradox* (Washington DC: National Research Council, 1987).

10 Nix, J., *Farm Management Pocketbook* (London: Wye College, 1989).

11 Tarrant, J., Barbier, E., Greenburg, R.J., Higgins, M.L., Lintner, S.F., Mackie, C., Murphy, L. and van Veldhuizen, H., *Natural Resources and Environmental Management in Indonesia* (Jakarta, Indonesia: US Agency for International Development, 1987).

12 Repetto, R., *Paying the Price: Pesticide Subsidies in Developing Countries* Research Report 2, (Washington: World Resources Institute, 1985).

13 Kenmore, P., Litsinger, J.A., Bandong, J.P., Santiago, A.C. and Salac, M.M., "Philippine rice farmers and insecticides: thirty years of growing dependency and new options for change", in: Tait, E.J. and Napompeth, B. (eds), *Management of Pests and Pesticides: Farmers' Perceptions and Practices* (London: West View Press, 1987).

14 Tarrant et al., 1987, *op. cit.*

15 Norton, G.A. and Mumford, J.D., "Decision making in pest control", *Adv. Appl. Biol.* 8 (1983) pp. 87–119; Loevinsohn, M.E., "The Ecology and Control of Rice Pests: With Reference to the Intensity and Synchrony of Cultivation", PhD Thesis (University of London: Imperial College, 1984).

16 Norton and Mumford, 1983, *op. cit.*

17 Mumford, J.D., "Perceptions of losses from pests of arable crops by some farmers in England and New Zealand", *Crop Protection* 1 (1982) pp. 283–8.

18 Mumford, 1982, *op. cit.*

19 Pingali, P.L. and Carlson, G.A., "Human capital, adjustments to subjective probabilities and the demand for pest control", *Am. J. Agric. Econ.* 67 (1985) pp. 853–61.

20 Mumford, 1982, *op. cit.*

21 Kenmore et al., 1987, *op. cit.*

22 Norton and Mumford, 1983, *op. cit.*

23 Zaidi, I.H., "Farmer perception and management of pest hazard. A pilot study of a Punjabi village in lower Indus Region", *Insect Sci. Applic.* 5 (1984) pp. 187–201.

24 Norton and Mumford, 1983, *op. cit.*

25 Morita, K., "The disease and insect pest occurrence forecast program in Japan", paper presented to 11th Session of the FAO/UNEP Panel of Experts on Integrated Pest Control, Kuala Lumpur (Rome: FAO, March 1982).

26 Fagoonee, I., "Pertinent aspects of pesticide usage in Mauritius", *Insect Sci. Applic.* 5 (1984) pp. 203–12.

27 RCEP, 1979, *op. cit.*

28 Fenemore, P.G. and Norton, G.A., "Problems of implementing improvements in pest control: a case study of apples in the UK", *Crop Protection* 4 (1985) pp. 51–70.

29 Tait, E.J., "Pest control decision making on brassica crops", *Adv. Appl. Biol.* 8 (1983) pp. 121–88.

30 Pimentel, D., Terhune, E.C., Dritschilo, W., Gallahan, D., Kinner, N., Nafus, D., Peterson, R., Zareh, N., Misiti, J. and Haber-Schaim, O., "Pesticides, insects in foods, and cosmetic standards", *BioScience* 27 (1977) pp. 178–85.

31 Pimentel et al., 1977, *op. cit.*

32 RCEP, 1979, *op. cit.*

33 Matthews, G., *Pesticide Application Methods* (London and New York: Longman, 1979).

34 ICAITI, *An Environmental and Economic Study of the Consequences of Pesticide Use in Central American Cotton Production* (Guatemala City, Guatemala: Instituto Centroamericano de Investigacion y Technologia Industrial, 1977).

35 Bull, D., *A Growing Problem, Pesticides and the Third World Poor* (Oxford: Oxfam, 1982); Matthews, G.A. and Clayphon, J.E., "Safety precautions for pesticide application in the tropics", *PANS* 19 (1973) pp. 1–12.

36 Staiff, D.C., David, J.E. and Stevens, E.R., "Evaluation of various clothing materials for protection and worker acceptability during application of pesticides", *Arch. Environ. Contam. Toxicol.* 11 (1982) pp. 391–8; Adamis, Z., Antal, A., Fuzesi, I., Molnar, J., Nagy, L. and Susan, M., "Occupational exposure to organophosphorus insecticides and synthetic pyrethroid", *Int. Arch. Occup. Environ. Health* 56 (1985) pp. 299–305.

37 Jones, R.D., "Organophosphorus poisoning at a chemical packaging company", *Br. J. Indust. Med.* 39 (1982) pp. 377–81.

38 Bonsall, J.L., "Measurement of occupational exposure to pesticides", in: Turnbull, G.J. (ed.), *Occupational Hazards of Pesticide Use* (London: Taylor and Francis, 1985).

39 Kurtz, P.H., Shaw, G., Kelter, A. and Jackson, R.J., "Assessment of potential acute health effects in agricultural workers exposed during the application of chlordimeform", *J. Occup. Med.* 29 (1987) pp. 593–5.

40 Jeyeratnam, J., Lun, K.C. and Phoon, W.O., "Survey of acute pesticide poisoning among agricultural workers in four Asian countries", *Bull. WHO* 65 (1987) pp. 521–27.

41 Fagoonee, 1984, *op. cit.*

42 Bull, 1982, *op. cit.*

43 Richards, R.P., Kramer, J.W., Baker, D.B. and Krieger, K.A., "Pesticides in rainwater in the northeastern United States", *Nature* 237 (1987) pp. 129–31.

44 Anderson, A., "It's raining pesticides in Hokkaido", *Nature* 320 (1986) p. 478.

45 Glotfelty, D.E., Seiber, J.N. and Liljedhal, L.A., "Pesticides in fog", *Nature* 325 (1987) pp. 602–605.

46   Strachan. W.M.J. and Edwards, C.J., "Organic pollutants in Lake Ontario", in: Nriagu, J.O. and Simmons, M.S. (eds), *Toxic Contaminants in the Great Lakes* (New York: John Wiley and Sons, 1984).

47   Richards et al., 1987, *op. cit.*

48   Wauchope, R.D., "The pesticide content of surface water draining from agricultural fields – a review", *J. Env. Quality* 7(4) (1978), pp. 459–72.

49   Hallberg, G.R., "Agricultural chemicals in groundwater: extent and implications", *Am. J. Altern. Agric.* 2 (1978) pp. 3–13.

50   National Research Council, *Alternative Agriculture, Committee on the Role of Alternative Farming Methods In Modern Production Agriculture*, (Washington DC: National Academy Press, 1989).

51   Baker, D.B., "Regional water quality impacts of intensive row-crop agriculture: Lake Erie basin case study", *J. Soil. Water Conserv.* 40 (1985) pp. 125–32.

52   ENDS, "Surveys of pesticides, chlorinated compounds in surface waters" 150 (1987) pp. 6–7.

53   ENDS, "New solvent spills hits East Anglian aquifer", 149 (1987) p.5.

54   WAA, *Water Pollution from Farm Waste. 1985, 1986* (London: Water Authorities Association, 1986, 1987).

55   Beyer, W.N. and Gish, C.D., "Persistence in earthworms and potential hazards to birds of soil applied DDT, dieldrin and heptachlor", *J. Appl. Ecol.* 17 (1980) pp. 295–308.

56   Buck, N.A., Estesen, B.J. and Warr, G.W., "DDT moratorium in Arizona: residues in soil and alfalfa after 12 years", *Bull. Environ. Contam. Toxicol* 13 (1982) pp. 61–72; Cooke, B.K. and Stringer, A., "Distribution and breakdown of DDT in an orchard soil", *Pesticide Science* 13 (1982) pp. 545–51.

57   Newton, I., "Uses and effects on bird populations of organochlorine pesticides", in: Jenkins, D. (ed.), *Agriculture and the Environment*, Proceedings of the thirteenth ITE Symposium 28–29 February and 1 March 1984, (Swindon:NERC/ITE, 1984).

58   Shin, Y.O., Chodan, J.J. and Wolcott, A.R., "Absorption of DDT by soils, soil fraction and biological materials", *J. Agric. Food Chem.* 18 (1970) pp. 1129–133.

59   Wheatley, G.A., "The assessment and persistence of residues of organochlorine insecticides in soils and their uptake by crops", *Ann. appl. Biol.* 55 (1965) pp. 325–29.

60   Lawrence, A.R. and Foster, S.S.D., *The Pollution Threat from Agricultural Pesticides and Industrial Solvents: a Comparative Review in Relation to British Aquifers.* Hydrogeological Report of the British Geological Survey no. 87/2 (Oxfordshire: Wallingford, BGS 1987).

61   Lawrence and Foster, 1987, *op. cit.*; Holden, P.W., *Pesticides and Groundwater Quality. Issues and Problems in Four States* (Washington DC: National Academy Press, National Research Council, 1986).

62   Holden, 1986, *op. cit.*

63   Lawrence and Foster, 1987, *op. cit.*; Warner, M.E., *An Environmental*

Risk Index To Evaluate Pesticide Programs in Crop Budgets (Ithaca, New York: Cornell University, Dept. of Agric. Econ., 1985).

64 Holden, 1986, *op. cit.*; Nielson, E.G. and Lee, L.K., "The Magnitude and Costs of Groundwater Contamination from Agricultural Chemicals", Economic Research Service, Agric. Econ. Rep. **576** (Washington: USDA, 1986).

65 HC, *The Effects of Pesticides on Human Health*, vol. 1, Report and Proceedings of the House of Commons Select Committee on Agriculture (London: HMSO, 1987).

66 Lawrence and Foster, 1987, *op. cit.*; Headworth, H.G., "Contamination of groundwater from diffuse sources arising from farming activities", *J. IWEM* (Oct 3, 1989) pp. 517–21; Croll, B.T., "Pesticides and other organic chemicals. Symposium on Catchment Quality Control", *J. IWEM* (April 1988).

67 HC, 1987, *op. cit.*

68 Lawrence and Foster, 1987, *op. cit.*; HC, 1987, *op. cit.*

69 Lawrence and Foster, 1987, *op. cit.*

70 Zaki, M.H., Moran, D. and Harris, D., "Pesticides in groundwater: the aldicarb story in Suffolk County, New York", *Am. J. Publ. Health* **72** (1982) pp. 1391–95; Warner, 1985, *op. cit.*

71 Holden, 1986, *op. cit.*; Zaki et al., 1982, *op. cit.*

72 Holden, 1986, *op. cit.*

73 Warner, 1985, *op. cit.*

74 Nielson and Lee, 1986, *op. cit.*; Holden, 1986, *op. cit.*

75 Holden, 1986, *op. cit.*

76 Flint and van den Bosch, 1981, *op. cit.*

77 CDFA, in: Flint and van den Bosch, 1981, *op. cit.*; Johansen, C.A., "Pesticides and pollinators", *Annual Review of Entomology* **22** (1977) pp. 177–92.

78 Johansen, 1977, *op. cit.*

79 Johansen, 1977, *op. cit.*

80 Gilbert, 1987, *op. cit.*

81 Johansen, 1977, *op. cit.*

82 Shires, S.W., "Pesticides and honey bees. Case studies with Ripcord and Fastac", *Span* **26** (1983) pp. 118–20; Murray, A., "Acute and residual toxicity of a new pyrethroid insecticide, WL 85871, to honey bees", *Bull. Environ. Contam. Toxicol.* **34** (1985) pp. 560–64.

83 Sotherton, N.W., Moreby, S.J., and Langley, M.G., "The effect of the foliar fungicide pyrazophos on beneficial arthropods in barley fields. *Ann. appl. Biol.* **111**(1987), pp. 75–87.

84 Edwards, C.A. and Thompson, A.R. "Pesticides and the soil fauna", *Residue Reviews* **45** (1973) pp. 1–79.

85 WHO, *DDT and its derivatives – environmental aspects*, Environmental Health Criteria 83 (Geneva: WHO, 1989).

86 Royal Society of Chemistry, *The Agrochemicals Handbook* (Nottingham: 1987); Madge, D.S., "Influence of agricultural practice on soil inver-

tebrate animals", in: Stonehouse, B. (ed.), *Biological Husbandry* (London: Butterworth, 1981); Edwards, C.A., "Changes in agricultural practice and their impact on soil organisms", in: Jenkins, D. (ed.), *Agriculture and the Environment* (Swindon: NERC/ITE, 1984).

87   Eigsackers, H. and van der Drift, J., "Effects on the soil fauna", in: Andus, L.J. (ed.), *Herbicide Physiology, Biochemistry, Ecology* (New York: Academic Press, 1976).

88   Somerville, L. and Greaves, M.P. (eds), *Pesticide Effects on Soil Microflora* (London: Taylor and Francis, 1987); Greaves, M.P., "Side-effects testing: an alternative approach", in: Somerville and Greaves (eds), 1987, *op. cit.*

89   Leake, C.R. and Arnold, D.J., "Nitrogen transformations: practical aspects of laboratory testing", in: Somerville and Greaves (eds), 1987, *op. cit.*

90   Horemans, S., De Coninck, K., Dressen, R. and Vlassak, K., "Symbiotic nitrogen fixation", in: Somerville and Greaves (eds), 1987, *op. cit.*

91   Haley, T.J., "Review of the toxicology of paraquat", *Clin. Toxicol.* **14** (1979) pp. 1–46; Curry, J.F., "The effects of different methods of new sward establishment and the effects of the herbicide paraquat and dalapon on the soil fauna", *Pedobiologia* **10** (1970) pp. 329–61; Riley, D., Wilkinson, W. and Tucker, B.V., "Biological unavailability of bound paraquat residues in soil", in: Kaufman, D.P. et al. (eds), *Bound and Conjugated Pesticide Residues*, ACS Symposium Series no. 29 (1976).

92   WHO, 1989, *op. cit.*

93   Anderson, J.M., "Assessment of effects of pollutants on physiology and behaviour", *Proc. Roy. Soc. Lond. B* **177** (1971) pp. 307–320.

94   Anderson, J.M., "Effect of sub-lethal DDT on the lateral line of brook trout *Salvelinus fontinalis*", *J. Fish Res. Bd. Can.* **25** (1968) pp. 2677–82; Anderson, J.M. and Peterson, M.R., "DDT: sublethal effects on brook trout nervous system", *Science* **164** (1969) pp. 440–41.

95   Sanders, J.W., "Mass mortalities and behaviour of brook trout and juvenile Atlantic salmon in a stream polluted by agricultural pesticides", *J. Fish. Res. Bd. Can.* **26** (1969) pp. 695–9.

96   Barnes, J.M. et al., quoted in Crosson, P.R. and Brubaker, S. 1982. *Resource and Environmental Effects of US Agriculture* (Washington DC: Resources For The Future, 1979).

97   Glynn, P.W., Howard, L.S., Concoran, E. and Freay, A.D., "The occurrence and toxicity of herbicides in reef building corals", *Mar. Poll. Bull.* **15** (1984) pp. 370–74.

98   Young, A., *A General Review of the Agriculture of Norfolk* (London: Board of Agriculture, 1804).

99   Sheail, J., *Pesticides and Nature Conservation. The British Experience 1950–1975* (Oxford: Clarendon Press, 1985); Potts, G.R., *The Partridge. Pesticides, Predation and Conservation* (London: Collins, 1986).

100   Flickinger, E.L., "Effects of aldrin exposure on snow geese in Texas rice fields", *J. Wildl. Manage.* **43** (1979) pp. 94–101; Flickinger, E.L. and

King, K.A., "Some effects of aldrin-treated rice on Gulf Coast wildlife", *J. Wildl. Manage.* **36** (1972) pp. 706–727.

101 Stanley, P.I. and Bunyan, P.J., "Hazards to wintering geese and other wildlife from the use of dieldrin, chlorfenvinphos and carbophenothion as wheat seed treatments", *Proc. R. Soc. Lond.* B **205** (1979) pp. 31–45.

102 Hamilton, G.A., Hunter, K., Ritchie, A.S., Ruthven, A.D., Brown, P.M. and Stanley P.I., "Poisoning of wild geese by carbophenothion-treated winter wheat", *Pesticide Science* **7** (1976) pp. 175–83.

103 Stanley and Bunyan, 1979, *op. cit.*

104 Hardy, A.R. and Stanley, P.I., "The impact of commercial agriculture use of organophosphorus and carbamate pesticides on British wildlife", in: Jenkins, D. (ed.) *Agriculture and the Environment*, Proceedings of the thirteenth ITE Symposium, 28–29 February and 1 March (Swindon: NERC/ITE, 1984).

105 Potts, 1986, *op. cit.*

106 Barker, R.J., "Notes on some ecological effects of DDT sprayed on elms", *J. Wildl. Manage.* **22** (1958) pp. 269–74

107 Scott, T.G., Willis, Y.L. and Ellis, J.A., "Some effects of a field application of dieldrin on wildlife," *J. Wildl. Manage.* **23** (1959) pp. 409–27; Luckmann, W.H., and Decker, G.C., "A 5-year report of observation in the Japanese beetle control area at Sheldon, Illinois", *J. Econ. Entomol.* **53** (1960) pp. 821–27.

108 Lockie, J.D., Ratcliffe, D.A. and Balharry, R., "Breeding success and dieldrin contamination of golden eagles in west Scotland", *J. App. Ecol.* **6** (1969) pp. 81–89; Newton, I., "Birds of prey in Scotland: some conservation problems", *Scot. Birds* **7** (1972) pp. 5–23.

109 Marquiss, M., Ratcliffe, D.A., and Roxburgh, "The number, breeding success and diet of Golden Eagles in southern Scotland in relation to changes in land use", *Biol. Conserv.* **34** (1985) pp. 121–40.

110 White, D.H., King, K.A., Mitchell, C.A., Hill, E.T. and Lamont, T.G., "Parathion causes secondary poisoning in a laughing gull breeding colony", *Bull. Environ. Contam. Toxicol.* **23** (1979) pp. 281–84.

111 *Farmers Weekly*, (London) 23 March 1990 p.19.

112 Mendelssohn, H. and Paz, U., "Mass mortality of birds of prey caused by azodrin, an organophosphorus insecticide", *Biol. Conserv.* **11** (1977) pp. 163–70.

113 Newton, 1979, *op. cit.*

114 MAFF/ADAS, "Secondary toxicity to owls from difenacoum", *Research and Development Report: Pesticide Science 1981*, Ref. Book of MAFF **252** (London: HMSO, 1982) pp. 36–38; Mendenhall, V.M. and Pank, L.F., "Secondary poisoning of owls by anticoagulant rodenticides", *Wildl. Soc. Bull.* **8** (1980) pp. 311–15.

115 Shawyer, C.R., *Rodenticides: a Review and Assessment of their Potential Hazard to Non-target Wildlife with Special Reference to the Barn Owl* (Tyto alba), Report to the Hawk Trust (London: The Hawk Trust 1985).

116 Merson, M.H., Byers, R.E. and Kankeinen, D.E., "Residues of the

rodenticide brodifacoum in voles and raptors after orchard treatment", *J. Wildl. Manage.* **48** (1984) pp. 212–16.

117 Duckett, J.E., "Barn owls (*Tyto alba*) and the second generation rat-baits utilised in oil palm plantations in Peninsular Malaysia", *Planter Kualar Lumpur* **60** (1984) pp. 3–11.

118 Shawyer, C., *The Barn Owl in the British Isles* (London: The Hawk Trust, 1987).

119 Shawyer, 1987, *op. cit*; Smal, C.M., "The diet of the barn owl *Tyto alba* in southern Ireland, with reference to recently introduced prey species – the Bank Vole – *Clethrionomys glareolus*", *Bird Study* **34** (1987) pp. 113–25.

120 Shawyer, 1987, *op. cit.*

121 Advisory Committee on Pesticides, *Annual Report 1984* (London: HMSO 1985); Duckett, 1984, *op. cit.*

122 Jefferies, D.J. and Davis, B.N.K., "The dynamics of dieldrin in soil, earthworms and song thrushes", *J. Wildl. Manage.* **32** (1968) pp. 441–56.

123 Henny, C.J., Blus, L.J., Kolbe, E.J. and Fitzner, R.E., "Organophosphate insecticide (famphur) topically applied to cattle kills magpies and hawks", *J. Wildl. Manage.* **49** (1985) pp. 648–58.

124 Cramp, S., Conder, P.J. and Ash, J.S., *Deaths of Birds and Mammals from Toxic Chemicals, Jan-June 1961*, the second report of the joint committee of the British Trust for Ornithology and the Royal Society for the Protection of Birds on toxic chemicals, in collaboration with the Game Research Association (Sandy: RSPB, 1962); Turtle, E.E., Taylor, A., Wright, E.N., Thearle, R.J.P., Egan, H., Evans, W.H. and Soutar, N.M., "The effects on birds of certain chlorinated insecticides used as seed dressings", *Journal Sci. Food Agric.* **14** (1963) pp. 567–77.

125 Blackmore, D.K., "The toxicity of some chlorinated hydrocarbon insecticides to British wild foxes (*Vulpes vulpes*)", *J. Comp. Path. Ther.* **73** (1963) pp. 391–409; Jeffries, D.J., "Causes of badger mortality in eastern counties of England", *J. Zool., London* **157** (1969) pp. 429–36.

126 Sheail, 1985, *op. cit.*

127 Jefferies, D.J. and Pendlebury, J.B., "Population fluctuations of stoats, weasels and hedgehogs in recent years", *J. Zool., London* **156** (1968) pp. 513–17.

128 Mason, C.F., Ford, T.C. and Last, N.I., "Organochlorine residues in British otters", *Bull. Environ. Contam. Toxicol.* **36** (1986) pp. 656–61.

129 McDonald, S.M., "The status of the otter (*Lutra lutra*) in the British Isles", *Mammal Rev.* **13** (1983) pp. 11–23.

130 WHO, 1989, *op. cit*; Jefferies, D.J., "Organochlorine insecticide residues in British bats and their significance", *J. Zool., London* **166** (1972) pp. 245–63.

131 Stebbings, R.E., *Conservation of European Bats* (London: Christopher Helm, 1988); Racey, P.A. and Swift, S.M., "The residual effects of remedial timber treatments on bats", *Biol. Conserv.* **35** (1986)

pp. 205–214; Mitchell–Jones, A.J., Cooke, A.S., Boyd, I.L., and Stebbings, R.E., "Bats and remedial timber treatment chemicals – a review", *Mammal Rev.* **19** (1989) pp. 93–110.

132 Andreasen, J.K., "Insecticide resistance in mosquito fish of the Lower Rio Grande Valley of Texas – an ecological hazard?", *Arch. Environ. Contam. Toxicol.* **14** (1985) pp. 573–77.

133 Rosato, P. and Ferguson, D.E., "The toxicity of endrin-resistant mosquito fish to eleven species of vertebrates", *BioScience* **18** (1986) pp. 783–4; Finley, M.T., Ferguson, D.E. and Ludke, J.L., "Possible selective mechanisms in the development of insecticide-resistant fish", *Pest. Monit. J.* **4** (1970) pp. 212–18.

134 Vermeer, K., Risebrough, R.W., Spaans, A.L. and Reynolds, L.M., "Pesticides effects on fishes and birds in rice fields of Surinam, South America" *Environ. Pollut.* **7** (1974) pp. 217–36.

135 Everaarts, J.M., Koeman, J.H. and Brader, L., "Contribution à l'étude des effets sur quelques éléments de la faune sauvage des insecticides organo-chlores utilisés au Tchad en culture cotonnière", *Coton. Fibr. Trop. Bull. Analyt.* **26** (1971) pp. 385–94.

136 Kiff, L.F., "Changes in the status of the peregrine in North America. An overview", in: Cade, T.J., Enderson, J.H., Thelander, C.G. and White, C.M. (eds), *Peregrine Falcon Populations. Their Management and Recovery* (Boise, Idaho: The Peregrine Fund, Inc. 1988); Ratcliffe, D.A., *The Peregrine Falcon* (Berkhampstead: Poyser, 1980).

137 Ratcliffe, 1980, *op. cit.*

138 Kiff, 1988, *op. cit.*

139 Hickey, J., "Some recollections about eastern North America's peregrine falcon population crash", in: Cade et al. (eds), *op. cit.*

140 Hickey, 1988, *op. cit.*

141 Stafford, "The heron population of England and Wales, 1928– 1970", *Bird Study* **18** (1971) pp. 218–21.

142 Reynolds, C.M., "The census of heronries 1969–73", *Bird Study* **21** (1974) pp. 129–134; Reynolds, C.M., "The heronries census: 1972–1977 population changes and a review", *Bird Study* **26** (1979) pp. 7–12.

143 Jefferies, D.J., and Prestt, I., "Post-mortems of peregrines and lanners with particular reference to organochlorine residues", *British Birds* **59** (1966) pp. 49–64.

144 Murton, R.K. and Visozo, M., "Dressed cereal seed as a hazard to woodpigeons", *Ann. Appl. Biol.* **52** (1963) pp. 503–517; Jefferies and Prestt, 1966, *op. cit.*

145 Jefferies, D.J., Stainsby, B. and French, M.C., "The ecology of small mammals in arable fields drilled with winter wheat and the increase in their dieldrin and mercury residues", *J. Zool., London* **17** (1973) pp. 513–39.

146 Jefferies et al., 1973, *op. cit.*

147 Ratcliffe, D.A., "Broken eggs in peregrine eyries", *British Birds* **51** (1958) pp. 23–6.

148 Peakall, D.B., Reynolds, L.M. and French, M.C., "DDE in eggs of the peregrine falcon", *Bird Study* 23 (1976) pp. 183–6; Ratcliffe, 1980, *op. cit.*

149 Hickey and Anderson, 1968, *op. cit.*

150 Newton, I., *Population Ecology of Raptors* (Berkhamsted: Poyser, 1979).

151 Hickey and Anderson, 1968, *op. cit.*

152 WHO, 1989, *op. cit.*

153 WHO, 1989, *op. cit.*

154 Lundholm, E., "Thinning of eggshells in birds by DDE: mode of action on the eggshell gland", *Comp. Biochem. Physiol.* 88c (1987) pp. 1–22; Peakall, D.B., "*p,p'*-DDE: Effect on calcium metabolism and concentration of estradiol in the blood", *Science* 168 (1970) pp. 392–4.

155 Ratcliffe, D.A., "Changes attributable to pesticides in egg breakage frequency and eggshell thickness in some British birds", *J. Appl. Ecol.* 7 (1970) pp. 67–107; Newton, I., "Breeding of sparrowhawks (*Accipiter nisus*) in different environments", *J. Anim. Ecol.* 45 (1976) pp. 831–49.

156 Ratcliffe, D., 1970, *op. cit.*; Ratcliffe, 1980, *op. cit.*; Newton, 1974, *op. cit.*; Newton, 1979, *op. cit.*

157 Cooke, 1973, *op. cit.*

158 Newton, I., and Bogan, J., "The role of different organochlorine compounds in the breeding of British sparrowhawks", *J. Appl. Ecol.* 15 (1978) pp. 105–116.

159 Lincer, J.L., "DDE-induced eggshell thinning in the American kestrel: a comparison of the field situation and laboratory results", *J. Appl. Ecology* 12 (1975) pp. 781–93; Porter, R.D., and Wiemeyer, S.N., "Dieldrin and DDT: effects on sparrowhawk eggshells and reproduction", *Science* 165 (1969) pp. 199–200.

160 WHO, 1989, *op. cit.*

161 Mahoney, J.J., "DDT and DDE effects on migratory condition in white-throated sparrows", *J. Wildl. Manage.* 39 (1975) pp. 520–7; Fox, G.A., Gilman, A.P., Peakall, D.B. and Anderka, F.W., "Behavioural abnormalities of nesting Lake Ontario herring gulls", *J. Wildl. Manage.* 42 (1978) pp. 477-83.

162 Newton, 1979, *op. cit.*

163 Jefferies and Pendlebury, 1968, *op. cit.*; Cooke, A.S., "Indications of recent changes in status in the British Isles of the frog and toad", *J. Zool. London.* 167 (1968) pp. 161–78.

164 Prestt, I. and Jeffries, D.J., "Winter numbers, breeding success, and organochlorine residues in the great crested grebe in Britain", *Bird Study* 16 (1969) pp. 168–85.

165 Prestt, I., "Organochlorine pollution of rivers and the heron (*Ardea cinerea* L.)", Pap. Proc. Tech. Meet. Int. Un. Conserv. Nat. Nat. Resourc. 11th, New Delhi 1969, (Morges: IUCN, 1970) Vol. 1, pp. 95–102; Cooke, A.S., Bell, A.A. and Prestt, I., "Eggshell characteristics and incidence of shell breakage for grey herons *Ardea cinerea* exposed to environmental pollutants", *Environ. Pollut.* 11 (1976) pp. 59–84.

166 Nisbett, I.C.T. "The relative importance of DDE and dieldrin on the decline of the peregrine falcon populations", in: Cade et al., (eds), 1988, *op. cit.*; Ratcliffe, 1980, *op. cit.*; Newton, I., *The Sparrowhawks* (Berkhamsted: Poyser, 1986); Cade, T.J., Lincer, J.L., White, C.M., Roseneau, D.G. and Swartz, L.G., "DDE residues and eggshell thinning changes in Alaskan falcons and hawks", *Science* 172 (1971) pp. 955–7; Peakall, D.B. and Kiff, L.F., "Eggshell thinning and DDE residue levels among peregrine falcons *Falco peregrinus*: a global perspective", *Ibis* 121 (1979) pp. 200–204; Peakall, D.B. and Kiff, L.F., "DDE contamination in peregrines and American kestrels and its effect on reproduction" in: Cade et al., (eds), 1988, *op. cit.*; Fyfe, R.W., Temple, S.A., and Cade, T.J., "The 1975 North American peregrine falcon survey", *Can. Field. Nat.* 90 (1976) pp. 228–73; Risebrough, R.W. and Peakall, D.B., "The relative importance of the several organochlorines in the decline of the peregrine falcon populations", in: Cade et al., (eds) 1988 *op. cit.*

167 Nisbett, 1988, *op. cit.*

168 Jefferies et al., 1973, *op. cit.*

169 Newton, 1972, *op. cit.*

170 Newton, 1986, *op. cit.*

171 Newton, 1984, *op. cit.*

172 Conrad, B., "Die Giftbelstung der Vogelwelt Deutschlands", *Vogel-kundlicte Bibliotek* vol. 5 (Greven: Kilda Verlag, 1979); Henny, C.J., "Birds of prey, DDT and tussock moths in Pacific Northwest", *Trans. N. Am. Wild. Nat. Resource Conf.* 42 (1977) pp. 397–411; Newton, 1986, *op. cit.*

173 Klass, E.E. and Belisle, A.A., "Organochlorine pesticide and poly-chlorinated biphenyl residues in selected fauna from a New Jersey salt marsh – 1967 *vs.* 1973," *Pesticide Monitoring J.* 10 (1977) pp. 148–58.

174 Blus, L.J., Lamont, T.G. and Neely, B.S., "Effects of organochlorine residues on eggshell thickness, reproduction and populations status of brown pelicans in South Carolina and Florida, 1969–76", *Pest. Monit. J.* 12 (1979) pp. 172–84.

175 Haseltine, S.D., Heinz, G.H., Reichel, W.L. and Moore, J.F., "Organochlorine and metal residues in eggs of waterfowl nesting on islands in Lake Michigan of Door County, Wisconsin, 1977–78", *Pest. Monit. J.* 15 (1981) pp. 90–97.

176 Newton, 1984, *op. cit.*

177 Ratcliffe, 1988, *op. cit*

178 Newton, 1988, *op. cit.*

179 Potts, 1986, *op. cit.*

180 Potts, 1986, *op. cit.*; Potts, G.R., "Insecticides and breeding success of partridges and pheasants", *Game Conservancy Review of 1989* (1990) pp. 74–7.

181 Potts, 1990, *op. cit*

182 Rands, M.R.W., (in press) quoted in Sotherton, N.W., "The cereals

and gamebirds research project: overcoming the indirect effects of pesticides", in: Harding, D.L.J. (ed.) *Britain Since Silent Spring* (London: Institute of Biology, 1988).

183 Rands, M.R.W. and Sotherton, W.N., "Pesticide use on cereal crops and changes in the abundance of butterflies on arable farmland in England", *Biol. Conserv.* **36** (1986) pp. 71–82.

184 Rands and Sotherton, 1986, *op. cit.*

185 Green, R., "Factors affecting the diet of farmland skylarks, *Alauda arvensis*", *J. Anim. Ecol.* **47** (1978) pp. 913–28.

186 Flegg, J.J.M., "Biological factors affecting control strategy", in: *Bird Problems in Agriculture*, (Croydon, Surrey: British Council for Crop Protection, 1980) pp. 7–19.

187 Greaves, M.P., "Long-term effects of herbicides on soil microorganisms", *Ann. appl. Biol.* **91** (1979) pp. 129–31.

188 Barrett, G.W., "The effects of an acute insecticide stress on a semi-enclosed grassland ecosystem," *Ecology* **49** (1968) pp. 1019–1035.

189 Mauk, W.L. and Olsen, L.E., "Toxicity of natural pyrethrins and five pyrethroids to fish", *Arch. Environ. Contam. Toxicol.* **25** (1976) pp. 18–29; Stephenson, R.R., "Aquatic toxicology of cypermethrin I. Acute toxicity to some freshwater fish and invertebrates in laboratory tests", *Aquatic Toxicol.* **2** (1982) pp. 175–85.

190 Crossland, N.O., *Laboratory to Environment*, Proc. V International Congress of Toxicology, Brighton July 16–21, 1989, pp. 184–192 (1989).

191 Crossland, N.O., "Aquatic toxicology of cypermethrin II. Fate and biological effects of pond experiments", *Aquatic Toxicol.* **2** (1982) pp. 205–222.

192 Crossland, N.O., Shires, S.W. and Bennett, D., "Aquatic toxicology of cypermethrin III. Fate and biological effects of spray drift deposits in fresh water adjacent to agricultural land" *Aquatic Toxicol.* **2** (1982) pp. 253–70.

193 Kingsbury, P.D., "Effects of an aerial application of the synthetic pyrethroid permethrin on a forest stream", *The Manitoba Entomologist* **10** (1976) pp. 9–17.

3 Pesticides and Human Health

Pesticides, as the preceding chapter has shown, are a serious hazard to wildlife. At high dosages they not only kill insects and other invertebrates, but birds and mammals as well. And at lower dosages they inflict a range of serious, sublethal effects. In particular, they adversely affect reproductive processes and significantly alter behavioural patterns. In the face of this evidence, it seems reasonable to assume that human beings are similarly at risk. Surprisingly, as this chapter shows, the hazard is less than might be expected.

We begin by discussing the evidence for illnesses and deaths caused by the predominant pesticides of the 1950s and 1960s – the organochlorines and phenoxy herbicides. We then discuss the impact of the apparently safer modern pesticides. The evidence comes from laboratory and epidemiological studies of specific pesticides or classes of pesticides. We next turn to more general evidence for pesticide effects, expressed in the form of mortality and morbidity statistics. In the remainder of the chapter, we describe the levels of pesticides currently found as residues in food and in human tissues, and discuss the likely consequences for health.

DDT and the organochlorines

Following their release for commercial sale in the late 1940s, the organochlorines became the most commonly used pesticides in agriculture and for malaria control. Their great virtue for pest control lay in their ability to persist under most environmental conditions. Treatments could be infrequent and hence costs were low. But their persistence had its drawbacks. They began to build up in the environment, in the soil, in food chains and eventually, because they are fat soluble, in the tissues of birds and mammals, including humans.

The cyclodiene insecticides known as the drins (aldrin, dieldrin and endrin) are highly toxic and endrin is one of the most toxic of insecticides. But most of the organochlorines are only moderately toxic (Table 3.1). Indeed DDT (dichlorodiphenyltrichloroethane), perhaps the most notable of the organochlorines, is about as hazardous an acute poison as aspirin. Where the ambiguity lies is in their chronic effects. As we saw in the last chapter, they can severely affect reproductive processes and behaviour in birds. Yet in humans there is little evidence of a hazard to health, except at very high dosages.

DDT and mammals

DDT exemplifies the contradictions. In laboratory mammals it affects the nervous system and liver. It can cause death at very high dosages yet in those that survive, the symptoms of poisoning disappear within 24 hours.[1] And over the longer term, rats and mice fed diets high in DDT for several generations have shown no effects on reproduction, lactation or survival of progeny.[2] Neither has DDT been found to be mutagenic.

The only evidence of chronic harm from DDT is in some strains of mice where changes occur in the liver cells leading to the formation of certain tumours when fed DDT in amounts of 5 mg/kg per day or more. However, more than 30 years after these tumours were observed, there is still considerable controversy over their nature.[3] They are correlated with the dosage of DDT, but only arise in some strains of mice, and only in male mice. They possibly occur in rats but not in other mammals. Whether the tumours are invasive or benign is not clear. As the World Health Organization Task Group on DDT put it, "although there is persuasive evidence that these multinodular tumours of mice ... are carcinomas, there is equally convincing evidence that they are not and the views of highly qualified pathologists ... remain diametrically opposed."[4]

Occupational exposure

The evidence of harm to ourselves is equally negative. In the 1950s and 1960s, workers manufacturing and formulating DDT pesticides were heavily exposed, as were spray operators in malarial control programmes. The doses received were of the order of 0.5 mg/kg body weight per day over several years, producing levels of storage in fat tissues of 100–250 mg/kg.[5] Volunteers have also been administered

Table 3.1   Approximate acute oral toxicities to rats of some common pesticides

Extremely toxic $LD_{50} < 10\,mg*$	Highly toxic $10\,mg < LD_{50}$ $< 50\,mg$	Moderately toxic $50\,mg < LD_{50}$ $< 500\,mg$	Slightly toxic $LD_{50} > 500\,mg$
Insecticides: Organochlorines			
endrin	aldrin	lindane	
	endosulfan	(γ-HCH)	
	dieldrin	DDT	
	PCP	heptachlor	
		chlordane	
		campheclor	
		(toxaphene)	
Insecticides: Organophosphates			
phorate	dichlorvos	diazinon	fenitrothion
mevinphos	chlorfenvinphos	quinalphos	malathion
parathion	carbophenothion	ethion	trichlorfon
azinphos methyl	methyl parathion	pyrazophos	dimethoate
	demeton-S-methyl	phosalone	fenchlorphos
	monocrotophos	chlorpyriphos	pirimphos-methyl
	methamidophos	triazophos	
	leptophos		
	dichloronat		
Insecticides: Carbamates			
aldicarb	methomyl	propoxur	carbaryl
carbofuran		pirimicarb	thiobencarb
Insecticides: Pyrethroids			
		deltamethrin	permethrin
		cypermethrin	
		fervalerate	
Herbicides			
		2,4-D	simazine
		2,4,5-T	propanil
		paraquat	atrazine
		dinoseb	MCPA
		ioxynil	mecoprop (MCPP)
			alachlor
			diuron
Fungicides			
		nabam	tecnazene
			quintozene
			thiram
			iprodione
			benomyl

continued

Table 3.1   Continued

Extremely toxic $LD_{50} < 10\,mg*$	Highly toxic $10\,mg < LD_{50}$ $< 50\,mg$	Moderately toxic $50\,mg < LD_{50}$ $< 500\,mg$	Slightly toxic $LD_{50} > 500\,mg$
Rodenticides brodifacoum difenacoum bromadiolone			
Inorganic products	thallium sulphate calcium arsenate		Bordeaux mixture aluminium metham sodium
Others			phosethyl (Fosetyl-Al)
	nicotine famphur DNOC	binapacryl DBCP EDB (bromoethane)	propargite daminozide rotenone (derris)

* LD_{50} values are mg per kg body weight.

Source: Royal Society of Chemistry, *The Agrochemicals Handbook* (Nottingham: RSC, 1987); Matthews, G.A., *Pesticide Application Methods* (London and New York: Longman, 1979).

similar doses, although over shorter periods. But in all these situations there is no epidemiological evidence of damaging effects.[6] One groups of workers studied in the USA were exposed to so much DDT that they were permanently coated with a layer of concentrated DDT dust, yet no correlation was detected between exposure and abnormality of the nervous system or of liver function.[7] These dosages, although high, are still ten times less than the levels that monkeys, dogs and rats can withstand without showing an effect. Dermatitis was commonly observed in spray operators but eventually was traced to the solvents used to make up the pesticide solutions rather than the DDT itself.

DDT and the general public

DDT and some of its derivative compounds are found in almost all people throughout the world. Most, though, are exposed to levels 200–1000 times less than in those occupationally exposed – in all there is no evidence of adverse effects (Table 3.2). In the numerous epidemiological studies that have taken place over the past 30 years,

Table 3.2   Effects of various doses of DDT on humans

Dose	Observation
Single Dose (μg/kg)	
16,000–286,000*	Prompt vomiting, some convulsions
6,000–10,000	Moderate poisoning
Repeated exposure (μg/kg/day)	
1,500	Administered as therapy for 6 months – no adverse effect
500	Administered to volunteers for 21 months – no adverse effect
500	Exposure of workers for 6.5 years – no adverse effect
250	Exposure of workers for 25 years – no adverse effect
2.5	Intake of population in USA, 1953–54 – no adverse effect
0.2	Intake of population in USA, 1969–70 – no adverse effect

* High unknown doses have caused death in a few instances.

Source: WHO, *DDT and its Derivatives* (Geneva: WHO, 1979).

most have found no relationship between the amounts of DDT stored in the body and cause of illness or death.[8] But there is some evidence of greater DDT storage in people dying of cirrhosis, hypertension and certain forms of liver cancer. The question, though, is whether the concentration of DDT is a cause or an effect.

The most widely quoted study which apparently implicates DDT was carried out in a Miami hospital in the 1960s.[9] Autopsies were conducted on 271 individuals who had died from various causes and these revealed that for certain liver diseases the levels of DDT were two to four times those of healthy individuals. Liver damage was also found to be correlated with high DDT concentrations in patients who had died of cancer and hypertension in Hawaii.[10] But in a later study of individuals who had died of liver cirrhosis in Vancouver, Canada, while the levels of DDT in the livers were significantly higher than for a control group, the correlation was also with the lipid content of the liver.[11] When the data were corrected for lipid content there was no difference between the cirrhotic and control individuals (Table 3.3). DDT becomes readily concentrated in lipids and these, in turn, become concentrated in damaged livers. The Vancouver study showed

Table 3.3   DDT and lipid levels in individuals with and without cirrhosis of the liver in a hospital in Vancouver, Canada

	Mean levels ($\mu g/kg$)	
	Cirrhotic individuals	Control individuals
Adipose tissue		
Total DDT	3681.48	4248.38
Brain tissue		
Total DDT	34.92	46.52
Liver specimens		
Total DDT	473.09*	273.64
% lipid	7.97*	5.08
Total DDT correlated for lipid content	120.04	72.97

* Difference from controls will only occur by chance in five in a hundred instances.

Source: Oloffs, C.P. et al., "DDT, dieldrin and heptachlor epoxide in humans with liver cirrhosis", Clin. Biochem 7 (1974) pp. 297–306.

no elevated levels of DDT in adipose or brain tissue of the cirrhotic patients. While the DDT levels were relatively high in the damaged livers they were still at least ten times less than in people exposed occupationally to DDT who have shown no signs of these diseases. It would seem that DDT concentration in the liver is a consequence of diseases with other causes, rather than being a cause itself.

Finally, national statistics provide no evidence of a correlation between DDT use and liver cancer, the most likely related disease. Over the period of greatest use of DDT, the total death rates of cancer of the liver and its biliary passages declined markedly in the USA, from 8.4/100,000 in the mid-1940s, to 5.6 in 1972, when DDT was banned, and in the early 1980s was between 2 and 4 for most sectors of the population.[12]

The World Health Organization in its comprehensive report on DDT published in 1979 concluded that "the safety record of DDT is phenomenally good."[13] There has been no subsequent evidence to question this conclusion.

Phenoxy herbicides

While the organochlorine story has proven, eventually, to be relatively straightforward, the picture for phenoxy herbicides remains inconsistent and confusing. The first phenoxy herbicides, 2,4-D, 2,4,5-T and

MCPA, were introduced for agricultural use in the mid-1940s. By the 1960s they were the most important single class of herbicide, being used for weed control on over 25 million hectares of US agricultural land, and also as defoliants by the US Armed Forces in Vietnam and Cambodia. Production and use in the USA then declined markedly in the early 1970s, from an annual 20 million kg per annum to only 400,000 in 1974.[14] By this time 2,4-D and 2,4,5-T use was permitted solely on rangelands and forests.

Phenoxy herbicides are of relatively low toxicity, similar to DDT with an acute LD_{50} of 100–500 mg/kg (Table 3.1). This is probably because they tend to be excreted rapidly in the urine without any change in form.[15] There is no evidence to indicate that 2,4,5-T, 2,4-D and MCPA cause cancer, but 2,4,5-T has been shown to be teratogenic, that is, it causes deformities of the foetus, in some, but not all, experimental animals. It causes congenital malformations in rats, mice and hamsters, but not in rabbits, sheep or monkeys. In rodents it has also been shown to kill foetuses.[16] But, as we have already pointed out, such experiments do not necessarily provide a useful guide to the likely impact on humans: aspirin at high doses can cause foetal malformations in rodents, yet it is used widely by humans with no such ill effects.[17]

Miscarriages in Oregon

The first, apparently clear, evidence that phenoxy herbicides were harmful to humans resulted from widespread spraying of 2,4,5-T against weeds in forest areas in the USA. In 1979 an unusually large incidence of miscarriages (spontaneous abortions) was reported in the western state of Oregon, apparently linked to this spraying. The US Environmental Protection Agency (EPA) was asked to investigate and confirmed that a correlation existed. They found the incidence of miscarriages in a regularly sprayed forest area, the Alsea Basin, which is close to the coast of Oregon, to be significantly higher than in both an adjacent urban location and in a rural control area on the eastern border of the state, both unaffected by 2,4,5-T.[18] The ALSEA II study, as it was called, also revealed a correlation between 2,4,5-T spraying in the spring and a peak of miscarriages three months later (Figure 3.1). Shortly after the study was complete the EPA suspended clearance for some uses of 2,4,5-T.

However, none of these correlations have survived subsequent analysis of the data.[19] The June peak was because of a single year's figures: in the June of 1976 there were 10 miscarriages compared with 3 in most of the other years. Further statistical analysis revealed no

Figure 3.1   2,4,5-T spraying and index of miscarriages in Alsea study area, Oregon

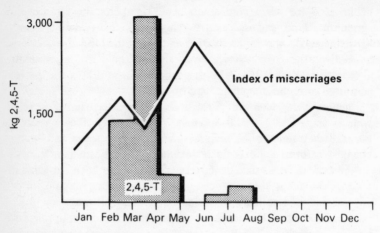

Source: Witt, J.M., *A discussion of the suspension of 2,4,5-T and the EPA Alsea II study* (Corvallis: Oregon State University, 1980).

Figure 3.2   Monthly hospitalized miscarriages in Alsea study area, 1972–77

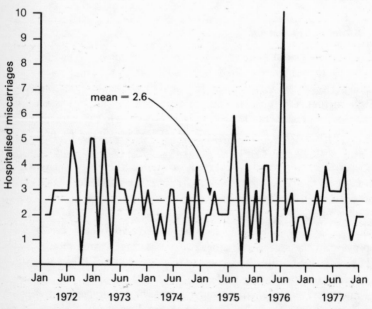

Source: Wagner, S.L., Witt, J.M., Norris, L.A., Higgins, S.F., Agresti, A. and Ortiz, M., *A scientific critique of the EPA Alsea II study and report* (Corvallis: Oregon State University, 1979).

seasonal pattern (Figure 3.2). Furthermore, comparisons with the rural and urban control areas were invalidated because the study recorded only hospitalized miscarriages, and made no correction for marked differences in the proportion of mothers going to hospital. The rate of hospitalization was much higher, 70 per cent, in the Alsea Basin, than in the urban control area, where it was 30 per cent.

When the miscarriage rate was recalculated as a proportion of live births and corrected for hospitalization, the urban area had a higher rate than the study area and all three were below the national average (Table 3.4). A re-analysis, which identified women by the postal zip code of their residence and then classified them according to whether 2,4,5-T had been applied three months previously in the zip code area, indicated no significant effects on the outcome of pregnancy (Table 3.5).

Table 3.4 Rates of miscarriage (spontaneous abortion) in Oregon

	*Miscarriages (spontaneous abortions) as % of live births**
Study area (Alsea basin)	11.4
Urban control	14.0
Rural control	9.3
USA	15–25

* corrected for birth rates and hospitalization rates
Source: Witt, J.M., *A discussion of the suspension of 2,4,5-T and the EPA Alsea II study*, (Corvallis: Oregon State University, 1980).

Table 3.5 Pregnancy outcome as a function of exposure to 2,4,5-T three months previously in zip code of residence

	Hospitalized miscarriages (spontaneous abortions)	*Live births*
Exposed	62	920
Unexposed	112	1743
Chi-square = 0.08, which is not significant		

Source: Agresti, A., *Analysis of association between 2,4,5-T exposure and hospitalized spontaneous abortions*, (Corvallis: Oregon State University, 1979).

Other studies have confirmed the lack of effect of phenoxy herbicides on reproduction and prenatal toxicity. For instance, neither the children of US and Australian soldiers who had served in Vietnam, nor the children of pesticide sprayers in New Zealand were found to have an excess risk associated with the exposure of their fathers to the herbicides.[20] In Britain, some evidence does point to increased birth defects among the children of fathers in occupations such as agriculture and forestry, although other studies are negative.[21] Clearly many factors in agriculture and forestry, other than the use of herbicides, can be involved.

Rare cancers

Although the link with miscarriages proved to be without substance, there is emerging epidemiological evidence that phenoxy herbicides may be responsible for the production of certain rare cancers. The studies were initiated when it was discovered that patients at a cancer clinic suffering from soft tissue cancers in Sweden had previously been exposed to phenoxy herbicides. Individuals with the cancers were matched with randomly chosen healthy individuals of the same age, sex, place of residence and so on.[22] The aim was to see if the two groups differed in their history of exposure to phenoxy herbicides, and this was confirmed, implying a raised risk of contracting soft tissue cancer from such exposure (Table 3.6). The relative figures are very small, but statistically significant.

Table 3.6 Soft tissue tumours and exposure to phenoxy herbicides in southern Sweden. One hundred and ten individuals with tumours (Cases) were each matched with two healthy individuals (Referents) of the same age, sex and from the same municipality and then classified according to whether they had been exposed to phenoxy herbicides

| | | Exposed | | |
	Not exposed	Phenoxy acids without dioxin contamination (e.g. 2,4-D, MCPA)	Phenoxy acids with possible dioxin contamination (e.g. 2,4,5-T)	All
Cases	96	7	7	14
Referents	214	4	1	5
Relative risk*		4.2	17.0	6

* The relative risk is defined as the ratio of risk among the exposed to the risk among the non-exposed (see Miettinen, 1972)

Source: Eriksson, M. et al., "Soft-tissue sarcomas and exposure to chemical substances: a case reference study", *Br. J. Indust. Med.* **38** (1981) pp. 27–33; Miettinen, O., "Components of the crude risk ratio", *Ann. J. Epidemiol.* **96** (1972) pp. 168–172.

A similar study was also conducted to investigate the link with malignant lymphoma cancers, notably Hodgkin's disease and non-Hodgkin's lymphoma. Again a statistical increase in risk was found which rose with duration of exposure to the herbicides, although there was no significant difference between the two cancers.[23] However, studies of this type can be criticized on a number of grounds: in particular, patients' recall of past events may have been affected by newspaper publicity or previous interviews. There is also a possibility of unconscious bias on the part of the interviewers.[24]

Subsequently, a much more extensive investigation was conducted into over 350,000 Swedish men employed in agriculture and forestry. But it failed to find any significant excess of soft tissue cancers in this group, when compared to other occupational groups.[25] There was also no change observed in relative risk over the period 1961–1979, despite a steady growth of phenoxy herbicide use from 1947 until restrictions were imposed in the 1970s. There are, of course, many conflicting factors involved. Swedish agricultural workers, as a group, are characterized by decreased cancer risk and are known to under-utilize health services, both factors possibly masking a raised risk.[26] There are also uncertainties associated with the diagnosis of soft tissue tumours.[27] Given the rarity of the diseases even one or two misdiagnoses can greatly alter the statistics. A more fundamental issue is that the cancers, although occurring in related tissues, are of very disparate types and it is difficult to see a connecting link that implicates 2,4,5-T.

Following the Swedish study, other countries have looked for a similar link. In Washington State, in the USA, where phenoxy herbicides are also heavily used, the incidence of the cancers among occupations likely to be exposed was found to be no greater than for other occupations.[28] Another study found no association between soft tissue cancers and previous military service in Vietnam, where many military personnel were exposed to the defoliant, Agent Orange, which contains both 2,4-D and 2,4,5-T.[29] Similarly, in New Zealand and Australia, also heavy users of phenoxy herbicides, no deleterious effects on human health have been detected.[30]

Then, in 1983, a considerably more convincing version of the Swedish study was carried out in Kansas in the USA.[31] Kansas is a major wheat producing state, with heavy usage of 2,4-D. The study examined the histories of the total number of cases of these cancers occurring in the state in the late 70s and early 80s: 200 men diagnosed with soft tissue sarcoma, 173 men with Hodgkin's disease and 200 out of the 297 men with non-Hodgkin's lymphoma. This constitutes a much larger sample than for the Swedish studies. As before, the cases were matched with similar individuals from the general population. Very detailed questions were asked about the history of herbicide use, method of application and about the use of insecticides and fungicides.

There were questions, too, on possible confounding factors, such as the presence of immune altering conditions, coffee consumption and smoking.

The results showed that men exposed to herbicides, specifically 2,4-D for more than 20 days a year had a sixfold increase in risk of non-Hodgkin's lymphoma, relative to non-farmers, and an eightfold increase for men who applied the herbicides themselves (Table 3.7). The level of risk was associated with the duration and frequency of use and it was also evident that farmers who did not use protective equipment or who applied herbicides with backpack or hand sprayers were at greater risk. However, neither of the other two cancers showed any correlation with herbicide exposure. More recently, there has been a follow-up study in Nebraska, which confirmed the findings: exposure to 2,4,5-T for more than 20 days per year increased the risk of developing non-Hodgkin's lymphoma threefold.[32]

Table 3.7   Non-Hodgkin's lymphoma in relation to duration and frequency of herbicide use

	No. of controls	No. of cases	Odds ratio (95% confidence interval)
Non-farmers	286	37	1.0
Farmers	662	133	1.4 (0.9, 2.1)
Duration of herbicide use (years)			
0	470	93	1.3 (0.8, 2.1)
1–5	53	9	1.3 (0.6, 3.1)
0–15	58	12	1.6 (0.7, 3.4)
>16	57	16	2.0 (1.0, 4.0)
Unknown	24	3	–
Frequency of herbicide use (days per years)			
0	497	94	1.3 (0.8, 2.0)
1–5	102	19	1.4 (0.7, 2.6)
6–10	29	6	1.6 (0.5, 4.3)
11–20	13	5	2.6 (0.8, 8.8)
>21	12	7	6.0 (1.9, 19.5)
Unknown	9	2	–

Source: Hoar, S.K. et al., "Agricultural herbicide use and risk of lymphoma and soft-tissue sarcoma", *J. Am. Med. Assn.* 256 (1986) pp. 1141–7.

Dioxin

There is potentially also a health hazard from the impurities, especially chlorinated dibenzodioxins and dibenzofurans, that may be present in commercial formulations of phenoxy herbicides. The most common impurity is 2,3,7,8-TCDD, usually referred to as dioxin. Until the introduction in the 1970s of stricter standards, 2,4,5-T could contain considerable amounts of dioxin. The highest values found in the UK were 28 mg/kg, and in the USA 100 mg/kg, although now levels of contamination are below 0.01 mg/kg.[33] Dioxin is fat soluble, and hence persistent; and is known to cause birth defects and cancer in some animals, though its effects vary greatly among species.[34] (See Table 1.2.)

Human populations have been exposed to high dosages of dioxin on several occasions: the American forces in Vietnam involved in the spraying of Agent Orange which contained 2,4,5-T and 2,4-D contaminated with dioxin; the victims of an industrial accident at Seveso in Italy, where dioxin was released to the atmosphere; and several groups of workers in manufacturing industry. The disfiguring skin disease, chloracne, is a common symptom of exposure and this may be accompanied by neurological and behavioural disorders and by effects on the immune system.[35] These symptoms can persist for several years, but studies of affected populations have not, as yet, found clear evidence of links with cancer, foetal abnormalities or mortality generally.[36]

Bans and restrictions

In 1972 the US Environmental Protection Agency banned DDT and subsequently banned or tightly restricted the use of other organochlorines. By 1976 only toxaphene was still in general use. Following the events in Oregon of 1979, the EPA also banned certain uses of 2,4,5-T and a total ban was imposed in 1983.

In the UK, DDT was finally banned in 1984 while other organochlorines are confined now to certain restricted uses. There were repeated calls for the banning of 2,4,5-T in the late 1970s and early 1980s. The Agricultural Workers Trade Group continued to allege poisoning of workers as a result of exposure from use, storage and disposal. In response, the Advisory Committee on Pesticides (ACP) reviewed available evidence on three separate occasions. Its conclusion was that harm would not occur from the herbicide when used for recommended purposes in the recommended way. At the time of writing, 2,4,5-T and 2,4-D continue to be cleared for certain uses in the UK under the Control of Pesticides Regulations 1986.[37]

In many developing countries, however, organochlorines are still widely used. In 1985, India consumed 10,000 tonnes of DDT and 3000 t of aldrin and dieldrin, while in Mexico the consumption was 4000 t and 1000 t respectively.[38]

Organophosphates and Carbamates

Following the phasing out of organochlorine insecticides in the industrialized countries, the organophosphates became the most commonly used class of insecticide. There are about 100 different kinds of organophosphate and together with two other classes, the carbamates and synthetic pyrethroids, they now constitute some 75–80 per cent of world consumption of insecticides.[39]

Short-term effects

The acute toxicity of organophosphates ranges from extreme to slight (Table 3.1). Massive single exposures, resulting from spillage or deliberate or accidental ingestion, may be fatal. However they persist in the body for relatively short periods of time, being rapidly broken down by various enzymes and excreted. Thus, in theory, they present a much lower chronic risk. The difference between these compounds and the organochlorines has been expressed as follows:

[D]amages inflicted by the organochlorines typically are subtle, diffused widely, both geographically and among affected individuals, and long term. Damages by the organophosphorus and carbamate compounds typically are sharp, localized and short term. They have many of the characteristics of industrial accidents.[40]

Worldwide, there have been many thousands of cases of acute poisoning from organophosphates, in particular due to parathion and methyl parathion.[41] In Japan in the 1960s, there were over 3000 accidental and occupational poisonings from parathion, including nearly 200 deaths.[42]

For the most part the effects of high doses, albeit often very unpleasant, appear short term. Both organophosphates and carbamates affect insects and ourselves by reacting with the enzyme, acetyl cholinesterase (AChE), which plays a role in the orderly transmission of nerve impulses.[43] The normal function of AChE is to terminate the transmission of a nervous stimulus. Organophosphates inhibit AChE, so resulting in continuous and excessive nervous stimulation. The first symptoms of poisoning are headaches, giddiness, nausea and blurred vision. Later, tachycardia (an abnormally rapid heart action), convulsions and, in extreme cases, respiratory failure occur. The early symptoms can easily be confused with other causes, leading to problems in detecting organophosphorus poisoning in hospital records.

Workers who do not take adequate safety precautions to prevent exposure are likely to receive doses sufficient to cause short-term intoxication. The best documented cases come from malarial control programmes: in Pakistan more than 2000 spraymen were poisoned following the replacement of DDT with the organophosphate, malathion.[44] The route of exposure tends to be via bare arms and hands. In other control programmes, acute poisoning has not occurred because safety procedures were rigorously followed: there was regular washing, prohibition of smoking and eating before washing, provision of clean uniforms every day and baths each evening.[45]

But not everyone finds it practicable to be this cautious. Even in the industrialized countries, organophosphates can poison farm workers. Part of the reason is that in hot conditions organophosphates become oxidized to more volatile and toxic products. Thus, the hazards may arise most acutely a few days after application, as occurred in California when workers mistakenly entered a field too soon after the spraying (Box 3.1). In the UK, organophosphate sheep dips frequently cause intense headaches and nausea. As one farmer from Devon remarked

Box 3.1   A poisoning incident among farm workers resulting from exposure to mevinphos

---

Salinas Valley, California, 1981
29 of a team of 44 lettuce harvesters reported these symptoms after entering a field sprayed with mevinphos:

More than 75%	Eye irritation
25–50%	Visual disturbance, dizziness, nausea, fatigue
0–25%	Chest pain, skin irritation, sweating, diarrhoea

22 of the workers reported three or more of the above symptoms

---

Sources: CDC, "Outbreak of severe dermatitis among orange pickers – California", MMWR 35 (1985) pp. 465–7; CDC, "Acute poisoning following exposure to an agricultural insecticide – California", MMWR 34 (1984) pp. 464–6.

"I never handled the dip without the gloves, but you cannot rig up a complete mask and shield because it is so hot in the summer."[46]

There is also a potential hazard from using impure pesticide products and from mixing pesticides. Malathion and certain other organophosphates are metabolized by means of carboxyesterase enzymes. These can be inhibited by impurities, such as isomalathion or trimethyl phosphorothiolates that occur in malathion formulations, or by simultaneous exposure to other pesticides (Table 3.8).

Table 3.8 Combined effect of fenchlorphos and malathion on anti-cholinesterase activity

Dose (mg/kg)		
Fenchlorphos	Malathion	% inhibition of AChE
0	200	13
30	0	1
30	200	61

Source: Murphy, S.D., "Mechanisms of pesticide interactions in vertebrates", *Res. Rev.* **25** (1969) pp. 201–221.

Delayed neuropathy

Most symptoms of organophosphorus poisoning only last a few days, but they do not necessarily occur soon after exposure.[47] Several compounds produce a delayed neurotoxicity. (Table 3.9). The delay can be up to four weeks, the first signs being tingling and burning in the hands and feet, followed by weakness in the lower limbs and, eventually, paralysis. A few cases have occurred among workers manufacturing the compounds listed but most poisonings have resulted from accidental or deliberate ingestion in amounts that would have been fatal, but for medical intervention.

Long-term effects

Little is known of the longer-term effects on ourselves of the commonly used organophosphorus and carbamate pesticides. Laboratory tests have revealed evidence of possible carcinogenicity in some organophosphorus compounds, notably parathion, but no evidence of mutagenicity in mammals. Teratogenicity has been observed in pigs dosed with trichlorfon, but this may have been a particularly susceptible herd since congenital tumours had been observed previously.[48]

Table 3.9 Organophosphorus pesticides reportedly causing delayed neuropathy in humans

Pesticide	Number of cases
Mipafox	2
Leptophos	8
Methamidophos	9
Trichlorfon	Many
Trichlornat	2
EPN	3 (moderate effects)
Chlorpyrifos	1

Source: WHO, *Organophosphorus Insecticides: A General Introduction* (Geneva: WHO, 1986) (citing original sources).

In general, there is no clear evidence of adverse effects on health from long-term exposure at levels where the enzyme acetyl cholinesterase is not affected. Severe behavioural effects – impairment of memory and speech, tendencies to depression, anxiety and irritability – occur in individuals where AChE is affected, but there is no substantiated evidence that such effects occur at lower doses. Complaints from workers occupationally exposed are common, but these reports are difficult to evaluate and complicated by the presence of other factors.[49]

Other pesticides

Insecticides and nematocides

Most of the newer insecticides are intrinsically safer. The synthetic pyrethroids have low persistence and low toxicity to mammals, yet are selectively toxic to a wide range of insects and at much lower rates than established products.[50] As they are also biodegradable, they do not leave residues that could accumulate in biological systems. Two compounds, permethrin and cypermethrin, are possible carcinogens; otherwise there is no evidence of potential harm to humans from pyrethroids.

One nematocide, dibromochloropropane (DBCP), has caused severe problems, however. It is known to be carcinogenic in laboratory animals and causes infertility in humans. Male factory workers engaged in the manufacture of DBCP have become infertile, while field operators have shown signs of depressed sperm counts.[51] In Costa Rica, where

DBCP was used extensively against nematodes in banana plantations, some 500 men have been diagnosed as sterile. Although many of the cases are still subject to lawsuits, about 300 of the most seriously affected have already been paid some compensation.[52] It was banned from production and its use heavily restricted in the USA in 1977, yet imports to Costa Rica continued until late 1978.

Herbicides and fungicides

The only highly toxic herbicide of the post-war years has been paraquat.[53] Its LD_{50} in rats can be as low as 80 mg/kg when absorbed through the skin. It is selectively accumulated in the lungs and severe poisoning results in pulmonary oedema – excessive fluid in the lungs – and eventually death. At lower levels of exposure, paraquat may produce skin irritation, rashes and blistering and damage to the nails. Eyes that are splashed may also be seriously damaged.

Deaths from occupational exposure are rare, however, either in those formulating the product or among agricultural workers. Between 1956 and 1973 no agricultural workers in the USA died from paraquat poisoning.[54] There were 4 deaths in 1974 but it is not clear whether these were occupational, suicidal or accidental. Most cases of injury are due to exposure of the skin from leaking spray machines, in particular knapsack sprayers (Table 3.10). Paraquat is commonly used for weed control in sugar cane or rubber estates in the tropics. Studies of workers subject to long exposure have revealed a fairly high incidence of nail damage and loss, skin and eye irritation, but

Table 3.10 Exposures of humans to paraquat using different application methods

	Dermal exposure (mg/hour)	Respiratory exposure (mg/hour × 10^{-3})
Hand-held knapsack	66 (12.1–169.8)	0.45–1.3
Vehicle mounted	0.4 (0.1–3.4)	0–2
Aerial		
Flag	0.1–2.4	0–47
Pilot	0.5–0.1	0–0.6
Mixer/loader	0.18	1.3–1.5

Source: WHO, Paraquat & Diquat (Geneva: WHO, 1984). Using data from different sources.

no more serious effects.[55] Typically, skin lesions affect the index, middle and ring fingers of the working hands, suggesting leakage from knapsack sprayers. Where deaths have been reported, workers have often suffered from prior dermatitis or damage to the skin, for instance due to scratching from the trees where spraying is being carried out. Most cases of paraquat poisoning are due to suicides or ingestion of the poison from unlabelled or mislabelled bottles.

Most modern fungicides and herbicides are either non-toxic or slightly toxic to humans. One possible exception is the herbicide atrazine, which accounts for almost 25 per cent of all herbicides applied to crops in the US. It has low toxicity to humans, but there is evidence it may be transformed metabolically by plants to form a substance which is mutagenic.[56] There are also claims that it can be transformed in the human stomach to its N-nitroso derivative. As a class, such N-nitroso compounds are carcinogenic (see Chapter 5). Another herbicide, propanil, which is used on rice, is reported to be metabolized by micro-organisms in the soil to a compound very similar to dioxin.[57]

Carcinogenicity

The health hazard which is most difficult to assess, and the most controversial, is carcinogenicity. In general, international reviews, particularly those of the World Health Organization, conclude that pesticides pose little or no carcinogenic hazard. However, the US government takes a considerably more conservative and cautious approach. This is partly because of the requirement of the Delaney Clause in the Federal Food, Drug and Cosmetic Act 1954 which bans all compounds in processed food, including pesticides and food additives, that have been found to "induce cancer."[58] (See Chapter 10.)

Oncogenic pesticides

The controversy arises over interpretation of the Delaney Clause. The US Environmental Protection Agency (EPA) takes it to imply a restriction on all tumour forming compounds, whether the tumours are benign or malignant. Such compounds are termed oncogenic, while truly carcinogenic compounds are only those that cause malignant tumours. The EPA will also accept as sufficient evidence the results from a single experiment that represents rather special circumstances.

Very rarely are animals other than mice or rats tested. Furthermore, no account is taken, as far as the Delaney Clause is concerned, of the actual level of risk of tumour formation. Production of a tumour, of any kind, in a single experiment is enough to classify a compound as oncogenic.

So far the EPA has identified 53 such oncogenic pesticides (Table 3.11). Most are the older arsenic based inorganics and other pesticides registered before 1970, but there are a number of modern compounds on the list. In some cases the basis for the finding is very clear. Benomyl, a widely used fungicide, has been shown to produce malignant tumours in rats and mice at all doses down to 500 ppm. However, in other instances the evidence is more problematic. The EPA has determined Fosetyl-Al as a possible human carcinogen and banned registration on the basis of one study where kidney tumours appeared when animals were fed at 35,000 ppm and also tumours of "questionable significance" at 8000 ppm. Because Fosetyl-Al has very low acute toxicity, the experimental animals can take these very high dosages – feeding at 35,000 ppm represents a quarter of the animal's total diet. However, despite these extreme circumstances the compound has to be classified as oncogenic since the EPA requires testing to the maximum tolerated dose, however high this may be.

In the case of permethrin, a widely used synthetic pyrethroid, the evidence is also contentious. In six long-term mouse and rat studies an increase in malignant tumours over the background level was evident only in the lungs of female mice from one test. On this basis it was classed as a possible human carcinogen and registration denied.

Levels of risk

Although prevented from use on crops that are processed, oncogenic pesticides may be given registration on food crops that are consumed raw, but here the determining factor is the dietary risk, measured as:

$$\frac{\text{human}}{\text{dietary risk}} = \frac{\text{food}}{\text{consumption}} \times \frac{\text{pesticide}}{\text{residue}} \times \frac{\text{oncogenicity}}{\text{potential}}$$

Inevitably there are many uncertainties in this calculation. The risks are likely to be overstated because of the extrapolation from high dose effects in rats and mice to low dose effects in humans, which ignores the likelihood of thresholds or other differences in the pattern of response. The calculation also assumes that all crops are treated and residues are at the maximum permitted under registration.

Table 3.11 Oncogenic pesticides as determined by the US Environmental Protection Agency. Risk and human carcinogenicity given where known

Compound	Risk	Human carcinogenicity*
INSECTICIDES/ACARICIDES		
Inorganic		
Calcium arsenate	–	
Copper arsenate	–	
Lead arsenate	–	
Sodium arsenate	–	
Organochlorines		
Lindane	–	
Toxaphene	–	
Organophosphates		
Acephate (Orthene)	3.73/100 thousand	NA
Amitraz (Baam)	–	
Azinphos-methyl (Guthion)	1.68/thousand million	Not classifiable
Chlordimeform (Galecron)	3.22/10 thousand	Probable
Chlorbenzilate	–	
Cyromazine (Larvadex)	3.58/10 million	NA
Dicofol (Kelthane)	–	
Methomyl (Lannate)	–	
Parathion	1.47/100 thousand	Possible
Tetrachlorvinphos	–	
Carbamates		
Thiodicarb (Larvin)	–	
Pyrethroids		
Permethrin (Ambush, Pounce)	4.21/10 thousand	Possible
Cypermethrin (Ammo, Cymbush)	3.73/million	Possible
FUNGICIDES/BACTERICIDES		
Benomyl (Benlate)	1.13/10 thousand	Possible
Captatol (Difolatan)	5.94/10 thousand	Probable
Captan	4.74/10 thousand	Probable
Chlorothalonil (Bravo)	2.37/10 thousand	NA
Folpet	3.24/10 thousand	Probable
Fosetyl-Al (Aliette)	3.24/100 million	Possible
Mancozeb (Dithane M.45)	3.38/10 thousand	Probable
Maneb	4.42/10 thousand	Probable
Metiram	1.15/10 thousand	Probable
O-Phenylphenol	9.99/100 thousand	NA
PCNB	–	
Thiophanate-methyl	–	

continued

Table 3.11 Continued

Compound	Risk	Human carcinogenicity
FUNGICIDES/BACTERICIDES – continued		
Zineb	7.17/10 thousand	Probable
Ethylene oxide	–	
HERBICIDES		
Acifluorten (Blazer)	–	
Alachlor (Lasso)	2.42/100 thousand	Probable
Arsenic acid	–	
Asulam	–	
Diallate	–	
Diclotop methyl (Hoelon)	2.04/million	NA
Ethalfluralin (Somalan)	3.56/million	NA
Glyphosate	2.73/10 million	Possible
Linuron (Lorox)	1.52/thousand	Possible
Methanearsonic acid	–	
Metolachlor (Dval)	1.44 million	Possible (pending)
Oryzalin (Surflan)	1.14/100 thousand	Possible
Oxadiazon (Ronstar)	1.21/100 thousand	Possible
Paraquat (Granoxone)	–	
Pronamide (Kerb)	7.77/million	Possible
Terbutryn	2.86/10 million	Possible
Trifluralin (Treflan)	–	

* **Human carcinogenicity according to EPA**

Human carcinogen – sufficient evidence from epidemiological studies to support a causal association between exposure to agents and cancer

Probable human carcinogen:
(1) sufficient evidence of carcinogenicity from animal studies with limited evidence of carcinogenicity from epidemiological studies
(2) with inadequate or no epidemiological data

Possible human carcinogen – limited evidence of carcinogenicity in absence of human data

Not classifiable as to human carcinogenicity – inadequate or no human and animal data for carcinogenicity

Evidence of non-carcinogenicity in humans – no evidence of carcinogenicity in at least two adequate animal tests in different species in adequate epidemiological and animal studies (this is based on available evidence and does not mean that the agent will not be a carcinogen under any circumstances)

Source: NRC, *Regulating Pesticides in Food, The Delaney Paradox* (Washington DC: National Research Council, 1987).

Furthermore, it is based on a daily consumption of residues for a 70 year lifetime. Equally, though, there is the possibility of underestimates due, in part, to lack of full information on all the active ingredients and their contaminants and on possible synergistic actions.

The risks for 28 out of 53 compounds are listed in Table 3.11. The highest level of recorded risk is 7.17 per ten thousand for zineb. That of Fosetyl-Al is about 1 in 100 million. These should be compared with the 2.5 per 10, that is, 1 in 4, risk of lifetime cancer for members of the US population. The risk from carcinogenic pesticides is miniscule in comparison to that of other causes of cancer.

However, these findings on oncogenicity are beginning to have a major impact on pesticide use. Although only 53 active ingredients have been identified as oncogenic, in total they comprise a very high proportion of the pesticides currently used in the USA. For instance, about 220 million kg of herbicides are applied annually and of this amount 135 million kg represent compounds that the EPA considers to be oncogenic. For fungicides the proportion of oncogenic compounds is 32–34 million kg out of the total of 36 million kg. In the case of insecticides, the percentage of oncogenic insecticides in terms of kg applied is very small, primarily because the two most commonly used, permethrin and cypermethrin, are applied at very low rates per acre. But on an area treated basis the proportion is higher – 35–50 per cent.[59]

Mortality and morbidity statistics

In the first part of the chapter we have focused on the laboratory, clinical and epidemiological evidence linking deaths and illnesses to specific pesticides and classes of pesticides. This is the most direct source of evidence for cause–effect relationships. However, more indirect information is available from the regional and national statistics on mortality and morbidity that most countries keep as a matter of routine. These usually record pesticide poisonings as a separate category, although the data tend to be highly variable in quality and consistency.

National and state records

The most reliable data are for accidental deaths on farms. In the UK, the Agricultural Inspectorate of the Health and Safety Executive (HSE) investigates incidents reported to them by farmers and members of the public, and also incidents they come across while conducting routine farm visits. Their records show there were no fatalities on the farm from non-fumigant pesticides in the 1980s, except for a recent case of a fatality of a child following a fall into a sheep dip. During the 1980s there was only one death resulting from the use of

fumigant pesticides. Fatal accidents from other causes on the farm –
due to machinery, falls into slurry pits and even killings by bulls are far
more frequent (Table 3.12).

Table 3.12   Verified fatal accidents on farms in the UK, 1978–85

	1978	1979	1980	1981	1982	1983	1984	1985*
Slurry pits								
Drowning	1	2	1	0	2	1	4	–
Asphyxiation	0	0	0	2	0	3	1	–
Tower silos								
Asphyxiation	1	3	1	–	2†	–	–	–
Animals	4	5	6	2	3	2	5	–
Pesticides	0	0	0	0	0	0	0	–
Fumigants	1	2	1	0	0	0	0	–
Machinery	43	44	31	38	33	33	29	–
Total**	73	94	78	72	68	64	67	65

*   All data for 1985 not yet available
** Other causes include drowning in water, falls and falling objects, diseases, electric
     accidents plus others
†   2 is total for 1981–84
Sources: Health and Safety Executive, *Agricultural Health and Safety* (London: HMSO,
1981, 1983, 1985, 1986); HSE, *Health and Safety Statistics 1984–85* (London: HMSO,
1987).

The pattern is similar in the USA, where records are kept by the
EPA and individual states. They reveal that very few deaths occur
from pesticide use on the farm: in California, for example, there were
six deaths between 1978 and 1985 resulting from exposure to pesticides,
but 130 due to tractor accidents while conducting farm work.[60] In the
1980s there were eight deaths in California (Box 3.2).

In contrast to the precision of the California records there is considerable confusion over records kept by various agencies in the UK. The
National Poison Information Service (NPIS), for instance, recorded
three accidental deaths in 1980 (Table 3.13), but the Ministry of
Agriculture, Fisheries and Food and the Medical Research Council
are quoted as stating the number of fatalities for that year to be 11 and
4 respectively.[61]

Non-fatal poisoning occurring on and close to farms is relatively well
reported. In the UK records are kept by the Agricultural Inspectorate
and show that the proportion of non-fatal farm accidents attributed
to pesticides is very small: during the 1980s there were some 10–20
incidents annually (0.018–0.036 per 100,000 population) out of a total
of over 4000 farm accidents. However, the figures are considerably

Box 3.2 Circumstances of occupational pesticide-related mortality in California in the 1980s

---

1981 2 deaths in 2 incidents

An employee working at a potato sorting job accidentally drank from a labelled, one gallon container of disinfectant and died.

A store clerk was killed by a thief who threw chloropicrin at him.

1982 2 deaths in one incident

One employee cleaning a portable storage tank contaminated with ethylene dibromide was overcome; the manager went into the tank to rescue him; both received dermal and lung exposure and died.

1985 2 deaths in 2 incidents

A pest control operator spraying chlorpyrifos in a confined space was exposed to pesticide and toxic solvent leaking from the spray gun. Both chemicals suspected, but not confirmed, of causing death.

A work crew entered a tomato field in violation of the 24 hour re-entry interval regulation. One became ill, collapsed outside the field, and was taken to hospital in Mexico, where he died.

1986 2 deaths in 2 incidents

A helicopter carrying close to a full load of methomyl caught fire and crashed while manoeuvering an 180° turn; the doors of the helicopter had been removed previously, and spray drift may have entered the cockpit.

A crop duster aircraft crashed during application of mevinphos and methomyl; cause of death not confirmed as autopsy not performed because of possibility of exposure to toxic pesticides.

Pesticides were not confirmed as cause of death in either case.

Each year a further 2 to 7 deaths are recorded from suicide attempts, from people entering fumigated premises, or from accidental ingestion of liquids.

Sources: CDFA, *Summary of illnesses and injuries reported in California by physicians as potentially related to pesticides* (Sacramento: California Dept. of Food and Agriculture, 1981–90).

higher if poisoning of the general public is taken into account, as well as incidents that are reported as likely but not confirmed (Table 3.14). In 1988, for example, 43 people were categorized as "likely or confirmed" poisoned by pesticides: this produces a total rate of 0.08 per 100,000 population.

Table 3.13 Number of deaths in England and Wales resulting from accidental poisoning by pesticides 1970–83 (note that the basis of reporting changed in 1979)

Year	Number of deaths from accidental poisoning by pesticides, fertilizers or plant food	Year	Number of deaths from accidental poisoning by agricultural and horticultural chemical and pharmaceutical preparations other than plant foods and fertilizers
1970	2	1979	3
1971	6	1980	3
1972	6	1981	10
1973	4	1982	2
1974	8	1983	2
1975	8		
1976	7		
1977	3		
1978	1		

Source: Gilbert, D.G.R., "Pesticide Safety Policy and Control Arrangements in Britain", PhD Thesis (University of London, 1987).

The rate of poisonings is much higher in California, although this may be partly due to the thoroughness of the records kept by the Californian Department of Food and Agriculture.[62] Any employed person may visit a practising physician for a free examination and the physician is required by law to report any illness or injury suspected of being related to pesticide exposure. In addition, the professional fee is paid by the appropriate insurance company or the State itself once the report to the County Agricultural Commissioner (CAC) is submitted. The CAC then informs the Health and Safety Branch of the CDFA. The records reveal an annual rate of 1000–1500 cases of poisoning (Table 3.15). Given a total population of 26 million (390,000 fieldworkers) this produces a rate of 3.8–5.8 per 100,000.

The highest risk categories among Californians are the applicators of pesticides and other farm fieldworkers (Figure 3.3). But in the UK at least half the people affected in 1988 were walking, cycling or jogging past the field being sprayed, perhaps reflecting a greater rural population density and more intensive use of the countryside for recreation.[63]

These figures for farm poisoning are dwarfed, though, by poisonings in the house and garden. In California the records kept by the Poison Information Centers of the inquiries made by physicians and the

Table 3.14 Incidence of non-fatal poisoning by pesticides and complaints by the public in the UK

Year	Farmers and agricultural workers	Confirmed incidents of non-fatal poisonings*	Members of public	Number of complaints by public alleging poisoning by spray drift**
1975	18			
1976	4			
1977	12			
1978	15			
1979	8		5	
1980	20		10	
1981	21		5	
1982	23		5	
1983	8		4	88
1984	10		10	127
1985		58†		94
1986		39		43
1987		22		89
1988	8		14	90

† Data not disaggregated.
* The Health and Safety Executive categorizes all investigated poisoning incidents as confirmed, likely, unlikely, unconfirmed. These data represent only confirmed incidents. During the 1980s HSE investigated between 150–240 incidents annually. Often incidents involve more than one person: in 1988 13 farmers and agricultural workers and 21 members of the public were poisoned.
** Complaints against both ground and aerial spraying

Sources: Health and Safety Executive, *Pesticide Incidents Investigated in 1988* (London: HMSO, 1989); HM Agricultural & Factory Inspectorate, HSE, *Health and Safety Statistics 1985–86* (London: HMSO, 1988); Gilbert, 1987, *op. cit.*

general public reveal that most pesticide poisoning incidents are non-occupational and occur in the home and garden.[64] Annually some 12–17,000 people are poisoned at home, at least half of whom are children less than 6 years of age. Yet of the 250–350 million kg of pesticides used annually in the state, only 12 per cent are for use at home, compared with 55 per cent in agriculture. In the UK the information for home and garden poisoning is inconsistent and patchy, again partly because responsibility for records rests with several government agencies.[65] The Home Accident Surveillance System (HASS), using a sample of 20 hospitals that offer a 24 hour accident and emergency service, reported over 100 incidents of pesticide poisoning in 1981. On this basis, the national incidence is probably some 20–25-fold greater.[66] However, over the period

Table 3.15   Cases of occupational pesticide poisoning in California, 1961–88

	Number of cases of definite, probable or possible occupational poisoning (1, 2)	Number of occupational deaths
1961	911	NR
1966	1347	NR
1971	1447	NR
1974	1157	0
1975	1343	1
1976	1452	0
1977	1531	0
1978	1194	0
1979	1019	0
1980	1355	0
1981	1093	2
1982	1117	2
1983	979	0
1984	952	0
1985	1268	2
1986	1065	2
1987	1507	0
1988	2016	0

NR = not recorded
1 Incidents are classified into one of five classes:
  (i) definite, where the symptoms are confirmed by medical and physical evidence
  (ii) probable, where there is a close correspondence between pattern of exposure and symptoms, but where medical and/or physical evidence may not be available
  (iii) possible, where there is some correspondence but some ambiguities
  (iv) unlikely, where the signs and symptoms are not typical of the exposure suspected, but pesticide poisoning cannot be disproved
  (v) unrelated, where there is no pesticide-caused illness or injury.
2 Changes occur in the recording program from year to year, so making exact comparison difficult. For example, in 1961 eye injuries were not recorded; and in mid-1987 incidents arising from poisoning by disinfectant anti-microbials were recorded for the first time, so elevating averages. Nonetheless there are some significant years: in 1985 there was a significant increase in field workers affected by drift.

Source: CDFA, *Summary of illnesses and injuries reported by Californian physicians as potentially related to pesticides* (Sacramento: California Department of Food and Agriculture, 1975–90).

1972 to 1982, the then Department of Health and Social Services (DHSS) recorded only about 850 inpatient discharges annually from National Health hospitals following treatment for pesticide poisoning. Probably the most accurate estimates come from the National Poisons Information Service (NPIS). In 1985, they recorded 1,846 new cases of acute or suspected acute poisoning – of which 640 required hospital

Figure 3.3 Categories of agricultural and related workers and the general public reporting pesticide illnesses in California (1988–89) and the UK (1988)

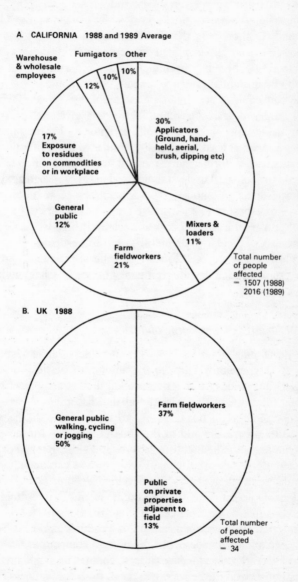

A. CALIFORNIA   1988 and 1989 Average

Warehouse & wholesale employees 12%

Fumigators 10%

Other 10%

30% Applicators (Ground, hand-held, aerial, brush, dipping etc)

17% Exposure to residues on commodities or in workplace

General public 12%

Farm fieldworkers 21%

Mixers & loaders 11%

Total number of people affected
= 1507 (1988)
   2016 (1989)

B. UK 1988

Farm fieldworkers 37%

General public walking, cycling or jogging 50%

Public on private properties adjacent to field 13%

Total number of people affected
= 34

Sources: CDFA, 1989, *op. cit.*; HSE, 1988, *op. cit.*

treatment. They also estimated that 800 to 1,000 cases could be added to this figure based on the number of inquiries made to regional poisons centres. Of the 1846 cases, approximately 69 per cent resulted from garden products and 31 per cent from pesticides in industry and agriculture. Various lobby groups in the UK, such as Friends of the Earth, the Soil Association and the London Food Commission, have also compiled dossiers of individual cases to support their claim that there is considerable under-reporting.[67] But the value of such circumstantial evidence remains contentious.

The collection of accurate data is complicated by the difficulty of establishing a causal connection between a given set of symptoms and pesticide poisoning. Many mild symptoms of acute poisoning in humans appear, at least superficially, similar to those of influenza, hay fever, or stress.[68] Furthermore, medical practitioners often have an in-adequate toxicological understanding and may not recognize symptoms of mild pesticide poisoning.[69] To attribute long-term effects – such as cancer – to exposure to a particular pesticide appears to be especially difficult, unless the effects occur at a relatively high frequency and are specific to a particular pesticide or group of pesticides. People using pesticides may be exposed to a wide range of products, and records of the products used and the frequency of use by each employee are rarely kept.

Greater hazards in developing countries

In the developing countries, mortality and illness due to pesticides are much more common relative to the amount of pesticide used. Lack of legislation, widespread ignorance of the hazards involved, poor labelling, inadequate supervision and the discomfort of wearing full protective clothing in hot climates, greatly increase the hazard both to agricultural workers and to the general public.[70] Moreover, many pesticides known to be highly hazardous and either banned or severely restricted in the industrialized countries, such as parathion, mevinphos and endrin, are widely available in developing countries and used without adequate precautions. In 1988 the Food and Drug Administration of the USA found that 5 per cent of some 10,000 imported foods when tested were found to contain residues of products banned in the USA, indicating continued widespread use of such compounds.[71]

The latest global estimates suggest about half a million cases of unintentional pesticide poisoning in the developing countries and 2300 deaths, compared to 360,000 cases in the industrialized countries and one thousand deaths.[72] But there are few reliable statistics in the developing countries for pesticide poisoning. Many records, for instance, do not distinguish between accidental poisoning and self-administration. One apparently good set of records for occupational pesticide poisoning is from Thailand. This shows a marked fall in the percentage of fatalities but an increase in incidents over the past decade, although this could be due to increased reporting of less severe cases (Figure 3.4).

Figure 3.4   Accidental pesticide poisoning in Thailand, 1972–84

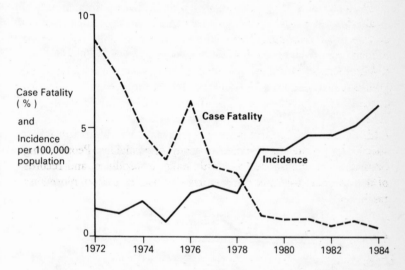

Source: Levine, R.S., *Assessment of Mortality and Morbidity due to Unintentional Pesticide Poisonings*, Document No. WHO/VBC/86.926 (Geneva: WHO, 1986).

In Sri Lanka, 11,000–15,000 people are admitted to hospital each year with pesticide poisoning, of whom about 1000 die, more than the total fatalities due to five major diseases, including malaria.[73] But 75 per cent of these mortalities are suicides, the remaining accidental poisoning giving a rate of about 23/100,000 population. In countries that distinguish between accidental poisoning and self-administration it appears that many accidental fatalities occur as a result of people mistaking pesticides for beverages. This has been particularly documented in the countries in the Pacific, where unlabelled containers, or the consumption of drinks contaminated by the container, have been the most important cause of pesticide related fatalities. In many countries severe poisoning also arises from misuse, for instance from attempting to control lice by applying paraquat to the skin or hair.

The rate of poisoning in Sri Lanka is reflected in several other national statistics. In Syria in 1971 there were 1064 pesticide poisonings (16.3/100,000), with 167 deaths (2.6/100,000). In central America (Nicaragua, Guatemala and El Salvador) pesticide application to cotton produces 3–4000 poisonings annually (23/100,000).[74] There the poisoning is highly seasonal, occurring in October to December at the time of most intensive pesticide use on cotton (Figure 3.5). The majority of those poisoned are temporary workers, living within 100 metres of the cotton fields in poor conditions where the only source of water is the irrigation channels which are heavily contaminated by pesticides.

Figure 3.5   Average monthly pesticide poisoning of agricultural workers in El Salvador, 1969–74

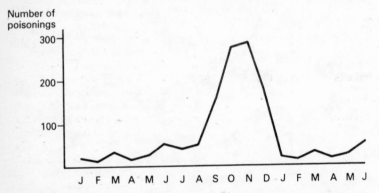

Source: Davies, J.E., Smith, R.F. and Freed, V., "Agromedical aproach to pesticide management", *Ann. Rev. Entomology* **23** (1978), pp. 353–366.

Even these figures may be underestimates. There is considerable anecdotal evidence from health workers of high levels of poisoning among rural populations in developing countries.[75] The most serious episodes have usually resulted from consumption of contaminated foodstuffs or treated cereal seeds (Table 3.16). One of the worst cases occurred in Iraq in 1971–72. Imported wheat and barley seed intended for sowing had been treated with methyl mercury fungicide; but much of the seed arrived too late for sowing. Warning labels on some sacks were in English or Spanish and rural families ate the seed and fed it to their livestock. Officially over 6000 people were poisoned and nearly 500 killed, but an unofficial estimate put the figures at over ten times these levels.[76] There have also been several cases of poisoning due to eating pesticide-contaminated wheat in India, most recently in 1990 at a wedding party where about 150 people died.[77]

Table 3.16 Examples of episodes of pesticide poisoning in developing countries

Country	Year	Cases	Deaths	Comments
Guyana[1]	1966	88	10	Flour contaminated with parathion during international transport
Qatar and Saudi Arabia[2]	1967	800	NR	Flour contaminated with endrin during international transport
Jamaica[1]	1968	NR	18	Flour contaminated with parathion during international transport
Iraq[3]	1971–2	6000	500	Treated seed corn consumed as food
Jamaica[1]	1976	79	17	Flour contaminated with parathion during international transport
Pakistan[4]	1976	2810	5	Poor safety practice for new pesticide (malathion) in malaria control programme
Indonesia[5]	1983	168	96	Eight episodes of poisonings from consumption of food (various pesticides)
Pakistan[6]	1984	194	19	Sugar contaminated with endrin during in-country transport
Sierra Leone[7]	1986	49	14	Flour contaminated with parathion during in-country transport

NR = not recorded

Sources:
1 Singh, P.D.A. and West, M.F., "Acute pesticide poisoning in the Caribbean", *W.I. Med. J.* **34** (1985) pp. 75–83.
2 Weeks, D.E., "Endrin food-poisoning. A report on four outbreaks caused by two separate shipments of endrin-contaminated flour", *Bull. WHO* **37** (1967) pp. 499–512.
3 Bakir, F., Damhiji, S.F., Amir-Zaki, L., Murtadha, M., Khalidi, A., Al-Rawi, N.Y., Tikriti, S., Dhahir, H.I., Clarkson, T.W., Smith, J.C. and Doherty, R.A., "Methyl mercury poisoning in Iraq", *Science* **181** (1973) pp. 230–41.
4 Baker, E.L., Zack, M., Miles, B., Alderman, L., Warren, M., Dobbin, R.D., Miller, S. and Teeters, W.R., "Epidemic malathion poisoning in Pakistan malaria workers", *The Lancet*, **i** (1978) pp. 31–4.
5 Directorate of Hygiene and Sanitation, Jakarta, in: *IOCU – The Pesticide Poisoning Report*. A Survey of some Asian Countries (Malaysia: IOCU, 1984).
6 Center for Disease Control, "Acute convulsions associated with endrin poisoning – Pakistan", *MMWR* **33**(1984) pp. 687–8, 693; Rowley, D.L., Rab, M.A., Hardjotanajo, W., Liddle, J., Saleem, M., Sokal, D., Falk, H. and Head, S., "Convulsions caused by pesticide poisoning in Pakistan" *Pediatrics* **79** (1984), pp. 928–934.
7 Etzel, R.A., Forthal, D.N., Hill, R.H. and Denby, A., "Fatal parathion poisoning in Sierra Leone", *Bull. WHO* **65** (1987) pp. 645–9.

Much information on pesticide poisoning comes from hospital admissions and yet poisoning is far more common among rural populations that are poorly served by hospitals. Even for hospital cases, there may be considerable misdiagnosis, producing both under- and over-estimates. An example was the episode of presumed thallium poisoning in Georgetown, Guyana in late 1986 and 1987. Thallium sulphate had been used as a rodenticide in sugar plantations and sporadic cases of poisoning had been recorded in previous years. During the episode blood tests indicated several hundred people were affected, but subsequent analysis of the samples and interviewing of patients could not confirm even one case of poisoning. The episode was eventually recorded as an "epidemic of false positives."[78]

Mortality in the Philippines

Perhaps the most compelling evidence that mortality and illness from pesticides are much more common in the developing countries than previously supposed, comes from a recent study in Central Luzon, in the Philippines.[79] This is an intensive rice growing region that has greatly benefited from the Green Revolution packages of high-yielding seeds, improved irrigation and the provision of agrochemicals. The increase in pesticide use began in the early 1970s, in response to the introduction of the new varieties and a government credit scheme and as a counter to a growing incidence of pest and disease outbreaks. Between 1970 and 1974 the value of insecticides applied to rice increased by over 250 per cent, although thereafter it remained fairly constant due to rising prices and scarcity of credit. In the study Loevinsohn examined mortality statistics in several contrasting rural and urban municipalities for diagnosed pesticide poisoning and also for other conditions that could be the result of such poisoning.[80] Organochlorines such as endrin and HCH can cause convulsions, so that poisoning may be misdiagnosed as epilepsy, brain tumours or strokes. Similarly, poisoning by organophosphates, such as parathion, can be misdiagnosed as cardiovascular or respiratory diseases.

The study detected a 27.4 per cent increase between 1961–1971 and 1972–1984 of non-traumatic mortality rates among rural males aged 15–54 years, although it decreased in children and women (Figure 3.6). The increase closely coincided with the growth in pesticide use. When the figures were broken down they revealed that deaths in the rural areas diagnosed as poisoning increased by 247 per cent and those from associated conditions by 41 per cent between the two periods, yet mortality from all other causes, except cancer, decreased by 33.7 per

Figure 3.6 Three-year moving averages of age-adjusted non-traumatic mortality among men and women aged 15–54 years in three rural municipalities in Nueva Ecija, Central Luzon

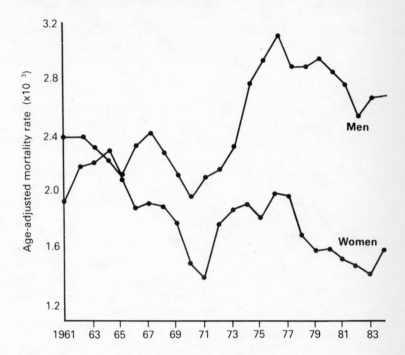

Source: Loevinsohn, M.E., "Insecticide use and increased mortality in rural central Luzon, Philippines", *The Lancet* i (1987), pp. 359–362.

cent. In the case of stroke, mortality increased for all men in both the urban and rural areas, but significantly the increase was greater among younger men who are generally at low risk of stroke. Following the 1982 ban on endrin, mortality attributed to stroke decreased for all men, but the decrease was significantly greater among the younger men in rural areas. The study also revealed that mortality rates had originally peaked each year during the wet season in August, the month of greatest insecticide use. But after double-cropping became widespread a second mortality peak appeared in February, at a time when insecticides are used on the newly cultivated dry-season crops (Figure 3.7).

These correlations are highly suggestive of occupational exposure to insecticides. Other factors may have been important: falling rural incomes, increased stress during land preparation, greater use

Figure 3.7 Ratio of observed-to-expected number of deaths among men aged 15–54 years in rural Cabanatuan, Nueva Ecija
1975 = period of intensive insecticide use and predominantly single-cropping
1976–82 = period of intensive insecticide use and predominantly double-cropping

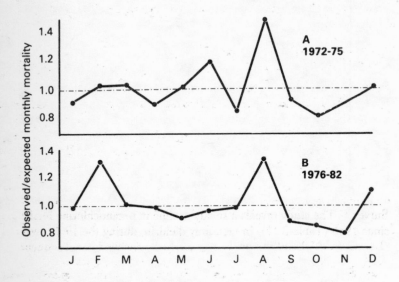

Source: Loevinsohn, M.E., 1987, *op.cit.*

of tobacco, and more efficient reporting. Nonetheless, Loevinsohn maintains these do not account for the selectiveness of the increases in mortality by age, sex, month and place of residence. If the findings of the Luzon study are correct, they imply many thousands of deaths a year in the Philippines alone and, until further studies are completed, the assumption must be that pesticide poisoning in many developing countries is at a similarly high level.

Pesticide residues in foods

Apart from accidental poisoning, the general public is primarily at risk from pesticides as residues in food. There is a growing body of evidence on the risks involved, but knowledge is still far from adequate.

The hazard posed by residues is related to the Acceptable Daily Intake (ADI) of a compound which is determined by the FAO/WHO

Codex Alimentarius Commission (CAC). The ADI is calculated at 100 times lower than the amount which would cause the least detectable effect if that level were ingested regularly throughout life. It is a conservative estimate since the detectable effect need not be deleterious and there is, in any case, a large margin of error. In most situations, even ingesting substantially more than the ADI is unlikely to cause harm.

Dietary levels

In the UK, the level of exposure to residues of the general population is assessed by means of the *Total Diet Study* which began in 1966.[81] Foodstuffs are purchased from a wide variety of retail outlets and the levels of residues estimated after preparation and cooking in the usual way. The food is divided into 20 food groups – bread, meat, offals, poultry, fish, fresh fruit, milk and so on – and the daily intake is then computed knowing the contribution of these groups to the typical diet, as found in the National Food Survey and the National Household Survey.[82] The study reveals a steady decline in organochlorine intake since 1966 (Table 3.17). In fact, only dieldrin, during the 1960s, was close to the ADI and the intake has markedly declined in subsequent years. The figures, though, are based on relatively small samples.

Table 3.17 Comparison between Acceptable Daily Intakes (ADI) and intakes computed from residues found in the *Total Diet Study* (μg/person/day) in the UK

	DDT + TDE + DDE	Dieldrin (HEOD)	Lindane (gamma HCH)
Acceptable Daily Intake (ADI)*	350.0	7.0	700.0
Years			
1966–7	44.0	6.6	6.6
1970–1	15.0	2.1	5.5
1974–5	12.0	1.9	4.4
1975–7	5.0	2.3	3.9
1979–80	3.0	1.6	3.0
1981	2.5	0.8	2.1
1984–5	0.5	0.5	0.5

* ADI based on average body weight of 70 kg

Sources: MAFF, *Report of the Working Party on Pesticide Residues*; Food Surveillance Paper no 25 (London: HMSO, 1989); MAFF, 1986, Paper no 16; MAFF, 1982, *Paper no. 9*.

The Food and Drug Administration in the USA has been conducting similar studies since the early 1950s, collecting foodstuffs from up to 27 cities for the Market Basket Survey.[83] Daily intakes of residues are computed using the average residue concentrations and the typical diet for adults, toddlers (2 years old) and infants (6 months). In the 1950s average daily intake of total DDT reached 286 μg/person, falling to 87 μg by the early 1960s as a result of bans on direct applications to livestock, and to 15 μg by 1970.[84] Since then daily intakes have fallen

Table 3.18 Daily intake of residues in the USA computed from *Total Diet Studies*

	$\mu g/individual/day$			
	DDT	Dieldrin	Lindane	Malathion
Adults				
ADI (70 kg b.w.)	350.0	7.0	700.0	1400.0
1976	4.4	2.8	1.1	9.0
1977	3.2	1.6	1.0	10.8
1978	4.9	1.2	0.8	10.0
1979	6.5	1.1	1.1	18.6
1980	2.4	1.5	1.0	14.2
1981–2	2.4	1.1	0.7	17.0
Toddlers (2 years)				
ADI (13.7 kg b.w.)	68.5	1.4	137.0	274.0
1976	1.4	0.6	0.3	2.0
1977	7.5	0.6	0.5	2.9
1978	1.4	0.5	0.5	4.1
1979	1.2	0.5	0.5	3.6
1980	0.7	0.6	0.5	3.2
1981–2	1.3	0.3	0.3	2.6
Infants (6 months)				
ADI (8.2 kg b.w.)	41.0	0.8	82.0	164.0
1976	0.6	0.2	0.1	0.7
1977	0.8	0.3	0.3	0.5
1978	0.8	0.4	0.3	2.7
1979	0.9	0.4	0.3	1.0
1980	0.3	0.3	0.2	1.6
1981–2	0.9	0.2	0.2	1.5

ADI = Acceptable Daily Intake based on average body weight (b.w.)

Source: Podrebarac, D.G., "Pesticide, heavy metal and other chemicals residues in infant and toddler total diet samples (V)", *J. Assoc. Off. Anal. Chem.* **67** (1984a) pp. 166–75; Podrebarac, (IV). *J. Assoc. Off. Anal. Chem.* **67** (1984b) pp. 176–85; Gartrell, M.J. et al., "Pesticides, selected elements and other chemicals in infant and toddler total diet samples", *J. Assoc. Off. Anal. Chem.* **69** (1986a,b) pp. 123–45, 146–59; Johnson, R.D. et al., "Pesticide, heavy metal and other chemical residues in infant and toddler total diet samples (III)", *J. Assoc. Off. Anal. Chem.* **67** (1984) pp. 145–54.

further, to a level comparable with those in the UK, and have remained relatively constant since 1976 (Table 3.18). Again, dieldrin has been the closest to the ADI. In adults it was 40 per cent of the ADI in 1976, falling to 16 per cent in 1982. Residues in infants have been greater, not falling below 25 per cent of ADI, and were as high as 50 per cent during 1978–9.

Individual state authorities in the USA also carry out monitoring surveys. One example is the Illinois survey of fat samples taken from cattle. This has revealed a very dramatic difference between the rapid decline in DDT since the early 1970s and that of aldrin/dieldrin and heptachlor which did not begin to fall until the 1980s (Figure 3.8).

Figure 3.8 Proportion of cattle fat samples from Illinois containing organochlorine residues, 1972–82

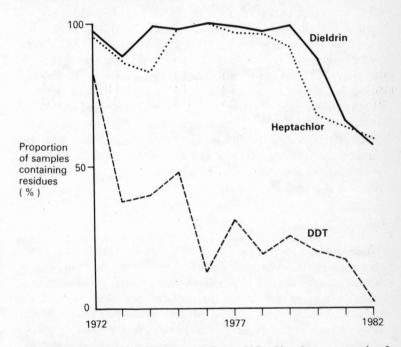

Source: Steffey, K.L., Reynolds, J.D. and Pettry, H.B., "An eleven-year study of chlorinated hydrocarbon insecticide residues in bovine fat in Illinois 1972–1982", *J. Environ. Sci. Health* B19 (1984), pp. 773–783.

Not surprisingly, because they are less persistent, levels of organophosphate residues have always been lower than organochlorines. In the 1966–1967 UK survey, only 20 out of 462 individual food samples contained organophosphates, primarily malathion on cereals. This pattern continued in later years; contamination, when present, was by malathion, phosalone or ethion on cereals or fruit, and produced intakes far below the ADIs. Organophosphates could not be detected in 141 of 144 samples of the 1981 study, and in 197 of 200 samples in 1984–85.[85] Several other carbamate, synthetic pyrethroid and fungicide compounds have also been detected in the total diet studies, but again all at a level considerably less than that liable to exceed ADI values. For example, the average daily intake of the fungicide tecnazene was 0.43 μg, some 100 times less than the ADI.[86] There is a similar pattern in the USA. Even where there are small increases in intake, such as of malathion, the levels are still approximately 100 times less than the ADI.

In the developing countries, however, daily intakes in total diets are often very high. Diet studies in five provinces of India have revealed intakes exceeding the ADI (Table 3.19). The main sources are wheat flour and other cereals. These supply 88 per cent of total DDT intake and 97 per cent of total HCH in Lucknow, and 78 per cent of DDT, 88 per cent HCH and 65 per cent of malathion in Calcutta. The burdens reflect the importance of cereals in the Indian diet: they constitute 73 per cent by weight of the total food consumed, compared with only 19 per cent in the USA.[87] However, a change in proportions of different foodstuffs consumed by Indians does not necessarily reduce body burdens. In Calcutta, 380 g of either vegetables or animal products is sufficient to reach the ADI for malathion, compared with an intake of 630 g of cereals.[88]

Individual foods

While total diet surveys provide a good estimate of the average intake, they mask variations between individual diet components and hence do not account for the risk to people who have dietary patterns different from the average or consume quantities of local produce containing high residues. For this purpose Maximum Residue Levels (MRLs) – also known as "tolerances" – have been recommended by various authorities. The MRLs of the Codex Alimentarius Commission (CAC) of FAO/WHO reflect the maximum levels likely to occur following application of a pesticide according to good agricultural practice. The MRLs of the European Commission (EC) are generally lower, tending to reflect the actual levels in commodities traded in Europe. For example, the CAC MRLs for DDT and dieldrin in vegetables and milk are ten times that of the EC; and the CAC MRC for dichlorvos in vegetables is five times that of the EC.[89]

Table 3.19 Comparison between Acceptable Daily Intakes and intakes of residues* in the five States of India

Location	DDT	Pesticide Lindane (γ-HCH) (μg/person/day)	Malathion
ADI (50 kg b.w.)	250	500	1000
Uttar Pradesh, 1984 (Lucknow)	200	1293	NR
Karnataka, 1982 (Mysore)	248	1323	NR
	0–11	173–1215	NR
	0	76–157	NR
Punjab, 1978	65	162	NR
West Bengal, 1975–6 (Calcutta)	1486	1666	1361
Andhra Pradesh, 1972 (Hyderabad)	358	NR	NR

NR = not recorded
* Dietary intakes based upon typical diets as computed by Gopalan et al., 1977 (from Kaphalia et al., 1985)

Source: Kaphalia, B.S., Siddiqui, F.S. and Setu, T.D., "Contamination levels in different food items and dietary intake of organochlorine residues in India", Ind. J. Med. Res. 81 (1985) pp. 71–8; Joia, B.S., Chawla, R.P. and Kalra, R.C., "Residues of DDT and HCH in wheat flour in Punjab", J. Ecol. 5 (1978) pp. 120; Lakshimanarayan, V. and Krishna Menon, P., "Exposure of general population of Hyderabad to DDT", J. Food Sci. Technol. 19 (1972) p. 82; Mukherjee, D., Roy, B.R., Chakraborty, J. and Ghosh, B.N., "Pesticide residues in human foods in Calcutta", Indian, J. Med. Res. 72 (1980a) pp. 577–82; Sowbhagya, H.B., Devi, A.V. and Viswesariah, K., "Chlorinated insecticide residues in certain food samples", Indian J. Med. Res. 78 (1983) pp. 403–6.

In the UK although the great majority of residues detected are at very low levels, the MRLs are exceeded in a few cases (Table 3.20). High residues on fruit and vegetables are of particular concern since they are often consumed with little preparation. Two lettuce samples have been found to contain over 100,000 μg/kg of thiram, some 30 times greater than the EC MRL; and more than 50 per cent of potato samples contained the post-harvest treatment agent, tecnazene, at above the MRL.[90]

Unexpectedly, DDT was detected in several home produced products as late as 1981–84, and exceeded EC MRLs on lettuces, mushrooms, cabbage and gooseberries. The European Commission's

Table 3.20 Examples of products in the UK in which pesticide residues exceeded European Community or Codex Alimentarius Commission – maximum residue limits (MRLs)

Product	Pesticide residue	Year of survey	Total samples	Proportion exceeding MRL (EC or CAC)	
Fruit and vegetables	All	1981–84	1649	1.8%	EC/CAC
Soft fruits	All	1982	137	55.2%	EC/CAC
Lettuce	Thiram	1979–80	103	42.0%	EC
	Iprodione	1979–80	217	20.0%	CAC
	Dimethoate	1979–80	199	1.0%	EC
	Quintozene	1979–80	98	16.3%	CAC
	HCB*	1979–80	64	25.0%	CAC
Lettuce					
(UK produced)	All	1981–82	–	2.0%	EC/CAC
(imported)	All	1981–82	–	0.7%	EC/CAC
Nuts	Bromine	1984	45	40.0%[†]	CAC[†]
Brassicas/carrots	DDT	1981	13	30.7%	EC
	DDT	1982–83	121	4.9%	EC
Strawberries	DDT	1985	236	0.4%	EC/CAC
Brassicas	DDT	1985	197	4.0%	EC
Brassicas	DDT	1987	225	1.0%	EC
Apples/pears/plums	Propargite	1982	24	8.3%	EC
Potatoes	Tecnazene	1985–86	67	55.2%	CAC
Maize (imported)	Dieldrin	1981	80	2.5%	CAC
Lamb	Lindane	1984	500	0.8%	CAC
Chicken	Dieldrin	1984–85	122	2.5%	EC/CAC
Pork/poultry	DDT	1985–87	26	77.0%	EC
(imported from China)	α-HCH	1985–87	26	85.0%	EC

* HCB is a contaminant of Quintozene
[†] There is no MRL for bromine, but the Guideline level of 0.01 mg/kg was exceeded in 40% of samples

Sources: MAFF, 1986, *op. cit;* MAFF, 1989, *op. cit.*

Directive 79/117 prohibited the marketing and use of DDT from 1st January 1981 (with some derogations granted which did not apply to the above crops). A further survey was carried out in 1983–84 and again DDT was found to exceed the MRL for the same products, and also for apples, brussels sprouts, cabbages and strawberries. As a consequence, DDT's clearance was withdrawn for all products by the UK Advisory Committee on Pesticides as from 1st October 1984. Yet it continued to be detected on strawberries, brussels sprouts and cabbage.[91] In 1985 4 per cent of brassicas sampled contained residues above MRL although it had declined to 1 per cent by 1987. Evidently use of DDT has continued despite restrictions and eventual bans, presumably because growers are finishing up old stock.

Other examples of contamination include glasshouse grown lettuce, tomato, cucumber and celery with over 100,000 $\mu g/kg$ of bromide following soil fumigation with methyl bromide. High residues of organochlorines have also been detected in oils manufactured from marine fish livers. The levels were high enough that children consuming 10 ml daily would have an intake approaching the ADI for dieldrin.[92]

Surprisingly, the latest survey conducted in the UK has discovered pesticide residues in a number of "health-food" or "organic" products.[93] No organophosphate residues were detected in a number of "organically-grown" wholeflour samples, but 7 of 12 samples of bread labelled as "organically-grown" contained pirimphos-methyl and malathion. The levels of the former were such that consumption of 1.4 kg of bread in a day would result in exceeding the ADI. Residues of organochlorines were also detected in herbal teas and peanut butter, but not in excess of MRLs. Of greatest concern, though, were residues in nuts and nut products: 40 per cent of samples contained residues of bromine resulting from the use of the fumigant methyl bromide, and all residues detected exceeded the CAC guideline level.

Recently there has been considerable public concern over the use of a growth regulater, daminozide (Alar), which is sprayed on apples after flowering to help the fruit set. The practice is widespread in the UK and USA but serious doubts as to its safety were raised in 1989. Daminozide is made from unsymmetrical dimethylhydrazine (UDMH). Both are oncogenic, with UDMH producing tumours in mice at much lower doses than daminozide.[94] UDMH remains a contaminant of daminozide formulations but can also be produced from daminozide during cooking. In the USA the Natural Resources Defense Council claimed that the risk of cancer was much greater, particularly in children, than was accepted by the Environmental Protection Agency. However in the UK, the Advisory Committee on Pesticides has estimated that even when worst case assumptions are combined – the highest reported residues and consumption, all apples having been treated and all apple products made from Alar-treated apples – there is no significant risk (Table 3.21).

Much of the serious contamination of individual products arises because of incorrect pesticide application. For instance, in 1985 spraying of watermelons with the insecticide aldicarb led to the

Table 3.21   Estimation of maximum consumer intakes for daminozide and UDMH

	Highest reported intake mg/kg body weight/day
Daminozide	
Infants	
apple	0.054
fruit desserts	0.033
apple juice	0.043
Adults	
apples, pears	0.087
Lowest dose causing tumours in mice	1483.000
UDMH	
Infants	
apple	0.00008
fruit desserts	0.005
apple juice	0.003
Adults	
apples, pears	0.0001
Lowest dose causing tumours in mice	4.8

Source: MAFF, *Evaluation of fully approved or provisionally approved pesticide products. Daminozide, November 1989* (London: MAFF, Pesticides Safety Division, 1989).

largest recorded outbreak of foodborne pesticide illness in North America.[95] About 1170 probable cases of poisoning were registered along the Pacific coast, from California to Alaska. Residues of 0.2 ppm are known to cause illness: in some cases the watermelons contained as much as 2.7 ppm. Aldicarb is not approved for use on watermelons and the contamination was probably because of illegal spraying. Aldicarb residues on hydroponically-grown cucumbers have also caused outbreaks of illness – in 14 Nebraskan consumers during 1977–78 and 85 Canadians in 1985.[96]

The most common cause of serious contamination, though, is post-harvest treatment of crops, particularly the use of fumigation during storage. This is the probable origin of pesticide residues in "health foods" or "organic" products. Cereals, for example, are commonly fumigated against insects and mites and sometimes samples have been found in the UK with residues above the MRL. Potatoes, too, are commonly treated with sprout suppressants and fungicides in storage, although this is not particularly hazardous since residues are mostly removed during washing and peeling.

Developing country foods

The major hazard in the developing countries lies in locally marketed food. Leafy vegetables are often sprayed twice a week and may come to market with a high degree of contamination, especially during the dry season.[97] Over 50 per cent of green leafy vegetables collected around Calcutta during the four dry winter months (November–February) contained residues, although during the rainy season (July–October) this fell to only 8 per cent, presumably because of the washing effect of rainfall. In Indonesia, cabbages and mustard greens have been found to contain from 75,000 to 350,000 μg/kg of quinalphos, 14,000–41,000 μg/kg of methamidaphos and 20,000–29,000 μg/kg of parathion. These are values many times in excess of human tolerance limits for organophosphate pesticides.[98] Similar levels of contamination have been recorded from Africa. The concentrations in vegetables from southern Nigeria were some two orders of magnitude greater than those from the Indian studies referred to earlier.[99]

Fish, particularly those living in paddy fields, may be an important source of residues in the diet.[100] Estimates based on the levels in fish and average daily fish intake in five villages in Malaysia revealed low intakes of HCH and DDT, but high intakes of dieldrin/aldrin, varying from 23 per cent to 44 per cent of ADI. Fortunately, the fish with highest residues were found in villages with low fish consumption. A worst case combination of the highest consumption and highest residues would lead to 88 per cent of the ADI being reached for dieldrin/aldrin. And this, of course, does not take account of residues in other components of the diet, such as rice. In Africa, too, residues of organochlorines in edible freshwater fish are often sufficiently high that only a small quantity consumed could exceed the ADI. Thus consumption of a 70 g fish containing 5000 μg/kg DDT would equal the ADI of 350 μg for an adult of 70 kg weight (Table 3.22).

Elsewhere food crops have been contaminated by nearby spraying of cash crops. In Central America in the 1970s high residues in food were associated with heavy pesticide spraying of cotton.[101] Fish, in particular, were highly contaminated with DDT at 630–8260 μg/kg. Residues in cows' milk were also present in high concentrations, at 2450–36,050 μg/kg, with samples from Masaya in Nicaragua containing a massive 73,420 μg/kg. Levels in milk from Guatemala are clearly linked to proximity of cotton, with concentrations rising following the beginning of pesticide treatments in August, after the July planting (Figure 3.9). Residues of DDT in most staples, though, were generally much lower, usually in the range 5–10 μg/kg for maize,

Table 3.22 Residues in freshwater fish and vegetables from some regions of Africa

Food	Location	DDT	Dieldrin (μg/kg)	Lindane (γ-HCH)
Fish	Lake Tanganyika	450–2390	–	–
Fish	Lake Nkuru	60–27000	–	–
Fish	Lake McIlwaine	10–20	–	–
Fish	South African rivers	3790–9180	–	–
Fish	Blendel State, Nigeria	80–4300	–	80–4360
Fish	Ibadan, Nigeria	50–2200	500–10200	10–3520
Spinach	Southern Nigeria	1330	–	1230
Cabbage	Southern Nigeria	2900	–	640
Onion	Southern Nigeria	4370	–	650
Carrot	Southern Nigeria	1100	–	1680
Cucumber	Southern Nigeria	1050	–	670
Lettuce	Southern Nigeria	970	–	1570

Sources: Atuma, S.S., "Residues of organochlorine pesticides in some Nigerian food material", *Bull. Environm. Contam. Toxicol.* **35** (1985) pp. 735–8; Atuma, S.S. and Okor, D.I., "Pesticide usage in Nigeria – Need for a baseline study", *Ambio* **14** (1985) pp. 340–1; Atuma, S.S. and Eigbe, C.O., "Organochlorine residues in freshwater fishes in Nigeria", *Intern. J. Environ. Studies* **24** (1985) pp. 251–4.

Figure 3.9 Total concentration of DDT in cows' milk from farms located within a cotton growing area or far away, Guatemala, 1975–76

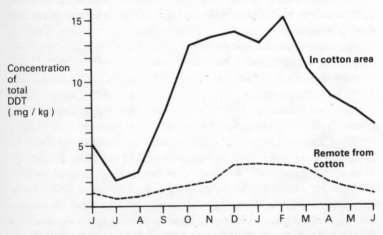

Source: ICAITI, *An environmental and economic investigation of the consequences of pesticide use in Central American cotton production* (Guatemala City: Instituto Centroamericano de Investigacion y Technologia Industrial, 1977).

30–180 for edible green vegetables, 11–15 for beans, 7–230 for fruit and 160–880 for rice.

The high residue levels in developing country foodstuffs are frequently exported. Much of the beef from Central America is exported to the USA and, in the 1970s, some 13 per cent was rejected because of residues of DDT at up to 6290 μg/kg. Again the contamination was related to spraying of nearby cotton: the levels from non-cotton areas were some five times less than those from cotton growing regions. In the UK fruit and vegetables are often rejected by inspectors at ports because they have higher residue levels than locally grown produce.[102] In one instance, two batches of citrus contained the fungicide 2–phenylphenol at 40–80 per cent greater than the CAC MRL. Another case was imported rabbit, pork and poultry from the People's Republic of China, which contained high levels of DDT and HCH.

Pesticide residues in humans

Blood and tissue analysis

There is considerable evidence that residues of organochlorine pesticides are widespread in human populations, although in the industrialized countries the levels have been declining for at least two decades (Figure 3.10). The most recent studies suggest typical concentrations of less than 5000 μg/kg for DDT and its derivatives in human tissue.[103] The decline in DDT appears to have begun before the imposition of restrictions and the withdrawal from use in the 1970s and 1980s. However, other organochlorines, such as dieldrin, although present at much lower levels, appear to be more persistent and are declining more slowly.

There are variations in residue burdens both within and between countries. Residents of agricultural areas may contain relatively higher burdens. Thus residues of DDT in the fat of people living in northeast Louisiana exceeded 10,000 μg/kg in 1980, although this declined to 4100 μg/kg by 1984.[104] Some countries have particularly high average residues: for Hungary and Poland in 1979, the average DDT levels were 18,300 and 17,200 μg/kg in human fat.[105] Maximum values may also be much higher than the average. In a survey of UK residents during 1982–3 the maximum was some 3.5 times greater than the average of 1440 μg/kg.[106] According to this survey, above average concentrations were especially found in people aged over 60. A five

Figure 3.10   Organochlorine residues in human fat tissue in the USA and UK, 1955–83

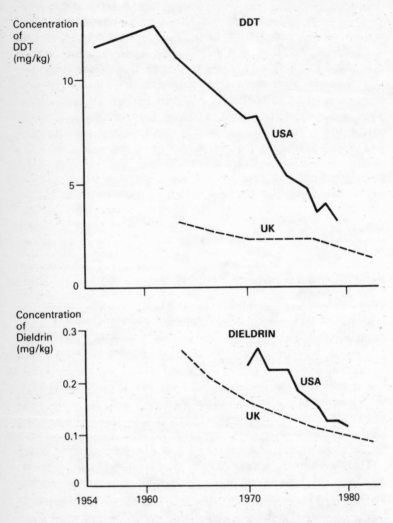

Sources: Abbott, D.C., Goulding, R. Homes, D.L. and Hoodless, R.A., "Organochlorine pesticide residues in human fat in the UK, 1982–1983", *Human Toxicology* 4 (1985), pp. 435–445; Kutz, F.W., Strassman, S.C. and Yobs, A.R., "Survey of pesticide residues and their metabolism in humans", in: Watson, D.R. and Brown, A.W.A. (eds), *Pesticide Management and Insecticide Resistance* (New York: Academic Press, 1977); CEQ, *Environmental Quality* (Washington DC: Council on Environmental Quality, 1983).

day old infant was also found to have 220 μg/kg of DDE and 80 μg/kg of HCH in its fat tissue.

In the developing countries, there is considerable variation in reported levels. Several studies from Nigeria, Zaire, India and Central America have found no levels of DDT exceeding 6500 μg/kg.[107] An investigation in Calcutta indicated that organochlorines were highest in the 40–60 year age group, and lowest in those aged less than 20 years, but mean concentrations of DDT did not exceed 600 μg/kg fat tissue.[108] The greatest concentration of lindane (gamma HCH) was 1500 μg/kg. The levels are also found to vary with the seasons, being highest in the dry winter months when leafy vegetables are most likely to be contaminated (see p 137) (Table 3.23).

Table 3.23   Comparison between detection rates of pesticides in foodstuffs and human tissues according to season. Study conducted Calcutta, 1975–6

Season	Detection rates for pesticide residues (%)*		
	All foods	Green leafy	Human tissues
Winter (November to February)[†]	31.3	53.3	32.6
Rainy (July to October)[†]	16.6	8.3	14.3

* The most common pesticides detected were DDT, lindane and malathion
† Probability that the differences between winter and rainy seasons have arisen by chance is less than 2 in a hundred.

Source: Mukherjee et al., 1980a, 1980b, *op. cit.*

But there have also been reports of very high levels, particularly in the 1960s and 1970s. In India and Pakistan levels in excess of 20,000 μg/kg DDT were detected, with some individuals containing 150,000 μg/kg.[109] During the early 1960s civil servants in Delhi were found to contain an average of 26,000 μg/kg of DDT and 1700 μg/kg of lindane.[110] The same study also found two children aged three and seven years at death with DDT concentrations of 291,000 and 180,000 μg/kg respectively. In Nicaragua, DDT in the blood of people living in a cotton growing region during the 1970s was some seven times more concentrated than in those from urban areas, and in 1980 another of the world's highest DDT levels, 97,000 μg/kg, was detected there.[111]

Residues in human milk

One of the most potentially serious hazards is the presence of organochlorine residues in human milk that is breast fed to infants. (In this chapter we exclusively refer to concentrations of residue in whole milk. To convert from $\mu g/kg$ of whole milk to $\mu g/kg$ on a fat basis multiply by a factor of 25.) Organochlorines are lipid soluble and human milk contains a higher concentration of lipids than human plasma, so increasing the risk of high residue levels.[112] International standards of 50 μg DDT/kg of whole cows' milk have been set by the FAO/WHO Codex Alimentarius Commission; for dieldrin the standard is 6 and lindane 10.[113] These standards have commonly been exceeded in many countries (Table 3.24).

In western Europe, levels of DDT in milk fell from 100–300 $\mu g/kg$ to less than 100 in the 1970s and levels in North America are comparable.[114] Nevertheless a recent US study detected dieldrin in more than 80 per cent of the 1436 samples collected.[115] Highest mean concentrations occurred in the southeastern states, reaching a maximum of 12,300 $\mu g/kg$ in one sample, perhaps because of the larger proportion of homes treated with dieldrin for termite control.

In eastern Europe, levels have generally remained high, DDT being in the range 250–550 $\mu g/kg$.[116] Levels are also often high in Asia, Africa and Latin America: average concentrations of DDT during the mid-1970s to mid-1980s have been of the order of 150–500 $\mu g/kg$. They are particularly high in regions which are heavily sprayed for mosquito or tsetse fly control. In Guatemala in the early 1970s values of 2–3500 $\mu g/kg$ were recorded; and more recently, in 1983–5, a study in Kenya recorded maximum values from various regions of the country in the range of 1000–2800 $\mu g/kg$.[117] The highest concentration in Kenya was in a woman from Rusinga Island in Lake Victoria, where no agricultural pesticides were used. Nevertheless, agricultural spraying can be important. In tea and pyrethrum growing regions concentrations may also be very high.

In Papua New Guinea milk from women in a community using both agricultural pesticides and participating in a malarial control programme contained an average of 290 $\mu g/kg$ of DDT, whereas that from a region not using pesticides contained only 3.2 $\mu g/kg$.[118]

Another factor is the source of food. In Guatemala levels were higher in the breast milk of urban mothers because their food largely came from lowland areas where pesticide use on cotton and coffee was heavy (Table 3.25). Diet is also important in the developed countries. The milk of vegetarian women in the USA contains lower levels of organochlorine residues, presumably because of lower consumption of fats compared with the general population.[119]

Despite these high residue levels, there have, as yet, been no

Table 3.24 Some examples of organochlorine residues in human milk (μg/kg whole milk)

		DDT		DIELDRIN	
US Food and Drug Administration Action Level for cows' milk		50		7.5	
FAO/WHO CAC MRL for cows' milk		50		6.0	
		Mean	*Maximum*	*Mean*	*Maximum*
Europe					
UK[1]	1965	78	250	–	–
UK[2]	1979–80	46	229	2.2	14.9
Scotland[3]	1979–80	128	–	–	–
Scotland[3]	1983–4	47	250	2.0	6.0
Denmark[4]	1982	40	117	1.4	16.5
Poland[5]	1970	280	–	–	–
France[5]	1971–2	130	–	–	–
Netherlands[5]	1969	108	–	–	–
North America					
USA[5]	1962	370	–	–	–
USA[6]	1970–1	170	–	–	–
Texas[6]	1970	108	–	–	–
Pennsylvania[6]	1970	90	–	–	–
Colorado[6]	1972	30–500	–	–	–
Arizona[6]	1972	100–500	–	–	–
Mississippi[6]	1973	22	–	–	–
Tennessee[6]	1974	75	–	–	–
Arkansas and Mississippi[6]	1974	447	–	–	–
USA, SE States[7]	late 1970s	–	–	242	12,300
USA, NE States[7]	late 1970s	–	–	98	12,300
USA, New York[1]	1984	31	170	–	–
Canada[6]	1969	139	–	–	–
Canada[8]	1983	25–44	–	–	–
South America					
Mexico[9]	1981	270	–	–	–
Argentina[9]	1974	140	–	–	–
Chile[9]	1974	250	–	–	–
Guatemala[9]					
La Bomba	1973	590 •	3500	–	–
Guatemala City	1976	230	–	–	–
Guatemala[10]	early 1980s	345	–	–	–
Nicaragua[9]	mid-1970s	500	–	–	–

continued

Table 3.24 Continued

		Mean	Maximum	Mean	Maximum
Asia					
India, Punjab[10]	1979–80	380	–	–	–
India[9]	1981	510	–	–	–
India[9]					
Karnal	1984	190	281	–	–
Bangalore	1984	53	166	–	–
Calcutta	1984	114	140	–	–
Bombay	1984	224	431	–	–
Papua New Guinea[11]	1970	290* 3**	–	–	–
Israel[12]	1984	89	–	–	–
Iraq[13]	1983–4	145	718	30	809
Japan[5]	1970–2	20–108	–	–	–
Japan[14]	1979	37	–	–	–
Africa					
Kenya[15]	1983–5	90–170	1000–2800	2–30	70–100
Zaire[14]	early 1980s	60	–	–	–

*   sprayed region
** non-sprayed region

Sources:
 1 Bush et al., "Polychlorinated biphenyl congeners (PCBs), *p,p'*-DDE and hexa-chlorobenzene in human milk in three areas of upstate New York", *Arch. Environ. Contam. Toxicol.* **14** (1985) pp. 443–50.
 2 Collins, G.B. et al., "Organochlorine pesticide residues in human milk in Great Britain 1979–80", *Hu. Toxicol.* **1** (1982) pp. 425–31.
 3 MAFF, *Report of the Working Party on Pesticide Residues (1982–5)* (London: HMSO, 1986).
 4 Anderson, J.R. and Orbaek, K., "Organochlorine contaminants in human milk in Denmark. 1982", *Ambio* **13** (1984) pp. 266–9.
 5 WHO, *DDT and its Derivatives*, Environ. Health Criteria 9 (Geneva: WHO, 1979).
 6 Dillion, J.C. et al., "Pesticide residues in human milk", *Fd. Cosmet. Toxicol.* **19** (1981) pp. 437–42.
 7 Savage, E.P. et al., "National study of chlorinated hydrocarbon insecticide residues in human milk, USA", *Am. J. Epidemiol.* **113** (1981) pp. 413–22.
 8 Mes, J. et al., "Polychlorinated biphenyls and organochlorine pesticides in milk and blood of Canadian women during lactation", *Arch. Environ. Contam. Toxicol.* **13** (1984) pp. 217–23.
 9 Ramakrishnan, N. et al., "Organochlorine pesticide residues in mother's milk: a source of toxic chemicals in suckling infants", *Hu. Toxicol.* **4** (1985) pp. 7–12.
 10 UNEP, *Environmental Data Report* (Oxford: Basil Blackwell, 1987).
 11 Hornabrook, R.W. et al., "DDT residues in human milk from New Guinea natives", *Med. J. Aust.* **1** (1971) pp. 1297–300.
 12 Weisenberg, E. et al., "Polychlorinated biphenyls and organochlorine insecticides in human milk in Israel", *Arch. Environ. Contam. Toxicol.* **14** (1985) pp. 517–21.
 13 Al-Omar, M. et al., "Organochlorine residues in human milk from Baghdad", *Bull. Environ. Contam. Toxicol.* **35** (1985) pp. 65–7.
 14 WHO, *The Quantity and Quality of Breast Milk*, (Geneva: WHO, 1985).
 15 Kanja, L. et al., "Organochlorine pesticides in human milk from different areas of Kenya, 1983–1985", *J. Toxicol. & Environ. Health* **19** (1988) pp. 449–64.

recorded instances of infants suffering ill-health from ingesting milk containing pesticide residues. There is a potential hazard, but clearly if infants were not breast fed they would continue to ingest residues through ordinary dietary food stuffs just as do their mothers.[120]

Table 3.25   Organochlorine residues in the milk of rich and poor urban mothers and rural mothers in Guatemala, late 1970s

	DDT	Dieldrin	Lindane (γ-HCH)
		(μg/l)	
Rich urban	216	3.2	24
Poor urban	228	2.3	15
Rural	40	1.3	5

Source: WHO, *The Quantity and Quality of Breast Milk* (Geneva: WHO, 1985).

Summary

There is no doubt that pesticides are hazardous. At very high dosages many are lethal to both laboratory animals and ourselves, and can cause severe illness at sublethal levels. But just how serious is the hazard from medium to low dosages is open to question. For instance, despite years of experimentation, the only known chronic effect of DDT on laboratory animals is to produce tumours in certain strains of mice, but whether the tumours are benign or malignant is still not known.

In the 1950s, 1960s and 1970s organochlorine insecticides were in widespread use in the industrialized countries and high levels of exposure were common in those engaged in their manufacture, in agricultural workers and, because of the presence of residues in foods, among the general public. Nevertheless, there is very little evidence of serious ill-health, other than as a result of accidental exposure to high dosages. The concentration of organochlorines in the livers of patients dying of cancers, cirrhosis and other liver diseases, appears to be a result rather than a cause of these conditions. Overall, liver cancer rates have declined in the industrialized countries over the period of greatest organochlorine use. The herbicides 2,4,5-T and 2,4-D were also commonly used in that period and were originally thought to be a cause of miscarriages. Subsequent, more thorough, studies suggest a link with increased incidence of a certain rare cancer, non-Hodgkin's lymphoma, but not with miscarriages or other reproductive effects.

Other pesticides appear to be intrinsically less hazardous, although the organophosphates, in particular, may produce severe acute poisoning. They are more acutely toxic than organochlorines but since they are not stored in body tissues are probably less hazardous over the long term and there is little evidence of chronic effects. Two highly hazardous pesticides are the nematocide, DBCP, which causes infertility in humans and the herbicide, paraquat, which may be carcinogenic and mutagenic. However, most synthetic pyrethroids and modern herbicides and fungicides have very low toxicity and no known health effects.

What is controversial is the extent of carcinogenicity among pesticides. The World Health Organization believes there is little risk of carcinogenicity but the US Environmental Protection Agency has identified 53 compounds as causing either benign or malignant tumours. Most of these are older compounds but some are products developed since 1970. In many cases the evidence for carcinogenicity is very slender and the highest levels of risk are only of the order of 1–10 per ten thousand, compared with the 1 in 4 lifetime risk of cancer from all causes in the USA. However, the 53 compounds constitute a major proportion of current pesticide use in the USA. Over half of herbicide use and over 80 per cent of fungicide use involves oncogenic compounds.

Pesticide residues in average diets in the industrialized countries are all well below Acceptable Daily Intakes (ADI). Only in the case of dieldrin in the 1960s were average intakes close to the ADI. Levels of organophosphate and other newer pesticides are at least 100 times less than the ADI. But levels in certain individual foodstuffs, particularly fruit and vegetables are, on occasions, unacceptably high and are thought to pose a risk to humans. In a few instances, for example aldicarb residues in watermelons, they have been known to cause illness. High levels of organochlorines in human milk are also worrying although there is no evidence linking such residues with ill effects. The levels of organochlorines in food and in human tissues, including human milk, are rapidly declining in industrialized countries now that they are banned or severely restricted. What is not known, however, is whether there is any long term effect of chronic exposure to organophosphates.

The major hazard lies in accidents. Even here, fatalities at work are very rare – one a decade in the UK; eight a decade in California and there are many other more common causes of death. There is, though, a relatively high incidence of ill health among those engaged in applying pesticides. But the principal danger is to the general public and particularly to children and others who accidentally encounter pesticides stored in and around the home. More than half of poisonings recorded by hospitals in the UK and Poison Information Centers in California are of children under the age of six. Although, in this respect, pesticides are no different from hazardous medicines, they are often not perceived as being in the same category and are less carefully guarded.

The systems for recording pesticide poisoning vary within and between countries, and are difficult to compare. Very approximately there are 2000 to 3000 cases of pesticide poisoning in the UK each year, giving a rate of 4–6 per 100,000. For the USA, the estimate is some 45,000 cases a year or 18 per 100,000.[121] Overall the hazard in the industrialized countries presented by pesticides is not very different from that of other manufactured chemicals, such as pharmaceuticals. Nonetheless, there continues to be considerable public concern over the risks arising from exposure to pesticides, in particular through accidental spraying and spray drift, or from residues in foodstuffs.

The overall situation is considerably worse in the developing countries. Poisoning is more common (20+ per 100,000), in particular because of lack of knowledge, poorer working and living conditions and the convenience of pesticides as a means of suicide. Residue levels are often well above the ADIs. There is now growing anecdotal and circumstantial evidence of very high levels of mortality and morbidity among rural populations exposed to pesticide applications.

References

1 WHO, *DDT and its Derivatives*, Environmental Health Criteria 9 (Geneva: World Health Organization, 1979); Hayes, W.J., "Pharmacology and toxicology of DDT", in: Muller, P. (ed.), *DDT: The inseccology and toxicology of DDT*", in: Muller, P. (ed.), DDT: The Insecticide Dichlorodiphenyltrichloroethane and its Significance (Basel: Berghauser Verlag, 1959).

2 Ottoboni, A., "Effect of DDT on reproduction in the rat", *Toxicol. appl. Pharmacol.* **14** (1969) pp. 74–81; Keplinger, M.L., Deichmann, W.B. and Sala, F., "Effect of combinations of pesticides on reproduction in mice", in: Deichmann, W.B. (ed.), *Pesticides Symposia* (Miami: Halos and Assoc., 1970).

3 IARC, *The Evaluation of the Carcinogenic Risk of Chemicals to Man, some Organochloride Pesticides* (Lyon: International Agency for Research on Cancer, 1974); WHO, 1979, *op. cit.*

4 WHO, 1979, *op. cit.*

5 Laws, E.R. Jr., Curley, A. and Biros, F.J. "Men with intensive occupational exposure to DDT; a clinical and chemical study", *Arch. Environ. Health* **15** (1967) pp. 766–775.

6 Laws et al., 1967, *op. cit*; WHO, *Safe use of pesticides*, WHO Technical Report Series no. 513 (1973).

7 Ortelee, M.F., "Study of men with prolonged intensive occupational exposure to DDT", *Ann. Med. Assoc. Arch. Indust. Health* 18 (1958) pp. 433–40.

8 WHO, 1979, *op. cit.*

9 Deichmann, W.B. and Radomski, J.L., "Retention of pesticides in human adipose tissue – Preliminary report", *Ind. Med. Surg.* 37 (1968) pp. 218–19; Radomski, J.L., Deichmann. W.B. and Chizer, E.E., "Pesticide concentrations in the liver, brain and adipose tissue of terminal hospital patients", *Food Cosmet. Toxicol.* 6 (1968) pp. 209–20.

10 Cassarett, L.J., Fryer, G.C., Yauger, W.L. and Klemmer, H.W., "Organochlorine pesticide residues in human tissues – Hawaii", *Arch. Environ. Health* 17 (1968) pp. 306–311.

11 Oloffs, C.P., Hardwick, D.F., Szeto, S.Y. and Moerman, B.G., "DDT, dieldrin and heptachlor epoxide in humans with liver cirrhosis", *Clin. Biochem.* 7 (1974) pp. 297–306.

12 Muir, C., Waterhouse, J., Mack, T., Powell, J. and Whelan, S. (eds) *Cancer Incidence in Five Continents* vol. V (Lyon: International Agency for Cancer Research, 1987); WHO, 1979, *op. cit.*

13 WHO, 1979, *op. cit.*

14 IARC, IARC Monographs on the Evaluation of the Carcinogenic Risk of Chemicals to Humans. *Some Halogenated Hydrocarbons and Pesticide Exposures* (Lyon: IARC, 1986).

15 ACP, *Further Review of the Safety for Use in the UK of the Herbicide 2,4,5-T* (London: Advisory Committee on Pesticides MAFF, 1980).

16 ACP, *Review of the Safety for Use in the UK of the Herbicide 2,4,5-T* (London Advisory Committee on Pesticides: MAFF, 1979); ACP, 1980, *op. cit.*

17 Wilson, J.G., Ritter, E.J., Scott, W.J. and Fradkin, R., "Comparative distribution and embryotoxicity of acetylsalicylic acid in pregnant rats and rhesus monkeys", *Toxicol. Appl. Pharmacol.* 41 (1977) pp. 67–78.

18 Environmental Protection Agency, *The Biologic and Economic Assessment of 2,4,5-T: a Report of the USDA-EPA-States RPAR Assessment Team* C/DC: Washington 1979).

19 Witt, J.M., "A discussion of the suspension of 2,4,5-T and the EPA Alsea II study", Special Report, unpublished (Corvallis: Oregon State University, 1980); Agresti, A., *Analysis of Association between 2,4,5-T Exposure and Hospitalised Spontaneous Abortions* (Corvallis: Environmental Health Sciences Centre, Oregon State University, 1979); Wagner, S.L., Witt, J.M., Norris, L.A., Higgins, J.E., Agresti, A. and Ortiz, M., *A Scientific Critique of the EPA Alsea II Study and Report* (Corvallis: Environmental Health Sciences Centre, Oregon State University, 1979).

20 Donovan, J.W., MacLennan, R. and Adena, N., "Vietnam service and the risks of congenital anomalies: a case control study", *Med. J. Aust.* 140 (1984) pp. 394–7; Smith, A.H., Matheson, D.P., Fisher, D.O. and

Chapman, C.J., "Preliminary report of reproductive outcomes among pesticide applicators using 2,4,5-T.", *NZ Med. J.* **93** (1981) pp. 177–9.

21 Balarajan, R. and McDowell, M., "Congenital malformations in agricultural workers", *The Lancet* **i** (1983) pp. 1112–13; Golding, J. and Sladden, T., "Congenital malformations and agricultural workers", *The Lancet* **i** (1983) p. 1393.

22 Hardell, L. and Sandstrom, A., "Case-control study: Soft-tissue sarcomas and exposure to phenoxyacetic acids or chlorophenols", *Br. J. Cancer* **39** (1979) pp. 711–17; Eriksson, M., Hardell, L., Berg, N.O., Moller, T. and Axelson, O., "Soft-tissue sarcomas and exposure to chemical substances: a case reference study", *Brit. J. Indust. Med.* **38** (1981) pp. 27–33.

23 Hardell, L., Ericksson, M., Lenner, P. and Lundgren, E., "Malignant lymphoma and exposure to chemicals especially organic solvents, chlorophenols and phenoxy acids. A case-control study", *Br. J. Cancer* **43** (1981) pp. 169–76.

24 Coggon, D. and Acheson, E.D., "Do phenoxy herbicides cause cancer in man?" *The Lancet* **i** (1982) pp. 1057–59; Colton, T., "Herbicide exposure and cancer", *J. Am. Med. Assn.* **256**, (1986) pp. 1176–78.

25 Wiklund, K. and Holm, L.E., "Soft tissue sarcoma risk in Swedish agricultural and forestry workers", *J. Nat. Cancer Inst.* **76** (1986) pp. 229–34.

26 Wiklund, K., "Swedish agricultural workers. A group with a decreased risk of cancer", *Cancer* **51**, (1983) pp. 566–8.

27 Fingerhut, M.A., Halperin, W.E., and Honchar, P.A. "An evaluation of reports of dioxin exposure and soft tissue sarcoma pathology among chemical workers in the United States", *Scan. J. Work Environ. Health* **10** (1984) pp. 299–303; Honchar, P.A. and Halperin, W.E., "2,4,5-T, trichlorophenol and soft-tissue sarcoma", *The Lancet* **i** (1981) pp. 268–9.

28 Milham, S., "Herbicides, occupation and cancer", *The Lancet* **i** (1982) pp. 1464–5.

29 Kang, H.K., Weatherbee, L., Breslin, P.P., Lee, Y. and Shepard, B.M., "Soft tissue sarcomas and military service in Vietnam: a case comparison group analysis of hospital patients", *J. Occup. Med* **28** (1986) pp. 1215–18.

30 McQueen, E.G., Veale, A.M.O., Alexander, W.S. and Bates, M.N., *2,4,5-T and Human Birth Defects* (New Zealand Department of Health: Reports of the Division of Public Health, 1977); Milby, T.H., Husting, E.L., Wharton, M.D. and Larson, S., *Potential Health Effects Associated with the Use of Phenoxy Herbicides* (Berkeley, CA: A report for the National Forest Products Association by the Environmental Health Associates Inc, 1981); Smith, A.H., Fisher, D.O., Pearce, N. and Chapman, C.J., "Congenital defects and miscarriages among New Zealand 2,4,5-T sprayers", *Arch. of Environ. Health* **37** (1982) pp. 197–200; Smith, A.H., Pearce, N.E., Fisher, D.O., Giles, H.J., Teague, C.A. and Howard, J.K., "Soft tissue sarcoma and exposure to phenoxy

herbicides and chlorophenols in New Zealand", *J. Nat. Cancer Inst.* **73** (1984) pp. 1111–17; Pearce, N.E., Sheppard, R.A., Smith, A.H. and Teague, C.A., "Non-Hodgkin's lymphoma and farming: an expanded case control study", *Int. J. Cancer* **39** (1987) pp. 155–61.

31 Hoar, S.K., Blair, A., Holmes, F.F., Boysen, C.D., Robel, R.J., Hoover, R. and Fraumeni, J.F., "Agricultural herbicide use and risk of lymphoma and soft-tissue sarcoma", *J. Am. Med. Assn.* **256** (1986) pp. 1141–47; Colton, 1986, *op. cit.*

32 Hoar, S.K., Weisenberger, D.D., Babbitt, P.A., Saal, R.C., Cantor, K.P. and Blair, A., "A case-control study of non-Hodgkin's lymphoma and agricultural factors in eastern Nebraska", *Am. J. Epidmiol.* **128** (1988) p. 901.

33 IARC, 1986, *op. cit.*; ACP, 1980, *op. cit.*

34 Hay, A., *The Chemical Scythe – Lessons of 2,4,5-T and Dioxin* (New York: Plenum Press, 1982); Lowrance, W.W., *Public Health Risks of the Dioxins* (Los Altos, California: Kaufmann, 1984); Kimbrough, R.D., "The epidimiology and toxicology of TCDD", *Bull. Environ. Contam. & Toxicol.* **33** (1984) pp. 636–47; Royal Commission on Environmental Pollution, *Managing Waste: the Duty of Care*, 11th Report, (London: HMSO 1985).

35 Hay, 1982, *op. cit.*

36 Health and Safety Executive, English translation of the final report of the Italian Parliamentary Commission of Enquiry on the escape of toxic substances on 10 July 1976 at the ICMESA Establishment, (London: 1980); Hay, A. and Silbergeld, E., "Assessing the risk of dioxin exposure", *Nature* **315** (1985) pp. 102–103; Hay, A., 1982, *op. cit.*; Zack, J.A. and Gaffey, W.R., in: Tucker, R.E., Young, A.L. and Gray, A.P. (eds), *Human Environmental Risks of Chlorinated Dioxins and Related Compounds* (New York: Plenum Press, 1983); Gough, M., "Dioxin exposure at Monsanto", *Nature* **318** (1985) p. 504; Tschirley, F., "Dioxin", *Scientific American* **254** February (1986) pp. 21–7; Mastroiacovo, P., Spagnolo, A., Marni, E., Meazza, L., Bertollini, R., Segni, G., "Birth defects in the Seveso area after TCDD contamination", *J. Am. Med. Assn.* **259** (1988) pp. 1670–72.

37 MAFF/HSE, *Pesticides 1986, Pesticides approved under the Control of Pesticides Regulations 1986*, Reference Book 500 (London: HMSO, 1986); Gilbert, D.G.R., "Pesticide safety policy and control arrangements in Britain", PhD Thesis (Imperial College, University of London: Centre for Environmental Technology, 1987); ACP, 1979, *op. cit.*; ACP, 1980, *op. cit.*; ACP, 1982, *op. cit.*

38 FAO, *Production Yearbook* (Rome: FAO, 1986).

39 Herve, J.J., "Agriculture, public health and animal health usage", in: Leakley, J.P. (ed.), *The Pyrethroid Insecticides* (London: Taylor & Francis, 1985).

40 Crosson, P.R. and Brubaker, S., *Resource and Environmental Effects of US Agriculture* (Washington: Resources for the Future, 1982).

41 Namba, T., Nolte, C.T., Jackrel, G. and Grob, D., "Poisoning due to organophosphate insecticides: acute and chronic manifestations", *Am. J. Med.* **50** (1971) pp. 475–92.

42 Namba, T., "Relative toxicity of malathion", *New England J. Med.* **290** (1974) p. 347.

43 Derache, R., *Organophosphorus Pesticides. Criteria (dose/effect relationship) for Organophosphorus Pesticides.* Report of a Working Group of Experts prepared for the Commission of European Communities Directorate-General for Social Affairs, Health and Safety Directorate. (Oxford: Pergamon Press, 1977).

44 Baker, E.L., Zack, M., Miles, J.W., Alderman, L., Warren, M., Dobbin, R.D., Miller, S. and Teeten, W.R., "Epidemic malathion poisoning in Pakistan malaria workers", *The Lancet*, **i** (1978) pp. 31–34.

45 WHO, *Field Surveys of Exposure to Pesticides – Standard Protocol* (Geneva: WHO, 1982).

46 *Farmers Weekly* "Farmer: I had to stop", 24 November (1989) p. 17.

47 Johnson, M.K., "Delayed neurotoxicity induced by organophosphorus compounds", in: Holmstedt, B., Lauwerys, R., Mercier, M. and Roberfroid, M. (eds), *Mechanisms of Toxicity and Hazard Evaluation* (Amsterdam: Elsevier, 1980).

48 IARC, "Dichlorvos", in: *Some Halogenated Hydrocarbons*, Monographs on the Evaluation of the Carcinogenic Risk of Chemicals to Humans (Lyon: IARC, 1979); IARC, *Miscellaneous Chemicals*, Monographs vol. 30 (Lyon: IARC, 1983); WHO, *Organophosphorus Insecticides: A General Introduction* (Geneva: WHO, 1986); Derache, 1977, *op. cit.*; Reuber, M.D., "Carcinogenicity and toxicity of malathion and malaoxon", *Environ. Res.* **37** (1985) pp. 119–53.

49 WHO, 1986, *op. cit.*

50 Leahey, J.P., 1985, *op. cit.*; Elliot, M., Janes, N.F. and Potter, C., "The future of pyrethroids in insect control", *Ann. Rev. Entomol.* **23** (1978) pp. 443–69.

51 Whorton, D., Krauss, R.M., Marshall, S. and Milby, T.M., "Infertility in male pesticide workers", *The Lancet* **ii** (1977) pp. 1259–61; Glass, R.I., Lyness, R.N., Mengle, D.C., Powell, K.E. and Kahn, E., "Sperm count depression in pesticide applicators exposed to dibromochloropropane", *Am. J. Epidem.* **109** (1979) pp. 346–51; Kahn, E. and Whorton, D., Letter to the editor – re "Sperm count depression in pesticide applicators exposed to dibromochloropropane." *Am. J. Epidem.* **112** (1980) pp. 161–4; Glass, R.I., Reply to Kahn, E. and Whorton, D., 1980, *Am. J. Epidem.* **112**, (1980) pp. 164–5.

52 SLB, "Banana workers suffer from exposure to DBCP pesticides". *SLB* **1** (1987) pp. 138–39.

53 WHO, *Paraquat & Diquat* (Geneva: WHO, 1984).

54 Hayes, W.J. and Vaughn, W.K., "Mortality from pesticides in the United States in 1973 and 1974", *Toxicol. and Appl. Pharmacol.* **42** (1977) pp. 235–252.

55 Swan, A.A.B., "Exposure of spray operators to paraquat", *Br. J. Indust. Med.* **26** (1969) pp. 322–9; Hearn, C.E.D. and Keir, W., "Nail damage in spray operators exposed to paraquat", *Br. J. Indust. Med.* **28** (1971) pp. 399–403.

56 Plewa, M.J. and Gentile, J.M., "Mutagenicity of atrazine: a maiz-microbe miossay", *Mutation Research* **38** (1976) pp. 287–92.

57 Hsia, M.J.S., "The worse for biodegration", *Science News* **114**(13) (1973).

58 NRC, *Regulating Pesticides in Food. The Delaney Paradox* (Washington DC: National Research Council, 1987).

59 NRC, 1987, *op. cit.*

60 CDFA, *passim, Summary of Illnesses & Injuries Reported by California Physicians as Potentially Related to Pesticides 1972–1990* (Sacramento, CA: California Department of Food and Agriculture).

61 House of Commons, *The Effects of Pesticides on Human Health* vol. 1, Report and Proceedings of the House of Commons Select Committee on Agriculture (London: HMSO, 1987).

62 CDFA, *passim, op. cit.*

63 HSE, *Pesticide Incidents Investigated in 1988* (Liverpool: Health and Safety Executive, 1989).

64 CDFA, *passim, op. cit.*

65 Gilbert, 1987, *op. cit.*

66 Gilbert, 1987, *op. cit.*

67 Gilbert, 1987, *op. cit.*; Friends of the Earth, *Pesticide Residues* (London: FAO, 1985); London Food Commission, *Pesticide Residues* (London: 1986); Dudley, N., *Spray Drift: an Investigation by the Soil Association* (Haughley, Suffolk: Soil Association Ltd, 1984); Tait, E.J., "Pest control decision making on brassica crops", *Adv. appl. Biol.* **8** (1983) pp. 121–88; NUAAW, *Not One Minute Longer. The 2,4,5-T Dossier* (London: National Union of Agricultural and Allied Workers, 1980); NUAAW, *Pray Before you Spray* (London: National Union of Agricultural and Allied Workers, 1981).

68 Gilbert, 1987, *op. cit.*

69 HC, 1987, *op. cit.*

70 WHO, *Safe Use of Pesticides*, 9th Report of the WHO Expert Committee on Vector Biology and Control, Tech. Rep. Series 720 (Geneva: WHO, 1985); Bull, D., *A Growing Problem. Pesticides and the Third World Poor* (Oxford: Oxfam, 1982); Warren, M.C., Ruebush, T.K., Hobbs, J.H., Hippolyte, R. and Miller, S., "Safety measures associated with the use of organophosphate insecticides in the Haitian malaria control programme", *Bull. WHO* **63** (1985) pp. 345–51; ICAITI, *An Environmental and Economic Study of the Consequences of Pesticide Use in Central American Cotton Production* (Guatemala City, Guatemala: Instituto Centroamericano de Investigacion y Technologia Industrial, 1977).

71 GAO, *Export of unregistered pesticides is not adequately monitored by EPA* (Washington: U.S. General Accounting Office, 1989); *Farmers Weekly*, 23 March (London, 1990), p. 14.

72 Levine, R.S., *Assessment of mortality and morbidity due to unintentional pesticide poisonings*. Working paper presented to Consultation on Planning Strategy for the Prevention of Pesticide Poisoning, doc. no. WHO/VCB/86.926 (Geneva: World Health Organistion, 1986).

73 Jeyaratnam, J., Seneviratne, R.S., de, A. and Coppleston, J.F., "Survey of pesticide poisoning in Sri Lanka", *Bull. WHO* 60 (1982) pp. 615–19.

74 Copplestone, J.F., "A global view of pesticide safety", in: Watson, D.L. and Browne, A.W.A. (eds), *Pesticide Management and Insecticide Resistance* (New York: Academic Press, 1977); ICAITI, 1977, *op. cit.*

75 Bull, 1982, *op. cit.*

76 Bull, 1982, *op. cit.*; Bakir, F., Damhiji, S.F., Amin-Zahi, L., Murtudha, M., Khalidi, A., Al-Rawi, N.Y., Tikriti, S., Dhahir, H.I., Clarkson, N.W., Smith, S.L. and Doherty, R.A. "Methyl mercury poisoning in Iraq", *Science* 181 (1973) pp. 230–41.

77 Bhat, R.V., "Pesticides: a necessary evil", *Medico Friends Circle Bulletin (Poona)* 19 (1981) p. 1; Sharma, M., Manjunatu, T.N., Wajh, S. and Prakash, S. "The Basti tragedy", *Health for the Millions* 16 (1990) pp. 19–20 (Voluntary Health Association of India).

78 CDC, "Thallium poisoning: an epidemic of false positives, Georgetown, Guyana", *MMWR* 36 (1987) pp. 481–8.

79 Loevinsohn, M.E., "Insecticide use and increased mortality in rural central Luzon, Philippines", *The Lancet* i (1987) pp. 1359–62.

80 Loevinsohn, 1987, *op. cit.*

81 MAFF, *Report of the Working Party on Pesticide Residues: 1985–1988.* Food Surveillance Paper no.25 (London: HMSO, 1989); MAFF, *Report of the Working Party on Pesticide Residues 1982–1985.* Food Surveillance Paper no.16 (London: HMSO, 1986); MAFF, *Report of the Working Party on Pesticide Residues: 1977–1981.* Food Surveillance Paper no.9 (London: HMSO, 1982).

82 MAFF, 1989, *op. cit.*; 1986, *op. cit.*; 1982, *op. cit.*

83 WHO, 1979, *op. cit.*; Gartrell, M.J., Craun, J.C., Podrebarac, D.S. and Gunderson, E.L., "Pesticides, selected elements and other chemicals in infant and toddler total diet samples, October 1980 – March 1982", *J. Assoc. Off. Anal. Chem.* 69 (1986a) pp. 123–45; Gartrell, M.J., Craun, J.C., Podrebarac, D.G. and Gunderson, E.L., "Pesticides, selected elements and other chemicals in adult total diet samples, October 1980 – March 1982", *J. Assoc. Off. Anal. Chem.* 69 (1986b) pp. 146–59; Podrebarac, D.G., "Pesticide, heavy metal and other chemical residues in infant and toddler total diet samples (V) October 1977 – September 1978", *J. Assoc. Off. Anal. Chem.* 67 (1984a) pp. 166–75; Podrebarac, D.S., "Pesticide, metal and other chemical residues in adult total diet samples (IV) October 1977 – September 1978", *J. Assoc. Off. Anal. Chem.* 67 (1984b) pp. 176–85; Johnson, R.D., Manske, D.D., New, D.H. and Podrebarac, D.S., "Pesticide, heavy metal and other chemical residues in infant and toddler total diet samples (III) August 1976 – September 1977", *J. Assoc. Off. Anal. Chem.* 67 (1984) pp. 145–54.

84 WHO, 1979, *op. cit.*

85 MAFF, 1989, *op. cit.*; 1986, *op. cit.*

86 MAFF, 1989, *op. cit.*

87 Kaphalia, B.S., Siddiqui, F.S., and Seth, T.D., "Contamination levels in different food items and dietary intake of organochlorine pesticide residues in India", *Indian J. Med. Res.* 81 (1985) pp. 71–8; Gartrell et al., 1986a, b *op. cit.*

88 Mukherjee, D., Roy, B.R., Chakraborty, J. and Ghosh, B.N., "Pesticide residues in human foods in Calcutta", *Indian J. Med. Res.* 72 (1980) pp. 577–82.

89 CAC, *Codex Maximum Limits for Pesticide Residues.* vol. XIII (Rome: FAO & WHO, 1986); European Community, Council Directive 76/895/EEC, OJ L340 (1976) pp. 26–31; EC, 86/363/EEC, OJ L221 (Brussels: EEC, 1986) pp. 43–7.

90 MAFF, 1986, *op. cit.*; 1989, *op. cit.*

91 MAFF, 1989, *op. cit.*

92 MAFF, 1986, *op. cit.*

93 MAFF, 1989, *op. cit.*

94 MAFF, *Evaluation of Fully Approved or Provisionally Approved Pesticide Products. Daminozide, November 1989* (London: Pesticides Safety Division, MAFF, 1989).

95 Centers for Disease Control, "Aldicarb food poisoning from contaminated melons – California", *MMWR* 35 (1986) pp. 254–8; Green, M.A., Heumann, M.A., Wehr, M., Foster, L.R., Williams, L.P., Polder, J.A., Morgan, C.L., Wagner, S.L., Wanke, L.A. and Witt, J.A., "An outbreak of watermelon-borne pesticide toxicity", *Am. J. Pub. Health* 77 (1987) pp. 1431–34.

96 Green et al., 1987, *op. cit.*

97 Mukherjee, D., Ghosh, B.N., Chakraborty, J. and Roy, B.R., "Pesticide residues in human tissues", *Indian. J. Med. Res.* 72 (1980) pp. 583–7.

98 Darma, G., *Residu Pesticidas dalam Sayuran-Sayuran Tanah Air* (Jakarta, Indonesia: Wahana Link Kungan Hidup, 1984).

99 Atuma, S.S., "Residues of organochlorine pesticides in some Nigerian food materials", *Bull. Environ. Contam. Toxicol.* 35 (1985) pp. 735–8.

100 Chen, D.F., Meier, P.G. and Hilbert, M.S., "Organochlorine pesticide residues in paddy fish in Malaysia and the associated health risk to farmers", *Bull. WHO* 62 (1987) pp. 251–3.

101 ICAITI, 1977, *op. cit.*

102 MAFF, 1989, *op. cit.*

103 Abbott, D.C., Goulding, R., Holmes, D.C. and Hoodless, R.A., "Organochlorine pesticide residues in human fat in the United Kingdom 1982–1983", *Human Toxicol.* 4 (1985) pp. 435–45; Bush, B., Snow, J. and Koblintz, R., "Polychlorobiphenyl (PCB) congeners, p,p'-DDE and hexachlorobenzene in maternal and fetal cord blood from mothers in upstate New York", *Arch. Environ. Contam. Toxicol.* 13 (1984) pp. 517–27.

104 Holt, R.L., Cruse, S. and Greer, E.S., "Pesticide and polychlorinated

biphenyl residues in human adipose tissue from northeast Louisiana", *Bull. Environ. Contam. Toxicol.* **36** (1986) pp. 651–5.

105 Abbott et al., 1985, *op. cit.*

106 Abbott et al., 1985, *op. cit.*

107 Atuma, S.S. and Okor, D.I., "Pesticide usage in Nigeria – need for a baseline study", *Ambio* **14** (1985) pp. 340–41; Tite, M., Wassermann, M., Pines, A., Cucos, S., Nzuzi, N., Lema, Y. and Wassermann, D., "Teneurs en insecticides organochlores et diphenyls polychlores chez la population générale du Zaire", *J. Toxicol Med.* **2** (1982) pp. 259–64; Gupta, S.K., Srivastava, N., Patel, J.S., Shah, M.P., Jani, J.P., Chatterjee, S.K. and Kashyap, S.K., "Organochlorine insecticide residues in fat of people from urban centres of India II", *Pesticides* **16** (1982) pp. 11–13; ICAITI, 1977, *op. cit.*

108 Mukherjee et al., 1980b, *op. cit.*

109 Mughal, H.A. and Rahman, M.A., "Organochlorine pesticide content of human adipose tissue in Karachi", *Arch. Environ. Health* **27** (1973) pp. 396–8.

110 Dale, W.E., Copeland, M.F. and Haynes, W.J., "Chlorinated insecticides in the body fat of people in India", *Bull. WHO* **33** (1965) pp. 471–7.

111 ICAITI, 1977, *op. cit.*; SACT (Sociedad Alemán de Cooperación Técnica), *Reporte del Laboratorio Ecotoxicologico del GTZ* (Managua, Nicaragua: MIDINRA, 1980).

112 WHO, *The Quantity and Quality of Breast Milk. Report on the WHO Collaborative Study on Breast-Feeding* (Geneva: WHO, 1985).

113 CAC, 1985, *op. cit.*

114 WHO, 1985, *op. cit.*

115 Savage, E.P., Keefe, T.J., Tessari, J.D., Wheeler, H.W., Applehans, F.M., Goes, E.A. and Ford, S.A., "National study of chlorinated hydrocarbon insecticide residues in human milk, USA", *Am. J. Epidemiol.* **113** (1981) pp. 413–22.

116 WHO, 1985, *op. cit.*; Ramakrishnan, N., Kaphalia, B.S., Seth, T.D. and Roy, N.K., "Organochlorine pesticide residues in mother's milk: a source of toxic chemicals in suckling infants", *Human Toxicol.* **4** (1985) pp. 7–12.

117 Ramakrishnan et al., 1985, *op. cit.*; Campos, M. and Olszyna-Marzys, A.F., "Contamination of human milk with chlorinated pesticides in Guatemala and in El Salvador", *Arch. Environ. Contam. Toxicol.* **8** (1979) pp. 43–58; Kanja, L., Skare, J.U., Nafstad, I., Maitai, C.K., Lokken, P., "Organochlorine pesticides in human milk from different areas of Kenya, 1983–1985", *J. Toxicol. and Environ. Health* **19** (1986) pp. 449–64.

118 Hornabrook, R.W., Dyment, P.G., Gomes, E.D. and Wiseman, J.S., "DDT residues in human milk from New Guinea natives", *Med. J. Aust.* **1** (1972) pp. 1297–1300.

119 Hergenrather, J., Hlady, G., Wallace, B. and Savage, E., "Pollutants in breast milk of vegetarians", *New Eng. J. Med.* **304** (1981) p. 792.

120 Dillon, J.C., Martin, G.B. and O'Brien, H.T., "Pesticide residues in human milk", *Food Cosmet. Toxicol.* **19** (1981) pp. 437–42; WHO, 1985, *op. cit.*

121 Pimentel, D., Andour, D., Dyson-Hudson, A., Gallahan, D., Jocobson, S., Irish, M., Kroog, S., Moss, A., Schreiner, I., Shepard, M., Thompson, T. and Vinzart, B., "Environmental and social costs of pesticides: a preliminary assessment", *OIKOS* **34** (1980) pp. 126–140.

4 Fertilizers and the Environment

Fertilizers, in contrast to pesticides, are not deliberately designed to kill life and are not directly toxic either to wild animals and plants or to ourselves. They are contaminants of the environment, rather than pollutants. Under certain conditions, though, they play an important role in chemical reactions in the environment that do result in significant pollution. Nitrates and phosphates can result in eutrophication of rivers, lakes and coastal waters; nitrates are converted inside ourselves and other animals to produce nitrites that are toxic; and nitrous oxide, given off to the atmosphere, takes part in both the depletion of the ozone layer and global climatic warming.

In this chapter we examine the causes of fertilizer contamination and discuss the relative importance of fertilizers, natural mineralization of soil nitrogen, livestock wastes and domestic sewage in contributing to rising nitrate concentrations in surface- and groundwater. We end with a description of eutrophication in various parts of the world.

Fertilizer use

There has been a dramatic increase in worldwide fertilizer use since the mid-1940s (Figure 4.1). In the most intensively farmed countries of western Europe and eastern Asia national average nitrogen (N) fertilizer rates to arable land are 120–550 kg N/ha (Table 4.1). These figures reflect the rates applied to most arable fields. Elsewhere average rates – calculated by dividing annual consumption by hectares of arable land – are much lower but mask the occurrence of highly intensive fertilizer use in certain regions. Thus in the USA the average is only 75 kg N/ha, but rates for maize, rice and cotton in the most intensive arable areas, such as in parts of Arizona, California, Florida, Illinois, Indiana, Nebraska and Ohio, are 140–200 kg/ha, similar to those in western Europe.[1]

In the developing countries, average fertilizer rates are a great deal

Figure 4.1 Consumption of nitrogen fertilizer, 1946–89

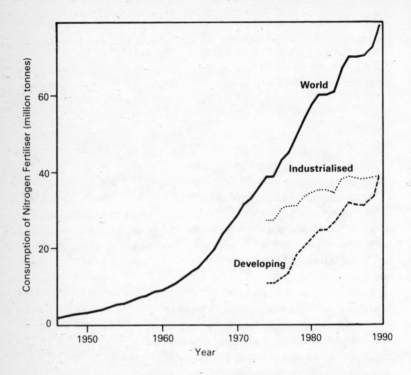

Sources: FAO, *Fertilizer Yearbooks* (Rome: Food and Agriculture Organisation, 1951–88);
USDA, *Agricultural Resources Inputs Situation and Outlook Report* (Washington DC:
Economic Research Service, 1990)

lower. The annual application to arable and permanent crops in Asia
is currently about 30 kg N/ha, in Latin America 15 kg N/ha and in
Africa only 4 kg N/ha, and much of the land receives no inorganic
fertilizer at all. None the less, the developing countries have shown
the highest rates of growth in recent years: annual consumption of
nitrogen fertilizer has more than tripled since 1975 and between
1989 and 1994 is expected to grow by a further 25 per cent.[2] Much of
this growth has been associated with the Green Revolution, which
began to affect many developing countries in the early 1960s. It
brought about major changes in farming practices, centred on the
use of new cereal varieties capable of producing high yields when
subject to heavy fertilizer application. Recommended rates for the
new rice varieties are 120–175 kg N/ha and for wheat, 120–160
kg N/ha.[3] As a consequence, average fertilizer applications in the

Table 4.1 National average nitrogen fertilizer applications to arable land and permanent crops in selected countries, 1986

Countries over 500 kg N/ha
  Netherlands (557)
  Singapore (550)

Countries 400–500 kg N/ha
  Bahrain (470)

Countries 300–400 kg N/ha
  Martinique (315)

Countries over 200–300 kg N/ha
  Egypt (260)
  Korean DPR (253)
  Belgium/Luxemburg (247)
  UK (238)
  Federal Republic of Germany (212)

Countries 100–200 kg N/ha
  Korean Rep (195)
  Saudia Arabia (154)
  Japan (145)
  China (138)
  France (135)
  Surinam (135)

Countries 50–100 kg N/ha
  Cuba (99)
  Mauritius (92)
  USA (75)
  Indonesia (64)
  Malaysia (57)
  Mexico (54)
  Sri Lanka (53)
  Fiji (50)

Countries 0–50 kg N/ha
  Bangladesh (46)
  Colombia (40)
  India (39)
  Philippines (31)
  Zimbabwe (30)
  Kenya (27)
  Chile (20)
  Thailand (13)
  Nigeria (6)

Note: all countries applying more than 200 kg N/ha are included in this list

Sources: FAO, *Fertiliser Yearbook* vol. 37 (Rome: FAO, 1988); Vroomen, H., *Fertiliser Use and Price Statistics, 1960–1988* (Washington DC: US Department of Agriculture, 1990).

intensive cereal cropping regions of the developing countries are fast approaching those of the developed countries.

The increase in worldwide fertilizer use has had enormous benefits in terms of food production. Although at the macro-level it is difficult to separate out the relative impact on production of fertilizers and other inputs, studies of Asian rice production indicate that fertilizers as a whole have contributed about 24 per cent of the growth in output since the mid-1960s, the remainder being mostly due to new varieties, irrigation and capital investment.[4] The combined consequences have certainly been dramatic. Global food production per capita has risen by 14 per cent since 1964.[5] In western Europe average national cereal yields are now of the order of 5 tonnes/ha, with individual farm records of some 15 tonnes/ha, while continuous cultivation under heavy fertilizer use in the developing countries can produce even higher yields. Food production per capita in Asia and Latin America has grown by 24 per cent and 11 per cent respectively, although it has fallen by 17 per cent in Africa (Figure 4.2).

Figure 4.2   Food production per capita for Asia, Latin America and Africa (production per capita in 1964 taken to be 100)

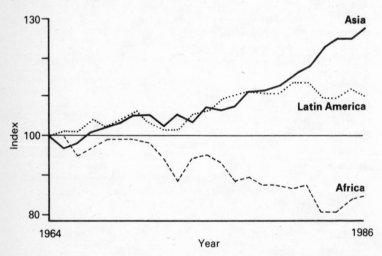

Source: FAO, *Production Yearbooks* (Rome: Food and Agriculture Organisation, 1965–86).

The causes of fertilizer contamination

If all the fertilizer applied to a field were to be taken up by the crop plants and, then, all used for harvestable crop growth, there would be no contamination of the surrounding environment. But, invariably, a significant proportion is lost. Part of the reason is excessive application of fertilizer but, more importantly, a combination of crop, soil and climatic factors prevent uptake from being complete.

Excessive use of fertilizers

Farmers often apply more than the optimum quantity of fertilizer required to maximize crop production or profit. Part of the reason is the unpredictability of the outcome. As many experiments have demonstrated, there is massive variation in the response to fertilizers, depending upon the site and crop, and the amount, type and mode of fertilizer applied.[6] Figure 4.3 shows the variability among closely related crops while Table 4.2 describes the responses in the same

Figure 4.3 Responses of various temperate vegetables to nitrogen fertilizer application

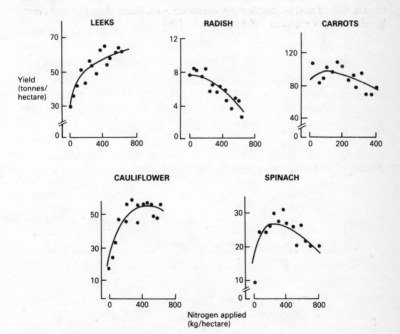

Source: Greenwood, D.J., Cleaves, T.J., Turner, P.K., Hunt, J., Niendorf, K.B. and Lognens, S.M.H., "Comparison of the effects of nitrogen fertiliser on the yield, nitrogen content and quality of 21 different vegetable and agricultural crops", *J. of Agric. Sci.* **95** (1980) pp. 471–485.

Table 4.2 Response of grassland to nitrogenous fertilizer in different regions of England and Wales. Regional means for four harvest years

| | N applied (kg per ha per year) | | | | |
| | 0 | 150 | 300 | 450 | 600 |
Geographical region	Annual dry matter yield (tonne ha)				
North-east	3.19	4.87	10.17	11.33	11.49
South-east	1.74	4.98	7.60	9.27	9.73
Midlands	3.02	7.21	10.20	11.56	12.15
South-west (including South Wales)	1.89	5.29	9.78	11.93	13.29
Wales	4.30	8.25	11.67	13.35	13.06

Source: Spedding, C.R.W., Walsingham, J.M. and Hoxey, A.M., *Biological Efficiency in Agriculture* (London: Academic Press, 1981).

crop under different conditions. Despite this variability, in all crops the percentage recovery of nitrogen – that is the amount removed in the harvest – declines as the level of fertilizer nitrogen is increased above an optimum value (Table 4.3). The problem is that, in practice, it is extremely difficult to determine where the optimum lies without extensive trials on each and every field. Soil testing can provide useful information on the reserves of nitrogen but estimation of its availability to the crop throughout the growing period is necessarily crude.[7] Most recommendations for fertilizer use are, thus, relatively imprecise. Inevitably, farmers tend to play safe and overfertilize, particularly where crop returns to added fertilizer are high.

Table 4.3 Nitrogen balance in a corn crop fertilized with four rates of nitrogen over a three-year period

Annual treatment (kg N ha/yr)	Total amount of N added 1973–5 (kg N/ha)	N removed in corn (kg N/ha)	N loss from tile drain (kg N/ha)	N remaining in 0–3 metres of soil profile autumn, 1975 (kg N/ha)
20	60	105	41	54
112*	336	167	53	100
224	672	166	93	425
448	1344	196	180	770

* Recommended rate

Source: Gast, R.G., Nelson, W.W. and Randall, G.W., "Nitrate accumulation in soils and loss in tile drainage following nitrogen applications to continuous corn", *J. Environ. Qual.* 7 (1978) pp. 258–61.

As with pesticides, the common practice of subsidizing fertilizer prices may also be contributing to excessive use. Cheap fertilizers encourage farmers to be unconcerned that extra applications may not be worthwhile. Since the Green Revolution, many developing countries have maintained prices to farmers artificially low to encourage greater fertilizer use on high yielding varieties. In Indonesia, for example, the effective subsidy is 68 per cent of the world price and, as a consequence, the average input of nitrogen fertilizer to arable land is higher than most other South East Asian countries.[8] (See Table 4.1.)

Plant uptake and nitrogen losses

The efficiency of nitrogen fertilizer uptake by plants can be measured either by comparing the amount of nitrogen in the harvest of a crop receiving fertilizer with a crop that is unfertilized, or by using a radioactive, N^{15} labelled, fertilizer. Using the first method, the percentage recovery is given as:

$$\text{percentage recovery of N} = \frac{\begin{array}{c}\text{N harvested in} \\ \text{crop receiving} \\ \text{fertilizer N}\end{array} - \begin{array}{c}\text{N harvested in} \\ \text{crop receiving} \\ \text{no N}\end{array}}{\text{fertilizer N added}} \times 100$$

Nitrogen recoveries calculated in this way range from 20 to over 100 per cent in temperate climates.[9] The range reflects a great variety of experimental conditions. Recoveries fall rapidly above an optimum rate of application (Table 4.3). This method of estimation also does not take account of the uptake of soil organic nitrogen which has been mineralized. About a third of the nitrogen assimilated comes from this source. The more precise method of tracing radioactive labelled nitrogen reveals lower recoveries for the same field. Nevertheless, in experiments conducted under ideal conditions with fertilizer applications at the optimum, recoveries measured in this way can be very high. For instance, winter wheat in the UK fertilized at the standard rate of 190 kg/ha recovered over 97 per cent, leaving only 1–5 kg of nitrogen as nitrate in the soil.[10]

Various factors, including rainfall, irrigation, soil and crop type, the mode of application and the nature of the fertilizer added, affect the efficiency of uptake of fertilizer N. Early sowing, for instance, increases the recovery in temperate cereal crops by extending the opportunity for N uptake. It also increases if early growth is vigorous, if rainfall and, therefore, leaching is low, or if there is little nitrogen already present in the soil.[11]

Recoveries for cut grass (excluding stubble and the roots), are somewhat higher than for arable crops. The recovery is usually around 65 per cent when fertilizer nitrogen is given within the normal growing season for grass and application rates do not exceed 400 kg N /ha annually.[12]

Recovery rates are lower in the tropics. Maximum recovery in dryland crops is 50–60 per cent of applied nitrogen, but seldom more than 30–40 per cent for rice.[13] The unique anaerobic conditions of paddy fields result in heavy losses of nitrogen, particularly through volatilization as ammonia. Even under highly controlled conditions and with the best agronomic practices, recoveries remain low in tropical conditions.

Overall, these figures suggest a high proportion of the applied nitrogen fertilizer can end up as an environmental contaminant. For industrialized nations it is probably over 50 per cent, taking into account the crops grown, the ratio of arable to grassland and the degree of over-fertilization. It is likely to be higher, on average, in the developing countries.

Fertiliser versus soil organic N

It is important, however, to recognize that not all the nitrogen lost from crop fields and ending up contaminating the environment derives from fertilizer.[14] A significant proportion comes from the natural stores of organic N in the soil.

Topsoils can contain large quantities of N in an organic form – as high as 5000 kg/ha in temperate arable soils. This is derived from the breakdown by microbial organisms of organic matter – plant and animal remains. There is also a small input of N from rainfall and of N fixed from the atmosphere by certain micro-organisms. Nitrogen in its organic form in the soil humus is immobilized and hence is unavailable for crop growth. But 2–3 per cent a year is mobilized by microbial organisms – mineralized – and released as ammonium, which plants can readily take up. Although this is only a small percentage, it can amount to 150 kg/ha a year in soils rich in organic N.

Losses of nitrogen from the field

Some of the nitrogen that is not taken up by the crop may remain there for future uptake. Some is carried away in run-off, either in soil sediments through erosion or dissolved as nitrate in the water. Some is leached down through the soil, either reaching surface waters via the field drains or going deeper to groundwater aquifers. The rest is lost to the atmosphere as nitrogen, ammonia or oxides of nitrogen (Figure 4.4).

Figure 4.4   The soil nitrogen cycle

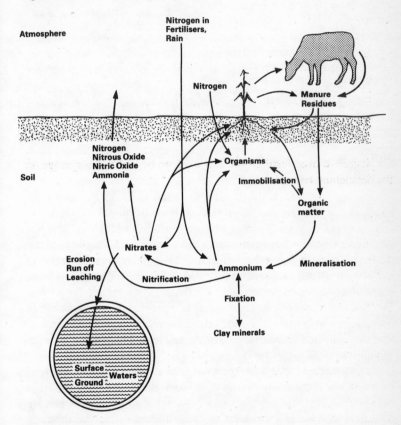

Source: simplified from Brady, N., *The Nature and Property of Soils* (New York: Macmillan, 1984).

Losses through erosion can be considerable. In the USA about 20 per cent is carried away through wind erosion and 80 per cent in water borne sediments. In total, about 4.5 million tonnes of N are lost annually in this way.[15] Leaching losses are usually greater than losses as gases. On average, 0.5–2 per cent of applied nitrogen is lost as nitrous oxide and 5–15 per cent as ammonia (see Chapter 7, pages 325–7 and 329–30). But if the soil is poorly drained and conditions favour bacterial production of gases, the losses may be considerably greater than from leaching (Table 4.4).

Table 4.4   Comparison of leaching and gaseous losses of fertilizer nitrogen from maize fields on the North Carolina coastal plain

	Well drained soil	Poorly drained clay soil
Fertilizer nitrogen input (kg N/ha)	160	196
Proportion lost to leaching (%)	29	8
Proportion lost as gas by denitrification (%)	0	31

Source: Gambrell, R.P., Gilliam, J.W. and Weed, S.B., "Nitrogen losses from soils of North Carolina coastal plain", *J. Environ. Qual.* 4 (1975) pp. 317–23.

Measurement of run-off and leachate losses

The critical questions, though, concern the amounts of nitrogen lost in run-off and leachate. Unfortunately estimates vary widely. Losses can be measured in a number of ways, each having different assumptions and different sources of error.[16] One approach is to take soil samples at different depths and then extract the nitrogen with a salt solution. The drawback is that even within a field there is great variation in soil structure and large numbers of samples are required to obtain representative measurements. An alternative is to sample tile drains. But again this may not be representative since water may flow outside the drains. There are also difficulties in relating measurements of samples collected at intervals to the overall loss, which depends more on the volume of water flow.

An approach that is more precise is to construct a physical lysimeter. This commonly consists of a block of soil isolated from the surrounding field by an impermeable material to prevent dispersion of water, with arrangements at the base for collecting the drainage water. The main problem is that the edges of the lysimeter may affect drainage pathways so that the lysimeter can be unrepresentative of real pollutant flows.

At a much larger scale, samples can be taken from a whole catchment but, unless the catchment is strictly confined and land management practices are fairly uniform, it is difficult to relate nitrate in drainage to specific practices. Finally, sampling can be taken from deep cores sunk through the unsaturated and saturated zones above underground aquifers. These will produce profiles of the pattern of downward movement of leachates, although there remains the difficulty of estimating the rates of flow through different strata. One ingenious approach has been to use tritium as a marker. In 1963 and 1964 the fall-out from thermonuclear tests led to significantly high concentration of radioactive tritium in the rainfall. Movement of the tritium can be easily measured down the profile and provides an estimate of the infiltration of rainwater that fell in those years.[17]

However, accurate predictions of downward movement are complicated by dispersion and dilution of the nitrate and the likelihood of it being denitrified by bacterial action.[18] All of these methods have been used to estimate nitrate losses and the following paragraphs summarize what is currently known.

Natural ecosystems

In natural ecosystems, with an undisturbed plant community, there is very little nitrogen loss because the input to the soil from rainfall and natural fixation is roughly balanced by the amount taken up by living, active roots. A detailed study of the Hubbard Brook catchment in New Hampshire, USA, revealed that the mean nitrate concentration in streams in the undisturbed catchment was only 3 mg/litre.[19] (In the next two chapters we exclusively refer to concentrations in terms of nitrate levels. In other sources they may be given as nitrate-nitrogen concentrations, that is, only the amount of nitrogen present rather than the total nitrate. To convert from nitrate to nitrate-N multiply by a factor of 0.2226. For example: 100 mg nitrate = 22.6 mg nitrate-N; 45 mg nitrate = 10 mg nitrate-N.) Typical leaching losses for coniferous forests are 0.5–1.5 kg N/ha per year and for deciduous forests 3–4 kg N/ha.[20] But increased mineralization and nitrification following clear cutting produce dramatically greater losses. In one North American hardwood forest nitrate losses rose to 342 kgN/ha a year after clear felling.[21]

Arable and grassland

Losses similarly increase if the soil is cultivated. Ploughing in of natural vegetation or crop residues results in the release of substantial amounts of nitrate as soil bacteria break down the organic matter. Some of the clearest information on the effects of cultivation comes from the Broadbalk experiment at Rothamsted in the UK, which has been running for over 100 years. In one set of plots, winter wheat has been cultivated without fertilizer. Drainage concentrations here are about 18 mg nitrate/litre with an annual loss of 45 kg N/ha. These levels are doubled with the use of farmyard manure, and doubled again when fertilizers are applied in the autumn (Table 4.5).

Table 4.5 Nitrate in drainage water from Broadbalk field growing winter wheat at Rothamsted in the UK

	Nitrate concentration (mg/l)	Nitrogen loss (kg N/ha)
None	18	45
Farmyard manure (35 tonne/ha)	22	58
48 kg N/ha of ammonium fertilizer applied in autumn	40	102
96 kg N/ha of ammonium fertilizer	71	180
144 kg N/ha of ammonium fertilizer	90	225

Note: Experiments conducted 1866–81

Source: Wild, A. and Cameron, K.C., "Soil nitrogen and nitrate leaching", in: Tinker, P.B. (ed.), *Soils and Agriculture* (Oxford: Blackwell Scientific Publications, 1980).

There is considerable variation in estimates of leachate losses from arable land, partly because of the disparities between different methods of measurement, but also because of the great range of factors involved. Drainage data from intensively managed arable fields indicate average annual concentrations of 45–90 mg/l nitrate (Table 4.6) and annual

Table 4.6 Nitrate concentrations in drainage waters in southern and eastern England

Site	Period	Nitrate concentration (mg/l)		
		Minimum	Maximum	Mean
Rothamsted clay loam	1	17	347	44
Saxmundham sandy-clay loam	2	2	292	52
Woburn loamy sand	3	5	150	59
Broom's Barn clay loam	1	51	161	81
Saxmundham: arable	4	38	146	98
grass/lucerne		3	67	17

Periods:
1: Jan 1970–Feb 1974   3: Mar 1970–Nov 1974
2: Feb 1968–Nov 1974   4: 14 Dec 1973–20 Feb 1974

Source: Wild and Cameron, 1980, *op. cit.*

Table 4.7 Leaching losses of nitrate from varied cropping systems and fertilizer rates

Crop land	Soil type	N applied (kg/ha/yr)	Average N leached (kg/ha/yr)
Maize, carrots[1]	Sandy soil	396	155
Lemons[1]	Sandy soil	26	46
Dates[1]	Sandy soil	149	62
Cotton[1]	Clay soil	492	71
Milo[1]	Clay soil	224	119
Cotton[1]	Clay soil	169	35
Potatoes[2]	Sandy soil	0	43
	Sandy soil	80	47
Winter rye[2]	Sandy soil	0	61
	Sandy soil	80	74
Oats[2]	Sandy soil	0	60
	Sandy soil	80	60

1 Experiment in California using tile drains
2 Experiment in Germany using lysimeters

Source: Letey, J., Blair, J.W., Devitt, D., Lund, L.J. and Nash P., "Nitrate-nitrogen in effluent from agricultural tile drains in California", *Hilgardia* 45 (1977) pp. 289–319; Pfaff, C., "Das verhalten des Stickstoffs im Baden nach langjuhrigen Lysimeter versucher". *Z. Acker-Plazenbau* 117 (1983) pp. 77–9.

losses varying from 35 to 155 kg N/ha (Table 4.7). At the lower end of the range these losses are similar to those recorded in the unfertilized plots of the long running Broadbalk experiment. Indeed in several instances in Table 4.7, losses from both fertilized and unfertilized plots are similar. It seems likely that much of the loss originates with the soil and organic N rather than fertilizer, at least under optimal rates of application. This is generally borne out by the results of lysimeter studies which indicate that less than 10 per cent of the nitrogen applied to arable land is lost by leaching.[22] In a three year experiment using lysimeters cropped with spring barley, the addition of 150 kg N/ha lead to an increase in leaching of only an extra 13 kg/ha, compared to cropping with no fertilizer (Table 4.8). This represents less than 10 per cent of the applied N, although it amounts to about 30 per cent of the total amount of nitrate leached. In a similar experiment, but using labelled N^{15} fertilizer, only 6 per cent of the applied N ended up in the leachate (Table 4.9).

By comparison with arable crops, the losses of nitrogen from grasslands are generally lower. This is primarily because the well distributed and extensive root systems of perennial grasses are able to absorb nutrients throughout the year, but also because grassland

Table 4.8   Nitrate lost in leaching from spring barley receiving different quantities of added nitrogen fertilizer

Fertilizer application (kg/ha)	Nitrogen lost in leachate (kg/ha)	Amount of applied nitrogen lost in leachate
0	31	0%
150	44	10%

Source: Royal Commission on Environmental Pollution, *Agriculture and Pollution* 7th Report (London: HMSO, 1979) using data from Shaw, K. (1978) and Shaw, K. and Jones, E. (1976).

produces subsoil conducive to dinitrification.[23] In the relatively dry southeast of England, for example, leaching losses from cut grassland are only 2–5 per cent of fertilizer additions of 250–400 kg N/ha, giving rise to concentration of nitrate in drainage water of less than 20 mg/l and annual losses of about 40 kg N/ha.[24] Losses under legume pastures are higher, though, primarily because the N fixed by the root nodules is released when the nodules are sloughed off, or when roots and plants die back.[25] In an unfertilized clover sward losses were 30 kg N/ha rising to 131 kg when the clover died.[26]

Losses from grassland may be high in regions of heavy rainfall. In Lancashire in the UK where annual rainfall is about 1500 mm, 10–40 per cent of the 250 kg of annually applied nitrogen is leached from grassland.[27] Because grassland in Britain is mostly located in the wetter, western regions, the overall quantities of nitrogen lost from grassland may actually be similar to those from arable.

Grassland under light, extensive grazing experiences little increase in loss – only 1–6 kg N/ha under upland pastures grazed by sheep.[28] But losses can approach those of arable land if grazing is intensive. In

Table 4.9   Nitrogen loss in drainage from lysimeters cropped with barley

	Fertilizer rate (kg N/ha/yr)		
Fertilizer N applied (kg N/ha/yr)*	0	80	120
Mean loading loss (kg N/ha/yr)	83	74	83
Total leaching loss (June, 1977–81) (kg N/ha)	332	297	335
Recovery of ^{15}N labelled nitrogen (June, 1977–81) in leachate (% of applied)	–	6.6%	6.3%

* ^{15}N fertilizer applied in first year only

Source: Dowdell, R.J., Webster, C.P., Hill, D. and Mercer, E.R., "A lysimeter study of the fate of fertiliser nitrogen in spring barley crops grown in shallow soil overlying chalk: crop uptake and leaching losses", *J. Soil Sci.* **35** (1984) pp. 169–83.

one experiment leaching from grazed pasture was shown to be five to six times greater than from grassland cut for silage or hay.[29] Plots of grassland received an average of 420 kg N/ha/year and losses from the grazed pasture were 162 kg N/ha, giving rise to nitrate concentrations in soil water of between 180 and 288 mg/l at six metre depth.

Animals are inefficient converters of plant nitrogen to protein. As a result, less than 20 per cent of the nitrogen applied to grassland is recovered in animal products, the remainder being returned to the soil surface in faeces and urine. This creates local hot spots of nitrogen equivalent, in the case of sheep, to 500 kg N/ha and as high as 950 kg N/ha for cattle.[30] Such concentrations are too much to be taken up by grasses. The alternative to grazing is to cut the grass for silage or hay and feed to livestock indoors, but this may only delay the leaching problem. If the slurry or farmyard manure produced by livestock fed on silage or hay is applied to the fields, leaching losses can be of the order of 150 kg N/ha.

In the UK and the USA the present levels of fertilizer added to grassland are relatively low. However experiments indicate large potential returns from high levels of fertilization. Maximum yields of grass and animal production are not attained until applications are in excess of 400 kg N/ha. If fertilizer rates approach this level and grassland becomes more intensively grazed, then leaching could rise considerably approaching that of arable land. As one experiment has shown, leaching increases from 8 to 142 kg N/ha when fertilizer applications rise from 250 to 500 kg/ha.[31]

Factors affecting losses

These brief summaries give a picture of the average nitrogen losses, but they mask the high variability in loss that commonly occurs. Among the critical variables are the rainfall, the soil type, cultivation and cropping practices and the nature and rates of application of fertilizers and manures.

Rainfall, season and irrigation

The amounts of nitrogen lost through run-off and leaching depend critically on the quantity of water moving across and down through the soil. Key factors are the amount and intensity of rainfall and the amount of water already present in the soil. In temperate regions the heaviest losses occur in late autumn, winter and early spring when there is little crop growth and hence little uptake of nitrate, but when the rainfall is greatly in excess of the losses of moisture due to evaporation and transpiration.[32] The detailed pattern of seasonal changes are shown in Figure 4.5. Heavy rainfall in the autumn produces high concentrations of nitrate in the drainage water, but because soil moisture is still in deficit there is little total drainage flow. Later in winter and early spring, once the field capacity has been reached, the drainage volume increases and reflects the rainfall. It is at times of peak drainage that the major nitrate losses occur. In late spring with new growth, the losses once again decline.

This seasonal pattern is clearly reflected in the nitrate concentrations of the River Thames in England which, in its upper reaches, runs through agricultural land (Figure 4.6). These data also show the influence of drought: concentrations were low during the long drought of 1975–76, but peaked again after the autumn rains of 1976. Much of the applied fertilizer had not been used because of poor crop growth and was, therefore, available for leaching. In one experimental lysimeter under grassland, 184 kg of the 250 kg nitrogen applied were lost in the year after the drought, compared with the loss of only 6 kg characteristic of a normal year.[33]

Thus, spring application of fertilizers usually produces little leaching, although it can be high if rainfall coincides with a period of low growth, particularly when spring is late. In general however, losses will be considerable when fertilizer is applied in the autumn to autumn sown crops that do not take up the fertilizer until the following spring. Drainage water from below winter wheat grown on clay may contain more than 220 mg nitrate/l during November–December, with a maximum of 420 mg/l, although by February–March the concentration may fall to between 4 and 22 mg/l.[34] Not all of this is directly attributable to fertilizer application, though. In the autumn continuing warmth and increasing moisture stimulate soil bacteria to produce nitrate from the reserves of organic nitrogen in the soil, and the reserves will be particularly large if previous fertilizer application has produced high yields and crop residues rich in nitrogen.[35]

The pattern of rainfall is also crucial in tropical regions. In the seasonal tropics, in particular, leaching is encouraged by the alternation of the extremes of the wet and dry seasons. There is a slow build up of nitrate in the top soil during the dry season as a result of mineralization of organic nitrogen. This is followed by a rapid and short increase at the onset of the rains and then a decline as nitrate is flushed into both surface and ground water.[36] The magnitude of the losses varies with the frequency and intensity of rainfall. Mineralization is greater during conditions of alternate soil wetting and drying; short droughts during

Figure 4.5 Seasonal changes in rainfall, tile drainage, nitrate content of drainage, and the total quantity of nitrate lost in drainage from arable and grassed fields

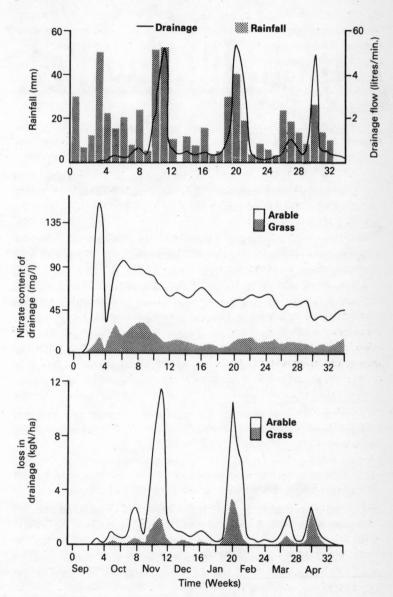

Source: Haynes, R.J. and Cameron, K.C., "Retention and movement of nitrogen in soils", in: Haynes, R.J. (ed.) *Mineral Nitrogen in the Plant–Soil System* (Orlando: Academic Press, 1986) using data from Williams (1975).

Figure 4.6   Nitrogen loads in the River Thames at Walton

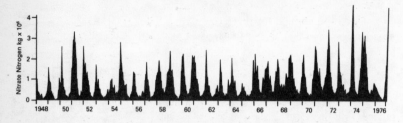

Source: Royal Commission on Environmental Pollution, *Agriculture and Pollution*, 7th Report (London: HMSO, 1979).

the rainy season lead to more nutrient flushes. As a result the losses can be considerable. Heavy rainfall of more than 2500 mm on porous soils in Colombia causes losses of more than 200 kg N/ha beneath pastures.[37]

The seasonal tropics are also the main sites of large scale irrigation. Over 80 per cent of the increase, since 1970, in the global area under irrigation, now 270 million hectares, has occurred in tropical countries.[38] Some of the highest cereal yields in the world are produced under irrigation in the tropical dry season when the light intensity is greatest. Dry season rice in India yields, on average, 1–1.5 t/ha more than the wet season at a given level of applied nitrogen, and dry season nitrogen recommendations are on average double, at 80–120 kg N/ha.[39] As a consequence, these regions will continue to be the focus for intensifying nitrogen fertilizer use, while at the same time being subject to some of the world's highest leaching rates. The effect of the seasonal nature of the climate is compounded by the use of irrigation water which provides a direct conduit for nitrate to surface and groundwater.[40]

Soils, plant cover and cultivation

Soil structure is important since it determines whether water runs off or passes downwards through the soil. Leaching tends to be greater in light soils, and in coarsely structured soils with high infiltration rates. Clays, on the other hand, are more likely to lose nitrates through run-off, although the total loss of run-off and leachate may be no different.[41]

Nitrate loss also depends upon the plant cover and the pattern of cultivation. Experiments measuring the concentration of nitrate during single storms at a farm in New York State indicated that water from bare fallow contained between 65–125 mg/l, while from cereal crops it was 4–75 mg/l and from pasture only 4 mg/l.[42] On bare fallows virtually all the applied fertilizer can be lost. Lysimeter measurements on a bare sandy loam recorded annual loss of 57–84 kg N/ha without fertilizer application but over 200 kg N/ha when fertilizer had been applied at 224 kg N/ha.[43]

Nitrate leaching is also invariably high when grassland is converted to arable by ploughing.[44] Great quantities of organic matter are turned into the soil and their subsequent mineralization produces large amounts of nitrate. Figure 4.7 shows the peaks of nitrate concentrations in a borehole under chalk, each peak corresponding to a previous ploughing of grassland. Some 100 kg N/ha may be

Figure 4.7 A profile of nitrogen concentration in a deep borehole in chalk

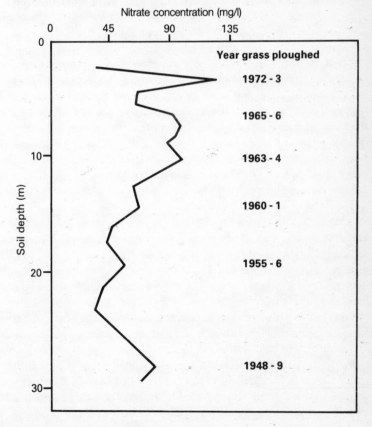

Source: Haynes, R.J. and Cameron, K.C., 1986, *op. cit.* using Young et al., 1976.

leached from the root zone over successive winters following an initial ploughing of grassland over chalk.[45] And at a site at Rothamsted, almost 4000 kg N/ha were lost, mainly as nitrate, during the first 18 years after ploughing, an average of 220 kg/year.[46] Losses can be particularly high when leguminous leys are ploughed in to the soil.

Fertilizers

Finally, leachate losses are strongly influenced by when and how fertilizers are applied. As we have already seen, timing of application in relation to rainfall, season and crop growth is crucial. Autumn applications in temperate climates result in especially serious losses. On the other hand, greater uptake results from split applications and the use of slow release compounds. Incorporation also produces less loss than broadcasting the fertilizer, but deep applications can result in high leachate losses. Up to 96 per cent of nitrate fertilizers, which are more mobile, together with 60–80 per cent of urea, may be lost if they are deep-placed in soils with a high percolation rate.[47]

There is also evidence that the addition of nitrogen fertilizer increases the mineralization or uptake of native soil nitrogen.[48] This has been demonstrated by various experiments using radioactively labelled nitrogen. The nitrogen in the fertilizer becomes partly immobilized in the soil and hence unavailable, while more of the native soil nitrogen is either mineralized or, at least, taken up by plants. The process is complex, however, and various factors are involved. It may be that the effect largely derives from changes in microbial activity, which in turn are the result of altered pH and salt concentrations brought about by the addition of inorganic fertilizers.

That fertilizers contribute significantly to nitrate losses is indisputable, but clearly they are only part of a complex interaction in which rainfall, soil type, plant cover, and cultivation practices and the organic nitrogen in the soil play equally, if not more, important roles. Much depends on the circumstances. If fertilizer rates are optimal and other conditions are favourable, then added fertilizers may contribute little to nitrate leaching. But excessive applications can directly result in heavy losses, especially when rainfall, soils and the absence of plant growth are conducive to high nitrate leaching.

In this respect application of manures and slurries is little different.[49] Losses can be 20–30 per cent of applied N if such wastes are applied in the autumn to fallow land.[50] Losses can also be especially high if crops are irrigated with sewage effluent.[51]

Nitrate in surface waters

So far we have primarily discussed the results from "micro" level studies in experimental fields where nitrate losses are estimated from lysimeters or from drainage samples. Most of these studies have involved fertilizer applications at near optimal levels and, as a consequence, have recorded relatively low percentage losses of added nitrogen. However, when measurements are made for whole catchments it is clear that overall nitrate losses are considerable. In the UK, for instance, estimates of mean annual concentrations for drainage from intensively managed arable catchments are of the order of 200 mg nitrate/litre, with much higher concentrations for short periods.[52] This has led a number of authors to conclude that between a third and a half of the fertilizer nitrogen applied annually to arable land in the UK is leached below the rooting depth each year.[53] Such a conclusion is apparently supported by the dramatic increase in nitrate concentrations in surface waters that has occurred over the past three decades. While part of this is due to increasing domestic sewage, the most rapid rises have been in areas of intensive agriculture. Fertilizers are the only source of nitrogen that has had a comparable increase (Table 4.10), but nevertheless the question is whether the rise is due to greater fertilizer use, involving excessive or ill-timed applications, or to changing patterns of cultivation, in particular the widespread conversion of grassland to arable that has occurred over the same period.

Table 4.10   Sources of nitrogen in England and Wales 1938–81

	Nitrogen fixation	Rainfall	Livestock excreta	Human excreta	Fertilizers
	(thousand tonnes/year)				
1938–9	1180	260	610	170	50
1940–9	1200	240	540	180	90
1950–9	1290	260	670	200	180
1960–9	1270	260	780	220	490
1970–2	1230	240	810	230	730
1980–1	NR	NR	600	NR	1150

NR = not recorded

Source: Croll, B.T. and Hayes, C.R., "Nitrate and water supplies in the United Kingdom", *Environ. Pollut.* **50** (1988) pp. 163–87.

Rising nitrate concentrations in rivers

Analysis of rivers in the United Kingdom shows, despite considerable year to year variation, a progressive increase in nitrate concentration over the past 30 to 40 years[54] (Figure 4.8). Concentrations and rates of increase are highest in the east and centre of the country corresponding to areas of intensive arable cropping. Several important rivers have mean values greater than 50 mg/l, the European Community limit (Figure 4.9). The River Thames, which provides the major supply of water for London, has increased its mean annual nitrate concentration from 11 mg/l in 1928 to 35 mg/l in the 1980s[55] and some model predictions suggest it will exceed 50 mg/l by the mid-1990s.[56] Following the 1976 drought, measurements at abstraction points for drinking water supplies showed nitrate concentrations in UK rivers increasing over the past 30 years at a rate of 0.1–1.1 mg/l/year. However, there are some signs of a plateau being reached in recent years.

Figure 4.8 Changing nitrate concentrations in five rivers of the UK. Averages are five-year means.

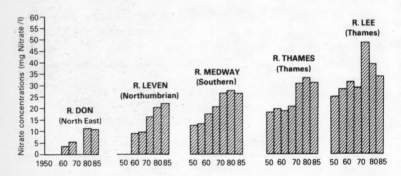

Source: Department of the Environment, *Digest of Environmental Protection and Water Statistics* (London: HMSO, 1990).

This increase in river nitrate concentrations has been reflected in the nitrate levels of reservoirs. The average annual concentration in the Farmwood Reservoir, which draws water from the River Thames, has risen from 9 to 27 mg/l between 1961 and 1981.[57] However, the problem is less serious in reservoirs, since natural denitrification usually occurs from early summer through to the late autumn, in some cases giving a 50 per cent reduction in nitrate.

In the United States, although many rivers are also showing increasing trends in nitrate contamination, the majority are still substantially

Figure 4.9 Proportion of rivers in each Water Authority region of the UK exceeding a nitrate concentration of 20 mg/l. Data from the DOE Harmonised Monitoring Scheme which samples rivers with median flows in excess of 2 metres/second

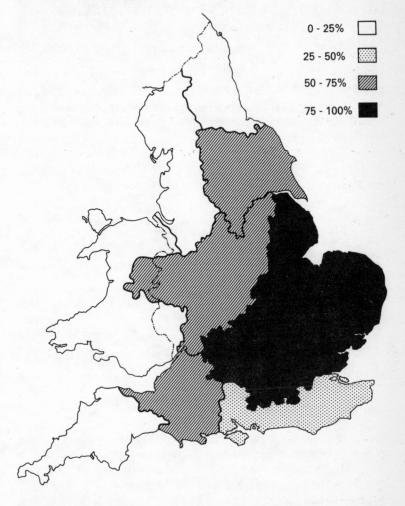

Source: Department of the Environment, *Nitrate in Water*, Pollution Paper 26 (London: HMSO, 1986).

below 45 mg/l.[58] A recent survey of some 380 river stations throughout the country found increasing trends of nitrate at about 30 per cent of the stations, with declines in less than 1 per cent, mostly in the southwest (Figure 4.10). Nevertheless, concentrations were generally low; 75 per cent of the stations contained less than 4 mg/l. Where increases are particularly marked is in the central Corn Belt. The nitrate content of the Mississippi, at the point where it leaves the Corn Belt, doubled between the mid-1950s and the mid-1970s and levels in the Illinois have increased by about one quarter during this period. They now vary from 11–14 mg/l in the uppermost regions to less than 0.1 mg/l at the mouth.[59] Other major rivers, for instance the Delaware, San Joaquin and Ohio Rivers, also show increasing trends, although concentrations still fall between 2 and 7 mg/l.

Figure 4.10   Trends in nitrate concentrations in rivers of USA, 1974–81
Upward arrow = increase; downward arrow = decrease; dot = no trend; dashed lines = regional drainage basins

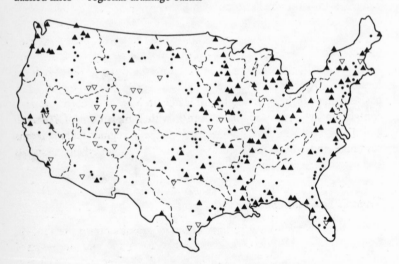

Source: Smith, R.A., Alexander, R.B., and Wolman, M.G. "Water quality trends in the nations' rivers", *Science* **235** (1987), pp. 1607–1615.

However, high levels have been reported for some rivers. In the Great Miami and the Scioto, which drain the intensively cultivated agricultural areas of Iowa, the levels of the former reached 47 mg/l in 1981, and of the latter 20 mg/l in 1977.[60] Levels in the Iowa and Cedar Rivers, both of which drain into the Mississippi, increased from 4–6 mg/l in the early 1970s to 24 mg/l by 1980, with a maximum recorded in 1978 of 59 mg/l.[61]

Fertilizers, sewage or nitrogen deposition?

How much of the nitrate in the rivers is due to land run-off or from sewage effluent is not clear, however. One estimate for the UK suggests that, leaving aside the amount of nitrate entering rivers from aquifers, 40–50 per cent of the nitrate derives from treated sewage and 50–60 per cent from land drainage.[62] On the other hand, the pronounced seasonality of the nitrate levels in the rivers can only be accounted for by land run-off during the winter months. In the UK the rivers with the higher concentrations of nitrate (in the centre and east of the country) are on average 5 mg/l more concentrated in winter (October–March) compared with annual median values, and in the Anglian region, where arable cropping is most intensive, the difference is 10 mg/l. This is also true in the USA. For instance, in the Sangamon River Watershed in Illinois, nitrate levels rise from 4 mg/l in the autumn to 40 mg/l in the spring.[63]

Much depends on the location of the river basin (Figure 4.11). In the USA, increasing nitrate levels appear to be mostly associated with fertilizer use and livestock density, but in the forested basins of the Midwest and East, atmospheric deposition of nitrogen derived from fossil fuel burning is playing an important role. Yet again, in other basins sewage is the most important factor. In New York State, streams contain on average 9–35 mg nitrate/l, with a maximum of 70 mg/l, and the highest concentrations occur in those in regions lacking mains sewerage and where the surface water is contaminated by cesspools and septic tank effluents.[64]

Tropical and subtropical rivers

There are few reports of serious nitrate contamination in developing countries, though this may merely reflect a lack of investigation. Ten of the major rivers of Asia, including the Yangtze, Yellow and Pearl Rivers in China, the Banjir Kanal, Sunter and Surabaya in Indonesia, the Kinta and Klang in Malaysia and Chao Phrya and Prasal in Thailand, average only 3.1 mg/l of nitrate with a maximum, reached in the Yellow River, of 10 mg/l.[65] In India, a nationwide survey of 350 streams found none with concentrations greater than 10 mg/l,[66] while in Sri Lanka tap water from streams contains an average of only 0.04 mg/l and a maximum of 0.1 mg/l.[67] The Mahaweli River, the basin of which covers 15 per cent of the area of the island, contains an average of 1.1 mg/l in the 30 km above Kandy rising to 2.4 mg/l in the 180 km below the city. However, Kandy Lake does contain some hot spots of nitrate – up to 45 mg/l, and the canal draining into the lake was found to contain concentrations as high as 310 mg/l.[68] Fertilizers, though, are not to blame, the contamination being caused by effluent from pit

182 Unwelcome Harvest

Figure 4.11 Trends in total nitrate concentrations in US rivers, 1974–81
The Grand River of Mississippi drains intensively cultivated land and received increased inputs of nitrogen fertilizer throughout the 1970s.
The Monongahela Basin of Pennsylvania is largely forested and received increased atmospheric deposition of nitrate during the 1970s.
Point source loads of nitrogen to the North Platte River of Nebraska decreased significantly during the late 1970s as a result of improved municipal waste treatment.

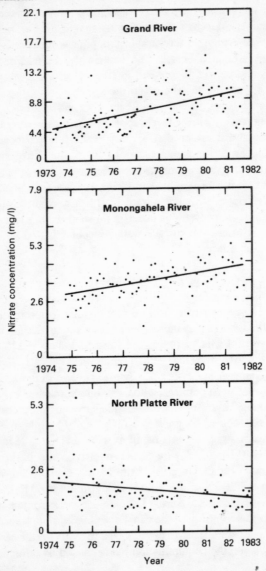

Source: Smith, R.A., et al., 1987, *op. cit.*

latrines and by slum-dwellers using the canal directly for defecation. Sewage effluents have also been the major source of high nutrient levels in rivers and lakes in Zimbabwe and Zambia.[69] Water near Kafue township in Zambia, for instance, contains more than 200 mg nitrate/l.

As yet there is little evidence of rising nitrate levels due to fertilizer use. An eight year study of water draining a sugar estate in Zimbabwe found only negligible contamination by nitrate, despite an annual application of about 130 kg N/ha fertilizer.[70] However, streams near a fertilizer factory at Que Que in Zimbabwe were found to have concentrations of up to 11,500 mg/l.[71]

Nitrate in groundwater

Of greater consequence is nitrate contamination of groundwater, both in developed and developing countries. In the USA over half the population rely upon groundwater as their primary source of drinking water; the comparable figure for the UK is about 30 per cent. In many localities, in both countries, nitrate levels are high and rising fast.[72] There are similarly high levels in certain localities in the developing countries.

Groundwater contamination in the UK

The principal groundwater sources in the UK are underground aquifers of chalk or sandstone which frequently underlie areas of intensive arable production (Figure 4.12). Water travels downwards relatively slowly in chalk, taking up to 40 years for nitrate applied at the surface to reach the aquifer. The shortest transit time occurs in limestone, commonly taking only a few years; sandstones fall between the two, with a time of 10–20 years.[73] However, local factors are also of importance. High rainfall, a shallow unsaturated zone or strong fissuring of the rock overlying the aquifer can produce rapid transit times (Figure 4.13). In the UK, the most severely contaminated aquifers are those in the Jurassic limestone area of Lincolnshire which is characterized by extensive rock fissuring. East Anglia, where groundwater is the main source of drinking supplies, receives some of the highest fertilizer applications in the country. Over the last 10 to 15 years, groundwater nitrate concentrations in many places have risen to levels which may intermittently or continuously exceed the European Community limit of 50 mg nitrate/l.[74] In 1970, 60 groundwater sources exceeded this limit and 16 sources had to be

Figure 4.12 Outcrops of the major aquifers in England and Wales

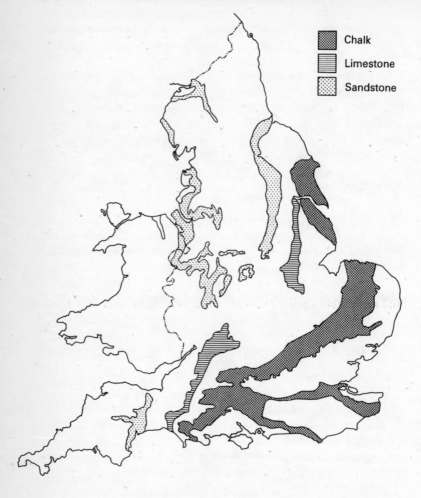

Source: Department of the Environment, *Nitrate in Water* (London: HMSO, 1986).

permanently closed (Table 4.11). The number of sources exceeding the limit has subsequently risen to 90 in 1980, 105 in 1984 and 142 in 1987.[75] At present about one and a half million people, mostly in eastern and central England, receive water which occasionally exceeds the EC limit.[76]

A recent report of the Nitrate Co-ordination Group concludes that in the drier parts of England (central and eastern) many groundwater concentrations are likely to exceed 100 mg nitrate/l in the long term

Figure 4.13   Representation of a typical groundwater system

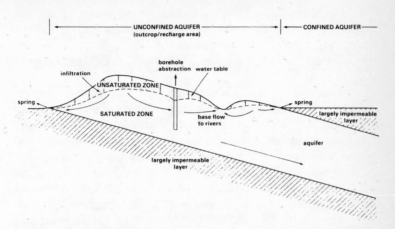

Source: Department of the Environment, *The Nitrate Issue*. A Study of the Economic and other Consequences of Various Local Options for Limiting Nitrate Concentrations in Drinking Water (London: HMSO, 1988).

and many other aquifers, with the exception of those from high rainfall areas in the west, are likely to stabilize between 50 and 100 mg/l.[77] Although in some places these high nitrate concentrations may be the result of urban wastes, the evidence convincingly points to leaching from arable land as the major source of contamination.[78]

Table 4.11   Underground sources of drinking water in the UK where nitrate levels exceeded 50 and 100 mg/l in 1979–81

	Total abstraction (Ml/d)	No. of sources over 100 mg/l	No. sources over 50 mg/l	Proportion of sources over 50 mg/l (%)
Thames	1400	0	24	2
Southern	890	0	15	2
Severn Trent	860	0	58	7
Anglian	630	16*	120	16
Wessex	450	0	3	1
North West	390	0	0	0
Yorkshire	320	0	21	7

* Subsequently taken out of supply
(Ml/d) = (megalitres/day)

Source: ENDS, "Nitrate spurs action on farming practices", *ENDS*, **111** (1984) pp. 6–7.

Sampling boreholes in Britain

The evidence largely derives from an extensive programme of sampling from boreholes into the chalk, sandstone and limestone in Britain, which reveals very strong correlations between high nitrate concentrations in the unsaturated zones of the aquifers and the history of land use above.[79]

Each borehole sampled produces a characteristic nitrate profile that reflects the historical pattern of land use (Figure 4.14). For instance in the profile A, where arable crops are periodically interrupted by grass leys, the nitrate concentrations show a pattern of peaks and troughs corresponding to the sequence of arable and grassland. For the most part, nitrate concentrations are around 50 mg nitrate/l but peak at over 100 mg corresponding, on the assumption of a downward movement of about one metre per year, to the ploughing up of the leys.[80] The low nitrate concentrations characteristic of the lower part of the profile correspond to when the site was permanent grassland, prior to 1949. Under the triassic sandstone the nitrate profile (B) is more irregular, probably due to the greater heterogeneity of sandstone, and the correlation is not so clear.

Profiles under unfertilized grassland show values less than 26 mg/l.[81] Concentrations between 22 and 45 mg/l are similarly characteristic of fertilized grassland receiving about 250 kg N/ha, but they may be as high as 440 mg when the grass has received more than 400 kg N/ha (Figure 4.15).

However, high nitrate concentrations are also present under fields that have been continuously arable, without previous ploughing of grassland or planting of temporary leys. Figure 4.16 shows the profile through South Yorkshire triassic sandstone in an area which has had continuous arable cropping since 1935, and probably for the whole of this century. At the bottom of the profile, nitrates are present at 45 mg nitrate/l, probably reflecting leaching rates of 25 kg/ha during the period before 1940 when fields were predominantly fertilized with organic manures.[82] Steadily increasing nitrate, chloride and sulphate above 40 metres appears to correspond to the introduction of such inorganic fertilizers as sodium nitrate, potassium chloride and ammonium sulphate. Leaching rates then rose to approximately 40 kg N/ha. Finally, there is a particularly dramatic increase in nitrate levels beginning, on the basis of the tritium marker, in the late 1960s and corresponding to the introduction of highly intensive fertilizer regimes.

Under long-standing arable fields in the drier eastern parts of England there is a characteristic large "nitrate front" around 3–8

Figure 4.14 Nitrate profiles in chalk (A, C, E) and triassic sandstone (B, D, F) beneath arable land with grass leys and fertilized and unfertilized permanent grassland in the UK

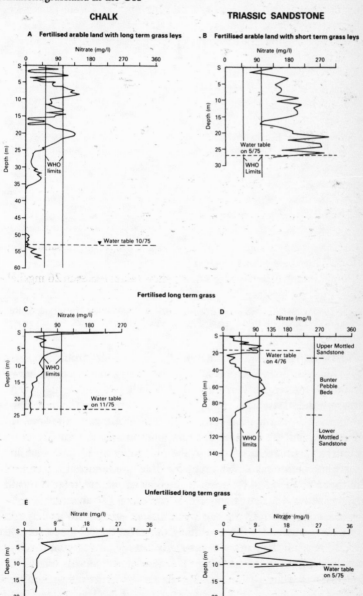

Source: Young, C.P. and Gray, E.M., *Nitrate in Groundwater – the Distribution of Nitrate in Chalk and Triassic Sandstone Aquifers*, Water Research Centre Technical Report TR69 (1978).

Figure 4.15   Nitrate profiles from the unsaturated zone of the chalk beneath unfertilized and fertilized grassland

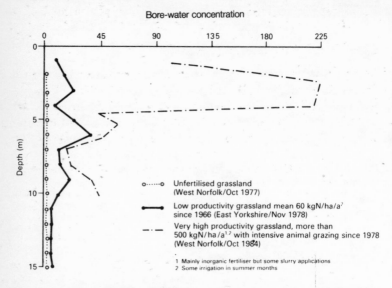

Bore-water concentration

o······o   Unfertilised grassland
(West Norfolk/Oct 1977)

•——•   Low productivity grassland mean 60 kgN/ha/a[2]
since 1966 (East Yorkshire/Nov 1978)

— · —   Very high productivity grassland, more than
500 kgN/ha/a[1,2] with intensive animal grazing since 1978
(West Norfolk/Oct 1984)

1 Mainly inorganic fertiliser but some slurry applications
2 Some irrigation in summer months

Source: Foster, S.S.D., Bridge, L.R., Geake, A.K, Lawrence, A.R. and Parker, J.M., *The Groundwater Nitrate Problem. A Summary of Research on the Impact of Agricultural Land-Use Practices on Groundwater Quality Between 1976–1985*, Hydrogeology Report No.86/2 (Wallingford: British Geological Survey, 1986).

metres below ground (Figure 4.17). The results from the analysis of tritium through such profiles indicate rates of movement between 0.3 and 1 metres per year through the chalk and 1–2 metres per year through the triassic sandstone. If both the nitrate and the tritium move uniformly down the profile, then the current nitrate front is indicative of a large increase in nitrate leaching since around the late 1960s. This may, in part, have been due to the ploughing up of grassland and a move to continuous arable cropping. But this occurred rather earlier in the late 1950s and early 1960s. The increasing intensity of fertilizer use provides a closer fit and a more universal explanation.

The concentrations present in these fronts are usually well in excess of EC recommended limits, although at lower depths they decrease to 45–90 mg/l. If the pattern of movement of the nitrate front continues, we can expect it to continue to move down slowly through the unsaturated zone of the aquifer to the groundwater, resulting in a progressive rise in nitrate concentration in well or spring supplies over the next 10 to 20 years. Computer models based on these data suggest that pumped groundwater in many areas will exceed 90 mg/l within the next 20 years and then stabilize at around 145 mg.[83] These predictions are relatively insensitive to future trends in land use and fertilizer application rates, since the sources of nitrate are in the past.

Groundwater contamination in the USA

In the USA the greatest risks of groundwater contamination occur in the central Great Plains, the Palouse and Columbia basin of Washington, parts of Montana and Southwestern Arizona, the irrigated fruit, vegetable and cotton growing regions of California; part of the Corn Belt, southeast Pennsylvania and parts of Maryland and Delaware.[84] In

Figure 4.16   Chemical profiles from outcrop area in South Yorkshire triassic sandstone in 1980

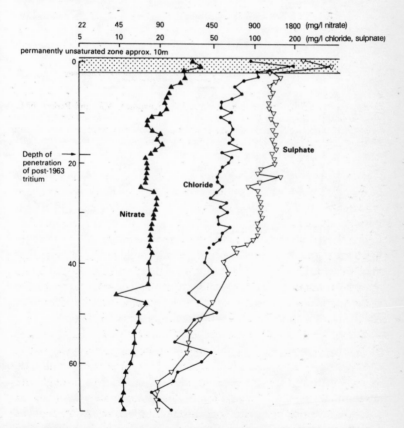

Source: Foster, S.S.D., Cripps, A.C. and Smith-Carrington, A., "Nitrate leaching to groundwater", *Phil. Trans R. Soc. Lond. B* **296** (1982), pp. 477–489

Figure 4.17 Profile for an individual long-standing arable field on Cambridge chalk

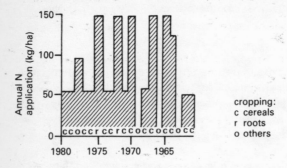

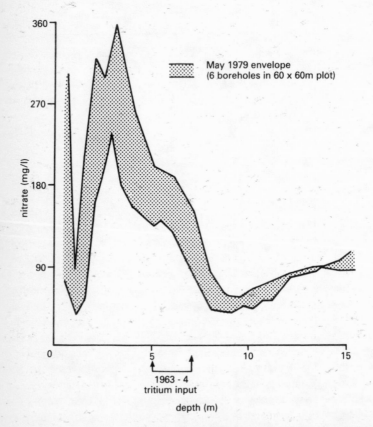

Source: Foster, S.S.D., Cripps, A.C. and Smith-Carrington, A., "Nitrate leaching to groundwater", *Phil. Trans. R. Soc. Lond. B* **296** (1982) pp. 477–489.

1984 a particularly comprehensive collection of data was undertaken by the US Geological Survey.[85] Records over a 25 year period up to 1984 were obtained from nearly 124,000 wells. Out of these, some 7900 wells were shown to exceed the drinking water standard of 45 mg nitrate/l. Half are in Texas, while almost 600 are in Arizona (Figure 4.18). The most widespread contamination occurs in Rhode Island, with 36 per cent of sampled wells exceeding 45 mg/l, and in Kansas, with 20 per cent. However, this does not represent a random survey of wells. Some wells were sampled because of suspected contamination, and there is little consistency of sampling between states.[86] The estimate of 6.4 per cent of wells nationwide containing 45 mg/l nitrate may well overstate the problem.

In another nationwide survey, conducted between 1981–4, the American Water Works Association[87] recorded 23 per cent out of 1583 drinking water wells with nitrate concentrations exceeding 45 mg/l and 10 per cent greater than 90 mg/l. In all, 87 counties were found to contain at least a quarter of their wells with levels greater than 45 mg/l. A third survey, the Environmental Protection Agency's extensive *Rural Water Conditions Survey*, found only 2.7 per cent of wells supplying rural homes in excess of 45 mg/l.[88] Nevertheless, local surveys in high risk areas reveal very high percentages of wells exceeding 45 mg/l (Table 4.12).

Shallow drinking wells, which are common in rural areas, present the greatest risk because the frequent lack of intermixing between different layers of the aquifer results in high nitrate concentrations in the surface layers. In Illinois, 23 per cent of shallow wells exceeded 45 mg/l, whereas only 2 per cent of wells more than 30 metres deep exceeded the limit.[89] A similar picture emerges from surveys in Wisconsin and Arkansas.[90]

Most of these "hot spots" are linked to fertilizer use. In the Santa Maria Valley of California, an intensive vegetable, field and fruit crops growing area, nearly 40 per cent of nitrogen fertilizer leaches below the root zone and nitrate concentrations in the groundwater average 55 mg/l.[91] A second hot spot, in the northeast of Long Island, New York, has levels up to 75 mg nitrate/l, apparently caused by intensive potato cultivation that receives some 225 kg N/ha annually.[92] Experiments indicate that maximum yields are achieved with 170 kg/ha at most, leaving an excess to be leached to the aquifer.

Most regions characterized by high fertilizer applications and intensive irrigation – California, Washington, Texas, Kansas and Oklahoma, for instance – have high nitrate levels in the groundwater, but this is not invariably so. In Florida, a state with much intensive agriculture, only 2 per cent of more than 3000 wells sampled contain

Figure 4.18   Number of well water supplies exceeding 45 mg nitrate for each state in the USA. Of the 123,656 wells sampled, 7,914 contained more than 45 mg/l

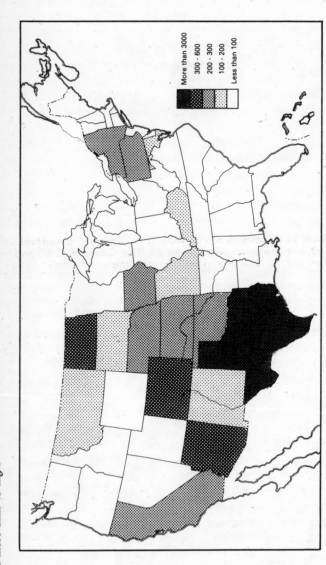

More than 3000
300 - 600
200 - 300
100 - 200
Less than 100

Source: Conservation Foundation, *Groundwater Protection* (Washington DC, 1987), using data from US Geological Survey 1985.

Table 4.12 Incidence of groundwater wells exceeding 45 mg/l in various counties and states of the USA

Location	Year	Proportion of wells exceeding 45 mg/l	Total number of wells surveyed
Iowa, north central[1]	1982–3	25%	170
Wisconsin, Rock County[2]	1980	27%	406
Delaware, Sussex County[3]	1976–7	20%	815
Nebraska, Holt County[4]	1976	19%	308
Nebraska, Platte Valley[5]	1975–6	11%	53
New York, Suffolk County[6]	1975	35%	37
Arkansas, Washington County[7]	1974	17%	58
Wisconsin, central[8]	1973	47%	36
Texas, Runnels County[9]	1973	88%	230
Illinois, Washington County[10]	1970	81%	221
New York, Nassau County[11]	1969	5%	370
Missouri[12]	1969	27%	5000
Illinois[13]	mid-1960s	5%	8844

Sources:
1 Baker, J.L., Kanwar, R.S. and Austin, T.A., "Impact of groundwater drainage wells on groundwater quality", *J. Soil and Water Conserv.* **40** (1985) pp. 516–20.
2 Zaporozec, A., "Nitrate concentrations under irrigated agriculture", *Environ. Geol.* **5** (1983) pp. 35–8.
3 Robertson, F.N., "Evaluation of nitrate in groundwater in the Delaware Coastal plain", *Ground Water* **17** (1979) pp. 328–37.
4 Exner, M.E. and Spalding, R.F., "Evolution of contaminated groundwater in Holt County, Nebraska", *Wat. Resources Res.* **15** (1979) pp. 39–47.
5 Spalding, R.F. and Exner, M.E., "Aerial, vertical and temporal differences in groundwater chemistry: 1. Inorganic constituents", *J. Environ. Qual.* **9** (1986) pp. 466–80.
6 Meisinger, J.J., "Nitrogen application rates consistent with environmental constraints for potatoes on Long Island", *SEARCH Agriculture* **6** (1976) pp. 1–9.
7 Wagner, G.H., Steele, K.F., MacDonald, H.C. and Coughlin, T.L., "Water quality as related to linears, rock chemistry, and rain water chemistry in rural carbonate terrain", *J. Environ. Qual.* **5** (1976) pp. 444–51.
8 Saffigna, P.G. and Keeney, D.R., "Nitrate and chlorine in groundwater under irrigated agriculture in central Wisconsin", *Ground Water* **15** (1977) pp. 171–7.
9 Kreitler, C.W. and Jones, D.C., "Natural soil nitrate: the cause of the nitrate contamination of groundwater in Runnels County, Texas", *Ground Water* **13** (1975) pp. 53–61.
10 Dickey, E., Lembke, W.D., Peck, G., Stone, G. and Walker, W.H., "Nitrate levels and possible sources in shallow wells", in: *Proc. 2nd Allerton Conf. Environ. Qual. and Agric.*, Spec. Publ. 26 (Urbana: University of Illinois, 1972).
11 Smith, S.O. and Baier, J.H., *Report on Nitrate Pollution of Groundwater, Nassau County, New York* (Mineolo, NY: Nassau Co. Dept Health, Bureau of Water Resources, 1969).
12 Smith, G.E., "Nitrate pollution of water supplies", *Trace Subst. Environ. Health* **3** (1970) pp. 273–87.
13 Larson, T.E. and Henley, L., *Occurrence of Nitrate in Well Water*, Research Rep. No. 1 (Urbana: University of Illinois Water Resources Center, 1966).

more than 45 mg/l.[93] On the other hand, fertilizers are not necessarily the cause of groundwater contamination. In Missouri, for example, animal waste and septic tank drainage are the principal sources.[94]

A more complex example is Runnels County, Texas where, by the early 1970s, nitrate concentrations in groundwater had risen to an average of 250 mg/l, with a maximum of 3100 mg/l.[95] Fertilizer use in the area is minimal and it seems that the original source of the nitrate must have been extensive ploughing up of grassland in the early part of this century. In the mid-1950s fields were terraced to improve soil moisture retention which, according to local farmers, has caused the water table to rise by up to six metres. This increased infiltration and the subsequent rise in groundwater has leached nitrates to the aquifer.

Leaching, however, is only one pathway for groundwater contamination. An even more rapid route is via drainage wells that transfer sub-surface water directly to the aquifer. In Iowa there are between 500 and 1000 of these wells, some up to 90 metres in depth, penetrating the sandstone and limestone bedrock aquifers. A survey found four of these drainage wells containing more than 45 mg/l, with a maximum of 150 mg during 1981–82.[96] If drinking water wells are nearby then they may be seriously contaminated (Table 4.13).

Irrigated agriculture is also an important source of nitrate in groundwater. In the Central Platte Valley and in Holt County, Nebraska, nitrate concentrations have risen to about 60 mg/l, and in some locations up to 180 mg/l.[97] These regions are characterized

Table 4.13 Concentration of nitrate in farm wells from three regions of Iowa containing differing numbers of agricultural drainage wells, 1982–3

	Region		
	A	*B*	*C*
Number farm wells	47	66	57
Number drainage wells	38	24	0*
Average nitrate concentration in farm wells (mg/l)	48.3	38.5	13.3
Maximum concentration measured	415	364	210†
Percentage of farm wells with concentration greater than 45 mg/l	37%	30%	9%

* C had 13 drainage wells 1.5 km to the west of the region
† This value is for a single well less than 2 km from the drainage wells

Source: Baker et al., 1985, *op. cit.*

by centre pivot irrigation systems that use pumped groundwater, and by high applications of nitrogen fertilizer. Any water not used by the crops is able to leach out nitrate on the return journey to the aquifer, whereupon it again may be pumped to the surface. Irrigation is also thought to be the dominant influence in Central Wisconsin, where aquifers contain nitrate concentrations up to 250 mg/l.[98]

Finally, livestock wastes are equally important. In Colorado the amount of nitrogen to a depth of nearly seven metres below irrigated agriculture was almost double that below dryland crops, but feedlots produced several times more contamination than either irrigated or dry crops.[99] In the semi-arid regions of eastern New Mexico, it is dairy farms rather than feedlots or irrigation that are critical.[100] Similarly at one hot spot in the Chino Basin, California the water table underlying crop land averages 200 mg/l, but the contamination appears to be from dairy farm wastes.[101] One reason for high contamination under dairy farming is the need for large quantities of washwater in dairying operations.

Tropical and subtropical groundwater

There are increasing reports of nitrate contamination of groundwater in the tropics but, as with surface waters, the causes are usually factors other than fertilizers. In India, a nationwide survey of 3000 dug wells found about 20 per cent in excess of 50 mg/l and 3 per cent over 100 mg/l, though deep aquifers mostly contained less than 10 mg/l.[102] Most regions are affected. For instance in the semi-arid region of Agra, 40 per cent of the drinking water sources exceed the standard of 45 mg/l, and in parts of Tamil Nadu and Kerala more than 50 per cent of domestic wells contain median concentrations of more than 50 mg/l, and in some cases exceed 1500 mg/l.[103] At all sites, though, concentrations are greater in wells in villages compared to those in the fields, suggesting that contamination mainly comes from domestic excreta leaching to the groundwater.

Africa and Latin America present similar pictures. In the Shemankar River basin of Central Nigeria, where some 50 per cent of village wells exceed concentrations of 45 mg/l, the maximum value in the villages of 400 mg/l contrasts strongly with a maximum of only 6 mg/l from wells situated in fields.[104] And in Botswana, nitrate levels as high as 600 mg/l have been recorded in village water supplies, where the sources are principally septic tanks and pit latrines. Contaminants may reach the water very rapidly: one measurement showed that the transit time between a pit latrine and a borehole 25 metres away was only 4 hours.[105] In one study of a central Indian village a nitrate plume containing concentrations of about 900 mg/l was discovered. It was centred on the village, and stretched out in the direction of groundwater flow. To the north concentrations fell to 45 mg/l within 50 metres, but to the south, the direction of flow, these levels were not reached for a distance of some 500 metres.[106]

Very high levels of contamination also occur under densely populated urban areas that are unsewered. In Bermuda concentrations up to 180 mg nitrate/l derive from cesspits and soakaways.[107] A similar situation occurs in the city of Buenos Aires, where septic tank discharge is believed to be the major source, together with wastes from food industries.[108]

Sometimes, though, livestock rather than human wastes is the main factor. High nitrate levels in granite aquifers in parts of Ghana appear to be caused by dense cattle populations around wells that have been sunk into highly permeable deposits.[109] This is also the case in the state of Haryana, India, where nitrate concentrations commonly exceed 500 mg/l and have reached 1900 mg/l.[110] Large numbers of cattle regularly congregate around water sources, while pigeons living in the sides of the wells also appear to be contributing to the contamination. There is a similar situation in the semi-arid regions of southern Africa.[111] In the Transvaal the groundwater is of ancient origin with nitrate levels naturally as high as 100 mg/l, but the water available to wells often exceeds 250 mg/l, and in one case reached 630 mg/l.[112] Once again the most probable source of the contamination is livestock wastes. Drinking troughs tend to be located close to the supplying well, either within confined enclosures or on the open range, and accumulations of livestock can be very dense.

Although fertilizers are rarely to blame for nitrate contamination in developing countries, there are examples of where they can create serious problems under tropical conditions. In the Canary Islands, a province of Spain located off the coast of West Africa, many groundwater supplies below agriculture are seriously contaminated because the poor volcanic soils require both heavy nutrients and irrigation.[113] In Gran Canaria, the most populated of the islands, 12 per cent of groundwater supplies exceed 60 mg nitrate/l, with the most serious problems occurring in water under banana groves. Shortage of space on the islands has encouraged particularly intensive agriculture with nitrogen fertilizer applications on bananas of 600 kg/ha/year. Concentration of nitrate beneath the groves is about 180 mg/l, with a range of 70–265 mg/l. On Tenerife, the water from galleries in the volcanic rocks in the higher parts of the island are relatively free of contaminants, but those from lower altitudes, which are viewed as a future drinking water resource, contain concentrations ranging from 10 to 100 mg/l. By contrast, concentrations in water from a third island, Lanzarote, where there is no irrigated agriculture, are between 5 and 10 mg/l. Although not, as yet, constituting a problem, the irrigation return water in some of the Hawaiian islands, similarly of volcanic origin and intensively cultivated, is also elevated above background levels.[114]

Neither the Canary Islands nor Hawaii are developing countries, but they illustrate the potential for serious contamination when high inputs of nitrogen fertilizer are applied in the tropics. In some respects, the potential problem is greater than in the industrialized, temperate countries. Especially in countries with pronounced seasonal climates, the high soil temperatures during the dry season may enhance mineralization of soil nitrogen, which is then leached out rapidly during the subsequent heavy rains. Fertilizers applied before, or at the beginning of, the rainy season are likely to result in heavy contamination.

The consequences of fertiliser contamination

The nutrients contained in fertilizers will not only promote the growth of crops but also of wild plants, including weeds in the fields, wild flowers, shrubs and trees in nearby hedgerows, as well as algae and aquatic plants in rivers, lakes, estuaries and, even, the sea. In some situations this inadvertent fertilizing may be beneficial, increasing fish populations, for example, as occurred in the River Ganga in India. There an outfall of organic effluents resulted in nearby deoxygenation of the river but, once mineralization had occurred further downstream, an abundant fishery developed.[115] In general, though, levels of nutrients in excess of those normally present in natural ecosystems will result in considerable disturbances to plant and animal communities, and these may be undesirable from the viewpoint of conservation, aesthetics or recreation. Damage usually results from nitrogen and phosphorus in excess; there do not appear to be any undesirable effects of potassium in the environment.

Eutrophication

The effects of added nutrients are most apparent in the aquatic environment. Rivers and lakes often undergo a process of nutrient enrichment. In many geological situations, rivers tend to be poor in nutrients (oligotrophic) near their sources in the uplands, and as they flow down through the lowlands to the sea they become progressively nutrient rich (eutrophic), because organic debris and soil washes or drains into them from the land through which they flow. Similarly, upland lakes tend to be oligotrophic. They have clear water with small populations of flora and fauna while lowland lakes are more eutrophic with turbid water and a richer plant and animal life.[116] Algae are a particularly good indicator of the nutrient supply in lakes and rivers: the higher the level of nutrients, the greater is the algal population.

The addition of fertilizers or sewage effluent greatly accelerates this process of nutrient enrichment, or eutrophication. Algae multiply, producing a dense population that reduces light to the aquatic plants beneath, which may then die. In turn, invertebrates, fish and birds that depend directly and indirectly on the plants may disappear. In deep, stratified lakes the dense algal populations may sink to the lower layers and, there, are decomposed microbially, removing oxygen from the water in the process. This can lead to a rapid decline in the populations of fish such as salmon and other aquatic fauna. Fish tolerant of lower oxygen concentrations may increase, but under extreme circumstances the body of water may become virtually lifeless (Fig. 4.19).[117]

Algal toxins

The dense growths of algae may also be a nuisance and a health hazard. Unpleasant odours are produced from decaying algae deposited in windrows along lake margins. Excessive algal growth in reservoirs can block filters in water treatment plants and generate unpleasant tastes and odours in drinking water.[118] Certain algae can also produce potent toxic compounds, that poison fish and other animals.[119] Toxins produced by the alga *Prymnesium*, for instance, can kill fish in certain circumstances.[120] Livestock also have died after drinking from lakes containing toxic algae, pigs being particularly susceptible.[121] Neurotoxins produced by blue-green algae (cyanobacteria) can arrest respiratory action within 10 to 30 minutes, and cattle have been so rapidly intoxicated that they have died before being able to move from the water's edge. Another group, the hepatotoxins, kill more slowly: within 1 to 6 hours, following symptoms of lethargy, pallor and, finally, haemorrhaging of the liver.[122]

The toxins are also hazardous to ourselves. Swimmers coming into contact with dense windrows of toxic blue-green algae may suffer from itching, reddening of the skin, eye irritation, and sometimes

Figure 4.19 Process of eutrophication in north temperate lakes. Benthic animals are those living at the bottom of lakes; coregonid fish include whitefish; cyprinid fish include carp, bream, roach; percid fish comprise the perches

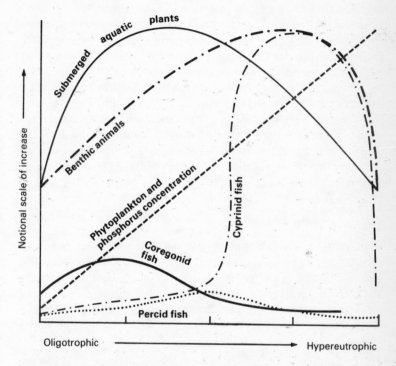

Source: Moss, B., *Ecology of Fresh Waters. Man and Medium* (2nd edition) (Oxford: Blackwell Scientific Publications, 1988).

cramps and vomiting, although this rarely lasts more than 24–48 hours.[123] There is also circumstantial evidence of chronic effects. In New South Wales, Australia, people drinking water extracted from a reservoir containing dense populations of the alga *Microcystis* showed a significant increase in the activity of certain liver enzymes indicative of toxic liver injury, compared with an adjacent population that drank from another source.[124] Algal growth in water supplies have also been linked to gasteroenteritic and hepatoenteritic illnesses in water consumers in Harare (then Salisbury), Zimbabwe in the 1960s and in Palm Island, Queensland in the late 1970s. However, such algal growth is usually associated with contamination from sewage effluent and it is more likely that the symptoms are a product of other micro-organisms or toxins.

More recently, exceptional growths of a toxin-producing flagellate alga, *Chrysochromulina*, have occurred in the sea around Scandinavia and also off Hong Kong.[125] Many fish have died both in fish farms and in the open sea: some 600 tonnes of caged fish were killed in Swedish and Norwegian waters in 1988. A mild, wet winter in Scandinavia may have resulted in greater run-off from agricultural land, producing higher than usual nutrient concentrations. But other factors such as warmer water and changes in salinity, and record winds that mixed nitrogen efficiently into deeper layers of water, may have been equally important. Lakes and reservoirs in the UK often experience widespread growths of toxic blue-green algae in the summer. In 1989, 44 reservoirs, lakes and ponds were closed to the public when a number of dogs and many lambs died after drinking water at the Rutland Water reservoir.[126] High temperatures and light intensities together with calm conditions resulted in heavy algal concentrations in the surface layers.

Causes of algal population growth

Both nitrogen and phosphorus are necessary for algal population growth, but algae require about 10–20 times as much nitrogen as phosphorus and, since this ratio is usually exceeded in most temperate water bodies, it is phosphorus, rather than nitrogen that is usually the limiting factor.[127] Even so, further addition of nutrients, whether phosphorus or nitrogen, is not by itself sufficient to cause rapid algal

Table 4.14 Phosphate loadings to water courses from different sources for various countries of Europe

	UK	Italy	Germany	Nether-lands	Denmark	Ireland
Total phosphate load (thousand tonnes per year)	57.1	58.7	82.4	20.7	11.2	8.7
Proportion of total (%)						
Agriculture	17	1	17	15	25	34
Animal farms	17	13	16	26	35	36
Domestic point sources	59	62	59	53	35	26
Industry	6	6	6	5	4	3
Non-cultivated land	1	2	2	1	1	1

Source: Vighi, M. and Chiaudani, G., "The impact of agricultural loads on eutrophication in EEC surface waters", in: Winteringham, F.P.W. (ed.), 1985, *Environment and Chemicals in Agriculture* London: Elsevier Appl. Science Publishers, 1985)

growth. Other factors such as the topography of the water body, the season and the overall composition of the fauna and flora may be critical.[128]

In most places, the source of phosphorus is domestic sewage rather than fertilizers or farm waste (Table 4.14). Nevertheless, in countries such as Denmark and Ireland, where the human population is relatively low and livestock numbers are high, the contribution from agricultural sources can be over 60 per cent. Nutrients deposited in precipitation may also be important. Lake Tahoe, an oligotrophic lake in the Sierra Nevada mountains of the western USA, has shown a steady increase in algal biomass together with a decline in water transparency over the past 2–3 decades.[129] The nitrogen input comes from rain and snow, while the phosphorus is derived from fertilizers used on golf courses and on private lawns in the developments along the shoreline (Table 4.15). A further source of nutrients is on-farm agricultural processing, particularly of plantation crops such as oil palm, rubber and sugar cane in developing countries (see Chapter 6, page 309–12).

Table 4.15   Sources of nutrients to Lake Tahoe watershed, western USA

Source	Nutrient	
	Nitrogen	Phosphorus
Fertilizers (%)	35	90
Precipitation (%)	65	10
Total input (tonnes per year)	230	30

Source: Loeb, S.L., "Algal biofouling of oligotrophic Lake Tahoe: causal factors affecting production", in: Evans, L.G. and Hogland, K.D. (eds), *Algal Biofouling* (Amsterdam: Elselvier, 1986).

Eutrophication in the tropics and subtropics

Dense algal populations are an especially common feature of many tropical and subtropical rivers and lakes, often arising naturally at certain times of the year. Although abundant light and warmth favour algal growth, the critical factor, as in temperate regions, is the supply of nutrients.[130] Whether nitrogen or phosphorus is limiting, however, varies from place to place depending upon the nature of the soils and the underlying geology.

Inorganic nitrogen, as in temperate regions, comes from a number of different sources. Mineralization of organic material derived from waterside vegetation and from aquatic plants and animals is important.

It is particularly apparent during the filling of artificial reservoirs when the flooded vegetation generates large quantities of nutrient and growths of algae. Sometimes, extensive blooms of surface plants, such as water hyacinth and water cabbage, are produced. These disrupt fishing and navigation, and also intercept light, producing severe oxygen depletion and widespread fish kills. During the filling stage of Lake Kariba on the Zambia–Zimbabwe border, the aquatic fern, *Salvinia*, covered an area of 1000 km^2, some 20 per cent of the lake's surface.[131] Such highly eutrophic conditions are usually temporary, however, and reservoirs eventually stabilize to more oligotrophic systems.

But the most important source of nutrients is human waste. Mineralization of such wastes proceeds much faster than in temperate regions, due to the higher temperatures and the greater abundance of bacteria, so that there is more opportunity for rapid algal growth. An example of a coastal lake severely affected in this way is Laguna de Bay in the Philippines. It extends over 90,000 hectares and is surrounded by a dense industrial and agricultural population. Fertilizer use is increasing in the surrounding rice fields since they are mostly planted to high yielding varieties. But fertilizers are not the major source of nutrients for the lake. Losses of nitrogen in the irrigation water are less than 7 kg N/ha per crop after a fertilizer application of 60 kg N/ha, although losses can be high in the dry season, when fertilizer is broadcast and irrigation water flow continuous (Table 4.16). At present human wastes produce a nitrogen loading five times as great as from other sources.[132] Dense algal populations are frequent as are fish kills, severely damaging an otherwise thriving fish-pen industry.

Eutrophication is also common, on a smaller scale, within flooded paddy fields.[133] Fertilizer nitrogen stimulates algal growth and this can remove up to 30 per cent of the added nitrogen, so making it unavailable for the rice crop.[134] On the other hand not all algal growth is unwelcome. Nitrogen fixing blue-green algae subsequently incorporated in the soil significantly add to the available nitrogen (see Chapter 11).

The strong seasonality of many tropical climates makes rivers and lakes particularly prone to eutrophication. Many rivers have a distinct cycle of flows dictated by the pattern of rainfall, with average maxima often two orders of magnitude greater than the minima.[135] At the onset of the rains, inorganic soil nitrogen that has been slowly accumulating during the dry season is flushed into the nearby water.[136] But often, the first rains also contribute large quantities of suspended material which intercepts light and limits photosynthesis so delaying algal growth. Peak algal production in the White Nile, for instance, does not occur

Table 4.16 Losses of nitrogen in irrigation water from paddy fields around Laguna de Bay, and estimates of total nitrogen loads to the lake

	Total N in outflow from paddy (kg N/ha)	Contribution of fertilizer applied in paddy to total N in outflow
Wet season		
Broadcast fertilizer	5.6	61%
Incorporated fertilizer	3.7	32%
Dry season		
Broadcast fertilizer	6.8	77%
Incorporated fertilizer	3.8	59%
	Total annual N load to Laguna de Bay (tonnes N)	
From human wastes	1400	
From rice paddy*	400	

* Assuming 40,000 ha of irrigated paddy with 2 crops per year and an average loss of 5 kg N/ha in water outflow

Source: Edra, R.B., "Laguna de Bay – an example of a fresh and brackish water fishery under stress of the multiple-use of a river basin", *FAO Fish Rep.* **288** (1983) pp. 119–24; Singh, V.P., Wickham, T.H., Corpuz, I.T. and Early, A.C., "Nitrogen losses in run-off from irrigated rice fields", *Prog. Water Tech.* **11** (1979) pp. 315–25.

until after the flood waters, high in both nutrients and sediment, have subsided.[137] Rivers with these regimes are thus often most at risk when droughts produce extended periods of low flow. Tropical lakes that are most susceptible to disruption by added nutrients are those with currently low production, despite advantageous temperature and light conditions. Lowland Malaysian lakes sited on old weathered soils that are very poor in nutrients fall in this category.[138]

The Norfolk Broads

In the United Kingdom, severe damage to recreation and amenity has resulted from nutrient inflows to the Norfolk Broads.[139] The Broadland was created between the ninth and fourteenth centuries by the extensive extraction of peat for fuel; in time the peat pits became shallow lakes, the Broads, linked by sluggish rivers and dykes. Prior to AD 1800, the Broads had a phosphorus concentration of about 10–20 μg/litre and were characterized by clear water, small populations of planktonic algae, a low-growing carpet of water plants and rich fish populations.[140] From about 1800, drainage and agricultural development increased nutrient levels, phosphorus rising to about 80 μg/litre. Algal populations increased, as did the growth of tall, rank water weeds. Despite these changes, the fishery remained highly productive.

The major deterioration has come relatively suddenly in the last three decades, primarily as a result of a greatly increased input of nutrients. Phosphorus has come from septic tanks and sewage treatment works, and nitrogen from field drainage and silage effluent (Table 4.17). Phosphorus levels in the waters are now typically 150–300 μg/l, sometimes reaching 2000 μg/l. The nutrients, combined, have stimulated algal growth. The increase in nitrate has also had a direct effect: the floating mats of reeds fringing the water courses have grown excessively, becoming top-heavy and liable to collapse.[141]

Table 4.17   Sources of nutrients in the River Bure in the Norfolk Broadland

| | Tonnes annually | |
	Phosphorus	Inorganic nitrogen
Catchment	4.5 (22%)	504.0 (94%)
Sewage treatment works	16.1 (78%)	32.3 (6%)

Source: Moss, B., Balls, H., Bosher, I., Manson, K. and Timms, M., "Problems in the construction of a nutrient budget for the River Bure and its Broads (Norfolk) prior to its restoration from eutrophication", in: Round, F.E. (ed.), *Algae and the Aquatic Environment* (Bristol: Biopress Ltd, 1988), pp. 326–53.

The Broads are now characterized by turbid water and declining fishery. However, painstaking work by Moss and his colleagues has shown that nutrient inflows are not the only cause of the changes (Figure 4.20). When they converted one of the Broadland dykes into a series of experimental ponds and fertilized them with phosphate and ammonium nitrate they found, unexpectedly, that neither did large algal populations result nor was aquatic plant growth reduced. However, they had also removed the fish populations from the ponds. When the fish were added algal populations grew rapidly. The fish were found to prey on large water fleas (*Cladocera*), such as daphnia, which in turn graze on the algae. In the Broads, generally, the numbers of these water fleas have dramatically declined. Previously they were able to escape fish predation by taking refuge beneath the cover of submerged water plants. They may have also suffered from the intensive use of organochlorine pesticides in the 1950s and 1960s.[142] Sediment cores have revealed peaks of DDT derivatives at the time when the major changes in the Broads were ocurring.

To restore the Broads would seem to depend on getting the phosphorus level below 50 μg/l. However, experiments in which

Figure 4.20 Some of the key processes involved in ecosystem changes in the Norfolk Broads

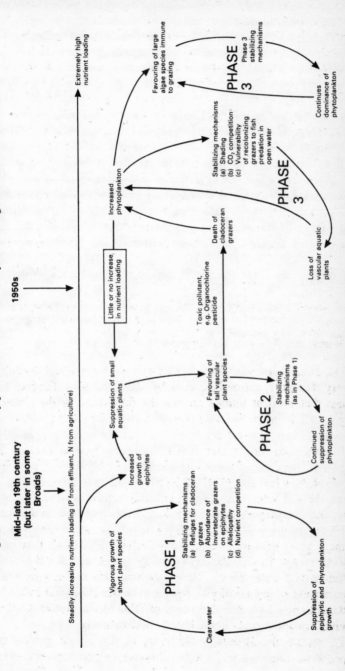

Source: after Moss, B., "Water pollution and the management of ecosystems: a case study of science and scientist" in: Grubb, P.J. and Whittaker, J.B. (eds), *Toward a More Exact Ecology* (Oxford: Blackwell Scientific Publications, 1989).

nutrient inflows have been excluded have only been partly successful. Although rising nutrient levels may have brought about the degradation of the Broads, building back the original complex interrelations will take more than a simple lowering of nutrient loading.[143]

The Great Lakes

A survey carried out in the US in the early 1970s found that some 65 per cent of 800 lakes were eutrophic and another 4 per cent were hypertrophic, that is, with very murky water and extremely high levels of plant biomass.[144] However, the problem is probably not as severe as the survey suggests. Lakes classified as eutrophic under the Environmental Protection Agency (EPA) definition can still provide reasonable recreational value, such as for swimming and fishing.[145] There is, indeed, a continuum in lake fertility and classification depends, in part, on human perceptions. Many lakes

Figure 4.21 Seasonal changes in phytoplankton in inshore waters of Lake Erie

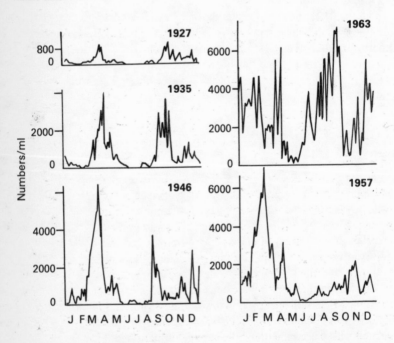

Source: Moss, B., *Ecology of Fresh Waters. Man and Medium.* (Oxford: Blackwell Scientific Publications, 1980).

classified as eutrophic by the EPA might be regarded as oligotrophic in the UK.

Nevertheless, severe human-induced eutrophication does occur, especially in the Great Lakes. The most severely affected are Lakes Erie and Ontario. The other major lakes – Huron, Michigan and Superior – are mainly oligotrophic, except in certain partly enclosed bays lying near to major cities. Most of the changes in chemical characteristics of the Great Lakes began around the end of the nineteenth century, coincident with a rapid increase in population, but severe eutrophic conditions did not occur until the 1960s.[146] In Lake Erie depletion of oxygen occurred in the inshore waters as a result of both algal growth and the high oxygen demand of the sediments.[147] The latter, in particular, has had a serious effect upon benthic (dwelling on the lake-bed) organisms, many of which include fish in the early stages of their life-cycles. The composition of the plankton in the inshore waters of the lake has also dramatically changed. There have been increases in copepods and in phytoplankton generally, while the large populations of diatoms in the late summer have been progressively replaced by blue-green algae (Figure 4.21).

In all the lakes the composition of the fish populations has changed, although overall fishery yields have only declined in Lakes Huron and Ontario. In Lake Erie the original fishery of lake trout, herring, whitefish, sauger and blue pike has been replaced by a less diverse, lower quality fishery, exploiting species such as yellow perch, white bass, rainbow smelt and alewife[148] (Figure 4.22). However, eutrophication is not the only cause. Selective fishing, invasion of marine species such as the sea lamprey and modification of tributary rivers have all played a role.[149] The decline of the lake herring in Lakes Huron and Michigan coincided with the establishment of the alewife; predation by the lamprey destroyed the lake trout; and the near-extinction of the sturgeon was caused by overfishing.[150]

As in the case of the Norfolk Broads, municipal sewage appears to be as, if not more, important a source of nutrients as agricultural run-off. Similarly, the principal cause of the accelerated eutrophication is the excessive loadings of phosphorus.[151] Thus, despite a steady increase in nitrate concentration from 0.33 to 1.38 mg/l between 1906 and 1976, Lake Superior remains oligotrophic because phosphorus inputs are low.[152] Where phosphorus inputs are high, attempts to reduce them have centred on point sources, such as wastewater flows. In Lake Erie, this has led to a decline in phosphorus loading from 12000 tonnes/year in 1970 to 4500 tonnes/year in 1980. Non-point source loading, typically from agriculture, was much lower during this period,

Figure 4.22   Commercial fish production in Lake Michigan

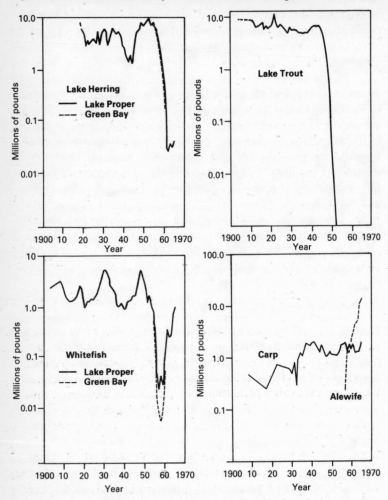

Source: Beeton, A.M., "Changes in the environment and biota of the Great Lakes", in: *Eutrophication: Causes, Consequences, Correctives* (Washington DC: National Academy of Sciences, 1969).

between 600 and 1200 tonnes/year, of which 90 per cent was estimated to be of rural origin.[153]

Coastal waters

Shallow marine environments are particularly susceptible to nutrient enrichment producing rapid growth in algal populations. Boston harbour, on the eastern coast of the USA, is a notable example: dense growths of algae were recorded there as early as the 1880s.[154]

Harbours

Nutrient contamination of harbours, though, is largely a product of urban wastes. And this is true of both temperate and tropical regions. In the Lac de Tunis, a coastal water body between the city of Tunis and the Mediterranean Sea, extreme eutrophication caused by urban wastes leads, during the summer, to a cycle of algal growth, anaerobic conditions, fish kills and releases of hydrogen sulphide.[155] Other seriously affected harbours include Portland, San Francisco and Tampa in the USA, Aarhus, Copenhagen and Gdansk on the Baltic Sea, and Bombay, Colombo and Madras on the Indian Ocean. Nonetheless, agricultural wastes can sometimes be important: when duck farm wastes were removed from inputs into Great South Bay, New York, the result was a decline in green algae content.[156]

Chesapeake Bay

Nutrients from agricultural land are likely to be more important in larger coastal bays fed by extensive catchments, such as the Chesapeake Bay on the east coast of the USA. In recent years there has been a considerable reduction in water clarity in the bay, accompanied by an increase in algal populations and a decline in submerged aquatic vegetation. There have also been prolonged periods of low dissolved oxygen in the deep layers, causing the loss of oysters and other benthic organisms.[157]

The changes have been caused by the increased inputs of nutrients to the bay, that occurred in most coastal areas in the USA during the late 1970s.[158] In the Chesapeake Bay the nitrogen load rose 29 per cent between 1974 and 1981. Both nitrogen and phosphorus have played a role but which is the critical factor is a matter of controversy. In the Bay there is a complex seasonal pattern of nutrient levels in the water and the sediments which is difficult to analyse. Nitrate concentrations in the water are highest in winter and early spring, and lowest in summer and early autumn, while the reverse is true of phosphorus.[159] Winter rainfall washes nitrate from the land into rivers which eventually flow into the Bay. This is also the time when phosphorus settles into the sediments in the Bay. In the late spring, though, nitrogen levels decline as temperature increases, denitrification occurs and organisms begin to use up the nitrogen for growth. The denitrification is a consequence of decreasing oxygen levels in the deep layers which forces bacteria to change to nitrate as a source of oxygen. The low oxygen levels, however, also create conditions ideal for the release of phosphorus from the sediments. This would normally lead to rapid algal growth but because nitrogen is limiting this only occurs if further nitrogen is added.[160] Thus, while phosphorus is the more important limiting nutrient in the upstream freshwater river areas, in the Bay itself nitrogen loading is probably the critical factor in producing the algal blooms. As a control measure the States of Maryland in 1985 and Virginia in 1987 have banned the use of phosphorus in detergents but this is unlikely to be enough. Reduction of nitrogen loading may also be required.

The North Sea

Dense populations of planktonic algae have also become more frequent in the coastal waters around the UK and in the North Sea generally.[161] They have been particularly common in the shallow coastal waters extending from Norway to France. They are associated with high concentrations of nitrate and phosphate, which tend to build up in coastal inlets characterized by restricted water exchange with the open seas.[162] Off Denmark dense growths of dinoflagellate plankton have been associated with a high incidence of fish and invertebrate mortalities in 1981 and 1985.

Another recent trend has been the greater intensity and duration of populations of the flagellate alga, *Phaeocystis*, in the southern part of the North Sea.[163] This alga is characterized by producing large quantities of mucilagenous material that foams. And as a result many of the beaches of northern France, the Netherlands and West Germany are covered for short periods, especially during April to late June, with a layer of foam up to two metres thick, causing a serious nuisance. Algal growth seems to be linked to the increasing discharge of nitrogen and phosphorus by rivers into the North Sea, but it is not known which of the two nutrients is most critical. One study of an algal population off the coast of the Netherlands found phosphorus to be clearly limiting,[164] while another off the Belgian coast observed nitrogen limitation.[165]

Water flowing into the North Sea from the English Channel is poor in nutrients but successive discharges of continental rivers lead to a progressively heavier contamination (Table 4.18). Along the continental coast concentrations have increased by up to four times

Table 4.18 Nitrogen loading of water flowing northwards in the eastern North Sea and the impact upon nitrate concentration and algal populations

River or nutrient measurement station* (km from Seine)		Cumulative increase in total nitrogen output (thousand tonnes per year)	Maximum nitrate concentration (mg/l)	Maximum algal concentration (mg chlorophyll a per litre)
Seine	0 km	90		
Station A			56.3	5
Somme	165 km	102		
Station B	245 km		100.6	13
Yser	330 km	106		
Station C	370 km		251.6	35
Scheldt	390 km	141		
Rhine	460 km	549		
Station D	535 km		442.7	40
Lake Ijssel	665 km	615		
Station E	665 km		503.1	70
Ems	800 km	657		
Weser	895 km	699		
Elbe	935 km	950		

* River outputs and nutrient measurement stations (A to E) from south to north, proceeding down list

Source: Lancelot, C. et al., "*Phaeocystis* blooms and nutrient enrichment in the continental coastal zones of the North Sea", *Ambio* **16** (1987) pp. 38–46.

since the 1960s.[166] How much is due to agriculture and how much to sewage and domestic sources is open to dispute, however.

Coral reefs

Recently, concern has been growing about the likely impact of nitrogen and phosphorus upon coral reef environments. Although reefs are mostly characterized by low levels of both nutrients, phosphorus concentration appears to be the most critical factor. In Discovery Bay, Jamaica nitrates from groundwater in concentrations of between 4 and 10 mg/l are a significant source of nitrogen for the reef but so far there are no signs of degradation.[167] However, if sewage high in phosphorus were to contaminate the bay, then eutrophication could well result. In the Pacific such eutrophication has already become a problem. Before 1950 Kaneohe Bay, Hawaii supported a diverse coral fauna and the reefs were well developed, but by 1970 virtually all the coral had died in about 900 hectares of the southern part of the bay.[168] Here, treated sewage inputs to the bay increased the phosphorus burden, leading to invasions of algae which formed blankets over large areas of the reef, so blocking light and reducing the available oxygen. The coral was also damaged directly by a combination of increased freshwater run-off and sediments from terrestrial sources. In general silt-laden run-off is the most important threat to coral reefs, but other problems have come from sugar mill wastes and seepage from cesspools and latrines.

Summary

Fertilizers are not directly toxic to wildlife. They are environmental contaminants rather than pollutants, but under certain conditions they can give rise to eutrophication of rivers, lakes and coastal waters that causes environmental harm.

Contamination of the environment arises because not all the fertilizer applied is taken up by crop plants and removed at harvest. Fertilizer use has grown dramatically in recent years with average rates in the industrialized countries of 120–550 kg N/ha. Excessive use has been encouraged by generous subsidies and by the difficulties in calculating what should be optimal applications. But the proportion of fertilizer, in particular nitrogen fertilizer, that is taken up by plants and recovered in the harvest is also affected by a great variety of crop, soil and water climate factors. Although under ideal conditions recovery can be over 90 per cent, in practice it ranges from 20 to 70 per cent. Losses are high under heavy rainfall, especially in late autumn and winter in temperate countries where fertilizer has been applied in early autumn and there is little crop growth. In the tropics losses may be much higher. In rice paddies recoveries are only 30–40 per cent. In the seasonal tropics the alternation of dry and wet seasons results in build-up of nutrients and heavy losses with the onset of the monsoon. Losses are increased under irrigation which is common in such regions.

In natural ecosystems, the process of mineralization of organic nitrogen in the soil results in average annual losses of only 0.3–4 kg N/ha. These increase under cultivation rising to about 45 kg N/ha without fertilizer, about double that amount when farmyard manure is applied, and double again when fertilizers are applied in the autumn.

Under arable crops losses of nitrogen, as nitrate, through leaching and run-off average 35–155 kg N/ha. Losses from grassland are generally lower, except when grass is heavily fertilized or is intensively grazed with livestock. There is still considerable dispute, however, over the relative contributions to these losses from applied nitrogen fertilizer as opposed to cultivation practices and mineralization of soil nitrogen. Most micro-level studies under controlled conditions, with near optimal rates of application, suggest only 10 per cent of applied nitrogen is lost by leaching and run-off. But estimates for drainage from whole catchments under intensive agriculture give losses of the order of 200 mg nitrate/l suggesting that between a third and a half of the applied nitrogen is being lost.

There is widespread evidence of rapidly rising nitrate concentrations, over the past three decades, in both surface and groundwater, in regions of intensive agriculture. In the UK several rivers have concentrations approaching 50 mg nitrate/l and this value has already been exceeded in a high proportion of groundwater sources in the eastern region of the country. Profiles from boreholes reveal a "nitrate front" some 3–8 metres below the surface and moving downward at about one metre per year. One source has been the extensive ploughing up of grassland in the late 1950s and early 1960s with consequent heavy mineralization of organic soil nitrogen. But high N levels are also present in profiles under land which has been continuously cultivated to arable crops and increasing fertilizer applications appear to be the main source. A similar pattern is emerging in many parts of the USA. Heavy fertilizer use is clearly implicated in some regions, although in others domestic sources or livestock waste appear to be the main cause. In the developing countries heavy contamination of groundwater is common in many places, but primarily as a result of domestic sewage. However the experience in the Canary Islands, where nitrate levels in groundwater under fertilized fields are often over 100 mg/l, shows the potential for contamination from fertilizers in tropical countries.

Fertilizers can damage wild plants by causing excessive growth, but the most serious environmental problem in which fertilizers may be implicated is the eutrophication of rivers, lakes and coastal waters. Nitrate and phosphate are responsible for generating dense algal growth with consequent shading out of other aquatic plants, losses of fish and other aquatic life. Serious cases of eutrophication have occurred in the Great Lakes of the USA, in the Norfolk Broads in the UK and in a number of tropical rivers and lakes. Various coastal waters, including the Chesapeake Bay in the USA and parts of the North Sea, have also experienced massive growths of algal populations. But while nitrate from land drainage is an important factor, phosphate derived from domestic effluents is often the immediate cause.

References

1 FAO, *Fertilizer Yearbook 1987*, no. 37 (Rome: FAO, 1988); USDA, *Agricultural Resources. Inputs Situation and Outlook Report*, Economic Research Service, AR-17 (Washington DC: US Department of Agriculture, 1990).

2 USDA, 1990, *op. cit.*; FAO, *Fertilizer Yearbooks* (Rome: FAO, 1973–88).

3 Stangel, P.J., "Nitrogen requirement and adequacy of supply for rice production", in: *Nitrogen and Rice* (Los Banos, Philippines: International Rice Research Institute, 1979); Roy, R.N. and Seetharaman, S., *Wheat*, 2nd edn (New Delhi: Fertilizer Association of India, 1977).

4 Herdt, R.W. and Capule, C., *Adoption, Spread and Production. Impacts of Modern Rice Varieties in Asia* (Los Banos, Philippines: International Rice Research Institute, 1983).

5 FAO, *Production Yearbooks* (Rome: FAO, 1973–88).

6 Batey, T., "Some effects of nitrogen fertilizer on winter wheat", *J. Sci. Fd Agric.* 27 (1976) pp. 287–97; Greenwood D.J., "Modelling of crop response to nitrogen fertilizer", *Phil. Trans. R. Soc. Lond. B* 296 (1982) pp. 351–62.

7 Brady, N., *The Nature and Property of Soils* (New York: Macmillan, 1984).

8 Tarrant, J., Barbier, E., Greenburg, R.J., Higgins, M.L., Lintner, S.F., Machie, C., Murphy, L. and van Veldhuizen, H., *Natural Resources and Environmental Management in Indonesia* (Jakarta, Indonesia: US Agency for International Development, 1987).

9 Greenwood, D.J., Cleaver, T.J., Turner, P.K., Hunt, J., Niendorf, K.B. and Loguens, S.M.H., "Comparisons of the effects of nitrogen fertilizer on the yield, nitrogen content and quality of 21 different vegetable and agricultural crops", *J. agric. Sci. Camb.* 95 (1980) pp. 471–85; Dowdell, R.J., "Fate of nitrogen applied to agricultural crops with particular reference to denitrification", *Phil. Trans. R. Soc. B* 296 (1982) pp. 363–73.

10 Addiscott, T. and Powlson, D., "Laying the ground rules for nitrate", *New Scientist* 29 April (1989) pp. 28–9.

11 Powlson, D.S., Hart, P.B.S., Pruden, G. and Jenkinson, D.S., "Recovery of ^{15}N-labelled fertilizer applied in autumn to winter wheat at four sites in eastern England", *J. agric. Sci. Camb.* 107 (1986) pp. 611–20.

12 Morrison, J., Jackson, M.V. and Sparrow, P.E., "The response of perennial ryegrass to fertilizer nitrogen in relation to climate and soil", report of the Joint ADAS./GRI Grassland Manuring Trial – GM 20, Grassland Research Inst, Techn. Pre. no. 27 (1980); Reid, D., "The effects on long-term application of a wide range of nitrogen rates on the yields from perennial ryegrass sward", *J. agric. Sci. Camb.* 79 (1972) pp. 291–301; Whitehead, D.C., *The Role of Nitrogen in Grassland Productivity*, Commonwealth Agricultural Bureau, Farnham Royal, UK Bull. no. 48, Comm. Bur. Past. Fld. Crops (1970).

13 Prasad, R. and De Datta, S.K., "Increasing fertilizer nitrogen efficiency

in wetland rice", in: *Nitrogen and Rice* (Los Banos, Philippines: International Rice Research Institute, 1979); De Datta, S.K., *Principles and Practice of Rice Production* (New York: John Wiley & Sons, 1981).

14 Dowdell, 1982, *op. cit.*; Addiscott and Powlson, 1989, *op. cit.*

15 Haynes, R.J., and Cameron, K.C., "Retention and movement of nitrogen in soils", in: Haynes, R.J. (ed.), *Mineral Nitrogen in the Plant–Soil System* (Orlando: Academic Press, 1986).

16 Haynes and Cameron, 1986, *op. cit.*

17 Foster, S.S.D., "The chalk groundwater anomaly – a possible explanation", *Journal of Hydrology* 25 (1975) pp. 159–65; Young, C.P. and Gray, E.M., *Nitrate in Groundwater – the Distribution of Nitrate in Chalk and Triassic Sandstone Aquifers* 'Water Research Centre, Medmenham' Tech. Rep. TR 69 (1978).

18 Foster, S.S.D., Bridge, L.R., Geake, A.K., Lawrence, A.R. and Parker, J. M., "The groundwater nitrate problem. A summary of research on the impact of agricultural land-use practices on groundwater quality between 1976 and 1985", *Hydrogeol. Rep. 86/2 (British Geological Survey, (Wallingford: 1986); Geake, A.K., and Foster, S.S.D., "Sequential isotope and solute profiling in the unsaturated zone of British Chalk", Hydrological Sciences Journal* 34 (1989) pp. 79–95.

19 Royal Society, 1983, *The Nitrogen Cycle of the UK*, Study Group Report, (London: The Royal Society, 1983).

20 Gosz, J.R., "Nitrogen cycling in coniferous forests", in: Clark, F.E. and Rosswall, T. (eds), *Terrestrial Nitrogen Cycles: Processes, Ecosystem Strategies and Management Impacts*, (Stockholm ecology bulletin, 1981); Melillo, J.M., "Nitrogen cycling in deciduous forests", in: Clark and Rosswall (eds), *op. cit.*

21 Hornbeck, J.W., Likens, G.E., Pierce, R.S. and Borman, F.H., "Strip cutting as a means of protecting site and stream flow quality when clearcutting northern hardwoods", in: Bernier, B. and Winget, C.H. (eds), *Forest Soils and Forest Land Management* (Quebec: Les presses de l'Université Laval, 1975).

22 Atkins, S.F., "Nitrogen leaching from fertilizers: lysimeter trials: published results from Europe and USA", ICI Research and Development Department (unpublished) (1976); Wild, A. and Cameron, K.C., "Soil nitrogen and nitrate leaching", in: Tinker, P.B. (ed.), *Soils and Agriculture* (Oxford: Blackwell Scientific Publ., 1980).

23 Foster et al., 1986, *op. cit.*

24 Cowling, D.W. and Lockyer, D.R., "Response of perennial ryegrass to nitrogen in various periods of the growing season", *J. Agric. Sci. Camb.* 75 (1970) pp. 539–46; Dowdell, 1982, *op. cit.*

25 Guiot, J., "The nature and origin of leached nitrogen in cultivated land", in: Brogan, J.C. (ed.), *Losses and Surface Run-off from Landspreading of Manures* (The Hague: Martinus Nijhoff, 1981); Vallis, I., "Nitrogen relationships in grass/legume mixtures", in: Wilson, J.R. (ed.), *Plant Relations in Pastures* (Canberra: CSIRO, 1978).

26 Low, A.J. and Armitage, F.R., "The composition of the leachate through

cropped and uncropped soils in lysimeters compared with that of rain", *Plant Soil* 33 (1970) pp. 393–411.

27 Whithead, 1970, *op. cit.*

28 Crisp, D.T., "Input and output of minerals for an area of Pennine moorland. The importance of precipitation, drainage, peat erosion and animals", *J. Appl. Ecol.* 3 (1966) pp. 327–348; Bargh, B.J., "Output of water, suspended sediment, and phosphorus and nitrogen forms from a small catchment", *N.Z. J. Agric. Res.* 21 (1978) pp. 29–38.

29 Ryden, J.C., Ball, P.R. and Garwood, E.A., "Nitrate leaching from grassland", *Nature* 311 (1984) pp. 50–53; White, R.E., "Nitrate leaching from grassland", *Nature* 311 (1984) pp. 10.

30 Steele, K.W., "Nitrogen in grassland soils", in: Lynch, P.B. (ed.), *Nitrogen Fertilizers in New Zealand Agriculture* (Wellington: NZ Inst. Agric. Sci., 1982); Ryden et al., 1984, *op. cit.*

31 Garwood, E.A., Salette, J. and Lemaire, G., "The influence of water supply to grass on the response to fertilizer nitrogen and nitrogen recovery", in: Prins, W.H. and Arnold, G.H. (eds), *Proc. Int. Symp. Europ. Grassland Fed. on Role of Nitrogen in Intensive Grassland Production* (Wageningen: Pudoc, 1980).

32 Correll, D.L. and Dixon, D., "Relationship of nitrogen discharge to land use on Rhode River watersheds", *Agro-Ecosystems* 6 (1980) pp. 147–59; Wild and Cameron, 1980, *op. cit.*

33 Garwood, E.A. and Tyson, K.C., "High loss of nitrogen in drainage from soil under grass following a prolonged period of low rainfall", *J. Agric. Sci. Camb.* 89 (1977) pp. 767–8.

34 Harris, G.L., Goss, M.J., Dowdell, R.J., Howse, K.R. and Morgan, P., "A study of mole drainage with simplified cultivation for autumn-sown crops on a clay soil. 2. Soil water regimes, water balances and nutrient loss in drainage water, 1978–80", *J. Agric. Sci. Camb.* 102 (1984) pp. 561–81.

35 Croll, B.T. and Hayes, C.R., "Nitrate and water supplies in the United Kingdom", *Environ. Pollut.* 50 (1988) pp. 163–87; Dowdell, 1982, *op. cit.*

36 Sanchez, P.A., *Properties and Management of Soils in the Tropics* (New York: John Wiley and Sons, 1976).

37 Sanchez, 1976, *op. cit.*

38 Rangeley, W.R., "Scientific advances most needed for progress in irrigation", *Phil. Trans. R. Soc. Lond. A* 316 (1986) pp. 355–68.

39 Patnaik, S. and Rao, M.V., "Sources of nitrogen for rice production", in: *Nitrogen and Rice* (Los Banos, Philippines: IRRI, 1979).

40 Viets, F.G., Humbert, R.P. and Nelson, C.E., "Fertilizers in relation to irrigation", in: Hagan, R.M., Haise, H.R. and Edminster, R.W. (eds), *Irrigation of Agricultural Lands* (Madison: Am. Soc. Agron., 1967).

41 Harris et al., 1984, *op. cit.*; Wild and Cameron, 1980, *op. cit.*

42 Haith, D.A. and Dougherty, J.V., "Non-point source pollution from agricultural runoff", *J. Env. Eng. Divn. Am. Soc. Civ. Eng.* 102 (1976)

pp. 1055–69.

43 Morgan, M.F., Jacobson, J.G.M. and Street, D.E., "The neutralisation of acid forming nitrogenous fertilizers in relation to nitrogen availability and soil bases", *Soil Sci.* **54** (1942) pp. 127–48.

44 Foster et al., 1986, *op. cit.*

45 Cameron, K.C. and Wild, A., "Potential aquifer pollution from nitrate leaching following ploughing of temporary grassland", *J. Environ. Qual.* **13** (1984) pp. 274–8.

46 Addiscot and Powlson, 1989, *op. cit.*

47 Craswell, E.T. and Vlek, P.L.G., "Fate of fertilizer nitrogen applied to wetland rice", in: *Nitrogen and Rice* (Los Banos, Philippines: IRRI, 1979); Katyal, J.C., Singh, B., Vlek, P.L.G. and Craswell, E.T., "Fate and efficiency of nitrogen fertilizers applied to wetland rice. II. Punjab, India", *Fert. Res.* **6** (1985) pp. 279–90.

48 Haynes, R.J., "The decomposition process: mineralisation, immobilisation, humus formation, and degradation", in: Haynes, R. (ed.), *op. cit.*

49 Sherwood, M., "Leaching of nitrogen from animal manures under Irish conditions", in: Brogan, J.E. (ed.), *op. cit.*

50 Vetter, H. and Steffens, G., "Leaching of nitrogen after the spreading of slurry", in: Brogan, J.E. (ed.), *op. cit.*

51 Lund, L.J., Page, A.L., Nelson, C.O. and Elliot, R.A., "Nitrogen balances for an effluent irrigated area", *J. Environ. Qual.* **10** (1981) pp. 349–52.

52 RCEP, *Agriculture and Pollution*, Royal Commission on Environmental Pollution, 7th Report (London: HMSO, 1979).

53 Foster, S.S.D., Cripps, A.C. and Smith-Carrington, A., "Nitrate leaching to groundwater", *Phil. Trans. R. Soc. Lond. B* **296** (1982) pp. 477–89; Burns, I.G. and Greenwood, D.J., "Estimation of the year-to-year variations in nitrate leaching in different soils and regions of England and Wales", *Agric. Environ.* **7** (1982) pp. 35–45; Wilkinson, W.B. and Greene, L.A., "The water industry and the nitrogen cycle", *Phil. Trans. Roy. Soc. Lond. B* **296** (1982) pp. 459–75.

54 Department of the Environment, "Nitrate in Water. A report by the Nitrate Coordination Group", Department of the Environment Pollution Paper, No,26 (London: HMSO, 1986).

55 Thames Water Authority, *Annual Report and Accounts 1981–2* (London: Thames Water Authority, 1982); DOE, 1986, *op. cit.*

56 Onstad, C.A. and Blake, J., "Thames basin nitrate and agricultural relations", in: *Proc. of the Symposium on Watershed Management* (Boise: American Soc. of Civil Engineers, 1980) pp. 961–73.

57 Wilkinson, quoted in Royal Society, 1983, *op. cit.*

58 Smith, R.A., Alexander, R.B. and Wolman, M.G., "Water-quality trends in the nation's rivers", *Science* **235** (1987) pp. 1607–15; WRI/IIED, *World Resources Report* (Washington and London: World Resources Institute and International Institute for Environment and Development, 1987).

59 Kothandaraman, V., Sinclair, R.A. and Evans, R.L., *Water Chemistry of*

the Illinois Waterway, Circular 147, Illinois State Water Survey (Illinois: Dept. of Energy and Natural Resources, 1981).

60 Preul, H.C., Discussion, in: Jenkins, S.H. (ed.), *Int. Assn. on Water Pollution Research and Control. Water Pollution Research and Control.* Part 3, *Water Science and Technology* **14** (1982) pp. 915–18.

61 McDonald, D.B. and Splinter, R.C., "Long term trends in nitrate concentration in Iowa water supplies", *J. Am. Water Works Assn.* **74** (1982) pp. 437–40.

62 Owens, M., "Nutrient balances in rivers", *Proc. Soc. Wat. Treat. Exam.* **19** (1970) pp. 239–47.

63 Kohl, D.H., Shearer, G.B. and Commoner, B., "Fertilizer nitrogen: contribution to nitrate in surface water in a corn belt watershed", *Science* **174** (1971) pp. 1331–4.

64 Katz, B.G., Lindner, J.B. and Ragone, S.E., "A comparison of nitrogen in shallow groundwater from sewered and unsewered areas, Nassau County, New York, from 1952 through 1976", *Ground Water* **18** (1980) pp. 607–16.

65 UNEP, *Environmental Data Report* United Nations Environment Programme, Nairobi (Oxford: Blackwells, 1988–9).

66 Handa, B.K., "Effect of fertilizer use on groundwater quality in India", in: International Association of Hydrological Sciences, *Groundwater in Resources Planning vol. II*, (1983) pp. 1105–19, IAHS Publ. no. 142.

67 Dissanyake, C.B. and Weerasooriya, S.V.R., "Chemistry of tap water in Sri Lanka – implications and health", *Int. J. Environ. Studies* **27** (1986) pp. 57–69.

68 Weerasooriya, S.V.R., Senaratne, A. and Dissanayake, C.B., "The environmental impact of nitrate distributions in the lake–effluent system in Kandy, Sri Lanka", *J. Environ. Manage.* **15** (1982) pp. 239–50.

69 Marshall, B.E., "Lake McIlwaine after twenty-five years", *Zimbabwe (Rhodesia) Sci. News* **12** (1978) pp. 79–82; Iwugo, K.O., "The present status of the water pollution problems in the Kafue township area", *Zambian J. Sci. Tech.* **1** (1976) pp. 17–28.

70 Grant, P.M., "Agriculture and water pollution: the rate of artificial fertilizer in Rhodesia", *Zimbabwe (Rhodesia) Science News* **9** (1975) pp. 308–11.

71 Fullstone, M.J., "A review of the factors affecting the disposal of effluents containing nitrogen and phosphate in Zimbabwe", *Zimb. Agric. J.* **77** (1980) pp. 207–12.

72 Council on Environmental Quality, *Environmental Quality*, 10th Annual Report of the CEQ (Washington DC: GPO, 1979); DOE, 1986, *op. cit.*

73 DOE, 1986, *op. cit.*

74 DOE, 1986, *op. cit.*; Wilkinson and Greene, 1982, *op. cit.*; Foster et al., 1982, *op. cit.*

75 DOE, 1986, *op. cit.*; House of Lords, *Nitrate in Water*, Select Committee of the European Community, Seminar 1988–89, 16th Report, HL Paper 73 (London: HMSO, 1989).

76 House of Lords, 1989, *op. cit.*

77 DOE, 1986, *op. cit.*

78 Royal Society, 1983, *op. cit.*

79 Foster et al., *op. cit.*; Young and Gray, 1978 *op. cit.*; Young et al., 1976, *op. cit.*; Foster, S.S.D. and Young, C.P., "Effects of agricultural land use on groundwater quality, with special reference to nitrate", in: *A Survey of British Hydrology* (London: The Royal Society, 1981) pp. 47–59. Severn-Trent Water Authority, *Groundwater Pollution Investigations in North Nottinghamshire, Part I: Research Development Project Report* (Birmingham: Severn-Trent Water Authority, 1978).

80 Young and Gray, 1978, *op. cit.*

81 Young and Gray, 1978, *op. cit.*

82 Foster et al., 1982, *op. cit.*

83 Young et al., 1976, *op. cit.*; Wilkinson and Greene, 1982, *op. cit.*; DOE, 1986, *op. cit.*

84 Nielson, E.G. and Lee, L.K., *The Magnitude and Costs of Groundwater Contamination from Agricultural Chemicals: a National Perspective*, Resources and Technology Division, Economic Research Service, Agricultural Economic Report no. 576 (Washington: USDA, 1987).

85 USGS, *National Water Summary 1984, Hydrologic Events, Selected Water-Quality Trends, and Groundwater Resources*, US Geological Survey (Washington DC: US Government Printing Office, 1985).

86 Conservation Foundation, *Groundwater Protection* (Washington DC: CF, 1987).

87 AWWA, "An AWWA survey of inorganic contaminants in water supplies", a survey carried out by AWWA Inorganic Contaminants Committee, Water Quality Division, *J. Am. Water Works Assn.* 77 (1985) pp. 67–72.

88 Conservation Foundation, 1987, *op. cit.*

89 Larson, T.E. and Henley, L., *Occurrence of Nitrate in Well Waters* Univ. Illinois Water Resources Centre, Research Rep. no. 1 (Urbana, 1966).

90 Saffigna, P.G. and Keeney, D.R., "Nitrate and chloride in groundwater under irrigated agriculture in central Wisconsin", *Ground Water* 15 (1977) pp. 170–77; Wagner, G.H., Steele, K.G., McDonald, H.C. and Coughlin, T.L., "Water quality as related to linears, rock chemistry, and rain water chemistry in a rural carbonate terrain", *J. Environ. Qual.* 5 (1976) pp. 444–51.

91 Lund, L.J., Ryden, F.C., Miller, R.J., Laag, A.E. and Bendixen, W.E., "Nitrogen balances for the Santa Maria Valley", in: Pratt, P.E. (ed.), *National Conference on Management of Nitrogen in Irrigated Agriculture* (Riverside, CA: Univ. of California, Riverside, 1978).

92 Bouldin, D.R. and Selleck, G.W., "Management of fertilizer nitrogen for potatoes consistent with optimum profit and maintenance of groundwater quality", in: Loehr, R.C. (ed.), *Food, Fertilizer and Agricultural Residues* (Michigan: Ann Arbor Publ., 1937).

93 USGS, 1985, *op. cit.*

94 Martin, W.P., Fenster, W.E. and Hanson, C.D., "Fertilizer management for pollution control", in: *Agricultural Practices and Water Quality, Proceed-*

ings of a Conference Concerning the Role of Agriculture in Clean Water (Ames, Iowa: Iowa State University, 1970).

95 Kreitler, C.W. and Jones, D.C., "Natural soil nitrate: the cause of nitrate contamination of groundwater in Runnels County, Texas", *Ground Water* 13 (1975) pp. 53–61.

96 Baker, J.L., Kanwar, R.S. and Austin, T.A., "Impact of groundwater drainage wells on groundwater quality", *J. Soil and Water Conserv.* 40 (1985) pp. 516–20.

97 Martin, D.L. and Watts, D.G., "Potential purification of high nitrate groundwater through irrigation management", *Trans. Am. Soc. Agric. Eng.* 25 (1982) pp. 1662–7; Exner, M.E. and Spalding, R.F., "Evaluation of contaminated groundwater in Holt County, Nebraska", *Water Resources Research* 15 (1979) pp. 139–147.

98 Saffigna and Keeney, 1977, *op. cit.*

99 Stewart, B.A., Viets, F.R. Jr, Hutchinson, G.L. and Kemper, W.D., "Nitrates and other pollutants under fields and feedlots", *Environ. Sci. Tech.* 1 (1967) pp. 736–9.

100 Taylor, R.G. and Bigbee, P.D., "Fluctuations in nitrate concentrations utilised as an assessment of agricultural contamination to an aquifer of a semiarid climatic region", *Water Research* 7 (1973) pp. 115–61.

101 Ayers, R.S., "A case study – nitrates in the Upper Santa Ana river basin in relation to groundwater pollution", in: Pratt, P.F. (ed.), *National Conference on Management of Nitrogen in Irrigated Agriculture* (University of California: Department of Soil and Environmental Sciences, 1978).

102 Handa, 1983, *op. cit.*

103 Jacks, G. and Sharma, V.P., "Nitrogen circulation and nitrate in groundwater in an agricultural catchment in southern India", *Environ. Geol.* 5 (1983) pp. 61–4; Mallick, S. and Banerji, S., "Nitrate pollution of groundwater as a result of agricultural development in Indo-Ganga Plain, India", in: van Duijvenboorden, W., Glasbergen, P. and van Lelyveld, H. (eds), *Quality of Ground Water* Studies in Environmental Science (Netherlands: Elsevier Sci Publ. Co., 1981); Pal, B., "Potential hazards of nitrate and fluoride in underground waters", *Water Research* 17 (1983) pp. 353–4.

104 Langenegger, O., "High nitrate concentrations in shallow aquifers in a rural area of central Nigeria caused by random deposits of domestic refuse and excrement", in: van Duijvenboorden et al. (eds), 1981, *op. cit.*

105 Hutton, L.G. and Lewis, W.J., *Nitrate Pollution of Groundwater in Botswana* Sixth WEDC Conference, Water and Water Engineering in Africa (1980) pp. 1–4.

106 Cook, J.M. and Das, D.K., *Semra Village – Case Study of Groundwater Pollution in Central India* Report No. WD/OS/80/16, Indo-British Betwa Groundwater Project (London: Overseas Development Administration, 1980).

107 Foster, S., Ventura, M. and Hirata, R., *Groundwater Pollution. An*

Executive Overview of the Latin America-Caribbean Situation in Relation to Potable Water Supply (Lima, Peru: WHO, PAHO and CEPIS, 1987).

108 Foster et al., 1987, *op. cit.*

109 Akiti, in: Young, C.P., "Data acquisition and evaluation of groundwater pollution by nitrates, pesticides, and disease-producing bacteria", *Environ. Geol.* 5 (1983) pp. 11–18.

110 Kakar, Y.P., "Nitrate pollution in groundwater in southern and southwestern Haryana, India", in: van Duijvenboorden et al. (eds), 1981 *op. cit.*

111 Heaton, T.H.E., "Sources of nitrate in phreatic groundwater in the western Kalahari", *J. Hydrol.* 67 (1984) pp. 249–59; Adam, J.W.H., "Water aspects of nitrate in drinking-water and possible means of denitrification (literature review)", *Water SA* 6 (1980) pp. 79–84.

112 Heaton, T.H.E., Talma, A.S. and Vogel, J.C., "Origin and history of nitrate in confined groundwater in the western Kalahari", *J. Hydrol.* 62 (1983) pp. 243–62.

113 Custodio, E., Guerra, J.A., Jimenez, J., Medina, J.A. and Soler, C., "The effects of agriculture on the volcanic aquifers of the Canary Islands", *Environ. Geol.* 5 (1984) pp. 225–31.

114 Davis, S.N. and Suarez, J.J., "Chemical character of return irrigation water in tropical volcanic islands", *Environ. Geol.* 1 (1975) pp. 69–73.

115 Ray, P. and David, A., "Effect of industrial wastes and sewage upon the chemical and biological composition and fisheries of the River Ganga at Kanpur (UP)", *Environ. Health* 8 (1966) pp. 61–9.

116 Lund, J.W.G., "Primary production", *Water Treatment and Examination* 19 (1970) pp. 332–58; Rohlich, G.A. (ed.), *Eutrophication: Causes, Consequences, Correctives*, National Research Council, Publ. 1700, Washington (1969).

117 Moss, B., *Ecology of Fresh Waters, Man and Medium*, 2nd edn (Oxford: Blackwell Scientific Publications, 1988); Stewart, W.D.P., Preston, T., Peterson, H.G. and Christofi, N., "Nitrogen cycling in euthrophic freshwaters", *Phil Trans. R. Soc. Lond. B* 296 (1982) pp. 491–509.

118 Walker, W.N., "Significance of eutrophication water supply reservoirs", *J. Am. Water Works Assn.* 75 (1983) pp. 38–42; Collingwood, R.W., *Significance of Eutrophication in Britain and its Effects on Water Supplies*, Water Research Centre, Tech. Rep. no. 40 (1977); Palmer, C.M., *Algae in Water Supplies*, US Dept. of Health, Education and Welfare, Public Health Service, Publ. No. 657 (1962).

119 Carmichael, W.W. (ed.), *The Water Environment – Algal Toxins and Health* (NY and London: Plenum Press, 1981); Skulberg, O.M., Codd, G.A. and Carmichael, W.W., "Toxic blue-green algal blooms in Europe: a growing problem", *Ambio* 13 (1984) pp. 244–7; Francis, G., "Poisonous Australian lake", *Nature* 18 (1978) pp. 11–12.

120 Moss, B., Bales, M. and Irvine, K., *Food Web and Water Quality Relationships in the Saline Broads of the River Thorne, Norfolk*, Inst. Ital. Hydrobiol. (in the press); Otterstrom, C.V. and Steemann-Nielsen, E.,

"Two cases of extensive mortality in fishes caused by the flagellate *Prymnesium parvum* Carter", *Rept Danish Biol. Sta.* **44** (1940) pp. 5–24.

121   Case, A.A., "Some aspects of nitrate intoxication in livestock", *J. Am. Vet. Med. Assoc.* **130** (1957) p. 323; Reynolds, C.S., "Cattle deaths and blue-green algae: a possible instance from Cheshire, England", *J. Inst. Water Eng. Sci.* **34** (1980) pp. 74–6; Richards, D.S., Beattie, K.A. and Codd, G.A., "Toxicity of cyanobacteria blooms in Scottish freshwaters", *Environ. Tech. Letters* **4** (1983) pp. 377–82; DOE, 1986, *op. cit.*

122   Slatkin, D.N., Jones, R.D., Adams, W.H., Kycia, J.H. and Siegelman, "A typical pulmonary thrombosis caused by a toxic cyanobacteria peptide", *Science* **220** (1983) pp. 1383–5; Skulberg et al., 1984, *op. cit.*

123   Carmichael, B., 1982, *op. cit.*

124   Falconer, I.R., Beresford, A.M. and Runnegar, M.T.C., "Evidence of liver damage by toxins from a bloom of the blue-green alga, *Microcystis aeruginosa*", *The Med. J. Australia* **1** (1983) pp. 511–14.

125   ENDS, "Nitrogen inputs implicated in toxic algal blooms", **175** (1989) pp. 5–6; Rosenberg, R., "Silent spring in the sea", *Ambio* **17** (1988) pp. 289–90; Sangfors, O., "Are synergistic effects of acidification and eutrophication causing excessive algal growth in Scandinavian coastal waters", *Ambio* **17** (1988) p. 296.

126   ENDS, "Toxic algae spark blooming debate on eutrophication", **176** (1989) p. 9–11.

127   Lund, 1970, *op. cit.*

128   Lund, 1970, *op. cit.*; Manuel-Faler, C.Y., Minshall, G.W., Dunn, R.W. and Bruns, D.A., "In situ nitrogen enrichments in two Idaho (USA) streams", *Environ. Monit. and Assessment* **4** (1983) pp. 67–79.

129   Loeb, S.L., "Algal biofouling of oligotrophic Lake Tahoe: causal factors affecting production", in: Evans, L.G. and Hoagland, K.D. (eds), *Algal Biofouling, (Amsterdam: Elsevier Sci. Publ., 1986).*

130   Payne, A.I., *The Ecology of Tropical Lakes and Rivers* (Chichester: John Wiley and Sons, 1986); Moss, B., "Limitation of algal growth in some Central American waters", *Limnol. Oceanogr.* **14** (1969) pp. 591–601; Viner, A.B., "Response of a tropical mixed phytoplankton population to nutrient enrichments of ammonia and phosphate and some ecological implications", *Proc. R. Soc. Lond. B* **183** (1973) pp. 351–70; Wurtsbaugh, W.A., Vincent, W.F., Alfaro Tapia, R., Vincent, C.L. and Richerson, P.J., "Nutrient limitation of algal growth and N-fixation in a tropical alpine lake, Lake Titicaca (Peru/Bolivia)", *Freshwat. Biol.* **15** (1985) pp. 185–95; Grobelaar, J.V., "Availability to algae of nitrogen and phosphorus absorbed on suspended solids in turbid waters of the Amazon River", *Arch. Hydrobiol.* **96** (1983) pp. 302–16; Edra, R.B., "Laguna de Bay – an example of fresh and brackish water fishery under stress of the multiple-use of a river basin", *FAO Fish. Rep* **288** (1988) pp. 119–24.

131   Payne, 1986, *op. cit.*

132   Edra, 1983, *op. cit.*

133   Mikkelsen, D.S. and De Datta, S.K., "Ammonia volatilisation from

wetland rice soils", in: *Nitrogen and Rice* (Los Banos, Philippines: IRRI, 1979).

134 Craswell and Vlek, 1979, *op. cit.*

135 Payne, 1981, *op. cit.*

136 Sanchez, 1976, *op. cit.*

137 Sinander, F. and Kerin, A.G.A., "Primary production and respiration of the phytoplankton in the Blue and White Niles at Khartoum", *Hydrobiol.* **110** (1984) pp. 57–9.

138 Richardson, J.L. and Jin, L.T., "Algal productivity of natural and artificially enriched freshwaters in Malaya", *Verh. Internat. Verein. Limnol.* **19** (1975) pp. 1383–9.

139 Moss, B., "The Broads", *Biologist* **34** (1987) pp. 7–13.

140 Moss, 1987, *op. cit.*

141 Crook, C.E., Boar, R.A. and Moss, B., *The Decline of Reedswamp in the Norfolk Broadland: Causes, Consequences and Solution*, Broads Authority Research Series **6** (1984).

142 Moss, B., "Water pollution and the management of ecosystems: a case study of science and scientist", in: Grubb, P.J. and Whittaker, J.B. (eds), *Toward a More Exact Ecology* (Oxford: Blackwell Scientific Publ., 1989).

143 Moss, B. and Leah, R.T., *Broadland Research*, final report of the Nature Conservancy Council on experiments conducted at Hickling and Brundall Broads, Norfolk (1980).

144 CEQ, 1979, *op. cit.*

145 Crosson, P.R. and Brubaker, S., *Resource and Environmental Effects of US Agriculture* (Washington DC: Resources for the Future, 1982).

146 Beeton, A.M., "Eutrophication of the St Lawrence Great Lakes", *Limnol. Oceanogr.* **10** (1965) pp. 240–54.

147 Sly, P.G., "Lake Erie and its basin", *J. Fish Res. Board Can.* **33** (1976) pp. 355–70.

148 Leach, J.H. and Nepszy, S.J., "The fish community in Lake Erie", *J. Fish. Res. Board Can.* **33** (1976) pp. 622–38; Christie, W.J., "Changes in the fish species composition of the Great Lakes", *J. Fish. Res. Board. Can.* **31** (1974) pp. 827–54; Beeton, A.M., "Changes in the environment and biota of the Great Lakes", in: National Academy of Sciences, *Eutrophication: Causes, Consequences, Correctives*, Proc. of a Symposium (Washington: National Academy Press, 1969).

149 Moss, 1980, *op. cit.*

150 Beeton, 1969, *op. cit.*

151 CEQ, 1979, *op. cit.*; Schelske, C.L., "Role of phosphorus in Great Lakes eutrophication: is there a controversy?" *J. Fish. Res. Board Can.* **36** (1979) pp. 286–8.

152 Benett, E.B., "The nitrifying of Lake Superior", *Ambio* **14** (1985) pp. 272–5.

153 Forster, D.L., Logan, T.J., Yaksich, S.M. and Adams, J.R., "An accelerated implementation program for reducing the diffuse-source phosphorus load to Lake Erie", *J. Soil Water Conserv.* **40** (1985) pp. 136–41.

154 Agassiz, A., in: UNESCO, "Eutrophication in coastal marine areas and lagoons: a case study of 'Lac de Tunis'", UNESCO Reports in *Marine Science* 29 1984, report prepared by Kelly, M. and Naquib, M.

155 UNESCO, 1984, *op. cit.*

156 UNESCO, 1984, *op. cit.*

157 D'Elia, C.F., "Nutrient enrichment of the Chesapeake Bay", *Environment* 29 (1987) pp. 6–11, 30–33.

158 Smith et al., 1987, *op. cit.*

159 D'Elia, C.F., Sanders, J.G. and Boynton, W.R., "Nutrient enrichment studies in a coastal plain estuary: phytoplankton growth in large scale continuous culture", *Can. J. Fish. Ag. Sci.* 43 (1986) pp. 397–406.

160 D'Elia, 1987, *op. cit.*

161 DOE, 1986, *op. cit.*

162 National Agency for Environmental Protection, *The NPR Report, Report on Input of Nitrogen, Phosphorus and Organic Matter to Groundwaters, FreshWaters and Marine Surface Waters* (Denmark: NAEP, 1984).

163 Lancelot, C., Billen, G., Sournia, A., Weisse, T., Colijn, F., Veldhuis, M.J.W., Davies, A. and Wassman, P., "Phaeocystis blooms and nutrient enrichment in the continental coastal zones of the North Sea", *Ambio* 16 (1987) pp. 18–46; Cadee, G.C. and Hegeman, J., "Seasonal and annual variation of *Phaeocystis pouchetii* (Haptophyceae) in the westernmost inlet of the Wadden Sea during the 1973 period", *Neth. J. Sea Res.* 20 (1986) pp. 29–36.

164 Veldhuis, J.M.W., Colijn, F. and Venekamp, L.A.H., "The spring bloom of *Phaeocystis pouchetii* (Haptophyceae) in Dutch coastal waters", *Neth. J. Sea Res.* 20 (1986) pp. 37–48.

165 Lancelot et al., 1987, *op. cit.*

166 Lancelot et al., 1987, *op. cit.*

167 D'Elia, C.F., Webb, K.L. and Porter, J.W., "Nitrate-rich groundwater inputs to Discovery Bay, Jamaica: a significant source of nitrogen to local coral reefs?" *Bull. Mar. Science* 31 (1981) pp. 903–10.

168 Endean, R., "Destruction and recovery of coral reef communities", in: Jones, O.A. and Endean, E. (eds), *Biology and Geology of Coral Reefs* (New York: Academic Press, 1976); Banner, A.H. and Bailey, J.H., "The effects of urban pollution upon a coral reef system", *Hawaii Inst. Marine Biol. Tech. Rep.* 25 (1970).

5   Fertilizers and Health

While fertilizers cause relatively little harm to wildlife, at least in comparison to the damage caused by pesticides, they are hazardous, in certain circumstances, to human health. They result in our ingesting nitrate which, while not itself directly toxic, can be converted to nitrite that is implicated in a number of serious diseases.

In this chapter we examine four of these diseases – methaemoglobinaemia, and gastric, bladder and oesophageal cancer. The causal link between nitrate and methaemoglobinaemia is well understood, but there is still considerable dispute over the link with cancers, and we discuss the available evidence and the contradictions it contains. We end the chapter with a description of the effects of nitrate on the health of domestic livestock.

Methaemoglobinaemia

Nitrate is non-toxic to humans probably because when ingested in food and water it is quickly absorbed and excreted. However, if the conditions are right, nitrate can be reduced by bacteria in the gut or mouth to produce nitrite, which is capable of disrupting vital physiological processes. In particular, it is now well established that nitrite is a cause methaemoglobinaemia, often referred to as the blue-baby syndrome.[1] In this disease the capacity of the blood to carry oxygen is lessened, and affected people – normally infants – exhibit a slate-blue discolouration (cyanosis) of the skin, usually beginning around the lips, fingers and toes, and spreading to the face and body.

Under normal circumstances the haemoglobin in the blood passes through a cycle of uptake and release of oxygen (Figure 5.1). Oxygen is bound to haemoglobin to produce oxyhaemoglobin and a very small fraction of haemoglobin is oxidized to methaemoglobin. This process is normally well balanced, but it can be disrupted by the presence of alternative oxidizing agents, such as nitrite which preferentially binds

Figure 5.1 The oxidation and reduction cycles in the blood under normal conditions (A) and in the presence of nitrite (B). Under normal conditions the upper cycle dominates; in the presence of nitrite it is the lower that is dominant.

A : Normal conditions

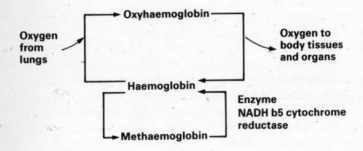

B : In the presence of nitrite

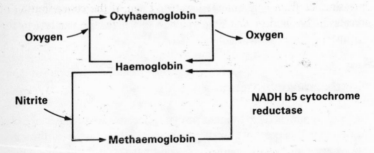

to the haemoglobin to form methaemoglobin. Less oxyhaemoglobin is produced and since methaemoglobin is incapable of binding oxygen there is less oxygen being transported in the blood stream. If between 10 and 25 per cent of the haemoglobin is converted to methaemoglobin then cyanosis occurs, although symptoms related to hypoxia (an acute deficiency of oxygen) do not set in until 30–40 per cent is converted. At over 70 per cent concentration of methaemoglobin, death usually results.[2] A number of chemicals, such as aniline dyes and sulphonamides, can act as oxidizing agents, but nitrite compounds are the most common cause of such acquired methaemoglobinaemia.[3]

Methaemoglobinaemia may also occur in individuals who are either deficient in the enzyme NADH b5 cytochrome reductase, which catalyses the reduction of methaemoglobin back to haemoglobin, or have structural abnormalities in haemoglobin that stabilize it in the oxidized state. In both these cases, though, the cause is hereditary rather than acquired and the condition remains a lifelong problem.[4]

Susceptibility of infants

For two reasons, acquired methaemoglobinaemia is largely confined to infants in the first few months of life.[5] Infants under four months of age have only 60 per cent of the enzyme NADH b5 cytochrome reductase compared with adults, so that the methaemoglobin is not readily reduced back to haemoglobin. They also have lower acidity of gastric juice. Although many strains of common bacteria, for example of *Escherichia*, *Staphylococcus*, *Pseudomonas* and *Clostridium*, are capable of reducing nitrate to nitrite, they can only operate in conditions of low acidity.[6] In normal adults the stomach is acidic and so bacteria are not present and there is no reduction of the nitrate. All the nitrate is absorbed before it reaches the lower intestine where the bacteria are present. But in infants, because the gastric juice is less acidic, the stomach tends to be colonized by bacteria from the mouth or the lower intestine, or from contaminated water. Then, if the concentration of nitrate in the food or drinking water is also high, the bacteria in the stomach will reduce it to nitrite.[7]

Methaemoglobinaemia is also commonly associated with diarrhoea. Infants suffering from diarrhoea usually have a less acid stomach than normal infants.[8] Moreover, some strains of acutely pathogenic organisms, such as *Vibrio*, *Salmonella* and *Shigella* that cause diarrhoea, cholera, and dysentery, can reduce nitrate. And it appears from recent studies of infants suffering from both diarrhoea and methaemoglobinaemia, but with no apparent significant dietary source of nitrate, that the diarrhoea creates conditions suitable for nitrate production inside the body.[9] But the mechanisms involved have not yet been identified.

A final factor is the much greater amount of fluid that is drunk by infants, which leads to potentially higher nitrate intakes. The total fluid taken in by an infant is up to ten times that of an adult per unit of weight.[10] Most recorded cases of methaemoglobinaemia have been caused by infants feeding on milk formulations which were prepared with water rich in nitrate. There is also a danger that preparatory baby foods may be made up from water which has been repeatedly boiled, so increasing the nitrate concentration. Even if, initially, the nitrate is not too high, thirty minutes of boiling can triple the concentration.[11]

Methaemoglobinaemia in the industrialized countries

Since methaemoglobinaemia was first recognized in 1945 by Comly, some 3000 cases have been reported worldwide, mainly in the period up to 1965.[12] In the USA, most of the 350 cases and 41 deaths occurred before 1950. To begin with the condition was particularly prevalent, or at least recognized, in southwestern Minnesota. A total of 139 cases were recorded between 1947 and 1949, with 14 deaths.[13] The incidence of cases was strongly correlated with high nitrate concentrations in drinking water, greater than 90 mg/l in all but two cases (Figure 5.2).

Although the evidence implicated nitrates, other factors were found to be important. In all the cases, the water supplies for each household were drawn from farm wells situated close to livestock yards, pigpens, privies or cesspools. Wells were poorly constructed, inadequately located and, thus, often contaminated with coliform bacteria. Fourteen percent of the infant cases had diarrhoea, and all were being fed exclusively on milk preparations. By contrast, there were no cases involving water from municipal wells, where only 3 per cent had nitrate concentrations greater than 45 mg/l.

All subsequent cases of methaemoglobinaemia in the USA have been linked, with one exception, to private water supplies,[14] despite the fact that many public supplies are routinely in excess of 45 mg nitrate/l. As a study in California showed, even with concentrations in public well water up to 130 mg/l, clinical methaemoglobinaemia is absent, although methaemoglobin levels were raised, particularly in infants with diarrhoea.[15] The crucial factor is bacterial contamination.

In central Czechoslovakia, a high incidence of methaemoglobinaemia in the 1950s and early 1960s was originally associated with nitrate concentrations in the water. But here, too, bacterial contamination was shown to be important, although it originated not from the drinking water but from the dried milk powder used to prepare infant feeds.[16] Methaemoglobinaemia became more frequent in infants as dried milk products became popular. All the brands contained bacterial microbes and, with one exception, the bacteria were capable of reducing nitrate to nitrite once in the stomach. The exception was a brand that inhibited microbial growth in the gut and so kept blood methaemoglobin levels low.

While feeding infants with milk powder formulations, directly or indirectly, increases the risk of methaemoglobinaemia, breast feeding confers a degree of protection. Nitrate does not become concentrated in human milk,[17] and breast feeding also confers a degree of resistance to diarrhoea.[18] Protection also comes from diets rich in vitamin C,

Figure 5.2 Maximum nitrate concentrations (mg/l) in well water (A) and distribution of cases of methaemoglobinaemia (B) in Minnesota, 1947–49

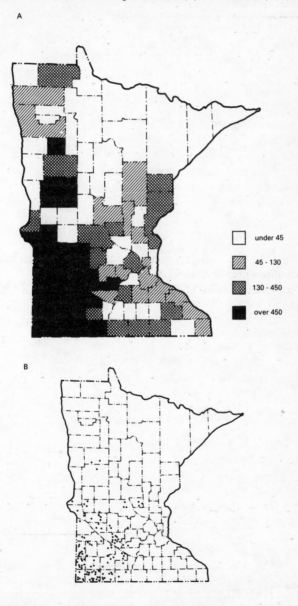

Source: Bosch, H.M., Rosenfield, A.B., Huston, R., Shipman, H.R. and Woodward, F.L., "Methaemoglobinaemia and Minnesota well supplies", *J. Am. Water Works Assn.* (February 1950) pp. 161–170.

since it takes part in the haemoglobin cycle, enhancing the reduction of methaemoglobin back to haemoglobin.[19] A study in Israel found no differences in concentration of blood methaemoglobin from infants in areas of high and low nitrate concentrations in drinking water, but most were breast fed and regularly consumed liquids rich in vitamin C, such as citrus and tomato juices.[20]

The disease is extremely rare in Britain where only 14 suspected cases have been recorded in the past 35 years, one of them fatal. The last confirmed case was in 1972. Even during the severe drought of 1976, when a number of water supplies in the UK contained nitrate concentrations of 50–100 mg/l, there were no reported cases. The low incidence is probably due to the rarity of private wells and the absence of bacterial contamination of drinking water.

The accumulated evidence, therefore, suggests that high nitrate concentrations in drinking water can result in clinical methaemoglobinaemia, but probably only in the presence of other factors. Feeding infants with baby foods or milk prepared with high nitrate water increases the risk, in particular where the milk powders enhance bacterial growth. Bacterial contamination of the water is also important and may be the key factor in determining whether serious methaemoglobinaemia occurs. High levels of vitamin C in the diet may provide protection.

In Minnesota the high frequency of cases and their geographic concentration in the southwest of the state led to medical practitioners and parents from farm households becoming familiar with the factors that were causing methaemoglobinaemia. As a result there was a marked reduction in cases during 1949. The UK Royal Commission on Environmental Pollution concluded that "whenever methaemoglobinaemia and the factors contributing to it have become widely known, the condition has become rare and fatalities have decreased to vanishing point."[21] However, in 1986 an infant died from methaemoglobinaemia in South Dakota, the first death in the USA for some 30 years.[22] The two month old baby had been drinking an infant formula mixed with water containing 650–700 mg nitrate/l. Other cases, but no deaths, have occurred in South Dakota in the 1980s, again with water contaminated by livestock and human wastes and having nitrate concentrations in excess of 600 mg/l.[23] Farm wells in the USA commonly have high concentrations of nitrate and heavy bacterial contamination.[24] A survey of more than 1000 wells in the Big Sioux river basin of South Dakota found 27 per cent had nitrate concentrations greater than 45 mg/l and about 30 per cent were contaminated with coliform bacteria.[25]

There have also been recent cases of methaemoglobinaemia in other industrialized countries. In Spain, for instance, mild cases occurred in 1982 linked to severe diarrhoea and water containing 76 mg nitrate/l.[26] However, the highest incidence in recent years has been in Hungary, where 1353 cases and 21 deaths were recorded between 1976 and 1982.[27] All those affected had been consuming water from privately dug wells drawing from shallow aquifers. Ninety three per cent of the supplies contained more than 100 mg nitrate/l and in the county of Bargana, in which 234 cases were recorded between 1968 and 1979, 60 per cent of the wells were severely contaminated with bacteria.[28]

A high risk in the tropics?

For a number of reasons, there may be a greater risk of methaemoglobinaemia in tropical countries. Infants drink more because of the high ambient temperatures, diarrhoea is very common and diets are poor in vitamin C.[29]

Nonetheless, there are very few records of methaemoglobinaemia in infants in tropical countries, probably because the condition is not recognized. Despite an exhaustive literature search we have found only one account: this refers to a high incidence of methaemoglobinaemia in infants from a rural area of Namibia.[30] Blood methaemoglobin was measured in nearly 500 infants younger than one year of age, and of these about 8 eight per cent showed levels of more than 5 per cent methaemoglobin. Because of the arid climate the rural population is almost entirely dependent upon ground wells for their drinking water and 40 per cent of the infants regularly consumed water at concentrations greater than 90 mg nitrate/l. One infant, close to death with a level of 35 per cent blood methaemoglobin, was found to have been consuming water containing 250 mg nitrate/l, an equivalent daily intake of 33 mg/kg body weight. The elevated blood methaemoglobin levels appeared to be associated with nitrate intake, and with the particularly low dietary intake of vitamin C (Table 5.1). However, there seemed to be no link with incidence of diarrhoea. The source of the high nitrate levels in the ground wells was not identified, although livestock waste is most likely.

In rare cases it appears that methaemoglobinaemia may be associated with the use of malarial prophylactic drugs.[31] The risk appears to be associated with individuals who only carry one of the genes coding for the enzyme, NADH b5 cytochrome reductase, that reduces methaemoglobin. Individuals lacking both genes suffer from hereditary methaemoglobinaemia, but individuals with only one gene show no symptoms. However, when six American soldiers suffering from cyanosis were evacuated from Vietnam in 1967–8 it was found that all lacked one of the genes but, in addition, were taking various combinations of anti-malaria drugs – chloroquine, primaquine and diaminodiphenylsulfone (DDI) – at normal doses. There was no link with intake of nitrate.[32]

Table 5.1 Effect of dietary vitamin C on the blood methaemoglobin levels in infants from high and low nitrate regions in Namibia

Regularity of vitamin C intake	Nitrate region	Methaemoglobin values		
		<2.1%	2.1–3%	>3%
None	High	54	12	38
	Low	104	8	16
Infrequent	High	38	8	25
	Low	107	13	16
Daily	High	17	0	1
	Low	19	4	3

High nitrate > 90 mg/l
Low nitrate < 90 mg/l
Significant interactions exist between vitamin C intake, area and methaemoglobin values – probability that interactions have arisen by chance is less than five in a hundred

Source: Super, M., Hesse, H. De V., MacKenzie, D., Dempster, W.S., Plessis, J. Du and Ferreira, J.J., "An epidemiological study of well water nitrates in a group of SW African/Namibian infants", *Water Research* 15 (1981) pp. 1265–70.

Despite the lack of evidence, methaemoglobinaemia may be more prevalent in developing countries than is supposed. It could be that its presence is masked by the far higher incidence of diarrhoea – currently accounting for some 5–10 million deaths a year. Infants may be dying from diarrhoea well before severe methaemoglobinaemia manifests itself.

Nitrates and cancers

The link between ingesting nitrate and development of cancer is still contentious. As in methaemoglobinaemia, the chain of events begins with the conversion of nitrate to nitrite by bacteria. However, this is then followed by the combination of the nitrite with amines and amides, derived from food and various environmental contaminants, to produce N-nitroso compounds, such as nitrosamines and nitrosamides. These are known to be powerful carcinogens in a wide variety of animal species.[33]

The experimental evidence

So far, the evidence for linking nitrates and nitrites with cancers largely derives from laboratory experiments with animals. On several occasions, animals fed with amines and nitrite together and – in one controversial experiment – nitrite alone, have been shown to develop tumours in a range of organs, notably the stomach, liver, oesophagus and bladder[34] (Table 5.2). In all these experiments N-nitroso compounds were produced. In humans there is now good evidence that N-nitroso compounds from smokeless tobacco cause oral cavity cancer, and animal evidence that tobacco N-nitroso compounds cause nasal cavity cancer.[35] But, as yet, there is no direct evidence from humans that N-nitroso compounds derived from the diet or formed within the body can cause cancer.

Table 5.2 Commonly occurring amines fed to rats in combination with nitrite and the sites of the induced tumours

Amine	Source	Site of induced tumour
Monuron	Herbicide	Stomach, liver
Oxytetracycline	Antibiotic drug	Liver
Tolbutamide	Drug	Stomach, liver
Morpholine	Foodstuffs; industrial materials	Liver
Lucanthone	NR	Liver
Methapyrilene	NR	Liver
Disulfiram	Anti-alcoholic drug; industrial materials	Oesophagus
Aminopyrine	Analgesic drug	Liver
Thiram	Fungicide	Stomach
Dimethyldodecylamine	Detergent	Bladder
Chlordiazepoxide	NR	Stomach

NR = not recorded

Source: Lijinsky, W., "Significance of *in vivo* formation of N-nitroso compounds", *Oncology* **37** (1980) pp. 223–6.

The internal production of N-nitroso compounds – the process of nitrosation – has been demonstrated in human volunteers fed a diet rich in nitrate and the amine known as proline. Nitrosation resulted in nitrosoproline (NPRO) which could be detected in the urine.[36] The process can occur in a number of different ways and is dependent on a variety of interlinked factors.[37] Common gut bacteria, including for example *Escherichia coli, Neisseria mucosa, Streptococcus* spp., *Proteus* spp., *Pseudomonas aeruginosa, Clostridia, Bacteroides* and *Bifidobacteria*, are important mediators of nitrosation, at least in animals.[38] Bacterial activity is, in turn, dependent on pH. In healthy young people, for instance, the low pH of the stomach creates conditions unsuitable for bacteria and this may be the reason why gastric cancer is more common in older individuals or in those suffering from malnutrition or pernicious anaemia, which reduce the acidity of the stomach.[39] However, some studies have found no evidence of a link between pH and nitrosation.[40] It also appears that the level of nitrite in the stomach is not necessarily critical. Large amounts of nitrite may not lead to nitrosation if other conditions are unfavourable.[41]

As in methaemoglobinaemia, vitamin C appears to play a protective role, inhibiting nitrosation and protecting cells from damage.[42] In people from a high-risk oesophageal cancer region of Henan province in China, markedly reduced quantities of N-nitroso compounds were excreted in their urine following ingestion of vitamin C.[43] Volunteers in Britain who were fed a salad meal high in nitrate and proline produced high levels of nitrosoproline (NPRO) in their urine, but this was significantly reduced after foods rich in vitamin C, such as raw green pepper, strawberries and blackcurrant drink, were included in the diet.[44] Complete inhibition of nitrosation is claimed to occur when there is a ratio of vitamin C to nitrite of 2:1, though other experiments have shown that the degree of inhibition depends upon presence of oxygen and certain anions, pH and temperature.[45]

Gastric cancer

The experimental evidence we have reviewed is certainly suggestive of a link between nitrate uptake and the incidence of certain cancers. At first sight a number of epidemiological investigations support this hypothesis. For instance, there is a general correlation between national rates of gastric cancer and nitrate intake per capita (Figure 5.3). The correlation also holds in particular localities. One of the highest gastric cancer rates in the world (150 per 100,000 population) occurs in the Andes of Colombia and is associated with a relatively high concentration of nitrate in the drinking water supply.[46] In Chile, the only country with natural deposits of nitrates and a heavy user of nitrate

Figure 5.3 Correlation between nitrate intake and gastric cancer mortality in 12 countries

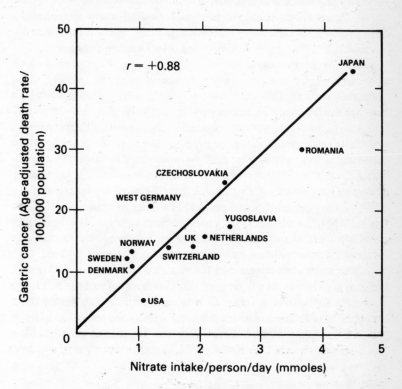

Source: Mirvish, S.S., "The etiology of gastric cancer", *Journal of National Cancer Institute* 71 (1983) pp. 629–647; using data of Hartman (1983).

fertilizer, there is also a general association between gastric cancer and agriculture.[47] But the correlations do not survive more detailed analysis.

The Worksop data

In the UK, the correlation was first observed in the population of a town in the midlands – the Borough of Worksop. Since at least 1953, the town's drinking water had contained over 90 mg nitrate/l, the highest level of any borough in the UK.[48] An analysis of the mortality from gastric cancer over the period 1963–71 showed it to be significantly higher than in nine neighbouring towns, the water supplies of which contained much lower nitrate concentrations (approximately 15 mg/l). These findings attracted considerable attention. But, for a variety of reasons, the correlation did not prove convincing. Although gastric cancer mortality in Worksop was elevated above the national average for both men and women, it was only significantly greater in women. Furthermore, mortality was also found to be significantly raised in two neighbouring towns, where the nitrate levels were low – in the men of Sutton-in-Ashfield and the women of Chesterfield.

Further analysis of the data has suggested that the apparent relationship was confounded by a number of factors (Table 5.3). In particular, four variables missing from the original analysis would all significantly contribute to higher numbers of expected deaths, and hence reduce the ratios of observed to expected mortality rates.[49] Most important, Worksop is a coalmining town and both miners and their wives are more likely to contract gastric cancer than the general population (for 1959–63 the ratio of observed per 100 expected for men was 149 and women 155). Second, risk of gastric cancer varies widely between social classes and this had not been taken into account. The ratios for class I (professionals) are 49 for men and 55 for women but for class V (manual workers) are 163 for men and 153 for women. Third, the census data used in the original study underestimated the number of women older than 65 years in Worksop. And finally, during the period 1963–71, gastric cancer mortality for women was particularly high (134) compared with the preceding and subsequent periods.

Table 5.3 Different estimates of gastric cancer mortality rates for the town of Worksop for 1963–71 (the national average is set at 100)

	Standardized mortality rate (observed per 100 expected)	
	Men	Women
Estimate of Hill et al. (1973)	108	160*
Estimate of Davies (1980) adjusted for social class, mining and more accurate population data	95	131[NS]

* Probability of difference arising by chance is less than one in a hundred
NS is not significantly different

Source: Hill, M.J., Hawksworth, G. and Tattershal, G. "Bacteria, nitrosamine and cancer of the stomach", *Br. J. Cancer* **28** (1973) pp. 562–7; Davies, J.M., "Stomach cancer mortality in Worksop and other Nottinghamshire mining towns", *Br. J. Cancer* **41** (1980) pp. 438–45.

When these factors are included the significant difference from neighbouring towns disappears. In particular, once the adjustment for mining is taken into account, comparison of mining and non-mining towns shows no evidence of differences in gastric cancer rates. The raised incidence of gastric cancer among coal miners is well known.[50] It may be a result of coal dust going from the lungs to the stomach where it becomes involved in the nitrosation process in the presence of nitrate.[51] But it is still not clear why miners' wives are at a high risk.

Negative correlations

More recent epidemiological evidence has not only failed to reveal a positive correlation between nitrate in drinking water and gastric cancer but, in some instances, has actually shown the reverse.[52] A study of mortality in 229 urban areas in the UK during 1969–73 revealed a negative association with concentrations of nitrate in drinking water. This was true of both sexes. When adjustments were made to ensure that results were not confounded by the different mortality rates typical of different social classes, the negative association remained significant (Table 5.4). It is also negative, although not significant, even in those urban areas with water exceeding the EEC guide level of 25 mg/l.

Table 5.4 Relationship between nitrate levels in drinking water and gastric cancer mortality in the UK, after adjustments made for confounding social factors

| | Regression coefficients | |
	Male	Female
All 229 urban areas	−1.19*	−2.06**
58 urban areas with nitrate above 25 mg/l	−0.05	−2.26

Regression coefficient = 0.00 if no association between nitrate levels and gastric cancer mortality. A negative value indicates high nitrate levels are associated with low gastric cancer mortality. Probability of difference arising by chance is less than five in a hundred (*) and less than one in a hundred (**)

Source: Beresford, S.A.A., "Is nitrate in the drinking water associated with the risk of cancer in the urban UK?" *J. of Epidemiol.* 14 (1985) pp. 57–63.

A study of gastric cancer mortality in East Anglia and Yorkshire has shown a tendency for districts supplied with higher levels of nitrate in their water to exhibit higher death rates from gastric cancer (Table 5.5). Nevertheless, the relationships were mostly non-significant, even when corrected for social class and proportion of miners in each region.[53]

Table 5.5   Gastric cancer mortality in 20 rural districts of East Anglia and 12 of Yorkshire in relation to levels of nitrate in drinking water

| | Ratio of observed per 100 expected | | | |
| | Males | | Females | |
Nitrate level	1969–73	1974–8	1969–73	1974–8
East Anglia				
0–25 mg/l	84**	90*	98	100
25–50	115	107	107	98
>50	137	129	92	105
Yorkshire				
0–25	97	99	102	88*
>25†	109	105	93	140

Probability of difference arising by chance is less than five in a hundred (*) and one in a hundred (**)

† number of deaths in 25–50 and >50 categories were small, thus data aggregated

Source: Fraser, P. and Chilvers, C., "Health aspects of nitrate in drinking water", *Science Total Environ.* **18** (1981) pp. 103–16.

Epidemiological studies have also been carried out on workers in the fertilizer industry, but again have failed to reveal any direct link between nitrogen fertilizers and cancer. An analysis of mortality rates found no differences between those workers from a 1961 cohort with high and low frequency of exposure to nitrate dust although in the 1971 cohort there was an elevated, but non-significant, risk (Table 5.6A).[54] A more specific study of a workforce in the northeast of England failed to find any evidence of significantly increased hazard in men exposed to substantial amounts of nitrate in the factory, though it does suggest a small excess of lung cancer in heavily exposed men (Table 5.6B). This is despite the fact that elevated levels of both nitrate and nitrite were found in the saliva of the men compared with both low exposed workers and the non-exposed local residents.[55] Ingestion of nitrate from the dust was occurring but there appeared to be no subsequent increased risk of gastric cancer.

National statistics

At the national level, too, if the correlations are considered over a reasonable time-span they turn out to be negative. Most developed countries have experienced at least a 30 per cent reduction in mortality from gastric cancer since the early 1950s, despite rapidly rising use of fertilizers (Figure 5.4). In the USA the reduction has been particularly

Table 5.6   Gastric cancer risk in workers from the UK fertilizer industry and concentrations of salivary nitrate and nitrite

A

Frequency of exposure to dust containing nitrate	Standardized mortality rate* (observed per 100 expected)			
	1961 cohort		1971 cohort	
	All deaths	All cancers	All deaths	All cancers
High	75	82	84	169
Low	81	74	24	42

B

Frequency to exposure to dust containing nitrate	Standardized mortality rate* (observed per 100 expected)				Saliva concentration (mmol/ml)	
	All deaths	All cancers	Stomach cancer	Lung cancer	Nitrate	Nitrite
High	88	115	97	169	212	129
Low	75	90	103	68	103	89
Very low (local residents)					64	68

* None of the differences significant at five in a hundred

Sources: A: Fraser, P., et al., "Census-based mortality study of fertiliser manufacturers", *Br. J. Indust. Med.* **39** (1982) pp. 323–9.
B: Al-Dabbagh, S., et al., "Mortality of nitrate fertilizer workers", *Br. J. Indust. Med.* **43** (1986) pp. 507–15.

large, by about 60 per cent since 1950.[56] Because of the very high fatality rate for gastric cancer – less than 10 per cent of patients survive five years from the time of diagnosis – mortality is a good index of incidence.[57]

Mortality rates are also falling in many developing countries (Table 5.7). This is probably due to better registration of cancer over time. In general, gastric cancer appears to be rare in Africa, SE Asia and parts of Central America, but is common in Chile, Colombia, Costa Rica and parts of Brazil, in Shanghai, and among the Chinese population in Singapore, though it is low among Singapore's Malay and Indian population[58] (Figure 5.5.) The reasons for this variability are not known, but in most cases the high rates seem unrelated to either fertilizer use or nitrate contamination of drinking water. Two apparent exceptions are in Chile and the Narino region of Colombia.

Figure 5.4 Age-adjusted incidence rates for gastric cancer in males and females in England and Wales, and mortality rates for the whole population in the USA, 1950–83

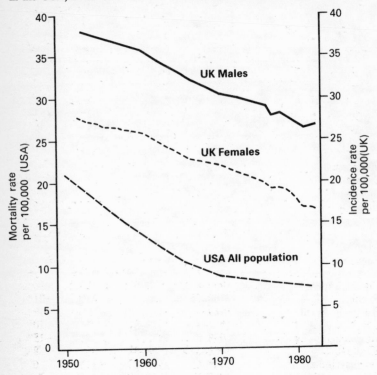

Sources: Office of Population Censuses and Surveys, *Cancer Statistics Registrations* (London: HMSO, 1972–82); Cohen, M.M. and Diamond, J.M., "Are we losing the war on cancer?", *Nature* **323** (1986) pp. 488–489.

Chile

Perhaps the most interesting, yet baffling, case is that of Chile, where the age adjusted mortality rates for gastric cancer are second only to Japan. Chile is also the only country in the world with natural deposits of nitrates, in the form of saltpetre.[59] It has a long tradition of heavy use of fertilizers. The nitrates are produced in the northern provinces and then shipped to the agricultural provinces in the centre. Although the current national average rate of application is only 12 kg N/ha, the average rates for the central provinces are, in some cases, over 80 kg/ha.[60]

Gastric cancer mortality rates are highest (median rate of 50.1/100,000)

Table 5.7 Changes in age-standardized rates of mortality and of incidence for gastric cancer in developing countries

Country	Period A	Period B	% Change in mortality A to B Males	Females
Costa Rica	1976	1983	− 8%	− 7%
Chile	1950–1	1982	−46%	−69%
Mexico	1960–1	1982	− 9%	−13%
Puerto Rico	1964–5	1983	−57%	−54
Uruguay	1976	1984	−44%	−59%
Venezuela	1960–1	1983	−32%	−37%
Hong Kong	1960–1	1985	−53%	−40%
Philippines	1964–5	1976	− 8%	− 6%
Singapore	1971	1985	− 7%	− 4%
Sri Lanka	1960–1	1980	−19%	−24%
Thailand	1964–5	1976	−23%	−25%

Cancer registry	Period A	Period B	% Change in incidence* A to B	
Ibadan, Nigeria	1960–5	1970–6	−11%	−20%
Recife, Brazil	1968–71	1980	+23%	−21%
Sao Paolo, Brazil	1969	1978	+ 8%	+17%
Cali, Colombia	1962–4	1977–81	− 9%	+10%
Kingston, Jamaica	1958–63	1973–7	−35%	−15%
Puerto Rico	1962–3	1978–82	−39%	−38%
Bombay, India	1964–6	1978–82	−11%	− 6%
Singapore (Chinese)	1968–72	1978–82	−16%	−14%
Singapore (Indian)	1968–72	1978–82	−40%	−23%
Singapore (Malay)	1968–72	1978–82	+ 2%	−30%

* Incidence is age standardized incidence, corrected to world population

Source: WHO, *World Health Statistics Annual* (Geneva: WHO, 1986); Segi, M. and Kurihara, M., Cancer Mortality for Selected Sites in 24 Countries (1960–61), no. 3 (Sendai, Japan: Dept. of Publ. Health, Tohoku Univ. School Medicine, 1964); Segi and Kurihara, no. 4 (1966); Segi and Kurihara, no. 5 (1969); Segi, M. (in collaboration with Hattori, H., Noye, H. and Segi, R.), *Age-adjusted Death Rates for Cancer for Selected Sites (A – Classification) in 40 countries in 1976* (Nagoya: Segi Inst. of Cancer Epidemiology, 1981); Logan, W.P.D., "Cancer of the oesophagus, stomach, intestine and rectum", International Mortality Patterns and Trends, World Health Stats. Rep. 28, pp. 458–501; Doll, R., Payne, P. and Waterhouse, J. (eds), *Cancer Incidence in Five Continents. IUCC Tech. Report 1* (Berlin: Springer Verlag, 1966); Doll, R., Muir, C. and Waterhouse, J. (eds), *Cancer Incidence in Five Continents. vol II* (Lyon: International Agency for Research on Cancer and International Association of Cancer Registries, IARC, 1970); Waterhouse, J., Muir, C., Correa, P. and Powell, J. (eds), *Cancer Incidence in Five Continents. vol. III* (Lyon: IARC, 1976); Waterhouse, J., Muir, C., Shanmugaratnam, K., Powell, J. (eds), *Cancer Incidence in Five Continents. vol IV (Lyon: IARC, 1982)*; Muir, C., Waterhouse, J., Mach, T., Powell, J. and Whelan, S. (eds), *Cancer Incidence in Five Continents. vol V* (Lyon: IARC, 1987).

Figure 5.5   Age-standardized incidence of gastric cancer in males and females at sites around the world

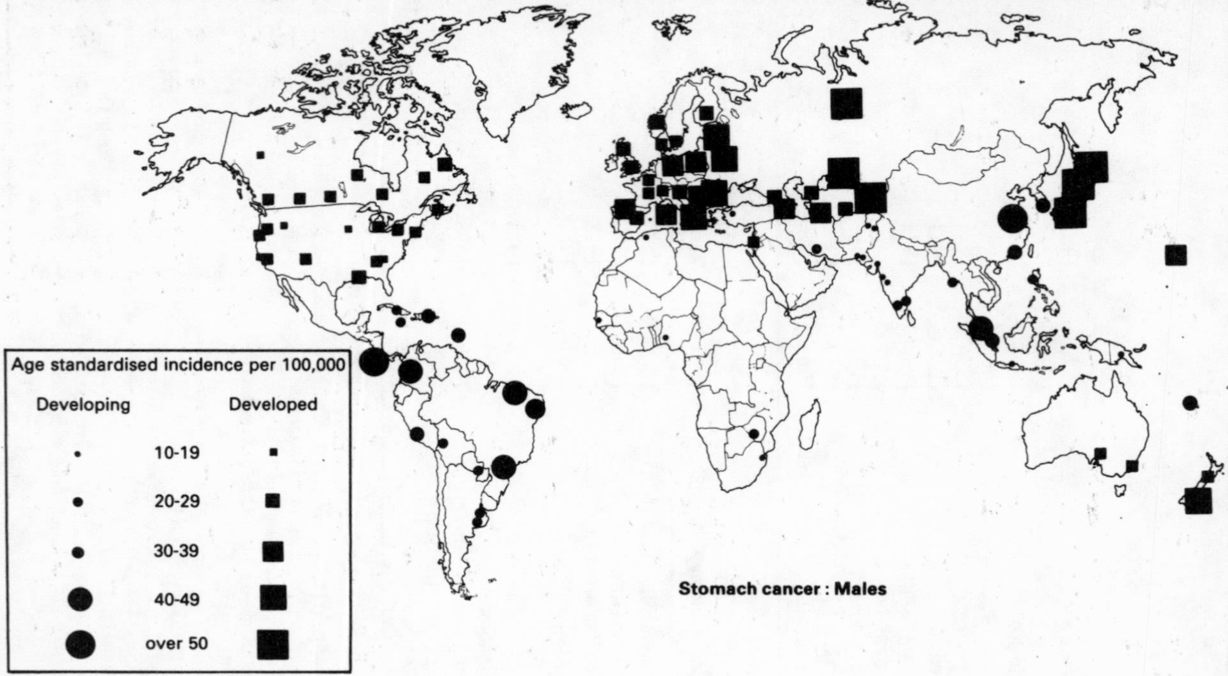

Stomach cancer : Males

Age standardised incidence per 100,000		
Developing	Developed	
10-19	·	▪
20-29	•	▪
30-39	•	◼
40-49	●	◼
over 50	⬤	◼

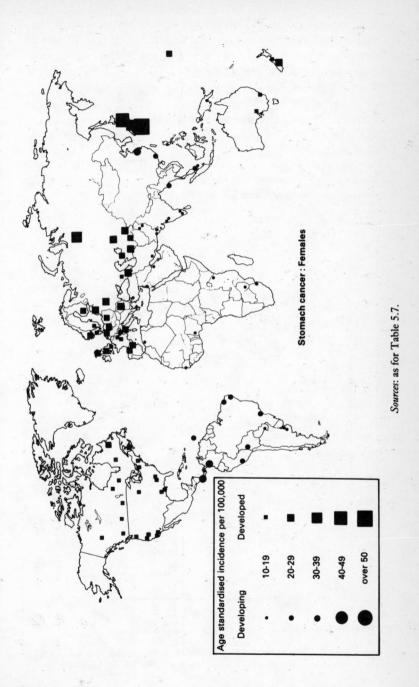

Stomach cancer : Females

Sources: as for Table 5.7.

in three agricultural provinces near the capital, Santiago, but decline towards the north and south to less than 25/100,000. Nitrates in drinking water are generally low (1.2–15.1 mg/l), although in areas near Santiago irrigated with municipal waste they may be as high as 60 mg/l.[61] But there is no correlation between gastric cancer and water nitrate concentrations.[62] The principal correlation appears to be with cumulative per capita exposure to nitrogen, calculated from the amount of fertilizer used in each province between 1945 and 1960 divided by the population (Figure 5.6).

Figure 5.6   Gastric cancer mortality and calculated per capita cumulative exposure to nitrogen by province, Chile, 1960

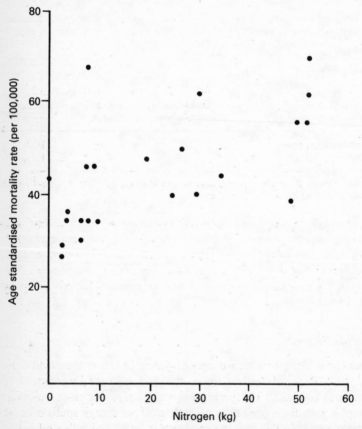

Source: Armijo, R. and Coulson, A.M., "Epidemiology of stomach cancer in Chile – the role of nitrogen fertilizers", *Int. J. Epidemiology* **4** (1975) pp. 301–309.

A later study[63] comparing hospital patients with gastric cancer and a set of controls appeared to confirm this association, revealing a significant correlation with agriculture as an occupation and length of residence in high risk areas (Table 5.8). Because the nitrate concentrations in the water were generally low in the agricultural areas it was suggested that the population was ingesting nitrate from vegetables. But it was then found that nitrate and nitrite levels in vegetables were high in both low and high cancer risk areas.[64] The highest nitrate levels occurred in beets, celery and radishes in the low risk areas, all with concentrations over 500 ppm. Moreover, when the urine of children aged between 11 and 13 was analysed, the nitrate levels were similarly found to be highest in the northern low risk areas.

Table 5.8 Comparison of years of location of residence (in high or low risk region) and years working in agriculture during first 25 years of life in people with gastric cancer and matched controls in Chile

| | | Average number of years | |
| | | Residence in | |
	Occupation in agriculture	high risk region	low risk region
Gastric cancer cases	3.4	6.6	10.8
Matched controls	2.8	4.6	13.1

Source: Armijo, R. et al., "Epidemiology of gastric cancer in Chile. I. Case-Control study", *Int. J. Epidemiol.* **10** (1981a) pp. 53–6.

The authors' suggested explanation for these paradoxical results is the presence or absence of trace elements: the northern areas not only have large deposits of nitrate but also high levels of arsenic in the drinking water which may block nitrosation. By contrast, the central areas are known to be deficient in selenium which may enhance nitrosation.[65]

Nariño, Colombia

One of the highest incidence rates of gastric cancer in the world (150 per 100,000 population) occurs in the Andes, in the Department of Nariño in Colombia. There a precursor stage of gastric cancer, chronic atrophic gastritis, is present in more than 50 per cent of adults over 40 years of age.[66] In this case the condition is associated with a relatively high level of nitrate in the drinking water supply. At the time of the study, about a third of the wells in the high risk areas had nitrate concentrations over 20 mg/l and a few had concentrations greater than 100 mg/l, although the levels were very low in surface waters.[67] However, the source of the nitrate levels in the wells is not known: although the area is predominantly agricultural, commercial fertilizers were not being used intensively at that time and had only been recently introduced.

When individuals in Nariño with gastric precancerous lesions were examined it was found that they had high concentrations of nitrite in their gastric juice.[68] People from the high risk area also had significantly higher salivary and urinary nitrate and higher salivary nitrite than those from low risk regions. Concentrations of urinary nitrate were also raised among people who did not drink contaminated water.[69] This has led to the suggestion that ingested nitrate in Nariño come not only from drinking water but also from grains and vegetable roots.[70] The fava bean, for instance, which is a common vegetable in Colombia, contains a compound that produces a potent mutagen when nitrosated in the presence of nitrite.[71]

Dietary factors

One explanation for the decline of gastric cancer in the developed countries is the reduced consumption of salt and of nitrate- and nitrite-preserved meats in recent years and, concurrently, the increased consumption of fruits and vegetables, providing high levels of vitamin C.[72] This argument has been strengthened by two recent studies. A comparative investigation of two high risk populations, one in Nariño, Colombia and the other in New Orleans, Louisiana, indicates that the high levels of fresh fruit and fresh green vegetables in the New Orleans' diet may have helped to suppress the reduction of nitrate.[73] In both populations, gastric pH rose in individuals with increasingly severe precancerous lesions. This would have created conditions ideal for reduction of nitrate to nitrite and thence to nitroso compounds, yet only in those subjects from Colombia did nitrite levels increase (Figure 5.7). The explanation may lie in the low intake of fresh fruit and vegetables in the Nariño population.

Bladder and oesophageal cancer

N-nitroso compounds have also been implicated as a cause of bladder and oesophageal cancers.[74] Bladder cancer is usually more common in industrialized than in developing countries and among males

Figure 5.7 Relationship between the severity of precursor gastric cancer lesions and nitrite concentrations in the stomachs of people from Nariño, Colombia and New Orleans, USA. One μmol nitrite is equivalent to 46 μg/l

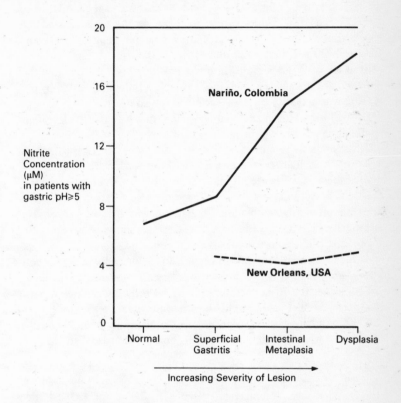

Source: Fontham, E., Zavala, D., Correa, P., Rodriguez, E., Hunter, F., Haenszel, W. and Tannenbaum, S.R., "Diet and chronic atrophic gastritis: a case control study", *J. National Cancer Institute* **76** (1986) pp. 621–662.

more than females: the age-standardized rates of incidence for males are typically 10–20/100,000 and 3–15/100,000 respectively; for females, though, they are below 5/100,000 worldwide. For oesophageal cancer, rates for males are similarly greater than for females: 5–20/100,000 compared with 1–10/100,000, and there are no overall differences between industrialized and developing countries.[75] There is no general evidence of a link with fertilizer nitrate but in certain localities in developing countries where these cancers are particularly common, this could be a factor.

Bladder cancer in Egypt

One country where bladder cancer is especially common is Egypt; it comprises about 30 per cent of all cancers in males and 12 per cent in females. However, it is not possible to calculate age-standardized incidence rates for bladder cancer in Egypt on the basis of available data.[76] Moreover the cancer strikes much younger, at age 40–50 compared with 20 years later in industrialized countries.[77] The causative agent in Egypt is not yet known, but it has long been evident that the incidence of the cancer is high in areas where human infection by the parasitic worm, *Schistosoma haematobium*, is also common.[78] The eggs of the worm are laid in the bladder wall, tending to cause ulceration which seems to increase the likelihood of a tumour.

Schistosomiasis is, however, not the only factor. In Egypt there is also a relatively high degree of bacterial infection of the bladder and many of these bacteria are nitrate reducing species.[79] In experimental animals they will not only reduce nitrate but also catalyse the process of nitrosation in infected bladders.[80] Patients with bladder cancer also tend to have high levels of urinary N-nitroso compounds.[81]

One area where schistosomiasis is endemic and there is a high risk of bladder cancer is the Qalyub region. In young men in this region there is a correlation between the quantities of N-nitroso compounds in their urine, the presence of reducing bacteria and infection with schistosomiasis[82] (Table 5.9). In one individual with more than 100,000 reducing bacteria per ml, the concentration of N-nitroso compounds was as high as 190 μg/l. These men also had average

Table 5.9 Concentrations of N-nitroso compounds (μg/l) in the urine of young Egyptian men, according to presence or absence of bacterial and schistosomiasis infection

	No bacterial infection	Infection by reducing strains of bacteria (more than 1000 per ml)	Infection by non-reducing strains of bacteria (more than 1000 per ml)
Schistosomiasis infection	21	36	14
No schistosomiasis infection	13	32	15

Source: Hicks, R.M. et al., "Association of bacteriuria and urinary nitrosamine formation with *Schistosoma haematobium* infection in the Qalyub area of Egypt", *Trans. R. Soc. Trop. Med. & Hyg.* 76 (1982) pp. 519–27.

urinary pH levels of between 5 and 7, conditions that are ideal for reducing bacteria, and high nitrate concentrations in the urine. The urine from over 50 per cent of the men contained between 75 and 300 mg nitrate/l, with a maximum value of 900 mg/l. Though the nitrate intake in the drinking water was found to be correlated with nitrate levels in the urine, more recent evidence has shown that infected bladders contain high nitrate content irrespective of nitrate intake.[83] It is possible that the schistosomiasis infection may be encouraging synthesis of nitrate inside the body. We have not been able to obtain data for nitrate contamination of water in Egypt, but Qalyub is in the Delta region, where annual nitrogen fertilizer applications are currently of the order of 260 kgN/ha.[84]

Pesticides may also be involved. Schistosomiasis and bladder cancer victims in countries such as Egypt are mainly agricultural workers or rural dwellers, and hence likely to be exposed to insecticides. Laboratory experiments with mice have shown several organochlorine, carbamate and organophosphorus insecticides to be capable of increasing the activity of the liver enzyme which activates N-nitroso compounds.[85]

Oesophageal cancer in China

Oesophageal cancer is very common in some provinces of northern China, where age adjusted mortality rates reach 150/100,000 for men. But, as with bladder cancer in Egypt, the precise causative factors have not been clearly identified.[86] The evidence, so far, rests on a number of correlations, not all of which are consistent. Several of these link the incidence of the cancer to various factors in the high risk area. For instance the content of nitrate, nitrite and amines in the diet can be relatively high. Pickled vegetables, in particular, contain high levels of nitrosamines and oesophageal cancer mortality is positively correlated with amount and frequency of consumption of pickled vegetables. Ground water nitrate concentrations are also highest in those regions with highest oesophageal cancer incidence, and there is a positive correlation between nitrate in well water, salivary nitrite and the degree of severity of oesophageal cancer. Finally, the concentration of N-nitroso compounds in the urine of inhabitants of the high risk region is some four times greater than of those in the low risk region.[87] But perhaps the most significant finding is that as oesophageal cancer progresses in patients, from the normal condition through mild to marked hyperplasia and finally to carcinoma, so the concentration of N-nitrosamines in the gastric juice increases (Table 5.10).

Table 5.10 Correlation between progress of oesophageal cancer and N-nitrosamine content of gastric juice in people from Lin-xian, China, a high-risk region

Condition	Concentration of N-nitrosamines in gastric juice (µg/l)
Normal	11.1
Mild hyperplasia	14.1
Marked hyperplasia	26.0
Carcinoma	46.7

Source: Lu, S.H. et al., "Determination of nitrosamines in gastric juice and urine", in Bartsch, H.H. et al. (eds), *Relevance of N-Nitroso Compounds to Human Cancer: Exposure and Mechanisms* (Lyon: IARC, 1987).

Further studies have indicated that high oesophageal cancer rates in China tend to be associated with a high nitrosation potential and low levels of vitamin C in the blood.[88] People from these high risk regions are also known to consume low quantities of fresh fruit and vegetables, and hence have a low vitamin C intake.[89]

The role of epidemiology

The poor evidence for the link between nitrate and cancer underlines the difficulty in reconciling conflicting data gathered at different levels of enquiry. Ideally the biochemical, experimental and epidemiological should reinforce one another. But if they do not, then policies have to based on the most relevant data available. This point is illustrated in a recent study by Forman and his colleagues.[90] They measured salivary nitrate and nitrite levels in people from low and high gastric cancer risk areas of Britain and found them to be negatively correlated (Table 5.11).

Table 5.11 Mean nitrate and nitrite concentrations (nmol per ml) in saliva of study populations in high and low gastric cancer risk areas in the UK

	Low risk (Oxford and Southeast)	High risk (Wales and Northeast)
Nitrate*	162.1	106.3
Nitrite*	100.2	67.0

* Probability that these differences have arisen by chance is less than one in ten thousand

Source: Forman, D. et al., "Nitrates, nitrites and gastric cancer in Great Britain", *Nature* 313 (1985a) pp. 620–25.

The study generated considerable controversy.[91] Critics claimed the results did not disprove the role of nitrate, nitrite and the nitrosation process in the causation of gastric cancer. They argued for many factors being involved in a long chain of effects. Correa,[92] for example, suggests that one of the preconditions is the creation of chronic atrophic gastritis (severe inflammation of the stomach with degeneration of functional activity), itself a product of irritants such as salt, and protein and vitamin deficiencies in the diet. This condition increases bacterial growth in the gut and hence the reduction of nitrate to nitrite (Figure 5.8). Forman and his colleagues replied, however, that they were making no claims about the role of nitrate in N-nitroso compound induced gastric cancer. They were simply saying that their "results in general weigh against the idea that environmental nitrates play a major role in determining the risk of gastric cancer in Britain."[93]

As they point out, epidemiology cannot unravel the complex bio-chemical pathways of a disease, but when control of an environmental factor such as nitrate in drinking water is proposed as a way of preventing the disease, then epidemiological evidence is the best way of testing whether it is likely to work. In this case, they conclude, expenditure might be better directed to other causative targets.

Nitrate restrictions in drinking water

The argument, however, is somewhat academic since strict limits on nitrate levels are now being enforced, at least throughout the industrialized countries. In 1962 the US Public Health Service set a drinking water standard of 45 mg of nitrate/l primarily because of the danger of methaemoglobinaemia in infants. This limit remains in force and is also the value for WHO guidelines in the International Standards for Drinking Water.[94] In Europe, the EC Directive on Quality of Water Intended for Human Consumption, has set a Maximum Admissible Concentration for nitrate of 50 mg/l (equivalent to 11.3 mg of nitrate-N/l) and a guide level of 25mg/l (= 5.65 mg nitrate-N/l).

Nitrate in food

The restrictions have primarily focused on nitrate contamination of drinking water. But this is not the only route for human uptake. Nitrates

Figure 5.8 Simplified version of Correa's model for the development of gastric cancer. The full version includes several other factors

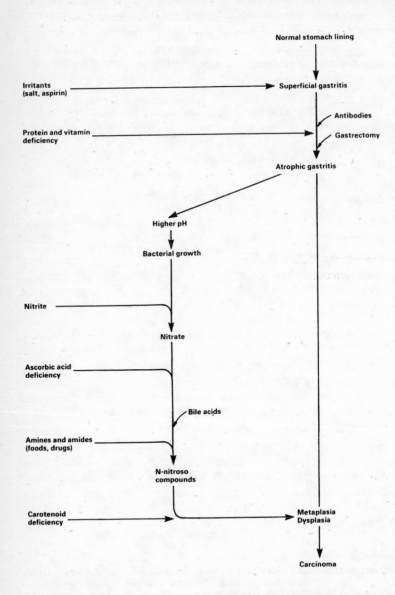

Source: Correa, P., "A human model of gastric carcinogenesis", *Cancer Research* 48 (1988) pp. 3554–3560.

derived from natural sources and from applied fertilizers will end up in crop harvests and, hence, in a variety of human foods. The special case of pickled vegetables in China has already been mentioned, and in many parts of the world dietary nitrate levels may be high.

Accumulation of nitrate

Nitrate is present in all plants but the concentrations vary from 1 to 10,000 mg/kg fresh weight. Once absorbed by the roots, nitrate is carried by the xylem tissues to the leaves and other parts where transpiration occurs.[95] Concentrations are thus likely to be high in foliage, but low in those parts of plants – stems, fruits, roots – that do not transpire. This contention is mostly supported by the evidence, though it is not known why some storage roots, such as beets, swedes and turnips, should contain large quantities of nitrate (Table 5.12).

How much nitrate ends up in the harvested crop depends on the amount of fertilizer nitrogen added, the intrinsic characteristics of the crop and a variety of environmental factors. In general, the more N applied, the higher the level in the crop.[96] But differences between crops determine how much nitrate is accumulated in relation to the optimum addition of nitrogen (Table 5.13). For root crops, nitrate

Table 5.12   Crops according to typical nitrate content

Crops usually accumulating less than 200 mg/kg fresh weight	Crops usually accumulating more than 1000 mg/kg fresh weight
Broad bean	Broccoli
Brussels sprout	Cabbage
Carrot	Celery
Cauliflower	Kale
French bean	Lettuce
Leek	Radish
Onion bulbs	Spinach
Parsnip	Swede
Pea	Turnip
Potato	
Sugar beet	
Sweetcorn	
Wheat	

Source: MAFF, *Nitrate, Nitrite and N-Nitroso Compounds in Food* (London: HMSO, 1987); NAS, *The Health Effects of Nitrate, Nitrite and N-Nitroso Compounds* (Washington DC: National Academy Press, 1981); Greenwood, D.J. and Hunt, J., "Effect of nitrogen fertiliser on the nitrate contents of field vegetables grown in Britain", *J. Sci. Food Agric.* 37 (1986) pp. 373–83.

Table 5.13   Nitrate content of crops grown under three different fertilizer regimes

| | Nitrate content (mg/kg dry matter) | | |
	Zero fertilizer	Optimum* fertilizer	Maximum** fertilizer
Lettuce	6600	15000	21160
Spinach	7620	17500	31770
Summer cabbage	434	15840	29510
Winter cabbage	8040	13620	15730
Red beet	1440	2550	13300
Swede	4300	3850	30630
White turnip	560	620	22730

* Optimum varied between 30–240 kg N/ha
** Maximum varied between 390–785 kg N/ha

Source: Greenwood, D.J. and Hunt, J., 1986, *op. cit.*

concentrations only increase markedly after very large quantities of fertilizer are applied. Seasonal factors may also be important. Lettuce accumulates increasing amounts of nitrate with increasing nitrate and ammonium fertilizer application, but the biggest difference is between spring and summer crops (Table 5.14). Sunlight appears to increase nitrate accumulation. Year to year variation can be high: spinach harvested at optimum maturity over a period of years varied in nitrate

Table 5.14   Accumulation of nitrate in lettuce during spring and summer under differing fertilizer regimes

| Fertilizer | Rate of application (kg N/ha) | Nitrate concentration in lettuce (mg/kg dry matter) | |
		Spring	Summer
No fertilizer	0	4430	18160
Sodium nitrate	56	8860	34550
	112	14176	48290
	224	49620	70440
Ammonium sulphate	56	10190	29680
	112	18160	35000
	224	21700	51390

Source: Maynard, D.N. et al., "Nitrate accumulation in vegetables", *Agron J.* **28** (1976) pp. 71–118.

by a factor of five despite identical amounts of applied fertilizer; and winter cabbage receiving optimum fertilizer varied in content by 15-fold.[97]

Other important physical factors include drought, which tends to increase nitrate accumulation, and irrigation which has the reverse effect. Trace elements in the soil may be important. For instance, nitrate content is controlled by the enzyme nitrate reductase, whose activity depends on the presence of molybdenum; nitrate concentrations in crops appear to be much higher in areas of molybdenum deficiency.[98] Finally, the form of fertilizer has an effect. Urea fertilizers tend to produce the least nitrate accumulation, ammonium compounds produce more, and greatest amounts result from nitrate products.[99]

Implications for methaemoglobinaemia

Vegetables high in nitrate were the indirect cause of about 50 cases of methaemoglobinaemia in the USA prior to 1973. In all cases infants under one year of age were affected and, in all but one case, the source was spinach or carrots.[100] The effects were often dramatic: the methaemoglobin level in one infant was raised to 60 per cent after consuming carrot juice containing over 500 mg/kg of nitrate and 700 mg/kg of nitrite. The carrots were grown in Florida. However, they had received no nitrogen fertilizers or subsequent added colouring or preservatives and the cause of high nitrate is not known.[101] Recently in France, four out of eight cases of methaemoglobinaemia in infants under two months of age were caused by regular consumption of carrot juice; one infant had 69 per cent blood methaemoglobin.[102]

Fresh spinach may contain relatively high levels of nitrate but usually no or little nitrite. The hazard arises from storage during which reductase enzymes will reduce nitrate to nitrite.[103] This is usually accelerated when the spinach is stored at room temperature, but some studies have recorded large accumulations of nitrite even when the vegetable is refrigerated.[104]

Drinking water versus food

Given the high levels of nitrate often present in food, the question is what proportion of intake derives from each source? The UK Steering Group on Food Surveillance[105] has produced calculations showing the average daily intake from food material to be 60 mg of nitrate, of which some 70–90 per cent is derived from vegetables (Table 5.15). Other studies of dietary nitrate intake in the US and several

Table 5.15 Estimated daily dietary intake of nitrate per person in the UK. Samples purchased and analysed in 1979

	Mean concentration (mg/kg)	Consumption of food (kg/person/day)	Nitrate intake (mg/person/day)
Cereals	8.8	0.23	2.0
Meats	3.6	0.15	0.5
Fish	55.0	0.02	1.1
Oils and fats	5.6	0.08	0.5
Fruits and sugars	13.3	0.17	2.3
Root vegetables	118.0	0.18	21.2
Other vegetables	219.0	0.11	24.1
Non-alcoholic beverages	14.0	0.12	8.3
Milk	1.5	0.40	0.6
Water	10–20	1.0	10–20
Beer	30.0	0.7	21.0

Source: MAFF, 1987, *op. cit.*

countries in Europe all lie in the range 50–90 mg/person/day. This similarity is rather surprising given the wide range of agricultural practices, analytical techniques and the composition and weights of diets (Table 5.16). But the estimates are broadly confirmed by studies of the amount of nitrate excreted in the urine. About 70 per cent of the dietary intake of nitrate is excreted, and a study of London residents found an average urinary concentration of 62 mg/day, representing a daily intake of 88 mg per person.

Table 5.16 Estimated dietary nitrate intakes reported for various countries

Country	Date of work	Total intake (mg/person/day)	Intake from water only (mg/person/day)
USA	1981	75	2
UK	1979	71–81	10–21
West Germany	1976	49*	**
Netherlands	1979–80	52	**
Sweden	1976	50	**
Switzerland	1980	91	19

* Not including contribution from water
** Data not given

Source: MAFF, 1987, *op. cit.*

As is evident from Table 5.16 the nitrate intake from water is normally considerably less than from food. Assuming an intake of 1 litre daily, water only contributes a further 10–20 mg/day to the average diet. Nevertheless the total nitrate intake will increase rapidly when nitrate concentrations in water are high. When nitrate exceeds 50 mg/litre in the drinking water the total intake is nearly doubled (Table 5.17).

Table 5.17 Mean dietary intakes (from water and food) calculated from urinary excretion for people in the UK consuming well-water containing different concentrations of nitrate

Well-water concentration (mg/l)	Dietary intake* (mg/day)
0	86
0–50	118
50–100	140
>100	260

* Assuming that 70 per cent of intake is excreted in urine

Source: Chilvers, C., Inskip, H., Caygill, C., Bartholomew, B., Fraser, P. and Hill, M., "A survey of dietary nitrate in well-water users", *Int. J. Epidemiol.* **13** (1984) pp. 324–31.

There are several special groups, apart from people consuming water highly contaminated with nitrate, who may ingest greater than average quantities of nitrate. Some vegetarians consume up to 0.6 kg of vegetables daily, which elevates total daily nitrate intake to some 110 mg, not including the contribution of water. Fresh milk is not a hazard primarily because it does not concentrate nitrate.[106] However, the nitrate intake from beer may be significant. Beers from the UK analysed in 1984–1985 contained an average of 30 mg/l.[107] Heavy beer drinkers consuming 4 pints (2.28 litres) a day could be adding an amount equivalent to that from the food intake.

In summary, for most people specific vegetable items are likely to be the largest single source of nitrate intake; for some, especially when the water contains nitrate levels in excess of 50 mg/litre, it will be drinking water. This provides a sound justification for a policy of restrictions on nitrate levels in drinking water. So far, though, there have been no restrictions on nitrates in food in the UK or USA.

Nitrates and livestock

Nitrates are hazardous to other vertebrate animals in much the same way as they are to ourselves. Methaemoglobinaemia can result, although again at fairly high levels of nitrate intake. Warm water fish in laboratory experiments can be killed by high nitrate concentrations in the water but the LD_{50} values are over 4000 mg nitrate/l and no adverse effects occur below 400 mg/litre.[108] As far as we are aware, there are no records of nitrate poisoning to wildlife in the field.

However, there is evidence of adverse effects on agricultural livestock. Ruminants, such as cattle and sheep, are able to rapidly metabolize and absorb nitrate and nitrite from the rumen, the extra "stomach" which contains large numbers of bacteria. Cattle also have the lowest methaemoglobin reductase activity, which further increases their susceptibility to poisoning.[109] Nevertheless, the LD_{50} for nitrate is still as high as 700–1000 mg/kg body weight and it appears that some animals develop a degree of tolerance over time.[110] Acute toxicity in cattle tends to occur with diets containing between 5000 and 10,000 mg/kg. Sheep can tolerate diets containing up to 10,000 mg/kg, though some have died at levels of 12,500.[111]

In non-ruminants, on the other hand, nitrate uptake does not appear to lead to elevated methaemoglobin production. Pigs only tend to be susceptible when nitrite is produced by bacteria in the food before consumption. Nitrite is some two and a half times more toxic to ruminants than nitrate, but some ten times more so for non-ruminants and high levels of administered nitrite have caused problems in pigs, poultry, rabbits and dogs.[112]

Nitrates in fodder and drinking water

Nitrate poisoning of livestock is not a new phenomenon. The earliest record appears to be from Kansas in the last century, when cattle died of methaemoglobinaemia after feeding upon maize stalks containing potassium nitrate.[113] The highest concentrations (up to 15,500 mg nitrate/kg) accumulated in maize grown on land formerly used as a cattle corral and pig yard. In the 1920s and 1930s, consumption of oat hay containing 4500–25,000 mg nitrate/kg led to cattle deaths in the High Plain of Wyoming.[114] More recently, some 225 cattle died in Nebraska in 1975 after feeding on weeds and wild hay harvested from a wetland pasture that had been fertilized with animal manures.[115] A further 42 cows aborted over the 3 weeks after the acute poisoning. The forage fed to the cattle was found to contain up to 40,000 mg/kg of nitrate, and the weeds, *Kochia* spp. and *Amaranthus* spp., up to 50,000 mg/kg.

Most poisoning from drinking water has been linked to nitrate concentrations of 300–675 mg/l, though several cattle died of anoxia in 1968 in Texas from consuming water containing an average of only 250 mg/l.[116]

Several factors affect the accumulation of nitrates in forage plants. The level of fertilizer N applied is important, though in many cases there is no simple relationship.[117] Other important factors include moisture conditions, amount of sunlight, the species of forage and even the use of herbicides. Many nitrate poisoning cases have occurred in semi-arid regions, or during drought conditions. A decline in moisture depresses the activity of the nitrate reductase enzyme which leads to nitrate accumulation. Cornstalk poisoning was common in Missouri during the drought of 1954, when many plants accumulated very high concentrations of nitrate (Table 5.18). Finally, even in the absence of fertilizers, certain wild plants can concentrate nitrates. This has been demonstrated in crops and pasture plants growing in the Florida Everglades and in Wisconsin peat marshes.[118]

Table 5.18   Nitrate content of some forage crops grown in the Missouri drought region during 1954

Forage	Nitrate (mg/kg)
Cornstalk (maize)	80,000
Corn silage	12,600
Alfalfa hay	
First cutting	1,550
Second cutting	4,100
Third cutting	2,850
Fourth cutting	680
Fifth cutting	3,350
Sorghum silage	5,400
Sweet potato vines	25,500
Pigweed	11,150

Source: Case, A.A., "Some aspects of nitrate intoxication in livestock", *J. Am. Vet. Med. Assoc.* **130** (1957) p. 323.

Herbicides also increase nitrate accumulation in some species of plants. Sublethal dosages of the herbicides 2,4-D, 2,4-T and MCPA applied to weeds caused some (*Impatiens biflora*, *Polygonum convolvulus* and *Eupatorium maculatum*) to accumulate nitrate to potentially lethal concentrations for browsing livestock, although others (*Chenopodium album*, *Cirsium arvense* and *Polygonum persicaria*) were unaffected or even lost nitrate.[119] Agricultural crops have also been known to accumulate nitrate following accidental treatment with herbicide. When several hundred hectares of sugar beet in South Dakota were sprayed with 2,4-D, the nitrate concentrations increased to up to 20 times the unsprayed, with a maximum concentration of over 50,000 mg/kg in the leaves.[120]

Chronic toxicity

While the acute effects of high nitrate and nitrite intakes are relatively well known, the consequences of chronic toxicity are difficult to assess. Some studies have reported slower growth, reproductive problems and lowered milk production in cattle fed on diets containing sub-acute concentrations of nitrate.[121] But in most instances the dosages are nearly acutely toxic.[122] At such dosages there is also some evidence of a decline in rate of conception, although there is no apparent effect on the oestrus cycle. Both milk and meat of heavily dosed cattle also had significantly higher concentrations of nitrate (Table 5.19). Only in some studies has milk production been significantly reduced, without keeping the cattle on the verge of collapse.[123] Although abortions in cattle are only induced at very high concentrations, there is one instance of an Aberdeen Angus herd, in apparent good health, giving birth to a number of calves that did not start respiring due

Table 5.19 Production and reproductive performance of dairy heifers fed various levels of nitrate in the diet

	Nitrate (mg/kg body weight)		
	0	440	660
Length oestrus cycle (days)	21	20.9	21.1
Number of services per conception*	1.3	1.4	2.6
Weight of calves (kg)	39	36	35
Number of abortions	0	1	2
Number of deaths	0	0	2
Average milk production (kg/day)	19.7	19.3	18.5
Milk composition** (mg nitrate/l)	5	9	15
Meat composition** (mg nitrate/kg)	5	16	21

Probability of difference arising by chance are less than five in a hundred (*) or five in a thousand (**)
Note that 440 mg nitrate/kg body weight in this experiment was approximately equivalent to 20,000 mg nitrate/kg in diet

Source: Davison, K.L. et al., "Reproduction, growth and lactation of heifers fed nitrate", *J. Anim. Sci.* **22** (1963) p. 835.

to severe methaemoglobinaemia.[124] The cattle had been feeding on hay containing 3700 mg/kg and silage at 4300 mg/kg of nitrate.

There are no reports of abortions in pigs and sheep, though there are some suggestions of reduced feed intake and growth. Pigs fed more than 11,000 mg/kg in the diet showed reduced weight, but even at 20,000 no reduction in reproductive performance.[125] Other studies have discovered no ill-effects, and it seems that it is nitrite in feed that is more likely to cause problems.[126]

Summary

Nitrate is clearly harmful to human beings in at least one respect. If taken in through the diet or via drinking water it may be converted to nitrite which can give rise to methaemoglobinaemia or the blue-baby syndrome. Infants are particularly susceptible for a variety of reasons. Their gastric juice is less acidic thus encouraging bacterial conversion of nitrate to nitrite, and they consume large quantities of fluid. Most recorded cases of methaemoglobinaemia have involved infants given milk formulations prepared with water rich in nitrate. Methaemoglobinaemia has been a serious problem in some regions of the industrialized countries but while fertilizer nitrate is an important factor, of at least equal importance is bacterial contamination of the drinking water. In the USA contaminated farm wells have been the principal source. Vitamin C provides a degree of protection and its presence in the diet together with an absence of bacterial contamination reduces the risk of methaemoglobinaemia, even when nitrate concentrations in drinking water are high. Since in developing countries, nitrate and bacterial contamination of drinking water from domestic sources and livestock are high and diets are lacking in vitamin C we might expect a high incidence of methaemoglobinaemia, but so far the condition is virtually unknown.

Far more problematic is the role of fertilizer nitrate in the production of cancer, especially gastric cancer. In the laboratory and in human volunteers nitrate may be converted to nitrite, which is then combined with amines and amides to produce N-nitroso compounds that are known to be carcinogenic. However, the link between nitrate in the diet or drinking water and the incidence of gastric cancer has not been established epidemiologically. Although nitrate intake per capita and national rates of gastric cancer are correlated, in certain regions of the world, with high nitrate intakes or high fertilizer use, the correlations do not survive detailed analysis. The first study to suggest a correlation, based on the borough of Worksop in England, has been found to be based on faulty analysis. Most recent studies in the developed countries have suggested a negative correlation between nitrate exposure and gastric cancer.

In most countries gastric cancer rates are declining despite rapid rises in fertilizer use. High rates occur in central Chile and the Nariño region of Colombia, but while in the former there is an association with overall fertilizer use but not with nitrate concentrations in drinking water, in the latter there is an association with drinking water but this does not seem to be related to fertilizer use. It seems that other factors, in particular the nature and content of the diet, are considerably more important. For bladder cancer, which is particularly prevalent in Egypt, and for oesophageal cancer, common in northern China, there is an association with the presence of N-nitroso compounds and possibly with nitrate in the drinking water or diet but, again, there are several complicating factors.

The known hazard of methaemoglobinaemia and the possibility of high nitrate concentrations resulting in human cancer have led to worldwide restrictions on nitrate levels in drinking water aimed to ensure they do not exceed 45–50 mg/l. Nitrate concentrations may also be high in human food, on average 50–90 mg per person per day. Certain vegetables can have very high nitrate concentrations and average intakes are higher for vegetarians and heavy beer drinkers, for instance. The contribution from drinking water, assuming an average water intake of 1 litre a day, is likely to be only a extra 10–20 mg a day, but when nitrate concentrations in drinking water are at or above 50 mg/litre the total intake doubles or more. In several instances, dietary nitrate, especially in infant foods containing spinach or carrots, has been a direct cause of methaemoglobinaemia.

Domestic livestock are affected in much the same way as human beings. Methaemoglobinaemia can be induced by levels of nitrate in the fodder of 5–10,000 mg/kg and acute toxicity has been reported on many occasions, although not necessarily as a result of high fertilizer N application. Little is known of the chronic effects of sub-acute dosages. Most instances of reproductive failure have been at dosages that are near-toxic.

References

1 Magee, P.N. "Nitrogen as a potential health hazard", *Phil. Trans. R. Soc. Lond. B* **296** (1982) pp. 543–50; RCEP, *Agriculture and Pollution*

Royal Commission on Environmental Pollution 7th Report (London: HMSO, 1979).

2 Maclean, D., "Methaemoglobinaemia", in: Parmeggiani, L. (ed.), *Encyclopaedia of Occupational Health*, vol. 2 (Geneva: International Labour Office, 1983).

3 Mansouri, A., "Methaemoglobinaemia", *Am. J. Med. Sci.* 289 (1985) pp. 200–209.

4 Cohen, R.J., Sacks, J.R., Wicker, D.J. and Conrad, M.E., "Methaemoglobinaemia provoked by malarial chemoprophylaxis in Vietnam", *New Eng. J. Med.* 279 (1968) pp. 1127–31; Mansouri, 1985, *op. cit.*

5 Taylor, N. "Medical aspects of nitrates in drinking water", *Wat. Treat. Exam.* 24 (1975) pp. 194–205; Walton, G., "Survey of literature relating to infant methaemoglobinaemia due to nitrate-contaminated ground water", *Amer. J. Public Health* 41 (1951) pp. 986–96.

6 Payne, W.J., "Reduction of nitrogenous oxides by micro-organisms". *Bact. Rev.* 37 (1973) pp. 409–52; Drasar, B.S. and Hill, M.J., *Human Intestinal Flora* (London: Academic Press, 1974).

7 Drasar and Hill, 1974, *op. cit.*

8 Marriott, W.M., Hartmann, A.F. and Senn, M.J.E., "Observations on the nature and treatment of diarrhoea and associated systematic disturbances", *J. Pediatr.* 3 (1933) pp. 181–91; Shuval, H.I. and Gruener, N., "Epidemiological and toxicological aspects of nitrates and nitrites in the environment", *Amer. J. Public Health* 62 (1972) pp. 1045–52.

9 Lee, K., Greger, J.L., Consaul, J.R., Graham, K.L. and Chinn, B.L., "Nitrate, nitrite balance and *de novo* synthesis of nitrate in humans consuming cured meats", *Amer. J. Clin. Nutr.* 44 (1986) pp. 188–94; Hegesh, E. and Shiloah, J., "Blood nitrates and infantile methaemoglobinaemia", *Clhin. Chim. Acta* 125 (1982) pp. 107–115; Yano, S.S., Danish E.H. and Hsia, Y.E., "Transient methaemoglobinaemia with acidosis in infants", *J. Pediatr.* 100 (1982) pp. 414–18; Bricker, T., Jefferson, L.S. and Mintz, A.A., "Methaemoglobinaemia in infants with enteritis", letter to editor, *J. Pediatr.* 102 (1983) p. 161; Hanukoglu, A., Fried, D. and Badner, D., "Methaemoglobinaemia in infants with enteritis", letter to editor, *J. Pediatr.* 102 (1983) pp. 161–2; Seeler, R.A., "Methaemoglobinaemia in infants with enteritis", letter to editor, *J. Pediatr.* 102 (1983) p. 162; Danish, E.H., "Methaemoglobinaemia in infants with enteritis", *J. Pediatr.* 102 (1983) pp. 162–3.

10 Burden, E.H.W.J., "The toxicology of nitrates and nitrites with particular reference to the potability of water supplies", *Analyst* 86 (1961) pp. 429–33.

11 Bosch, H.M., Rosenfield, A.B., Huston, R., Shipman, H.R. and Woodward, F.L., "Methaemoglobinaemia and Minnesota well supplies", *J. Am. Water Works Assn* (Feb 1950) pp. 161–70.

12 Comly, H.H., "Cyanosis in infants caused by nitrates in well water", *J. Amer. Med. Assn.* 129 (1945) pp. 112–16; WHO, *Health Hazards from*

Nitrates in Drinking Water, report on a WHO meeting, Copenhagen 5–9 March 1984 (Geneva: WHO, 1985).

13 Bosch et al., 1950, *op. cit.*

14 Vigil, J., Warburton, S., Haynes, W.S. and Kaiser, L.R., "Nitrates in municipal water supplies cause methaemoglobinaemia in infants", *Public Health Report* 80 (1965) p. 1119.

15 Shearer, L.A., Goldsmith, J.R., Young, C., Kearns, O.A. and Tamplin, B.R., "Methaemoglobin levels in infants in an area with high nitrate water supply", *Amer. J. Public Health* 62 (1972) pp. 1174–80.

16 Knotek, Z. and Schmidt, P., "Pathogenesis, incidence and possibilities of preventing alimentary nitrate methaemoglobinaemia in infants", *Pediatrics* 34 (1964) pp. 78–83.

17 Green, L.C., Tannenbaum, S.R. and Fox, J.G., "Nitrate in human and canine milk", *New Eng. J. Med.* 306 (1982) pp. 1367–68; Simon, C., Manzke, H., Kay, H. and Mrovetz, G., "Uber vorkommen, pathogenese und moglichkeiten zu prophylaxe der durch nitrit verursachten methamoglobinamie", *Z. Kinderheilk* 91 (1964) pp. 124–38.

18 Feachem, R.G. and Koblinsky, M.A., "Interventions for the control of diarrhoeal diseases among young children: promotion of breast-feeding", *Bull. WHO* 62 (1984) pp. 271–91.

19 Gibson, Q.H., "Reduction of methaemoglobin by ascorbic acid", *Biochem. J.* 37 (1984) pp. 615–18; Calabrese, E.J., Moore, G.S. and McCarthy, M.S., "The effect of ascorbic acid on nitrite-induced methaemoglobin formation in rats, sheep and normal human erythrocytes". *Regulatory Toxicol. & Pharmacol.* 3 (1983) pp. 184–8; Feachem and Koblinsky, 1984, *op. cit.*

20 Shuval and Gruener, 1972, *op. cit.*

21 RCEP, 1979, *op. cit.*

22 Johnson, C.J., Bonrud, P.A., Dosch, T.L., Kilness, A.W., Senger, K.A., Busch, D.C. and Meyer, M.R., "Fatal outcome of methaemoglobinaemia in an infant", *J. Am. Med. Assn.* 257 (1987) pp. 2796–97.

23 Busch, D. and Meyer, M., "A case of infantile methaemoglobinaemia in South Dakota", *J. Environ. Health* 44 (1982) p. 310.

24 Johnson et al., 1987, *op. cit.*

25 Meyer, M., "A summary of groundwater pollution problems in South Dakota", *State/EPA Task 2–3.1–11B* (Pierre: South Dakota: Dept. of Water and Natural Resources, Office of Water Quality, 1986).

26 Farre Sostres, I., Oliver Clapes, B., Sanchez Carranza, F., Grau Codina, I. and Perez del Pulgar, J., "Outbreak of methaemoglobinaemia in a group of infants due to an excessive content of nitrates in the water supplies", *Arch. Pediatr.* (Barcelona) 33 suppl. 1 (1982) pp. 85–94.

27 Deak, in: WHO, 1985, *op. cit.*

28 Steiner, J. and Buryevacz, J. "Trends of nitrate content in drinking waters", *Hidrologiai Kozlony* (Budapest) 61 (1981) pp. 193–201.

29 WHO, *Nitrates, Nitrites and N-Nitroso compounds.* Environmental Health Criteria no.5. (Geneva: WHO, 1978).

30 Super, M., Hesse, H. De V., MacKenzie, D., Dempster, W.S., Plessis, J. Du and Ferreira, J.J., "An epidemiological study of well-water nitrates in a group of SW African/Namibian infants", *Water Research* 15 (1981) pp. 1265–70.

31 Sankale, M. and Philippe, F., "Pathogénie iatrogène des antimalariques", *Médecine d'Afrique Noire* 33 (1986) pp. 129–39; Medina, M.I., Espinal, C.A., Arias, A.E., Arellaneda, O. and Baena, R. "Malaria en niños: discusión de algunos aspectos clínicos, diagnósticos y terapéuticos", *Biomedia* 3 (1983) pp. 125–9.

32 Cohen et al., 1968, *op. cit.*

33 Magee, P.N. and Barnes, J.M. "Carcinogenic nitroso compounds", *Adv. Cancer Res.* 10 (1967) pp. 163–246; Magee, D.N., Montesano, R. and Preusmann, R. "N-Nitroso compounds and related carcinogens", in: Searle, C.E. (ed.), *Chemical Carcinogens*, A.C.S. Monograph no. 173 (Washington DC: American Chemical Society, 1976); WHO, 1978, *op. cit.*

34 Lijinsky, W., "Significance of in vivo formation of N-Nitroso compounds", *Oncology* 37 (1980) pp. 223–6; Mirvish, S.S., "N-Nitroso compounds: their chemical and in vivo formation and possible importance as environmental carcinogens", *J. Toxicol. & Environ. Health* 2 (1977) pp. 1267–77; Newberne, P.M., "Nitrite promotes lymphoma incidence in rats", *Science* 204 (1979) pp. 1079–81.

35 Hecht, S.S. and Hoffmann, D., "The relevance of tobacco and specific nitrosamines to human cancer", *Cancer Surveys* 8 (1989) pp. 273–94; Preston-Martin, S. and Correa, P., "Epidemiological evidence for the role of nitroso compounds in human cancer", *Cancer Surveys* 8 (1989) pp. 459–74.

36 Ohshima, H. and Bartsch, H.H., "Quantitative estimation of endogenous nitrosation in humans by monitoring N-nitrosoproline excreted in the urine", *Cancer Research* 41 (1981) pp. 3658–62; Bartsch, H., O'Neill, I.K., and Shulte-Herman, R. (eds), *Relevance of N-Nitroso Compounds to Human Cancer: Exposure and Mechanisms*, IARC Scientific Publications no. 84 (Lyon: International Agency for Research on Cancer, 1987).

37 Tannenbaum, S.R., "Endogenous formation of N-nitroso compounds: a current perspective", in: Bartsch et al. (eds), *op. cit.*

38 Bartsch et al., 1987, *op. cit.*; Drasar and Hill, 1974, *op. cit.*; Suzuki, K. and Mitsuoka, T., "N-Nitrosamine formation by intestinal bacteria", in: O'Neill, I.K., von Borstel, R.C., Miller, C.T., Long, J. and Bartsch, H. (eds), *N-Nitroso Compounds: Occurrence, Biological Effects and Relevance to Human Cancer*, IARC Scientific Publications no. 57 (Lyon: IRAC, 1984); Hawksworth, G. and Hill, M.J., "Bacteria and the N-Nitrosation of secondary amines", *Br. J. Cancer* 25 (1971) pp. 520–26.

39 Hill, M.J. "Aetiology and micro-environment of gastric cancer", in: Felipe, M.E. and Jass, J.R. (eds), *Gastric Carcinoma* (Edinburgh: Churchill Livingstone, 1986); Stockbrugger, R.W., Eugenides, N., Bartholomew, B.A., Walters, C.L., Thompson, R.E.M., Hill, M.J. and

Cotton, P.B., "Cimetidine treatment, intragastric bacterial overgrowth and its consequences", *Gasteroenterology* **80** (1981) pp. 1295 (abstr.); Reed, P., Smith, P.L.R., Haines, K., House, F.R. and Walters, C.L., "Effect of cimetidine on gastric juice N-nitrosamine concentration", *Lancet ii* (1981a) pp. 553–6; Reed, P., Smith, P.L.R., Haines, K., House, F.R. and Walters, C.L., "Gastric juice and N-nitrosamines in health and gastrointestinal disease", *Lancet ii* (1981b) pp. 550–52; Eisenbrand, G., Adam, B., Peter, M., Malfertheiner, P. and Schlag, P., "Formation of nitrite in gastic juice of patients with various gastric disorders after ingestion of a standard dose of nitrate – a possible risk factor in gastric carcinogenesis", in: O'Neill, I.K. et al. (eds), 1984 *op. cit.*

40 Milton-Thompson, G.J., Ahmet, Z., Lightfoot, N.F., Hunt, R.H., Barnard, J., Brimblecombe, R.W., Moore, P.J., Bavin, P.M.G., Darkin, D.W. and Viney, N., "Intragastric acidity, bacteria, nitrite, and N-Nitroso compounds before, during and after cimetidine treatment", *Lancet i* (1982) pp. 1091–95.

41 Tannenbaum, 1987, *op. cit.*

42 Mirvish, S.S., "The etiology of gastric cancer", *J. Nat. Cancer Inst.* **71** (1983) pp. 629–47; Kawasaki, H., Morishige, F., Tanaka, H. and Kimoto, E., "Influence of oral supplementation of ascorbate upon the induction of N-methyl-N'-nitro-N nitroso-guanidine", *Cancer Letters* **16** (1982) pp. 57–63.

43 Lu, S.H., Ohshima, H., Fu, H.M., Tian, U., Li, F.M., Blettner, M., Wahrendorf, J. and Bartsch, H., "Urinary excretion of N-nitrosamino acids and nitrate by inhabitants of high and low-risk areas for oesophageal cancer in northern China: endogenous formation of nitrosoproline and its inhibition by vitamin C", *Cancer Res.* **46** (1986) pp. 1485–91.

44 Knight, T.M. and Forman, D., "The availability of dietary nitrate for the endogenous nitrosation of L-proline", in: Bartsch et al. (eds), 1987, *op. cit.*

45 Bartsch et al., 1987, *op. cit*; Licht, W.R., Tannenbaum, S.R. and Deen, W.M., "Use of ascorbic acid to inhibit nitrosation: kinetic and mass transfer considerations for an in vitro system", *Carcinogenesis* **9** (1988) pp. 365–72.

46 Cuello, C., Correa, P., Haenszel, W., Gordillo, G., Brown, C., Archer, M. and Tannenbaum, S., "Gastric cancer in Columbia I. Cancer risk and suspect environmental agents", *J. Nat. Cancer Inst.* **57** (1976) pp. 1015–20; Tannenbaum, S.R., Moran, D., Rand, W., Cuello, C. and Correa, P., "Gastric cancer in Colombia IV. Nitrite and other ions in gastric contents of residents from a high risk region", *J. Nat. Cancer Inst.* **62** (1979) pp. 9–12.

47 Armijo, R., Orellana, M., Medina, E., Coulson, A.H., Sayre, J.W. and Detels, R., "Epidemiology of gastric cancer in Chile: I – Case-control study", *Int. J. Epidemiol.* **10** (1981a) pp. 53–56; Armijo, R., Gonzalez, A., Orellana, M., Coulson, A.N., Sayre, J.W. and Detels, R., "Epidemiology of gastric cancer in Chile: II – Nitrate exposures and stomach cancer

frequency", *Int. J. Epidemiol.* **10** (1986) pp. 57–62; Armijo, R. and Coulson, A.M., "Epidemiology of stomach cancer in Chile – the role of nitrogen fertilisers", *Int. J. Epidemiol.* **4** (1975) pp. 301–309.

48 Hill, M.J., Hawksworth, G. and Tattershal, G., "Bacteria, nitrosamines and cancer of the stomach", *Br. J. Cancer* **28** (1973) pp. 562–7.

49 Davies, J.M., "Stomach cancer mortality in Worksop and other Nottinghamshire mining towns", *Br. J. Cancer* **41** (1980) pp. 438–45.

50 Falk, H.L. and Jurgelski, W., "Health effects of coal mining and combustion: carcinogens and cofactors", *Environ. Health Perspectives* **33** (1979) pp. 203–226.

51 Whong, W.Z., Long, R., Ames, R.G. and Ong, T.M., "Role of nitrosation in the mutagenic activity of coal dust: a postulation for gastric carcinogenisis in coal miners", *Environ. Res.* **32** (1983) pp. 298–304; Meyer, M.B., Luk, G.D., Sotelo, J.M., Cohen, B.H. and Menkes, H.A., "Hypothesis: the role of the lung in stomach carcinogenesis", *Amer. Rev. Respir. Dis.* **121** (1980) pp. 887–92.

52 Beresford, S.A.A., "Is nitrate in the drinking water associated with the risk of cancer in the urban UK?" *Journal of Epidemiol.* **14** (1985) pp. 57–63.

53 Fraser, P. and Chilvers, C., "Health aspects of nitrate in drinking water", *Science Total Environ.* **18** (1981) pp. 103–116.

54 Fraser, P., Chilvers, C. and Goldblatt, P., "Census-based mortality study of fertiliser manufacturers", *Brit. J. Indust. Med.* **39** (1982) pp. 323–9.

55 Al-Dabbagh, S., Forman, D., Bryson, D., Stratton, T. and Doll, R., "Mortality of nitrate fertiliser workers", *Br. J. Indust. Med.* **43** (1986) pp. 507–519.

56 Devesa, S.S. and Silverman, D.T., "Cancer incidence and mortality trends in the US 1935–74", *J. Nat. Cancer Inst.* **60** (1978) pp. 545–71.

57 Coggon, D. and Acheson, E.D., "The geography of cancer of the stomach", *British Medical Bull.* **40** (1984) pp. 335–41.

58 Parkin, D.M. (ed.) in association with Arslon, A., Bieber, A., Bouby, O., Muir, C.S., Owụr, R. and Whelan, S., *Cancer in Developing Countries* (Lyon: IARC, 1986). WHO, 1986, *op. cit.*; Muir et al., 1987, *op. cit.*

59 Armijo and Coulson, 1975, *op. cit.*

60 Zaldivar, R., "Nitrate fertilisers as environmental pollutants: positive correlation between nitrates ($NaNO_3$ and KNO_3) used per unit area and stomach cancer mortality rates", *Specialia* **33** (1977) pp. 264–5.

61 Schalscha, E.B., Vergara, I., Schirado, T. and Moraks, M., "Nitrate movement in a Chilean agricultural area irrigated with untreated sewage water", *J. Environ. Qual.* **8** (1979) pp. 27–30.

62 Zaldivar, R. and Wetterstrand, W.H., "Nitrate nitrogen levels in drinking water of urban areas with high- and low-risk populations for stomach cancer: an environmental epidemiology study", *Z. Krebsforsch. Klinische Onkologie* **92** (1978) pp. 227–34.

63 Armijo et al., 1981a, *op. cit.*

64 Armijo et al., 1981b, *op. cit.*

65 Armijo et al., 1981b, *op. cit.*; Shamberger, R.J., Tytko, S.A. and Willis, C.E., "Antioxidants and cancer Part VI. Selenium and age adjusted human cancer mortality", *Arch. Environ. Health* **31** (1976) pp. 231–5.

66 Cuello et al., 1976, *op. cit.*

67 Cuello et al., 1976, *op. cit.*

68 Tannenbaum et al., 1979, *op. cit.*

69 Hawksworth, G., Hill, M.J. and Cordillo, G. and Cuello, C., "Possible relationship between nitrates, nitrosamines and gastric cancer in southwest Columbia", in: Bogovski, P. and Walker, E.A. (eds), *N-Nitroso Compounds in the Environment*, Scientific Publ. no. 9 (Lyon: IARC: 1975).

70 Fontham, E., Zavala, D., Correa, P., Rodriguez, E., Hunter, F., Haenszel, W. and Tannenbaum, S.R., "Diet and chronic atrophic gastritis: a case-control study", *J. Nat. Cancer Inst.* **76** (1986) pp. 621–7.

71 Yang, D., Tannenbaum, S.R., Buchi, G. and Lee, G.C.M., 4-Chloro-6-methoxyindole is the precursor of a potent mutagen (4-chloro-6-methoxy-2-hydroxy-1-nitroso-indolin-3-one oxime) that forms during nitrosation of the fava bean (*Vicia faba*)", *Carcinogenesis* **5** (1984) pp. 1219–24.

72 Mirvish, 1983, *op. cit.*; RCEP, 1979, *op. cit.*; Risch, H.A., Jain, M., Choi, N.W., Fodor, J.G., Pfeiffer, C.J., Howe, G.R., Craib, K.J.P. and Miller, A.B., "Dietary factors and the incidence of cancer of the stomach", *Am. J. Epidemiol.* **122** (1985) pp. 947–57.

73 Fontham et al., 1986, *op. cit.*

74 Radomski, J.L., Greenwald, D., Hearn, W.C., Block, N.L. and Woods, F.M., "Nitrosamine formation in bladder infections and its role in the etiology of bladder cancer", *J. Urology* **120** (1978) pp. 148–50; Eisenbrand, G., Spiegelhalder, B. and Prussmann, R., "Nitrate and nitrite in saliva", *Oncology* **37** (1980) pp. 227–31.

75 Waterhouse, J., Muir, C., Shanmugaratnam, K., Powell, J. (eds), *Cancer Incidence in Five Continents*, vol. IV (Lyon: International Agency for Research on Cancer and International Association of Cancer Registries, 1982); Muir, C., Waterhouse, J., Mack, T., Powell, J. and Whelan, S. (eds), *Cancer Incidence in Five Continents, vol. V, IARC Scientific Publications no. 88 (Lyon:IARC, 1987); Howe, G.M. (ed.), Global Geocancerology. A World Geography of Human Cancers* (Edinburgh: Churchill Livingstone, 1987).

76 Parkin, D.M. (ed) *op. cit.*

77 Parkin, 1986, *op. cit.*

78 Hicks, R.M., "The canopic worm: role of bilharziasis in the aetiology of human bladder cancer", *J. Roy. Soc. Med.* **76** (1983) pp. 16–22.

79 Hicks, R.M., Ismail, M.M., Walters, C.L., Beecham, P.T., Rabie, M.F. and El Alamy, M.A., "Association of bacteriuria and urinary nitrosamine formation with *Schistosoma haematobium* infection in the Qalyub area of Egypt", *Trans. R. Soc. Trop. Med. & Hyg.* **76** (1982) pp. 519–27.

80 Hawksworth and Hill, 1971, *op. cit.*

81 El-Merzabani, M.M., El-Aaser, A.A. and Zakhary, N.I., "A study of the aetiological factors of bilharzial bladder cancer in Egypt. 1–Nitrosamines and their precursors in urine", *Eur. J. Cancer* 15 (1979) pp. 287–91; Hicks, R.M., Gough, T.A. and Walters, C.L., "Demonstration of the presence of nitrosamines in human urine: preliminary observations on possible aetiology for bladder cancer", in: Walker, E.A., Griciute, I., Castegnaro, M. and Lyle, R.E. (eds), *Environmental Aspects of N-Nitroso Compounds*, IARC Publ. No. 19 (Lyon: IARC, 1978).

82 Hicks et al., 1982, *op. cit.*

83 Tricker, A.R., Mosfafa, M.H., Spiegelhalder, B. and Preussmann, R., "Urinary excretion of nitrate, nitrite and N-nitroso comopunds in schistosomiasis and bilharzia bladder cancer patients", *Carcinogenesis* 10 (1989) pp. 547–52; Bartsch, H., Ohshima, H., Pignatelli, B. and Calmell, S., "Human exposure to endogenous N-nitroso compounds: quantitative estimates in subjects at high risk for cancer of the oral cavity, oesophagus, stomach and urinary bladder", *Cancer Surveys* 8 (1989) pp. 325–62.

84 FAO, *Fertiliser Yearbook 1987* vol. 37 (Rome: FAO, 1988).

85 Mostafa, M.H., El-Bassiouni, E.A., El-Sewedy, S.M., Tawfic, T. and El-Sebae, A.H., "Influence of pretreatment with various insecticides on the N-demethylation of dimethylnitrosamine", *Environ. Res.* 32 (1983) pp. 57–61.

86 Lu, S.H., Yang, W.X., Guo, L.P., Li, F.M., Wang, G.J., Zhang, J.S. and Li, P.Z., "Determination of N-nitrosamines in gastric juice and urine and a comparison of endogenous formation of N-nitrosoproline and its inhibition in subjects from high- and low-risk areas for oesophageal cancer", in: Bartsch et al. (eds), 1987 *op. cit.*; Wang, Y.L., Lu, S.H. and Li, M.M., "Determination of nitrates and nitrites in well water from Yaocun Commune, Linxien County, Henan Province", *Chin. J. Oncology* 1 (1979) pp. 201–205.

87 Lu et al., 1987, *op. cit.*

88 Chen, J., Ohshima, H., Yang, H., Li, J., Campbell, T.C., Peto, R. and Bartsch, H.H., "A correlation study on urinary excretion of N-nitroso compounds and cancer mortality in China: interim results", in: Bartsch et al. (eds), 1987, *op. cit.*

89 Lu et al., 1987, *op. cit.*

90 Forman, D., Al-Dabbagh, S. and Doll, R., "Nitrates, nitrites and gastric cancer in Great Britain", *Nature* 313 (1985a) pp. 620–25.

91 Tannenbaum, S.R. and Correa, P., "Nitrate and gastric cancer risks", *Nature* 317 (1985) pp. 675–6; Mirvish, S.S., "Gastric cancer and salivary nitrate and nitrite", *Nature* 315 (1985) pp. 461–2; Forman, D., Al-Dabbagh, S. and Doll, R., "Reply to Mirvish 1985", *Nature* 315 (1985b) p. 462; Forman, D., Al-Dabbagh, S. and Doll, R., "Reply to Tannenbaum & Correa", *Nature* 317 (1985c) p. 676.

92 Correa, P., "The gastric precancerous process", *Cancer Surveys* 2, (1983) pp. 437–450.

93   Forman et al., 1985a, *op. cit.*

94   WHO, 1985, *op. cit.*

95   Greenwood, D.J. and Hunt, J., "Effect of nitrogen fertiliser on the food nitrate contents of field vegetables grown in Britain", *J. Sci. Agric.* **37** (1986) pp. 373–383.

96   Maynard, D.N., Barker, A.V., Minotti, P.L. and Peck, N.H., "Nitrate accumulation in vegetables", *Agron. J.* **28** (1976) pp. 71–118; Greenwood and Hunt, 1986, *op. cit.*

97   Maynard et al., *op. cit.*; Greenwood and Hunt, 1986, *op. cit.*

98   MAFF, *Nitrate, Nitrite and N-Nitroso Compounds in Food*, the 20th report of the Steering Group on Food Surveillance, the Working Party on Nitrate and Related Compounds in Food, Surveillance Paper no. 20 (London: HMSO, 1987); Hewitt, E.J. and Smith, T.A., *Plant Mineral Nutrition* (New York: J. Wiley and Sons, 1975).

99   Maynard et al., 1976, *op. cit.*; Barker, A.V., Peck, N.H. and MacDonald, G.E., "Nitrate accumulation in vegetables. 1. Spinach grown in upland soils", *Agron. J.* **63** (1971) pp. 126–9; Peck, N.H., Barker, A.V., MacDonald, G.E. and Shallenberger, R.S., "Nitrate accumulation in vegetables. II. Table beets grown in upland soils", *Agron. J.* **63** (1971) pp. 130–32.

100 Luhrs, C.E., "Human health", in: *Hazardous Materials Advisory Committee Nitrogenous Compounds in the Environment*, EPA-SAB-730001 (Washington DC: Environmental Protection Agency, 1973).

101 Keating, J.P., Lell, M.E., Strauss, A.W., Zarkowsky, H. and Smith, G.E., "Infantile methaemoglobinaemia caused by carrot juice", *New Eng. J. Med.* **288** (1973) pp. 824–6.

102 Blanc, J.P., Teyssier, G., Geyssant, A. and Lauras, B., "Les methé-moglobinémies au cours des diarrhées aiguës du nourrisson", *Pédiatrie* **38** (1983) pp. 87–99.

103 Phillips, W.E.J., "Changes in the nitrate and nitrite content of fresh and processed spinach during storage", *J. Agric. Food Chem.* **16** (1968) pp. 88–91; Keating et al., 1973, *op. cit.*

104 Phillips, 1968, *op. cit.*

105 MAFF, 1987, *op. cit.*

106 Green et al., 1982, *op. cit.*; Simon et al., 1964, *op. cit.*

107 MAFF, 1987, *op. cit.*

108 Westin, D.T., "Nitrate and nitrite toxicity to salmonid fishes", *Prog. Fish. Cult.* **36** (1974) pp. 86–9; Trama, F.B., "The acute toxicity of some common salts of sodium, potassium and calcium to the common bluegill (*Lepomis macrochirus* Rafinesque)", *Proc. Acad. Nat. Sci., Philadelphia* **106** (1954) p. 185; Knepp, G.L. and Arkin, G.F., "Ammonia toxicity levels and nitrate tolerance of channel catfish", *The Prog. Fish Cult.* **35** (1973) p. 221.

109 Ridder, W.E. and Oehme, F.W., "Nitrates as an environmental, animal and human hazard", *Clinical Toxicol.* **7** (1974) pp. 145–59.

110 Ridder and Oehme, 1974, *op. cit.*; Emerick, R.J., "Consequences of high

nitrate levels in feed and water supplies", *Federation Proc.* **33** (1974) pp. 1183–7; Eppson, M.F., Glenn, M.W., Ellis, W.W. and Gilbert, C.S., "Nitrate in the diet of pregnant ewes", *J. Am. Vet. Med. Assoc.* **137** (1960) pp. 611–14; Wright, M.J. and Davison, K.L., "Nitrate accumulation in crops and nitrate poisoning in animals", *Adv. in Agronomy* **16** (1964) pp. 197–247.

111 Clarke, E.G.C. and Clarke, M.C., *Veterinary Toxicology* (London: Balliere Tindall, 1975); Eppson et al., 1960, *op. cit.*

112 Emerick, 1974, *op. cit.*; London, W.T., Henderson, W. and Cross, P. F., "An attempt to produce chronic nitrate toxicosis in swine", *J. Amer. Med. Assn* **150** (1967) pp. 398–402.

113 Mayo, N.S., *Kansas Agr. Expt. Station Bulletin* **49** (1895).

114 Wright and Davison, 1984, *op. cit.*

115 Hibbs, C.M., Stencel, E.L. and Hill, R.M., "Nitrate toxicosis in cattle", *Vet. & Human Toxicol.* **20** (1978) pp. 1–2.

116 Aldrich, S., "Perspectives on nitrogen in agriculture: food and production and environmental implications", paper presented at 1976 annual meeting of American Association for the Advancement of Science (1976); Kreitler, C.W. and Jones, D.C., "Natural soil nitrate: the cause of the nitrate contamination of groundwater in Runnels County, Texas", *Ground Water* **13** (1975) pp. 53–61.

117 ap Griffith, G. and Johnston, T.D., "The nitrate nitrogen content of herbage I", *J. Sci Food Agric.* **11** (1960) pp. 622–6; Wright and Davison, 1964, *op. cit.*

118 Kretschmer, A.E., *Agron. J.* **50** (1958) pp. 314–316.

119 Frank, P.A. and Grigsby, B.H., "Effects of herbicidal sprays on nitrate accumulation in certain weed species", *Weeds* **5** (1957) pp. 206–217; Willard, C.J., "Indirect effects of herbicides", Proc. North Cent. Weed Control Conf. (1950) pp. 110–12.

120 Stahler, L.M. and Whitehead, E.I., "The effect of 2,4-D on potassium nitrate levels in leaves of sugar beets", *Science* **112** (1950) pp. 709–51.

121 Case, A.A., "Some aspects of nitrate intoxication in livestock", *J. Am. Vet. Med. Assoc.* **130** (1957) p. 323; Muhrer, M.E., Garner, G.B., Pfander, W.H. and O'Dell B.L., "The effect of nitrates on reproduction and lactation", *J. Anim. Sci.* **15** (1956) p. 1291.

122 Davison, K.L., Hansel, W., McEntee, K. and Wright, M.J., "Reproduction, growth and lactation of heifers fed nitrate", *J. Anim. Sci.* **22** (1963) p. 835.

123 Case, 1957, *op. cit.*; Davison et al., 1963, *op. cit.*

124 Case, 1957, *op. cit.*

125 Eppson et al., 1960, *op. cit.*

126 Seerley, R.W., Emerick, R.J., Embry, L.B. and Olson, O.E., "Effect of nitrate or nitrite administered continously in drinking water for swine and sheep", *J. Anim. Sci* **24** (1965) pp. 1014–19; London et al., 1967, *op. cit.*

6 Farm Wastes

Farm wastes are the unwanted by-products of agricultural production. Since they are not removed in the final harvest they have to be left on the farm or disposed of elsewhere. Often the quantities are small and can be productively recycled but, under certain conditions, excessive amounts of waste are produced which can create serious environmental contamination. The most important categories of farm wastes are manures, slurries and gases from farm livestock, silage effluent and cereal straw, and the wastes arising from the on-farm processing of crops such as the oil palm.

Changes in farming patterns

Farm wastes have become a serious pollution problem as a direct consequence of an increasingly intensive and specialized agriculture. The traditional mixed farm is a closed system, generating few external impacts. Crop residues are fed to livestock or incorporated in the soil; manure is returned to the land in amounts that can be absorbed and utilized; trees bind the soil and provide valuable fodder and fuelwood. In this way the components of the farm are complementary in their functions. There is little distinction between products and by-products. Both flow from one component to another, only passing off the farm when the household decides they should be marketed (Figure 6.1).

But over the last half century, such highly integrated systems have largely disappeared, at least in the industrialized countries. Farms today are larger and fewer in number. In the USA the number of farms declined between 1945 and 1985 from 5.9 million to 2.2 million, while the total agricultural land remained constant at 138 million hectares.[1] In England and Wales the decline over the same period was from 363,000 to 184,000 while the total agricultural land has remained approximately at 19 million hectares.[2] Farms have also become more

Figure 6.1 Produce flow on a traditional mixed farm

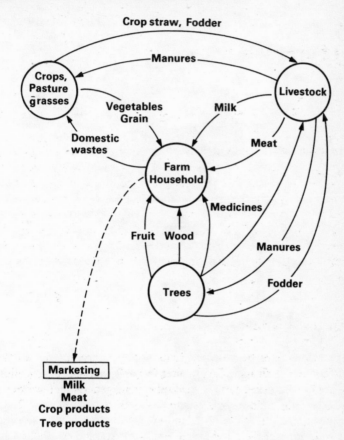

Note: This only depicts the flows of products and does not represent all interactions, for example, livestock for transport or ploughing; shading of crops by trees; nitrogen fixation by trees

specialized with crop and livestock enterprises separated. Livestock are often reared indoors on farms whose arable land is usually too small to provide sufficient useful uptake of the livestock wastes. Livestock enterprises have also become concentrated in well defined geographic regions, distant from the centre of arable cropping. In the UK, the east and south tends to be given over to cereal growing, while livestock predominate in the west and north (Figure 6.2). In the USA, cattle are heavily concentrated in four major areas, southern California and Arizona, the panhandles of Texas and Oklahoma, the central Corn Belt

Figure 6.2 Geographic specialization of agriculture in England and Wales

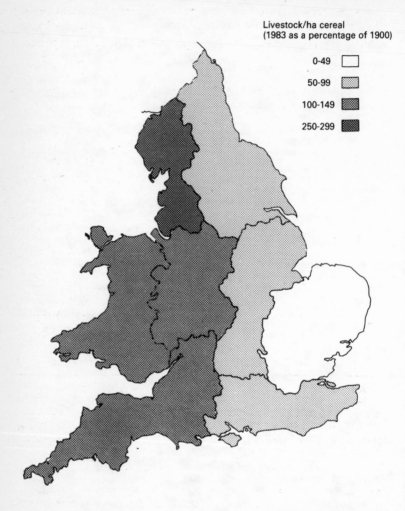

Livestock/ha cereal
(1983 as a percentage of 1900)

0-49	
50-99	
100-149	
250-299	

Source: Ministry of Agriculture, Fisheries and Food, *Agricultural Statistics* (London: HMSO, 1984 and 1900).

and an area from eastern Colorado through Nebraska to North Dakota. The changes are less marked in the developing countries, but stall-fed cattle and intensive pig and chicken raising are becoming common on the fringes of, and often deep inside, the rapidly growing urban centres.

This geographical specialization has been accompanied by the concentration of livestock into increasingly large herds (Table 6.1).

In the USA some 20 per cent of cattle are now raised in feedlots –
outdoor livestock farms that grow no crops. Cattle enter between the
ages of 7 and 12 months and are fed high-energy, purchased grain,
putting on some 200–350 kg in weight before slaughter a year later.[3]

Table 6.1 Indicators of the concentration of livestock into larger operations
and larger herds in both the USA and UK

	Proportion of all cattle sales in USA by source of operation	
	Small operations (<$100,000)	Large operations (>$500,000)
1969	64%	22%
1982	20%	62%

	Proportion of all pig sales in USA by source of operation	
	Small (<$100,000)	Large (>$100,000)
1969	88%	2%
1982	36%	18%

	Proportion of all pigs in UK by source of operation	
	Small herds (<200 pigs)	Large herds (>1000 pigs)
1981	12%	54%
1985	4%	63%

Source: Office of Technology Assessment, *Technology, Public Policy, and Changing
Structure of American Agriculture* (Washington DC: OTA, 1986); MAFF, *Annual Statistics*
(London: HMSO, 1981–5).

The economics of scale are so advantageous that feedlots have become
very large: of the 47,000 feedlots in the 13 states where cattle-raising is
most concentrated, just 75 feedlots have a total of 6.5 million cattle, an
average size of 87,000 animals each (Table 6.2). In the UK the average
size of British cattle herds increased by 25 per cent and pig herds by
50 per cent between 1978 and 1986.[4] These changes reflect a general
trend throughout farming: farm sizes have increased as the number
of holdings has declined. The amounts of manure produced are very
great and the arable land that could potentially use them is too far away.
For the farmer it is cheaper and easier to apply inorganic fertilizers on
the arable land and dispose of the livestock waste in other ways.

Table 6.2 Distribution of cattle in the 13 most cattle-populated states of the USA by feedlot operation size in 1989

	Feedlots less than 1000 head		Feedlots >1000 and <32,000 head		Feedlots >32,000 head	
	No. of lots	No. of cattle (1000s)	No. of lots	No. of cattle (1000s)	No. of lots	No. of cattle (1000s)
Arizona	7	15	5	112	3	214
California	9	4	38	393	8	553
Colorado	130	35	286	1180	9	1100
Idaho	45	14	58	603	–	–
Illinois	7850	491	50	129	–	–
Iowa	16250	1215	250	560	–	–
Kansas	1626	55	261	2811	13	1379
Minnesota	5945	435	55	90	–	–
Nebraska	8320	1240	475	3420	5	410
Oklahoma	223	20	23	365	4	380
South Dakota	4142	213	58	357	–	–
Texas	639	40	128	2245	33	2460
Washington	49	7	16	429	–	–
Total	45,235	3784	1703	12,695	75	6496

Source: National Agricultural Statistics Service, *Cattle on feed* (Washington DC: USDA, 1990).

Livestock wastes and slurry

Specialized livestock operations are a very potent source of pollution. The worst problems arise from the slurry systems of pig and dairy farms in the UK, and of beef-lots and veal and pig production units in the USA. In recent years, many of these have become essentially indoor systems. The livestock are housed in such a way that their faeces and urine fall through slatted floors into channels or pits from where they are periodically transferred into storage tanks or lagoons. The resulting nutrient load can be enormous: on the largest feedlots, with 900–2000 animals per hectare, assuming an average animal size of 450 kg, each excreting 0.17 kgN per day, the loading to each hectare is between 150–250 kg of nitrogen *per day*.[5]

The total national pollution load from livestock excretion is thus very large (Table 6.3). In the UK it is equivalent to 150 million people, about two and a half times the human population, while in the USA it is ten times greater, that is, equivalent to two billion people or 40 per cent of the world's population. As the Royal Commission on Environmental

Table 6.3 Total waste and nitrogen produced by confined livestock in the USA, 1978

	Total number (million)	Proportion confined (%)	Dry weight of wastes produced (million tonnes per year)	Total nitrogen produced (mt/yr)
Dairy cattle	19.8	65	17.9	0.71
Beef cattle	96.9	25	23.1	1.11
Pigs	57.6	80	5.5	0.34
Chickens and broilers	909.6	98	6.9	0.41
Turkeys and ducks	72.5	68	1.1	0.07
Horses, sheep and goats	21.0	18	6.3	0.11

Source: Fogg, C.E., "Confined livestock production: state-of-the-art", in: ASAE, *Livestock Waste: A Renewable Resource* (St Joseph, Michigan: American Society Agricultural Engineers, St Joseph, 1980).

Pollution put it "a modern farm of 40 hectares carrying a dairy herd of 50 cows and a pig population based on 50 sows has a potential pollution load equivalent to that of a village of 1000 inhabitants."[6] Large feedlots are comparable to small cities.

In the tanks or lagoons, the organic matter in the slurry undergoes anaerobic fermentation producing a number of gases – ammonia, hydrogen sulphide and the mercaptans and skatoles. These may be hazardous. Inside livestock housing they may become sufficiently concentrated to pose health threats to both farm workers and animals. Several of the gases also have particularly offensive odours that can be a nuisance to the public when they escape outside. And ammonia and methane are important pollutants of the atmosphere (see Chapter 7).

If the slurry is applied to land it may lead to excessive build-up of nutrients in the soil, or contaminate nearby watercourses. But even when properly applied, hazards may arise from micro-organisms such as *Salmonella* in the slurry or from metal salts originating in livestock feedstuffs (see Chapter 9 for full details).

Silage effluents

The practice of ensiling fodder is nearly as old as agriculture itself – whole crop cereals were ensiled in Egypt in 1000–1500 BC.[7] However, it did not become common until the last century and only in the last

20 years has silage replaced hay as a source of winter feed for livestock in Europe. When grass, maize or other fodder crops that are high in moisture content are left in the open they become rapidly degraded by aerobic bacteria. But if placed in a silo, in anaerobic conditions, the fodder instead undergoes fermentation to produce silage. This keeps well and is a highly valuable feed for livestock. With a good fermentation, the resulting silage has a nutritive value close to that of the fresh crop.[8]

In western Europe as a whole, the production of grass crop converted to silage has risen from 40 per cent to 57 per cent between 1975 and 1985.[9] In the UK the trend has been even steeper with production growing from about 9 million tonnes in 1970, to over 45 million tonnes in 1986 – some 70 per cent of total grass production[10] (Figure 6.3). There are several reasons for the rapid growth. Silage making is much less vulnerable to unpredictable weather conditions than is hay making,

Figure 6.3   Change in silage and hay production in the UK, 1970–86

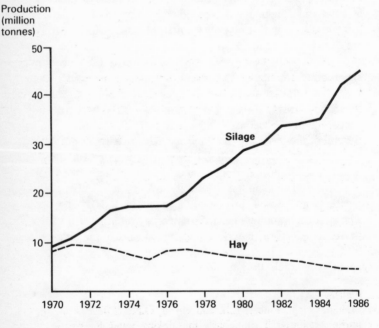

Source: Marks, H.F., *A Hundred Years of British Food and Farming* (London: Taylor and Francis, 1989), using data of MAFF, *Output and Utilisation of Farm Produce in the UK*(?).

which requires a spell of dry weather. Earlier cutting is also possible, allowing for quicker regrowth of grass and up to 2–3 cuts per year. Although in temperate regions the season for active grass growth is relatively short, there are surpluses over grazing needs in May and June, and in the early autumn, that can be cut and ensiled for winter feed. Silage is also a substitute for expensive feed concentrates, a benefit that is becoming increasingly important because of the recent enforcement of milk quotas in the European Community.[11]

In the USA, by contrast, the trend has been to increased hay and reduced silage production: the area of maize for silage fell from 3.3 million hectares in 1982 to 2.7 in 1989; hay acreage rose over the same period from 24 to 26 million hectares.[12]

Harvesting and storage

As good silage making depends on ensiling material with a high ratio of fermentable material to fibre, grass is harvested younger than for hay. Maize is also harvested earlier, when the grain is doughy and the leaves are just turning brown.[13] The crop is either directly carried to the silo, or cut and left in the field to wilt for a period. Generally a grass crop of 180–200 g dry matter (DM) per kg will wilt to 250 g DM/kg within 24 hours. Current recommendations are that the grass should be left to wilt for 24 hours after cutting, and at least for three to four hours.[14] However, under poor weather conditions this is frequently impossible and moreover, it is costly to take machinery twice to the same field. Often the silage crop has to be brought in, despite the high moisture content.

From the field the crop is taken to either a silage clamp or tower silo. A clamp is a three-walled bunker of rectangular shape, made of concrete, brick or even wood, which is filled from the open end and then sealed with plastic sheeting, weighted down with old tyres, bricks or timber. A tower silo is more elaborate. It is usually constructed of steel and concrete and is up to 20 metres in height and 5 metres diameter. Traditionally it was loaded by means of an elevator, requiring the manual distribution of material in the silo, but now blowers are more commonly used, so eliminating the need for farmworkers to go inside (Figure 6.4).

Once in the clamp or silo, and sealed from the air, the material undergoes fermentation, sometimes assisted by chemical additives. One of two types of fermentation can occur: lactic fermentation producing good quality silage, and clostridial or butyric fermentation resulting in a much poorer product.[15] For several hours after ensiling

Figure 6.4 Tower silo with top loader and unloader

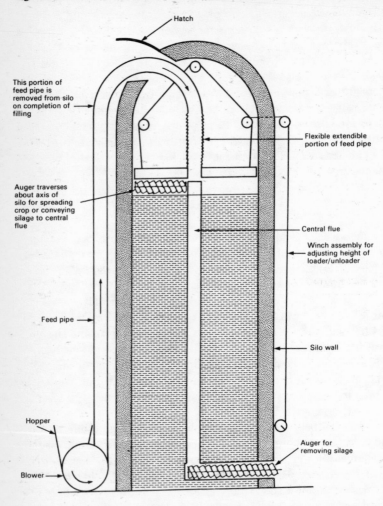

Source: Woolford, M.K., *The Silage Fermentation* (New York: Marcel Decker, 1984).

the crop continues to respire, using up all the available oxygen. Then bacteria multiply rapidly using sugars as a substrate, and producing lactic and acetic acids. This reduces the pH. However, if the dry matter (DM) content is low and too much moisture is present then clostridia bacteria may predominate, producing the weaker butyric acid and releasing carbon dioxide, so increasing the pH. This encourages the growth of bacteria that form amines, amides and ammonia and the silage is spoilt.

Production of effluents

Effluent begins to flow from the clamp or silo within 24 hours of ensiling, and can continue for several weeks. Much depends on the moisture content at the time of ensiling; effluent production is only insignificant when the DM is over 35 per cent (Table 6.4). Even at 15 per cent DM the total effluent produced will be 150–330 litres per tonne. The scale of effluent production is thus enormous: a farmer ensiling 700 tonnes at about 20 per cent DM has to contend with a peak effluent flow of 18,000 litres per day.

Table 6.4 Expected silage effluent production from ensiling grass in a clamp silo

Dry matter of grass (%)	Total effluent produced (litres/tonne of ensiled material)
35	0–10
25	10–110
20	60–220
15	150–330
10	400–500

Source: MAFF/ADAS, *Silage Effluent*, Farm Waste Management Booklet 2429 (Northumberland: MAFF, 1983).

This means that silage clamps and silos require large tanks to intercept the effluent before it escapes to contaminate nearby surface or groundwater. And since the tanks should have a capacity of at least one day's peak flow, a 1000 tonne silo with grass ensiled at 20 per cent DM, discharging 25 litres per tonne daily at the peak, needs to have an associated tank of at least 25 cubic metres. But in very wet years even this may be insufficient, and up to 40 cubic metres of storage may be necessary.

Silage effluent is very acidic, sometimes having a pH as low as 3.4. It can be very damaging to pastures and crops. In particular, some of the volatile fatty acids in the effluent of silage made from pea haulms will kill pasture grass and inhibit germination.[16] The effluent can also contain a number of hazardous substances. They include isoflavenoids and coumarin derivatives that behave like oestrogen hormones and thus can lower livestock fertility; nitrosamines, which are carcinogenic (see Chapter 5); residues of pesticides; microbial toxins; and ammonia and oxides of nitrogen.[17] These are mostly associated with poor quality silage, resulting from butyric fermentation. Nitrosamines, for instance, may be formed at a rate of 0.5 μg of N-nitrosamines per kg of silage but only when dry matter content is low.[18] The potential hazard is that dairy cattle feeding on silage may pass on these compounds in their milk.[19]

Health hazards from gases and dusts

The most serious hazards to human and animal health arise from the gases that are given off by stored manures or silage. Ammonia (NH_3) and hydrogen sulphide (H_2S) from manures frequently reach concentrations capable of inducing respiratory failure in humans and animals. For ammonia the recommended limit, set by the National Institute for Occupational Safety and Health (NIOSH) in the USA, is 50 ppm over a 5 minute period.[20] But even between 10 and 50 ppm headaches, nausea and dizziness may result; higher concentrations give rise to bronchitis, pulmonary oedema (lung tissue swollen with excess fluid), nausea and unconsciousness. At 500–1000 ppm, respiratory paralysis and death can occur. For hydrogen sulphide, the concentration ought not exceed 10 ppm in a 10 minute sampling period; at 50 ppm the danger is considerable and affected buildings have to be evacuated. H_2S has a characteristic odour of "rotten eggs" and can be readily detected at concentrations even as low as 0.2 ppm. However, at very high concentrations – 100 to 150 ppm – the sense of smell is completely inactivated and workers may unknowingly find themselves at risk.

Under normal conditions, gases from livestock waste are released slowly and adequate ventilation will usually ensure that toxic concentrations are quickly dispersed. But often ventilation is poor or the livestock density is too high for efficient dispersal. In swine units in Iowa it is common for one or more of the gases to exceed recommended limits at any given time, ammonia at 0–50 ppm in summer and 25–200 ppm in winter, while the H_2S concentration is at 0–10 ppm all year.[21] A further hazard is the displacement of oxygen, caused by a build-up of gases such as methane (CH_4) and carbon dioxide (CO_2). Methane is produced directly in the guts of ruminant livestock (see Chapter 7), and animals give off CO_2 during respiration. In one experiment, in an unventilated, enclosed space, pig respiration alone increased the CO_2 content to 15 per cent and depleted the oxygen to 10 per cent, in just eight hours.[22]

Nitrogen dioxide in silos

Gases are also produced during the process of silage fermentation, notably nitrogen dioxide (NO_2), nitric oxide (NO), carbon dioxide (CO_2), ammonia and various volatile organic acids. They are given off in a characteristic sequence: CO_2 concentrations rise first, accompanied by a fall in oxygen, and then followed by NO and NO_2, the latter rising to concentrations that may reach several thousand parts per million.[23] The highest concentrations are found close to the silage surface. In tower silos mixing of gases is often poor, resulting in very high concentrations in the part of the tower closest to the silage.

Nitrogen dioxide constitutes the greatest hazard to ourselves. Although the odour of NO_2 is perceptible at concentrations in air between 0.1–0.2 ppm, the sense of smell is lost when the concentration rises to 10–25 ppm. Moreover, the lack of immediate irritation of the upper respiratory tract allows workers to inhale NO_2 gas for some time without distress. Throat irritation does not occur until concentrations reach 60 ppm, and coughing not until 100 ppm. Nevertheless, before these levels are reached respiratory effects are occurring. Short-term exposure to 5 ppm NO_2 increases bronchial resistance and begins to impair lung function, while exposure to just 25–75 ppm for only an hour can induce pneumonia and bronchitis, although symptoms often do not appear until up to 30 hours after exposure. At higher concentrations, acute problems arise: 300–500 ppm NO_2 can cause rapid and fatal pulmonary oedema.[24] The adequate safety margin for workers is exposure for 15 minutes to a concentration of no more than 1 ppm NO_2.

Circumstances of accidents

There have been a number of deaths and other near-fatal incidents arising from exposure to toxic gases in the USA in recent years (Table 6.5). Wherever investigations were able to repeat the circumstances leading up to the deaths, the gas concentrations were found to exceed the limits set by the National Institute for Occupational Safety and Health (NIOSH). Most of the deaths appear to have occurred either during waste removal operations or when workers entered a slurry disposal tank to retrieve fallen objects or conduct maintenance. When wastes are moved from tanks to storage lagoons, or are prepared for land spreading, they usually have to be agitated to resuspend the semi-solid matter and prevent clogging of the pipes. This often requires workers to introduce a pump into the pit or tank, which

Table 6.5 Selection of accidents involving farm workers poisoned by gases arising from wastes on dairy and pig farms in various locations, USA

Site	Fatalities and illnesses	Circumstances	Gas and concentration
Iowa (1976)	1 fatality	Farmer attempting to unblock manure pipe during emptying operation collapsed	Assumed CH_4
Wisconsin (1977)	3 fatalities (1 farmer, 2 passing motorists)	Farmer entered recently emptied outdoor tank, collapsed; 2 successive rescuers also collapsed	Assumed CH_4
Wisconsin (1977)	1 fatality, 2 illnesses	16 year old farm worker cleaning inside building, 10 metres from a 500,000 litre tank undergoing agitation; collapsed after 10 minutes; 2 rescuers collapsed, recovered, escaped	Unknown
Iowa (1977)	1 fatality	4 year old boy entered slurry storage pit; found face down	Combination toxic gas and drowning
Iowa (1979)	2 short-term illnesses; 60 pig fatalities	Farmer's first attempt to empty slurry pit; pump activated to agitate wastes; pigs soon in respiratory distress; farmers entered building to investigate, came close to collapse	2 weeks later H_2S 3 ppm NH_3 3 ppm (agitation not repeated for fear of killing more pigs)
Iowa (1980)	1 short-term illness, 224 pig fatalities	Farmer's first attempt to empty new slurry storage tank; wastes agitated by pump; farmer returned after spreading first load on field; noticed peculiar odour, collapsed, escaped; pigs died; no ventilation in building	3 days later NH_3 50 ppm (agitation not repeated)

Table 6.5 Continued

Site	Fatalities and illnesses	Circumstances	Gas and concentration
Iowa (1980)	3 fatalities	Emptying slurry pit, but slurry too thick; 1000 litres of liquid added plus pump for agitation; son entered pit to unblock pipe, collapsed; father and other son each entered to rescue, but both collapsed	Agitation repeated: H_2S rose to 400 ppm (did not fall until after pump stopped); NH_3 and CH_4 not detected
Utah (1980)	3 fatalities, 2 illnesses	Cow kicked slurry storage tank lid into tank; father drained slurry to 45 cm, entered, collapsed; son entered to rescue, collapsed; town barber and sheriff arrived to help, former entered, collapsed; latter entered, collapsed; ambulance technician entered, collapsed too; barber and technician rescued and recovered	1 week later: CH_4 6360 ppm H_2S 76 ppm (estimated at time of accident to be 570 ppm)
1989*	2 fatalities	Farmer entered manure pit to clear obstruction from clogged pipe; overcome; brother entered pit, but also collapsed	Assumed CH_4
1989*	5 fatalities	Farmer entered pit to repair agitator shaft, overcome; each of 4 other victims entered one by one and were overcome; a tradesman working at the farm entered to attempt to rescue, overcome but rescued by an assistant; four victims died within an hour; one died six hours after removal	Assumed CH_4

Source: Donham, K.J., Knapp, L.W., Manson, R. and Gustafson, K., "Acute toxic exposure to gases from liquid manure", *J. Occup. Med.* **24** (1982) pp. 142–5; Morse, K.L., Woodbury, M.A., Rentmeester, K. and Farmer, D. "Death caused by fermenting manure", *J. Amer. Med. Assn.* **245** (1981) pp. 63–4; CDC, "Deaths associated with liquid manure systems' – United States", *MMWR* **30** (1981) pp. 151–7; Obsern, L.N. and Crapo, R.O., "Dung lung: a report of toxic exposure to liquid manure", *Annals of Internal Med.* **95** (1981) pp. 312–4; NIOSH, *Preventing Deaths of Farm Workers in Manure Pits* (Cincinatti: National Inst. for Occupational Safety and Health, US Dept. of Health and Human Services, 1990).
* Locations not recorded by NIOSH.

then circulates the wastes. It is a particulary hazardous operation. The circulation increases the contact of the wastes with the air, enhancing the volatilization of H_2S and NH_3. Resulting concentrations in the immediate vicinity can be very high.

Agitation of slurry containing just 2 mg/l of dissolved sulphides can generate nearby concentrations of 300 ppm of H_2S, and livestock wastes frequently contain sulphides at concentrations of 25 mg/l.[25] These concentrations usually do not last long, but are often sufficient to produce illness or death. Immediately after 3 deaths had occurred on an Iowa cattle farm in 1980, an investigation found ammonia at only 50 ppm but no signs of H_2S and methane. Yet one month later, when the circumstances of the deaths were reconstructed by agitating the liquid manure, the H_2S concentration rose very rapidly to 400 ppm. It did not fall until an hour after agitation had ceased.[26]

In the UK, as in the USA, asphyxiation incidents often occur while farm workers are carrying out cleaning operations in storage areas or are retrieving fallen tools. On one occasion two adults were asphyxiated in the same underground slurry reception tank which had become blocked; on another a worker died when he entered a slurry channel in a pig farrowing house.[27] Between 1981 and 1984, six farm workers died in this manner (see Table 3.12, p. 116). But the records of the Health and Safety Executive also reveal that drowning in slurry lagoons is an equally common hazard. Five of the seven deaths between 1982–84 were of children, usually in circumstances that appropriate fencing could have prevented.

The most dangerous situation in silos arises if the surface is concave, as NO_2 is heavier than air. At the edge of the tower, at head height, concentrations are likely to be low, creating a false sense of security but in the centre, at a height of about 30 cm above the surface, peak levels may be over 1000 ppm and as high as 4000 ppm NO_2.[28] Even good ventilation does not appear significantly to reduce the hazard. Farmworkers may have to enter silos to install or remove plastic sheeting, or for maintenance and repair of machinery, but, in practice, it is impossible to predict whether it is safe to enter or not.

The condition known as "silo-fillers disease" was reported first in the USA in 1914 when four farm workers died after entering a recently filled silo.[29] But the connection with NO_2 was not made until 1956, when several workers fell seriously ill with varying degrees of respiratory failure.[30] In one fatal case, reported in 1956, a young farmer was exposed when he climbed an enclosed ladderway to the top of his silo, which had been filled the previous day with maize. While climbing he noticed an irritating odour, accompanied by oppressive heat and humidity. Almost overcome, he was forced to climb down without accomplishing his intended task of opening the top door for ventilation. For two weeks he was affected by coughing and wheezing, listlessness, then shaking chills and fevers. The symptoms then increased alarmingly; he was admitted to hospital, but did not respond to treatment and died a month after the exposure to NO_2. All tissues in both lungs were found to have been severely damaged.

At least 65 cases of silo-fillers disease have been recorded in the USA up to 1978, though this may be a considerable underestimate.[31] A survey of more than 2000 Wisconsin farm operators revealed that 4.2 per cent had, at some time, developed symptoms of NO_2 induced pulmonary problems while working in or around freshly filled silos. In Wisconsin, alone, there are some 160,000 operators, suggesting that perhaps over 7000 may have been exposed to dangerous concentrations of NO_2.

In the UK, only fatalities are recorded. Between 1978–84 seven farmworkers were asphyxiated on farms in the UK after entering tower silos.[32] In one incident a worker entered an almost full silo of fresh silage. He was found asphyxiated; a second man entered the silo without venting the silo of gases, and also died.

Chronic health effects

While gases are the more important source of acute toxic incidents, dusts and other particular matter are the main cause of chronic health effects. Dusts that arise from manures may be fine enough to be taken into the lungs. They can contain high concentrations of protein, faecal matter, bacteria and fungi which cause irritation, infection and chronic lung disorders. It has long been known that farmers exposed, in grain silos and cotton ginning operations, to grain and cotton dust and to fungal spores, suffer from a variety of respiratory symptoms, ranging from chest tightness, bronchitis, coughing, wheezing, nasal and eye irritations, to obstructions of the lungs, pulmonary oedema and allergic reactions.[33] Today, livestock buildings have replaced silos and cotton ginning as the main source of these conditions.

One particular syndrome is hypersensitivity pneumonitis or farmers' lung – an extreme allergic reaction in which the lungs become hypersensitive to fungal spores and various protein-rich dusts. The symptoms are breathlessness, chills, fevers, cough and eventually long-term damage of the tissues.[34] Prevalence among farmers is high, varying between 200 and 8600 per 100,000 exposed population, and it is often a fatal condition.[35] In the UK, nine farm personnel died between 1981 and 1984 of farmers' lung. One fatality involved a worker becoming allergic to chicken faeces despite a "scrupulously clean poultry house and only spending 10 per cent of his time working in the building."[36]

The recent rapid growth in intensive livestock farming has meant an increasing number of farmers and farm workers are exposed, in livestock buildings, to a cocktail of gases, dusts, proteins from faecal matter, bacterial endotoxins, grain particles, pesticides, mites, insects and spores. In the USA there are thought to be a million such workers, half in the pig industry and the remainder involved in poultry, veal, beef or dairy operations.[37] A number of surveys suggest that at least 70 per cent of these workers suffer from chronic respiratory illnesses that include bronchitis, asthmatic attacks and episodes of farmers' lung.[38] For pig farmers the incidence of symptoms is significantly higher on farms where the pigs are kept inside (Table 6.6). Yet this practice is relatively young – the average exposure of Iowa workers sampled in 1984 was only 6 years. (Iowa has more than 14 million pigs, which is about a quarter of all pigs in the USA.) Compared with exposure times required for other occupational respiratory diseases, this is a very short time for symptoms to become manifest. Farm workers may also not be the only people affected. Veterinarians, for example, may develop various symptoms of chronic effects. Of 35 Iowa veterinarians spending, on average, 7 hours per week in pig-rearing buildings, 32 reported irritation, coughing, chest-tightness, excess phlegm and occasional nausea.[39]

Effects on livestock

High dust and gas concentrations may also harm or kill the livestock themselves. Several of the acute incidents recorded in Table 6.5 involved deaths or severe illness of livestock as well as farm workers. If ventilation is poor then dusts, and occasionally ammonia, are liable to exceed recommended standards.[40] This is particularly true for poultry in contact with their own wastes: dust levels in buildings where chickens are housed in wire cages are only 15–30 per cent of the levels that occur when chickens live on the floor.[41] Damping down the dust using water sprays results in a lower mortality.[42]

Confined livestock suffer, particularly, from chronic pneumonia caused by secondary bacterial infection acting on lungs that have been damaged by gases and dusts. Lung tissues in pigs can be disrupted by high concentrations of NH_3 (100 ppm), alone, or in combination with cereal dust.[43] At these concentrations NH_3 appears to have a direct impact upon growth of the pigs, although there is no effect at levels

Table 6.6 Comparison of chronic respiratory disease symptoms in 24 Iowa pig farmers working in confinement compared with 24 in non-confinement operations

	Confinement pig farmers	Non-confinement pig farmers
Subjects[†]		
Average age (years)	44.5	46.9
Time raising pigs (years)	24.7	20.3
Time with confinement buildings (years)	6.2	0
Symptoms*		
Chronic cough	33%	8%
Chronic phlegm	58%	21%
Chronic episodic cough with phlegm	29%	4%
Chronic wheezing, associated with cold	63%	29%
Frequent chest colds	46%	21%

[†] Individual pairs of farmers were matched according to age, sex, county of residence, smoking history and work history

* In all cases the difference in symptoms between the two groups of farmers was significant

Source: Donham, K.J., Zavala, D.C. and Merchant, J.A., "Respiratory symptoms and lung function among workers in swine confinement buildings: a cross-sectional epidemiological study", Arch. Environ. Health 39 (1984) pp. 96–101.

more commonly encountered (Table 6.7). Gases and dusts may also act synergistically: NH_3 at 50 ppm has no effect, alone, on pig growth, but when combined with 300 mg/m^3 of dust, the growth rate declines by 20 per cent.[44]

Bacterial contamination and antibiotics

A further hazard to livestock and farm workers arises from the high levels of bacteria commonly found in the atmosphere of livestock buildings.[45] Bacterial infections can pass readily from animal to animal in confined spaces, and to counter this the practice of routinely adding subtherapeutic levels of antibiotics to feed has become widespread. In the USA more than 75 per cent of all livestock have been fed antibiotics at some time in their lives. In 1985 4.5 million kg were used in agriculture, up from 0.2 in 1953, a level of consumption about the same, now, as for medicinal use in humans and animals.[46] The benefits are considerable: improved feed efficiency and growth rate, and a rapid check on diseases. Chickens, for instance, will gain weight as much as 10 per cent faster when fed antibiotics.[47]

Table 6.7   Impact of ammonia and dust upon the growth rate of pigs

	Ammonia concentration (ppm)	Dust concentration (mg/m³)	Average daily weight gain (kg/pig)
Experiments without dust			
	12	–	0.81
	61	–	0.79
	103	–	0.68†
Experiments with dust			
(i)	0	0	0.48
	50	0	0.50
	50	10	0.49
(ii)	0	0	0.52
	50	300	0.42*

† Impossible to calculate significance from available data
* Difference from control would arise by chance in less than 1 in 10 occasions

Sources: Stombaugh, D.P., Teague, H.S. and Roller, W.L., "Effects of atmospheric ammonia on pigs", *J. Anim. Sci.* **28** (1969) pp. 844–7; Curtis, S.E., Drummond, J.G., Grunloh, D.J., Lynch, P.B. and Jensen, A.H., "Relative and qualitative aspects of aerial bacteria and dust in swine houses", *J. Anim. Sci.* **41** (1975) pp. 1512–20.

But there are concerns that the routine use of antibiotics on livestock increases the incidence of resistant strains of bacteria and thus presents a hazard to those consuming meat and other livestock products. Livestock are, already, a major source of resistant salmonellae although, as yet, there are few documented incidents of transmission of resistant strains to human beings. In one case, 18 people in four midwestern states of the USA, who were infected with salmonella resistant to ampicillin, carbenicillin and tetracycline antibiotics, were found to have received the infection from beef hamburgers made from a cattle herd in South Dakota. The cattle had been fed subtherapeutic amounts of the antibiotic chlortetracycline.[48] Regulations have been proposed to stop the use on livestock of antibiotics that are commonly administered to human beings, such as penicillin and tetracycline, but this move is strongly opposed by livestock producers and antibiotic manufacturers.[49] In the UK antibiotics are only permitted for the treatment of sick animals.

The odour nuisance

The smell of farmyard manure is almost as old as farming itself. It is normally not perceived as offensive, but the odours arising from modern, intensive livestock operations are far removed from the traditional "good country smell".[50] The problem is primarily created by the storage of slurry. As it decomposes anaerobically it gives off a variety of compounds – over 77 in pig slurry – that have characteristically strong odours. They include volatile fatty acids, organic acids, phenols and organosulphide compounds – mercaptans and skatoles.[51] Emissions increase during storage, but once the slurry is spread on land it gradually oxidizes and the smell disappears.[52] The problem can be avoided by preventing anaerobic decomposition, for instance by spreading the slurry within one or two days of its production. Unfortunately, this is rarely practicable; farmers usually have to store wastes for some time before they can be spread.

As might be expected, odour complaints are most frequent when livestock or poultry production units are close to housing or shopping areas.[53] This may not necessarily be the fault of the farmer. In one recently documented case in Yorkshire, in the UK, a city council permitted housing development to within 20 metres of a pig farm.[54] The sloping grassland between the farm and houses was used to dispose of slurry and, on occasions, poor management permitted the slurry to run down the slope and into the gardens. Since 1982, Local Authority Environmental Health Officers (EHOs) in the UK have been recording the numbers of complaints the public have made about odours from livestock operations and each year 4–5000 people feel that a particular odour is sufficient of a nuisance to take the trouble to contact their local EHO (Table 6.8).

The majority of complaints concern odours from slurry and over half are related to pig raising operations. Once a complaint is recieved the EHO visits the site to decide whether the complaint is "justifiable". As no objective measure of odour exists, a subjective distinction such as this is felt necessary to screen out those complaints made by people who may be over-sensitive.[53] About a quarter to a third of all complaints are thought to be justified.

Surface water pollution

Slurry or silage effluent may contaminate surface waters either through accidental discharge from overfilled or defective tanks and lagoons, or through surface run-off following application to land. Run-off is especially pronounced when the land is sloping, waterlogged or frozen. Application to cracked dry soils carries the danger of direct

Table 6.8   Public complaints made to Environmental Health Officers over odours resulting from livestock operations in the UK

	Complaints*			
	1986–7		1987–8	
Source of complaints	Total	Proportion justifiable	Total	Proportion justifiable
Livestock housing	1559	21%	986	31%
Slurry stores and lagoons	1702	18%	780	39%
Slurry spreading	1602	32%	1405	40%
Animal feed preparation, especially swill boiling	356	22%	457	33%
Silage clamps	155	37%	118	70%
Total complaints	5374	24%	3746	37%

* Between 1982–6 the annual total of justifiable complaints varied between 1900 and 2400, which compares with 1300 and 1400 for 1986–7 and 1987–8

Source: IEHO, *Environmental Health Reports* (London: Institution of Environmental Health Officers, 1982–7); Mr J. Alexander, Institution of Environmental Health Officers, personal communication, 13 June 1990.

discharge into land drains or groundwater-bearing strata. In the case of silage effluent, because of its very low pH, it has to be spread carefully on farmland and needs to be diluted to avoid scorching of crops.

Pollution occurs because the slurry or silage effluent is rich in nutrients and organic matter. The nutrients encourage algal growth (see Chapter 4), while the organic matter is a source of food for bacteria. As the material is broken down, so the bacteria use up oxygen in the water and hence the strength of the pollutant is most appropriately measured by the biological oxygen demand (BOD) – the amount of oxygen removed by a given quantity of pollutant. The BOD of slurry or silage effluent is of the order of 10,000–80,000 mg/l and the bacterial breakdown may so deplete the oxygen content of waters that fish and other aquatic life die. These values for BOD are some 200 times greater than for domestic sewage and far higher than the general standard for treated sewage effluent (20 mg/l).

Dairies and fish farms

Dairying also presents a hazard because of the hypochlorite-based solutions used to sterilize milking parlours. If discharged to rivers these can significantly increase the chlorine content. Milk, itself, can also be a problem since it has a BOD of 120,000 mg/l. Dairy farmers sometimes have to dispose of excess milk, either because of overproduction during concentrated calving periods or because milk is contaminated by antibiotics after treatment for infections such as mastitis.

Fish farms contaminate watercourses through the disposal of unconsumed fish feed or of fish faecal wastes.[56] These have a high BOD and high nitrogen and phosphorus concentrations, and hence are liable to lead to eutrophication. The problem is particularly severe in the Jutland region of Denmark where trout farms are responsible for 30–35 per cent of the total organic matter load to freshwater – equivalent to the sewage load from a population of over half a million people.

Pollution incidents in surface waters

Pollution of watercourses is rapidly increasing in the industrialized countries, largely as a result of deliberate or accidental discharge of farm wastes (Box 6.1). In England and Wales the annual number of pollution incidents recorded by the water authorities more than doubled during the 1980s (Figure 6.5). Today, they comprise about 20 per cent of all water pollution incidents recorded by water authorities in England and Wales.[57] Most occur in the west and north of the country and 80 per cent derive from dairy or beef farms.

A number of factors have contributed to this steady rise.[58] The increases in intensive livestock farming and herd size have tended to occur without attendant improvements in collection, storage and disposal facilities. This has meant that many slurry storage lagoons have too small a capacity for the number of animals and many structures have been poorly designed or constructed to inadequate standards. Lagoons and tanks tend to age quickly due to the corrosive nature of the wastes. Many farms also lack the facilities to separate rainwater from yard washings and slurry lagoons, so that high rainfall often causes slurry stores and lagoons to overflow. Although heavy rainfall will also increase river flow and so dilute the pollution caused by farm wastes, its effect is usually minimal. Another factor is the decline in the practice of wilting grass before ensiling. This is partly because of the availability of chemical additives which enhance production of good quality silage from wet grass, and partly because advice in the farming press is often against wilting, in spite of evidence that wet material still leads to poor quality silage.[59] A final factor is the relatively low levels of fines on farmers prosecuted for causing pollution. In the UK

Box 6.1 Selection of accidental and intentional discharges of livestock wastes and silage effluent to watercourses in Britain

1985 Trent Mersey canal
Five years of recurring fish mortality was eventually traced to a slurry lagoon fitted with a valve that allowed a steady removal of top water. Discharges were made for 1–2 hours at six monthly intervals. The source of this type of pollution is very difficult to trace.

1985 Thames Region
Silage liquor entered a river causing fish mortality and closure of water treatment and supply works for three days. Farmer prosecuted.

1986 Wales
Wall of concrete slurry lagoon collapsed, releasing 1.25 million litres of slurry causing fish mortality. Contractor successfully prosecuted; accident was not farmer's fault.

1986 West Avon River, Cheshire
Large volume of slurry discharged to river killed trout and all other fish. Damaged limited by reoxygenation of river and removal of tanker loads of polluted water. The costs of remedial measures were more than £6000.

1987 Welshpool
Silage effluent entered drinking water supply reservoir, completely deoxygenating 40 million litres of water. Reoxygenation was required to restore aerobic conditions and prevent health hazard.

1987 River Alne, Northumberland
Slurry discharged from a holding tank, killed 4000 trout in a 10 km stretch of river. The incident was caused by a bull escaping from its enclosure and pushing past an operating lever that opened a drain valve on the storage tank.

1987 Tributary of River Exe
Spillage of 230,000 litres of slurry into river through partially opened valve. Discharged for many hours, killing fish and forcing closure of intake for city of Exeter's drinking water.

1987 Wessex region
Pig slurry contaminated a private water supply from a spring. The farm worker was instructed to dispose of slurry on a certain field; unable to negotiate entry to a field, he emptied two tanker loads into a ditch. The slurry flowed along the ditch and entered the spring source 200 metres distant.

1987 Yorkshire
Long history of silage effluent draining from one farm to river. Several previous prosecutions of farmer. 1987 prosecution, with £500 fine, resulted from pollution of 18 km of river and death of 20,000 fish.

1989 River Sapiston, Suffolk
13 million litres of pig effluent poured into river through breach in wall of slurry lagoon. Polluted 65 km of river, killing some 10,000 fish. Farmer fined £10,000, costs £38,000. Prosecuted in Crown Court, where higher fines can be set. Farmer had four previous convictions.

Sources: WAA, *Water Pollution from Farm Waste Surveys for 1985–1987* (London: Water Authorities Association, 1986–8); NRA, in *Farmers Weekly* 22 December (1989) p. 9.

Figure 6.5 Growth in number of pollution incidents of water courses in England and Wales arising from silage effluents, slurry stores and farmyard washings. The "other" category includes pollution from land run-off, treatment systems failure, sheep dip pesticides, vegetable washings and oil spillages

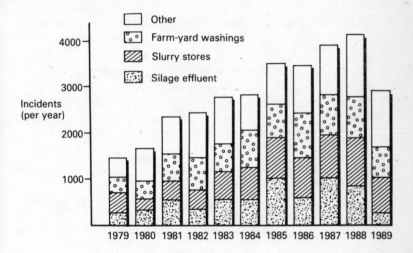

Source: National Rivers Authority, *Water Pollution from Farm Waste, 1989* (London: NRA, 1990); Water Authorities Association, *Water Pollution from Farm Waste, Surveys for 1985–1988* (London: WAA, 1986–9); MAFF Farm Waste Unit, London.

these have been of the order of £50–400 for first offences, although water authorities are increasingly willing to prosecute farmers for causing polluting incidents – between 1979 and the end of the 1980s the annual number of prosecutions rose from 38 to between 150 and 200.

to year variation, largely caused by variable rainfall. In the UK the summer of 1985 was cool and wet, leading to a large increase in incidents due to silage effluent and slurry run-off (see Figure 6.5). In the same year a long cold spring meant that animals were kept inside for longer than usual, causing overloading of many slurry stores, which then overflowed in the heavy summer rains. But even in a normal summer, if heavy rain happens to fall when slurry stores are full or during silage making, this can cause acute problems, as in 1987. The year of 1989 was notable for the smallest number of incidents for five years – it was also very hot and dry, and so farmers were able to let silage wilt with confidence.

The official figures may well be underestimates. Several local surveys suggest that farm waste disposal to watercourses in the UK is commonplace. For instance, in a dairy-specializing region of southwest Scotland, large numbers of farmers were found to be disposing of manurial liquids, silage effluents and washwater from farm yards and parlours, directly into watercourses (Table 6.9).[60]

Table 6.9 Disposal by farmers of wastes from dairying operations in southwest Scotland*

	Washwater from yards, dairies and parlours	Manure liquids	Silage effluent
Direct to watercourse	48%	34%	5%
To sedimentation tank, then to watercourse	21%	29%	4%
To slurry store	22%	9%	52%
To tank, then spread on land	4%	9%	28%
Natural seepage, soakaway	5%	19%	11%

* The survey sampled 155 farms, approximately one in ten of all in the region

Source: Brownlie, T.G. and Henderson, W.C., "A survey of waste management on dairy farms in southwest Scotland", *Agric. Wastes* **9** (1984) pp. 267–78.

The reason was the long delay between the time when slurry was mostly produced and when it could be applied to land. Conditions are optimal for spreading slurry during March–September, but it is between October and December that most slurry is produced (Figure 6.6). For five months of the year there is, therefore, an excess of production over application, yet average slurry storage capacity on the farms was only three months. Nine farms had no storage facilities at all, and a further 25 had only four weeks, capacity.

In another survey, the North West Water Authority visited all farms in four catchments in Cheshire, Cumbria and Lancashire in 1987. Despite advanced warning of visits, about 40–50 per cent of the farms were found to be causing pollution or likely to do so if no changes to facilities were made.[61] Similarly, when in 1990 the Severn Trent Water Authority surveyed 1000 dairy farms in the Midlands they found only a third were entirely satisfactory in their farm waste disposal arrangements.[62] Clearly, farm waste pollution is widespread and not only attributable to a minority of farmers.

Figure 6.6 Seasonal production of slurry and application to land on dairy farms in southwest Scotland

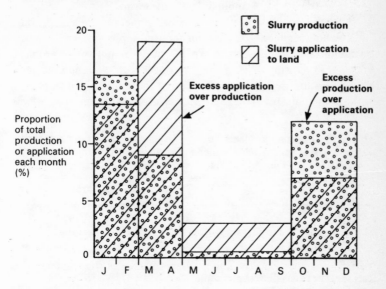

Source: Brownlie, T.G. and Henderson, W.C., "A survey of waste management on dairy farms in southwest Scotland", *Agric. Wastes* **9** (1984) pp. 267–278.

Catchment pollution

The overall effects of farm waste on watercourses are well illustrated by two catchments in the UK, one in the east of the country and one in the southwest. Both catchments are suffering from declining fish populations because of livestock waste pollution.

The Waveney Catchment, East Anglia[63]

This catchment, of 670 km², lies in the counties of Norfolk and Suffolk where the soils and climate are ideal for cereal growing. Since the turn of the century, the area planted to cereals has increased by about 35 per cent, mostly at the expense of grassland. The number of sheep in the two counties has fallen to only 150,000, although cattle have remained constant, at about 220,000.[64] None of these changes would suggest the possibility of serious pollution problems from livestock waste. However, the region has also become a centre for intensive pig farming, largely because of the local availability of cereals for feed and proximity to the coast for low-cost imported concentrate feeds.

The two counties have a population of over one million pigs producing, daily, 5–14 million litres of waste (5 million litres is based on the assumption of dry feeding alone and 14 million on a liquid feeding regime).[65] The catchment itself supports nearly a quarter of a million pigs and effluents from pig farms are now a serious problem. (Figure 6.7). During 1984–5 there were 60 acute pollution incidents reported for the river Waveney, a third of these due to effluents from pig farms (Table 6.10). The impact is measurable in terms of the

Table 6.10　Pollution incidents for the Waveney catchment in East Anglia, UK during 1984–5 and number of monitoring sites exceeding the 95 percentile value in 1984 of 1.5 mg NH_3-N/litre

	Incidents (1984 and 1985)
Pig effluent	19
Other farms wastes (slurries, yard washings, silage effluent)	20
Sewage treatment works and other organic sources	21
Number of sites exceeding 95 percentile	23
Total monitoring sites	30

* The 95 percentile value is the concentration which is exceeded for 5 per cent of the time

Source: Anglian Water Authority, *A study of the water quality and habitat features of the Rivers Waveney, Bure and Gipping fisheries*, Report No. ND/SR/I/86 (Norwich: Anglian Water, 1986).

ammonia concentrations in the river at its tidal limit near Lowestoft. These increased steadily from 0.08 mg NH_3-N/l in 1965 to 0.28 in 1985. The ammonia concentration is closely correlated to the density of pigs in the area drained by each tributary of the river (Figure 6.8). The greatest increase in pig numbers, from 250 to 640/km² between 1964 and 1984, occurred around Chickering Beck, and the two monitoring stations in this tributary also recorded the catchment's highest 95 percentile values for ammonia, 24 and 30 mg NH_3-N/l respectively.

The consequence of this pollution has been a dramatic decline in the productivity of the fishery. In 1978–81 the average fish biomass in the river was 18.4 g/m²; by 1985 it had declined to just 7.5 g/m². Fish have suffered from the lack of oxygen due to the high BOD of the effluents and from direct toxicity of the ammonium ions. An ammonia level of 1.5 mg NH_3-N/l as a 95 percentile value is the water quality guideline

Figure 6.7 Location of the Waveney Catchment in East Anglia, density of pigs by subcatchment and ammonia concentrations in watercourses

Source: Anglian Water Authority, *A survey of water quality and habitat features of the Rivers Waveney, Bure and Gipping fisheries* (Norwich: Anglian Warer, 1986)

Figure 6.8   Relationship between ammonia concentration and density of pigs in the Waveney catchment, 1984

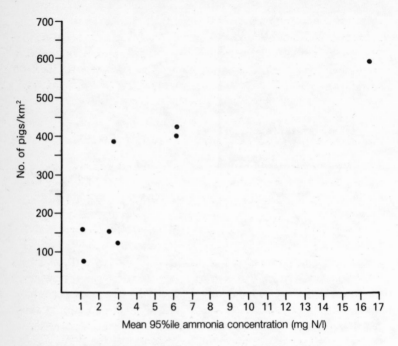

Source: Anglian Water Authority, 1986, *op.cit.*

set by the Anglian Water Authority for support of a fishery dominated by roach, bream, pike and perch, and this has been exceeded in many parts of the catchment. The toxicity to fish, though, depends upon the balance in water between the free or un-ionized ammonia (NH_3) and the ammonium ions (NH_4^+) and this balance is dependent on pH: as alkalinity increases, so more of the highly toxic NH_4^+ is produced. In some of the tributaries, concentrations of ammonia are at times toxic to adult roach: in May 1984 in Starston Beck, of the total ammonia concentration of 8 mg/l, 0.46 mg was un-ionized and the site was fishless during 1985. This level compares with a LC_{50} value for roach of 0.35 mg NH_3-N/l.[66] In the main river, although concentrations are not acutely toxic to adult fish, it seems likely that they are having an effect on the more susceptible young fish. Between 1981 and 1985 the proportion of the roach population younger than two years declined from 57 per cent to 39 per cent.

In addition to the decline in fish the abundance and richness of aquatic vertebrates has also fallen. The riverbed fauna became dominated by oligochaete worms, a good indicator of polluted conditions. A biotic index, based on the presence or absence of species of varying sensitivity to organic pollution, shows a significant relationship with ammonia concentration in the catchment.

Starting in 1986 the Anglian Water Authority mounted a campaign involving farm visits, increased publicity and prosecutions of the worst offenders.[67] As a result farmers have taken measures to improve their disposal operations and, since the beginning of 1987, ammonia concentrations in the catchment have been falling steadily.

The Torridge Catchment, southwest England[68]

This part of England, in contrast to East Anglia, is mainly a livestock region, based on pasture and rough grazing. One of the major catchments is the Torridge which covers an area of about 850 km² in northwest Devon. It, too, has undergone some significant changes in its agriculture. Since 1952, cattle numbers have increased by 85 per cent to 84,000 and sheep by 70 per cent to 140,000. The area under permanent grassland has increased by 67 per cent, to about 43,000 hectares, much of it fertilized, and the rough grazing has been improved by drainage, ploughing and reseeding. About five per cent of the total area was drained between 1971 and 1984 though, in some parishes, it was as much as 15 per cent. There has also been a dramatic increase in silage production – up threefold during the 1970s – at the expense of hay and feed concentrates, together with a greater use of winter housing. Silage now supplies some 75 per cent of winter forage.

The Torridge catchment is famous for its salmon, yet in recent years there have been steep declines in both salmon and sea trout catches and frequent reports of river foam, water colour changes, and algal blooms.[69] Initially, the decline in fish populations was thought to be a result of overfishing, but it seems more likely the result of a combination of factors. First, some of the soils contain salts of metallic suphides, which can be oxidized to release sulphuric acid. During the first extensive rainfall after dry weather this can lead to acid surges. Fish mortalities have been associated with such surges in 1976, 1978, 1983 and 1984. Second, drought conditions have become increasingly common; for example in 1984 the Torridge fell to less than 50 per cent of its 95 percentile flow. Such low flows allow a build up of nutrients, producing eutrophic conditions which threaten the survival of salmonid fish. The third factor is the increased clearance of riverbank vegetation and removal of trash dams, which act as spawning and nursery sites for fish. This results in longer periods of low flow and shorter periods of fast flow, both of which are also detrimental to salmonid fish. Fourth, is the increased inputs of nutrients from livestock wastes.

Which of these factors is most critical is not known. But the rapidly growing pollution load in the catchment is certainly having an effect. The BOD loading of the cattle in the catchment is equivalent to that of nearly 600,000 people; in contrast the actual human population served by the catchment's sewage treatment works is only 15,000. Of the reported pollution incidents since 1980, those originating from farms have shown the greatest increase (Table 6.11). Incidents have been caused by overfilled or defective storage lagoons and tanks, surface run-off or drainage after application of wastes to land, and leaking effluents from silage clamps. And a number of the incidents have been associated with serious fish kills: one in 1983, caused by liquid wastes from two farms, led to the deaths of many thousands of fish.

Table 6.11 Reported pollution incidents in the River Torridge catchment in the UK, 1980–5

| | | Sources of pollution | | | |
	Farms	Sewage treatment works	Trade pemises	Others[†]	Total
1980*	13	1	2	9	25
1981	22	7	13	18	60
1982	17	3	21	18	59
1983	68	8	28	25	139
1984	45	14	24	47	130
1985	63	4	14	29	110

* May–December only
† Includes storm overflows, tips, vehicle accidents, oil and other untraceable events

Source: South West Water Authority, *Environmental Investigation of the River Torridge* (?: South West Water, Dept. of Environmental Services, 1986).

As in the Waveney catchment the recorded incidents of livestock waste pollution are but the tip of the iceberg. A programme of on-farm inspection conducted by South West Water Authority in 1985 found that 25 per cent of farms were causing serious pollution, and a further 25 per cent were posing a high risk if heavy rainfall should occur. By the third visit none were still actively polluting, but since the campaign only visited 2,000 out of the 35,000 farms of the catchment it seemed likely that at least 7500 farms were still causing pollution by 1986.

Well and groundwater pollution

In addition to run-off and spillages to rivers, farm wastes can contaminate domestic wells and groundwater. However, the amounts of nitrate leached from applied manure or slurry are generally less than those from nitrogen fertilizer, and in total, livestock wastes are a less important cause of contamination compared with fertilizer applications to intensive arable agriculture (see Chapter 4). Nevertheless, in certain localities they can create serious problems. For instance slurry from intensive pig rearing can lead to raised groundwater nitrate concentrations, especially when units are sited on chalk, characterized by rapid fissure flow. In one site in Yorkshire, in the UK, applications of 150 m^3/ha of slurry per year, mostly outside the growing season, produced a nitrate concentration as high as 620 mg/l below the plant root depth, compared to the background concentrations of 25–35 mg/l, and moving downwards at about a metre a year.[70] Copper concentrations of up to six times the background level were also found throughout the 30 metres depth of the profile.

Local groundwater pollution from livestock wastes is particularly serious in parts of the USA. In Lancaster County of Pennsylvania, for instance, manure is applied at 100 tonnes/ha, supplying more nutrients than is required by the predominant maize crop, and the farmers add to this more than 100 kg/ha of inorganic nitrogen. Many of the wells in the county now exceed nitrate standards for drinking water.[71] In Sussex County, Delaware, high nitrate levels in drinking water wells result from the proximity to livestock farms, and in particular broiler farms (Table 6.12). It is estimated that the 140 million chickens in Delaware produce more solid waste each year than the entire city

Table 6.12 Contamination of wells by nitrate at four different types of location in Sussex County, Delaware, USA

Location of wells	Number of wells sampled	Average concentration of nitrate (mg/l)	Proportion of wells with concentration greater than 45 mg/l (%)
Farms	153	41.2	35
Municipal	568	30.3	19
Camp grounds	74	22.1	10
Woodland	20	12.8	5

Source: Robertson, F.N., "Evaluation of nitrate in groundwater in the Delaware coastal plain", *Ground Water* **17** (1979) pp. 328–37.

of New York.[72] Nitrate levels in wells closer than 150 metres to broiler farms are some 70 mg/l.[73] Similarly in Kansas, shallow wells closer than 50 metres to a beef feedlot contained concentrations up to 110 mg/l.[74] In California, beneath the dairy farm area of the Chino Basin, nitrate concentrations average 200 mg/l, although they fall in the deep aquifer to about 27 mg/l.[75] Often overflows or seepage from slurry lagoons is the principal cause of the problem. Groundwater in Virginia beneath old lagoons is highly contaminated with nitrate (up to 300–400 mg/l), though concentrations fall with increasing distance from the lagoon.[76] Contamination is often particularly severe with new slurry lagoons before they become fully sealed. On the Delamarva peninsula, Delaware, the number of pig slurry lagoons doubled in the decade up to 1984, and the nitrate concentrations in nearby wells increased rapidly after initial loading of each new lagoon, some reaching 35–40 mg/l, before eventually declining.[77] Similarly, nitrate concentrations in groundwater under newly constructed dairy slurry lagoons in Tennessee, increased to 90 mg/l over a period of 3–6 months, although they then declined as the lagoon began to self-seal.[78]

Because of the high density of animals in feedlots, pollution of the groundwater beneath is especially severe. In the South Platte valley of Colorado the total nitrogen beneath feedlots, to a depth of about seven metres, was found to be some three times greater than under irrigated crops, 5–6 times more than under dryland crops and 18 times more than under native grassland.[79] Nevertheless, the irrigation of fertilized crops remained the most serious contaminator of ground water because of the much greater land area involved. Despite the high levels of contamination caused by feedlots, it remains a relatively localized problem.

Livestock wastes are also an important source of phosphorus. As is clear from Table 4.14 (Chapter 4), phosphate loadings of watercourses derive as much from livestock waste as from arable agriculture. Spreading of manures or slurries or intensive stocking of animals often leads to phosphorus levels greater than the crop requires. In the UK the stocking rate for pigs at which waste is in balance with crop requirements is 10 animals/hectare, yet 75 per cent of all pig farms exceed this rate and 30 per cent of farms contain 50 or more pigs per hectare. Some wastes are disposed of to other farms, but there are still excess loadings to land on pig farms.

Phosphorus normally is resistant to leaching, being strongly bound to soil particles. But in the Netherlands a phosphorus front was recently found moving down through the soil beneath a farm carrying

80 pigs/ha.[80] It was estimated that the annual loading of 200 kg P/ha/year could contaminate the aquifer within 20 years.

Water pollution in developing countries

In Chapter 4 we showed that much of the nitrate pollution in developing countries arises from animal and human waste, rather than fertilizer. Contamination by livestock arises in a number of different ways. First, drinking wells attract large numbers of cattle. This is particularly true of semi-arid localities.[81] Excreta are deposited in the vicinity of the wells, so that during the rains the nitrate is readily leached to the groundwater. Often drinking troughs are placed close to domestic wells and in the state of Harayana, India, nitrate concentrations in such wells commonly exceed 500 mg/l and have reached 1900 mg/l.

Second, some developing countries are adopting intensive livestock rearing practices similar to those of the industrialized countries. In Mexico an increasing proportion of the 18 million pig population is being reared in confinement, with consequent growing problems of odour and waste disposal.[82] Pig farms are also causing nitrate pollution in Taiwan, and large quantities of waste have been generated in Kuwait by the poultry industry.[83]

Third, particularly acute problems are being caused by the livestock wastes generated by farms in urban areas. Cities such as Hong Kong and Singapore are characterized by limited land area, rapid urbanization, and a considerable increase in livestock production, in particular of pigs and poultry, to satisfy growing urban demand.[84] In Hong Kong, the numbers of pigs had increased to nearly half a million by 1977 together with 5.7 million poultry. In Singapore in 1979 there were 1.25 million pigs and 32 million poultry. Many of the rivers in the cities are heavily polluted and livestock wastes are a major contributing factor. Of the 400 km of rivers in Hong Kong, some 16 per cent in the 1970s were classified, according to bacteriological criteria, as grossly polluted and 24 per cent as polluted. The problem is particularly acute in the streams of the New Territories of Hong Kong where agricultural wastes contribute more than 67 per cent of the total pollutant load and estimates suggest that some 80 per cent of pig excreta escapes directly into streams without treatment[85] (Table 6.13). In Singapore pollution from wastes became so important that in 1975 one thousand hectares of the island were especially demarcated for large scale pig rearing and farmers relocated there from more sensitive areas.[86]

Table 6.13 Sources of pollutant load entering New Territories' streams, Hong Kong

Source	Contribution
Effluents from pig farms	54%
Solid wastes from poultry farms	13%
Domestic sewage, night soil and refuse	11%
Industrial effluents and wastes	22%

Source: Binnie and Partners (Hong Kong), *The New Territories Stream Pollution Study* (Hong Kong: Government Report for the Director of Public Works, 1973).

Micro-organisms in livestock waste

Besides its high BOD and nutrient content, livestock waste may contain micro-organisms harmful to other animals and to ourselves. Since animals may carry pathogenic bacteria and viruses without necessarily showing any symptoms, the hazard may be underestimated. In the UK a series of surveys carried out in the 1970s found that 20 out of 187 samples of cattle slurry, 12 out of 98 of pig slurry and 27 out of 64 of poultry manure, yielded salmonella on culture.[87] In Taiwan, a survey of pig farms found all wastes to be heavily contaminated with bacteria, in particular faecal coliforms and streptococci. Bacterial counts were more than 10^6 per 100 ml and as high as 10^9 in some cases.[88]

Foot-and-mouth disease, turberculosis and brucellosis can be easily spread by slurry application and, in the UK, the practice is banned in areas affected by these diseases. Government guidelines require that slurry be stored for at least four weeks and that a further four weeks should elapse between spreading on the land and grazing.[89] But the survival of pathogens in excreta varies considerably, and some organisms can survive this period (Table 6.14; see also Table 9.16). Survival is affected by the amount of organic material on which the bacteria can multiply, on temperature and sunlight, moisture, pH and availability of oxygen. The hazard may be greater in tropical and subtropical climates because of the rapid bacterial multiplication at high temperatures.

The hazard is also present in the run-off of wastes from intensive grazing on pastures.[90] When cattle were introduced to the rangelands and floodplain pastures in Idaho and Colorado, faecal bacterial contamination rapidly increased and only declined after the removal of the animals. However, total faecal coliform counts rarely exceeded 1000/100 ml and were typically around 100/100 ml,

Table 6.14   Survival of livestock pathogens in slurry and after spreading on land

Pathogen	Survival times (days)	
	In slurry	After spreading on pasture
Salmonella spp.	85–230	<30
Mycobacteria (tuberculosis and Johne's disease)	150–330	<30
Brucella	<30	<14
Leptospira	<3	<3
Listeria	NR[1]	<12
E. coli, Pseudomonas spp. and Klebsiella spp. (mastitis producing organisms)	<80	<10
Bacillus anthracis	many months	up to 40 years
Roundworms, tapeworms, liverfluke	many months	many months
Viruses	<100	<20

[1] No data for *Listeria* in slurry, but has survived in excreta for 500 days

Source: Williams, B.M., "The survival of pathogens in slurry and the animal health risks from disposal to land", *ADAS Quart. Rev.* **32** (1979) pp. 59–68.

much lower than those derived from spreading of wastes. Several studies of water quality in high-mountain watersheds in the USA have also revealed high bacterial concentrations in areas closed to both humans and agricultural livestock. It appears that the source of contamination is the large populations of game animals, including moose, elk and deer.[91] One group at risk from such contamination is people engaged in water-based recreation, and in the State of Ontario, Canada, recreational facilities at several reservoirs have had to be closed for this reason.[92]

The risk from pathogens may also be high in the intensive home gardens common in SE Asia. These highly integrated farming systems utilize the wastes of pigs, ducks, poultry, cattle or rabbits as a source of nutrients for crops and for raising fish and aquatic plants in small ponds.[93] Bacteria, viruses, amoebae and helminth parasites can all be transferred in this way to consumers of the fish or water-plants. Bacteria and viruses may survive for considerable periods in water, and fish cultured in excreta-laden ponds carry the pathogens passively in the gut, gills and on the skin. Some human pathogens, such as *Vibrio* spp. and *Salmonella* spp., are able to multiply in fish, and in Japan and the Philippines such infections have been clearly related to the use of untreated livestock manures.[94] The greatest risk is to fish-handlers, preparers of food and those who consume raw or inadequately cooked fish. Helminth parasites are also spread by the use of untreated livestock manures – once again the risk is to consumers of raw or inadequately cooked fish and water-plants, but also to field workers (Table 6.15).

Table 6.15   Cases and routes of infection of humans by helminth parasites following the use of livestock manures in aquaculture systems

Location	Infective helminth	Route of infection
Thailand	Opisthorcis viverrini (liver fluke)	Consumption of raw or inadequately cooked tilapia fish cultivated in excreta-laden water
Philippines	Echinostoma ilocanum (Garrison's fluke)	Consumption of raw or inadequately cooked freshwater snails
Philippines	Schistosoma spp. (Schistosomiasis)	Direct infection of aquaculture and rice-field workers following use of wastes from domestic animals
Southeast Asia	Schistosoma spp. (Schistosomiasis)	Consumption of giant Malaysian prawn, a predator of snails that are intermediate hosts
Asia	Fasciola hepatica (liver fluke) Fasciolepsis bushi (giant intestinal fluke)	Consumption of uncooked water plants, such as water chestnut or water spinach, that have intermediate stages of the parasite on surfaces

Source: Naegel, L.C.A., "A review of public health problems associated with the integration of animal husbandry and aquaculture, with emphasis on Southeast Asia", Biol. Wastes 31 (1990) pp. 69–83.

In addition to contamination from manures and grazing animals there can be a hazard present in the residues from the anaerobic digestion of wastes. The temperatures reached in digesters used for the commercial production of methane gas are usually not sufficiently high to inactivate many viruses. Bovine parvovirus, bovine enterovirus and porcine enterovirus all survive at temperatures below 50°C.[95] For instance, anaerobic digestion of pig wastes on a farm in Canada, where temperatures did not exceed 50°C, only partially reduced porcine viral infectivity. Re-feeding of residues to livestock can thus cause further spread of the pathogens.

Metals in slurry

To the list of potential contaminants of slurry must be added heavy metals derived from the additives used in pig feeds. Copper (Cu) is added to feed, at up to 250 ppm, to accelerate growth by increasing food conversion rates. Zinc (Zn) is added for the same purpose and to counteract the toxicity which might be caused by high copper concentrations.[96] But in each case, only 5–15 per cent of the metal additive is absorbed by the pig and the remainder is excreted.

Application of pig manure high in Cu and Zn can lead to accumulations of the metals in topsoil and parts of crops.[97] There is very little risk to animals from grazing on the herbage, but since they also consume significant quantities of soil while grazing (see Chapter 9) – for cattle from 1–10 pr cent of total dry matter intake and for sheep up to 30 per cent – high soil concentrations can be toxic, particularly if slurry is directly consumed.[98]

There is, also, a potential hazard to humans if pig slurry is applied to vegetables, as is common in countries such as Hong Kong. Accumulation is particularly high in carrots and other root crops. But the metal content of domestic sewage is usually higher than that of livestock slurry, and it represents a much greater hazard (see Chapter 9). Experiments in Hong Kong have shown that application of chicken and pig manures to vegetables produces fewer problems than sewage sludges and also gives better plant growth.[99] Vegetables accumulated the most Cu, lead (Pb), Zn and manganese (Mn) when treated with activated sewage sludge; least accumulation resulted from chicken manure and pig manure applications.

The hazard is increased if the slurry is stored for long periods before application, since the loss of moisture and decomposition of organic matter increases the concentrations of metals. However, the amounts of slurry which have to be applied to a pasture to reach levels of Cu toxic to both plants and animals are unlikely to be reached before quantities of N and P far in excess of requirements are added.[100] No serious effects resulting from application of pig wastes have been reported in the UK, though caution needs to be observed with grazing sheep because of their particular susceptibility to copper toxicity (see Chapter 9).

Processing wastes from plantation crops

A very significant source of wastes in developing countries are farms growing such tropical plantation crops as oil palm, rubber and sugar cane. The products are usually processed in mills and small factories situated on the plantation; all produce large amounts of liquid wastes that contaminate surface waters.

Palm oil and rubber in Malaysia

Malaysia is the world's largest producer of palm oil and also a significant rubber producer. It has some 180 palm oil mills, serving 750,000 hectares of plantation, and 250 rubber factories for a further two million hectares.[101] For the production of palm oil, fruit bunches are brought to the mill, sterilized and crushed hot in a continuous press. This produces 200 kg of oil for every tonne of fruit, plus a further 500 kg of solid waste and 300 kg of liquid sludge. In the production of rubber a number of washing, coagulating and acid treatment processes produce large quantities of liquid effluent.

In the country as a whole these mills and factories produce an enormous amount of waste: daily 80–100 million litres from the rubber industry and 7–10 million litres from palm oil production.[102] The levels of nitrogen compounds in the effluents are high but, because of the high organic content, it is the BOD and chemical oxygen demand (COD) that are most significant. The BOD from these two agro-industries is equivalent to the waste produced by a human

Table 6.16   The quality of typical effluents produced by palm oil and rubber mills in Malaysia

	Palm oil effluent[†]	Rubber effluent[*]
pH	3.5–4.5	3.5–6.0
BOD (mg/l)	25000	1500
COD (mg/l)	45000	3000
Ammoniacal nitrogen (mg/l)	30	100
Other nitrogen (mg/l)	800	160
Total solids (mg/l)	35000	1500
Suspended solids (mg/l)	25000	900
Oil and grease (mg/l)	8300	–

[†] Palm oil effluent also contains ash, starch and protein
[*] Rubber effluent also contains sulphuric and formic acid, uncoagulated latex and various proteins and carbohydrates

Source: John, C.K., "Treatment of agro-industrial wastes using water hyacinth", Wat. Sci. Tech. **17** (1985) pp. 781–90; Kirkaldy, J.L.R., "Treatment of oil palm sludge", in: Consumers Association of Penang, Development and the Environment Crisis, Proceedings of the 1978 Symposium on the Malaysian Environment in Crisis (Malaysia: Consumers Association of Penang, 1982); Sinnappa, S., "Treatment studies of palm oil mill waste effluent", in: Lohani, B.N. and Thani, N.C. (eds), Water Pollution Control in Developing Countries vol. II (Bangkok: AIT, 1978).

population of 37 million – more than twice the actual population of Malaysia (Table 6.16).

Impact on the environment

Because palm oil mills and rubber factories are so widespread – in small holdings and estates on almost 70 per cent of the country's cultivated lands – the impact on the environment of these wastes is also very extensive. By the mid-1970s, 42 of Malaysia's rivers were grossly polluted with no aquatic life and a further 16 were moderately polluted.[103] As effluents enter streams and rivers the impact is marked. Sinnappa described palm oil effluent entering a stream in Peninsular Malaysia as follows:

> The water in the stream is crystal clear until the entry point of the waste effluent. Thereafter, the colour turns muddy brown and a distinct foul odour is produced. Upstream ... the stream contains water weeds growing in abundance, but none of these were observed even up to a distance of 0.8 km ... No fish were observed downstream.[104]

The effluents increase the temperature, remove oxygen and make the stream more acidic (Table 6.17). Palm oil processing and discharge of effluents continues throughout the year; during the dry season there is greater likelihood of damage because river flows are low.

Table 6.17 Impact of palm oil mill effluent on a stream in Peninsular Malaysia

	Temperature of effluent or water (°C)	pH	BOD (mg/l)	COD (mg/l)	Total solids (mg/l)
Effluent					
As entered stream	37	4.5	11600	27000	17000
River					
Upstream of entry point	29	6.1	4	30	180
8 metres downstream	34	4.7	1000	3300	2000
800 metres downstream	29	4.7	800	1300	800

Source: Sinappa, S., 1978, *op. cit.*

Most effluents are discharged with little or no active treatment, although lagoon systems and ditches can greatly reduce the BOD and COD, and allow for sedimentation of some of the solids. They are frequently simple and inexpensive to construct, but have several disadvantages: they require a large area of land, which has to come from the productive farm or estate land currently planted to trees; they do not remove all the contaminants and they are a potent breeding ground for mosquitoes.[105] Alternative forms of treatment include anaerobic digestion for recycling of wastes as a source of feed for fish and livestock, and the use of water hyacinth (*Eichhornia crassipes*) to purify water (see Chapter 11).

Summary

Farm wastes have become an increasingly serious source of pollution following the demise of the traditional mixed farm. In the industrialized countries, farms are now larger and more specialized. Livestock and arable production tend to be geographically divorced from one another. Highly intensive beef-lots and pig and dairy farms produce pollutions loads equivalent to that of the domestic sewage of small cities. The switch from hay to silage production in Europe has also added considerably to the problem of farm waste disposal. Silage effluents are equivalent to slurry in biological oxygen demand, with values 200 times that of domestic sewage.

The most serious hazards to humans arise from the gases given off by slurry and silage. Hydrogen sulphide and ammonia occur in high concentrations, particularly during the removal or agitation of slurry and can cause the death of operators. Similarly, nitrogen dioxide build-up in silos can be lethal, and many silo workers suffer from serious pulmonary problems. The number of fatalities is low, about one a year in the USA and in the UK but, at least in the UK, higher than that caused by pesticides on the farm. Chronic respiratory illnesses, such as farmers' lung, can be caused by dusts and fungal spores arising from livestock wastes. In the USA as many as 70 per cent of the half million exposed workforce suffer from such illnesses. Livestock may also be affected.

Another potential health hazard arises from the administration of subtherapeutic dosages of antibiotics to livestock. In the USA more than 75 per cent of all livestock have been fed antibiotics at some time in their life. The risk lies in the transmission of antibiotic resistant micro-organisms to humans; in one documented case resistant salmonella infected people who had fed on hamburgers derived from antibiotic treated cattle. Finally, the odour from livestock wastes, and especially slurries, although not a health hazard, causes considerable nuisance.

Farm wastes are an increasing cause of water pollution incidents in industrialized countries. The most serious usually arise from accidental discharge caused by failure of holding tanks or spillover from tanks due to heavy rainfall. Wet years also increase the water content of silage, and result in large quantities of silage effluent. Immediate damage, including fish kills, can occur, but regular low level discharges and application of slurry of silage effluent to land will also result in long-term declines in aquatic life, especially fish populations. In the USA there are many instances of serious local contamination of wells and groundwater from livestock effluent, particularly in the vicinity of feedlots and dairy farms. This is also true in developing countries, particularly in semi-arid areas where cattle congregate around wells.

Finally, hazards from livestock waste may arise from the presence of bacteria and metals. Diseases such as foot and mouth, tuberculosis and brucellosis can be spread in slurry, and pig viruses can be recycled in the pig population through residues derived from anaerobic digesters using pig waste. Copper and zinc fed as additives may also contaminate pig wastes, although the overall hazard to treated crops is much less than from domestic sewage.

Apart from pollution arising from livestock wastes, there are problems associated, particularly in tropical countries, with the on-farm processing of plantation crops such as oil palm and rubber. The amounts of effluent produced are enormous – in Malaysia the equivalent in BOD to double that produced by the human population. Discharge of the wastes is highly detrimental to nearby surface waters.

References

1   USDA, *Economic Indicators of the Farm Sector: National Financial Summary, 1986*, ECIFS 6–2 Econ. Res. Service. (Washington DC: US Dept. of Agriculture, 1987).

2   Marks, H.F., *A Hundred Years of British Food and Farming* (London: Taylor & Francis, 1989).

3   NRC, *Alternative Agriculture* (Washington DC: National Research Council, 1989).

4   WAA, *Water Pollution from Farm Waste, 1987* (London: Water Authorities Association, 1988).

5   NRC, *Ammonia* (Washington DC: National Research Council, 1979).

6 RCEP, *Agriculture and Pollution*, Royal Commission on Environmental Pollution, 7th Report, Cmnd 7644 (London: HMSO, 1979).

7 Woolford, M.K., *The Silage Fermentation* (New York: Marcel Decker, 1984).

8 Woolford, 1984, *op. cit.*

9 ENDS, "UK lags in control of silage effluent", **152** (1987) p. 6.

10 Marks, 1989, *op. cit.*

11 WAA, *Water Pollution from Farm Waste, 1985* (London: Water Authorities Association, 1986).

12 USDA, *Crop Production Final Estimates* (Washington: National Agricultural Statistics Service, USDA, 1982–1990).

13 Woolford, 1984, *op. cit.*

14 MAFF/ADAS, *Silage Effluent*, Farm Waste Management Booklet 2429 (Northumberland: MAFF Publications, 1983).

15 Woolford, 1984, *op. cit.*

16 Clarke, E.G.C. and Humphries, D.J., "Toxic factors in pea haulm silage effluent: the factor affecting germination and growth in plants", *J. Sci. Food Agric.* **21** (1970) pp. 225–7.

17 Woolford, 1984, *op. cit.*

18 van Broekhaven, "Formation of volatile N-nitrosamines during the fermentation of grass silages", in: Prins, W.H. and Arnold, G.H. (eds), *The Role of Nitrogen in Intensive Grassland Production*, Proc. Internat. Symp. Europ. Grassl. Fed, Wageningen (Wageningen: Pudoc, 1980).

19 Juskiewicz, T. and Kowalski, B., "Passage of nitrosamines from rumen into milk in goats", in: Bogarski, P. and Walker, E.A. (eds), *N-nitroso Compounds in the Environment* (Lyon: IARC, 1974).

20 CDC, "Occupational fatality following exposure to hydrogen sulphide – Nebraska" *MMWR* **35** (1986) pp. 533–5.

21 Donham, K.J., Rubino, M., Thedell, T.D. and Kammermeyer, J., "Potential health hazards to agricultural workers in swine confirmation buildings", *J. Occup. Med.* **19** (1977) pp. 383–7.

22 Meuhling, A.J. "Swine housing and waste management: a research review", in: *Cooperative Extension Service* (Urbana: University of Illinois, 1969) pp. 65–78.

23 Commins, B.T., Raveney, F.J. and Jesson, M.W. "Toxic gases in tower silos", *Ann. Occupat. Hyg.* **14** (1971) pp. 275–83; Horvath, E.P., do Pico, G.A. Barbee, R.A. and Dickie, H.A., "Nitrogen dioxide induced pulmonary disease", *J. Occup. Med.* **20** (1978) pp. 103–110.

24 WHO, *Recommended Health-based Occupational Exposure Limits for Respiratory Irritants*, Report of a WHO Study Group, Technical Report Series no. 707 (Geneva: WHO, 1984).

25 Donham, K.J., Knapp, L.W., Monson, R. and Gustafson, K., "Acute toxic exposure to gases from liquid manure", *J. Occup. Med.* **24** (1982) pp. 142–5.

26 Donham et al., 1982, *Ibid.*

27 Health and Safety Executive, *Agricultural Black Spot, A Study of Fatal*

Accidents (London: HMSO, 1986).

28 Horvath et al., *op. cit.*; Commins et al., 1971, *op. cit.*

29 Hayhurst, E.R. and Scott, E., "Four cases of sudden death in a silo", *J. Amer. Med. Assn.* **63** (1914) pp. 1570–72.

30 Lowry, T. and Schuman, L.M., "Silo-fillers' disease: a syndrome caused by nitrogen dioxide", *J. Amer. Med. Assn.* **162** (1956) pp. 153–160; Grayson, R.R., "Silage gas poisoning: nitrogen dioxide pneumonia, a new disease in agricultural workers", *Ann. Internal. Med.* **43** (1956) pp. 393–408.

31 Horvath et al., 1978, *op. cit.*

32 Health and Safety Executive, 1986, *op. cit.*

33 Dosman, J.A., Graham, B.L., Hall, D., Loon, P.V., Bhasin, P. and Froh, F., "Respiratory symptoms and pulmonary function in farmers" *J. occup. Med.* **29** (1987) pp. 38–43; Popendorf, W., Donham, K.J., Easton, D.N. and Silk, J., "A synopsis of agricultural respiratory hazards", *Am. Ind. Hyg. Assoc. J.* **46** (1985) pp. 154–161.

34 do Pico, G.A., "Occupational Lung Disease in the Rural Environment", in: Gee, J.B.L. (ed.), *Occupational Lung Disease* (New York: Churchill Livingstone, 1984); Holt, P.F., *Inhaled Dust and Disease* (Chichester: J.Wiley and Sons, 1984); Crofton, J. and Douglas, A., *Respiratory Diseases*, 2nd edn (Oxford: Blackwells, 1975).

35 Popendorf et al., 1985, *op. cit.*

36 Health and Safety Executive, 1986, *op. cit.*

37 Donham, K.J., Zavala, D.C. and Merchant, J.A., "Respiratory symptoms and lung function among workers in swine confinement buildings: a cross-sectional epidemiological study", *Arch. Environ. Health* **39** (1984) pp. 96–101.

38 Donham et al., 1984, *op. cit.*; 1982, *op. cit.*; 1977, *op. cit.*

39 Donham et al., 1977, *op. cit.*

40 Jones, W., Morring, K., Olenchock, S.A., Williams, T. and Hickey, J., "Environmental study of poultry confinement buildings", *Am. Ind. Hyg. Assoc. J.* **45** (1984) pp. 760–66.

41 Clark, S., Rylander, R. and Larson, L., "Airborne bacteria, endotoxin and fungi in dust in poultry and swine confinement buildings", *Am. Ind. Hyg. Assoc. J.* **44** (1983) pp. 537–41.

42 Cravens, R.L., Beaulieu, H. and Buchan, R., "Characterisation of the aerosol in turkey rearing confinements", *Am. Ind. Hyg. Assoc. J.* **42** (1981) pp. 315–18.

43 Doig, P.A. and Willoughby, R.A., "Response of swine to atmospheric ammonia and organic dust", *J. Amer. Med. Assn.* **159** (1971) pp. 1353.

44 Curtis, S.E., Anderson, C.R., Simon, J., Jensen, A.H., Day, D.L. and Kelley, K.W., "Effects of aerial ammonia, hydrogen sulphide and swine-house dust on rate of gain and respiratory-tract structure in swine", *J. Anim. Sci.* **41** (1975) pp. 735–9; Stombaugh, D.P., Teague, H.S. and Proller, W.L., "Effects of atmospheric ammonia on pigs", *J. Anim. Sci.* **28** (1969) pp. 844–7.

45 Clark, et al., 1983, *op. cit.*; Curtis, S.E., Drummond, J.G., Grunloh, D.J., Lynch, P.B. and Jensen, A.H., "Relative and qualitative aspects of aerial bacteria and dust in swine houses", *J Anim. Sci.* **41** (1975) pp. 1512–20.

46 Institute of Medicine, *Human Health Risks with the Subtherapeutic Use of Pencillin or Tetracyclines in Animal Feed* (Washington DC: National Academy Press, 1989); NRC, 1989, *op. cit.*

47 Dafwang, I.I., Bird, H.R. and Sunde, M.L., "Broiler chick growth response to antibiotics, 1981–82" *Poultry Science* **63** (1984) pp. 1027–1032.

48 Holmberg, S.D., Osterholm, M.T., Senger, K.A. and Cohen, M.L., "Drug-resistant salmonella from animals fed antimicrobials", *New Eng. J. Med.* **311** (1984) pp. 617–22; Budiasky, S., "Jumping the smoking gun", *Nature* **311** (1984) p. 407; Levy, S.B., "Antibiotics in animals", *Nature* **313** (1985) p. 344.

49 Hays, V.W., Batson, D. and Gerrits, R., "Public health implications of the use of antibiotics in animal agriculture: Preface", *J. Anim. Sci.* **62** suppl. 3 (1986) pp. 1–4.

50 RCEP, 1979, *op. cit.*

51 Miner, J.R., "Controlling odours from livestock production facilities: state-of-the-art", in: ASAE, *Livestock Waste: A Renewable Resource* (St. Joseph, Michigan: ASAE, 1980).

52 Williams, A.G. and Evans, M.R., "Storage of piggery slurry", *Agric. Wastes* **3** (1981) pp. 311–21.

53 Miner, 1980, *op. cit.*

54 WAA, 1988, *op. cit.*

55 Mr J. Alexander, Institution of Environmental Health Officers, personal communication, 13 June 1990.

56 WAA, 1988, *op. cit.*; Willett, I.R. and Jakobsen, P., "Fertiliser properties of trout farm waste", *Agric. Wastes* **17** (1986) pp. 7–13; Warrer-Hansen, I., "Fish farms are having to watch their waste", *Fish Farming Int.* **5** (1978) p. 19.

57 WAA, *Water Pollution from Farm Waste, Surveys for 1985–1988* (London: Water Authorities Association, 1986–9); NRA, *Water Pollution from Farm Waste 1989* (London: National Rivers Authority, 1990).

58 WAA, 1986–9, *op. cit.*; NRA, 1990, *op. cit.*

59 WAA, 1986, *op. cit.*

60 Brownlie, T.G. and Henderson, W.C., "A survey of waste management on dairy farms in south-west Scotland", *Agric. Wastes* **9** (1984) pp. 267–78.

61 WAA, 1988, *op. cit.*

62 *Farmers Weekly* (London), April 1990, *passim.*

63 (principal source) Anglian Water Authority, *A study of the water quality and habitat features of the rivers Waveney, Bure and Gipping fisheries*, Report No. ND/SR/1/86 (Norwich: Anglian Water, 1990).

64 MAFF, *Annual Statistics* (London: HMSO, 1990); MAFF, *Annual Statistics* (London: HMSO, 1984).

65 RCEP, 1979, *op. cit.*

66 Solbe J.F. de L.G., Cooper, V.A., Willes, C.A. and Mallet, M.J., "Effects of pollutants in freshwaters on European non-salmonid fish 1: Non-metals", *J. Fish Biol.* **27** suppl. A (1985) pp. 197–207.

67 WAA, 1988, *op. cit.*

68 (principal source) South West Water Authority, *Environmental Investigation of the River Torridge* (South West Water, Dept. of Environmental Services, 1986).

69 SWWA, 1986, *op. cit.*

70 Joseph, J.B., "The effects of applying pig slurry to land over an unconfined aquifer", in: *International Conference of Groundwater and Man, Sydney, 1983*, vol. 2: Groundwater and Environment (Canberra: Australian Government Publ. Service, 1983).

71 Young, C.E., Crowder, B.M., Shortle, J.S. and Alwang, J.R., "Nutrient management on dairy farms in southeastern Pennsylvania", *J. Soil. Wat. Conserv.* Sept–Oct (1985) pp. 443–5.

72 Conservation Foundation, *Groundwater Protection* (Washington DC: Conservation Foundation, 1987).

73 Robertson, F.N., "Evaluation of nitrate in groundwater in the Delaware coastal plain", *Ground Water* **17** (1979) pp. 328–37.

74 Terry, R.V., Powers, W.L., Olsen, R.V., Murphy, L.S. and Rubison, R.M., "The effect of beef feedlot runoff on the nitrate-nitrogen content of a shallow aquifer", *J. Environ. Qual.* **10** (1981) pp. 22–6.

75 Ayers, R.S., "A case study – nitrates in the upper Santa Ana river basin in relation to groundwater pollution", in: Pratt, P.F. (ed.), *Nat. Conf. on Manage. of Nitrogen in Irrigated Agriculture* (Univ. of California, Dept Soil & Environ. Sciences, 1978).

76 Ciravolo, T.G., Martens, D.C., Hallock, D.L., Collins, E.R., Jr, Kornegay, E.T. and Thomas, H.R., "Pollutant movement to shallow groundwater tables from anaerobic swine waste lagoons", *J. Environ. Qual.* **8** (1979) pp. 126–30.

77 Ritter, W.E., Walpole, E.W. and Eastburn, R.P., "Effect of an anaerobic swine lagoon on groundwater quality in Sussex Country, Delaware", *Agric. Wastes* **10** (1984) pp. 267–84.

78 Sewell, J.I., "Dairy lagoon effects on groundwater quality", *Trans. ASAE* **21** (1978) pp. 948–52.

79 Stewart, B.A., Viets, F.G., Hutchinson, G.L. and Kemper, W.D., "Nitrate and other water pollutants under fields and feedlots", *Environ. Sci. Technol.* **1** (1967) pp. 736–9.

80 ENDS, "Piggery waste may spark new conflict between agriculture and environment", **146** (1987) p. 8.

81 Akiti, in: Young, C.P., "Data acquisition and evaluation of groundwater pollution by nitrates, pesticides and disease-producing bacteria", *Environ. Geol.* **5** (1983) pp. 11–18; Heaton, T.H.E., "Sources of the nitrate in phreatic groundwater in the western Kalahari", *J. of Hydrology* **67** (1984) pp. 249–59; Heaton, T.H.E., Talma, A.S. and Vogel, J.C., "Origin and

history of nitrate in confined groundwater in the western Kalahari", *J. of Hydrology* **62** (1983) pp. 243–62; Kakar, Y.P., "Nitrate pollution of groundwater in southern and south-western Haryana, India", in: Van Duijvenboorden, W., Glasbergen, P. and van Lelyveld, H. (eds), *Quality of Groundwater*, Studies in Environmental Science No.17 (Netherlands: Elsevier Sci Publ. Co., 1981).

82 Iniguez-Covarrubias, G., Franco-Gomez Ma De, J., Pena-Romero, M. and Ciurlizza-Guizar, A., "Evaluation of the protein quality of solids removed from hog manure slurry", *Agric. Wastes* **16** (1986) pp. 113–120.

83 Chung, K.T., Tseng, H.C., Lai, Y.F. and Sung, H.H., "Microbiological, physical and chemical studies of livestock-farm water in Taiwan", *Agric. Wastes* **14** (1985) pp. 1–18; Ilian, M.A. and Salman, A.J., "Feeding processed hatchery wastes to poultry", *Agric. Wastes* **15** (1986) pp. 179–86.

84 Wong, M.H., "Agricultural wastes and freshwater supply in Hong Kong", *Prog. Water Tech.* **11** (1979) pp. 121–3; Pescod, M.B., "Agricultural wastes in urban areas", in: Chan, M.W.H., Hoare, R.W.M., Holmes, P.R., Land, R.J.S. and Reed, S.B. (eds), *Pollution in the Urban Environment* (Amsterdam: Elsevier, 1979).

85 Wong, 1979, *op. cit.*

86 Taiganides, E.P., Chou, K.C. and Lee, B.Y., "Animal wastes management and utilisation in Singapore", *Agric. Wastes* **1** (1979) pp. 129–41; Pescod, 1985, *op. cit.*

87 Jones, P.W. and Matthews, R.R.J., "Examination of slurry from cattle for pathogenic bacteria", *J. of Hyg. Camb.* **74** (1975) pp. 57–64; Jones, P.W., Bew, J. and Burrows, M.R., "The occurence of salmonellas, microbacteria and pathogenic strains of *E. coli* in pig slurry", *J. of Hyg. Camb.* **77** (1976) p. 43.

88 Chung, et al., 1985, *op. cit.*

89 Williams, B.M., "The survival of pathogens in slurry and the animal health risks from disposal to land", *ADAS Quart. Rev.* **32** (1979) pp. 59–68.

90 Stephenson, G.R. and Street, L.V., "Bacterial variations in streams from a southeast Idaho rangeland watershed", *J. Environ. Qual.* **7** (1978) pp. 150–57.

91 Skinner, Q.D., Adams, J.C., Rechard, P.A. and Beetle, A.A., "Effect of summer use of a mountain watershed on bacterial water quality", *J. Environ. Qual.* **3** (1974) pp. 329–35; Stuart, D.G., Bissonnette, G.K., Goodrich, T.D., and Walter, W.D., "Effect of multiple use on water quality of high mountain watersheds: bacteriological investigations of mountain streams", *J. Appl. Microbiol.* **22** (1971) pp. 1048–1054; Walter, W.G. and Bottman, R.P., "Microbiological and chemical studies of an open and closed watershed", *J. Environ. Health* **30** (1967) pp. 157–63.

92 Thornley, S. and Bos, A.W., "Effects of livestock wastes and agricultural drainage on water quality: an Ontario case study", *J. Soil and Water*

Conserv. Jan–Feb (1985) pp. 173–5; Diesch, S.L., "Disease transmission of water-borne organisms of animal origin", in: Willrich, T.E. and Smith, G.E. (eds), *Agricultural Practices and Water Quality* (Ames: Iowa State University Press, 1970).

93   Naegel, L.C.A., "A review of public health problems associated with the integration of animal husbandry and aquaculture, with emphasis on southeast Asia", *Biol. Wastes* **31** (1990) pp. 69–83; Edwards, P., "A review of recycling organic wastes into fish, with emphasis on the tropics", *Aquaculture* **21** (1980) pp. 261–79.

94   Jacalne, A.V. et al., 1975, and Manlapiig, E.T., 1981, in: Naegel, 1990, *op. cit.*

95   Derbyshire, J.B., Monteith, H.D. and Shannon, E.E., "Virological studies on an aerobic digestion system for liquid pig manure", *Agric. Wastes* **18** (1986) pp. 309–12.

96   Wong, M.H., "Heavy metal contamination of soils and crops from auto traffic, sewage sludge, pig manure and chemical fertiliser", *Agric. Ecosyst. and Environ.* **13** (1985) pp. 139–49; Hanrahan, T.J. and O'Grady, J.F., "Copper supplementation of pig diets: the effect of protein level and zinc supplementation on the response to added copper", *Anim. Prod.* **10** (1968) pp. 423–32.

97   Jeffrey, J.J. and Uren, N.C., "The effect of the application of piggery effluent to soils and pastures", *Prog. Wat. Tech.* **11** (1979) pp. 275–82; Kornegay, E.T., Hedges, J.D., Martens, D.C. and Kramer, C.Y., "Effect on soil and plant mineral levels following application of manures of different copper contents", *Plant and Soil* **45** (1976) pp. 151–62; McAllister, J.S.V. "Spreading slurry on the land". *Soil Sci.* **123** (1977) pp. 338–43; Batey, T., Berryman, C. and Line, C., "The disposal of copper-enriched pig-manure slurry on grassland", *J. Br. Grassland. Soc.* **27** (1972) pp. 139–43.

98   Thornton, I., "Geochemistry applied to agriculture", in: Thornton, I. (ed.), *Applied Environmental Geochemistry* (London: Academic Press, 1983).

99   Cheung, Y.H. and Wong, M.H., "Utilisation of animal manures and sewage sludges for growing vegetables", *Agric. Wastes* **5** (1983) pp. 63–81.

100 Batey et al., 1972, *op. cit.*

101 John, C.K., "Treatment of agro-industrial wastes using water hyacinth", *Wat. Sci. Tech.* **17** (1985) pp. 781–90; Ching, L.W., "Recycling agricultural wastes as a method of controlling environmental pollution", in: Consumers Association of Penang, Development and the Environment Crisis, Proceedings of 1978 symposium on the Malaysian Environment in Crisis (Malaysia: Consumers Association of Penang, 1982).

102 Singh, M., Kadir, A.A., Ibrahim, A., Chin, P.S., Haridas, C.I., John, C.K., Dolmat, M.T., Karim, M.A., Kadir, M.A., Pee, T.H., Pushparajah, E., Sethu, S., Yong, W.M. and Isa, Z., "Rubber factory discharges and their impact on environmental quality", in: Consumers

Association of Penang, 1982 *op. cit.*; Ching, 1982, *op. cit.*; Chin, P.S., Singh, M.M., John, C.K., Karim, M.Z.A., Bakti, N.A.K., Sethu, S. and Yong, W.M., "Effluents from natural rubber processing factories and their abatement in Malaysia", in: Lohani, B.N. and Thani, N.C. (eds), *Water Pollution Control in Developing Countries vol. II* (Bangkok: Asian Institute of Technology, 1978).

103   Ching, 1982, *op. cit.*

104   Sinnappa, S., "Treatment studies of palm oil mill waste effluent", in: Lohani and Thani, 1978, *op. cit.*

105   John, 1985, *op. cit.*; Kirkaldy, J.L.R., "Treatment of oil palm sludge", in: Consumers Association of Penang, 1982, *op. cit.*

7 Agriculture as a Global Polluter

In the preceeding chapters we have concentrated on problems and impacts of a local or regional nature, mostly involving pollution of the water or land. Yet agriculture is also a major source of atmospheric pollution, with consequences that are both long term and global in dimension.

In this chapter we look at three major polluting gases produced by agriculture – methane, nitrous oxide and ammonia – and the various products of the burning of biomass. Separately, or in combinations, they contribute to acid precipitation, the depletion of the ozone layer and global warming.

Polluting gases

Crop plants and livestock interact continuously with the atmosphere: plants take up carbon dioxide during photosynthesis and produce oxygen, while both animals and plants take up oxygen and respire carbon dioxide. These natural activities, though, do not result in pollution, or even in significant contamination, as the gases in the atmosphere are in a state of dynamic natural balance. What is potentially harmful is the added burden of carbon dioxide produced when vegetation is burnt and of certain other gases, notably methane (CH_4), nitrous oxide (N_2O) and ammonia (NH_3), produced during the course of intensive agriculture.

All of these gases are generated in some quantity by natural processes, but agriculture has increased the rates of emission, slowly at first but now with significant effect as agriculture expands and intensifies. For instance, in Asia the area of irrigated paddy land has grown by 40 per cent since 1970, so contributing to increased production of methane and ammonia. Similarly, the worldwide growth in inorganic nitrogen fertilizer use – up from 20 to nearly 80 million tonnes annually since the mid-1960s – has contributed to a rapid rise in nitrous oxide production. Ammonia and methane emissions have grown with the intensification of livestock husbandry. And the clearance of forests and grasslands, as well as the burning of straw and other crop residues, has raised production of carbon and nitrogen oxides, together with smoke and particulates (Figure 7.1).

Figure 7.1   The principal atmospheric emissions from agriculture and their immediate impact

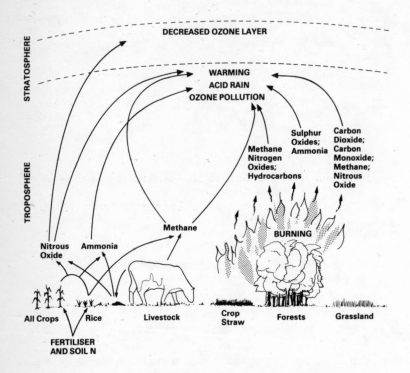

Methane (CH$_4$)

Agriculture is an important producer of methane, contributing about 45 per cent of total emissions (natural plus human-made) in 1990. Methane is produced by specialized bacteria in environments that are free of oxygen, and during the burning of biomass. Anaerobic conditions occur naturally in wetland ecosystems – swamps and marshes – and in their agricultural equivalent, the rice paddy. They also exist, on a much smaller scale, within the guts of cattle and other ruminants, as well as in wood-eating insects, such as termites.

Sources of methane

In normal, well-drained soils, aerobic bacteria break down organic matter to produce carbon dioxide and various oxides of nitrogen. By contrast, in flooded soil the decomposition is by anaerobic bacteria and the end products, in addition to carbon dioxide, include methane, hydrogen sulphide and various other gases.[1] Organic rich wetlands are particularly important sources of methane: emissions from the Amazonian floodplain, alone, are estimated to be 8–21 million tonnes annually.[2] Natural wetlands probably contribute 20 per cent to global methane emissions.

Rice paddies generate about the same amount and, together, natural wetlands and paddy produce about 40 per cent of methane worldwide (Table 7.1). Compared with wetlands, paddy fields are capable of producing double the maximum daily emission rates per unit area, though these high levels mostly occur in the first six weeks after the fields are flooded and are not sustained throughout the growing season.[3] However, there are a great many uncertainties in the estimates. Few experiments have been conducted in tropical conditions; and those that have measured methane emissions have

Table 7.1 Estimates of annual emissions of methane by source, 1990. The total source is not necessarily calculated from the sum of the indicated individual sources

	Emission of methane (million tonnes/year)	
	(1)	(2)
Rice paddies	25–170	60–140
Domestic ruminants	65–100	65–100
Natural wetlands	100–200	40–160
Termites	10–100	10–100
Fossil-fuel production	40–100	50–95
Biomass burning	20–80	50–100
Oceans and freshwaters	6–45	15–35
Landfills	20–70	30–70
Methane hydrate destabilization	0–100	–
Total (estimated range)	350–600	400–640

Source: (1) Watson, R. et al., "Greenhouse gases and aerosols", in: *The Scientific Assessment of Climate Change*, report to the Intergovernmental Panel on Climate Change (IPCC), Working Group 1, Section 1, Peer Reviewed Assessment for Working Group 1 Plenary, 25 April 1990 (Geneva: World Meteorological Organization, 1990); (2) Bouwman, A.F., "Land use related sources of greenhouse gases", *Land Use Policy*, April (1990) pp. 154–64.

produced widely divergent results.[4] For example, emissions may be increased by rising soil temperature, but it is not clear whether they are raised by the addition of inorganic fertilizers.

Methane production by livestock also results from the activity of anaerobic bacteria, breaking down organic matter in the animal's gut. The amounts produced are quite large: individual cattle, buffaloes and camels produce 35–55 kg/year; goats, sheep and horses 5–15 kg and pigs 1 kg.[5] Because of their large numbers – about 1.4 billion worldwide in 1988 – cattle and buffaloes produce about 80 per cent of all the methane emissions from animals.[6] Overall ruminant animals contribute about 15 per cent of total methane emissions.

The burning of agricultural wastes, fuelwood, vegetation during swidden (slash and burn) cultivation, and grasslands on savannas is a further important source of methane, probably about eight per cent of all emissions.[7] The principal non-agricultural sources, apart from natural wetlands, are releases during the production and burning of fossil fuels, and landfills of solid waste in the industrialized world.

Trends in atmospheric methane

Once in the troposphere, most methane is destroyed through photo-chemical oxidation by the hydroxyl (OH) ion. Some goes higher to the stratosphere and the remainder returns to the ground and is decomposed in aerobic soils. Until the industrial revolution, the production of methane by human activities was more or less balanced by its destruction, but this is no longer the case. Measurements of concentrations of gases trapped in the polar ice show a rapid rise in average methane levels from about the time of the industrial revolution. Over the past 150 years the concentration has increased from about 700 parts per billion by volume (ppbv) to a level of 1720 ppbv in 1990, presumably as a consequence of increased agricultural activity as well as the burning and mining of fossil fuels (Figure 7.2).[8]

The levels are also now significantly higher in the northern hemisphere than in the southern, reflecting the differences in the scales of agricultural and industrial activity. The global rate of increase in methane concentrations is about 1–2 per cent per year.[9] Future trends are difficult to predict because they are a function not only of the methane emissions themselves but also of the production of other gases, notably carbon monoxide (CO), nitrogen oxides (NO_x) and other hydrocarbons, which affect the concentration of the hydroxyl ion (OH) in the troposphere that, in turn, destroys methane. For instance, the recent growth in carbon monoxide emissions of about 0.6 – 1 per

Figure 7.2 Methane levels in air trapped in ice cores in Greenland and Antarctica

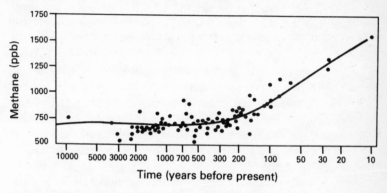

Source: Bolle, H.J., Seiler, W. and Bolin, B. "Other greenhouse gases and aerosols", in: Bolin, B. et al. (eds), *The Greenhouse Effect, Climatic Change and Ecosystems* (Chichester: John Wiley and Sons, 1986).

cent per annum will have reduced the availability of hydroxyl ions, and hence increased methane levels.[10] Nonetheless most methane sources are likely to continue to grow; under the 'business-as-usual' projection to the year 2050, estimates suggest that the methane concentration will rise by a further 55 per cent to 2694 ppbv.[11]

Nitrous oxide (N_2O)

Agriculture has a relatively smaller impact on the global cycle of nitrous oxide, but it is nevertheless important. Both the growth in nitrogen fertilizer use and the clearance of land have contributed to rising concentrations of N_2O in the atmosphere.

Sources of nitrous oxide

Nitrous oxide is produced naturally by the action of bacteria in soils and water and by the burning of biomass and fossil fuels containing nitrogen. The most important natural source, accounting for some 20–30 per cent of total global emissions, is bacterial action on natural nitrogen compounds in tropical soils.[12] Emissions are particularly high from soils covered by undisturbed tropical rainforest, producing, in the Amazon region, greater tropospheric N_2O levels than the global average.[13] Atmospheric emissions are usually much lower from temperate forests, although the amounts reaching surface waters can be high.[14] Cutting forests can cause an immediate increase in atmospheric emissions, but the amount of N_2O dissolved in soil water can multiply a hundred times and on reaching surface streams will also escape to the atmosphere.[15] After a time, however, the emissions decline.

In addition to breaking down natural soil nitrogen, bacteria will also liberate N_2O from nitrogen fertilizers. Soils which have been fertilized emit between two and ten times as much as unfertilized soils and pastures, though there is considerable variation in experimental results. One factor is the type of fertilizer. In temperate countries ammonium and urea compounds tend to produce the highest emissions with up to two per cent of added nitrogen lost as N_2O (Table 7.2). As yet there is insufficient experimental evidence of this behaviour under tropical conditions but, if urea is more prone to N_2O loss as the results suggest, this is significant since urea tends to be the preferred fertilizer in the developing countries. Over 70 per cent of total fertilizer consumption in Asia is of urea, and an increasing proportion of new manufacturing capacity in Asia is being devoted to urea production.[16] In Central and South America urea accounts for 50 per cent of fertilizer use, although it is less in Africa.[17]

In a similar fashion, livestock wastes are a source of N_2O: some studies have shown high and continuing losses when animal wastes and slurry are applied to land – in one case some 50 kg of nitrous oxide as nitrogen (N_2O-N) per hectare per year were emitted from a manured soil in Denmark.[18]

Trends in atmospheric nitrous oxide

As in the case of methane, analysis of air bubbles in the Antarctic ice reveals that nitrous oxide concentrations have increased since the industrial revolution – from 280–290 ppbv to about 310 ppbv in 1990 (Figure 7.3). At present, atmospheric N_2O is increasing at a rate of 0.2–0.3 per cent per year.[19] There is even more uncertainty over the relative contributions from different sources than for methane. Nitrogen fertilizers, for instance, contribute an estimated 5–20 per cent of total emissions. The most recent assessment, made by the Intergovernmental Panel on Climate Change Working Group 1 in 1990, has reduced considerably the previous limits of emissions from oceans and fossil-fuel and biomass burning.[20] But the estimate for total emissions of 14 million tonnes per year remains as before, since it is calculated from the atmospheric build-up and main known routes of

Table 7.2 The yield of gaseous nitrous oxide as a proportion of added nitrogen fertilizer to various soils

Yield of N_2O as percentage added of N

Fertilizer type:

Location	Nitrate	Ammonium sulphate	Ammonium nitrate	Anhydrous ammonia	Urea	Urea and ammonium nitrate
Tropics						
Brazil	0.5	0.09	—	—	—	—
Europe						
UK	–	–	1.3–1.6	—	—	—
Germany	0.001–0.7	0.07–0.38	–	—	—	—
Denmark	0.33	–	–	—	—	—
North America						
Iowa	0.01–0.04	0.11–0.18	—	–	0.12–0.14	—
New York	0.25	–	—	–	2.08	0.24–1.17
Colorado	–	0.38	—	–	0.6	–
Colorado	–	–	—	1.3	–	–
Utah	–	1.8	–	–	–	–
Ontario	–	–	0.25	–	–	–
Washington	–	–	–	0.011	–	–

Source: Keller, M., Kaplan, W.A., Wofsy, S.C. and Da Costa, J.M., "Emissions of N_2O from tropical forest soils: response to fertilisation with NH_4^+, NO_3^- and PO_4^{3-}", *J. Geophys. Res.* 93 (1988) pp. 1600–4, using various sources.

Figure 7.3 Nitrous oxide levels in air trapped in the Antarctic ice

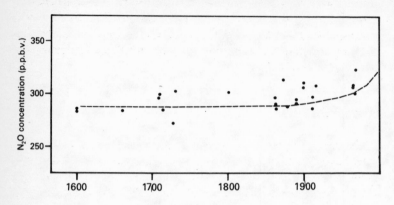

Source: Pearman, G.I. et al., "Evidence of changing concentrations of CO_2, NO_2, and CH_4 from air bubbles in Antarctic ice", *Nature* **320** (1986) pp. 248–250.

Table 7.3 Estimate of annual emission of nitrous oxide by source, 1970

	Emission of nitrous oxide (million tonnes/year)
Fertilizers	0.01–2.2
Biomass burning	0.02–0.2
Soils: tropical forests	2.2–3.7
temperate forests	0.7–1.5
Oceans	1.4–2.6
Fossil fuel use	0.1–0.3
Unaccounted sources	4
Total emission (calculated from atmospheric build-up and main sinks)	14

Source: Watson, R. et al., 1990, *op. cit.*; see Table 7.1.

destruction (or sinks). There is, thus, at least four million tonnes unaccounted for (Table 7.3).

The "business as usual" projections suggest an increase of about 15 per cent over current concentrations to 364 ppbv by the year 2050.[21] Although reductions in nitrogen fertilizer use could limit this trend, the very long atmospheric residence time of the gas – about 170 years – implies that an atmospheric steady state will only be approached some

150 to 200 years after the emission rates have become constant.[22] Furthermore, emissions will not be reduced by the destruction of tropical forests, since pastures recently converted from forest can be very significant sources of nitrous oxide.[23] Present trends are thus likely to continue for some time to come, whatever the changes in agricultural practice.

Ammonia (NH_3)

While agriculture plays an important, but not dominant, role in the production of methane and nitrous oxide, it is the principal source of atmospheric ammonia – emitted when nitrogen contained in fertilizers, or in the excreta of animals, is volatilized or when biomass is burnt.

Sources of ammonia

In the industrialized countries these sources are responsible for about 80–90 per cent of total emissions; the rest comes from industrial processes, coal combustion, traffic, human and wild animal wastes, and natural soils.[24] On a global scale animal wastes are still the largest source, at between 22 and 30 million tonnes, but biomass burning probably contributes 10–15 per cent of the total atmospheric burden, and volatilization of ammonia from fertilized rice paddies is a major source in some parts of the world.[25]

It has long been recognized that a high proportion of the total nitrogen in livestock waste is lost as ammonia.[25] In 1804 the British agricultural writer and farmer, Arthur Young, recommended that manures be used fresh and not left on dunghills:

He who is within the sphere of the scent of a dunghill smells that which his crop would have eaten if he would have permitted it. Instead of manuring his land, he manures the atmosphere; and before his dunghill is finished turning, he has manured another parish, perhaps another county.[26]

On grazed pasture the source of ammonia is urine and excreta produced by the animals while grazing, the ammonia being mostly volatilized in the first two weeks after the wastes are produced. But losses per hectare are higher when animal wastes are applied to land, often as high as 50 per cent of the nitrogen applied, and extremely high from open slurry lagoons, particularly if they are regularly agitated (Table 7.4).[27] Densely packed animal feedlots are also important sources because of the continuous physical disturbance of the wastes.[28]

Table 7.4 Losses of ammonia in livestock raising agriculture

	Losses of NH$_3$ (kg/ha/day)	Stepwise increase in ratio
Pasture	0.01–0.02	1
Pasture and manure	0.05–0.2	×5–10
Manure covered isle in dairy barn	0.5–1.0	×5–10
Beef feedlot	0.5–10.0	×1–10
Anaerobic pig slurry lagoon	17–100	×10

Source: Miner, J.R., "Controlling odours from livestock production facilities: state-of-the-art", in: *Livestock Waste: A Renewable Resource*, (St. Joseph, Michigan: International Symposium on Livestock Wastes ASAE Publications, 1980).

Ammonia volatilization following fertilizer application is less well understood. It is not yet clear which type of fertilizer or what mode of application results in the largest emissions. One set of studies in temperate climate indicates that urea produces the most ammonia, with up to 20 per cent of the applied nitrogen lost to the atmosphere, in contrast to ammonium nitrate where only 1–2 per cent is lost.[29] But, another study suggests that ammonium sulphate is the most productive, with losses of 15 per cent, followed by ammonium nitrate, anhydrous ammonia and urea all producing 10 per cent.[30] The circumstances favouring high losses – from both fertilizers and animal wastes – are known, however. They include hot and dry conditions, high wind speed and high soil pH. Because losses only occur soon after fertilizer is applied, they can be reduced by incorporating the fertilizer or immediately irrigating the land after application.

Ammonia losses are particularly high from fertilized paddy fields in the tropics and subtropics; the losses are usually 5–15 per cent but sometimes reach 40–60 per cent of the applied nitrogen.[31] Losses from applied urea are typically 10–50 kg N/ha and from ammonium sulphate 5–10 kg/ha, both rising to a maximum of 40–60 kg/ha. Again, a number of factors significantly affect the amount lost. If the crop is dense much of the ammonia may be reabsorbed by the leaves. On the other hand, because algal photosynthesis raises the water pH, high algal populations may increase losses.

Emission densities and trends

Regional ammonia emissions correlate closely with the density of livestock, in particular of cattle and buffaloes. The greatest losses occur from the large feedlot operations situated in the central and western USA (see Chapter 6). In the Chino–Corona regions of southern California, for instance, 160,000 head of cattle are concentrated in an area 12 by 12 km, producing ammonia and volatile amine concentrations 20–30 times greater than those of nearby non-dairy regions (Figure 7.4). Over 500 km² are enriched with NH_3.[32]

Figure 7.4 Atmospheric ammonia in relation to intensive dairying in southern California. Isopleths represent average absorption by acid traps in g/10 m²

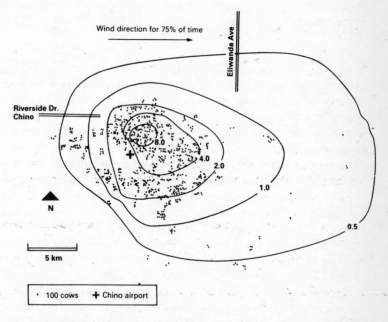

Source: Luebs, R.E., Davis, K.R. and Laag, A.E., "Enrichment of the atmosphere with nitrogen compounds volatised from a large dairy area", *J. Environ. Qual.* **2** (1973) pp. 137–141.

According to our calculations, based upon livestock emissions alone, the greatest total emissions occur in India, China, Brazil, the USA and Argentina, each producing more than one million tonnes annually (Table 7.5). But on a per unit area basis, small countries, such as the

Table 7.5 Emissions of ammonia from livestock waste in selected countries, measured in terms of nitrogen (i.e. NH_3-N)

Country	Total emissions of NH_3 (million tonnes)	Emission per hectare of arable and permanent pasture (kg/ha)
Emissions >30 kg/ha		
Netherlands	0.127	63.5
Bangladesh	0.53	55.0
Belgium	0.075	50.0
Egypt	0.12	48.6
Nepal	0.19	45.2
India	5.61	31.7
Emissions 20–30 kg/ha		
Denmark	0.084	30.0
F R Germany	0.357	29.8
Pakistan	0.72	28.8
Ireland	0.146	25.6
Japan	0.12	25.0
New Zealand	0.36	24.9
Cuba	0.13	24.5
Burma	0.23	23.0
Emissions 10–20 kg/ha		
UK	0.37	19.6
Guatemala	0.047	17.5
Uruguay	0.26	17.2
Panama	0.027	16.9
France	0.53	16.9
Poland	0.31	16.4
Fiji	0.004	16.1
Turkey	0.48	14.2
Colombia	0.47	13.8
Italy	0.22	12.7
Thailand	0.22	12.4
Brazil	2.60	11.3
Honduras	0.056	11.2
Venezuela	0.23	11.2
Reunion	0.0007	11.0
Mauritius	0.0012	10.9
Ethiopia	0.61	10.3
Emissions <10 kg/ha		
China	3.03	7.9
Tanzania	0.29	7.4
Mexico	0.69	6.9

continued

Table 7.5   Continued

Country	Total emissions of NH_3 (million tonnes)	Emission per hectare of arable and permanent pasture (kg/ha)
Emissions <10 kg/ha – Continued		
Nigeria	0.34	6.7
Argentina	1.09	6.5
Nicaragua	0.04	6.5
Madagascar	0.22	6.0
USA	2.24	5.2
Iran	0.30	5.1

Notes:
1 Emissions of ammonia are calculated on the following bases:
  (i)   Emission factors are assumed to be the same in temperate and tropical climates (this may not be the case as emissions rise as temperature increases).
  (ii) Emissions are assumed not to differ according to different management regimes, for animals grazing all year 35 per cent of N is lost as NH_3, for housed animals it is 45 per cent.
  (iii) Emissions from livestock waste are calculated by assuming each cow or buffalo emits 18.66 kg NH_3-N per year, each sheep or goat 2.89 kg and each pig 2.83 (see Kruse et al., 1989, 1986; Buijsman et al., 1987). Losses from other animals have not been accounted for.
  (iv) Livestock numbers are taken from FAO Production Yearbook, 1986; arable and permanent pasture area from same source.
  (v)   Emission totals for European countries from ApSimon et al., 1987.
2 Emissions do not include losses from human excreta and fertilizers. The former may be significant in China; the latter especially where crops are irrigated.
3 Emissions will be higher where manures are sun dried to make dung cakes for fuel; and will be lower where manures are quickly incorporated into the soil.

Sources: Calculated from data from FAO *Production Yearbooks*; Kruse, M., ApSimon, H.M. and Bell, J.N.B., *An emissions inventory for ammonia arising from agriculture in Great Britain* (London: Imperial College, 1986); Kruse, M., ApSimon, H.M. and Bell, J.N.B., "Validity and uncertainty in the calculation of an emission inventory for ammonia arising from agriculture in Great Britain", *Environ. Pollut.* 56 (1989) pp. 237–57; Buijsman, E., Maas, H.F.M. and Asman, W.A.H., "Anthropogenic ammonia emissions in Europe", *Atmos. Environ.* 21 (1987) pp. 1009–22; ApSimon, H.M., Kruse, M. and Bell, J.N.B., "Ammonia emissions and their role in acid deposition", *Atmos. Environ.* 21 (1987) pp. 1939–46.

Netherlands or Cuba, or those with only limited amounts of arable and pasture and specializing in livestock, such as Egypt and Panama, are the greatest producers. India, though, remains one of the largest emitters in total and by unit area. These data, it should be noted, are based on extrapolations from the estimated numbers of livestock and do not take various local factors into account. For example, ammonia emissions increase with rising temperature and soil alkalinity and thus the value of 55 kg NH_3-N/ha for Bangladesh may be a considerable underestimate, since the country has a large proportion of irrigated land, many soils are very alkaline and the climate is tropical.

The data also do not account for losses from inorganic fertilizers – which can be high from irrigated fields – or human excreta applied as fertilizer, and do not include losses from poultry and other animals.

Only in a few instances have detailed inventories been produced that take account of the relative contribution of different sources of ammonia and their pattern of distribution. In the UK it is estimated that some 350–370,000 tonnes of ammonia are emitted annually, and again livestock dominate: cattle contribute about 60 per cent, sheep a further 20 per cent and poultry, pigs, horses and fertilizers the remainder.[33] Emissions are particularly high in the west of the country, since this is where the highest cattle and sheep populations are located, and also in parts of East Anglia where there is a concentration of pig farms (Figure 7.5). Emissions also vary seasonally, being highest in the spring when the spreading of livestock wastes is common, and lowest in winter when the animals are mostly indoors. The average annual loss for arable and permanent pasture throughout the country is about 20 kg N/ha.

Ammonia emissions are likely to continue rising for the foreseeable future, primarily because of the rapid growth of livestock numbers and of irrigated land devoted to paddy. In Europe emissions are thought to have doubled since 1950, largely because of growing livestock numbers.[34] Worldwide, cattle and large ruminant numbers grew during the 1980s by 13 per cent to 1.4 billion. In Asia the area of irrigated rice alone grew by 40 per cent to 130 million hectares between 1970 and the mid-1980s.[35]

The products of burning

A further major source of global air pollution is the burning of vegetation, in particular during the clearing of forest, scrub and grassland to make way for agriculture. When vegetation is burned the carbon and sulphur is released, together with the accumulated nutrients – nitrogen, phosphorus and potassium. If the burn is carried out *in situ*, most of the potassium and phosphorus is returned to the soil, but the remaining constituents are emitted to the atmosphere in the form of carbon monoxide and carbon dioxide, nitrogen oxides, nitrous oxide and ammonia, methane and other hydrocarbons, as well as various sulphur products.

Figure 7.5 Ammonia emissions in England and Wales (as tonnes of ammonia as nitrogen NH$_3$-N) emitted per 100 km^2

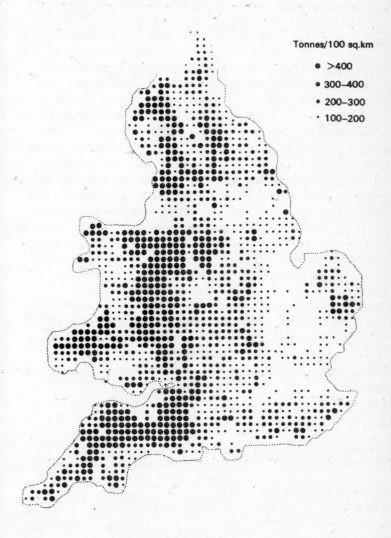

Tonnes/100 sq.km

● >400
● 300–400
· 200–300
· 100–200

Source: Kruse, M., ApSimon, H.M. and Bell, J.N.B., "Validity and uncertainty in the calculation of an emission inventory for ammonia arising from agriculture in Great Britain", *Environ. Poll.* 56 (1989) pp. 237–257.

This is not a new phenomenon; it even predates agriculture. Quite apart from natural fires caused by lightning and volcanic eruptions, hunter gatherers have long known how to create fire and to use it to improve grazing grounds. What has changed is the extent and amount of burning that goes on each year, as more and more land is cleared.

Land clearance

The largest clearance of land is still for shifting – or swidden – cultivation, the predominant form of agriculture in many upland regions of the tropics and subtropics. Primary or secondary forest or savanna land is cleared and as much of the dead plant material as possible is burnt on site. The soil, enriched by the potassium and phosphorous from the burnt vegetation, is then sown with a variety of crops. Yields are usually high in the first year but then decline as nutrients are depleted and weeds increasingly invade. Eventually the clearings are abandoned, to become covered by secondary vegetation which returns slowly to savanna or forest. The land may be cleared and burned again after a fallow time of five to ten years, depending upon such factors as soil fertility, population density and climate. Estimates are difficult to arrive at, but it is believed that 200–300 million people are supported by swidden, and they annually clear 20–100 million hectares of tropical forests and savanna.[36] The efficiency of burning is usually low and, despite the fact that burns are often repeated, only 25–75 per cent of the cleared biomass is finally burnt. Nevertheless, on these estimates between 0.9 and 2.5 billion tonnes of dry matter are burned as part of the swidden cycle each year (Table 7.6).

It is also common practice in savanna regions to burn dead vegetation in the dry season so as to enhance the growth of grasses and hence improve grazing. Much of the African savanna is burned at least once every three years, while in South America 20 per cent of the savanna – the *Cerrado* – totalling some 40,000 km^2, is subjected to fire each dry season.[37] Observations from the air indicate that plumes cover about five per cent of the *Cerrado* at any one time, and smoke, dispersed within a 3 km deep inversion layer, can cover the whole region.

In addition to swidden clearance – which is itself increasing because of population pressure and competing demands for marginal land – there has been rapidly growing clearance of forests and savanna to make way for permanent agriculture and livestock raising, as well as for settlements and highways. Some 8–15 million hectares are cleared annually for these purposes, with the increasing cattle population alone accounting for about half of global deforestation.[38] In the Amazon

Table 7.6 Global estimates for cleared area and burned biomass due to various activities

Activity	Cleared or burned area (million ha/yr)	Burned biomass (billion tonnes/yr)
Swidden (total)	20.5–61.5	0.9–2.5
Asia	10–30	
Africa	8–24	
Latin America	2.5–7.5	
Other deforestation (total)	8.8–15.1	0.55–0.9
Permanent agriculture and livestock	8.3–14.3	
Colonization	0.4–0.7	
Highways	0.1	
Wild fires in savanna and temperate and tropical forests		0.7–2.2
Burning of industrial and fuel wood		1–1.2
Burning of agricultural wastes		1.7–2.1

Source: Seiler, W. and Crutzen, P.J., "Estimates of gross and net fluxes of carbon between the biosphere and the atmosphere from biomass burning", *Climatic Change* 2 (1980) pp. 207–47.

region probably as much as 90 per cent of the burning is to open the land for livestock raising. The burns usually take place in the dry season, the plumes of smoke from individual fires joining to form very widespread layers of smoke (Figure 7.6).

Satellite images taken during the months of July and August in 1985 revealed over one thousand fires with smoke covering an area of 90,000 km2.[39] By August of 1987 the situation was much worse – a US satellite photographed some eight thousand separate fires, each at least a square kilometre in size and many larger, suggesting that the area burnt had doubled in two years.[40] Some plumes of smoke travel up to 1000 km from the point of origin, producing layers of smoke haze at altitudes between 1000 and 4000 metres. While the layers are usually only 100–300 metres thick, they extend over several hundred kilometres. Inside the plumes and haze layers the concentrations of CO, CO_2, NO and ozone (O_3) are all significantly raised over the regional background levels.[41]

Burning of wastes

The burning of farm wastes, especially cereal straw, is a further

Figure 7.6 Burning plumes observed by satellite over Brazil for the periods (a) 20–31 July 1985 and (b) 3–9 August 1985

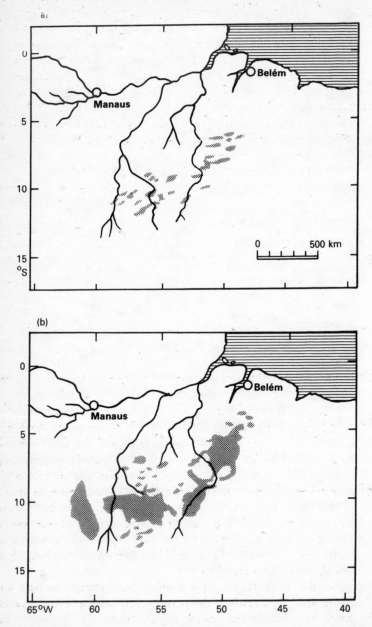

Source: Andreae, M.O. et al., "Biomass-burning emission and associated haze layers over Amazonia", *J. Geophys. Res.* **93** (1988) pp. 1509–1527.

contribution to the problem of atmospheric pollution. It has long been customary for farmers, throughout the world, to burn the cereal stubble after harvest but, in recent years, farmers in the industrialized countries have begun also to burn the straw. During the 1980s the straw was burned on some 25,000 farms in the UK – about 37 per cent of total cereals by area, though almost half of the total 13–15 million tonnes of straw produced. Only a very small proportion is ploughed into the soil (Table 7.7). Much of the burning is geographically concentrated in the southern and eastern arable regions of the UK (Figure 7.7). Straw burning is seldom practised in the USA, except for a specific need such as preparing for double-cropping of wheat land with soybeans.[42]

Table 7.7 Cereal straw disposal on farms in the UK, 1984

| | Cereal straw disposal (million hectares) | | |
	Baled and removed	Ploughed in or cultivated	Burned in field
Wheat	0.64	0.18	1.04
Winter barley	0.73	0.03	0.15
Spring barley and oats	0.56	0.15	0.07
Total	1.93	0.24	1.26
Proportion	56%	7%	37%
No. of farm holdings (thousand)	65.8	7.8	25.4

Source: Butterworth, B., *The Straw Manual* (London: E. and F.N. Spon, 1985).

In the developing countries, the most significant wastes are those of sugar cane and pineapple plantations, although rice straw is burned in some intensive lowland regions in Asia. Sugar cane and pineapple fields have long been burned in the Hawaiian Islands primarily to reduce the bulk of wastes and, in the case of sugar cane, to increase yields. Particularly serious pollutants are the particulates and dusts emitted, especially when sugar cane and pineapple wastes are burned. Cereal straw produces about 9 kg of particulates and dusts per tonne burnt, but the wastes of pineapple and sugar cane produce 65 and 680 kg per tonne respectively.[43]

For the temperate farmer it is quicker and cheaper to burn straw in the field, particularly as this permits early sowing of winter cereals, which have become increasingly popular in the UK. Yields of winter cereals increase with the length of the growing period, and this creates pressure to clear fields quickly after harvest. Because cereal cropping

Figure 7.7 Density of total cereal straw production in England and Wales.
Tonnes of dry matter per 10 × 10 km square grid

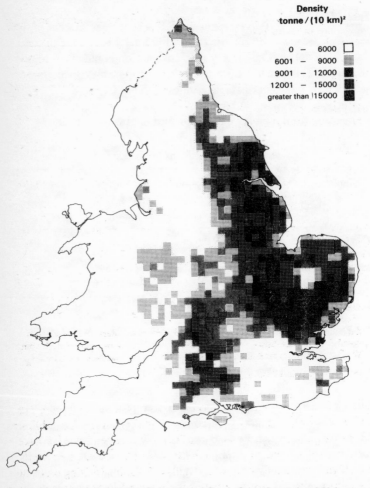

Source: Ministry of Agriculture, Fisheries and Food, *Straw Disposal and Utilisation: A Review of Knowledge* (London: MAFF, 1984).

and livestock raising are now mostly separated geographically, there is
little use for straw on the farm where it is produced. Straw is a bulky
product – its density is only 80–130 kg per cubic metre whereas the
weight of a cubic metre of water is 1000 kg – so the relatively high
handling and transport costs make it unprofitable for it to be sent to
distant livestock rearing regions.

The other advantages of burning in the field are the destruction of weed seeds and seedlings, and animal pests (Table 7.8). Burning

Table 7.8 Impact of removing or burning straw upon animals and weed populations in cereal fields in the UK

	Straw baled and removed	Straw burnt
Weeds		
Blackgrass seeds[1]		
Number viable seeds per m^2		
Ploughing	347	231
Direct drilling	3372	1016
Barren brome seeds[2]		
Number viable seeds per m^2, August	1895	1895
Number seedlings produced, December	1023	57[3]
Animals		
Collembola[4] (no./m^2)	2300	700
Spiders[4] (no./m^2)	85	25
Thrips[4] (no./m^2)	28	3
Insects[4] (no./m^2)	29	3
Deep burrowing earthworms[5] (g/m^2)	6	2.5

[1] *Alopecurus myosuroides*
[2] *Bromus sterilis*
[3] But each of these surviving seeds produced both more tillers and more seeds
[4] Number of surface-living arthropods ten months after straw removal or burning
[5] Weight of earthworms 4 months after third successive year of straw removal

Source: Butterworth, 1985, *op. cit.*

kills on average about 30 per cent of wild oats seeds (*Avena fatua*) and half of the seeds of blackgrass and barren brome, although those that remain can be at a considerable competitive advantage – surviving seeds tend to produce both more tillers and more seeds.[44] The high surface temperature also kills most animals living on or near the surface. But as organic matter is destroyed in the process, there is an adverse effect on deep-living earthworm populations which, in turn, produces a deterioration in soil structure. There are several other major disadvantages: wildlife, hedges and trees can be damaged; the high ash levels in the soil readily absorb herbicides, which significantly reduces effectiveness; and the absence of stubble may increase the risk of soil erosion from wind or water.

If we include agricultural wastes, then agriculture contributes actively 60–65 per cent of the annually burned biomass worldwide (see Table 7.6). The amounts of various gases produced, though, are not a simple function of this total burn. They vary from place to place, depending upon the type of material, and the rate and intensity of the fire. For example, savanna and grassland burns readily, but the burn in wet forest areas tends not to be so complete, resulting in some of the accumulated nitrogen and sulphur being incorporated into the soil in organic form. Estimates for the total emissions from biomass burning are given in Table 7.9.

On a world-wide basis the industrialized countries, particularly in North America, are responsible for most of the burning of agricultural wastes. Of the remaining, some 55 per cent is burned in Asia, 30 per cent in Africa and 15 per cent in Latin America. The countries having the greatest individual impact are Brazil, Colombia and Indonesia, followed by Thailand, Ivory Coast, Zaire, Philippines, Peru, Ecuador and Mexico.[45]

Table 7.9 Global emission of carbon, nitrogen, sulphur and particulate matter from biomass burning

Product	Emission (million tonnes)
Carbon dioxide(CO_2)	1000–2000 mt C
Carbon monoxide(CO)	260 mt C
Methane (CH_4)	20–100 mt C
Nitrogen oxides (NO_x)	7.6 mt C
Nitrous oxide(N_2O)	0.02–0.2 mt N
Ammonia (NH_3)	3.3 mt N
Sulphur oxides(SO_x)	2.6 mt S
Particulate and elemental carbon	31 mt

Sources: Watson et al., 1990, *op. cit.*; Andreae, M.O. et al., "Biomass burning emissions and associated haze layers over Amazonia", *J. Geophys. Res.* **93** (1988) pp. 1509–27; Bouwman, A.F., "Land use related sources of greenhouse gases, *Land Use Policy* April (1990) pp. 154–64.

The impact of global air pollution

The various gases we have discussed so far, either individually or in combination, have a number of important effects. They may simply create a nuisance or, more seriously, contribute to acidification of soil and water, depletion or addition to ozone, and global warming.

Burning as nuisance

The burning of vegetation and agricultural wastes often has serious, although local, undesirable effects. Fires may get out of control, affecting nearby settlements or destroying valuable watersheds or other natural habitats. Smoke and particulates may also create a considerable nuisance, if not a hazard, to local communities. In the early 1980s, the summer combustion of 6–7 million tonnes of cereal straw in the UK produced 18,000 tonnes of black smoke.[46] In national terms, this represented less than 10 per cent of the estimated total production of black smoke by the combustion of coal every year. But since straw burning was concentrated in a limited period of time and in certain parts of the country, the ensuing levels of local pollution were generally worse than would be tolerated in industrial regions.[47]

Smoke and smuts cause substantial annoyance to local residents and to those visiting the countryside. Fires may also get out of control, damaging trees, hedges and wildlife and endangering crops, buildings and people. One market gardener, in Leicestershire in the UK, lost 25,000 cauliflowers when they were destroyed by smuts from a neighbour's straw fire. Road traffic also can be endangered and serious accidents may occur if the smoke covers roads. Detailed records of such accidents are not recorded but examples of major incidents reported in the press are listed in Table 7.10.

The level of nuisance can be gauged from Table 7.11 which records the complaints made to Local Authorities in the UK over straw burning

Table 7.10   Selection of accidents in the UK caused by smoke from straw burning

Year	Location of accident	Number of vehicles involved	Number injured	Number killed
1979	Sussex	2	–	–
	Kent	2	2	–
1980	Cambridgeshire	16	14	–
	Berkshire	30	11	–
1983	North Yorkshire	9	3	2
	Cleveland	8	–	–
1984	Wiltshire	9	–	–
1985	Bedfordshire	10	11	–
1989	Oxfordshire	32	14	–

Source: Conway, G.R., "Agricultural pollution", in: Conway, G.R. (ed.), *The Assessment of Environmental Problems* (London: Imperial College, 1986); National Society for Clear Air, *The NSCA Surveys of Straw/Stubble Burning* (Brighton: NSCA, 1985–9).

Table 7.11 Complaints to local authorities in the UK over straw burning, 1984 to 1989

	1984*	1985	1986[†]	1988[†]	1989*
Char and smut fall-out and smoke general nuisance	2558	605	172	160	1635
Threat/damage to property	118	28	13	13	142
Threat/damage to wildlife and habitats	146	14	7	7	154
Effects on human health	124	35	12	8	311
Reduced visibility on roads	154	73	39	35	223
Total	3100	765	243	223	2465

* Some local authorities received so many complaints in 1984 and 1989 that they stopped counting – these are not included
[†] No survey was conducted for 1987

Source: National Society for Clean Air, *The NSCA Surveys of Straw/Stubble Burning* (Brighton: NSCA, 1984–9).

between 1984 and 1989.[49] The first and last years in the series were particularly bad years: both were hot and dry and, although most farmers burned in general compliance with straw and stubble burning codes, complaints were common. Smoke, soot and charred straw from fierce fires during the prolonged dry spells caused widespread nuisance. In 1984 fire brigades answered more than 500 calls to deal with out-of-control fires, in just the three counties of Cambridgeshire, Essex and Hertfordshire. Between 1985 and 1988 there were far fewer complaints, partly because it was frequently too wet to burn the straw and also because the Straw and Stubble Burning Code of the National Farmers Union was apparently proving effective, as was the liaison between environmental health officers and farmers. However, a massive rise in complaints in 1989 cast serious doubt upon the effectiveness of the voluntary controls. In one locality a fire brigade was fighting 13 fires simultaneously. A pilot reported seeing a plume of stubble smoke on a cross-channel flight "carrying over the channel to the low countries and beyond".[49] As a consequence a complete ban on straw-burning was announced by MAFF in the winter of 1989 to take effect from 1992.

Acidification

Not all the ammonia that is produced by livestock or fertilizers stays long in the atmosphere, nor is it necessarily harmful. Much is rapidly absorbed by vegetation and by water surfaces. Actively growing plants generally absorb ammonia when the atmospheric concentration is greater than 1.5–4 ppb and, at high concentrations, some plants can derive as much as half of their nitrogen from this source.[50]

Local impacts

Nevertheless, there are significant adverse consequences of ammonia emissions. Acidification of the air, soil and water is primarily a consequence of the release of sulphur dioxide and nitrogen oxides from the burning of fossil fuels (see Chapter 8). But ammonia also plays a role, either independently or in combination with sulphur dioxide.

Often concentrations are high close to the emitting source (Figure 7.8). In northeast Colorado, absorption traps sited nearly half a

Figure 7.8 Ammonium concentration in open field precipitation (––– μmol) and forest soil (—— μmol per kg dry weight) as a function of distance to chicken farms

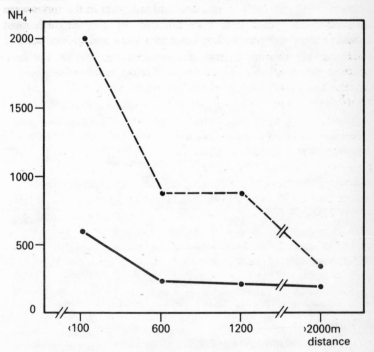

NH$_4^+$

Source: Roelofs, J.G.M., Kempers, A.J., Houdijk, A.L.F.M. and Jansen, J., "The effect of airborne ammonium sulphate on *Pinus nigra var. maritima* in the Netherlands", *Plant and Soil* **84** (1985) pp. 45–56.

kilometre from a feedlot containing 90,000 head of cattle collected, on average, 73 kg NH_3-N/ha/year, with individual weekly values closest to the feedlot as high as 5.7 kg/ha. But the depositions rapidly declined to only 39 kg per year at 2 km distance, and only 4 kg for a control site unaffected by feedlots or cities.[51] The effects are more extensive in regions where total ammonia emissions are high. In the Netherlands, where there are high densities of livestock and the spreading of liquid manure on land is a common practice, deposition can be as high as 60 kg N/ha/year.[52]

Though understanding of the impacts is still incomplete, there is increasing evidence that such ammonia deposition is disrupting plant life. In particular, it is now believed that ammonia emissions may be a partial cause of the serious forest die-back that has occurred in Europe in recent decades.[53] A number of different mechanisms have been proposed that implicate ammonia. For instance, ammonia absorbed into the leaves may cause losses of magnesium, calcium and potassium leading to deficiencies and premature leaf shedding.[54] A second hypothesis is that ammonia deposition causes leaching of these elements from the soil, so inhibiting nutrient uptake. It is known that the soil solution of severely damaged pine forests in the Netherlands contains higher concentrations of ammonium ions and lower concentrations of magnesium, calcium and potassium ions than is present in healthy forests (Table 7.12). Absorption by plants of nitrogen as ammonia may also reduce frost hardiness.

Table 7.12 Chemical composition and pH of soil solutions from healthy and severely damaged forests of *Pinus nigra* var. *maritima* in the Netherlands

| | Concentration (μ mol per kg dry soil) | | | | | |
	NH_4*	Mg*	Ca*	K	Al	pH
Healthy	334	77	153	137	191	4.1
Severely damaged	509	26	43	60	183	4.1

* Differences between content of ammonium, magnesium and calcium in healthy and damaged will arise by chance on less than 5 in a 100 occasions

Source: Roelofs, J.G.M. et al., "The effect of air-borne ammonium sulphate on *Pinus nigra* var. *maritima* in the Netherlands", *Plant and Soil* 84 (1985) pp. 45–56.

Impacts are also detectable on the composition of plant communities, especially on nutrient-poor soils. The balance of heathland communities of the heather *Calluna vulgaris* and grasses *Molinia caerulea* and *Festuca ovina* is disrupted by the addition of nitrogen.[55] When nutrient supply is poor, *Calluna* is a better competitor for nutrients than *Molinia* and *Festuca*; but in experiments in which the quantity of available nutrients is increased, the biomass of grasses increases much more rapidly than that of the heather, with the result that *Calluna* loses the advantage to the grasses. Heathlands receiving just one dose of nitrogen are unaffected, but continuous addition results in growing dominance by grasses. This out-competition by grasses only occurs in mature stands of *Calluna* when the input of nitrogen is high, and in young ones that have recently been burned or suffered attack by heather beetle (Table 7.13). Thus low, but repeated, inputs of nitrogen in the form of atmospherically deposited ammonia can change a heathland to an acid grassland. In the Netherlands some 80 km² of heathland have become dominated by grassland over the past few decades.[56]

Table 7.13   Impact of nitrogen on the displacement of the heather, *Calluna vulgaris*, by the grass, *Festuca ovina*, in a heathland community in the Netherlands. Nitrogen was added in 1969–72; the community structure observed in 1981

| | *Proportion of cover by* Festuca ovina *(%)* | | |
| | *One application of N* | *Repeated applications of N* | |
Annual input of nitrogen (kg N/ha)		*Young stand of* Calluna	*Old stand of* Calluna
0	4	12	5
1.7	11	22	4
7	15	36	26
28	15	66	50

Source: Heil, G.W. and Diemont, W.H., "Raised nutrient levels change heathland into grassland", *Vegetatio* **53** (1983) pp. 113–20.

Watercourses too may be affected. Seeley Lake in Colorado, situated 2 km from the very large feedlot described above, absorbed sufficient NH_3 to raise the nitrogen concentration in the water by 0.6 mg/l annually.[57] This is sufficient, as we have seen in Chapter 4, to lead to eutrophication. These instances suggest the impacts may be more widespread than is generally supposed, both in the industrialized countries and in tropical and subtropical regions, and particularly in those localities with high ruminant densities or intense paddy rice cultivation.

Longer-term hazards

More complex still is the role of ammonia in atmospheric chemistry and the longer-term consequences (Box 7.1). The average lifetime of

---

Box 7.1 The chemical reactions occurring in clouds between the pollutant gases ammonia, sulphur dioxide and nitrogen oxides

1 Ammonia and sulphur dioxide are dissolved in the water droplets to form ammonium (NH_4^+) ions, hydroxyl (OH^-) ions, and sulphate (SO_4^{2-}) ions:

$$NH_3 + H_2O = NH_4^+ + OH^-$$
$$SO_2 + 2OH^- = SO_4^{2-} + 2H^+$$

2 Nitrogen dioxide is oxidized to nitric acid, and nitric oxide to nitrous acid in the gas phase of the clouds (note: the OH is not from the dissociation of NH_3 in equation 1):

$$NO_2 + OH^- = HNO_3$$
$$NO + OH = HONO$$

3 The nitrous acid may be oxidized in the water droplets by OH from the NH_3 dissociation (equation 1):

$$HONO + OH = HNO_3 + H^+$$

4 The ammonium and sulphate ions combine to form aerosols of ammonium sulphate:

$$2NH_4^+ + SO_4^{2-} = (NH_4)_2SO_4$$

5 The ammonia and HNO_3 combine to form aerosols of ammonium nitrate:

$$NH_3 + HNO_3 = NH_4NO_3$$

---

ammonia in the atmosphere is very short – only 7–14 days – but as it is very water soluble it quickly dissolves in droplets of mist, cloud or rain in the troposphere.[58] The resulting solution contains both ammonium ions (NH_4^+) and hydroxyl ions, so making the clouds alkaline. The hydroxyl ions, in turn, combine with any sulphur dioxide present to form sulphate ions, which readily associate with ammonium ions to form ammonium sulphate. Ammonium nitrate aerosols can also be formed as a result of reactions in both the liquid and gas phases, beginning with nitric oxide and nitrogen dioxide.

Confirmation of the removal in this way of sulphur dioxide (SO_2)

from the atmosphere by NH_3 has come from observations made from
specially equipped aircraft in the UK.[59] Two such flights over the west
of Britain took paths perpendicular to, and downwind of, an industrial
plume that originated in the Midlands and was carrying SO_2. This
plume moved westwards over the intensive cattle farming regions of
Cheshire and North Wales, where NH_3 emissions are on average 3–4
times greater than elsewhere in the UK. The oxidized plume picked
up the ammonia, then the SO_2 was oxidized to sulphate ions, and
these, in turn, were neutralized by the ammonium ions. By the time
the air mass had reached the coast the total amount of sulphur present
had halved – the remainder had been deposited either as SO_2 or as
SO_4 (Table 7.14). If this effect is widespread it may account for the
phenomenon of declining atmospheric SO_2 levels in such countries as
the former German Democratic Republic, where both SO_2 and NH_3
emissions were rising in the mid-1980s.[60]

Table 7.14 Conversion of SO_2 to sulphate over an ammonia producing
region of the UK

Constituents of plume	Concentration of constituents of plume (measured as flux of S or N in tonnes per hour)	
	Border of England and Wales	Welsh Coast
SO_2	84	24
SO_4	6	18
NH_4	3.5	18
Total sulphur (t/hour)	90	42

Source: Bamber, D.J. et al., "Air sampling flights round the British Isles at low altitudes:
SO_2 oxidation and removal rates", *Atmos. Environ.* **18** (1984) pp. 1777–90; ApSimon,
J.N., Kruse, M. and Bell, J.N.B., "Ammonia emissions and their role in acid deposition",
Atmos. Environ. **21** (1987) pp. 1939–46.

Although removal of sulphur dioxide from the atmosphere in this way
reduces the potential for long distance acid deposition, it is not
necessarily to be welcomed. The resulting aerosols reduce atmospheric
visibility and acidify the soil. Ammonium sulphate has potentially twice
as great an acidifying effect on the soil as sulphuric acid (H_2SO_4) alone.
As bacteria break down the ammonium sulphate in the soil, so the two
ammonium ions associated with each sulphate ion are nitrified to form
two nitric acid (HNO_3) molecules, and in the process two hydrogen
ions (H^+) are released. (Acidity is created by the release of hydrogen
ions (H^+), otherwise known as protons. A measure of the acidity is the

pH which is the negative logarithm of the concentration of hydrogen ions.) A further source of acidity comes from plant roots themselves: as each NH_4^+ ion is taken up so the root must maintain its ionic balance by releasing a H^+ ion.[61]

As is, by now, well known, acidification of soils and water can have serious consequences on the environment.[62] In freshwater, high hydrogen ion concentrations and consequent increases in aluminium ions can be toxic to fish and other aquatic organisms. Many lakes in Europe and North America are now devoid of their original fauna as a result of soil acidification. Trees are also thought to have suffered damage from acidification, though the mechanisms involved are complex and, as yet, not fully understood. Forest decline is now significant over large areas of Europe and North America. Acid deposition also directly damages agricultural crops and reduces yields (see Chapter 8).

Ozone (O_3)

The effects on ozone of the various gases produced by agricultural activities are, in one sense, paradoxical. In the lower layers of the atmosphere – the troposphere – various gases including carbon monoxide and methane interact to increase ozone concentrations, while in the upper atmosphere – the stratosphere, that extends from 10 to 50 km above the earth's surface – some gases, notably methane and nitric oxide, have the reverse effect.

Ozone increases

The atmospheric chemistry in both cases is complex. In the troposphere, ozone is formed when carbon monoxide or reactive hydrocarbons, such as methane, are oxidized in the presence of sunlight and high levels of nitric oxide and nitrogen dioxide (collectively referred to as NO_x).[63] It is a process that occurs only during the daytime, driven by ultraviolet radiation. At night the lack of ultraviolet light allows the process to be reversed; ozone (O_3) breaks down to oxygen (O_2) and is also directly deposited on the ground. However, the reversal is not necessarily complete and with increasing production there is a growing accumulation. Various mathematical models suggest that the tenfold increase in NO_x concentration, from 0.02 to 0.2 ppbv, which occurred between 1860 and 1985 in Europe should have resulted in a growth of tropospheric ozone from 10 to 27 ppbv, a figure that agrees well with the increase that has actually occurred (see Chapter 8).

Daytime and seasonal increases can be particularly marked in the subtropics and tropics and especially close to cities, where there is an abundant supply of hydrocarbons derived from vehicles (see Chapter 8). But levels can be high in rural areas too: in Brazil concentrations of ozone over the Amazon Basin are usually 10 to 15 ppb, but during the season for burning vegetation, they can rise to 40 ppb (Figure 7.9). A similar effect occurs as a result of burning savannas.

Figure 7.9 Comparison of surface ozone concentrations for three sites in Brazil. At S.J. Campos there is burning of vegetation; at Cuiabá and Manaus there is no burning

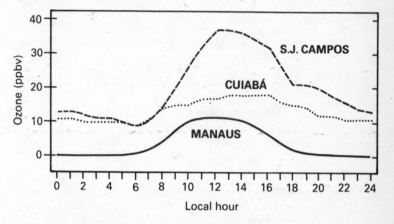

Source: Kirchhoff, V.W.J.H. "Surface ozone measurements in Amazonia", *J. Geophys. Res.* **93** (1988) pp. 1469–1476

Increasing ozone in the lower levels of the atmosphere can be directly damaging to plants. It may contribute to the death of trees now widely occurring in Europe and North America and also may damage agricultural crops and reduce yields (see Chapter 8).

Ozone depletion

The main concentrations of ozone, though, are not in the troposphere but in the stratosphere. There the ozone forms a distinctive layer, comprising about 90 per cent of all the ozone present in the atmosphere (Figure 7.10). Just how much is present, however, depends on a dynamic balance between ozone production and destruction which, in turn, is a function of the interaction of complex physical

Figure 7.10   Ozone volumes in the atmosphere

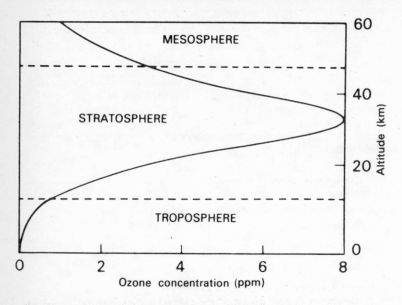

Source: UK Stratospheric Ozone Review Group, *Stratospheric Ozone* (London: HMSO, 1987).

and chemical processes. Ozone is produced in the stratosphere as a result of the action of ultraviolet light on oxygen. It is then broken down through the catalytic action of a variety of molecules including chlorine (Cl), bromine (Br), the hydroxyl ion (OH) and nitric oxide (NO) (see Box 7.2). A major source of the chlorine is now known to be the class of compounds referred to as chlorofluorocarbons (CFCs) that are extensively used as aerosol propellants and refrigeration coolants, and in foam packaging and insulation. When the CFCs are transported into the stratosphere above 20 km, ultraviolet radiation breaks them up to release chlorine. The hydroxyl ion is derived from methane and water vapour, while the nitric oxide comes mainly from nitrous oxide and, hence, both are partly products of agricultural activities.

Just what is the relative importance of these various gases in the destruction of ozone is still uncertain. However, it is clear that nitric oxide, and hence nitrous oxide (N_2O), are particularly significant. Current estimates suggest that a 20 per cent increase in N_2O concentration would result in a 2 per cent reduction in stratospheric ozone.[64] But there remain a great many uncertainties. For instance, the catalytic molecules that destroy ozone are themselves

Box 7.2 The basic chemical reactions in the ozone layer of the stratosphere

The chemical reactions are very complex but can be summarized as follows:

Ozone production
Ultraviolet light breaks up oxygen molecules into oxygen atoms which react with further oxygen molecules to form ozone (O_3)

$$O_2 + \text{ultraviolet light} \rightarrow O + O$$

$$O + O_2 + M \rightarrow O_3 + M$$

where M is a third molecule, usually N_2 or O_2

Ozone destruction
Ozone is broken down into oxygen molecules through the action of a variety of catalytic molecules

$$X + O_3 \rightarrow XO + O_2$$
$$\underline{XO + O \rightarrow X + O_2}$$
$$\text{net } O + O_3 \rightarrow 2O_2$$

where X can be H, OH, NO, Cl or Br
  OH can be derived from methane and NO derives from the breakdown of N_2O, both emitted partly by agricultural activity.
  In the destruction of ozone the catalytic molecule is regenerated and so can repeat the cycle. This may occur several thousand times before the catalytic molecule is finally removed.

For example:
$$Cl + O_3 \rightarrow ClO + O_2 \qquad\qquad NO + O_3 \rightarrow NO_2 + O_2$$
$$\underline{ClO + O \rightarrow Cl + O_2} \qquad\qquad \underline{NO_2 + O \rightarrow NO + O_2}$$
$$\text{net } O + O_3 \rightarrow 2O_2 \qquad\qquad \text{net } O + O_3 \rightarrow 2O_2$$
$$\text{(Cl and ClO are conserved)} \qquad \text{(NO and } NO_2 \text{ are conserved)}$$

Source: UK Stratospheric Ozone Review Group, *Stratospheric Ozone* (London: HMSO, 1988).

eventually removed from the stratosphere to the troposphere, and are then washed out in rainfall. Methane is important in this removal process. For instance, it removes the chlorine as hydrochloric acid. Thus methane plays several important, and contrary, roles in ozone atmospheric chemistry: it contributes to ozone production in the troposphere yet it causes ozone destruction in the stratosphere through its production of hydroxyl ions; and yet again helps to remove the chlorine that destroys ozone.[65]

Considerable effort has gone into modelling these processes but the computations involved are daunting. A fully comprehensive model would contain over 30 constituents and 200 reactions and these would have to be replicated for different altitudes in the atmosphere, for different latitudes and for different times of the year.[66] The models are inevitably simplified and the results thus open to considerable debate.

During the early 1980s the models indicated a likelihood of only small changes in stratospheric ozone as a result of increased emissions of ozone-destroying gases. Yet in 1985 the British Antarctic Survey team, stationed at Halley Bay and led by Farman, reported that there existed a startling springtime "ozone hole" over the Antarctic.[67] Direct observations had picked up what theorists had failed to predict. Since then the springtime hole has remained constant in extent, covering the Antarctic continent, and equivalent roughly to 5 per cent of the earth's surface area. The hole has, however, rapidly deepened each Antarctic spring – the most severe depletions occurred in 1987 and 1989 when at altitudes of between 14–18 km the concentration of ozone was, on occasions, 95 per cent less than normal (Figure 7.11).[68] The hole is confined by a vortex of swirling wind which begins to fall apart after the spring in late October or November, allowing ozone-depleting air

Figure 7.11   Stratospheric ozone levels over Halley Bay, Antarctica

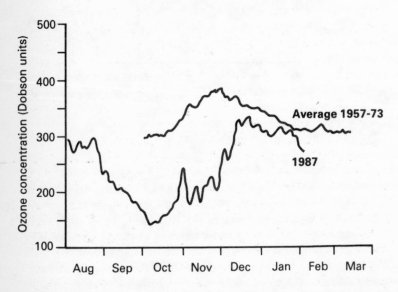

Source: UK Stratospheric Ozone Review Group, *Stratospheric Ozone* (London: HMSO, 1988).

to spread across the southern hemisphere. In 1987 record low ozone levels were measured in Australia and New Zealand.[69]

It is now apparent that the effect is not confined to the southern hemisphere. In the Arctic, an unexpectedly large amount of reactive chlorine has been observed, creating the potential for significant ozone loss, and there is evidence of reductions in ozone over Europe and North America since 1970, about 1 per cent per decade.[70] The downward trend in the winter is greater and appears to be accelerating. Depletion is largest between latitudes 53°N and 64°N – which includes most of the UK – and amounts to 7 per cent between December and February.[71] Based on the 1989 observations of reactive chlorine and nitrogen molecule content, now as high as those observed over the Antarctic, it has been predicted that in February of 1989 10–25 per cent of ozone may have been lost.[72] If the hole over the Antarctic were to be repeated in the northern hemisphere, it would extend over the whole of the Arctic Ocean plus large parts of Greenland, Norway, Canada and the Soviet Union.

Ultraviolet light and human health

The importance of the ozone layer is that it is an effective screen of ultraviolet light. Virtually all UVC light (at wavelengths of 240–290 nm) is eliminated by ozone, and only a small amount of UVB (at 290–320 nm) penetrates. Ozone is thus particularly important, as many organic molecules, notably DNA and proteins, can absorb and be destroyed by both UVB and UVC light. In practice, UVB has a range of impacts upon human health. In the short-term it causes sunburn and snow blindness and suppresses the immune system; in the long-term it causes both skin cancers and cataracts of the eye. A decline in total column ozone (ozone in the stratosphere and troposphere) is expected to lead to an increase in incidence of all these conditions.

The main hazard lies in the production of skin cancers, of which there are three kinds – basal cell carcinoma, squamous cell carcinoma (both non-melanoma types) and malignant melanoma. All become increasingly common in human populations receiving higher doses of UVB light.[73] Those people most at risk have white skins and live at high altitudes or low latitudes. However, there are some important differences between these cancers (Table 7.15). Non-melanoma cancers are the more common, and incidence is related to cumulative dose of UVB over a lifetime. Malignant melanomas are more likely to cause death, but risk is related to intermittent high doses of UVB plus a range of other factors, such as exposure to chemical carcinogens and viruses and genetic predisposition.

Table 7.15 Characteristics, incidence and mortality of skin cancers and impact of a decline in total column ozone

	Malignant melanoma skin cancer	Non-melanoma skin cancers (basal cell and squamous cell carcinomas)
Risk-related factors	Proportional to intermittent high doses and other factors	Proportional to cumulative lifetime UV dose
Incidence (population) Australia USA	40 per 100,000 10 per 100,000	820 per 100,000 625 per 100,000
New cases each year: USA	26,000	400,000
Deaths each year: USA	5800	6000
Incidence by age group	Most common in young adults (<40 years)	Most common in elderly
Mortality	High: about 25%	Low: 1–2%
Effect of a 5% decline in total column ozone (and 10% increase in UVB)	14–24% increase in incidence 2-10 increase in mortality	10–30% increase in incidence No change in mortality

Sources: Elwood, J.M., "Epidemiology of melanoma: its relationship to ultraviolet radiation and ozone depletion", in: Russell-Jones, R. and Wigley, T. (eds), *Ozone Depletion: Health and Environmental Consequences* (Chichester: J. Wiley and Sons Ltd, 1989); Russell-Jones, R., "Consequences for human health of stratospheric ozone depletion", in: Russell-Jones and Wigley (eds), *op. cit.*; US Environmental Protection Agency, *Assessing the risks of trace gases that can modify the stratosphere* (Washington DC: EPA Office of Air Pollution and Radiation, 1987).

Although the relationship between ozone depletion and UV penetration to the earth's surface is not simple, it is generally accepted that a 1 per cent decline in ozone will result in an increase of UVB of about 1.5–2 per cent.[74] A decline in total column ozone will thus result in significant growth in incidence of all skin cancers and mortality from malignant melanomas. For example, a 10 per cent decline in total column ozone would produce an extra 160,000 non-melanoma skin cancers in the USA each year, and an extra 8000 in the UK.[75]

UVB light also induces cataracts in the eye. Senile cataracts are very common – 600,000 operations are conducted annually in the USA – yet are probably an inevitable result of ageing as well as UV exposure.[76] Once again populations at lower latitudes are at greater risk. Estimates suggest an increase in cataract prevalence of about 2 per cent for each

1 per cent increase in UVB radiation – so a 10 per cent decline in total ozone would cause an additional 600,000 cataracts in the existing population of the USA between now and 2050, but 4.3 million in those people born between now and 2029.[77]

UV light and terrestrial and aquatic systems

Increased UVB light will also have an impact upon plants and animals in terrestrial and aquatic systems. So far, virtually all tests have been on agricultural crops, of which some two-thirds are sensitive to increased ultraviolet radiation.[78] The most sensitive are species in the legume, squash and cabbage families: UVB reduces leaf and stem growth and results in lower plant weights and yields. In other species, such as soybean, tomato and potato, the oil and protein content can also be significantly reduced. Members of the grass family, which includes cereals, are more tolerant. About half of coniferous tree seedlings tested are adversely affected. Because of these differences in tolerance between species it is predicted that changes in UVB radiation will modify distribution and abundance of plants, and result in changes of community structure and composition.[79]

Small increases in UVB radiation will also cause changes in aquatic communities, where fish, shrimp and crab larvae and plankton are known to be sensitive.[80]

In one laboratory-based study a 20 per cent increase in UVB radiation – which would probably accompany a 10 per cent decrease in total ozone – was predicted to kill eight per cent of the annual larval population of anchovy.[81] However, there have been few such studies and, although the effects are predicted to be large, they are as yet not fully quantified.

The greenhouse effect

As serious as the depletion of the ozone layer is the long-term effect of agricultural activities on the global climate. The atmosphere and the earth are heated by incoming solar radiation, but heat is lost through radiation from the earth's surface to the atmosphere and out to space. The incoming radiation is mainly visible and short-wave in character, while the outgoing is thermal and largely long-wave (Figure 7.12). Certain gases in the atmosphere, such as carbon dioxide, ozone, methane, nitrous oxide, CFCs and water vapour, only weakly absorb the short-wave radiation but strongly absorb the long-wave. In effect,

Figure 7.12 The Earth's heat balance

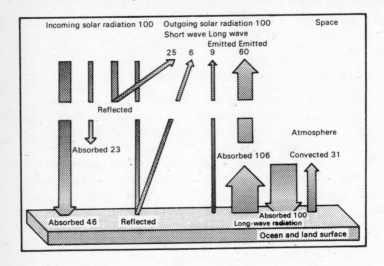

Source: UNEP/GEMS, *The Greenhouse Gases* (Nairobi: United Nations Environment Programme, 1987).

these gases trap the heat being radiated out from the surface of the globe, in a manner akin to that of a greenhouse.

The emissions of these gases are growing and are now known to be contributing to a warming of the earth's climate. More than 300 of the world's leading climate scientists who were part of the Intergovernmental Panel on Climate Change (IPCC), established by the UN General Assembly in 1988, have concluded that:

> We are certain that emissions resulting from human activities are substantially increasing the atmospheric concentrations of greenhouse gases: carbon dioxide, methane, CFCs and nitrous oxide. These increases will enhance the greenhouse effect, resulting on average in an additional warming of the earth's surface.[82]

Carbon dioxide is the most important greenhouse gas, contributing more than half of global warming. However, methane and nitrous oxide have contributed during the 1980s more than a fifth (Table 7.16). The increases in all these gases have already caused a temperature rise of 0.3–0.6°C this century. Based on the business-as-usual predictions the global temperature will rise by 0.3°C per decade (range

Table 7.16 Summary of the common greenhouse gases, rates of growth and contribution to global warming in the 1980s

	CO_2	CH_4	N_2O	CFCs
Annual increase (%)	0.5	1	0.8	4
Relative absorption of radiation compared with carbon dioxide	1	32	150	>10,000
Contribution to global warming in the 1980s	55	15	6	24

Source: Leggett, J., "The nature of the greenhouse threat", in: Leggett, J. (ed.), *Global Warming. The Greenpeace Report* (Oxford: Oxford University Press, 1990).

0.2–0.5), causing a mean sea level rise of about 6 cm per decade (range 2–10 cm).[83] But there are many uncertainties. Estimates are compli-cated by two factors – the residence times of gases in the atmosphere and the presence of various feedback mechanisms. Reducing emissions of these gases will not reduce concentrations immediately, as some persist for a long time in the atmosphere: for CO_2 and N_2O residence times are about 100 and 170 years respectively, although for methane only 8–12 years.

Potentially more important are the wide range of feedback mech-anisms. As in the depletion of the ozone layer the chemistry, physics and dynamics of the atmosphere are highly complex and as yet poorly understood. Some changes will encourage further warming, others will reduce the average temperature. Overall, though, these will probably act to increase, rather than decrease, greenhouse gas concentrations in a warmer world (Box 7.3). As the IPCC scientists have put it:

The complexity of the system means that we cannot rule out surprises.[84]

The consequences of global temperature increase are likely to be very serious, although they will vary from place to place and in ways that are not yet fully predictable.[85] Weather patterns will shift and sea levels will rise, initially from thermal expansion of the oceans and, perhaps eventually, as a result of melting of the polar ice caps. The greatest temperature changes will be at high latitudes, but water availability will worsen at low latitudes. Attendant on these changes in temperature will also be a growing likelihood of short-term extreme climatic events. Floods, droughts, hurricanes and severe freezes are all likely to become more common. Some of these may have a more serious and immediate impact upon the semi-arid tropics compared to either

Box 7.3 Summary of principal feedbacks in the greenhouse effect. Positive feedback mechanisms contribute to further warming, negative feedbacks act to cool the earth

Feedback	Positive or negative	Details
Water vapour	+ve	Warmer atmosphere will contain more water as evaporation rates are increased. Water vapour is a potent greenhouse gas.
Ice and snow	+ve	Less ice and snow will mean less reflection of incoming solar radiation. The darker surface absorbs more radiation.
Clouds	unknown	Can act as both +ve and −ve feedbacks. Current effect is to cool the earth.
Hydroxyl ions	unknown	Warmer atmosphere means more humidity and thus more OH ions. But the drain on OH will grow with increasing emissions of CH_4, CO, NO_x, NMHCs*, all of which are oxidized by, and destroy, OH. Result is unknown.
Aerosol particles	unknown	Sulphate and nitrate aerosols cool the earth. But these arise from acidification, which can damage ecosystems and reduce capacity to absorb CO_2.
Ocean temperature	+ve	As water temperature increases, solubility of CO_2 declines, so less CO_2 absorbed.
Ocean circulation	+ve	Plankton multiplier effect: increasing sea temperature stabilizes thermal stratification and prevents vertical mixing of water and nutrients. Less plankton growth means less CO_2 uptake.
Wind patterns and gas exchange	unknown	Wind patterns and speed help to determine exchange of gas between oceans and atmosphere.
Biochemical cycling of oceans	unknown	Balance of ocean dynamics could be disturbed. Unable to predict effects.
CO_2 fertilization	unknown	Increased CO_2 concentrations should promote increased photosynthesis and increased plant growth: a negative feedback. But uptake depends on well-being of forests threatened by air pollution, etc.
Eutrophication	−ve	Nitrogen and phosphorus fertilizers escaping from agriculture promote algal growth in surface waters. More growth takes up more CO_2.

Box 7.3 Continued

Feedback	Positive or negative	Details
Increased fertilizer usage or nitrogen from acid precipitation	+ve	Nitrogen competitively inhibits methane oxidization in soils, so reducing CH_4 consumption.
Temperature and plant respiration	+ve	As temperature increases respiration and photosynthesis increase. But respiration increases faster, and so contributes more CO_2 than is consumed.
Soil moisture	both	CO_2, N_2O and CH_4 uptake and absorption all influenced by temperature.
Vegetation distribution	unknown	Changes in temperature will affect distribution of vegetation. But unknown whether new ecosystems will migrate and adapt quickly enough.
Vegetation albedo	+ve	Poleward shift of vegetation will decrease reflectance of surface.
UVB and phytoplankton	+ve	Depletion of ozone layer and increased UVB penetration will decrease marine productivity.
UVB and terrestrial biota	+ve	Reduced plant productivity and less CO_2 uptake.
Rice paddies	+ve	Increased irrigation and rice paddy production will increase CH_4 emissions.
Methane in permafrost	+ve	Warmer, wetter soils in tundra regions will greatly increase methanogenesis and methane emissions.
Organic matter in permafrost	+ve	Higher temperatures mean accelerated microbial decomposition of abundant stores of organic matter.
Methane hydrates in permafrost	+ve	Methane hydrates, combinations of water crystals and methane gas trapped under pressure, occur below permafrost. Some of this vast reservoir could be released.
Offshore methane hydrates	+ve	Methane hydrates in sediments could be released by even a slight warming of Arctic water.

* *NMHCs are non-methane hydrocarbons*

Source: Leggett, J. "The nature of the greenhouse threat", in: Leggett, J. (ed.), *Global Warming. The Greenpeace Report* (Oxford: Oxford University Press, 1990).

the humid tropical or cool temperate regions, even though the latter may experience a greater rise in warmth. Crop and forage yields are more sensitive to changes in seasonal rainfall in the semi-arid tropics than in the humid regions – year-to-year variability tends to be greater and yields can be considerably lower in the driest years. During the 1980s, persistent droughts in the Sahel, north central India, northeast Brazil, south and eastern Africa and Australia led to hardship, famine, out-migration and forest fires. These may well become more frequent and widespread.

Buffering the world against such extreme events during the next century will require concerted action and practical recommendations from farm to national level, many of which will have to centre on both in-creasing and stabilizing crop productivity. Yet with current agricultural practices, production increases will lead to more atmospheric pollution. Although there is much that could be done to reduce agricultural emissions a great deal more investigation is still necessary to predict exactly the impact of a given measure on emissions. A reduction in biomass burning, however, will clearly reduce emissions and the contribution to tropospheric ozone production. Reducing methane emissions is more uncertain: changes to agronomic practice in paddy rice production and to livestock management, through the use of low-cellulose and high-cereal grain diets or methanogenesis-inhibiting feed supplements, could reduce emissions. Both ammonia and nitrous oxide emissions could be reduced by the choice of appropriate fertilizers and mode of application, and ammonia could be reduced by changes in storage practices and in the way livestock wastes are applied to land (see Chapter 11).

Summary

Agriculture is a major source of atmospheric pollution (Table 7.17). Paddy fields, the guts of livestock and the burning of vegetation, together, produce some 45 per cent of global methane emissions, which are currently 400–640 million tonnes annually and increasing at a rate of about one per cent per year. Methane contributes to increases in tropospheric ozone, to destruction of ozone in the stratosphere and also to global warming. In the 1980s methane produced by agriculture contributed about seven per cent to total global warming.

Agriculture is a less important, but nevertheless significant, source of nitrous oxide emissions, arising from nitrogen fertilizers, livestock waste and the burning of vegetation. About 14 million tonnes a year

Table 7.17 Contribution of agriculture to total production of globally important gases

	CH_4	N_2O	NH_3
Agricultural contributions to total emissions			
Paddy rice	21%	–	unknown
Livestock and wastes	15%	unknown	80–90%
Biomass burning	8%	5–20%	unknown
Fertilizers	–	5–20%	<5%
Total contribution	44%	10–25%	90%
Agricultural contribution to global warming	7%	0.6–1.5%	–

are produced, 10–25 per cent from agriculture. Levels are rising at about 0.2–0.3 per cent per year, driven mostly by increasing nitrogen fertilizer use. Nitrous oxide, through conversion to nitric oxide, contributes to depletion of stratospheric ozone. Nitrous oxide also absorbs radiation and hence contributes to global warming. In the 1980s nitrous oxide produced by agriculture contributed 0.6–1.5 per cent of total global warming.

The single main cause of global warming, however, is carbon dioxide, estimated to contribute about half of the projected warming over the next 50 years. Burning of biomass produces carbon dioxide equivalent to 50–100 per cent of that from burning of fossil fuels and, of the former, agriculture is responsible for 60–65 per cent. The principal sources are the practice of shifting, or swidden, cultivation and the annual burning of savanna lands and the clearing of forest and savanna for livestock and arable farming. Burning of agricultural wastes, in particular cereal straw and the residues of sugar cane and pineapples, can also cause a serious, but localized, nuisance.

Agriculture is also the principal source of ammonia emissions, arising when the nitrogen contained in fertilizers or livestock waste is volatilized, and when biomass is burnt. In the industrialized countries of Europe emissions from intensive livestock farming have doubled over the past 40 years. Emissions though are probably higher in a number of developing countries. Locally, ammonia depositions can damage plant growth, while on a larger scale atmospheric ammonia may be contributing to acid deposition.

References

1 Sanchez, P., *Properties and Management of Soils in the Tropics* (New York: John Wiley & Sons, 1976).

2 Devol, A.H., Richey, J.E., Clark, W.A. and King, S.L., "Methane emissions to the troposphere from the Amazon floodplain", *J. Geophys. Res.* **93** (1988) pp. 1583–92; Bartlett, K.B., Crill, P.M., Sebacher, D.I., Harriss, R.C., Wilson, J.O. and Melack, J.M., "Methane flux from the Central Amozonian flood plain", *J. Geophys. Res.* **93** (1988) pp. 1571–82.

3 Holzapfel-Pschorn, A. and Seiler, W., "Methane emissions during a cultivation period from an Italian rice paddy", *J. Geophys. Res.* **91** (1986) pp. 11803–814.

4 Ehrlich, A., "Agricultural contributions to global warming", in: Leggett, J. (ed.), *Global Warming. The Greenpeace Report* (Oxford: Oxford University Press, 1990).

5 Crutzen, P.J., Aselmann, I. and Seiler, W., "Methane production by domestic animals, wild ruminants, other herbivorous fauna, and humans", *Tellus* **38B** (1988) pp. 271–84.

6 FAO, *Production Yearbook 1988* (Rome: FAO, 1989); Bouwman, A.F., "Land use related sources of greenhouse gases", *Land Use Policy* April (1990) pp. 154–64.

7 Watson, R. et al., "Greenhouse gases and aerosols", in: *The Scientific Assessment of Climate Change*, report to the Intergovernmental Panel on Climate Change (IPCC), Working Group 1, Section 1. Peer Reviewed Assessment for Working Group 1 and Plenary, 25 April 1990 (Geneva: World Meteorological Organization, 1990); Bouwman, A.F., 1990, *op. cit.*

8 Watson et al., 1990 *op. cit.*; Blake, D.R. and Rowland, F.S., "Continuing worldwide increase in tropospheric methane, 1978–1987", *Science* **239** (1988) pp. 1129–31; Bolle, H.J., Seiler, W. and Bolin, B., "Other greenhouse gases and aerosols", in: Bolin, B., Doos, B.R., Jager, J. and Warwick, R.A., *The Greenhouse Effect, Climatic Change and Ecosystems, SCOPE no.* 29 (Chichester: J. Wiley & Sons, 1986).

9 Bouwman, 1990, *op. cit.*; Cicerone, R.J. and Oremland, R.S., "Biogeochemical aspects of atmospheric methane", *Global Biogeochem. Cycles* **2** (1988) pp. 299–327; Blake and Rowland, 1988, *op. cit.*; Bolle et al., 1986, *op. cit.*

10 Khalil, M.A.K. and Rasmussen, R.A., "Causes of increasing atmospheric methane: depletion of hydroxyl radicals and the risk of emissions", *Atmos. Environ.* **19** (1985) pp. 397–407.

11 Kelly, M., "Halting global warming", in: Legett, J. (ed.), 1990, *op. cit.*

12 Watson, et al. 1990, *op. cit.*; Keller, M., Kaplan, W.A. and Wofsy, S.C., "Emissions of N_2O, CH_4, and CO_2 from tropical forest soils", *J. Geophys. Res.* **91** (1990) pp. 11791–802; Matson, P.A. and Vitousek, P.M., "Cross-system comparisons of soil nitrogen transformations and nitrous oxide flux in tropical forest ecosystems", *Global Biogeochem. Cycles* **1** (1987)

pp. 163–70.

13 McElroy, M.B. and Wofsy, S.C., "Tropical forests: interactions with the atmosphere", in: Prance, G.T. (ed.), *Tropical Rain Forests and the World Atmosphere* (Colorado: West View Press, 1986).

14 Keller, M., Kaplan, W.A, Wofsy, S.C. and Da Costa, J.M. "Emissions of N_2O from tropical forest soils: response to fertilization with NH_4^+, NO_3^- and PO_4^{3-}", *J. Geophys. Res.* 93 (1988) pp. 1600–604; Keller et al., 1986, *op. cit.*; Livingston, G., Vitousek, P.M. and Matson, P.A. "Nitrous oxide flux and nitrogen transformations across a landscape gradient in Amazonia", *J. Geophys. Res.* 93 (1988) pp. 1593–9.

15 Bowden, W.S. and Bormann, F.H. "Transport and loss of nitrous oxide in soil water after clear-cutting", *Science* 233 (1986) pp. 867–9.

16 Prasad, R. and De Datta, S.K., "Increasing fertiliser nitrogen efficiency in wetland rice", in: *Nitrogen and Rice* (Los Banos, Philippines: IRRI, 1979).

17 FAO, *Fertiliser Yearbook* no 37. (Rome: FAO, 1988).

18 Ryden, J.C., "Denitrification loss from managed grassland", in: Golterman, H. (ed.), *Denitrification in the Nitrogen Cycle* (New York and London: Plenum Press, 1985). Christenssen, S., "Denitrification in an acid soil and effects of slurry and potassium nitrate on the evaluation of nitrous oxide and on nitrate-reducing bacteria", *Soil Biol. Biochem.* 17 (1985) pp. 757–64.

19 Watson et al., 1990, *op. cit.*; Rasmussen, R.A. and Khalil, "Atmospheric trace gases: trends and distributions over the last decade", *Science* 232 (1986) pp. 1623–24; Bolle et al., 1986, *op. cit.*; Pearman, G.I., Etheridge, D., de Silva, R. and Fraser, P.J., "Evidence of changing concentrations of CO_2, N_2O and CH_4 from air bubbles in Antarctic Ice", *Nature* 320 (1986) pp. 248–50.

20 Ehrlich, 1990, *op. cit.*; Watson et al., 1990, *op. cit.*

21 Kelly, 1990, *op. cit.*

22 Ko, M.K.W. and Sze, N.D., "A 2-D model calculation of atmospheric lifetimes for N_2O, CFC-11 and CFC-12", *Nature* 287 (1982) pp. 317–19; Bolle et al., 1986, *op. cit.*

23 Luizao, F., Matson, P., Livingston, G., Luizao, R. and Vitousek, P., "Nitrous oxide flux following tropical land clearing", *Global Biogeochem. Cycles* 3 (1989) pp. 281–5.

24 Kruse, M., ApSimon, H.M. and Bell, J.N.B., *An emissions inventory for ammonia arising from agriculture in Great Britain* (University of London: Imperial College Centre for Environmental Technology, 1986); Kruse, M., ApSimon, H.M. and Bell, J.N.B., "Validity and uncertainty in the calculation of an emission inventory for ammonia arising from agriculture in Great Britain", *Environ. Pollut.* 56 (1989) pp. 237–57; ApSimon, H.M., Kruse, M. and Bell, J.N.B., "Ammonia emissions and their role in acid deposition", *Atmos. Environ.* 21 (1987) pp. 1939–46; Buijsman, E., Maas, H.F.M. and Asman, W.A.H., "Anthropogenic NH_3 emissions in Europe", *Atmos. Environ.* 21 (1987) pp. 1009–22.

25 Galbally, I.E., "The emission of nitrogen to the remote atmosphere", in: Galloway, J.N., Charlson, R.J., Andreae, M.O. and Rodhe, H. (eds),

The Biogeochemical Cycling of Sulfur and Nitrogen in the Remote Atmosphere (Hingham, Mass.: D. Reidel, 1985); Andreae, M.O., Browell, E.V., Garstang, M., Gregory, G.L., Harriss, R.C., Hill, G.F., Jacob, D.J., Pereira, M.C., Sachse, G.W., Setzer, A.W., Silva Dias, P.L., Talbot, R.W., Torres, A.L. and Wofsy, S.C., "Biomass-burning emissions and associated haze layers over Amazonia", *J. Geophys. Res.* **93** (1988) pp. 1509–27.

26 Young, A. (1804), "Essay on Manures", in: Gazley, J., *A Biography of Arthur Young* (Pennsylvania: American Philosophical Society, 1973).

27 Muck, R.E, Guest, R.W. and Richards, B.K., "Effect of manure storage design on nitrogen conservation", *Agric. Wastes* **10** (1984) pp. 205–20; Ayers, R.S., "A case study – nitrates in the upper Santa Ana River basin in relation to groundwater pollution", in: Pratt, P.F. (ed.), *Management of Nitrogen in Irrigated Agriculture* (Riverside: University of California, 1978).

28 Elliott, L.F, Schuman, G.E. and Viets, F.G. "Volatilization of nitrogen-containing compounds from beef cattle areas", *Soil Sci. Soc. Amer. Proc.* **35** (1971) pp. 752–5.

29 Ryden, J.C., Whitehead, D.C., Lockyer, D.R., Thompson, R.B., Skinner, J.H. and Garwood, E.A., "Ammonia emission from grassland and livestock production systems in the UK", *Environ. Pollut.* **48** (1987) pp. 173–184.

30 Buijsman et al., 1987, *op. cit.*

31 Fillery, I.R.P. and Vlek, P.L.G. "Reappraisal of the significance of ammonia volatilisation as an N loss mechanism in flooded rice fields", *Fert. Res.* **9** (1986) pp. 79–98; Mikkelson, D.S. and De Datta, S.K., "Ammonia volatilisation from wetland rice soils", in: *Nitrogen and Rice* (Los Banos: IRRI, 1979).

32 Luebs, R.E., Davis, K.R. and Laag, A.E. "Enrichment of the atmosphere with nitrogen compounds volatilised from a large dairy area", *J. Environ. Qual.* **2** (1973) pp. 137–41.

33 Kruse et al., 1986, *op. cit.*

34 ApSimon et al., 1987, *op. cit.*

35 FAO, *Production Yearbooks* (Rome: FAO), *passim.*

36 Seiler, W. and Crutzen, P.J. "Estimates of gross and net fluxes of carbon between the biosphere and the atmosphere from biomass burning", *Climatic Change* **2** (1980) pp. 207–47; Greenland, D.J. and Okigbo, B.N., "Crop production under shifting cultivation and the maintenance of soil fertility", Symposium on potential productivity of field crops under different environments 1980 (Los Banos, Philippines: IRRI, 1983).

37 Delany, A.C., Haagensen, P., Walters, S. and Wartburg, A.F., "Photochemically produced ozone in the emission from large-scale tropical vegetation fires", *J. Geophys. Res.* **90** (1985) pp. 2425–29.

38 Seiler, W. and Crutzen, P., 1980, *op. cit.*

39 Andreae et al., 1988, *op. cit.*

40 Rocha, J., "Ozone fears as Amazon forest burns", quoting Paul Crutzen

and Richard Stolarski, *The Guardian* 18 April (1988) p.6.

41 Andreae et al., 1988, *op. cit.*; Delany et al., 1985, *op. cit.*; Kirchhoff, V.W.J.H., "Surface ozone measurements in Amazonia", *J. Geophys. Res.* 93 (1988) pp. 1469–76; Browell, E.V., Gregory, G.L., Harriss, R.C. and Kirchhoff, V.W.J.H., "Tropospheric ozone and aerosol distributions across the Amazon Basin", *J. Geophys. Res.* 93 (1986) pp. 1422–30.

42 Larry van Meir and Robert Bohall, USDA, Washington, personal communication, 3 August 1990.

43 Daniels, A., "Diffusion and emission of smoke from agricultural burning in Hawaii", *Water, Air and Soil Pollution* 34 (1987) pp. 111–24; Stern, A.C., Boubel, R.W., Turner, D.B. and Fox, D.L., *Fundamentals of Air Pollution*, 2nd edn (London: Academic Press, 1984).

44 Butterworth, B., 1985, *The Straw Manual* (London: E. and F.N. Spon, 1985).

45 Seiler, W. and Crutzen, P., 1980, *op. cit.*; Detwiler, R.P. and Hall, C.A.S., "Tropical forests and the global carbon cycle", *Science* 239 (1988) pp. 42–7.

46 Larkin, S.B.C., Lee, M., McInnes, G., Sharp, V. and Simmonds, A.C., *The Management of Air Pollution and Other Factors Relating to the Practice of Straw and Stubble Burning*", WSL Report Lr 518 (AP) (Stevenage: Warren Spring Laboratory, 1985).

47 RCEP, *Managing Waste: The Duty of Care*, 11th Report (London: HMSO, Royal Commission on Environmental Pollution, 1985).

48 NSCA, *The NSCA Surveys of Straw/Stubble Burning* (Brighton: National Society for Clean Air, 1984–9).

49 NSCA, 1989, *op. cit.*

50 Lockyer, D.R. and Whitehead, D.C. "The uptake of gaseous ammonia by the leaves of Italian ryegrass", *J. Experim. Botany* 37 (1986) pp. 919–27.

51 Hutchinson, G.L. and Viets, F.G. "Nitrogen enrichment of surface water by absorption of ammonia volatilized from cattle feedlots", *Science* 166 (1969) pp. 514–15.

52 van Breeman, N., Burrough, P.A., Velthorst, E.J., van Dobben, M.F., Dewit, T., Ridders, T. and Reijnders, H.F.R., "Soil acidification from atmospheric ammonium sulphate in forest canopy throughfall", *Nature* 299 (1982) pp. 548–50.

53 Roelofs, J.G.M., Kempers, A.J., Houdijk, A.L.F.M. and Jansen, J., "The effect of air-borne ammonium sulphate on *Pinus nigra* var. *maritima* in the Netherlands", *Plant and Soil* 84 (1985) pp. 45–56; Nihlgard, B. "The ammonia hypothesis – an additional explanation to the forest dieback in Europe", *Ambio* 14 (1985) pp. 2–8; van der Eerden, L.J., Harsema, H. and Klarenbeek, J.V., "De relatie tussen bedricjfsomvag en de kans op beschadiging van gewassen dondom intensieve veehouderijdedrijven", in: *NH₄ Tagung Groenveld, Baarn 1985* (Utrecht: Staatsbosbeheer, Rijksdenst 1985).

54 Roelofs et al., 1985, *op. cit.*

55 Heil, G.W., Werger, M.J.A., de Mol, W., van Dam, D. and Heijne, B.,

"Capture of atmospheric ammonium by grassland canopies", *Science* **239** (1988) pp. 764–5; Heil, G.W. and Diemont, W.H., "Raised nutrient levels change heathland into grassland", *Vegetatio* **53** (1983) pp. 113–20; Heil, G.W. and Bruggink, M., "Competition for nutrients between *Calluna vulgaris* (L.) Hull and *Molinia caerulea* (L.)", Moensh. *Oecologia* **73** (1987) pp. 105–107.

56 Heil and Diemont, 1983, *op. cit.*

57 Hutchinson and Viets, 1969, *op. cit.*

58 Hahn, J. and Crutzen, P.J., "The role of fixed nitrogen in atmospheric photochemistry", *Phil. Trans. R. Soc. Lond. B* **296** (1982) pp. 531–41.

59 Bamber, D.J., Clark, P.A., Glover, G.M., Healey, P.G.W., Kallend, A.S., March, A.R.N., Tuck, A.F. and Vaughan, G., "Air sampling flights round the British Isles at low altitudes: SO_2 oxidation and removal rates", *Atmos. Environ.* **18** (1984) pp. 1777–90; ApSimon et al., 1987, *op. cit.*

60 Moller, D. and Schieferdecker, H., "A relationship between agricultural ammonia emissions and atmospheric sulphur dioxide over industrial areas", *Atmos. Environ.* **19** (1985) pp. 695–700.

61 Bell, J.N.B., Imperial College, London, personal communication, 28 June 1990.

62 Ashmore, M., Bell, N. and Garretty, C., *Acid Rain and Britain's Natural Ecosystems* (London: Imperial College Centre for Environmental Technology, 1988); NRC, *Acid Deposition: Long Term*, National Research Council (Washington DC: National Academy Press, 1986); Bell, J.N.B., "Effects of acid deposition on crops and forests", *Experimentia* **42** (1986) pp. 363–71.

63 Ehhalt, D.H. "Methane in the global atmosphere", *Environment* **27** (1985) pp. 6–12, 30–33.

64 UNEP/GEMS, *The Ozone Layer*, UNEP/GEMS Environmental Library no.2 (Nairobi: UNEP, 1987).

65 UK SORG, *Stratospheric Ozone*, Stratospheric Ozone Review Group prepared at the request of the Dept. of the Environment and the Meteorological Office (London: HMSO, 1988).

66 UK SORG, 1988, *op. cit.*

67 Farman, J.C., Gardiner, B.G. and Shanklin, J.D., "Large losses of total ozone in Antartica reveal seasonal ClO_x/NO_x interaction", *Nature* **315** (1985) pp. 207–10.

68 UK SORG, 1988, *op. cit.*; UK SORG, *Stratospheric Ozone* (London: HMSO, 1990).

69 Farman et al., 1985, *op. cit.*; UK SORG, 1988, 1990, *op. cit.*; UK SORG, *Stratospheric Ozone* (London: HMSO, 1987). Stolarski, R.S., Krueger, A.J., Schoeberl, M.R., McPeters, R.D., Newman, P.A. and Alpert, J.C., "Nimbus 7 satellite measurements of the springtime Antarctic ozone hole", *Nature* **322** (1986) pp. 808–11; Hofmann, D.J., Harder, J.W., Rolf, S.R. and Rosen, J.M., "Balloon-borne observations of the development and vertical structure of the Antarctic ozone hole in 1986", *Nature* **326** (1987) pp. 59–62; Heath, D.F., Bhartia, P.K. and Schlesinger,

B.M., "Large scale perturbations of stratospheric ozone during the period of slowly varying changes in solar UV spectral irradiance and the eruption of El Chichon: 1978–1983", *EOS* 66 (1985) p. 1009.

70 WMO, "Scientific Assessment of Stratospheric Ozone: 1989", vol. I, Global Ozone Research & Monitoring Project Report No. 20 (Geneva: World Meteorological Organisation, 1989); SORG, 1990, *op. cit.*

71 UK SORG, 1988, *op. cit.*

72 McKenna, D.F., Jones, R.L., Poole, L.R., Solomon, S., Fahey, D.W., Kelly, K.K., Proffitt, M.H., Brine, W.H., Loewenstein, M. and Chan, K.R., "Calculations of ozone destruction during the 1988–89 Arctic winter", *Geophys. Res. Lett.* 17 (1990) pp. 553–6.

73 Russell-Jones, R., "Consequences for human health of stratospheric ozone depletion", in: Russell-Jones, R. and Wigley (eds), *Ozone Depletion Health and Environmental Consequences* (Chichester: John Wiley & Sons, 1989); Elwood, J.M., "Epidemiology of melanoma: its relationship to ultraviolet radiation and ozone depletion", in: Russell-Jones and Wigley (eds), *op. cit.*; US Environmental Protection Agency, *Assessing the Risks of Trace Gases that can Modify the Stratosphere* vols I–V, US EPA/400/1–87/001 AE (Washington DC: Office of Air and Radiation, 1987).

74 Russell-Jones, 1989, *op. cit.*

75 Russell-Jones, 1989, *op. cit.*

76 Russell-Jones, 1989, *op. cit.*

77 EPA, 1987, *op. cit.*

78 Worrest, R.C. and Grant, L.D., "Effects of ultraviolet-B radiation on terrestrial plants and marine organisms", in: Russell-Jones and Wigley (eds), *op. cit.*

79 Gold, W.G. and Caldwell, M.M., "The effects of ultraviolet-B radiation on plant competition in terrestrial ecosystems", *Physiol. Plantarum* 58 (1983) pp. 435–44.

80 Worrest and Grant, 1989, *op. cit.*

81 Hunter, J.R., Kaupp, S.E. and Taylor, J.H., "Assessment of the effects of UV radiation on marine fish larvae", in: Calkins, J. (ed.), *The Role of Solar Ultraviolet Radiation on Marine Ecosystems* (New York: Plenum Press, 1982).

82 Intergovernmental Panel on Climate Change, *Scientific Assessment of Climate Change*, report of Working Group 1, and accompanying Policymakers Summary (Geneva: World Meteorological Organisation, 1990a).

83 IPCC, 1990a, *op. cit.*

84 IPCC, 1990a, *op. cit.*

85 Parry, M., *Climate Change and World Agriculture* (London: Earthscan Publications Ltd, 1990); Intergovernmental Panel on Climate Change, *The Political Impacts of Climate Change: Impacts on Agriculture and Forestry* (Geneva and Nairobi: World Meteorological Organisation and United Nations Environment Programme, 1990b).

8 The Impact of Air Pollution on Agriculture

So far in this book, we have presented the evidence for agriculture as a polluter of our environment. Yet agriculture also suffers from pollution, in particular from pollutants in the air derived from industrial and urban activity, and from agriculture itself. Crops and livestock may be damaged by concentrated pollutants emitted by nearby industries, for example sulphur dioxide from power stations or fluorides from brick factories. Equally, though, agricultural production is at risk from moderately raised levels of pollutants in the ambient air of rural areas, as a result of long distance dispersal from industrial, urban or agricultural origins.

The air pollutants that are most damaging to agriculture are sulphur dioxide (SO_2) and the oxides of nitrogen (NO_x), which can be categorized as acid pollutants, and ozone (O_3) together with other photochemical oxidants. Fluorides used to be major pollutants but, at least in the industrialized countries, are of diminishing importance. Each of these pollutants is relatively easy to measure and monitor but still not enough is known of the effects on crops and livestock.

We begin this chapter with a discussion of the problems of experimentation on pollution effects. We then describe the present sources and trends of the most important pollutants and what is known of their impact, both individually and in combination. The last section of the chapter is devoted to the topic of radiation, whose impact on agriculture has been demonstrated in dramatic fashion by the Chernobyl accident.

The experimental evidence for damage

The nature and amount of damage caused to crop plants by air pollutants depends on three key factors – the inherent toxicity of the particular pollutant gas, the proportion that is taken up by the plants and their physiological reaction. These, in turn, are affected by the environment in which the crop is growing, including the presence of other pollutants.

Early research was principally concerned with acute injury, that is, damage produced by high doses. The best documented responses are effects on plant foliage – distinctive patterns of necrosis (death of cells) and chlorosis (loss or destruction of photosynthetic pigment). These are often, but not invariably, associated with air pollution and it is sometimes difficult to be certain of the cause of the injury. For instance, a disease of alfalfa, known as white spot, can be caused by a high concentration of SO_2, or by water stress, or by leafhopper attack. Similarly, temperature and wind extremes can cause a burn on the leaf margins of many plants that is similar to injury by fluoride.[1] Nevertheless, acute injury remains much better understood than the chronic effects produced by exposure to low or medium levels of pollutants over long periods of time.

Problems of experimentation

In addition to visible damage, air pollutants also affect growth and yield of plants. These can be measured and, indeed, in the last 20 years such measurement has become highly sophisticated. Nonetheless, it is still difficult to relate causes and effects in an accurate manner. Part of the problem lies in exactly replicating field conditions. In the early experiments, plants were grown in greenhouses with filtered or unfiltered air, but the micro-environment and, in particular, the aerodynamics close to and within a crop are rarely the same as those outside. Subsequently, various complex environments have been designed to achieve more realistic air flows, but the most successful has been the relatively straightforward, open-top chambers into which treated or ambient air is drawn at the base and then expelled through the top, leaving the plants otherwise exposed to the environment (Figure 8.1).

Even with open-top chambers, however, it is difficult to ensure that conditions inside are similar to those outside, apart from the pollution treatments. The first investigations, in the UK, of the effect on barley of SO_2 and hydrogen fluoride (HF) emitted from brickworks used enclosed chambers, the plants being ventilated with either ambient (polluted) air or filtered (clean) air.[2] But inside the chambers, humidity and temperature were higher and light intensity lower than outside. Plants inside developed 20 days ahead of those outside and even plants grown in filtered air had twice the level of sulphur in their leaves as plants grown outside. The experimental design was changed.

Figure 8.1 Open-top chamber for use in experiments on effects of air pollution on plant growth

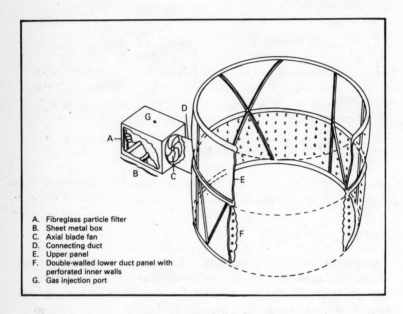

A. Fibreglass particle filter
B. Sheet metal box
C. Axial blade fan
D. Connecting duct
E. Upper panel
F. Double-walled lower duct panel with perforated inner walls
G. Gas injection port

Source: Heck, W.W., Cure, W.W., Rawlings, J.O., Zaragoza, L.J., Heagle, A.S., Heggested, H.E., Kohut, R.J., Kress, L.W. and Temple, A.J., "Assessing impacts of ozone on agricultural crops" *J. Air Poll. Cont. Assoc.* 34 (1984) pp. 729–735.

Open-top chambers were substituted, and ventilated with ambient or filtered air that was passed into the chamber at a sufficient rate to ensure that ambient air from above could not enter.[3] The unfiltered air reduced straw and grain yields, yet still the yields of barley grown on identical plots outside the chambers were significantly higher than yields in the chambers, whether in filtered or unfiltered air (Table 8.1). As in the enclosed chambers used previously, the barley plants in the chambers were developing more rapidly: for example, reaching the stage at which stamens produce pollen 7–8 days earlier.

It is also difficult to measure the actual dose of the pollutant in the chambers to which the plants are exposed. Two workers, Unsworth and Mansfield[4], puzzled by the differences in published experiments on the effects of SO_2 on perennial ryegrass (*Lolium perenne*), suggested that the SO_2 concentration to which plants were being exposed in the chambers was actually substantially lower than the inlet concentrations quoted in the reports. In particular, they criticized one closed-top design as producing fluxes of SO_2 to the grass leaves well below

Table 8.1 Yields of barley grown in the field or in chambers with filtered (clean) or unfiltered (polluted with SO_2 and HF) air in the Bedfordshire brickfields of the UK

| | Inside chambers | | |
	Filtered	Unfiltered	Unenclosed
Number shoots per m^2	1068	884	1255
Number ears per m^2	628	600	966
Total dry weight (g/m^2)	1242	952	1403
Grain dry weight (g/m^2)	525	413	595

Source: Buckenham, A.H. et al., "Effects of aerial pollutants on the growth and yield of spring barley", *Ann. Appl. Biol.* **100** (1982) pp. 179–87.

the presumed concentrations.[5] Ideally the presumed concentration of pollutant at the exit should be the same as at the inlet, but the exit concentration tends to fall if the flow of air is low or if there is a large leaf area of plants in the chamber.

Minor aspects of environmental design can also be important. Open-top chambers, for example, often permit outside air to enter during turbulent and windy conditions. The growing of plants in containers may also place an artificial constraint on root growth that can, in turn, aggravate the effect of the SO_2.[6] And the method of watering in the chambers or glasshouses can be significant. Misting instead of using subirrigation has been found to enhance chronic damage, partly because moisture on the leaves increases the uptake of pollutant gases. In climates such as those of Britain, where dew or rainfall keeps foliage of crops wet for some 30 per cent of the time, this may be a critical factor in determining the degree of damage.

Experiments also need to reproduce the temporal pattern of pollution produced by industrial and urban sources. There are several critical questions. How important are the peak levels of pollutants as compared to the normal exposure? Does constant exposure produce the same effect as a variable exposure with the same overall mean? What is the effect of combinations of pollutants that commonly occur in the field?

The length of exposure to pollution may also be important. Experiments tend to be of relatively short duration, which is less of a problem for annual crops, but is a major drawback in studies of pollution effects on perennials. The longest experimental fumigation of trees has been seven years, but this is still only a small proportion of a lifespan and leaves many questions unanswered.[7] For instance, a pollutant dose may predispose a tree to damage by another cause at a later time. This has still to be investigated.

Not surprisingly the results of apparently similar experiments can differ greatly (Figure 8.2) and this has led to considerable discussion over experimental protocols.[8] Far too often the results are misleading because, for one reason or another, the experiment is not realistic. For instance, concentrations of gases are used that are much higher than usually encountered. But the commonest criticism of the published work is that the details of the experiment are not fully described, so making it difficult fully to assess the realism and produce valid comparisons. Often information on such variables as growing conditions, density of planting, concentration over time of the pollutant, the presence of other pollutant gases, and details of the micro-environment are lacking.

Figure 8.2   Relationship between total SO_2 dose and percentage reduction in shoot dry weight of spaced *Lolium perenne* plants compared with clear-air controls in a variety of experiments

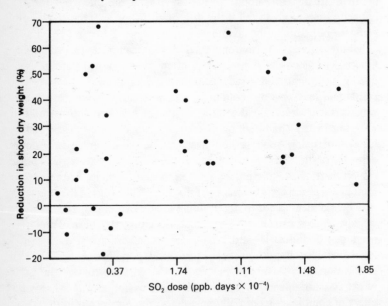

Source: Bell, J.N.B., "Sulphur dioxide and the growth of grasses" in: Unsworth, M.H. and Ormrod, D.P. (eds), *Effects of Air Pollution in Agriculture and Horticulture* (London, Butterworth, 1982), using data of Bell and Clough, 1973; Ashenden et al., 1978, 1979a, b; Ayazloo and Bell, 1981.

Environmental and genetic factors

A further complicating factor, still imperfectly understood, is the influence of climate and soils on the sensitivity of plants to pollutants.

Mediating the effect are two key physiological processes: the metabolic rates of plants and the opening and closure of the stomata – the apertures in the plant leaf surface through which gases, such as SO_2, gain entry to the inside of leaves. High metabolic rate and a wide stomatal aperture are both favoured by the same conditions – moderate temperatures, high light intensity and humidity, adequate soil moisture and nutrients – and the effect in both cases is, in general, to increase the sensitivity to SO_2 and NO_x. If the metabolic rate is high the response time of the plant can be very rapid, so leading to acute injury. Necrosis due to fluoride, for example, is more pronounced at higher temperatures. But chronic SO_2 injury is probably worse under slow growing conditions.[9]

The effects of humidity on stomatal opening have been demonstrated experimentally on green beans. A rise in relative humidity from 35 per cent to 75 per cent increases uptake of SO_2 and ozone by two to three fold.[10] On the other hand, water stress and drought cause stomatal closure, which results in lower levels of damage. Findings on the effects of nutrients are more conflicting: optimum nutrient supply can induce greater sensitivity by increasing physiological activity which then promotes pollutant uptake, but it may also speed recovery after exposure.

Crops in the tropics are likely to be most sensitive to pollutants when a high metabolic rate is combined with open stomata. This will happen when there is adequate soil moisture (the crops are irrigated) and adequate nutrients (the crops are fertilized), when the light intensity is high (during the cloudless dry season), or when the humidity is high (during the wet season). Plants differ in their photosynthetic systems, producing different intermediate compounds in the pathway from fixing CO_2 to producing carbohydrates. In this respect they are either C_3 plants or C_4 plants. Rice, wheat, barley, potato, cassava and soybean are C_3 plants; maize, millet, sorghum and sugar cane are C_4 plants. C_3 plants tend to be more susceptible than C_4 plants, and since rice is a C_3 plant, there is considerable potential for air pollution damage in irrigated rice lands close to industrial and urban areas.

Finally, there are genetic factors that complicate the picture. In some plants, resistance to damage may be conferred by specific genes: sensitivity to ozone in onions, for instance, is controlled by a single gene which codes for stomata to close after exposure.[11] Stomata in plants without the gene remain open and allow more pollutant to enter.

Acid pollution

Three important gases produce acid when dissolved in water – sulphur dioxide (SO_2), nitrogen dioxide (NO_2), and nitric oxide (NO), the latter two being referred to collectively as the nitrogen oxides, NO_x. From the air they are deposited onto farmers' fields, directly in the form of *dry deposition*, or from rain or snow as *wet deposition*, commonly referred to as *acid rain*, or they are captured by plants from cloud or fog, as *occult deposition*. Acidity is generally defined as deposition having a pH value below 5.6 – under normal conditions carbon dioxide combines with water in the air to form a dilute solution of carbonic acid, which has a pH of 5.6.

Sources of sulphur dioxide

Sulphur dioxide is produced naturally in abundance, as anyone who stands on the lip of an active volcanic crater will soon appreciate. Other natural sources of sulphur are sea spray, soils and plants (mainly as hydrogen sulphide, H_2S) and the burning of biomass (mainly as sulphur dioxide, SO_2). But, today, emissions from human activity roughly equal those of nature, both being about 80 million tonnes of sulphur annually.[12] The primary source is the burning of fossil fuels containing sulphur. In the industrialized countries about 70 per cent of emissions arise from power generating stations, and only a small proportion of the remainder from domestic and commercial premises. But in countries such as China, domestic coal burning stoves are a significant source. Most of the emissions arise in western and central Europe, in the east of North America and in parts of Asia. But in a few highly industrialized regions of the developing countries, such as parts of southeastern Brazil, sulphur emission density may be comparable to that of the industrialized countries.[13]

The highest ambient concentrations of SO_2 occur in and around cities and near centres of industrial activity (Figure 8.3a,b), though levels in many industrialized countries have been falling in recent years. In London, for example, both the concentration and incidence of winter peaks have fallen since the early 1960s. The average of the highest daily concentrations measured at different sites is now of the order of 75 ppb, down from 500 ppb in the 1960s (see Box 8.1 for description of the different measures of pollutant gas concentrations).

The adoption of efficient dispersion mechanisms has reduced the severity of SO_2 pollution close to its sources, but this may have been at the expense of increased ambient levels over a much larger

Figure 8.3a   Sulphur dioxide emissions in 127 × 127 km grid squares in North America, 1970–75. Units are thousand tonnes SO_2/year

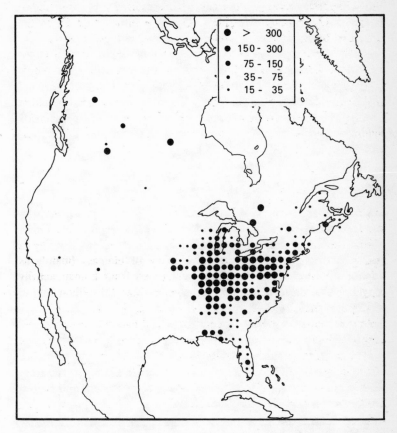

Source: Ottar, B., Dovland, H. and Semb, A. "Long range transport of air pollutants and acid depositions" in: Treshow, M. (ed), *Air Pollution and Plant Life* (New York: John Wiley and Sons, 1984).

area. Where there is a heavy population density and industry is concentrated, such as in western Europe and eastern North America, ambient concentrations are high over a substantial proportion of the region. More than 1.3 million hectares of agricultural land in northwestern Europe, representing one per cent of the total land area, is currently subject to annual mean SO_2 concentrations above 38 ppb.[14] In the UK, annual mean concentrations vary between 3.7 and 15 ppb depending on locality, but rural areas near large industrial conurbations may experience winter means of 19–38 ppb. In the USA

Figure 8.3b   Sulphur dioxide emissions in 150×150 km grid squares for Europe, 1978. Units are thousand tonnes SO_2/year

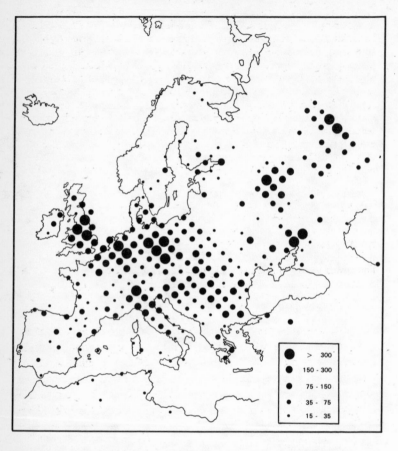

Source: Ottar et al., 1984, *op. cit.*

ambient annual mean SO_2 concentrations are currently of the order of 8–10 ppb, but in the heavily populated midwest and northeast and near point sources in Utah and New Mexico are 15–25 ppb.[15] There may, also, be considerable short-term fluctuations – maximum hourly concentrations of SO_2 may rise to 30 times the annual mean.

In the developing countries, high levels of SO_2 are not so widely dispersed. They tend to be concentrated in and around cities where most values are similar to those of the industrialized countries (Table 8.2). Some of the highest levels in the world occur in southern China. The widespread burning of coal, particularly in domestic stoves and

Box 8.1   Measures of concentration for gaseous pollutants

Concentrations of gaseous pollutants can be expressed either on a volume to volume basis, such as parts per billion (ppb), or on a mass to volume basis, such as micrograms per cubic metre ($\mu g/m^3$). The former is best suited to descriptions of ambient pollutant concentrations and is independent of temperature and pressure, whereas the latter is used in physiological and biochemical studies aimed at describing plant response to specific amounts of pollutant, or for evaluating dosages and fluxes. For simplicity, concentrations in this chapter are solely presented as ppb.

The conversion of ppb to $\mu g/m^3$ or vice versa depends upon temperature, pressure and molecular weight of the gas. Conversion factors are given below for the most common gases, assuming a temperature of 20°C (i.e. 293 Kelvin) and a pressure of 1 atmosphere and that the gases obey the ideal gas law ($P_1V_1/T_1 = P_2V_2/T_2$).

To convert ppb SO_2 to $\mu g/m^3$ multiply by 2.67
To convert ppb NO_2 to $\mu g/m^3$ multiply by 1.91
To convert ppb NO to $\mu g/m^3$ multiply by 1.25
To convert ppb HF to $\mu g/m^3$ multiply by 0.83
To convert ppb O_3 to $\mu g/m^3$ multiply by 2.00
To convert ppb PAN to $\mu g/m^3$ multiply by 4.37
To convert $\mu g/m^3$ to ppb use reciprocal of above values.

small-scale industry, produces 15–18 million tonnes of SO_2 annually for the country as a whole. Adverse meteorological conditions for dispersion and low smoke stacks cause serious pollution close to where the coal is burnt, particularly in winter when large amounts of domestic coal are burnt. The problem is particularly acute in the south because local coal contains between 3–5 per cent sulphur, much more than that of the north.[16] Annual concentrations in the southern cities of Chongqing and Guiyang are 100–150 ppb.[17]

In most developing countries, however, increased SO_2 levels are usually very localized. Industrialization close to the international agricultural research centre, the International Crop Research Institute for the Semi-Arid Tropics, ICRISAT, at Hyderabad, in India, produces potentially phytotoxic levels of several hundred ppb of SO_2, occasionally peaking at 1000 ppb.[18] Yet parts of the research station site, only 1–3 km from the sources, experience background levels of only 5 ppb of SO_2.

Sources of nitrogen oxides

The primary natural sources of nitrogen oxides are lightning and

Table 8.2 Sulphur dioxide in the air of urban areas

Top ten polluted cities[1]	Average SO_2 concentration[2] (ppb)	P_{98} concentration[3] (ppb)
Milan	62	182
Shenyang	61	316
Tehran	48	120
Seoul	43	161
Rio de Janeiro	40	124
Sao Paolo	32	37
Xian	30	107
Paris	30	90
Beijing	30	138
Guangzhou	26	85
Selected from Third World		
Santiago	24	64
Manila	22	60
Calcutta	21	51
Shanghai	20	52
New Delhi	15	74
Medellin	15	24
Caracas	12	21
Bombay	10	17

[1] Not included in this list are the two cities of Guiyang and Chongqing, where average SO_2 concentrations are 147 and 97 ppb (Zhao and Xiong, 1988, *op. cit.*)
[2] Average of annual means of 1980–4
[3] The P_{98} value (98 percentile) indicates that less than two per cent of daily averages (less than seven days per year) exceed the value given. Those listed are for the most recently recorded year: for some cities P_{98} values have been greatly exceeded in previous years: Milan 268 in 1982; Tehran 231 in 1982; Sao Paolo 96 in 1980; Bombay 57 in 1981

Source: UNEP, *Environmental Data Report* (Oxford: Blackwell, 1990).

microbial activity in soils, that oxidize atmospheric and soil nitrogen. Emissions from human activity are about double those from natural sources, producing a combined global total of 25–100 million tonnes annually.[19] The major source is the combustion of fossil fuels but, in contrast to SO_2, a large proportion comes from burning gasoline in motor vehicles. In the UK and the USA electric power generating stations and vehicles each produce between 30 and 40 per cent of total emissions.[20] Also important is the burning of biomass, and this is the main NO_x source in developing countries. NO_x is given off when fuelwood is burnt domestically and when trees and other vegetation are burnt during forest clearance or savanna burning. In Venezuela the burning of 15 million hectares of savanna each year produces some

27,000 tonnes of NO_x. This then oxidized to nitrate and nitric acid and deposited as acid rain during the first rains after the dry season.[21]

The global pattern of emissions is similar to that of SO_2. Ambient levels of NO_x in the industrialized countries usually match those of SO_2 with slightly greater concentrations of NO_x. For rural conditions in the UK the ratio is commonly 1.1 parts of NO_x to 1.0 part of SO_2.[22] China is not as important a producer of NO_x as it is of SO_2, although Beijing has relatively high emissions because of the growing number of motor vehicles.

Trends of emissions

The trends of SO_2 emissions are markedly different in the developed and developing countries. In the former the trend is downward: pollution control measures are responsible for a major reduction in emissions (Figures 8.4). But in the developing countries the trend is

Figure 8.4 Trends in emissions of sulphur dioxide and nitrogen oxides in the USA and UK, 1970–88

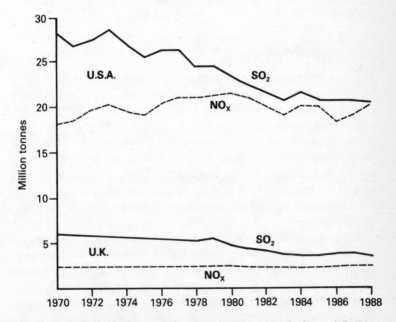

Sources: US Environmental Protection Agency, *National Air Quality and Emissions Trends Report* (Washington DC: EPA, 1990); Department of the Environment, *Digest of Environmental Protection and Water Statistics* (London: HMSO, 1990).

markedly upward. Although the data are far less complete, it is clear that the greatest rates of increase of SO_2 emissions in recent years have occurred in countries that are rapidly industrializing. Patterns of fuel consumption and of the growth of industrial processes producing significant SO_2, such as ore-smelting, suggest that the greatest increases have occurred in Asia, notably in China and Indonesia, in parts of North Africa and the Middle East and in Mexico, Brazil and Venezuela.[23] Inevitably as such industrialization continues, many developing countries will soon conform to the industrialized country pattern of widely dispersed regions of high SO_2 concentrations.

Unlike SO_2, the trends for NO_x production in the industrialized countries are not declining (see Figure 8.4). In the UK, for example, emissions in 1988 were the highest since 1979, mostly because of increasing numbers of motor vehicles.[24] Globally, the number of motor vehicles has grown from 53 million in 1950 through 195 million in 1970 to 386 million in 1986.[25] Although about 70 per cent are in North America and Western Europe, the greatest future growth is likely to occur in developing countries. As in the case of SO_2, this is where NO_x emissions will increase most dramatically. In Venezuela, for example, annual anthropogenic emissions of NO_x have grown from 50,000 tonnes in 1970 to 120–140,000 in 1984.[26]

Patterns of acid deposition

In Europe the highest acidity in rainfall occurs mainly over Germany, Poland, Czechoslovakia and the Netherlands, while in North America it is in the northeastern USA, at the border with Canada (Figure 8.5). These areas are both close to large sources of emissions and in the path of the dominant winds that bring emissions from other industrial and urban areas. The distance travelled can be considerable: SO_2 generated in Great Britain, for example, follows the predominant winds to end up as acid rain in Scandinavia; and acid pollutants produced in the east coast of the USA fall in Bermuda, 1000 km away.[27]

How much acidity reaches the ground is also affected by whether the deposition is dry or wet. In the UK the maximum concentration of human-made sulphur in rainfall occurs in the east of the country, which is in the path of the dominant westerly winds. But because more rain falls in the west and north this is where wet deposition – that is the amount per unit area – is greatest (Figure 8.6A, B). In the east and south, dry deposition accounts for more than 75 per cent of the total sulphur deposited. In tropical countries, the total deposition of acidic pollutants is likely to be greater because of higher rainfall and because moisture is often repeatedly recycled in a restricted locality – in the Amazon basin rainwater falls, evaporates, and falls again several times before it is eventually transported from the basin.[28]

Acid rainfall is particularly acute in southwestern China, where

Figure 8.5   The pH of wet deposition over Europe, 1978–82 (A) and North America, 1983 (B, overleaf)

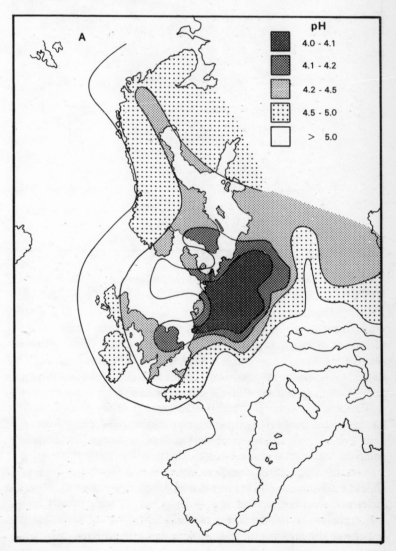

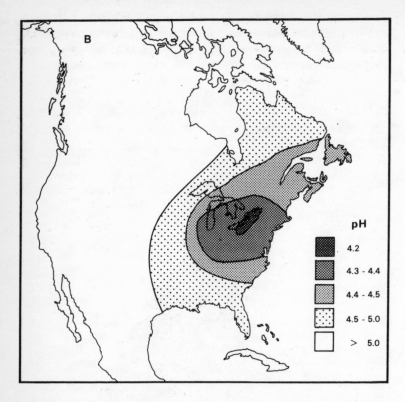

Source: United Nations Environment Programme, *Environmental Data Report* (Oxford: Blackwell, 1987).

the source is locally generated SO_2 (Table 8.3). In Guizhou and Sichuan Provinces, to the south and north of the Yangtze River, some 40,000 km² now receive rainfall of a pH less than 4.5.[29] Raised SO_2 concentrations occur in the cities, such as Guiyang and Chongqing, but even 10–20 ppb in remote rural areas of these provinces is common. This highly acidic rainfall arises partly because the local coal contains 3–5 per cent of sulphur, and partly because the meteorological conditions of most of the cities are unfavourable to pollutant dispersal – most are located in valleys with weak winds and where temperature inversions are common (see page 397). At Guiyang itself, rainfall pH is less than 4.0 from September to January inclusive, when the weather is cold and clear. Despite equally high SO_2 emissions in the north, the rainfall acidity is much lower, partly because of the presence of alkaline soils that give off large quantities of ammonia which serve to buffer the acidity (Table 8.4).

The effects on crop plants of acid pollution can be conveniently divided into those resulting from dry deposition and those from acid rain.

Figure 8.6   Concentration (A) and deposition (B, overleaf) of sulphur in the UK, 1986

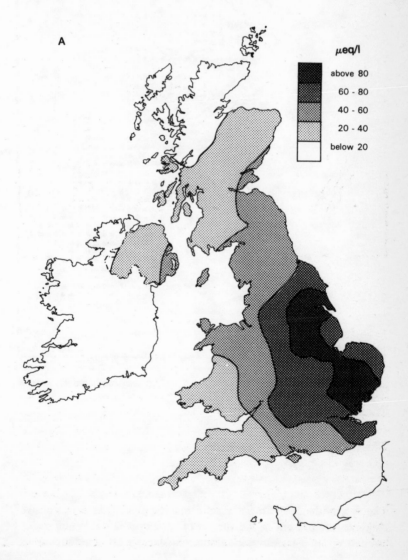

Source: Irwin, J.G. and Williams, M.I., "Acid Rain: chemistry and transport", *Environ. Pollut.* **50** (1988) pp. 29–59.

The effects of dry deposition

Acute injury

The first evidence of air pollution damaging plants was the extensive visible injury present in the vicinity of smelters. At the beginning of this century, in Tennessee and California, damage extended over areas

Table 8.3   The acidity of rainfall recorded from various parts of the tropics and subtropics

Location	pH of rainfall	
	Average	Range
Australia		
Katherine	4.8	4.0–5.4
Jabiru	4.4	3.9–5.4
Western Australia	5.0	NR
Groote Eylandt	4.3	NR
Brazil	5.1	4.7–5.7
China		
Guizhou and Sichuan	4.05	4.0–4.1
Beijing and Tianjin	6.5	6.3–6.8
Hangzhou	5.1	NR
Fuzhou	4.5	NR
Nanjing	6.4	NR
Costa Rica	5.3	4.8–6.3
Trinidad	5.8	5.3–6.4
Uganda	7.9	5.7–9.8
Venezuela		
San Carlos	4.7	4.0–6.7
Camburito	4.4	3.0–5.5
La Paragua	4.8	4.0–5.6
Joaquin del Tigre	5.1	4.2–5.8
Parupa	5.0	4.5–5.6

NR = not recorded

Source: Rodhe, H. and Herrera, R. (eds), *Acidification in Tropical Countries*, SCOPE Report no. 36 (Chichester: John Wiley and Sons, 1988).

as large as 200–750 km², with the land virtually barren close to the smelter.[30] Visible injury took the form of necrosis of plant tissue – typically the leaves died from the tip of the plant downwards – but only occurred when SO_2 levels exceeded 500 ppb for a few hours. It was closely correlated with yield loss.

Since that time field observations at these sites have shown a considerable range of sensitivity among crop plants to acute dosages of SO_2 (Table 8.5). Field trials in the vicinity of smelters and fumigation chamber experiments have also revealed more of the detailed relationships between concentration, length of exposure and damage. For susceptible species, thresholds for production of more

Table 8.4 Comparison of factors contributing to pH of rainfall in two areas of China

	Southwest China (Guizhou and Sichuan Provinces)	Northeast China
Sulphur content of coal	3–5%	1%
Emissions of SO_2 (million tonnes/year)	2.02	NR
Average SO_2 concentration in large cities (ppb)	100–200	30–60
Average pH of rainfall	4.0–4.1	6.3–6.8
Average ammonia concentration (ppb)	0.8–5	23–44
Soil pH	5–6	7–8

NR = not recorded

Source: Zhao, D. and Xiong, J., "Acidification in southwestern China", in: Rodhe and Herrera (eds), *op. cit.*; Galloway, J.N., Zhao, D., Xiong, J. and Likens, D.E., "Acid rain in China, United States and a remote area", *Science* **236** (1988) pp. 1559–62.

Table 8.5 Relative sensitivity of various species to SO_2 exposure. From observations of visible injury around power plants in Tennessee and nickel smelters in Sudbury

Sensitive*	Moderately sensitive*	Relatively resistant*
Sunflower	Red clover	Apple
Blackberry	White clover	Black cherry
Grape	Carrot	Peach
Soybean	Blueberry	Red mulberry
Squash	Persimmon	Corn
Alfalfa	Beans	Cotton
Barley	Strawberry	Irish potato
Buckwheat		Walnut
Rye		Rape
		Cabbage

* Sensitive – damage occurs when the one hour mean concentration is less than 500 ppb
Moderately sensitive – damage occurs when the one hour mean is 600–800 ppb
Relatively resistant – damage occurs only when the one hour mean exceeds 800 ppb

Source: Roberts, T.M., Darrall, N.M. and Lane, P., "Effects of gaseous air pollutants on agriculture and forestry in the UK", *Adv. appl. Biol.* **9** (1983) pp. 1–142.

than 5 per cent foliar injury are 500 ppb for one hour, decreasing to 180–250 ppb for 6–8 hours.[31]

NO$_x$ is also acutely toxic at high concentrations, for instance causing chlorosis on orange trees at 500 ppb and growth reductions in tomato and beans at 100–300 ppb.[32] Although these values are higher than would regularly occur in rural areas, excepting sites close to busy roads, they are significant for the cultivation of glasshouse crops. It is common practice to burn hydrocarbon fuels, such as propane or kerosene, in glasshouses to provide heat and also to enrich the atmosphere with CO_2, so increasing plant growth rates. However, NO_x gases are also generated in the process. Levels typically vary through the day and can at times be very high, 1000 ppb being recorded when flueless heaters are in use. This is sufficient to reduce the yields of tomatoes.[33]

Chronic injury

In the 1920s the first tall smokestacks were constructed for smelters, power stations and other industrial plants. Today, virtually all such plants in North America and western Europe have tall stacks and, as a result, local levels of pollution have been greatly reduced. The copper/nickel smelter at Sudbury, Ontario, for instance, formerly caused severe local damage within a radius of 15 km, but the massive 341 metre smokestack built in the early 1970s has given much better control and wider dispersion.[34] Annual emissions of SO_2 are now about 1.27 million tonnes, half the value before the smokestack, and some 97 per cent of the sulphur is carried further afield than 60 km. In the UK maximum concentrations at ground level around major 2000 MW coal-fired power stations now rarely exceed 120 ppb for hourly sampling.[35]

Taller smokestacks have thus alleviated the problems close to source, but they have widened the area of higher background pollution. The question now is: what are the effects on crops of the low to moderate concentrations of pollutants that are typical today of rural areas in the industrialized countries? Experimental work using both field exposure systems, in which SO_2 is released from pipes standing in fields, and open-top chambers have shown that growth and yields of cereals and vegetables are affected by low levels of SO_2. Barley, for example, was found by Baker and colleagues to start under-yielding as the SO_2 concentration rose above 40 ppb, losing 0.3–0.7 tonnes/ha in yield per 10 ppb increase in concentration.[36] In some experiments these yield reductions have been accompanied by growth reductions, and in others by better growth and increased tillering compared with plants grown at more than 80 ppb SO_2.[37] Growth reductions have also occurred in radish and alfalfa following exposure to less than 50 ppb SO_2.[38] But the most complete information, at present, relates to grasses.

Injury to grasses

Most agricultural grasses are perennials, and hence may experience pollution over long periods of time, making them, in theory, more vulnerable to chronic damage. But the evidence is conflicting. Measurements in the field suggest that substantial effects are occurring in localities where the annual mean SO_2 concentration does not exceed 55 ppb.[39] On the other hand, analysis of 32 experiments involving exposures of perennial ryegrass (*Lolium perenne*) to constant levels of SO_2 does not reveal any correlation between dose and response measured by changes in shoot weight (see Figure 8.2). The correlation exists only if exposures of less than 40 days or more than 160 days are omitted.[40] Then there is some evidence of a broad dose–response relationship (Figure 8.7). Only 20 per cent of the observations below 44 ppb showed yield losses whereas they occurred in 80 per cent of observations above 86 ppb. In all the experiments there is considerable variability in response. This is particularly important at low levels of exposure, that is, less than 50 ppb, typical of ambient levels in the rural areas of Europe, the USA and parts of China. It suggests that damage is occurring in such situations but that a variety of factors may be involved.

One such factor is the variability of exposure. The majority of these experimental fumigations have used constant concentrations of gases but fluctuating concentrations could give rise to different effects on plants, if periods of low concentrations between the peaks allow time for recovery, or if the peaks are large enough to exceed thresholds for effects on particular metabolic processes. But where this has been investigated, the results are conflicting. Fluctuating treatments of SO_2 caused a 25–30 per cent decline in *L. perenne* leaf dry weight compared with only 10 per cent under constant concentration; yet in another experiment on a different grass, Timothy (*Phleum pratense*), there was no significant difference in effects.[41]

Confounding factors

Perhaps the most important confounding factor is the rate of growth of the plant. Not only does SO_2 affect this, but the growth rate, in turn, determines the nature of the SO_2 effect. There is, now, good evidence that SO_2 induced injury is greatly enhanced when plants are growing slowly. This explains why ambient air concentrations as low as 10–20 ppb during winter have been found to cause significant growth reductions in several grass species after only 28 days.[42] Table 8.6 shows clearly that a significant reduction in growth of Timothy

Figure 8.7   Effects of long-term exposure (20–200 days) to SO_2 on the grass *Lolium perenne*

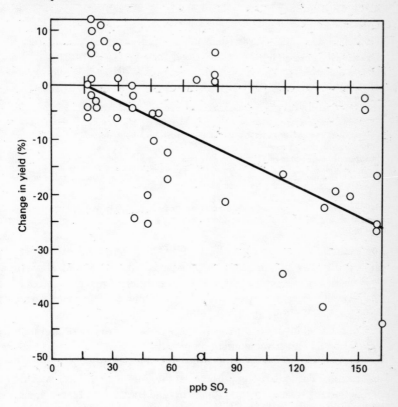

Source: Roberts, T.M., "Long-term effects of sulphur dioxide on crops: an analysis of dose-response relations", *Phil. Trans. R. Soc. Lond. B* **305** (1984) pp. 299–316.

grass only occurred when it was grown under a winter regime. Low light intensity, short days and low temperature produce slow growth which makes the plants more vulnerable to SO_2.[43] This winter effect may subsequently be reversed during the period of rapid spring and summer growth, when the presence of SO_2 may stimulate growth (Figure 8.8).

As might be expected, stress is also important. Stress factors may have a greater impact in the presence of SO_2: for instance, winter wheat plants exposed to 20–60 ppb/hour in the field were found to suffer more frost damage than those relatively free of SO_2.[44] Or the stress itself may magnify the impact of SO_2: frequent defoliation,

Table 8.6 Effect of light regime on growth of Timothy grass *(Phleum pratense)* grown in either clean or polluted air

	Summer light regime[1]	Winter light regime[2]
Dry weight in clear air (g)	0.735	0.030
Dry weight in SO$_2$ air[3] (g)	0.704	0.015
Significance of difference between growth in pollutant and clean air	NS	**

[1] Photosynthetic active radiation 480 μlx m^2/sec for 16 hour/day
[2] Photosynthetic active radiation 125 μlx m^2/sec for 12 hour/day
[3] 12 ppb SO$_2$ for 35 days
**difference will occur by chance on less than one in a hundred occasions

Note: μlx is a measure of illuminance (*E*), where one lux (lx) is equal to a flux density of 1 lumen/m^2

Source: Davies, T., "Grasses more sensitive to SO$_2$ pollution in conditions of low irradiance and short days", *Nature* **284** (1980) pp. 483–5.

for example, increases the effect of SO$_2$. In one field experiment the productivity of pure swards of ryegrass and cocksfoot (*Dactylis glomerata*) was assessed at three sites in northern England subject to ambient SO$_2$ levels, varying from 10 to 34 ppb.[45] The swards were defoliated by cutting at different times of the year. In most cases, but not all, defoliation during periods of slow growth or frequent defoliation had an adverse effect on growth.

Finally, SO$_2$ effects are influenced by the dynamics of the crop population. Particularly important is the inter- and intra-specific competition between plants for light and nutrients. Here, again, the investigations have been carried out predominantly on grasses and the results show that as a population of plants, initially spaced at regular intervals, develops into a grass sward, the impact of the SO$_2$ is ameliorated. There are two possible explanations: either the SO$_2$ dose per plant is reduced because of changing gradients of SO$_2$ concentration within the canopy, or competition serves to select tolerant individuals at the expense of those that are more sensitive to SO$_2$.[46]

Genetic tolerance to SO$_2$ certainly occurs in grasses and other crops. Populations of grasses with a history of SO$_2$ pollution have a greater tolerance to SO$_2$ than those from unpolluted sites or than bred cultivars.[47] Tolerance can arise very rapidly – within four years in the presence of 45 ppb.[48] The evidence for tolerance is obtained by taking plants from polluted and unpolluted sites and then exposing them to SO$_2$. If tolerance exists, the plants from the former localities lose less overall weight and have a higher proportion of live to dead

Figure 8.8 Seasonal differences in the effects of SO_2 and $SO_2 + NO_2$ on the growth of grasses

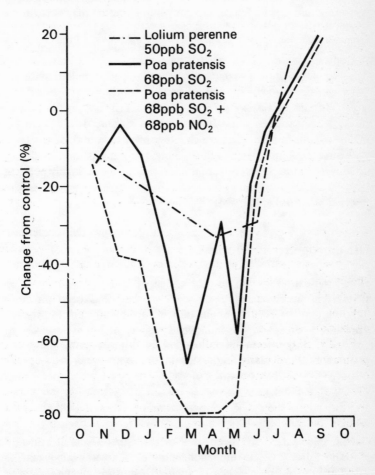

Source: Roberts. T.M. 1984 *op. cit.*, data from Colvill et al., 1983, for *L. perenne* and Whitmore and Mansfield, 1983, for *P. pratensis*

leaves.[49] The reasons for tolerance are complex, but changes in stomatal resistance appear to be an important component.[50] Tolerant plants, however, perform less well in clean air and one consequence is a constantly shifting mosaic of tolerant and less tolerant strains as SO_2 concentrations vary from locality to locality.[51] It is one of the main reasons why it is impossible to generalize on the effect of SO_2 on grassland productivity as a whole.[52] Tolerance may well reduce the overall impact but much depends on how quickly new sources of pollution are arising, and how much time plant populations have to become tolerant. In areas that are rapidly industrializing or have rapidly expanding motor vehicle use, the growth in pollution may outstrip the development of tolerance.[53]

These confounding factors will have different effects in tropical and subtropical countries. High mean temperatures and irrigation produce high year round growth so that an increased impact of pollution during periods of slow growth will not arise. Many of the new high-yielding cereal varieties mature very rapidly – 95 to 110 days in the case of the new rice varieties – and so may escape chronic damage. On the other hand, since perennials are able to grow year round, they may be more susceptible to chronic effects. Potentially at risk are the diverse multilayered home-gardens commonly located close to highly polluted urban areas in developing countries, but, as yet, they have not been reported as suffering damage.

The damage from acid rain

So far, most investigation into the effects of acid rain has focused on forests and watercourses. Such work as there has been on crops indicates that the concentrations of acids are insufficient to produce acute injury except in the immediate vicinity of intense sources of emissions. Most experimental reports of foliar injury are for pH values of less than 3.5, a concentration in rainfall rarely achieved even in the northeast of the USA (Figure 8.9).

Experimental results

Various approaches have been used to study the effects of acid rain on crops; they include the application of simulated acid rain to potted plants in greenhouses or in field exposure chambers, or to field grown crops. There are, inevitably, many confounding factors: field grown crops also receive ambient rain and other pollutants, and there are problems of overwatering and poor temperature control. As a consequence, there is a considerable range in size and direction of effects at any given pH.[54] For instance, while artificial rain at pH 3–4, compared to a control value of pH 5.6, will decrease by up to 75 per cent the yield of root crops such as radish, carrot and beet and, by causing foliar damage, will decrease the yield and marketability of leafy crops such as spinach and mustard green, it may, at the same time,

Figure 8.9 Comparison of acidity of ambient rain at two sites in the northeastern USA with acidity causing foliar injury to experimental vegetation growth in greenhouses or chambers

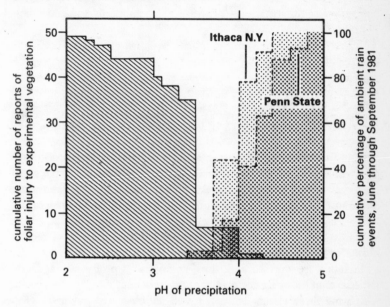

Source: Jacobson, J.S., "Effects of acidic aerosol, fog mist and rain on crops and trees", *Phil. Trans. R. Soc. Lond. B* **305** (1984) pp. 327–338.

cause visible foliar injury in tomatoes yet increase tomato yields. Yields may also be increased in other fruit crops, such as green peppers and strawberries, as may the productivity of forage crops such as alfalfa and some grasses. The only general conclusion is that broadleaf plants are more susceptible than grasses, and root and leafy vegetables are more susceptible than forage, grain and fruit crops.[55]

It is also clear that responses can differ between cultivars of the same crop species (Table 8.7). Susceptible varieties of soybeans produced fewer numbers of pods per plant, possibly as a result of lower flower pollination, and had less pod retention or inadequate development of young pods. Again, though, experimental results are often conflicting. One study found Golden Delicious apple trees to be more susceptible than McIntosh to acid rain, but in other tests, the opposite was found.[56] Even where there is a relationship between pH and damage, it is not necessarily linear. Apple seedlings showed dry weight reductions between pH 2.3–3.0 and between 4.3–5.6, but not between 3.3–4.0.[57] There are many possible reasons for this variability,

Table 8.7   Effect of acid rain on yield of four commercial varieties of soybean

		Soybean yield (% yield at pH 5.6)			
Soybean Cultivar	*pH*	*5.6*	*4.4*	*4.1*	*4.3*
Amsoy		100	89	90	88
Asgrow		100	86	88	91
Corsoy		100	86	87	92
Hobbit		100	91	94	83

Source: Evans, L.S., Lewin, K.F., Owen, E.M. and Santucci, K.A., "Comparison of yields of several cultivars of field-growth soybeans exposed to simulated acidic rainfalls", *New Phytol.* **102** (1986) pp. 409–17.

ranging from different experimental designs, measurement procedures and techniques of statistical analysis, to variability of response of individual plants and cultivars. As with the work on dry deposition, different experiments are often not at all comparable. The use of pH 5.6 as a control value may also bias the results – natural rainfall events sometimes occur at lower pH. It is unlikely that the pH of rain in northeast USA would be near 5.6, even if emissions of anthropogenic pollutants were stopped and, thus, comparisons probably exaggerate the effects of reducing the acidity of precipitation.[58]

Leaving these effects aside, it is still not clear why any given crop should show either an increase or decrease in productivity in the presence of acid rain. As Irving has concluded:

> the net response of a crop to acidic deposition is the result of the interaction between the positive effects of sulphur and nitrogen fertilization, the negative effects of acidity, and the interaction between these factors and other environmental conditions such as soil type and presence of other pollutants.[59]

In developing countries

There is little direct evidence of damage from acid rain to crops in developing countries and most comes from southern China. Around Chongqing, large areas of paddy have suddenly turned yellow following rainfall of pH 4.5; and in Chongqing itself vegetation has been damaged by rain of pH 4.1. Field experiments on wheat, in the same region, also showed that rainfall of less than pH 3.5 during middle to late stages caused acute injury and reduced yields.[60]

Despite the paucity of evidence of damage, many tropical and subtropical countries may be at greater risk than temperate countries from environmental acidification. This is because their soils are already acidic and are unable to buffer any further additions of acidity. Further acidification can lead to an increase in the weathering rate of soil minerals, increased leaching of bases that would otherwise offset acidification, and the bringing into solution of potentially toxic trace metals. Aluminium, for example, precipitates at pH values greater than 6.0, but as the pH falls, it becomes more soluble and available to plant roots. Aluminium in acid soils disrupts the metabolic processes of roots and inhibits their growth. Those soils considered to be most at risk are the Oxisols, Inceptisols, Spodosols and Ultisols that are common in southern China, southeast Asia, southwest India, equatorial Africa, and southeast Brazil through the Amazon basin to northern Venezuela.[61]

Ozone as a pollutant

The ozone that exists in the upper regions of the atmosphere – in the stratosphere – is beneficial, shielding the earth from harmful ultraviolet radiation, but ozone in the lower regions – in the troposphere – acts as a pollutant. There it is produced by complex photochemical reactions involving NO_x, carbon monoxide, methane and hydrocarbons (see Chapter 7). Nitrous oxide and methane are products of agricultural practices, but nitrogen oxides and the other key constituents are primarily emitted by motor vehicles and the combustion of biomass and fossil fuels. The origins of ozone pollution thus lie, on the one hand, in urban areas and, on the other, in those rural areas where savanna and forest burning is occurring.

Meteorological conditions over cities

Many cities experience the right meteorological conditions for ozone production: clear skies and still dry weather permit sunlight to react with the precursor pollutants, such as NO_x, carbon monoxide and hydrocarbons, to produce ozone and other oxidants. But the process is assisted when temperature inversions arise in the atmosphere over cities.

There are three kinds of inversion of relevance to ozone production.[62] The first are nocturnal inversions, created by differential cooling during hot weather. Typically, in the late afternoon, after the hottest part of the day, the air temperature at the ground begins to fall, at first slowly, but then, after sunset, increasingly rapidly as heat is radiated from the surface to the colder night sky. Away from the ground the temperature also falls, but more slowly (Figure 8.10). The colder air at the surface is heavier and becomes trapped inside the layer of warm overlying air. The temperature inversion, so created, is very stable: if air passes above the inversion it cools, becomes more dense and so sinks back. But then at sunrise the ground and the adjoining air heat up quickly and the inversion breaks down. In terms of ozone pollution it has three effects. It traps pollutants and smoke at ground level during the night and early morning; it isolates ozone in the upper warmer layer so reducing the opportunity for direct deposition to the ground at night; it rapidly brings pollutants, including ozone, back from higher altitudes to the surface during the day.

Figure 8.10 The formation of a temperature inversion in late summer at Oak Ridge, Tennessee

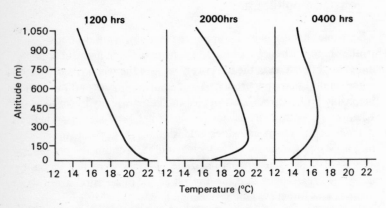

Source: Wanta, R.C., "Meteorology and air pollution", in: Stern, A.C. (ed.), *Air Pollution* 2nd edition (New York: Academic Press, 1968).

Nocturnal inversions are common inland in hot, cloudless climates, typically occurring in valleys and basins, sheltered from the wind. In wind-free, hot desert areas they are particularly frequent; in Guiyang in southwest China inversions are created every day between October and May, coinciding with the season of greatest SO_2 concentrations and rainfall acidity.[63]

The other types of inversion are longer lasting. The first is the trade-wind or subtropical inversion that arises over coastal cities of western continents as a result of high pressure areas over the ocean, which push warm air over the adjoining land. The Los Angeles inversion is an example. It is usually very persistent, forming a lid for the pollutants from the city – "viewed from above the Los Angeles area looks as though it is covered by a lake of brownish smog, the surface being as sharp and distinct as a water surface. The clear air of the inversion layer is in marked contrast to the murky layer below."[64] The second type of semi-permanent inversion occurs when warm air from deserts is driven over a basin containing a city, so trapping the cooler air beneath. It is characteristic of Mexico City, during December to February.

Both Los Angeles and Mexico City are infamous for their photochemical smogs, which contain elevated levels of ozone as well as associated oxidants such as peroxyacetyl nitrate (PAN). In Los Angeles the four million private cars consume 30 million litres of gasoline daily; Mexico City has a million fewer cars but combustion is very inefficient due to the high altitude.

Ambient levels of ozone

Ozone is typically generated in plumes of air contaminants originating in urban areas, but often at a considerable distance from the source (Box 8.2). This explains why, in southeast England, higher maximum concentrations more regularly occur in rural areas than in the centre of London.[65] Plumes downwind of large North American cities produce

Box 8.2   An ozone episode

Early on a sunny, warm and relatively still day a parcel of clean air passes over an isolated urban or industrialized centre. It picks up NO_x and hydrocarbons, produced by motor vehicles and small industries. The most reactive hydrocarbons begin to be photochemically oxidized and, in the presence of NO_x, start to produce ozone. As the parcel moves away from the town and into the rural areas, the emissions decrease. But ozone levels within the parcel continue slowly to increase over the next ten or so hours. The extent of net ozone production is only finally limited by the approach of sunset. After sunset ozone production stops, and chemical destruction and dry deposition to the ground of the ozone begins to dominate. But above the nocturnal temperature inversion layer ozone cannot be deposited, so at high concentrations some will survive to dawn. The following dawn, the inversion breaks up, bringing ozone down from aloft quickly during the morning while the photochemical reactions are re-established. Ozone concentrations then increase again. On subsequent days ozone production contiues until all the hydrocarbons are depleted.

Source: PORG, UK Photochemical Oxidants Review Group, *Tropospheric Ozone* (Ruislip, Middlesex: Department of Environment, 1987).

elevated ozone concentrations of between 130 and 200 ppb, often at distances of 100–300 km.[66] For example, plumes originating over New York in the summer of 1975, produced levels of 250–300 ppb in Connecticut at 125 km distance, and 100–150 ppb northwest of Boston at 300 km distance.[67] But large urban centres are not the only sources: even quite small cities can produce elevated levels of O_3 in rural areas, though the minimum population size required to raise O_3 concentration above 40 ppb is 100,000.[68]

Prior to the 1970s it was not thought that ozone could occur above

Figure 8.11   Number of exceedences of 60 ppb hourly average tropospheric ozone concentrations during summer (April–September) 1988

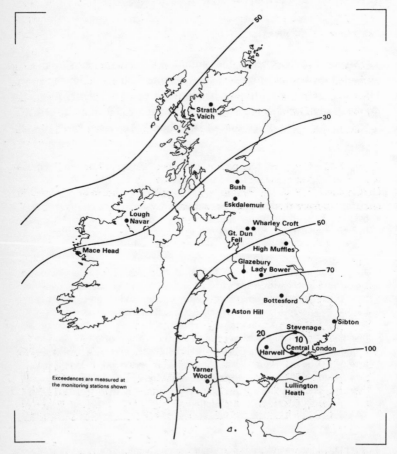

Source: Department of the Environment, 1990, *op.cit.*, using data from Warren Spring Laboratory, Department of Trade and Industry.

the maximum natural levels of 20–40 ppb prevalent in the rural areas of Europe.[69] But then a program of systematic monitoring in the UK revealed that ozone regularly exceeds 40 ppb in summertime. For instance, maximum levels of 250 ppb were recorded during the dry hot summer of 1976.[70] In rural areas, high concentrations arise on days that are hot, dry and calm, typically peaking around midday and then falling at night. The highest values occur in the southeast of the country (Figure 8.11). There, in 1988, the 60 ppb hourly WHO health guideline was exceeded on more than 100 occasions between April and September. The contours show a marked gradient, which suggests that air from Europe is also bringing pollutants.[71]

High ozone levels similarly arise over a wide area of North America.[72] Background concentrations are typically 20–60 ppb, but many cities show much greater levels: in the Los Angeles basin hourly peaks can reach 600 ppb, and the 120 ppb hourly Federal ozone standard value is exceeded some 350 times annually[73] (Figure 8.12). Between 1973 and 1982 the two sites of San Bernadino and Upland each exceeded the standard on average some 650 times annually. Over the USA as a whole, the 120 ppb standard for ozone is exceeded at some 40 per cent of monitoring sites yearly.[74]

Severe photochemical smogs are common in urban areas in the

Figure 8.12 Comparison of peak ozone concentration in London (UK) with other cities in North America, Japan and Europe
Dotted line = US secondary standard (120 ppb ozone not to be exceeded for one hour on more than one day per annum)

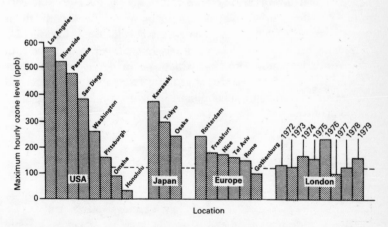

Source: Roberts, T.M., Darrall, N.M. and Lane, P., "Effects of gaseous air pollutants on agriculture in the UK", *Adv. Appl. Bio.* **9** (1983) pp. 1–142

tropics and subtropics, for example in Mexico City, Sao Paolo, Cairo and New Delhi. In the Middle East, in particular, climatic conditions coupled with fast industrial expansion are conducive to ozone production. Levels in Baghdad may exceed 100 ppb during the afternoons and can reach almost 300 ppb.[75] A contributing factor in such regions may be fugitive emissions of hydrocarbons from oil fields, refineries and fuel tanks.

Tropical rural areas may also experience high ozone levels, arising directly from photochemical reactions involving the products of biomass burning or the natural emissions of volatile hydrocarbons from forest vegetation (see Chapter 7). Ozone concentrations are particularly high in the Brazilian atmosphere following the burning of savanna during the dry season.[76]

Trends of ozone production

Ambient levels of ozone in the troposphere over Europe may have doubled in the last century, from 11 ppb to about 24 ppb, today, at remote sites.[77] Most of the increase has probably occurred in recent decades: the longest set of records comes from the former East Germany, and indicates a doubling since the mid-1950s. There has also been a shift in seasonal pattern. A small spring maximum has been replaced by a much stronger maximum that peaks in May and extends well into summer.

Motor vehicles are the largest source of chemically reactive hydrocarbons, but because ozone monitoring began in the early 1970s, and hence coincided with the oil crisis and a slowing in the rate of increase of fuel consumption, the data do not unequivocally show correlations between ozone levels and the growth in motor vehicles.[78] Nevertheless, in general, we can expect ozone levels to continue to increase with the growth in motor vehicles, particularly in developing countries where the number of vehicles is growing faster than elsewhere and the optimal meteorological conditions for ozone production are more common.

Damage from ozone

There is, of course, a directly injurious effect of photochemical smog, since it reduces the amount of light reaching plants and hence interferes with photosynthesis.[79] If the visibility declines to only 10 km at the latitude of the northeastern United States, the amount of photosynthetically active radiation (PAR) – between wavelengths of 0.35 and 0.72 μm – reaching plants will be reduced to 20–30 per cent of that during clear conditions. The effect on yield, though, depends on the kind of crop plant. C_3 plants reach saturation of photosynthesis at about one third full sunlight, so that reductions in PAR may have little effect. On the other hand, C_4 plants (such as maize and sugar cane) increase their net photosynthesis up to very high levels of irradiance, and any reduction in PAR may lower yields.

Direct, visual crop damage caused by ozone and peroxyacetyl nitrate (PAN) was first recorded in the Los Angeles basin in 1944.[80] The symptom was a characteristic pattern of flecking or stippling of the leaves – the small white areas corresponding to dead cells. It was first recognized on leafy vegetable and field crops, one of which, tobacco, was so sensitive that a common variety had to be withdrawn from commercial use.[81] Most early cases occurred on crops grown close to cities both in Europe and North America, as well as in Bogota in Colombia and São Paolo in Brazil.[82]

As with acid pollutants, there is a great deal of variation of response both within and between crop species (Table 8.8). Legumes are particularly sensitive while crucifers contain a large number of resistant species. Plants characteristic of cultivated and calcareous soils tend to be more sensitive than those of acid and nutrient-poor soils, and hence the grasses *Agrostis*, *Avena*, *Phleum* and *Catapodium* are highly sensitive while *Molinia*, *Nardus* and *Deschampsia* are resistant.[83]

To protect crops from episodes of acute pollution the US government set an air quality standard for ozone in 1979 of 120 ppb for a one hour limit, not to be exceeded more than once per year. However, it is now clear that this will not protect all crop plants. Levels well below the air quality standard will reduce crop growth and yields, without necessarily causing visible injury. A wide variety of species have shown yield reductions of 10–50 per cent at constant ozone concentrations of only 60–100 ppb (Table 8.9). Fruits, cereals, root crops and vegetables are all affected. Ozone in the Los Angeles basin has caused premature leaf fall and fruit drop on orange and lemon trees, reducing yields by approximately 50 per cent, while yields of grapevines have been reduced by 12–60 per cent.[84] Recent studies on four cultivars of a hard red wheat commonly cultivated in the USA have shown some loss at even 40 ppb ozone.[85] All four had declining yields with increasing concentration, the losses varying between 20–80 per cent at 100 ppb.

Experiments on commercial cultivars of rice have found that ozone at ambient concentrations affects most of the components of yield – it reduces seed weight, the number of spikelets per panicle, the height of

Table 8.8 Ozone sensitivity of agricultural crops grown in temperate regions

Highly sensitive	Slightly to moderately sensitive	Resistant
White and red clover*	Barley*	Sugar beet
Pea*	Wheat*	Oilseed rape
Alfalfa*	Rye*	Kale
Spinach*	Oat	Brussels sprout
Radish*	Bean*	Lettuce
Grape vine*	Maize	Cabbage
Hop	Fescue	Cauliflower
Broccoli	Ryegrass	
Timothy grass	Potato	
Tobacco*	Swede	
	Turnip	
	Carrot	
	Onion*	
	Parsnip*	
	Watermelon*	
	·Peanut*	
	Tomato*	
	Soybean*	

* Visible leaf injury to these crops have been observed in the field

Sources: Ashmore, M.R., "Effects of ozone on vegetation in the UK", in: Grennfelt, P. (ed.), *Proc. int. workshop on the eval. and assess. of effects of photochem. oxidants* (Gothenburg: SERI, 1984); Roberts, T.M. et al., 1983, *op. cit.*; Krupa, S.V. and Manning, W.J., "Atmospheric ozone: formulation and effects on vegetation", *Environ. Pollut.* **50** (1988) pp. 101–37.

the plants and the straw weight, and increases the number of sterile seeds and panicles.[86] (Figure 8.13). These data suggest that in the Sacramento Valley, California, where the ambient concentrations of ozone are 50 ppb, the cultivar M9 is already suffering yield losses of some 7 per cent. But in the area around Tokyo, where ozone concentrations regularly reach 200 ppb, rice crop losses could range between 12–29 per cent depending upon cultivar sensitivity. There have been no experiments on rice in developing countries. But ozone injury has been observed on potatoes in Punjab and tobacco grown in industrialized parts of Taiwan that experience winter temperature inversions.[87]

Contributing factors

Stomatal opening increases uptake of ozone and thus high temperature and humidity will increase sensitivity to ozone, but there are a number

Table 8.9 Loss in yield of selected crops grown under differing ozone concentration regimes compared with controls grown at a 7-hour seasonal daytime mean of 25 ppb ozone

Crop	(Variety)	Loss in yield at each ozone concentration	
		60 ppb	90–100 ppb
Maize	(Pioneer 3780)	5%	17%
Maize	(Coker 16)	4%	8%
Maize	Common response	3%	13%
Soybean	(Corsoy)	22%	47%
Soybean	(Davis)	12%	26%
Soybean	Common response	17%	30%
Kidney bean	(California Light Red)	7%	15%
Lettuce	(Empire)	23%	49%
Cotton	Common response	10%	20%
Barley	(Poco)	0.5%	3%
Peanut	(NC-6)	25%	53%
Sorghum	(Dekalb 28)	3%	7%
Spinach	(America)	18%	40%
Tomato	(Murrieta)	4%	16%
Turnip	(Just Right)	31%	66%
Wheat	(Blueboy 11)	10%	22%
Wheat	(Coker 47–27)	14%	30%
Wheat	(Oasis)	9%	19%
Wheat	(Vona)	48%	71%
Wheat	Common response	11%	27%

Source: Heck, W.W., "Defining gaseous pollution problems in North America", in: Koziol, M.J. and Whatley, F.R. (eds), *Gaseous Air Pollutants and Plant Metabolism* (London: Butterworths, 1984); Heck, W.W. et al., "Assessment of crop loss from ozone", *J. Air Pollut. Control Assoc.* 32 (1981) pp. 353–61.

of factors that have the opposite effect. Increasing soil moisture stress causes stomata to close, and plants then suffer less damage. This has been experimentally demonstrated in soybeans, green beans and alfalfa,[88] though a linear decrease in soybean seed yield with increasing ozone, regardless of soil moisture, has also been shown to occur.[89] The problem, of course, is that the water stress may be so severe that plants suffer yield loss anyway.

Of particular importance is the episodic nature of the pollution, which is often not reflected in experiments. When a plant suffers from stress, quantities of the plant hormone ethylene (C_2H_4) are produced.[90] The hormone accelerates the abscission of leaves damaged by the stress and hence increases leaf fall. An experiment on pea seedlings showed that continuous low levels of ozone stimulated little

Figure 8.13 Response of the rice cultivar M9 to ozone pollution. Exposures were for 5 hours each day for 5 days each week for 15 weeks

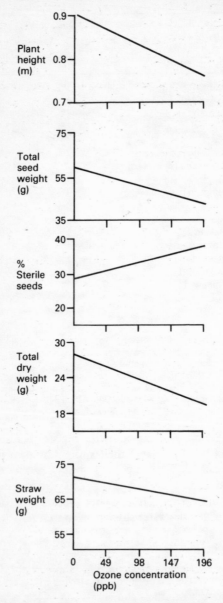

Source: Kats, G., Dawson, P.J., Bytnerowicz, A., Wolf, U.W., Thompson, C.R. and Olszyk, D.M., "Effects of ozone and sulphur dioxide on growth and yield of rice", *Agric. Ecosyst. Environ.* **14** (1985) pp. 103–117.

production of ethylene and caused no damage; but one large dose of ozone significantly raised the level of the hormone and damage resulted. It seems that plants are likely to be more susceptible to ozone injury if high ozone concentrations occur infrequently – a situation that commonly occurs in the field.

Genetic tolerance is also important, not only in tobacco. For instance, tolerance in alfalfa is manifest in how severe an effect ozone has on the regrowth following cutting. All cultivars may show declines in growth rate due to the ozone but, after cutting, some respond with greater photosynthetic rates during regrowth.[91] In general, crop cultivars developed in regions with a history of elevated ozone levels tend to be more tolerant than those developed in cleaner areas. This has been documented for alfalfa, beans, cotton, potatoes and sugar beet. Examples of cultivar differences in potatoes are shown in Table 8.10. The five most sensitive cultivars were developed in the mid-west and south of the USA, which have less of an ozone problem than the Atlantic coastal region. In the 1970s tolerance became of economic importance in Virginia. Farmers had changed from Pungo to higher yielding varieties such as Norchip, La Chipper and Alamo, but these then suffered from severe ozone damage and yield losses of up to 50 per cent. As a consequence they returned to sowing Pungo and Superior.[92]

Table 8.10   Yield responses of potato cultivars to ozone pollution developed in different parts of the USA but grown in Beltsville, Maryland

Cultivar	Proportion of yield in unfiltered air to filtered air (%)	Site where cultivar developed
Katahdin	128	Maryland
Penn 71	107	Pennsylvania
Pungo	102	Virginia and Maryland
Norgold Russett	100	North Dakota
Superior	96	Wisconsin
Kennebec	92	Maine and Maryland
Wanseon	80	Maine and Maryland
Norchip	74	North Dakota
La Chipper	73	Lousiana
Alamo	66	Texas and Maryland
Haig	63	Nebraska
Norland	50	North Dakota

Source: Heggestad, H.E. and Bennett, J.H., "Impact of atmospheric pollution in agriculture", in: Treshow, M. (ed.), *Air Pollution and Plant Life* (Chichester: John Wiley and Sons, 1984).

The geography of damage

In mapping the extent of ozone damage, advantage has been made of the high sensitivity of certain tobacco varieties. One cultivar, Bel-W3, has a threshold for visible injury of only 40–50 ppb and is thus a good indicator of potential subacute damage to other crops. In the British Isles the amount of leaf injury was recorded at weekly intervals at some 60 sites during 1977 and found to correlate with sunshine as well as the upwind proximity of urban sources. As Figure 8.14 indicates, few parts of the country were free of damage.

Figure 8.14   Distribution of ozone in the UK based on the degree of visible injury on *Nicotiana tabacum*, cv. Bel W3, at 53 sites

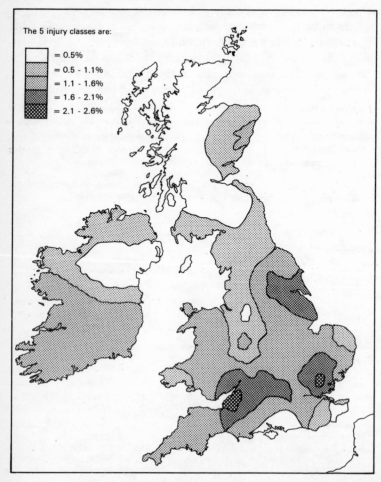

Source: Roberts, T.M. et al., 1983, *op. cit.*, redrawn from Ashmore, M. et al., 1979 *op. cit.*

In the USA damage has been mapped by the National Crop Loss Assessment Network (NCLAN), established in 1980.[93] This uses open-top chambers at a number of sites to evaluate the chronic effects of ozone, and other pollutants, on crops. The results suggest that there are significant losses of yield from ozone at concentrations below current air quality standards. Similar results have been obtained from the European Communities Open-Top Chamber Programme[94] (Table 8.11).

As yet, there have been few comparable exercises in developing countries, although favourable conditions for pollution damage exist both around many large cities and in rural areas where biomass

Table 8.11 Summary of results of open-top chamber experiments conducted at various sites in Europe in 1987–8 as part of the European Communities Research Project on Open-Top Chambers

Location	Average ambient ozone concentrations (ppb)	Effect of unfiltered air on crops
UK (Silwood Park, Ascot)	21	No effect on yield of *Vicia* beans, but reduced rate of crop development; greater population size of aphids
UK (Nottingham)	20–24	No effect on yields of *Vicia* beans, but changes in plant physiology
Belgium	20	Reduction in root weight, straw yield and grain weight of spring wheat
Sweden	35–50	Reduction in yield of spring wheat
France	30–50	Reduction in yield of *Phaseolus* beans
Switzerland	35–40*	Inhibition of powdery mildew (*Erysiphe graminis*) infection on spring wheat; stimulation of rust, *Septoria nodorum*, infection; reduction in yield of spring wheat
Denmark	40*	Reduction in yields of spring wheat
Germany	9.5–12	No effect on yields of spring or winter cereals
Eire	20–30	No effect on yields of *Vicia* beans or spring barley

* These experiments also used open-top chambers in which extra ozone was added, producing even greater reductions in yield

Source: Bonte, J. and Mathy, P., *The European Communities Research Project on Open-Top Chambers Results on Agricultural Crops 1987–88* (Brussels: CEC, 1989).

burning is common. Open-top chambers have been established in Mexico, China and Taiwan, but with limited success.[95] Yield loss in developing countries may well be common.

Fluoride pollution

There are several other pollutants in the air that may have an adverse impact on agriculture. Of these, fluorides are probably the most important. They are among the most toxic of gases to plants but, unlike acid pollutants and ozone, they only occur at high concentrations close to industrial sources.

Sources of fluorides

Fluorine is typically emitted as hydrogen fluoride (HF) from brick, glass and tile works, steelworks, potteries, aluminium smelters, phosphate fertilizer factories and some other industries. Not all fluoride, though, originates from human-made sources: soils may naturally contain high fluoride levels. Crops grown on soils in Tennessee can contain 300 ppm fluoride, enough to harm grazing livestock.[96]

Before the introduction of pollution controls in the UK and the USA, fluoride concentrations around industrial sources were high, typically 10–50 ppb.[97] Concentrations are now much lower. For instance, around the Stewartby brickworks in the UK mean fluoride levels are 0.08–0.56 ppb, although the decline is largely attributable to reduced output and the closure of neighbouring works.[98] In the USA levels around sources now rarely exceed a few ppb over short periods.

Accumulation by plants

An effect peculiar to fluoride is the way it is taken up and accumulated by plants. Hydrogen fluoride enters principally through the leaf stomata, though some soluble forms penetrate the leaf cuticle directly.[99] Once inside, fluoride moves with the transpiration stream to the tip and margins of the leaves where it accumulates. Concentrations in the tip or margins can be 100 times greater than elsewhere in the leaf.[100] The fluoride accumulates in the leaf chloroplasts, inhibiting action of certain key enzymes and so reducing photosynthesis.[101] Chlorosis and necrosis occur beginning at the leaf tips and margins with the highest accumulations. There is no natural mechanism of detoxification and the more that is taken up, the more is accumulated.

Hence damage is correlated less with the concentration of fluoride in the air and more with the amount accumulated in the tissue.

For vegetation far from emitting sources the hazard arises from long-term exposures to very low levels, and hence perennials and trees are more likely to suffer damage than annuals. Conifers accumulate fluoride steadily as they age: at five months Douglas Fir, Lodgepole Pine and Ponderosa Pine contain 28 ppm on average in needles, but by 17 months this rises to 102 ppm and at 29 months to 233 ppm.[102] The tea family is a particularly efficient accumulator of fluoride.[103]

One of the most notable fluoride emitting industrial sources has been the Colombia Falls aluminium smelter in north-west Montana, USA. It began operations in 1955 and by the late 1960s it was emitting 3.4 tonnes of fluoride daily, though this had fallen to 1.1 tonnes by 1971.[104] The emissions produced raised levels of fluoride in grasses, shrubs and coniferous trees over an area of 87,000 hectares (Figure 8.15). The highest concentrations, of more than 1000 ppm, and the most severe damage occurred in the 260 ha around the plant; but visual injury to conifers was evident over the 28,000 ha where average levels in the vegetation was greater than 30 ppm. Similar acute damage caused by fluoride emissions has occurred at Spokane, Washington; The Dalles, Oregon; and Georgetown Canyon, Idaho.[105]

Damage to crops

Although industrial emissions are much lower today, typical levels around emitting sources are still sufficient to reduce crop yields, despite the absence of visible signs of injury (Table 8.12). In general, levels of up to 2.4 ppb do not affect agricultural field crops, but will damage ornamentals and certain conifers, and also reduce the yields and quality of soft and stone fruits.[106] Levels above 3.6 ppb may damage some cereals and other crops. Yield reductions have been noted for wheat, barley, maize, sorghum, oats and pasture grasses, as well as for alfalfa, peas, onion, potato and clover.[107]

Hydrogen fluoride also interferes with pollen germination and pollen-tube growth. Exposure at the critical time during pollination to concentrations as low as 1 ppb for four days can reduce wheat grain yields by 20–30 per cent.[108] And significant reductions in yield of apricot, cherry, strawberry and pear fruits can occur following exposure during flowering.[109] The fluoride in the nectar and pollen can also pass to bees and other pollinators which are particularly susceptible to fluoride poisoning. Beekeepers have suffered economic losses in areas close to fluoride emitters.[110]

Figure 8.15 Fluoride pollution at Columbia Falls, Montana, USA. A total of 87,000 ha are contained within the 10 ppm contour; 50,000 in the 20; 8,000 in the 60; 2,850 in the 100 and 260 in the 600 contour

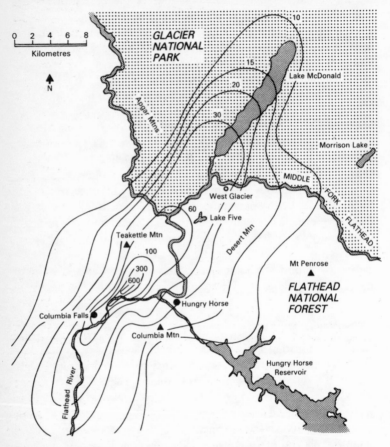

Source: Carlson, C.E., "Fluoride pollution in Montana", *Fluoride* 6 (1973) pp. 127–137.

Furthermore, fluoride may directly damage fruits, such as peach, apricot and cherry.[111] Even though concentrations rarely exceed a few ppm in the tissue, this is enough to cause premature ripening of the fruit along the suture line. Affected areas become overripe and rot before the rest of the fruit ripens. The condition is called soft suture or suture red-spot and was first recognized in peaches earlier this century when fluoride sprays were tested as insecticides.

Table 8.12 Relative susceptibilities of North American agricultural plants to foliar injury produced by atmospheric fluoride

Susceptible	Intermediate	Tolerant
Apricot	Apple	Alfalfa
Barley (young plant)	Barley (mature plant)	Bean
Crabgrass (*Digitaria*)	Cherry	Cabbage
Grape	Clover	Carrot
Peach (fruit)	Grapefruit	Cauliflower
Plum	Green pepper	Celery
Sorghum	Johnson Grass	Coffee
Sweet corn	Lemon	Cotton
	Maize	Cucumber
	Mulberry	Eggplant
	Oat	(aubergine)
	Orange	Onion
	Peach (foliage)	Pea
	Rice	Pear
	Rye	Potato
	Spinach	Ryegrass
	Sweet potato	Soybean
	Tomato	Squash
	Walnut	Strawberry
	Wheat	Sugar cane
		Sunflower
		Tobacco

Source: Weinstein, L.H., "Fluoride and plant life", *J. Occup. Med.* **19** (1977) pp. 49–78.

Pasture and livestock

Accumulation of fluoride in forage presents a particular risk to grazing cattle and sheep. Prolonged ingestion of excessive amounts can cause fluorosis, which is characterized by damage to the teeth and bones and eventually by lameness, an inability to feed, and diminished milk yield.[112] Mottling of the teeth, one of the earliest signs of poisoning, occurs in cattle when the diet contains 20 ppm of fluoride. The full symptoms begin at over 50 ppm.

A number of cases of fluorosis were recorded in Britain in the 1950s but the problem seems, now, to have declined. Only 12 cases were reported between 1974 and 1979. However, one incident was particularly serious: close to an aluminium smelter in Scotland 31 cattle and sheep with severe skeletal damage had to be slaughtered after eating forage containing more than 45 ppm fluoride.[113] Wild animals can also suffer harm: in the two National Parks close to the Colombia Falls smelter in Montana, deer that were feeding on forage high in fluoride have suffered mottling, black discolouration and softening of the teeth, skeletal disorders and lameness.[114]

Very high levels in forage can occur close to smelters and other sources, but usually rapidly decline with distance. For instance, fluoride levels were 500 ppm within a 100 metre radius of an aluminium smelter in New South Wales, Australia, but down to 150 ppm at 350 metres.[115] Restricting livestock from these relatively small high concentration areas is usually sufficient to prevent fluorosis.

Forage grasses with more upright growth tend to be more susceptible than those with lower, spreading growth. Typically the terminal shoots of the former are killed, so encouraging the laterals to grow more vigorously and produce a bush-like growth. Fluoride concentration in forage grasses usually varies seasonally, being high in winter and low in spring/summer, partly because although the leaves grow in spring the absolute quantity of fluoride does not change.[116] However, the winter peak may be more directly a consequence of domestic burning of coal and of the higher rainfall; wet leaves retain particulate matter containing fluorides.[117] Dead leaves also tend to have higher fluoride levels than living leaves, and during winter a sward of grass contains a higher proportion of dead leaves.

Silkworms

There are few reports of fluorides affecting agriculture in developing countries. A notable instance is the serious damage to sericulture from small rural industries in China.[118] Emissions from brick kilns, phosphate fertilizer plants and coal burning cause fluoride to accumulate in mulberry leaves which, when passed onto the larvae of the silkworm, depresses their feeding rate, softens the silkworm cuticle, reduces the growth rate and increases mortality. The concentration of ambient fluoride is strongly correlated with fluoride content in the mulberry leaves and this, in turn, is strongly negatively correlated with silk yield (Figure 8.16). Similar effects are probably occurring in other developing countries, both on silkworms and other livestock. The paucity of reports is presumably due to a lack of investigation.

Particulate matter

Another problem for agriculture is the presence of particles, mainly dusts and soot, in the air. Coal burning produces very high levels of

Figure 8.16 Correlation between fluoride content of mulberry leaves and silk yield of cocoons in China

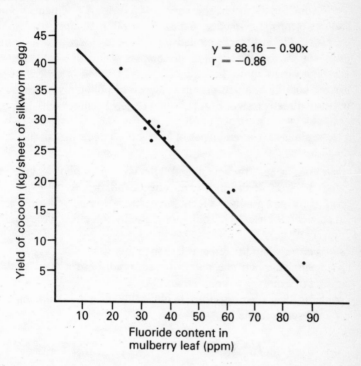

$$y = 88.16 - 0.90x$$
$$r = -0.86$$

Source: Wang, J.-X. and Bian, Y.-M., "Fluoride effects on the mulberry silkworm system", *Environ. Pollut.* **52** (1988) pp. 11–18.

suspended particulates although in Europe and North America ambient levels have generally declined following legislation on domestic and industrial combustion, and crops are only affected close to sources. More important, today, are the effects of local deposition of dust from cement works, motorway construction, power stations and quarries, and from the traffic on motorways. Soot or dust may affect plant growth by reducing the rate of photosynthesis and by wedging open stomata or abrading the cuticle, so increasing water loss. Usually, though, the loss to the farmer arises because high value produce, such as fruit, vegetables and horticultural crops, are rendered unsaleable. The problem may be exacerbated in arid or semi-arid parts of the world where concentrations of inert dusts, originating from desert ecosystems, may also be high.

Mixtures of pollutants

We have considered, so far, the effects of individual pollutants upon agricultural crops. In practice, damage can often be attributed to a single cause. Nevertheless polluted air usually consists of a mixture of gases which may affect plants in complex ways. One explanation for the high variability we have described as common in experiments is that the conditions often permit presence of pollutants other than those being directly tested. SO_2 pollution effects become confounded, for example, by the presence of NO_x.

In these situations several types of interactive effects may occur:

- *synergistic*, when the combined effect of pollution is greater than the sum of the individual effects (often a combination of pollutants may produce effects when the individual pollutants are at concentrations which would normally have no effect if they were present alone);[119]
- *antagonistic*, when the effect is less than this sum;
- *predisposition*, when one pollutant may predispose a plant to the impact of exposure to another; and
- *desensitization*, when exposure to one pollutant reduces the impact of a subsequent one.[120]

Sulphur dioxide and ozone

The first clear demonstration of an interaction between two pollutants was when O_3 and SO_2, combined, were found to cause visible foliar injury on a sensitive cultivar of tobacco.[121] Concentrations which alone would have produced no injury, together led to 15 per cent of the leaves being injured. Subsequently a wide range of similar plant reactions have been observed. Synergistic injury occurs on tobacco, radish and cucumber, while antagonistic responses may be present in white bean and soybean.[122] Sometimes even the symptoms produced by the mixture are different from those resulting from the individual gases. Thus a mixture of SO_2 and O_3 produced a chlorotic response in white bean quite unlike the necrotic lesions typical of the effect of either of the gases alone.[123] Nevertheless, a combined effect is not universal. Experiments on winter wheat have found no interactions between SO_2 and O_3 on either photosynthesis or yield (Table 8.13). Usually the synergism is only manifest at low to medium levels of contamination. At high levels the effect is usually dominated by the most abundant contaminant.

Table 8.13 Yields of winter wheat (tonnes/hectare) exposed to ozone and sulphur dioxide in the northeastern USA in open-top chambers, 1983

Sulphur dioxide 4 hour mean (ppb)	Ozone 7 hour mean (ppb)				
	27	57	76	96	Mean
0	4.9	3.8	2.8	2.0	3.4
39	3.4	4.4	3.6	2.5	3.5
166	4.6	3.9	2.0	2.1	3.2
363	4.6	3.5	2.9	2.6	3.3
Mean	4.4	3.9	2.8	2.3	

Source: Kohut, R.J., Amundson, R.G., Lawrence, S.A., Colavito, L., van Leuken, P. and King, P., "Effects of ozone and sulphur dioxide on yield of winter wheat", *Phytopath.* 77 (1987) pp. 71–79.

Sulphur dioxide and nitrogen oxides

Contradictory results are also a feature of experiments with mixtures of SO_2 and NO_x. The gases have been shown to act synergistically in inducing foliar injury in soybean, radish, tomato, beans and oats[124] but, in an extensive survey of nearly 90 wild species indigenous to the southwestern desert areas of the USA, no evidence was found of anything other than additive effects.[125] In the case of pasture grasses, exposure to concentrations of 68 ppb of SO_2 and/or NO_2 has resulted in synergistic growth reductions in cocksfoot (*Dactylis*), ryegrass (*Lolium*), timothy (*Phleum*) and meadow grass (*Poa*).[126] But the complexity of responses is demonstrated by a long-term experiment using mixtures of SO_2 and NO_2 on smooth meadow grass (*Poa pratensis*).[127] During the winter, treatment with NO_2 alone stimulated growth and SO_2 alone had little effect, and the mixture produced a substantial negative effect. However, in the summer all treatments had recovered and even began to surpass the control treatment (Figure 8.17).

There have been some attempts to uncover the biochemical basis of synergism. In one experiment in which the grasses *Dactylis* and *Lolium* were exposed over 1–2 weeks to 250 ppb of NO_2 it was found that the activity of the nitrate reductase enzyme, which helps to break down the NO_2, was significantly increased.[128] Treatment with SO_2, alone, had no effect on this enzyme but when grasses were fumigated with SO_2 in combination with NO_x, the presence of the SO_2 completely prevented the increase in enzyme activity. The grasses were thus unable to detoxify the NO_2 and hence were damaged.

Figure 8.17 Reduction in dry weight of *Poa pratensis* compared with controls after exposure to weekly mean concentrations of 62 ppb NO_2, 62 ppb SO_2 or 62 ppb of both

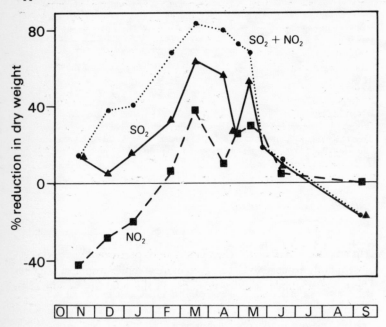

Source: Whitmore, M.E. and Freer-Smith, P.H., "Growth effects of SO_2 and/or NO_2 on woody plants and grasses during spring and summer", *Nature* **300** (1982) pp. 55–57.

Three gases together ($SO_2 + NO_x + O_3$)

Few experiments have considered the effects of ozone in the presence of mixtures of SO_2 and NO_x, a situation commonly found in rural areas of Europe and North America. The results are variable and complex.[129] For instance, a clear synergistic interaction has been demonstrated in peas, but in radish only additive effects occurred (Table 8.14). One question is whether the diurnal pattern of build-up of the different gases in the environment has any significance. In many situations, NO_2 increases in ambient air in the morning and is then followed by a rise in O_3. Experiments on wheat and radish using this sequence have found that NO_2 on its own stimulates growth, while ozone alone reduces growth, but NO_2 before O_3 appears to sensitize these crops to increased harmful effect, resulting in a greater reduction in growth of leaves and roots.[130]

Table 8.14   Effects on plants of the addition of ozone to SO_2/NO_2 mixtures

	Pollutant gas mixtures*		
	$SO_2 + NO_2$	O_3	$SO_2 + NO_2 + O_3$
Pea			
Proportion of leaves showing necrosis	0%	2%	18%
Radish			
Proportion of leaves showing necrosis	11%	45%	57%
Change in hypocotyl dry weight compared with control plants	−11%	−20%	−35%

* For pea, gas concentrations were 110 ppb SO_2, 210 ppb NO_2 and 110 ppb O_3
  For radish, gas concentrations were 40 ppb SO_2, 40 ppb NO_2 and 40 ppb O_3

Source: Bell, J.N.B., "Air pollution problems in Western Europe", in: Koziol and Whatley (eds), *Gaseous Air Pollutants and Plant Metabolism* (London: Butterworths, 1984).

In another experiment, when beans were pretreated with NO_2 and subsequently exposed to O_3, an even more complex response occurred. There was a simple additive response in the total dry weight of the above ground parts of the bean plants. NO_2 alone increased the weight while O_3 reduced it and the mixture produced the arithmetic sum of these effects. But the effect was less than additive for green leaf dry weight and the production of dying leaves (Table 8.15). Depending on mixtures and sequencing of exposure, synergistic, antagonistic and additive effects have all been demonstrated.[131]

Table 8.15   Effects of NO_2, O_3 and $NO_2 + O_3$ sequential exposure on growth of *Phaseolus* beans. Data are percentage changes from control after 40 days

	Exposure	Change in total dry weight	Change in green leaf dry weight	Senescence* index
NO_2	100 ppb 0900–1200 h daily	+28	+ 4	+16
O_3	100 ppb 1200–1800 h daily	−69	−88	+76
$NO_2 + O_3$	In sequence: NO_2 in morning, O_3 in afternoon	−41	−67	+58

* Ratio of senesced (dead) leaf weight/total leaf weight

Source: Runeckles, V.C., "Impact of air pollutant combinations on plants", in: Treshow, M. (ed.), 1984, *op. cit.*

Mixtures with fluorides

Mixtures of HF with SO_2 and with O_3 also cause variable interactions. O_3 has been shown to decrease the accumulation of fluoride in alfalfa and rye grass, but had no effect on tomato, maize, bean, mint and *Phleum* and *Dactylis* grasses. In some cases SO_2 concentrations of 80 ppb in the presence of only 0.8 ppb HF resulted in greater than additive injury to barley and maize.[132]

Gases, pests and diseases

Not only may pollutant gases interact with one another, they may also encourage or suppress the growth of various pests and pathogens, so increasing in certain cases the amount of crop damage that would occur if only the gas or the pest or pathogen were present alone.

It has been long recognized that there is an interaction between pests and point sources of air pollution. Surveys have indicated that areas downwind of London and also in the proximity of heavy industry contain consistently higher infestations of black bean aphids (*Aphis fabae*) on field beans than would be otherwise expected.[133] Support for this comes from experiments that have demonstrated that SO_2 increases the rates of growth of aphids: those on polluted plants gain biomass at a rate 12 per cent greater than those on unpolluted plants. As a consequence, peas grown in air containing 45 ppb SO_2 are attacked earlier by Pea Aphids, and accumulate a greater population of aphids over the growing season (Figure 8.18). SO_2 alone has little effect on pea growth and yields but aphids alone have an effect and the combination of SO_2 and aphids produces an even greater reduction (Table 8.16). The effects, however, mostly occur at SO_2 levels greater than 45 ppb, though over very short periods, and thus they are unlikely to occur in more remote rural areas. The impact of SO_2 on aphids is now known to be a universal phenomenon – it has been demonstrated with a wide range of plant hosts and aphid species.[134]

Aphid populations have also been found to be much greater on plants. As a consequence, peas grown in air containing 45 ppb SO_2 are attacked earlier by pea aphids, and accumulate a greater population Ozone, too, appears to enhance attack by insects: in combination with whitefly at only 20 ppb it doubles the injury of beans, where neither alone has much effect (Figure 8.19). Mexican bean beetles prefer feeding on soybean foliage subject to ozone pollution at 30–60 ppb, and tomato pinworms develop faster and survive longer on tomato plants injured by ozone.[136] In the UK aphids on black beans grew more quickly and survived better when exposed to air containing just 21 ppb

Figure 8.18 Effect of adding SO_2 to ambient air on the density of pea aphids on pea plants grown in greenhouses. Ambient air, 1.5 ppb SO_2; ambient air + SO_2 45 ppb SO_2

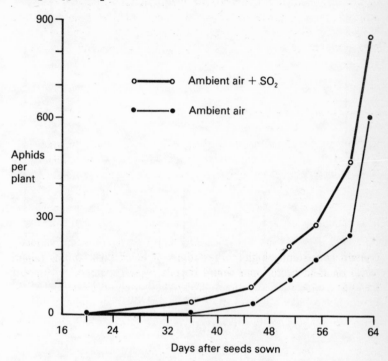

Source: Warrington, S., Mansfield, T.A. and Whittaker, J.B., "Effects of SO_2 on the reproduction of pea aphids, *Acyrthosiphon pisum*, and the impact of SO_2 and aphids on the growth of peas", *Environ. Pollut.* 48 (1987) pp. 285–294.

Table 8.16 Effect of SO_2 and pea aphids on growth of peas

	Mean pea weight (mg)	Shoot dry weight (g)	Mean no. pods per plant
Ambient air*	126.4	11.0	3.6
Ambient air + SO_2 (45 ppb)	130.0	10.1	3.9
Ambient air + aphids	85.3	8.7	3.3
Ambient air + SO_2 + Aphids	79.8	7.3	3.0

* ambient air contained concentrations of the following pollutants: 1.5 ppb SO_2, 7.5 ppb NO_2, 17 ppb O_3

Source: Warrington, S., Mansfield, T.A. and Whittaker, J.B., 1987, *op. cit.*

Figure 8.19   Leaf injury on bush bean (*Phaseolus vulgaris* L. cv. Pure Gold Wax) exposed to ozone and white-fly

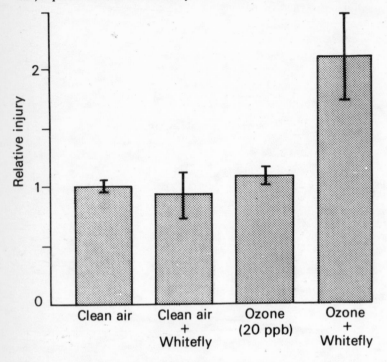

Source: Unsworth, M., "Adding ethylene to injury", *Nature* **327** (1987), pp. 364–365, using data from Rosen and Runeckles, 1976.

of ozone compared with filtered air.[137] These levels of ozone, unlike those in the SO_2 experiments, are commonly found in rural areas. It seems likely that the impact of ozone on plant–pest relationships is widespread.

In a similar fashion, synergy may involve fungal pathogens. Fungal parasites of plants are divided in two groups depending upon whether they can live in the absence of the living plant host: powdery mildew, smuts and rusts grow and reproduce only on living hosts and are termed *obligate*; the *non-obligate* fungi can live on both dead and living host tissue. The incidence of diseases caused by obligate fungi is usually reduced by ozone or SO_2.[138] In the case of SO_2 this may be because of the fungicidal properties of sulphur. Nevertheless, this cannot be the explanation for the ozone effect. Young wheat plants fumigated with moderate amounts of ozone develop far fewer pustules of the wheat brown rust, *Puccinia recondita*, compared with those grown in filtered air (Table 8.17). The concentrations of ozone used were not sufficient to cause direct damage to the plants, and all were healthy at the time of inoculation with the pathogen. The impact also varies with the pathogen: powdery mildew (*Erysiphe graminis*) on barley increases in severity during the season when exposed to 32 ppb of SO_2, but leaf-blotch fungus (*Rhynchosporium secalis*) declines.[139] In some instances, the synergy may simply be the result of a stress effect. Lesions caused by the non-obligate fungus *Alternaria* very rarely occur on undamaged tobacco leaves, but are much more common on ozone-damaged foliage.[140]

Table 8.17 Effect of ozone fumigation on wheat before inoculation with the brown rust *Puccinia recondita*

	Proportion of leaves in each infection class (%)			
Percent cover of leaves with Puccinia pustules	*Ozone air (85 ppb for 25 hours)*	*Filtered air*	*Ozone air (105 ppb for 49 hours)*	*Filtered air*
0	90	38	68	34
1–25	10	24	27	44
26–45	0	23	4	15
>46	0	15	1	7

Source: Dohmen, G.P., "Secondary effects of air pollution: ozone decreases brown rust disease potential in wheat", *Environ. Pollut.* 43 (1987) pp. 189–94.

Beneficial effects of air pollutants

Although the harm caused by air pollutants to crops and livestock is our primary concern, it is important to recognize that under certain circumstances the damage may be outweighed by significant benefits. Both nitrogen and sulphur are essential ingredients for crop growth. In the case of NO_x the contribution of nitrogen to plant growth is probably greatly outweighed by normal fertilizer inputs.[141] But, there is good evidence of atmospheric sulphur compounds alleviating deficiency in crops grown on sulphur deficient soils: prolonged exposure to air containing about 19 ppb will improve yields.[142] In the USA sulphur deficiencies have been identified in over half the states[143] while in the British Isles sulphur deficiencies are only marginal, tending to occur only in Ireland where sulphur deposition is low. However, declining use of sulphate fertilizers in favour of nitrate and urea has meant that some crops, such as oil seed rape, benefit from the annual deposit of 20–50 kg S/ha in the UK.[144] Sulphur deficiency is also present in many other parts of the world and, in particular, in sub-Saharan Africa.

Average SO_2 concentrations in rural Britain of 11 ppb will contribute about 3 kg S/ha annually to the soil.[145] High yielding wheat and grassland requires about 10–30 kg/ha annually, though brassicas and legumes may remove up to 50 kg S/ha, and sugar cane as much as 100 kg S/ha. The average contribution of sulphur from SO_2 is thus not insignificant and in areas of Britain where SO_2 levels are low (less than 5 ppb), and annual sulphur deposition in precipitation is less than 10 kg S/ha, there are many reports of crops responding to sulphur fertilizers.[146] Sulphur deficiency has become more likely in the industrialized countries with the increasing substitution of ammonium nitrate and urea for ammonium sulphate in high grade fertilizers. If sulphur deposits from the atmosphere were to be decreased significantly, that is, to less than 15 kg S/ha, it would become necessary to apply sulphur fertilizers more extensively.

Radioactivity and agriculture

Radioactivity in the environment arises naturally from such sources as granite rocks, and the effects on plants and animals will be common to both wild and domesticated species. There is, indeed, a potentially beneficial effect on all forms of life in that background radiation, by inducing mutations in genetic material, provides the basis for significant natural and artificial selection, out of which new varieties and breeds emerge.

Direct effects of radiation

Radiation does, however, directly damage organisms through the dissipation of its energy in biological tissues, creating chemically reactive ions and radicals. These disrupt and transform normal chemical processes, so producing adverse effects on cells, tissues and even entire organisms. The dose of radiation (see Box 8.3) lethal to an organism varies according to the group of organisms – in general mammals and birds are the most sensitive, micro-organisms the most resistant (Figure 8.20).

The sensitivity of plants to radiation depends upon two factors: the amount of genetic material present in the cells, and the metabolic activity of the cells when receiving the dose. Plants with large chromosomal volumes have a large target for absorbing radiation –

Box 8.3   The various measures of radioactivity and dose

There is a bewildering range of measures for radioactivity, exposure and dose.

A One **becquerel** (Bq) is equivalent to one nuclear disintegration of any kind per second, so:

one gamma ray emitted in one second is 1 Bq

One **rutherford** = 1 million Bq

One **curie** = 37 billion Bq (3.7×10^{10} Bq)

B But these measures do not reflect the dose absorbed by biological tissues, so:

One **roentgen** is the amount of radiation that produces 2.58×10^{-4} coulombs of elecrical charge in one kg of dry air, or

one **rad** (radiation absorbed dose) is the amount of radiation that deposits 0.01 joules of energy in each kg of material or tissue receiving the radiation

one hundred rads = one **gray**

During the Chernobyl accident all workers receiving 6–16 gray died within 9–28 days, those receiving 4–6 all died within 14–49 days.

C Yet these measures are still insufficient. Grays and rads do not take account of the fact that different kinds of radiation* have different effects on biological tissues according to penetrating power, energy and the absorbing power of the tissue, so for a measure of dose equivalence:

one **roentgen–equivalent–man** is one **rem**

one **rem** produces the same biological effect as one roentgen of X-rays, or 8 billion Bq/kg

100 rems = one **sievert**

Rems and sieverts do not measure radioactivity, but accumulated dose. Most people receive about 0.002 sieverts per year (0.2 rem), with probably the same effect on cancer risk as smoking one cigarette every ten days, but 10 sieverts (1000 rem) in a few minutes would cause death.

D The **becquerel, gray** and **sievert** are the terms in current usage under the SI classification

* There are three main types of radiation, *alpha*, *beta* and *gamma*.

thus coniferous trees, especially the genera *Pinus*, *Picea*, *Albies* and *Pseudotsuga*, are very sensitive to low levels. For these trees, growth is inhibited at doses of 1.5–3 sieverts (Sv), and the lethal dose is

Figure 8.20 Approximate acute lethal dose ranges for various groups of organisms

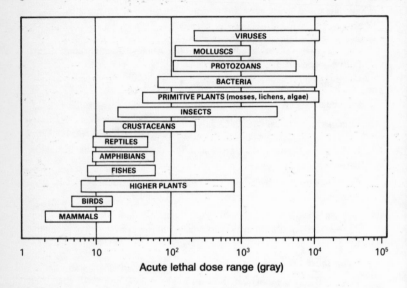

Source: Hutchinson, T.C., Harwell, M.A., Cropper, W.P., and Grover, H.D., "Additional potential effects of nuclear war on ecological systems", in: Harwell, M.A. and Hutchinson, T.C. (eds.), *Environmental Consequences of Nuclear War* (New York: John Wiley and Sons, 1985); using data from Whicker and Shultz, 1982.

4–9.5 Sv.[147] By comparison, the growth of deciduous trees is not usually inhibited until they are exposed to 15–100 Sv. In general, cereal crops and grasses are as tolerant as deciduous trees. Sensitivity is also increased by metabolic activity – dormant seeds are much more resistant than actively dividing cells.

There are also serious chronic effects. At a lower, but continuous, exposure to radiation, whole plant and animal communities may be disrupted or even destroyed. One of the best known experimental treatments of a natural community is in Long Island, New York, where an oak-pine forest at the Brookhaven National Laboratory was exposed to a source of radiation from 1961.[148] Gamma radiation – particles which penetrate substances readily, from a 3.5×10^{14} Bq source of caesium-137 in the forest created a concentric pattern of damage as the intensity of exposure decreased with distance from the source. Close by the source, exposure was 2–20 Sv per day, producing a central devastated zone with only lichens surviving (Table 8.18).

Since these measurements were made the circle of damage has
expanded as the dose has accumulated over the years.

Table 8.18   Effects of a single source of gamma radiation on an oak-pine
forest in Long Island, New York, after irradiation for 6 months

Distance from source (metres)	Dose received (sieverts per day)	Vegetation present
0–15	>2	No higher plants Few mosses and lichens
15–22.5	1.5–2	Sedges, dominated by *Carex pennsylvanica*
22.5–32.5	0.4–1.5	Shrubs, dominated by *Vaccinium* and short species of oak (*Quercus ilicifolia*)
32.5–50	0.16–0.40	Tree-sized oaks (*Quercus alba* and *Q. coccinea*)
50–110	less than 0.02	Oak-pine (*Pinus rigida*) zone with some damage, but no mortality
>110		No damage

Source: Woodwell, G.M., "The biotic effects of ionising radiation", *Ambio* 11 (1982)
pp. 144–8; Woodwell, G.M., "Radiation and patterns of nature", *Science* 156 (1987)
pp. 461–70.

Uptake of radioactive isotopes

Although this experiment graphically describes the potential impact
of ionizing radiation on agriculture, such radiation levels only occur
where nuclear weapons are tested and hence damage to crops and
livestock is extremely rare. Even when there is a serious release of
radioactive material, such as following the Chernobyl accident in the
USSR, there is surprisingly little direct harm to plants and animals.
Nevertheless, they readily absorb radioactive isotopes which end up as
contaminants of our food.

The transfer of radionuclides from the environment to plants
depends upon the mobility of the elements and the type of soil. Of
particular importance are those radionuclides with long half-lives. The
half-life is the time required for a given amount of the material to decay
away to only half the amount: the half-life for caesium (^{134}Cs) is 2 years
and for ^{137}Cs 30 years, but for iodine (^{131}I) it is only eight days. In
general, soils with a high clay content tend to lock up radionuclides;
they are more likely to be taken up from sandy or acidic soils (Table

8.19). The proportion of radionuclides passed from one stage of the food chain to another – measured as the transfer coefficient – is usually less than one, implying that there is little concentration up the chain. However, for some very mobile elements this is not the case – technetium-99, for example, is readily transferred even in clay soils to the straw of wheat plants, producing a concentration some 20–70 times greater than in the soil.[149] The ^{99}Tc, though, remains in the straw. For most radionuclides, grain accumulates 10–50 times less than the straw.

Table 8.19   Transfer of caesium-137 from various soils to winter wheat

Soil type		Activity (Bq/g)	Transfer coefficient*
Clay	Straw	4.0	0.05
	Grain	2.6	0.03
Sandy loam	Straw	9.9	0.12
	Grain	2.3	0.03
Organic	Straw	3.7	0.04
	Grain	2.2	0.03

* Transfer coefficient is the proportion of caesium in the plant, straw or grain, to the amount in the soil

Source: Grogan, H.A., Mitchell, N.G., Minski, M.J. and Bell, J.N.B., "Pathways of radionuclides from soils to wheat", in: Coughtrey, P.J., Martin, M.H. and Unsworth, M.H. (eds), *Pollutant Transport and Fate in Ecosystems* (Oxford: Blackwell, 1987).

Nuclear accidents

Three accidents provide most of our current knowledge of the potential consequences for agriculture of relatively high levels of radionuclides released to the environment. The first occurred in October 1957 and was the result of a fire in the air-cooled graphite reactor at Windscale (now called Sellafield) in Cumbria, northwest England. The fire released large amounts of volatile fission products over the course of two days, which were then deposited over much of England and parts of Europe.[150] Iodine-131 was taken up by cattle feeding on contaminated grassland and passed to milk. Radioactive iodine readily accumulates in milk, and once ingested, further accumulates in the thyroid gland, leading to a raised risk of cancer. In parts of northwest England, milk distribution was stopped for more than six weeks. But no damage to crops or livestock was reported and there were no other restrictions on food distribution.

The second accident was in a nuclear waste reprocessing plant in the Cheliabinsk province of the USSR. No official statements have been made, but careful piecing together of evidence from a multiplicity of sources has led Medvedvev, Trabalka and others to conclude that the accident so severely contaminated the area to the east of Kyshtym that canals were built to divert water around contaminated lakes and villages and agriculture was abandoned.[151] The accident is thought to have released more than 3.7×10^{16} Bq of strontium-90 alone.

By far the most notorious accident was at the Chernobyl nuclear reactor complex in the Ukraine, USSR, on 26 April, 1986. An explosion, fire and resultant melt of the core of the reactor caused the release of an unprecedented amount of radioactivity into the atmosphere over central Europe. Some 3×10^{17} Bq of iodine-131 and 4×10^{16} Bq of caesium-137 were released.[152] The majority of the fall-out occurred in the region around the plant: 5–10 km from the reactor the maximum radiation level reached was 0.01 sievert/hour, compared to normal background levels that were 50,000–100,000 times lower.[153] The ground to the north, northwest and northeast of the plant was severely contaminated, the plume affecting the Ukrainian, Belorussian and Russian republics before moving northwards to the Baltic and Scandinavia. Above-background levels were eventually recorded even in North America, where milk was contaminated by ^{131}I in areas where summer rainfall was high, such as California and Oregon.

The accident caused the deaths of some workers at the plant, and necessitated the evacuation of about 135,000 other people living close to the reactor. The Chernobyl area is not a major food producing region, largely consisting of peat bogs and marshes, and agriculture is confined to dairy farming and potato cultivation. But normal agricultural activity is now not permitted in a zone stretching 80 km to the north and west of the plant. Within this zone farmers may not graze cattle; nor can humans consume milk. The only crops grown are those exhibiting low radionuclide uptake. Moreover, the farmers are still thought to be at "grave risk to their health".[154]

The immediate impact on regions distant from Chernobyl was also significant. Ripening durum wheat in Greece was severely contaminated, as was tea growing in northern Turkey. In many parts of central and southern Europe vegetables had to be destroyed because of high contamination. But two of the most severe and long-term impacts occurred in northern Europe, and those most affected were farmers and pastoralists living in remote and marginal areas.

Reindeer in Scandinavia

The most dramatic impact was on the reindeer of northern Scandinavia, which are the major source of livelihood for the nomadic Lapp tribes. At the time of the accident the herders were in the high mountain pastures but when they brought reindeer in for slaughter later in the summer, carcasses containing up to 20,000 Bq/kg were found (in Sweden and Norway the maximum stipulated limits are 300 and 600 Bq/kg respectively). Of the 21,000 reindeer slaughtered in October of 1986, only 500 were fit for human consumption. By 1988 as much as 80 per cent of the total reindeer population of Scandinavia had been seriously contaminated.[155]

Reindeer become contaminated by feeding on lichens and mosses, which are particularly good at trapping airborne contaminants, in this case the caesium radionuclides from Chernobyl. Since the accident the contamination has declined only very slowly. It takes nine years for lichens to shed half their load of caesium, so that if a reindeer with 8000 Bq/kg today continues to eat lichen, it would die of old age before concentrations came down to 1000 Bq/kg. Some reindeer meat is thus unlikely to be acceptable for human consumption for "several decades" to come. However, if alternative sources of winter food can be found, such as hay – which is currently too costly – then levels in individual animals will fall more rapidly.

Hill-sheep in northwest Britain

Britain received radioactive fallout about one week after the accident. As the plume passed over, 0.7–0.8 per cent of the total caesium and iodine released during the accident was deposited. The north and west of the country suffered the worst effects, as the heavy rainfall washed out ^{137}Cs, ^{134}Cs and ^{131}I; elsewhere ^{131}I was deposited dry.[156] Before the accident caesium concentrations in vegetation were typically less than 5 Bq/m^2, and in lowland Britain the extra burden of caesium was less than that already accumulated in soil and vegetation due to nuclear weapons testing. But in the uplands of the north and west the concentrations of caesium reached several thousand Bq/m^2 (Table 8.20). The caesium and iodine were taken up by grass and other fodder and ended up in milk and in meat.

Iodine concentrations in milk over the whole country increased to 40–100 Bq/litre 9–12 days after the accident; for caesium the highest levels occurred in the north and west. Nevertheless, these were not sufficient to cause a ban on consumption. More significant was the

Table 8.20 Deposition of radioactive iodine and caesium to grasslands in Britain and resultant concentrations in cows' milk

Site	Iodine-131 Deposition to grass (Bq/m²)	Iodine-131 Concentration in milk (Bq/l)	Caesium-137 Deposition to grass (Bq/m²)	Caesium-137 Concentration in milk (Bq/l)
Dry areas				
Berkshire	242	38	20	2
Cleveland	70	14	17	NR (10–18)
Oxfordshire	459	37	22	13
Light rainfall				
Cheshire	325	11	93	14
Dorset	64	52	25	4
Essex	1345	71	285	18
Kent	2346	82	NR	10
Lancashire	1327	49	358	48
Heavy rainfall				
Cumbria	2246	110	1334	128
Dumfries and Galloway	610	151	598	171
Gwynedd	1009	74	1235	124
Highlands	3604	61	1164	24
Orkney	3159	127	682	71
Strathclyde	3445	61	2285	68
West Yorkshire	1259	NR (30–40)	680	NR (13–40)

NR = not recorded
NR (10–18) = not recorded (range of values from neighbouring counties)

Source: Clark, M.J. and Smith, F.B., "Wet and dry deposition of Chernobyl releases", *Nature* 332 (1988) pp. 245–9.

contamination of the sheep meat. Caesium concentrations reached 2450 Bq/kg, and in June 1986 the government banned the movement and slaughter of sheep in Cumbria and North Wales, and then in parts of southern Scotland. The sheep themselves have not been at risk since the doses received were too low to cause birth defects in lambs or infertility in ewes. However, concentrations were above the WHO "action level" of 1000 Bq/kg indicating a risk to human health and, indeed, had been so for more than a month before the ban. A major objective of the ban had been to safeguard consumers and maintain their confidence in lamb as a food. However, the ban caused lamb prices throughout the UK to fall by a quarter to a third as demand rapidly declined. Supermarkets, recognizing that their customers would avoid lamb whether it posed a risk or not, stopped buying lamb.

The ban was not expected to last for long, largely because it was thought that caesium would bind to soil particles, thus removing it from the biological cycle. However, the concentration in the vegetation did not decline. Sheep moved to lowland uncontaminated pastures were able to eliminate some of their caesium body burden; but if they returned to contaminated pastures the burden once again increased. Vegetation also showed great variability in the quantity of caesium present; mosses in the same square metre, for instance, often carried ten times the radioactivity of grasses. Upland soils are largely acidic and rich in organic material, but contain little clay that can bind the Cs. It is thus not readily immobilized, and when grasses begin to grow in the spring, it is taken up again from the soil and transfers to the sheep.

The original predictions of rapidly declining contamination have proven inaccurate. This is partly because they were based on experiments in lowland soils high in clay content, and also because they failed to predict that concentrations in lichens and mosses would increase. Furthermore, immediately after the accident the caesium deposited on forage plants was in an insoluble form and hence when ingested by sheep was not readily absorbed from the gut. Once it had been taken up by plants, however, it was more available for absorption. In March 1988, some 322,000 sheep were restricted on 860 farms in Cumbria, North Wales, southern Scotland and Northern Ireland, and by March 1990, restrictions were still in force on 750 farms. In Cumbria, the area where some of the highest levels of Cs deposition occurred, the last time a farm was freed from restrictions was in September 1986.[157]

Farmers have suffered in a number of ways. They are unable to move sheep from one pasture to another without their being first scanned to check for levels of contamination. Extra labour is required to look after sheep that must remain on high pastures, and to bury animals that have died on the farm. Extra capital is also required to buy uncontaminated feed that can be fed to sheep before sale and so reduce the level of caesium in meat. Most hill farms have only a small proportion of low pasture, yet sheep must graze here or be fed forage for at least six weeks before concentrations fall below 1000 Bq/kg and can then be sold. Farmers receive compensation of £1.30 per animal tested before going to the market. But sheep or lambs previously contaminated always fetch lower prices at market.

There are several possible options for reducing the caesium burden in hill sheep. One is to add feed supplements, such as prussian blue, to remove radioactivity. Another is to add calcium, phosphorus or clay material to the soil – plants take up Ca and P in preference to Cs, and clay could help bind the Cs. Thirdly, hot spots of radioactivity on the pastures can be identified and fenced off. But all these have drawbacks – the prussian blue option is only at the laboratory stage, the addition of clay, Ca and P would cause major ecological disruption, and the identification of hot spots has so far either proven too costly or is not an option for some farmers whose entire farms are hot spots. Caesium is recycling at a rate that continues to keep sheep on the hill pastures contaminated beyond the 1000 Bq/kg limit, and the contamination is showing no signs of decreasing.

Summary

Air pollution can cause serious losses to crop and animal husbandry, although the levels of loss under different circumstances are difficult to assess experimentally. Especially, in crop experiments, there are problems of ensuring comparability of environmental conditions, and of separating out the interactions with soil and climatic factors.

Sulphur dioxide (SO_2) and nitrogen oxides (NO_x) are prime causes of acid pollution. This is prevalent in industrialized countries, particularly in northern Europe and northeastern USA, primarily as a result of the burning of fossil fuels, and also in the industrialized regions of certain developing countries such as China and Brazil.

Dry deposition of SO_2 and NO_x can cause injury and loss of yield to crops at acute exposures of about 500 ppb, although some crops are sensitive at exposures as low as 100 ppb. There have been many experiments on the effects of low doses on arable crops and perennial grasses but with conflicting results. In particular, the effects are highly variable at doses comparable with those currently present in rural areas. Damage appears to be more likely under conditions of slow growth in winter and when the plants are subject to stress. Genetic tolerance can quickly evolve.

Experimental evidence on the effects of acid rain on crops is also conflicting, but, in general, obvious injury only occurs at pH levels of less than 3.5, which are rarely encountered.

Ozone (O_3) pollution of the troposphere is of increasing importance in both the industrialized and developing countries, as a result of the rapid growth in the use of motor vehicles. Although primarily of urban origin, ozone pollution may spread extensively over rural areas producing concentrations in excess of 100 ppb. In Brazil, and some other countries, high ozone concentrations may also result from biomass burning.

Direct visible injury and loss of yield occur in a wide variety of crops under ambient ozone levels. Oranges, lemons, grapes and wheat have shown loss of 12–80 per cent at levels of 100 ppb and less. Rice is probably suffering loss of 7 per cent at the prevailing 50 ppb in California and up to 30 per cent at 200 ppb in Japan. Widespread monitoring in Europe and USA using open-top chambers is revealing losses of yield in field crops at hourly mean ozone concentrations of 30 ppb and more. There is also evidence of considerable genetic variability in tolerance among cultivars.

Emissions of fluorides from such sources in brickworks and aluminium smelters have been greatly reduced in recent years, but are still sufficiently high around the emitting sources to cause damage. Fluorides are accumulated in leaves and also interfere with pollination and fruit production. Exposure of only 1 ppb at a critical period has reduced wheat yields by 20–30 per cent but in general damage to agricultural crops occurs at concentrations greater than 3.6 ppb. Build-up of fluorides in pasture grasses may have particularly serious effects on livestock, producing skeletal damage when levels in the grass are of the order of 45 ppm or more.

Mixtures of pollutants may produce synergistic or antagonistic effects, or one gas may predispose or desensitize a plant to the effect of the other. The experimental results are, however, complicated and, in some cases, conflicting and it is currently impossible to predict what type of interaction will happen when a given crop is subjected to a given combination of pollutants. Gaseous pollutants may also stimulate more serious attack by pests such as aphids and whitefly and by non-obligate fungi, but protect against some fungi, such as mildews.

Damage from radiation to crops or livestock at the levels emitted from nuclear power stations and by nuclear weapons testing appears to be negligible. Of greater concern is the accumulation of radionuclides, particularly of iodine and caesium, in livestock grazing on pastures contaminated by fallout from accidents such as Chernobyl in 1986. In the UK caesium levels in sheep reached 2450 Bq/kg soon after the Chernobyl accident and have remained high because levels have not declined in the pasture as rapidly as expected. Restrictions were still in force on 750 farms some four years after the accident.

In the tropics and subtropics, although air pollution has not become as widespread as in the industrialized countries, there is a potential for serious damage to crops and livestock. Daytime temperature and sunlight intensity are often high year round, so increasing the activity of photochemical processes, and soils in many parts of the tropics are particularly sensitive to pollutant damage. Where rainfall is high, wet deposition of sulphur and nitrogen compounds is common and in some regions, wind direction also tends to be unchanged over extended periods of time, so making areas downwind of emitting sources subject to continuously elevated ambient concentrations and deposition of pollutants. Biomass burning is an important source of trace gases, but very little is known, as yet, of the effects of air pollutants in these regions.

References

1 Heck, W.W. and Brandt, C.S., "Effects on vegetation: native crops and forests", in: Stern, A.C. (ed.), *The Effects of Air Pollution* vol. II (New York: Academic Press, 1977).

2 Brough, A., Parry, M.A. and Whittingham, C.P., "The effect of low concentrations of ambient pollutants on the growth and yield of crops", in: Ministry of Agriculture, Fisheries and Food, *Inorganic Pollution and Agriculture* Ref. Book 326 (London: HMSO, 1980).

3 Buckenham, A.H., Parry, M.A.J. and Whittingham, C.P., "Effects of aerial pollutants on the growth and yield of spring barley", *Ann. appl. Biol.* **100** (1982) pp. 179–87.

4 Unsworth, M.H. and Mansfield, T.A., "Critical aspects of chamber design for fumigation experiments on grasses", *Environ. Poll. (A)* **23** (1980) pp. 115–20.

5 Lockyer, D.R., Cowling, D.W. and Jones, L.H.P., "A system for exposing plants to atmospheres containing low concentrations of sulphur dioxide", *J. Experiment. Bot.* **27** (1976) pp. 397–409.

6 Bell, J.N.B., "Effects of acid deposition on crops and forests", *Experientia* **42** (1986) pp. 363–71.

7 Bell, 1986, *ibid.*

8 Cowling, D.W., Lockyer, D.R., Chapman, P.F. and Koziol, M.J., "Assessment of the concentration of SO_2 to which plants are exposed in a system of chambers", *Environ. Pollut.* **26** (1981) pp. 1–13; Unsworth and Mansfield, 1980, *op. cit.*; Bell, J.N.B., "Sulphur dioxide and the growth of grasses", in: Unsworth, M.H. and Ormrod, D.P., *Effects of Gaseous Air Pollution in Agriculture and Horticulture* (London: Butterworths, 1982).

9 Bell, 1982, *op. cit.*; Bell, J.N.B., Rutter, A.J. and Relton, J., "Studies on the effects of low levels of sulphur dioxide on the growth of *Lolium Perenne*", *L.J. New Phytolo.* **83** (1979) pp. 627–44; Davies, T., "Grasses more sensitive to SO_2 pollution in conditions of low irradiance and short days", *Nature* **284** (1980) pp. 483–5.

10 McLaughlin, S.B. and Taylor, G.E., "Relative humidity: important modifier of pollutant uptake by plants", *Science* **211** (1981) pp. 167–9.

11 Heck and Brandt, 1977, *op. cit.*

12 Möller, D., "Estimation of the global man-made sulphur emission", *Atmos. Environ.* **18** (1984a) pp. 19–27; Möller, D., "On the natural sulphur emission", *Atmos. Environ.* **18** (1984b) pp. 29–39; Varhelyi, G., "Continental and global sulphur budgets I. Anthropogenic SO_2 emissions", *Atmos. Environ.* **19** (1985) pp. 1029–40.

13 Moreira-Nordemann, L.M., Forti, M.C., Di Lascio, V.L., do Espirito Santo, C.M. and Danelon, O.M., "Acidification in southeastern Brazil", in: Rodhe, H. and Herrera, R. (eds), *Acidification in Tropical Countries*, SCOPE Report no. 36 (Chichester: John Wiley and Sons, 1988).

14 Fowler, D. and Cape, J.N., "Air pollutants and agriculture and horticulture", in: Unsworth, M.H. and Ormrod, D.P. (eds), *Effects of Gaseous Air Pollution in Agriculture and Horticulture* (London: Butterworths, 1982).

15 EPA, *National Air Quality and Emissions Trends Report, 1988* (Washington DC: US Environmental Protection Agency, 1990).

16 Galloway, J.N., Zhao, D., Xiong, J. and Likens, G.F., "Acid rain: China, United States and a remote area", *Science* **236** (1987) pp. 1559–62.

17 Zhao, D., Xiong, J., Xu, Y. and Chan, W.H., "Acid rain in southwestern China", *Atmos. Environ.* **22** (1986) pp. 349–58; Zhao, D. and Xiong, J., "Acidification in southwestern China", in: Rodhe and Herrera (eds), 1988 *op. cit.*

18 Colls, J.J. and Harris, D., "Air pollution assessment at the International Crops Research Institute for the Semi-Arid Tropics, India", *Environ. Technol. Lett.* **8** (1987) pp. 653–6.

19 Logan, J.A., "Nitrogen oxides in the troposphere: global and regional budgets", *J. Geophys. Res.* **88** (1983) pp. 10785–807.

20 Department of Environment, *Digest of Environmental Protection and Water Statistics* (London: HMSO, 1990).

21 Sanhueza, E., Cuenca, G., Gomez, M.J., Herrera, R., Ishizahi, C., Marti, J. and Paolini, J., "Characterisation of the Venezuelan environment and its potential for acidification", in: Rodhe and Herrera (eds), 1988 *op. cit.*

22 Bell, J.N.B., "Air pollution problems in Western Europe", in: Koziol, M.J. and Whatley, F.R. (eds), *Gaseous Air Pollutants and Plant Metabolism* (London: Butterworths, 1984).

23 Hameed, S. and Dignon, J., "Changes in the geographical distributions of global emissions of NO_x and SO_x from fossil-fuel combustion between 1966 and 1980", *Atmos. Environ.* **22** (1988) pp. 441–9; Varhelyi, 1985, *op. cit.*

24 Department of Environment, 1990, *op. cit.*

25 Renner, M., "Rethinking the role of the automobile", *Worldwatch Paper 84* (Washington: Worldwatch Institute, 1988).

26 Sanhueza et al., 1988, *op. cit.*

27 Jickells, T., Knapp, A., Church, T., Galloway, J. and Miller, J., "Acid rain on Bermuda", *Nature* **297** (1982) pp. 55–7.

28 McDowell, W.H., "Potential effects of acid deposition on tropical ter-
    restrial ecosystems", in: Rodhe, H. and Herrera, R. (eds), 1988 *op. cit.*
29 Zhao and Xiong, 1988, *op. cit.*
30 Haywood, J.K., "Injury to vegetation and animal life by smelter fumes",
    J. Am. Chem. Soc. **29** (1907) pp. 998–1009; Hedgcock, G.G., "Injury by
    smelter smoke in southeastern Tennessee", *Wash. Acad. Sci. J.* **4** (1914)
    pp. 70–71.
31 Roberts, T.M., Darrall, N.M. and Lane, P., "Effects of gaseous air
    pollutants on agriculture in the UK", *Adv. appl. Biol.* **9** (1983)
    pp. 1–142.
32 Thompson, C.R., Hensel, E.G., Kats, G. and Taylor, U.C., "Effects
    of continuous exposure of navel oranges to NO_2", *Atmos. Environ.* **4**
    (1970) pp. 344–55; Spierings, F.H.F.G., "Influence of fumigations with
    NO_2 on growth and yield of tomato plants", *Neth. J. Plant Pathol.* **77**
    (1971) pp. 194–200; Taylor, O.C. and Eaton, F.M., "Suppression of
    plant growth by nitrogen dioxide", *Plant Physiol.* **41** (1966) pp. 132–5.
33 Mansfield, T., "Nitrogen oxides: products of combustion processes that
    constitute a serious hazard to crops", in: MAFF, *Inorganic Pollution and
    Agriculture*, Ref. Book 326 (London: HMSO, 1980).
34 Hutchinson, T.C., "The ecological consequences of acid discharges
    from industrial smelters", in: D'Itri, F. (ed.), *Acid Precipitation, Effects
    on Ecological Systems* (Michigan: Ann Arbor, 1982).
35 Roberts et al., 1983, *op. cit.*
36 Baker, C.K., Colls, J.J., Fullwood, A.E. and Seaton, G.G.R., "Depression
    of growth & yield in winter barley exposed to sulphur dioxide in the field",
    New Phytol. **104** (1986) pp. 233–41; Baker, C.K., Fullwood, A.E. and
    Colls, J.J., "Tillering and leaf area of winter barley exposed to sulphur
    dioxide in the field", *New Phytol.* **107** (1987) pp. 373–85.
37 Baker et al., 1987, *op. cit.*; Pande, P.C. and Mansfield, T.A., "Responses
    of winter barley to SO_2 and NO_2 alone and in combination", *Environ.
    Pollut. A* **39** (1985) pp. 281–91.
38 Halbwachs, G., "Organismal responses of higher plants to atmospheric
    pollutants: sulphur dioxide and fluoride", in: Treshow, M. (ed), *Air
    Pollution and Plant Life* (Chichester: John Wiley and Sons, 1984).
39 Bell, 1984, *op. cit.*
40 Mansfield, T.A. and Freer-Smith, P.H., "Effects of urban air pollution
    on plant growth", *Biol. Rev.* **56** (1981) pp. 343–68.
41 Roberts, T.M., "Long-term effects of sulphur dioxide on crops: an
    analysis of dose-response relations", *Phil. Trans. R. Soc. Lond. B* **305**
    (1984) pp. 299–316; Jones, T. and Mansfield, T.A., "Studies on dry
    matter partitioning and distribution of ^{14}C-labelled assimilates in plants
    of *Phleum pratense* exposed to SO_2 pollution", *Environ. Pollut.* **28** (1982a)
    pp. 199–207.
42 Bell, 1984, *op. cit.*
43 Jones, T. and Mansfield, T.A., "The effect of SO_2 on growth and
    development of seedlings of *Phleum pratense* under different light and

temperature environments", *Environ. Pollut. A* 27 (1982b) pp. 57–71.

44 Baker, C.K., Unsworth, M.H. and Greenwood, P., "Leaf injury on wheat plants exposed in the field in winter to SO_2", *Nature* 299 (1982) pp. 149–50.

45 Ashenden, T.W., "Effect of ambient levels of air pollution on grass swards subjected to different defoliation regimes", *Environ. Pollut.* 45 (1987) pp. 29–47.

46 Bell, 1982, *op. cit.*

47 Ayazloo, M. and Bell, J.N.B., "Studies on the tolerance to sulphur dioxide of grass populations in polluted areas, 1. Identification of tolerant populations", *New Phytol.* 88 (1981) pp. 203–22.

48 Wilson, G.B. and Bell, J.N.B., "Studies on the tolerance to sulphur dioxide of grass populations in polluted areas. III. Investigations on the rate of development of tolerance", *New Phytol.* 100 (1985) pp. 63–77.

49 Ayazloo and Bell, 1981, *op. cit.*

50 Ayazloo, M., Garsed, S.G. and Bell, J.N.B., "Studies on the tolerance to sulphur dioxide of grass populations in polluted areas II. Morphological and physiological investigations", *New Phytol* 90 (1982) pp. 109–26.

51 Bell, J.N.B., Ayazloo, M. and Wilson, G.B., "Selection of sulphur dioxide tolerance in grass populations in polluted areas", in: Burnkamm, R., Lee, J.A. and Seaward, M.R.B. (eds), *Urban Ecology* (Oxford: Blackwell Sci. Publ., 1982).

52 Bell, 1982, *op. cit.*

53 Bell, J.N.B., Ashmore, M. and Wilson, G.R., (in press) "Ecological, genetic & chemical modifications of the atmosphere", in: Taylor, G.F. (ed.), *Plant Ecology, Genetics and Air Pollution Stress* (New York: Springer Verlag, 1991).

54 Bell, 1986, *op. cit.*; Jacobson, J.S., "Effects of acidic aerosol, fog, mist and rain on crops and trees", *Phil. Trans. R. Soc. Lond. B* 305 (1984) pp. 327–38.

55 Lee, J.J., "The effects of acid precipitation on crops", in D'Itri, F. (ed.), 1982, *op. cit.* Bell, 1986, *op. cit.*; Lee, J.J., Neely, G.E., Perrigan, S.C. and Grothams, L.C., "Effect of simulated sulphuric acid rain on yield, growth and foliar injury of several crops", *Environ. Exp. Bot.* 21 (1981) pp. 171–85.

56 Proctor, J.T.A., "Effect of simulated sulphuric acid rain on apple tree foliage, nutrient content, yield and fruit quality", *Environ. Exp. Bot.* 23 (1983) pp. 167–74; Forsline, P.L., Musselmann, R.C., Kender, W.J. and Del, R.J., "Effects of acid rain on apple productivity and fruit quality", *J. Proc. Ann. Hort. Soc.* 10 (1983) pp. 70–74.

57 Forsline et al., 1983, *op. cit.*

58 Jacobson, 1984, *op. cit.*

59 Irving, P.M. (1983), quoted in Bell, 1986, *op. cit.*

60 Zhao and Xiang, 1988, *op. cit.*

61 Rodhe, H., Cowling, E., Galbally, J.N. and Herrera, R., "Acidification and regional air pollution in the tropics", in: Rodhe and Herrera, (eds),

1988, *op. cit.*

62 Perkins, H.C., *Air Pollution* (Tokyo: McGraw-Hill Kogakusha, 1974); Wanta, R.C., "Meteorology and air pollution", in: Stern, A.C. (ed.), *Air Pollution*, 2nd edn (New York and London: Academic Press, 1968); Neilburger, M., Ediger, J.G. and Bonner, W.D., *Understanding our Atmospheric Environment* (California: W.H. Freeman and Co., 1973).

63 Zhao and Xiong, 1988, *op. cit.*

64 Neilburger et al., 1973, *op. cit.*

65 PORG, UK Photochemical Oxidant Review Group, *Ozone in the UK* (South Ruislip: Department of the Environment, 1987).

66 Krupa, S.V. and Manning, W.J., "Atmospheric ozone: formation and effects on vegetation", *Environ. Pollut.* **50** (1988) pp. 101–37.

67 Spicer, C.W., Joseph, D.W., Sticksel, P.R. and Ward, G.F., "Ozone sources and transport in the Northeastern United States", *Environ. Sci. Tech.* **13** (1979) pp. 875–85.

68 Ashmore, M.R., Bell, J.N.B. and Reily, C.L., "The distribution of phytotoxic ozone in the British Isles", *Environ. Pollut. B* **1** (1980) pp. 195–216.

69 Bell, 1984, *op. cit.*

70 RCEP, *Tackling Pollution – Experience and Prospects*, Royal Commission on Environmental Pollution (London: HMSO, 1984).

71 Department of Environment, 1990, *op. cit.*

72 Heck, W.W., "Defining gaseous pollution problems in North America", in: Koziol and Whatley (eds), *op. cit.*

73 Walker, H.M., "Ten-year ozone trends in California and Texas", *J. Air Pollut. Control Assoc.* **35** (1985) pp. 903–12.

74 PORG, 1987, *op. cit.*

75 Kanbour, F.I., Faiq, S.Y., Al Taie, F.A., Kitto, A.M.N. and Bader, N., "Variation of ozone concentrations in the ambient air of Baghdad", *Atmos. Environ.* **21** (1987) pp. 2673–9.

76 Rodhe et al., 1988, *op. cit.*

77 Volz, A. and Kley, D., "Evaluation of the Montsouris series of ozone measurements in the nineteenth century", *Nature* **332** (1988) pp. 240–42; Penkett, S.A., "Increased tropospheric ozone", *Nature* **332** (1988) pp. 200–205; PORG, 1987, *op. cit.*

78 Penkett, S.A., "Ozone increases in ground-level European air", *Nature* **311** (1984) pp. 14–15.

79 Gerstl, S.A. and Zardecki, A., "Effects of aerosols on photosynthesis", *Nature* **300** (1982) pp. 436–7.

80 Middleton, J.T., "Photochemical air pollution damage to plants", *Ann. Rev. Plant Physiol.* **12** (1961) pp. 431–48.

81 Krupa and Manning, 1988, *op. cit.*

82 Went, F.W., *Proc. 3rd National Air Pollution Symposium*, Pasadena, California (1955) pp. 8–11.

83 Ashmore, M.R., "Effects of ozone on vegetation in the UK", in: Grennfelt, P. (ed.), *Proc. int. workshop on the evaluation and assessment*

of the effects of photochemical oxidants on human health, agricultural crops, forestry, materials and visibility (Gothenburg: Swedish Environ. Res. Inst., 1984).

84 Thompson, C.R. and Taylor, O.C., "Effects of air pollutants on growth, leaf drop, fruit drop, and yield of citrus trees", *Environ. Sci. Technol.* 3 (1969) pp. 934–40; Thompson, C.R., Hensel, E. and Kats, G., "Effects of photochemical air pollutants on Zinfandel grapes", *Hort. Sci.* 4 (1969) pp. 222–4.

85 Kohut, R.J., Amundson, R.G., Laurence, J.A., Colavito, L., Van Leuken, P. and King, P., "Effects of ozone and sulphur dioxide on yield of winter wheat", *Phytopath.* 77 (1987) pp. 71–74.

86 Kats, G., Dawson, P.J., Bytnerowicz, A., Wolf, J.W., Thompson, C.R. and Olszyk, D.M., "Effects of ozone or sulphur dioxide on growth and yield of rice", *Agric. Ecosyst. and Environ.* 14 (1985) pp. 103–17.

87 Babawale, O.M., "Evidence of ozone injury to a crop plant in India", *Atmosph. Environ.* 20 (1986) pp. 1501–03; Street, O.E., Sung, C.H., Wu, H.Y. and Menser, H.A., "Studies on weather fleck of tobacco in Taiwan", *Tobacco Science* 15 (1971) pp. 128–31.

88 Amundsen, R.G., Raba, R.M., Schoettle, A.W. and Reich, P.B., "Response of soybean to low concentrations of ozone II, Effects on growth, biomass, allocation and flowering", *J. Environ. Qual.* 15 (1986) pp. 161–67; Tingey, D.T., Thutt, G.L., Gumpertz, M.L. and Hogsett, W.E., "Plant water status influences ozone sensitivity of bean plants", *Agric. Environ.* 7 (1982) pp. 243–54; Temple, P.J., Benoit, L.F., Lennox, R.W., Reagan, C.A. and Taylor, "Combined effects of ozone and water stress on alfalfa yield", *J. Environ. Qual.* 17 (1988) p. 108.

89 Heggestad, H.E., Anderson, E.L., Gish, T.J. and Lee, E.H., "Effects of ozone and soil water deficit on roots and shoots of field-grown soybeans", *Environ. Pollut.* 50 (1988) pp. 259–78.

90 Mellhorn, H. and Wellburn, A.R., "Stress ethylene formation determines plant sensitivity to ozone", *Nature* 327 (1987) pp. 417–18; Unsworth, M., "Adding ethylene to injury", *Nature* 327 (1987) pp. 364–5.

91 Cooley, D.R. and Manning, W.J., "Ozone effects on growth and assimilate partitioning in alfalfa, *Medicago sativa* L.", *Environ. Pollut.* 49 (1988) pp. 19–36.

92 Heggestad, H.E. and Bennett, J.H., "Impact of atmospheric pollution on agriculture", in: Treshow, M. (ed.), 1984, *op. cit.*

93 Heck, W.W., Taylor, O.C., Adams, R., Bingham, G., Miller, J., Preston, E. and Weinstein, L., "Assessment of crop loss from ozone", *J. Air Pollut. Control Assoc.* 32 (1982) pp. 353–61; Heck, 1984, *op. cit.*

94 Bonte, J. and Mathy, P., *The European Communities Project on Open-Top Chambers, Results on Agricultural Crops 1987–1988* (Brussels: Commission of European Communities, 1989).

95 Bell, J.N.B., Imperial College London, personal communication, 1 September 1990.

96 Suttie, J.W., "Effects of fluoride on livestock", *J. occup. Med.* 19 (1977)

pp. 40–48.

97 Heggestad and Bennett, 1984, *op. cit.*

98 ENDS, "Reassuring study on fluoride pollution in the Bedfordshire brickfields", **155** (1987) pp. 6–7.

99 Weinstein, L.H., "Fluoride and plant life", *J. occup. Med.* **19** (1977) pp. 49–78.

100 Halbwachs, 1984, *op. cit.*

101 Weinstein, 1977, *op. cit.*; Heggestad and Bennett, 1984, *op. cit.*

102 Kay, C.E., Tourangeau, P.C. and Gordon, C.C., "Industrial fluorosis in wild male and whitetail deer from Western Montana", *Fluoride* **8** (1975) pp. 182–91.

103 WHO, *Fluorine and Fluorides*, Environ. Health Criteria 36 (Geneva: WHO, 1984).

104 Carlson, C.E., "Fluoride pollution in Montana", *Fluoride* **6** (1973) pp. 127–37.

105 Miller, P.R., "Concept of forest decline in relation to western US forests", in: MacKenzie, J.J. and El-Ashry, M.T. (eds), *Air Pollution's Toll on Forests and Crops* (New Haven: Yale Univ. Press, 1989).

106 Unwin, R.J., "Atmospheric fluoride pollution in the UK and possible effects upon agricultural and horticultural crops", *ADAS Quart. Rev.* **39** (1980) pp. 271–83.

107 Halbwachs, 1984, *op. cit.*

108 MacLean, D.C. and Schneider, R.F., "Effects of gaseous hydrogen fluoride on the yield of field-grown wheat", *Environ. Pollut. A* **24** (1981) pp. 39–44.

109 Bonte, J., "Effects of air pollutants on flowering and fruiting", in: Unsworth, M.H. and Ormrod, D.P. (eds), 1982, *op. cit.*

110 WHO, 1984, *op. cit.*; Carlson, 1973, *op. cit.*

111 Heggestad and Bennett, 1984, *op. cit.*

112 Shupe, J.L., Ammerman, C.B., Peeler, H.T., *Effects of Fluorides in Animals* (Washington DC: National Academy of Sciences, 1974); Suttie, 1977, *op. cit.*

113 Royal Commission on Environmental Pollution, RCEP, *Agriculture and Pollution*, 7th Report (London: HMSO, 1979); Gilbert, D.L., "Environmental effects of airborne fluoride from aluminium smelting at Invergordon, Scotland 1971–1983", *Environ. Pollut. A* **39** (1985) pp. 293–302.

114 Kay et al., 1975, *op. cit.*

115 Murray, F., "Response of grapevines to fluoride under field conditions", *J. Amer. Soc. Hort. Sci.* **108** (1981) pp. 526–9.

116 Suttie, 1977, *op. cit.*

117 Craggs, C., Blakemore, J. and Davison, A.W., "Seasonality in the fluoride concentrations of pasture grass subject to ambient airborne fluorides", *Environ. Pollut.* **9** (1985) pp. 163–77.

118 Wang, Jia-Xi, and Bian, Yong-Mei., "Fluoride effects on the mulberry–silkworm system", *Environ. Pollut.* **52** (1988) pp. 11–18.

119   Roberts, 1984, *op. cit.*

120   Runeckles, V.C., "Impact of air pollutant combinations on plants", in: Treshow, M. (ed.), 1984, *op. cit.*

121   Menser, H.A. and Heggestad, H.E., "Ozone and sulphur dioxide synergism: injury to tobacco plants", *Science* 153 (1966) pp. 424–25.

122   Runeckles, 1984, *op. cit.*

123   Hofstra, G. and Ormrod, D.P., "Ozone and sulphur dioxide interaction in Whitebean and Soybean", *Can. J. Plant Sci.* 57 (1977) pp. 1193–8.

124   Marie, B.A. and Ormrod, D.P., "Tomato plant growth with continuous exposure to sulphur dioxide and nitrogen dioxide", *Environ. Pollut. A* 33 (1984) pp. 257–65.

125   Hill, A.C., Hill, S., Lamb, C. and Barrett, I.W., "Sensitivity of native desert vegetation to SO_2 and NO_2 combined", *J. Air Pollut. Control Assn* 24 (1974) pp. 153–7.

126   Ashenden, T.W. and Mansfield, T.A., "Extreme pollution sensitivity of grasses when SO_2 and No_2 are present in the atmosphere", *Nature* 273 (1978) pp. 142–3; Ashenden, T.W., "The effects of long-term exposures to SO_2 and NO_2 pollution on the growth of *Dactylis glomerata* L. and *Poa pratensis* L.", *Environ. Pollut. A* 18 (1979) pp. 249–58.

127   Whitmore, M.E. and Freer-Smith, P.H., "Growth effect of SO_2 and/or NO_2 on woody plants and grasses during spring and summer", *Nature* 300 (1982) pp. 55–7.

128   Wellburn, A.R., Higginson, L., Robinson, D. and Walmsley, C., "Biochemical explanations of more than additive levels of SO_2 and NO_2 upon plants", *New Phytol.* 88 (1981) pp. 223–37.

129   Bell, 1984, *op. cit.*

130   Runeckles, 1984, *op. cit.*

131   Bell, J.N.B., "Direct effects of air pollution on plants", in: Troganowsky, C. (ed.), *Air Pollutants Attacking Plants* (Weinheim: Verlag Chemie, 1985).

132   Runeckles, 1984, *op. cit.*

133   Dohmen, G.P., McNeill, S. and Bell, J.N.B., "Air pollution increases *Aphis fabae* pest potential", *Nature* 307 (1984) pp. 52–3.

134   Houlden, G., McNeill, S., Aminu Karo, M. and Bell, J.N.B., "Air pollution and agriculture aphid pests, I. Fumigation experiments with SO_2 and NO_2", *Environ. Pollut.* (in press).

135   Braun, S. and Fluckiger, W., "Increased population of the aphid *Aphis pomi* at a motorway. Part 3 – The effect of exhaust gases", *Environ. Pollut. A* 39 (1985) pp. 183–92.

136   Chappelka, A.H., Kraemer, M.E., Mebrahtu, T., Ranguppa, M. and Benepal, P.S., "Effects of ozone on soybean resistance to the Mexican bean beetle (*Epilachna varivestis* M.)", *Environ. and Experim. Bot.* 28 (1988) pp. 53–60; Trumble, J.T., Hare, J.P., Musselman, R.C. and McCool, P.M., "Ozone-induced changes in host-plant suitability: interactions of *Keiferia lycopersicella* and *Lycopersicon esculentum*", *J. Chem. Ecol.* 13 (1987) pp. 203–18.

137 Ashmore, M.R., Brown, V., Kristiansen, L. and Shah, B., "Effects of ambient air pollution, water stress and aphid pests on *Vicia faba*", in: Bonte, J. and Mathy, P. (eds), 1989, *op. cit.*

138 Heagle, A.S., "Interactions between air pollutants and parasitic plant diseases", in: Unsworth, M.H. and Ormrod, D.P. (eds), 1982, *op. cit.*

139 Mansfield, P.A., Bell, J.N.B., McLeod, A.R., Wheeler, P.J.W., "Effects of sulphur dioxide on the development of some major fungal diseases of winter barley in an open-air fumigation system", *Agric. Ecosys. and Environ.* (in press).

140 Ashmore et al., 1980, *op. cit.*

141 Bell, 1984, *op. cit.*

142 Cowling, D.W. and Lockyer, D.R., "Growth of perennial ryegrass (*Lolium perenne* L.) exposed to a low concentration of sulphur dioxide", *J. Exp. Bot.* 27 (1976) 411–17; Lockyer et al., 1976, *op. cit.*

143 Terman, G.L., *Atmospheric Sulphur – The Agronomic Aspects, Tech. Bull. No. 23* (Washington DC: The Sulphur Institute, 1978).

144 Bell, 1984, *op. cit.*

145 Cowling, D.W. and Koziol, M.J., "Mineral nutrition and plant response to air pollutants", in: Unsworth, M.H. and Ormrod, D.P. (eds), *op. cit.*

146 Roberts et al., 1983, *op. cit.*

147 Hutchinson, T.C., Harwell, M.A., Cropper, W.P. and Grover, H.D., "Additional potential effects of nuclear war on ecological systems", in: Harwell, M.A.and Hutchinson, T.C. (eds), *Environmental Consequences of Nuclear War*, vol. II SCOPE 28 (New York: John Wiley and Sons, 1985).

148 Woodwell, G.M., "The biotic effects of ionising radiation", *Ambio* 11 (1982) pp. 144–8; Woodwell, G.M., "Radiation and patterns of nature", *Science* 156 (1967) pp. 461–70; Woodwell, G.M. and Whittaker, R.H., "Effects of chronic gamma irradiation on plant communities", *Q. Rev. Biol.* 43 (1968) pp. 42–55.

149 Grogan, H.A., Mitchell, N.G., Minski, M.J. and Bell, J.N.B., "Pathways of radionuclides from soils to wheat", in: Coughtrey, P.J., Martin, M.H. and Unsworth, M.H. (eds), *Pollutant Transport and Fate in Ecosystems* (Oxford: Blackwell Sci. Publ., 1987).

150 Crick, M.J. and Linsley, G.S., *An Assessment of the Radiological Impact of the Windscale Reactor Fire, 1957*, National Radiological Protection Board Report (London: HMSO, 1983).

151 Medvedvev, Z., *Nuclear Disaster in the Urals* (New York: W.W. Norton, 1979); Trabalka, J.R., Eyman, L.D. and Auerback, S.I., "Analysis of the 1957–1958 Soviet nuclear accident", *Science* 209 (1980) pp. 345–53.

152 International Atomic Energy Agency, IAEA, *Vienna Safety Series 75 - INSAG - 1* (Vienna: IAEA, 1986).

153 Marples, D.R., *The Social Impact of the Chernobyl Disaster* (London: Macmillan Press, 1988).

154 Marples, 1988, *op. cit.*

155 Marples, 1988, *op. cit.*

156 Clark, M.J. and Smith, F.B., "Wet and dry deposition of Chernobyl releases", *Nature* 332 (1988) pp. 245–9; Fry, F.A., Clarke, R.H. and O'Riordon, M.C., "Early estimate of UK radiation doses from the Chernobyl reactor", *Nature* 321 (1986) pp. 193–5.
157 *Farmers Weekly* (London), 30 March 1990, pp. 20–21.

9   The Impact of Land and Water Pollution on Agriculture

Although pollution of land and water sometimes creates severe problems for agriculture, they are mostly local in their effect. Overall, the impacts are not as great as those from air pollution nor do they pose the same kind of growing, worldwide threat. In this chapter we examine, first, two aspects of land pollution – the effects of heavy metals and other elements on crops and livestock, and the special hazards created by the practice of applying sewage sludge to agricultural land. In the second part, we discuss the variety of pollutants contained in rivers, aquifers and other watercourses that are sources of agricultural water.

Heavy metals and other elements

Heavy metals such as copper, lead and cadmium, and other elements like fluorine, occur naturally in rocks of many kinds and through the normal processes of geological erosion come to be present in surface soils. As such, they are a natural part of the agricultural environment. Indeed, many are essential in small quantities for the growth of crops and livestock. It is for this reason that they are often referred to, in the agricultural literature, as "trace elements" or micro-nutrients. However, the optimal ranges for healthy growth are frequently narrow (Figure 9.1). Molybdenum, for example, may be beneficial to crops if added at levels of only 16–32 g/ha, but toxic if applied at 3.5–4.5 kg/ha.[1] Hence, soils are often deficient in heavy metals or contain them to excess – both states being potentially harmful. The term "heavy metal" has a variety of connotations. Strictly speaking heavy metals are simply the metallic elements of heavy molecular weight. "Trace element" is a more comprehensive term, since it includes the essential and non-essential, metallic and non-metallic elements which are normally present in relatively small quantities.

Our concern in this book is primarily with the problems of excess.

Figure 9.1   Deficient, normal and toxic levels in plants for five micro-nutrients
Mo = molybdenum; Cu = copper; B = boron; Zn = zinc; Mn = manganese

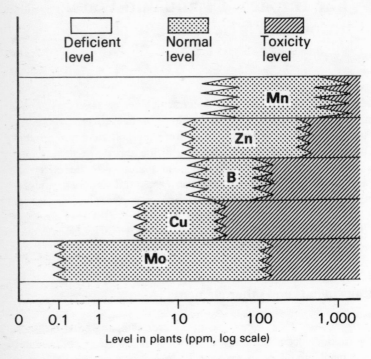

Source: Brady, N., *The Nature and Property of Soils* (New York: Macmillian,
1984).

(For an introduction to the literature on trace element deficiency see
Brady (1984) and Underwood (1977, 1981)[2].)[2] Such problems may
occur naturally since some rocks have particularly high concentrations
of heavy metals. The levels in the overlying soils or in sedimentary
soils downstream may then be high enough to cause damage to
crops or to livestock grazing on pastures. However, this naturally
occurring contamination may be augmented, sometimes in the same
area, by deposits of heavy metals arising from mining and smelting
activities. The most toxic elements to plants when present in excess are
cadmium (Cd), copper (Cu), lead (Pb) and zinc (Zn), but damage may
also be caused by arsenic (As), boron (B), chromium (Cr), fluorine (F),
mercury (Hg), manganese (Mn), molybdenum (Mo), nickel (Ni) and
selenium (Se).

Distribution of heavy metals

Metalliferous mining in the UK began in Roman or earlier times but reached a peak in the nineteenth century when Britain produced the major proportion of the world's copper, tin and lead. It is the legacy from this mining that presents a major hazard to agriculture in Britain today; metal mining now is a relatively minor activity, creating only very local problems. In the nineteenth century not only were large quantities of mining waste produced, but they were heavily contaminated. It was common for wastes to contain 10,000 ppm of the mined metal, resulting in sterile waste heaps on which virtually no vegetation could grow. Modern mining, by contrast, uses greatly superior separation techniques so improving the efficiency of extraction, although wastes still typically contain 1000 ppm.[3]

Table 9.1 shows the normal ranges of metals in British soils, and the high levels outside these ranges that can occur in natural metal-rich soils. Some 4000 km[2] of England and Wales are presently contaminated by past mining and smelting activities. We have very detailed knowledge of the distribution of the important heavy metals, thanks to the technique of geochemical mapping developed by Webb and Thornton.[4] This is based on sampling of stream sediments on the assumption that they represent a combination of the erosion products of the rock, the overburden and the soil upstream from the point of sampling. By adopting this approach the necessity of taking a very large number of samples to account for local variations in rock and soil type is avoided. Nonetheless, some 48,000 samples were needed to produce the maps (Figure 9.2).

In the USA three similar surveys of regional geochemistry are being conducted, primarily with the aim of locating areas of high mineral potential.[5] Initially the surveys are on a large scale, using a mapping unit of 1 by 2 degree quadrangles, that is, at 1:250,000. After the quadrangles with high potential are identified, stream sediments are then collected at 500–2000 sites, giving an average sampling density of one site per 10–50 km[2]. As yet the survey is only partly complete.

Elsewhere, geochemical maps are rare. They have been produced in a number of industrialized countries, such as Yugoslavia, as aids to mineral exploration.[6] But they are virtually non-existent for the developing countries. While in temperate regions the soils are relatively young and dominated by parent material, under tropical conditions weathering processes are often more vigorous. The relationships between the chemical composition of original parent materials and

Table 9.1 Trace elements and metals in soils derived from normal and geochemically anomalous parent materials in Britain

	Typical normal range in soil (ppm)	Metal rich soil (ppm)	Sources	Possible effects
As	<5–40	up to 2500 up to 250	Mineralization Metamorphosed rocks around Dartmoor	Toxicity in plants and livestock; excess in food crops
Cd	<1–2	up to 30 up to 20	Mineralization Carboniferous black shale	Excess in food crops
Cr	15–300	up to 3500	Ultrabasic rocks in Scotland	No known effect
Cu	2–60	up to 2000	Mineralization	Toxicity in cereal crops
F	20–500	10,000 or more	Mineralization	Fluorosis in livestock
Hg	0.008–0.19	1–7	Mineralization	No known effect
Mo	<1–5	10–100	Marine black shales of varying age	Molybdenosis or molybdenum induced hypocuprosis in cattle
Ni	2–100	up to 8000	Ultrabasic rocks in Scotland	Toxicity in cereal and other crops
Pb	10–150	10,000 or more	Mineralization	Toxicity in livestock; excess in foodstuffs
Se	<1–2	up to 7	Marine black shales in England and Wales	No effect
		up to 500	Namurian shales in Ireland	Chronic selenosis in horses and cattle
Zn	25–200 or more	10,000	Mineralization	Toxicity in cereal crop

As = Arsenic; Cd = Cadmium; Cr = Chromium; Cu = Copper; F = Fluorine; Hg = Mercury; Mo = Molybdenum; Ni = Nickel; Pb = Lead; Se = Selenium; Zn = Zinc.

Source: Thornton, I. et al., "The interactions between geochemical and pollutant metal sources in the environment: implications for the community", in: Thornton, I. and Howarth, R.J. (eds), *Applied Geochemistry in the 1980s* (London: Graham and Trotman, 1986).

soils may thus be obscured, and this presents considerable difficulties for accurate surveying.[7]

Mining and smelting

That mining damaged agriculture in Britain was apparent as early as the mid-eighteenth century. Borlase, a natural historian writing in

1758, recognized that "the sterility of the soil may be great where metals and minerals abound" and that the "acrimonial mineral juices" from mining "are mortal enemies to vegetation".[8] By the nineteenth century there were some 600 mines operating in a 1900 km² belt of the Cornish peninsula, primarily producing tin, copper and arsenic. Today there is still widespread contamination from this activity, adding to the natural burden of contamination from the high metal levels in

Figure 9.2   Distribution of arsenic (A), cadmium (B) and lead (C) in stream sediments in England and Wales

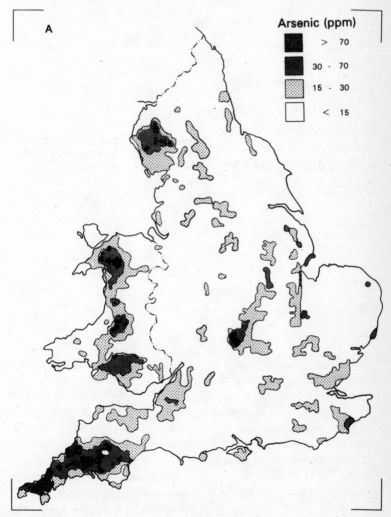

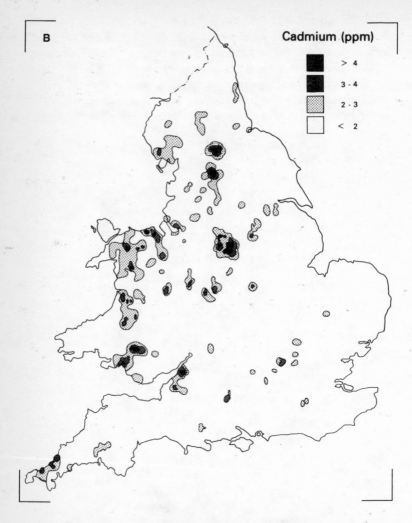

B

Cadmium (ppm)

> 4
3 - 4
2 - 3
< 2

the underlying rocks of the region. Alluvial soils downstream of Devon Great Consuls mine, once the largest copper mine in Europe, still contain mean concentrations of As and Cu 12–14 times and Pb and Zn 3–5 times greater than those upstream.

There was also extensive mining in other parts of the West Country of the UK and this, too, has left a legacy of contamination. Elevated levels of Cd, 40–600 ppm, together with extremely large amounts of zinc, usually at a Zn:Cd ratio of 100:1, remain in soils around Shipham in Somerset, where smithsonite (zinc carbonate) was mined from around 1700 to 1850.[9] At other sites in Cornwall, arsenic values are very

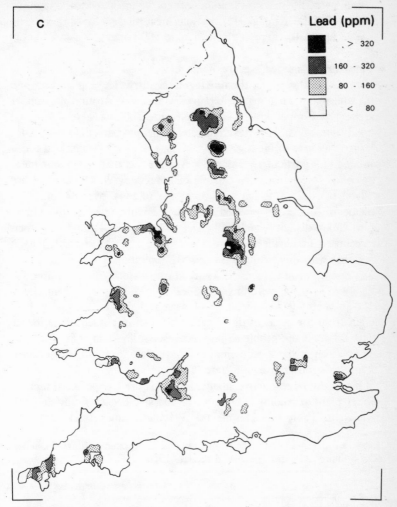

Source: Webb, J.S., Thornton, I., Howarth, R.J., Thompson, M.T., Lowenstein, P.L., *The Wolfson Geochemical Atlas of England and Wales* (Oxford: Oxford University Press, 1978).

high around the stacks of arsenic processing works that ceased working in 1890, though again the total area affected tends to be small. Current values of As and Cu peak at 14,000 ppm and 8000 ppm respectively.

The damage caused by smelters has also been long recognized: in the early nineteenth century, poisoning of livestock in Derbyshire was attributed to lead smelters.[10] The fumes produced by the smelters so contaminated the pastures that the owners were obliged to compensate farmers for the damage.[11] And soils near these old workings still contain up to 30,000 ppm Pb, with up to 8000 ppm of Zn and 34 ppm of Cd.[12]

In North America, severe damage was also caused by smelting operations at the end of the nineteenth century. The impact was, and still is at many locations, visible over wide areas. Around the copper smelters at Copper Hill, Tennessee, some 7000 ha were devastated and, at Ducktown, land near a smelter remained barren 50 years after closure, because of the high levels of As, Cu and Pb which had accumulated.[13] A particularly notorious example was the copper smelter at Anaconda, Montana, once capable of processing 9000 tonnes of ore daily.[14] In addition to massive discharges of SO_2, over 23 tonnes of arsenic trioxide were emitted each day. Pasture grasses and alfalfa up to 25 km distant contained between 20–78 ppm As, and one ranch is recorded as having suffered 1800 cattle and sheep mortalities.[15] Together with this airborne As and SO_2 pollution, tailings containing large quantities of Cu were discharged into watercourses required for irrigation. So great were the quantities that the copper concentrations were sufficient to kill seedlings of peas and maize at a distance of 26 km from the point of discharge. The smelter ceased operating in 1980 although the problems persist. Arsenic levels in soils are high, and children in the local community have significantly higher urinary As levels than do those elsewhere.[16]

One of the largest active smelters today is the Copper Cliff nickel-copper plant at Sudbury, Ontario. Its massive levels of emission are detailed in Table 9.2. Despite the 341 metre smokestack, levels of

Table 9.2   Annual emissions from Copper Cliff copper and nickel smelter near Sudbury, Ontario, Canada in the late 1960s

	Annual emissions (tonnes)
Sulphur dioxide (SO_2)	2,450,000*
Iron	12,000
Nickel	2400
Copper	1800
Lead	230
Zinc	140
Cobalt	53

* These emissions of SO_2 were reduced to about half by the early 1980s

Source: Hutchinson, T.C., "The ecological consequences of acid discharges from industrial smelters", in: D'Itri (ed.), *Acid Precipitation, Effects on Ecological Systems* (Michigan: Ann Arbor, 1982).

metals in nearby soils reach 4000 ppm Ni and 6500 ppm Cu.[17] Another major polluter is the ASARCO copper smelter at Tacoma, Washington which currently emits 280 tonnes As annually, through the smokestack and via fugitive emissions at ground level.[18]

Heavy metals and plants

Heavy metals, when present in trace amounts, play a crucial role in plant metabolism, indirectly affecting such processes as protein and chlorophyll synthesis, respiration and nitrogen fixation (Table 9.3). Their immediate effect is on certain key enzyme systems, for

Table 9.3   Beneficial effects of heavy metals when present in trace amounts

Micro-nutrient	Functions in higher plant processes
Zinc (Zn)	Formulation of growth hormones, promotion of protein synthesis, seed and grain maturation and production
Iron (Fe)	Chlorophyll synthesis, oxidation–reduction in respiration, constituent of certain enzymes and proteins
Copper (Cu)	Catalyst for respiration, enzyme constituent, chlorophyll synthesis, carbohydrate and protein metabolism
Boron (B)	Protein synthesis, nitrogen and carbohydrate metabolism, root system development, fruit and seed formation and water relations
Manganese (Mn)	Nitrogen and inorganic acid metabolism, carbon dioxide assimilation (photosynthesis), carbohydrate breakdown, formation of carotene, riboflavin, and ascorbic acid
Molybdenum (Mo)	Symbiotic nitrogen fixation and protein synthesis

Source: Brady, N., The Nature and Property of Soils (New York: Macmillan, 1984).

example those that facilitate the transformation of nitrate to amino acids and proteins. When heavy metals are present in appropriate amounts, the enzyme systems function efficiently, but if present to excess they are damaged, often irreversibly. There are two particularly important consequences: first, root growth is inhibited, which in addition to reducing the capacity of plants to take up nutrients, increases their susceptibility to drought damage; and second various forms of depigmentation or chlorosis occur in the leaves and other above-ground parts of the plants with a resultant loss of photosynthesis. Given the high levels of heavy metals in many soils, we might expect damage of this kind to be a widespread and serious problem. That it is not so is due to two reasons – uptake by plants is limited and many plants exhibit tolerance to heavy metals.

In general, the fraction of heavy metal in the soil that is taken up by the plant roots is very small, and even less reaches the above-ground stems and leaves. For instance, a large proportion of copper is bound up in the organic matter of soils and is unavailable for root uptake. Moreover, there is a progressive decline in the marginal uptake. With increasing copper levels in the soil a smaller fraction finds its way into the plant; a 5–10-fold rise in soil Cu causes only a twofold increase in Cu in pasture grasses.[19] In several areas of Wales contaminated by mine wastes, the concentration of Cu in grasses on the least contaminated soils was 62 per cent of the soil content (19 ppm), yet the proportion was only one per cent on soils containing 1400 ppm.[20] The same situation applies to many crops in the presence of cadmium and lead. Grasses growing on cadmium contaminated soil exhibit increasing uptake, but there is a clear threshold above which little or no further cadmium is taken up (Figure 9.3).

The concentrations of heavy metals in plants also tend to be seasonal, reaching a peak in the late winter to early spring of temperate

Figure 9.3 Content of cadmium in grass herbage in relation to the concentration in the soil

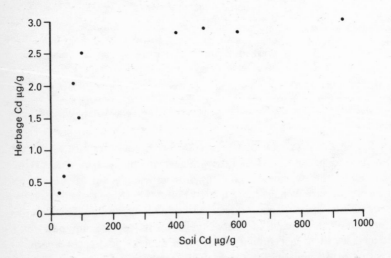

Source: Matthews, H. and Thornton, I. "Seasonal and species variation in the content of cadmium and associated metals in pasture plants at Shipham" *Plant and Soil* **66** (1982) pp. 181–193.

climates. This reflects a combination of factors. Aerial deposition of metal-rich particulates tends to occur in the winter months. Also at this time of year, phosphorus levels in the soil are lower, and so Pb and Cd are more mobile. And then with spring growth the metals previously bound in the roots move to the shoots. However, in late spring and early summer rapid growth dilutes heavy metal concentrations and the heightened metabolic activity also serves to keep metal burdens low.[21] In practice, it means that autumn sown crops are most vulnerable to high heavy metal levels in the soil while many spring sown crops can partly escape.

Tolerance to heavy metals varies between plant species and individuals, and may involve a variety of physiological processes each of which contributes to the total level of tolerance. The inheritance of tolerance is also a complex phenomenon, usually involving several genes.[22] In grasses, tolerant strains take up more metals in their roots than non-tolerant strains but, as yet, it is not clear how they render these high concentrations harmless. Specific new mechanisms of detoxification may be involved or normal metabolic pathways may have been modified. More likely, though, the metals are bound to cell walls or isolated in vacuoles, preventing them from further contact with metabolic processes.[23]

It is also evident that the form of contamination is important. For example, vines dressed with Bordeaux mixture (copper sulphate plus lime) for decades can survive in soils containing 200–300 ppm Cu. Yet, elsewhere, copper toxicity has been observed in vineyards and orchards when treated, for the first time, with copper-rich fungicides.[24]

Heavy metals and livestock

Animals, like plants, may benefit from heavy metals in trace amounts or suffer when they are in excess. Selenium is a necessary component of a key enzyme in muscles, and deficiency depresses the enzyme's activity, eventually causing muscle degradation.[25] Ruminants need cobalt in their diet to ensure a supply of vitamin B_{12}; cobalt is an essential component of the vitamin, which is synthesized by bacteria in the rumen. Some elements, such as iodine and fluorine, are necessary for animal growth but apparently have no beneficial effect on plants.

A wide variety of effects and symptoms in livestock are produced by both deficiencies and excesses (Table 9.4). Livestock poisonings have occurred on soils containing both naturally elevated and industrially contaminated levels of heavy metals. It is very difficult, though, to establish maximum tolerable limits to exposure, largely because

Table 9.4 Impact of metals on livestock when deficient or present in excess in the diet

Metal	Deficiency	Excess
Copper	Anaemia, bone disorders, depigmentation of hair and wool; in lambs swayback or lamkruis (neonatal ataxia); in calves stilted gait; in cattle diarrhoea (scouring)	Toxicity in ruminants anaemia, jaundice, disruption of oxygen transport in blood
Molybdenum	No effects observed	"Teart" – severe diarrhoea, discoloured coat, drop in milk yield in cattle (equivalent to low Cu)
Selenium	White muscle disease (degeneration of muscles) in young cattle and sheep	Acute: laboured breathing, diarrhoea, death. Chronic: "blind staggers" and "alakali disease" – weight loss, hair loss, abnormal growth of hooves, wandering, stumbling, impaired vision
Cobalt	Anaemia, loss appetite; induced lack of vitamin B_{12} (pining) in ruminants	Depression of body weight and appetite; anaemia
Zinc	Growth retardation, through reduced appetite and impaired food utilization; induced vitamin A deficiency, alopecia	Reductions in feed efficiency, abortions in sheep, disruption of iron metabolism in blood
Lead	None	Acute: anaemia, constipation, vomiting, renal damage, muscle discoordination, tremor
Cadmium	None	Reproductive disturbances, cardiovascular disorders and hypertension
Arsenic	None	Loss of condition, death

Sources: Lewis, G., "Geochemistry and animal health", in: Thornton and Howarth (eds), *op. cit.*; Thornton, I., "Soil-plant-animal interactions in relation to the incidence of trace elements disorders in grazing livestock", in: Suttie et al., *op. cit.*; WHO, *Selenium*, Environ. Health Criteria 58 (Geneva: WHO, 1987); Underwood, E.J., *Trace elements in Human and Animal Nutrition* (New York: Academic Press, 1977); Thomas, R., "Arsenic pollution arising from mining activities in south-west England", in: MAFF, 1980, *op. cit.*

tolerance to one metal frequently depends upon the presence of others.[26] For instance the role of copper is very important: it is itself toxic in large quantities, yet copper deficiency is often induced by many other elements.

Specific heavy metals

In the following sections we discuss the effects of four major heavy metal pollutants, lead, copper, zinc and cadmium, review the effects of other less important metal pollutants and, finally, describe the synergistic effects that can occur between heavy metals, particularly in the case of livestock poisoning.

Lead (Pb)

Sources

Lead has been mined for nearly 3000 years with the result that it is now widely dispersed throughout the world. In the Arctic ice, for instance, atmospheric deposits over this period have resulted in a 300-fold increase in concentration.[27] Emissions of lead in the USA have probably doubled the content of rural soils, while in inhabited areas the increase has been 2–200-fold.[28] The concentrations in British soils have risen on average by 20 ppm since 1700 (see Table 9.1), mostly as a result of mining and smelting emissions during the nineteenth century but also, following the introduction of leaded petrol in 1946, from vehicle emissions. The latter now contribute about 3 ppm to rural soils in the vicinity of roads and 10 ppm in towns.[29]

A typical example of contamination by mine workings is the Ceredigion mine in mid-Wales. Between 1750 and 1900 some 117,000 tonnes of Pb were lost during processing at the mine, representing 50 per cent of total output. The wastes were washed into streams and rivers, and contaminated 400 km^2 of catchment, largely consisting of a floodplain that lies downstream of the mine.[30] It continues to be a problem because on the floodplain the soils and riverbed materials are periodically redistributed as the river banks erode during heavy floods, so spreading the contamination.

Damage to plants

Compared to other metals, such as copper or cadmium, the pattern of lead uptake is rather more complicated. In general, the ratio of plant Pb to soil Pb declines with increasing soil content, for example for vegetables from 0.06 at 13 ppm Pb in soil to 0.003 at 4644 ppm Pb.[31] But there are exceptions. The relationship is sometimes linear: the lead content of radishes grown in rural areas was found to increase by 13 ppm per 1000 ppm rise in soil Pb, and by 22 ppm in urban soils.[32] And in alfalfa, Pb content rises relatively faster than the increase in soil content, a 10-fold soil increase resulting in a 27-fold increase in plant content. For grasses the relationship is not clear, probably because many experiments have used tolerant races of grass growing on highly contaminated soils. In some cases, levels in grasses have been found to be greater than in the soil.[33] Nevertheless, in one experiment, in which grass turf was transplanted to a site near a smelter, the lead content rapidly rose during the first month from 80 to 300 ppm and then showed little further change, suggesting that, at least in some situations, there are plateaux of lead concentrations.[34]

As with other heavy metals, concentrations are usually highest during the winter and early spring months, but fall rapidly just before grazing begins (Figure 9.4). The problem is thus most critical

Figure 9.4 Seasonal variations in the lead contents of pasture herbage growing in contaminated and uncontaminated soils in Derbyshire

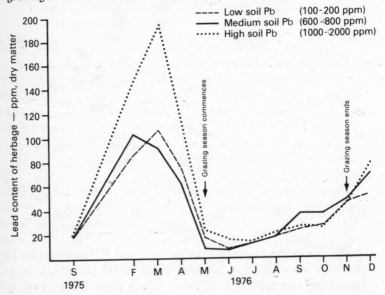

Source: Thornton, I., Abrahams, R.W., Culbard, E., Rother, J.A.P. and Olson, B.H., "The interaction between geochemical and pollutant metal sources in the environment: implications for the community", Thornton, I. and Howarth, R.J. (eds), *Applied Geochemistry in the 1980s* (London: Graham and Trotman, 1986).

on winter grown crops. In an area of high soil Pb (13,000 ppm) in the UK the lead content of vegetables was 5–11-fold greater for winter grown compared with summer grown crops (Table 9.5). All the winter crops exceeded the 1 ppm (fresh weight) UK general limit for foods, set by the Lead in Food Regulations 1979.[35] This value of 1 ppm would of course be considerably higher if content was measured by dry weight.)

Table 9.5   Change in lead content of vegetables grown during winter and summer on soils at Shipham, Somerset, containing 13500 ppm lead

| | *Lead concentration (ppm fresh weight)* | | |
	Winter crop	*Summer crops*	*Winter/summer ratio*
Brussels sprout	1.07	0.09	×11
Cabbage	1.47	0.24	× 6
Carrot	1.29	0.26	× 5
Kale	2.12	0.25	× 8
Leek	1.38	0.14	×10
Parsnip	1.64	0.25	× 7
Spinach	2.79	0.29	×10

Source: RCEP, *Lead in the Environment*, 9th Report, Royal Commission on Environmental Pollution (London: HMSO, 1983).

Contamination of crops from lead pollution is often serious in the vicinity of major roads. Grasses and vegetables growing within 50 metres of major roads in industrialized countries typically contain up to 200 times and 5–20 times more Pb, respectively, than at non-roadside sites.[36] The figures for grasses are of the order of 50–400 ppm Pb (dry weight) and for vegetables 25–100 ppm. Most Pb in grass and cereal leaves near roads is derived from the atmosphere, though soil splash during rainfall may be an important source of contamination. Again, the lead content is higher during winter.

These roadside effects are very localized, however, and are much less important for agriculture than the impact of contamination from mines and smelters.[37] Very high levels of contamination may occur: grasses close to a Toronto smelter contain up to 1000 ppm Pb, more than 20 times greater than levels in city parks.[38] Uptake of lead by plants in these situations depends on both soil contamination and continuing atmospheric deposition. Which plays the greatest role depends on various factors, in particular the ability of different crops to absorb Pb from the air. In an experiment in which soil Pb was held constant, concentrations in bean and lettuce leaves rose with increasing Pb in the air, but there was no change in tomatoes, carrots or potatoes.[39] Grass species with hairy leaf surfaces also tend readily to take up atmospheric lead. And age of plants is important. Young wheat plants near a lead smelter in the UK obtained more Pb from atmospheric deposition than from the soil, while for mature plants it was the reverse. The probable reason is that young plants have a higher proportion of surface area.[40]

The seasonality of contamination is illustrated by wild oats in the vicinity of a lead smelter, northeast of San Francisco. Concentrations of Pb in the above-ground portion of the plants rose from almost zero during May–June to peak at more than 500 ppm during the winter. Levels then continued to rise even after death of the grasses, when transfer of lead from the soil had presumably ceased. Part of the explanation lies in losses of dry weight and changes in mobility at the outset of winter, but the main reason appears to be that dead and desiccated tissue has more sites that can bind the metal. Concentrations in leaf litter, for instance, can be as high as 1000 ppm.[41]

Lead and livestock

Livestock readily take up lead. Blood lead content is generally higher in animals grazing contaminated sites; in sheep by UK roadsides blood Pb is more than four times that of animals from uncontaminated regions. Similarly, blood Pb in cattle from heavily contaminated farms (soil 1000–2000 ppm Pb) in Derbyshire was 30 μg/100 ml compared with 10 μg/100 ml on farms with low contamination (100–200 ppm).[42]

Nevertheless, few cases of acute poisoning of livestock result from grazing contaminated forage. One instance is the deaths of thirteen horses in California in 1969–70 while grazing on winter pasture in the region close to a lead smelter.[43] There have also been reports from old lead mining areas of the North Pennines in the UK of poor growth, lameness and deaths among lambs and calves, but in such cases accidental soil ingestion is suspected of being the important factor rather than the consumption of forage.[44] In cattle, soil constitutes some 1–10 per cent of total dry matter intake, though for sheep, which graze closer to the ground, this can rise to 30 per cent.[45] Soil ingestion is greatest in winter months and early spring, or during very dry summers, when grass is in short supply. Where soil concentrations are high, the effect can be significant: in the old lead mining district of Derbyshire, soil intake contributed more than 40 per cent of total Pb intake in cattle.

A more acute hazard to livestock may come from contaminated feed imported onto the farm. In late 1989 feed compounded in the Netherlands was so contaminated with lead that cattle on some 1500 farms in the west of England and 330 in the Netherlands were poisoned, causing the deaths of at least 90 animals in the two countries.[46] Marketing of meat and milk from English farms was restricted, and some 1.3 million litres of milk destroyed daily. The source of the lead was rice bran, originating clean from Burma, but becoming contaminated on board ship. Despite orders for its destruction, the bran somehow reached the compounding firm, and the feed so produced contained up to 1500 ppm of lead.

Finally, livestock are frequently poisoned when they chew or lick fences or gates or other surfaces that have been covered with paints containing lead. Young animals are more likely to do this, and for them the risk of lead poisoning is probably higher from this source than from contaminated soil or forage.[47]

Lead in human diets

Even if crop plants and livestock taking up lead are not adversely affected, high levels of lead may get into food for human consumption. For most people, food and drink form the major pathway for Pb uptake though, in extreme cases, this can be via inhalation of high Pb air, derived from petrol and industrial emissions. On average, 60–70 per cent of ingested and inhaled lead derives from food, but not all the lead originates with agriculture.[48] Food can be contaminated during processing, from the widespread use of Pb solder in cans or from using contaminated water.

Not all this ingested or inhaled lead is absorbed into the body. In adults only some 50 per cent is absorbed from the lungs and 10 per cent from the gut, although these rates rise to about 70 per cent and 50 per cent respectively in young children. Once inside the body most inorganic Pb becomes attached to red blood cells before distribution to other organs. It accumulates eventually in bones where it is mostly isolated and inert, but there is evidence of a slow transfer back to other organs, with serious toxic effects.[49]

Blood lead levels in humans are a function of uptake, with successive increments in exposure resulting in progressively smaller increases in the lead level. At present the average blood lead concentration in humans living in the UK is some 25 per cent of that at which features of unmistakable poisoning may occur. In general, blood lead levels are higher in cities compared with rural areas, and are higher

in cities with a great deal of traffic. With the recent switch to use of
unleaded petrol in some industrialized countries blood Pb levels appear
to have declined. In the USA, the decline may also be partly due to the
substitution of non-soldered cans as food containers.[50]

Copper (Cu) and zinc (Zn)

Sources

Copper in soils is usually present at 2–60 ppm, but this may be
exceeded in highly metalliferous regions, rising to 2000 ppm. Some
2 million tonnes of Cu are released each year as a result of human
activity, causing locally raised levels in terrestrial and aquatic environments.[51] The principal releases to the soil are from mine tailings, coal
fly ash residues, smelter slags and wastes, animal wastes and sewage
sludge. Much less is emitted to water, primarily from manufacturing
processes, domestic waste water and sewage sludge water. Emissions
to the atmosphere are from smelting, coal combustion and refuse
incineration.

The emissions of zinc are slightly more than those of Cu – annually
about 2.4 million tonnes.[52] The principal sources are also coal fly ash,
mine tailings and smelter wastes. Significantly more Zn than Cu is
contributed to the soil through animal, agricultural and food wastes.
Metal manufacturing processes are an important source for water,
while the source for atmospheric contamination is primarily Zn-Cd
smelting. Locally high soil levels can be caused by metalliferous
ores and industrial pollution, though the most common source is
the application of zinc-bearing sewage sludge.

Copper, zinc and plants

There is little risk of copper toxicity to plants, even though raised levels
may occur on the external surfaces of plants.[53] It is unusual for the
concentration to exceed 20–30 ppm (dry weight) in agricultural crops
but at higher concentrations crop growth can suffer.[54] By comparison
with other heavy metals, copper has low toxicity although it may have
a significant synergistic effect. Experiments on the growth of young
barley in solutions containing mixes of Cu, Ni and Zn show that
combinations of two metals synergistically interact to further reduce
yields (Figure 9.5).

Figure 9.5 Yield contours (0–100 per cent of maximum yield) of young barley grown in solutions of copper (Cu) and zinc (Zn), Cu and nickel (Ni), and Ni and Zn, as a function of tissue concentrations

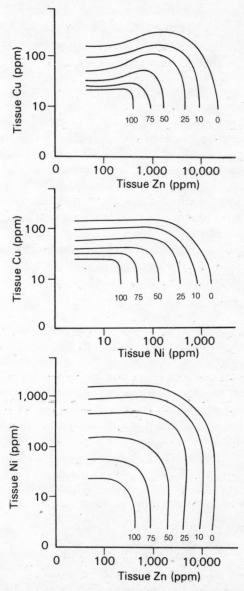

Source: Beckett, P.H.T., Davis, R.D. and Brindley, P., "The disposal of sewage sludge to farmland: the scope of the problem of toxic elements", *Water Pollution Control* **78** (1979) pp. 419–440.

There may also be indirect effects. For instance, copper taken up by cabbages and radishes grown on contaminated pig slurries is passed on to the caterpillars feeding on the plants.[55] Copper salts in the pig slurry can also kill earthworm populations, but they are only temporarily reduced provided concentrations of Cu do not reach 100 ppm in the soil, which usually occurs only when slurry is applied at many times the recommended rate.[56]

As a general rule, high zinc levels in soils result in high levels in plants, but uptake is affected by several factors, including the presence of other metals and pH. For example, heavy dressings with lime can greatly reduce levels of Zn in pasture.[57] Typical levels in plants are 25–35 μg/kg; they rarely exceed 200 μg/kg, unless there is severe industrial contamination.[58] In vegetables grown on soils treated with sewage sludge, concentrations vary between 3 and 20 μg/kg fresh weight for edible parts, though levels are higher in tops and leaves.[59] In the vicinity of smelters, such as the Avonmouth zinc smelter in the UK, aerial deposition may be more important than soil contamination. Green leaves collected less than 2 km from the smelter contained 3–4 times the zinc than controls up to 15 km away, and the outer leaves in turn contained 3–4 times the zinc than inner leaves.[60]

Copper, zinc and livestock

Sheep are particularly susceptible to copper poisoning, which can arise if diets contain as little as 8–11 ppm.[61] Sheep store copper in the liver from where it may be liberated to disrupt fatally the oxygen transport system in the blood. In pigs, excess copper can cause marked depression in feed intake and growth, leading to anaemia and jaundice, unless the diet is supplemented with zinc and iron.

One source of uptake for cattle is copper-containing salt licks; another is treatment with copper drenches. Feeds may be contaminated with copper compounds, and in the case of pigs, from copper supplements given as growth stimulants, should the diet not be adequately balanced with other interacting elements.[62] There are also records of sheep and cattle mortalities following the spraying of copper sulphate as a pesticide in orchards and vineyards.[63]

Pig slurry applied to pastures is also an important source of copper intake by cattle. If the slurry has been produced through anaerobic digestion it is likely to contain insoluble copper sulphides that are largely unavailable to livestock. But treatment by aerobic digestion generates copper salts that are available to pasture plants.

Compared with other metals, zinc is relatively non-toxic to live-stock.[64] Nevertheless toxicity can occur. Cattle and lambs fed diets containing 1000 ppm suffer reduced weight and depressed food consumption, while abortion occurs at even lower levels in pregnant ewes. High levels of zinc are known to have a toxic effect on rumen micro-organisms and this is probably the reason for the reduction in food utilization. The extent of tolerance, though, depends on the presence of calcium, copper, iron and cadmium in the diet, all of which interact with zinc during food absorption and utilization. Pigs and poultry are more tolerant than sheep and cattle. On diets of 1000 ppm zinc, pigs suffer no ill effects but at 4000 to 8000 ppm, growth and appetite are depressed, followed by the onset of arthritis, internal haemorrhages and then mortality. However, raising the dietary calcium level from 0.7 to 1.1 per cent protects against all these toxic effects.

Human diets

Both copper and zinc are necessary components of human diets; adequate daily intakes are 2 mg Cu and 5–15 mg Zn.[65] Food is the most important source of both elements. The highest levels of copper and zinc are found in animal livers, crabs, oysters and shellfish, all of which are usually minor items in the diet; the main sources in average diets are therefore meats, cereal products and milk.[66] Only those people consuming several hundred grams of crabs, oysters or liver daily would exceed the maximum acceptable daily intake for copper. Intakes may also be significantly increased where copper piping or tanks are used to convey drinking water that is acidic or soft. There are no records of copper or zinc poisoning in humans.

Cadmium (Cd)

Sources

Geologically, cadmium is normally associated with zinc and is not mined in its own right, being obtained indirectly as a by-product of zinc mining. Zinc and cadmium contamination thus often occur together, particularly near old mine workings. In Shipham, Somerset, where zinc was mined between 1700–1850, the soils typically contain 30–80 ppm Cd and 2500–60,000 ppm Zn, although in the worst affected area of some 8 km^2 the soils contain over 100 ppm Cd, peaking at 600 ppm.[67]

As with most other heavy metals, high levels can also occur naturally, in this case in soils underlain with carboniferous black shales, which may contain up to 200 ppm Cd.[68]

Cadmium also enters the environment as a result of smelting activities, as well as from its use in the electroplating industry, as a stabilizer in plastics, as a pigment in paints, in cadmium batteries, and as a contaminant in phosphate fertilizers and sewage sludge. About 30,000 tonnes are lost to the environment each year.[69]

Cadmium and plants

Cadmium is a relatively mobile element and thus taken up more readily than other metals, particularly by leafy plants. Crops vary, though, in the level of uptake. On soils with a history of sewage sludge application and containing 5–10 ppm Cd, levels in spinach can reach those in the soil, and in lettuce and radish may reach 50–60 per cent of the soil level, although in other vegetables the figure is less than 30 per cent.[70] The uptake also levels off at the very high soil concentrations typical of old mine workings (see Figure 9.3). On these soils, the roots are the site of heaviest metal burden: at Shipham the Cd content of the soil has been shown to be some six times greater than that in grass roots, which in turn is six times greater than that in stems and leaves.[71] Uptake as a result of airborne cadmium is only important close to smelters; ryegrass at 0.3 km distant from a smelter contained 50 ppm, but at 11 km the level was only 2 ppm.[72]

No phytotoxic effects of Cd have been observed in field conditions. But experiments have shown Cd to be toxic to many crop plants, reducing yields and inducing chlorosis in some species at quite low soil concentrations (Table 9.6). In general, vegetables are less tolerant than field crops; especially susceptible are leafy crops such as spinach and lettuce.[73]

Cadmium and livestock

Cadmium is highly toxic to animals, whether it is ingested, injected or inhaled.[74] Significant changes in structure and function occur in the liver, kidneys, gastro-intestinal tract, heart, testes, pancreas, bones and blood vessels. Moreover, it is impossible to state precise minimum levels or maximum safe dietary levels, because of the powerful interactions of cadmium with other elements, notably zinc, copper, iron, calcium and selenium. For example, the common manifestation of cadmium toxicity, anaemia, is partly due to cadmuim's antagonism to iron and copper.

Table 9.6 Amounts of cadmium added to a calcareous soil resulting in a 50 per cent reduction in yield of various crops

Cadmium concentration reducing yields by 50% (ppm)			
10–50	*50–100*	*100–200*	*>200*
Spinach	Carrot	Turnip	Squash
Soybean	Fieldbean	White clover	Tall fescue
Cress	Wheat	Table beet	Cabbage
Lettuce	Sudan grass	Alfalfa	Bermuda grass
Maize		Radish	Tomato
Upland rice			Paddy rice

Source: Page. A.L., El-Amanny, M.M. and Chang, A.L., "Cadmium in the environment and its entry into terrestrial food chain crops", in: Foulkes, E.C. (ed.), *Cadmium* (Berlin: Springer-Verlag, 1986).

Uptake by pasture of cadmium varies according to time of year and species and, as with lead, maximum levels in grasses tend to occur in late winter, before livestock are released onto pastures. There are considerable differences in uptake between different pasture species: grasses are unlikely to exceed 5 ppm but plants such as the daisy, dandelion and yarrow (members of the Compositae) can accumulate between 10–70 ppm in tissues without outward signs of damage, and hence present a hazard to cattle.[75]

Itai-itai disease

Perhaps the most serious problem arising from cadmium pollution of the environment is the contamination of food. Cadmium is virtually absent from the human body at birth, but accumulates with age, mostly in the liver and kidneys. At high levels the consequences can be very severe. During the 1950s in Japan, irrigation of ricefields using water contaminated by cadmium and other pollutants from industrial sources produced a serious condition known as itai-itai (*itai-itai* is the Japanese for "a cry of pain").[76] Uptake of cadmium by the rice plants resulted in concentrations in excess of 1 ppm Cd in the grain compared with 0.05–0.07 from non-polluted regions. People who fed on the rice suffered from intolerable pain, especially on movement. Bones bent, deformed, decalcified and easily fractured, and kidney function was disrupted. At least 100 people eventually died. Most affected were post-menopausal women, consuming diets high in rice and low in protein and calcium. It is thought that the disruption of the kidney function caused increased excretion of calcium, so further damaging bones already short of calcium. But other possibilities include disruption of calcium binding proteins and enzymes, either directly by cadmium or indirectly through the disruption of the activity of vitamin D, and inhibition of calcium uptake from the intestine.[77] The contamination has proved highly persistent. In the late 1970s some 2700 hectares of rice were still seriously affected and, even today, ten per cent of paddy soils and eight per cent of orchard soils in Japan continue to be severely contaminated.[78]

The general population is fortunately not exposed to such high concentrations of Cd in the diet. A recent comprehensive survey conducted in the USA by three agencies, the United States Department of Agriculture, the Food and Drug Administration and the Environmental Protection Agency, found mean levels of Cd in food crops to be less than 0.03 ppm, save for lettuce and spinach (Table 9.7). However these values are exceeded by crops grown in the Salinas Valley, California, a region of soils naturally elevated in Cd. In some samples concentrations above those from rice in Japan were found.[79]

Levels in excess of those in the polluted ricefields of Japan and the Salinas Valley occur in the garden soils of Shipham in the UK. In over 60 per cent of the gardens they are greater than 60 ppm Cd. But although some of the vegetables being grown there are consumed, the

Table 9.7 Concentrations of cadmium in various food crops grown in the major producing regions of the USA compared with concentrations occurring on naturally elevated soils in the Salinas Valley, California

| | Cadmium concentration (ppm)[1] | | | |
| | Countrywide survey | | Crops from Salinas Valley[2] | |
Crop	Average	Maximum	Average	Maximum
Lettuce	0.67	4.09	4.63	24.0
Spinach	0.85	2.56	3.09	3.8
Peanut	0.09	0.66	NM[3]	
Carrot	0.26	1.24	0.98	2.79
Onion	0.11	0.54	NM	
Potato	0.16	0.91	NM	
Tomato	0.27	0.75	2.57	4.12
Soybean	0.06	0.12	NM	
Sweet corn	0.01	0.16	NM	
Maize	0.01	0.32	NM	
Wheat	0.05	0.25	NM	
Rice	0.02	0.28	NM	

[1] Concentrations expressed on dry weight basis
[2] Cd concentrations in the soil of the Salinas Valley vary between 0.2–8.4 ppm
[3] NM = Not measured

Source: Page, A.L. et al., 1986, *op. cit.*

intakes by local inhabitants are, on average, only 200 μg Cd weekly, which is less than half of the WHO tolerable intakes (Table 9.8).[80] Both Zn and calcium levels are also high, and it is thought that they are interacting to afford some degree of protection, perhaps by saturating exchange sites on plant roots and human tissues, so reducing uptake of the cadmium.[81]

Table 9.8 Impact of elevated soil cadmium levels in Shipham on average intakes of cadmium in the diet and levels excreted in urine compared with a local uncontaminated village and the UK averages

	Cadmium in urine (nmol/g creatine)[1]	Average intake of cadmium[2] (μg per week)
Shipham	6.2	200
North Petherton[3]	5.5	NR
UK average	NR	140

[1] Significant difference between Shipham and North Petherton: the difference would arise by chance in less than 27 per thousand instances
[2] WHO tolerance intake is 400–500 μg/week
[3] North Petherton is a nearby uncontaminated town

Source: Barltrop D. and Strehlow, C.D., "Cadmium and health in Shipham", The Lancet ii (1982) pp. 1394–5.

One consequence of the itai-itai episode is that cadmium is now the most strictly regulated of heavy metals. Recently the International Agency for Research on Cancer re-evaluated Cd and classified it as a "substance probably carcinogenic to man".[82] The FAO/WHO Expert Committee (1972) has set an Acceptable Daily Intake (ADI) for cadmium of 0.057–0.071 mg. In Japan the average daily intake of cadmium is very close to this level at 0.056 mg, and there is evidence of fairly common renal dysfunction, particularly among people with poor diets.[83]

Most analyses of rice in developing countries have shown cadmium concentrations to be well below those which would give rise to intakes above the ADI.[84] However, one sample of rice from a textile industrial area in Majaraja, Indonesia, was found to contain 0.34 ppm Cd, sufficient to exceed the ADI if humans consume 0.3 kg rice daily. Contamination also appears to be serious in one locality in Zambia, where a zinc and lead refinery produced levels in maize meal of 0.9 ppm Cd and 28 ppm Pb. The contamination on the outer surface of the maize leaves was as high as 5 ppm Cd, 300 ppm Pb, 20 ppm Cu and 900 ppm Zn.[85]

Other metals

Effects on plants

Several other important toxic metals can be absorbed by plants, in amounts that depend on the species, degree of tolerance and availability of the metal in the soil. Generally, the higher the soil levels, the greater the accumulation, but concentration factors are usually low. For instance, barley grown on soils containing less than 50 ppm arsenic (As) contained between 0.01–0.05 ppm As, but on 250–350 ppm soils the concentration rose to only 0.15–0.35 ppm.[86] Nevertheless, pasture grasses on soils containing 1000 ppm contained up to 10 ppm As. Like copper, only small amounts of arsenic are usually taken up by grasses, although more tolerant races of *Agrostis* and *Holcus* have been shown to accumulate between 500–3500 ppm on mine spoil.[87] Arsenic tends to accumulate in the roots of crops, causing root rot that disrupts growth and reduces yields. Potato, carrot, tobacco, tomato and grasses are very tolerant; strawberry, maize, beet and squash are fairly tolerant; and beans, rice, onions, peas, cucumbers and legumes are very sensitive.[88]

Very high mercury concentrations in plants may also occur in the vicinity of industrial activity. For example, mercury levels in vegetables grown near an industrial centre of Alexandria in Egypt accumulated between 0.020–0.362 ppm, with the highest levels in leafy crops such as lettuce and cabbage.[89] And even higher concentrations have occurred in sites close to chloralkali works in the UK, 3–4 ppm in weeds and grasses.[90] One kilogramme of vegetables from Alexandria consumed in a week would exceed the acceptable levels of intake set by WHO. If food crops near to the chloralkali works were to be contaminated to a level similar to the grasses and weeds, then a mere 100 g of vegetables per week would give rise to the maximum tolerable dose in an individual.[91]

Some species of plants are particularly good at accumulating certain elements. Selenium (Se), for instance, has been found concentrated to over 50 ppm in certain plants.[92] One vetch, *Astragalus*, in the western USA has been recorded with up to 15,000 ppm Se. This is in an area where alkaline conditions combined with high soil levels of Se have prevented the growth of many other pasture plants. Se in acid soils is immobile, but in alkaline soils is in a soluble form and available to plant roots for uptake. In general, most grasses, clovers and vegetables do not show toxicity up to about 5 ppm of the selenium, while cereals and onions are even more tolerant, being able to absorb 30 ppm with no toxicity.[93]

Acute nickel (Ni) toxicity occurs in cereals in parts of Scotland where natural levels of Ni are high in basic igneous and serpentine rocks containing 50–400 ppm.[94] Oats are most severely affected. Beans and turnips accumulate the most Ni from the soil, and wheat and barley the least.

Effects on livestock

Livestock can also suffer from excesses of some of these elements. There are reports of loss of condition and deaths in livestock on arsenic polluted land in southwest England, mostly through consumption of grasses that have accumulated extremely high levels of arsenic.[95] Most serious though, are the effects of selenium on livestock. Consumption of plants that accumulate selenium, particularly in times of pasture shortage, can lead to laboured breathing, abnormal movement, diarrhoea and death. "Blind staggers" has been reported in animals that eat, over several weeks, only limited amounts of plants with accumulated selenium. It was a common condition in the semi-arid regions of the USA in the 1930s. The affected animals wander, stumble, have impaired vision, and eventually die from respiratory failure. Another condition arising from selenium poisoning is "alkali disease", in which animals lose hair and weight, and exhibit lameness and hoof malformations.

Soils originating from cretaceous shales in South Dakota, Wyoming and Nebraska in the USA can contain between 1 and 80 ppm of Se, levels associated with acute selenosis of cattle. In certain parts of India, particularly the northwestern states, soils may contain selenium concentrations of 2–10 ppm.[96] Here selenosis, known locally as "Degnala disease", is common among buffaloes. Affected animals have lesions, inflammation of joints, lameness, skin necrosis and deformation of hooves. Selenium has been shown to accumulate in major sources of fodder, including rice straw, berseem and lucerne. But some of the highest soil Se concentrations in the world occur in County Limerick in Ireland. There, 30–300 ppm of Se in soil have resulted in a pasture content of 150–500 ppm, producing serious livestock poisoning.[97]

In regions with high soil Se levels, irrigation may result in increased concentration of Se in drainage waters.[98] Until recently there was no significant evidence of hazard but in the San Joaquin Valley of California, Se salts in drainage water have passed to a nationally important wildlife reserve, the Kesterson Reservoir, producing concentrations of 60–430 mg/l.[99] This compares with the US drinking water standard for selenium of only 10 mg/l.[100] The result has been a high incidence of mortality, abnormal embryos and chicks in water birds, and the loss of all species of fish, save for mosquito fish. Irrigation water delivery to this reservoir has now been prohibited.

Synergistic effects

So far we have dealt with individual heavy metals and their effects. The picture is greatly complicated, though, by the frequent occurrence of synergism between metals. High levels of one metal may enhance the effect of another, or reduce its effect or even produce deficiency. Some of the most important synergistic interactions involve copper, molybdenum and cadmium and their effects on livestock. We will concentrate on these.

As we have indicated, sheep store copper in the liver. But the degree of storage is affected by the presence of other metals. Zinc, for instance, reduces copper storage in the liver, with the result that increasing zinc levels will produce less liver damage and fewer deaths in lambs when fed a diet containing 29 ppm Cu, a level that otherwise is toxic (Table 9.9). On the other hand, an excess of zinc or cadmium can reduce the availability of copper and hence effectively create a deficiency. This is particularly critical during pregnancy. The concentration of copper in the blood normally falls at this time because of the demands of the foetus, and any further reduction hazards foetal

Table 9.9 Effect of combinations of dietary zinc and copper on copper content of liver and liver damage of lambs

	Treatments		
Dietary intakes			
Copper (ppm)	29	29	29
Zinc (ppm)	43	220	420
Impact upon lambs			
Copper in liver (ppm)	436	209	176
Plasma arginase index*	0.40	0.15	0.14
Deaths by 24 weeks[†]	3	0	0

* Values greater than 0.15 are indicative of liver damage; index calculated by mg urea produced/ml plasma/hour
[†] Eight lambs tested in each treatment

Source: Bremner, I., Young, B.W. and Mills, C.F., "Protective effects of zinc supplementation upon copper toxicosis in sheep", *Br. J. Nutrition* **36** (1976) pp. 551–61.

development and birth. Zinc at 750 ppm in a diet was shown to induce late abortions in sheep and death in any surviving lambs, symptoms of the copper deficiency condition known as "swayback".[101]

A further set of interactions occurs with cadmium (Cd). Consumption by sheep of Zn and Cd combined at levels typically found in plants can depress the activity of a copper-containing enzyme, caeruloplasmin, in the blood plasma, and this can lead to the decline of copper in the liver and the development of a brittle, poorly-mineralized skeleton. Lamb foetuses and young lambs are not affected since cadmium does not transfer across the placenta and mammary gland.[102] But once lambs start to graze, a marked increase in retention of Cd in the liver occurs, which may then accelerate the loss of liver copper (Figure 9.6). In general, newly weaned lambs and calves are vulnerable even to low levels of Cd, particularly if Cu intake is low.

Molybdenosis and copper deficiency

Too much molybdenum (Mo) also induces copper deficiency. A variety of conditions linked to copper deficiency have been recognized since the nineteenth century. In cattle "teart", as it is sometimes known in England (it is also known as bovine hypocupraemia, molybdenosis, warfa, copper pine and peat scours), is characterized by loss of pigment, stilted gait, progressive malnutrition, anaemia and diarrhoea. In lambs the condition is known as "swayback", a similar nervous disorder that usually results in death.[103] That these symptoms are also related to the presence of molybdenum was first realized in the 1940s. At that time teartness occurred widely on 8000 hectares in Somerset where the Mo content in pasture grasses reached 20–50 ppm, some 6–7-fold greater than in non-teart pastures.[104] High molybdenum levels are typically found in soils overlying natural black shales.[105]

About this time Mo was also confirmed as the causal factor behind a similar and long standing condition among cattle in the San Joaquin Valley in California.[106] The condition was associated with neutral to alkaline soils, where Mo was present in soluble form, and linked to the occurrence of certain species of legumes, which were found to contain 80–200 ppm Mo dry weight, 6–8-fold more than grasses.

In addition to being naturally occurring, high molybdenum levels may arise from molybdenum containing fertilizers or as wastes from various industrial processes. The latter can result in forage containing up to 125 ppm.[107] In general, levels of more than 2 ppm Mo in pasture may be sufficient to induce copper deficiency in cattle and sheep. If Cu intake is normal, Mo is not harmful until levels of greater than 10 ppm

Figure 9.6   Influence of dietary cadmium given to ewes during pregnancy and lactation on cadmium and copper content on lamb livers

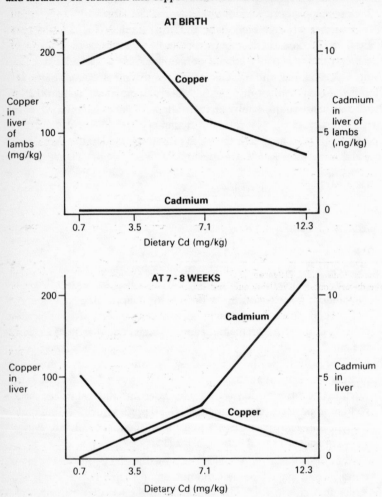

Source: Mills, L.F., Campbell, J.K., Bremner, I. and Quarterman, J., "The influence of dietary composition on the toxicity of cadmium, copper, zinc and lead to animals", in: *Inorganic Pollution and Agriculture*, MAFF Ref. 326 (London: HMSO, 1980).

are consumed, but if Cu intake is low then the critical concentrations fall to 3–10 ppm. Some 1700 herds of cattle in England and Wales were found to be deficient during 1979–80. Many of these were on Mo-rich soils, although other metals may be playing an important role.[108]

The mechanism of all these forms of molybdenosis poisoning also involves sulphur. On diets low in sulphur, Mo appears to have little effect on copper, but when sulphur is present at greater than 2 ppm dry matter, a strongly synergistic action between Mo and Cu occurs (Table 9.10). The simultaneous exposure of tissues to high levels of both Mo and S produces, in some way, an increased binding of Cu, with a consequent reduction in Cu availability. It is thus possible for increased sulphur deposition in forage, resulting from SO_2 emissions, to induce outbreaks of molybdenosis.

Table 9.10   Change in liver copper of growing cattle with different dietary content of molybdenum (Mo) and sulphur (S) over a 75-day period

Dietary Mo (ppm)	Dietary S (ppm)	Change in total liver Cu (mg)
< 0.5	1	+110
< 0.5	3	+114
5	1	+ 38
5	3	− 51

Source: Mills, C.F., Dalgarno, A.C., Bremner, I. and El-Gallad, I.T., "Influence of the dietary content of molybdenum and sulphur upon the hepatic retention of copper in young cattle", *Proc. Nutrition Soc.* **36** (1977) p. 105.

Conditions involving induced copper deficiency continue to be common today throughout the world. Swayback, for instance, has now been recognized in young goats in Karnal, India. Low blood copper levels are linked with consumption of berseem (alfalfa) containing as much as 20 ppm Mo.[109] The change from hay to silage feeding also reduces Cu availability, as does the tendency toward producing larger, more rapidly growing animals.[110] On the positive side, copper containing feeds are now readily available and can be used as remedies.

Selenium interactions

The final interaction of interest is the antagonism of selenium to other toxic metals.[111] Even at normal levels in the diet, Se can counteract the toxic effects of organic mercuric substances, and can divert Cd from target proteins to other less damaging sites. Other interactions are suspected, such as with Pb, but are at most weak.

Sewage pollution

The hazards of applying sewage effluent and sludge to agricultural land arise from contaminants such as heavy metals, organic compounds and pathogens, that in turn have come from domestic and industrial sources of sewage.

Sewage effluent and waste water

Applying domestic and industrial wastes to agricultural land is a very old practice. In China the systematic use of human excreta – night soil – as a fertilizer goes back several thousand years.[112] Sewage farms, in which crops were being grown on partly treated sewage effluent, had been established close to such cities as Edinburgh, London and Manchester by the seventeenth century.[113] And during the late nineteenth century they became increasingly common throughout Europe and North America. Over 5300 hectares close to Paris were being irrigated and in Berlin nearly 18,000 hectares, by the first decade of the twentieth century. In the USA sewage irrigation was first established in the 1870s in Massachussetts and Maine. And in developing countries, Bombay, Delhi and Mexico City were early adopters of sewage farms.[114] However, this practice soon ceased as the public became more aware of the potential health hazards. Odours too were a nuisance – early farms in Chicago and Los Angeles were soon abandoned as the suburbs came too close to the source of the odours.[115]

Sewage sludge

In the nineteenth century the pattern of waste disposal also began to change. Increasingly, domestic and industrial wastes were being collected together and treated in sewage works from which emerged two products – a harmless liquid that could be discharged to rivers or the sea and a solid material that settled out of the liquid and was termed sludge. In the UK, some 1.2 million tonnes of dry solids from sewage sludge are produced from industrial and domestic effluents annually: about 45–50 per cent of this is applied to agricultural land, some 30 per cent is dumped at sea and the remainder is dumped in landfill sites or incinerated.[116] In the USA about 7.7 million dry tonnes are produced annually, but the pattern of disposal is very different: 44 per cent is disposed to landfill, 22 per cent is incinerated, 6 per cent dumped at sea, 12 per cent sold or disposed of elsewere and countrywide only 16 per cent is applied to agricultural land.[117] However the USA has banned dumping at sea from the end of 1991; in the EC there is growing pressure for member states to do likewise. The states applying the most to land are New Jersey, Pennsylvannia, Ohio, Illinois, Michigan, Missouri, Wisconsin, and Minnesota.

In the past, applying sludge to land was seen as primarily of benefit to the farmer but, today, with rapidly growing quantities of sludge being produced, the principal justification is that it is a cheap means of disposal. The Yorkshire Water Authority in the UK has estimated in the late 1980s that disposal costs to land were of the order of £50 per tonne, comparing favourably with incineration at £107/t and sea disposal at £60/t.[118] To this can be added the benefits from improved soil fertility and increased crop yields, although compared with the results of applying modern synthetic fertilizers this is relatively small. In the UK, the use of sewage sludge represents a net benefit to agriculture of £1.5–2 million annually, but this is insignificant compared to the annual inorganic fertilizer bill of some £800 million.[119] Sludge is applied to only one per cent of agricultural land.

The nutrient content of sludge is low, typically of the order of 3–4 per cent nitrogen, 1.5–3.5 per cent phosphorus and 0.3 per cent potassium, though some sludges contain more than 10 per cent nitrogen and 8 per cent phosphorus.[120] And the availability of these nutrients is also variable. If the sludge is anaerobically digested, either for several months in open tanks or several weeks in heated enclosed tanks, the nitrogen is highly available in the form of ammonium compounds. But in untreated raw sludge, the nitrogen is mostly present in organic complexes and is only released slowly by the action of soil bacteria.[121] Since this tends to occur during the summer months it is of little value to cereal crops, which require nutrients during the early stages of growth. Sludge may also be beneficial as a soil conditioner because of its organic content but again, at the normal rates of application, typically 2–5 tonnes/ha in the UK, this is of relatively small consequence.[122] The benefits may be greater in semi-arid and sandy regions where sewage sludge can aid water retention and reduce water stress.

Heavy metals in sludge

Nutrients, though, are not the only contents of sewage sludge; it usually contains a large number of contaminants, in particular metals, organic compounds and pathogenic organisms. The metals are largely derived from industrial discharges, though some, such as boron, arise from domestic detergents. In the UK there has been a downward trend in the heavy metal content of sludge, as a result of improved pretreatment and a decline in the contaminating industries (Figure 9.7). Inevitably, some metals are more common in sludge than others but by comparison with other sources of metals in the UK, sludge is only a significant environmental contaminator in the case of cadmium and chromium (Table 9.11). In the USA, at typical rates of application

Table 9.11 Sources of metal inputs to agricultural land in the UK

| | *Proportion of each metal (%)* | | | | | | | | |
	As	Cd	Cr	Cu	Hg	Ni	Pb	Se	Zn
Atmosphere	89	50	45	77	37	93	92	91	90
Sewage sludge	3	14	30	6	5	7	5	2	5
Inorganic fertilizers	8	36	25	1	1	–	3	7	1
Pig slurry	–	–	–	16	–	–	–	–	–
Farm waste	–	–	–	–	–	–	–	–	4
Seed dressing	–	–	–	–	57	–	–	–	–

As = Arsenic; Cd = cadmium; Cr = chromium; Cu = copper; Hg = mercury; Ni = nickel; Pb = lead; Se = selenium; Zn = zinc.

Source: Water Research Centre, in HL, *Sewage Sludge in Agriculture* (London: House of Lords Select Committee, 1983).

to agricultural land, the total quantities of these metals annually applied per hectare are small – for chromium 0.2 kg/ha and for cadmium ten times less. More substantial are the inputs of iron, zinc and copper. In the Salem programme in Oregon some 90–95 per cent of the 120,000 cubic metres of liquid sludge produced each year by the city of Salem are digested and the solids applied to agricultural land within a 30 km radius of the plant (Table 9.12).[123]

There is also a special problem created by pig wastes. As we pointed out in Chapter 6, they may contain large quantities of Cu and Zn, resulting from additives in the pig diets, 80–95 per cent of which may be excreted. These wastes are usually applied directly to land, though in some cases they enter the sewage system.

Effects on plants

We have already discussed the damage that may be caused to plants and animals by heavy metals. The question posed by their presence in sewage sludge is whether this presents a special hazard

Figure 9.7   The trend in heavy metal content of sewage sludge in the UK, 1976–83

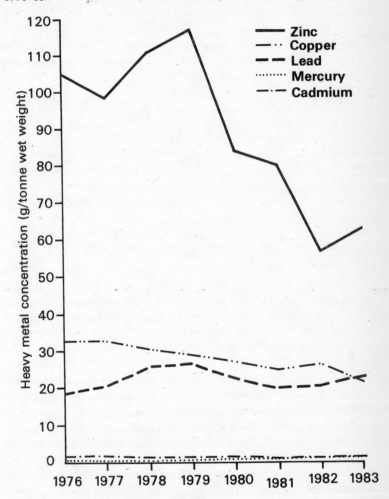

Source: Royal Commission on Environmental Pollution, *Managing Waste: the Duty of Care*, 11th Report (London: HMSO, 1985).

compared with other sources. Much of present day heavy metal contamination of agricultural land arises from past mining activities and the contribution of sewage sludge is comparatively small. However, application of sludge is a continuing process and thus results in a steady accumulation of metals. In this sense it is akin to the build-up

Table 9.12 Constituents of digested sewage sludge from Salem in Oregon and average annual loading to agricultural land. Sludge is applied once per year

Constituent	Average concentration in digested sludge (mg/kg dry weight)	Total annual loading per hectare (kg/ha)
Nitrogen	103,000	350
Phosphorus	20,000	68
Potassium	9,600	33
Zinc	980	3.33
Copper	470	1.60
Nickel	43	0.15
Cadmium	7	0.024
Iron	21,000	71.4
Barium	230	0.78
Chromium	60	0.20
Arsenic	0.1	0.0003
Cobalt	8	0.027

Source: EPA Office of Water, *Environmental Regulations and Technology, Use and Disposal of Municipal Wastewater Sludge* Office of Water (Washington DC: US Environmental Protection Agency, 1989).

arising from contemporary smelting or the deposition of lead alongside roads from passing motor vehicles. In general, heavy metals are not removed from soils by leaching or by plant uptake, so that repeated applications of sludge are likely to lead to cumulative and irreversible contamination.

There is also the question of whether heavy metals, when applied in this way, are reaching concentrations hazardous to crops and livestock and whether the sludge itself creates special conditions conducive to uptake. The evidence from the field is conflicting. Some experiments have found reduced yields associated with increased metal concentrations in treated soils (Table 9.13). However, the results of many of these experiments need to be treated with caution, in particular those using sludge spiked with inorganic metal salts.[124] In this technique, metals salts are added to uncontaminated sewage sludge and allowed to equilibrate over a period of weeks before drying and mixing with the soil. The major experimental advantage is the opportunity for adding precise quantities of single or mixed elements. But this may not represent the true availability of metals in sludge. For example, cadmium uptake from sludge spiked with cadmium sulphate is greater than that from sludge with naturally elevated levels, even after it is left for a year to come to equilibrium in the soil.[125] Other experiments have made use of growing plants in

Table 9.13 Yields of red beet and celery following application of sewage sludge containing various concentrations of metals

| | | Yield (tonnes/ha) | |
		Red beet	Celery
Control (No sludge)		46	60
Sludge*			
Uncontaminated		61	54
Zinc	8000 ppm	19	46
	16000 ppm	0	25
Copper	4000 ppm	45	61
	8000 ppm	17	62
Nickel	2000 ppm	24	46
	4000 ppm	0	18
Chromium	4400 ppm	71	62
	8800 ppm	62	57

* Applied at 125.5 tonnes dry matter/hectare

Source: Webber, J., "Effects of toxic metals in sewage on crops", *Water Pollut. Control*, (1972) pp. 405–13.

nutrient solution to which the metal salts have been added. But plants in these solutions take up more metal, even when concentrations are greater in the sludge.[126]

Whether the high organic matter content of sewage sludge has an effect is also in doubt. It may reduce pH and so increase uptake of metals. The concentration of metals released from sewage sludge or sludge-soil mixtures increases sharply below threshold pH values – pH 5.8–6.0 for Zn, 4.5–4.8 for Cu and 6.3 for Ni. As a result, at pH 7.0 more than four times the quantities of Zn and Ni are required to produce the same reductions in yield of beet and onions as at pH 6.2.[127] In general, there does appear to be a tendency for uptake to decline with increased levels of organic matter but, of course, any protective effect will be lost as the organic matter is decomposed.[128]

Long-term application can result in heavy accumulation. In Dayton, Ohio, USA use of sludge over 35 years has greatly elevated soil metal levels, yet the concentration in maize grain on contaminated sites is not significantly different from that from control sites (Table 9.14). The roots, stems, leaves and husks from plants growing in soils treated with sludge had higher concentrations than control plants. But here, and elsewhere, accumulation in the grain is very low even following application of highly concentrated sludges.[129]

Table 9.14   Levels of metals in soil and maize grain after 35 years of sewage sludge application in Dayton, Ohio

	Concentration in soil (ppm in top 30 cm)		Concentration in maize grain (ppm)	
	Control	Sludged	Control	Sludged
Cd	2	71	0.8	0.9
Cu	51	843	8	12
Ni	72	147	1	1
Pb	61	1015	<5	<5
Zn	158	2065	12	79

Cd = cadmium; Cu = copper; Ni = nickel; Pb = lead; Zn = zinc

Source: Kirkham, M. B., "Trace elements in corn grown on long-term sludge disposal site", *Environ. Sci. Technol.* **9** (1975) pp. 765–8.

Effects on livestock

There is also a risk to livestock from the application of sludge to pasture. Some grass species may retain considerable quantities of sludge on leaves following application, even after rainfall (Table 9.15).

Table 9.15   Retention of sewage sludge on leaves of tall fescue (*Festuca arundinacea*)

Interval following application (days)	Rainfall (mm)	Proportion of harvested forage consisting of sludge
14	27	15–22%
80	41	2–5%

Source: Chaney, R.L., Hornick, S.B. and Simon, P.W., "Heavy metal relationships during land utilisation of sewage sludge in the north-east", in: Loehr, R.C. (ed.), *Land as a Waste Management Alternative* (Ann Arbor, Michigan: Ann Arbor Sci. Publ., 1977).

Livestock can thus ingest significant amounts of metals either from direct grazing or from hay or silage. Certain types of forage harvester may also pick up slurry accumulated on the soil surface.[130] And livestock can take up metals through directly ingesting soil, since after sludge has been applied to grassland most metals remain in the top 5 cm of the soil.[131] Nevertheless, there are few recorded cases of livestock poisoning attributed to the application of sewage sludge. A notable exception was fluorine poisoning of cattle in the UK during the 1970s.[132]

Finally, there is some evidence of heavy metals in sludge having an indirect effect on soil micro-organisms. In experiments at the Woburn Experimental Farm in Bedfordshire, populations of bacteria and blue-green algae were depressed and fixed less nitrogen on soils that had, in the past, received applications of sewage sludge high in metals (Figure 9.8). Clover plants on sludged soil had lower yields, compared with plants treated with farmyard manure, and the nodules on the roots were small and ineffective at nitrogen-fixation.[133] A 50 per cent reduction in fixation occurred when soils contained 330 ppm Zn, 100 ppm Cu, 27 ppm Ni and 10 ppm of Cd.

Figure 9.8 Microbial biomass in soils treated with inorganic fertilizer or farmyard manure (O) compared with sludge containing heavy metals (●)

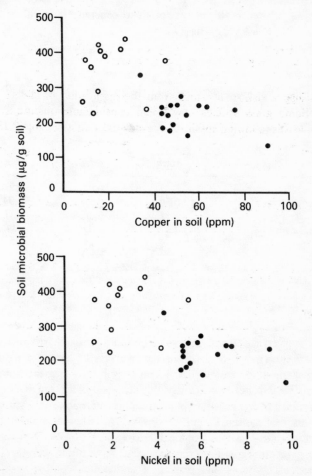

Source: Brookes, P.L. and McGrath, S.P., "Effects of metal toxicity on the size of the soil microbial biomass" *J. Soil Sci.* **35** (1984) pp. 341–346.

Organic compounds in sludge

In addition to heavy metals, sludge may contain organic compounds. Although many are degraded during treatment, the residues can be sufficient to produce adverse effects in crops, and, if taken up by plants, constitute a hazard to livestock or ourselves. Many kinds of organic compound are involved – dyes, inks, pesticides, oils, solvents and aromatic hydrocarbons.

Table 9.16 gives the levels of organochlorine compounds typically found in sewage sludge in the UK. The dieldrin, polychlorinated biphenyls (PCBs) and HCH were primarily from industrial sources, such as textile factories that process wool imported from countries where fleeces are still treated with dieldrin. In the 1970s, sludge containing 17 ppm dieldrin was found to concentrate in the milk of grazing cattle to a level of 30–47 ppm. But it is now very unlikely that sludge containing such high levels would be applied to agricultural land.[134]

Table 9.16   Organochlorines in sewage sludge in the UK, 1981–2. Results are from analysis of 444 sludges taken from representative sewage throughout the UK

	Concentration (ppm)		
	Mean	Median	Max
Aldrin	0.03	0.02	0.21
Dieldrin	0.50	0.13	52.94
Endrin	0.11	0.06	0.71
HCH (Lindane)	0.41	0.09	70.00
PCBs	0.34	0.14	21.50

Source: McIntyre, A.E. and Lester, J.N., *Analysis and incidence of persistent organochlorine micropollutants in sewage sludges*, Dept of Civil Engineering (London: Imperial College, 1984).

In most cases PCBs, organochlorines and aromatic hydrocarbons do not exceed 1–10 ppm in soils and are unlikely to present a hazard. Concern has been expressed over alkyl phenols and linear alkyl benzene sulphonates (LAS) that may be present in sludge at between 0.3–1.2 per cent of dry digested material.[135] These came into use during the 1960s as biodegradable alternatives for synthetic detergents that caused foaming in rivers. But whether such organic compounds cause harm is not clear. Most are not taken up by plants. However, recent experiments in the USA have found an increasing incidence of chromosomal breakages and mutant pollen grains in plants grown on soils containing an increasing amount of sludge and this may be a result of such contamination.[136] Other experiments have found that the germination of some cereals and grasses is retarded by the addition of sludge, and this effect probably results from volatile organic compounds rather than heavy metals.

Pathogens in sludges

The third major category of contaminants are pathogenic organisms. Raw sewage often contains bacteria, viruses and parasites (particularly the eggs of worms or protozoan cysts) which are not completely eliminated by sludge treatment. Some of these pathogens are able to survive for considerable periods in soil and on plants (Table 9.17).

Table 9.17 Survival times of various pathogenic organisms in soil and on plants

	Survival times at 20°C (days)			
	In soil		On plants	
Pathogenic organisms	Possible	Usual	Possible	Usual
Viruses				
Enterovirus	<100	<20	<60	<15
Bacteria				
Faecal coliforms	<70	<20	<30	<15
Salmonella spp.	<70	<20	<30	<15
Vibrio cholerae	<20	<10	<5	<2
Tubercle bacilli	<600	<180	<90	<90
Shigella spp.	–	–	<10	<2
Protozoa				
Entamoeba histolytica cysts	<20	<10	<15	<10
Helminths				
Ascaris eggs	many months		many months	
Taernia saginata eggs	–	–	<360	<90

Sources: Shuval H.I. et al., *Wastewater Irrigation in Developing Countries*, World Bank Tech. Paper no. 51 (Washington DC: The World Bank, 1986); DHSS, in HL, *Sewage Sludge in Agriculture* (London: House of Lords Select Committee on European Communities, 1983).

Two of the pathogens occurring in sludge in the UK can cause diseases in livestock and humans, namely *Salmonella* and the beef tapeworm (*Taenia saginata*).[137] The hazards, though, are apparently not very great. In the case of *Salmonella* there is some disagreement over the length of time required for *Salmonella* organisms to die once the sludge is applied; death within 16–32 days of application is most likely, though they survive up to 70 days if ponding of the sludge on a field has occurred, for example in the ruts of the tractor wheels.[138] But it seems unlikely that *Salmonella* populations ever reach hazardous levels. Experiments under controlled conditions have found that some 10 million bacteria are required to infect a cow; by contrast only 100–1000 per gram are likely to be present in treated sludge, even before the mandatory three week grazing interval begins.[139]

Few instances of Salmonellosis in cattle have resulted from the use of sludge, though outbreaks have occurred from the use of contaminated cattle slurry.[140] Much more important to cattle is the probability of *Salmonella* infection from animal protein feedstuffs.[141] And as a source of infection, sewage sludge is considerably less important than, say, eating raw shellfish raised in sewage polluted waters or drinking from private drinking water supplies contaminated by septic tank systems.[142]

A greater danger may be tapeworm infection. There were some 80–100 annual reports of human tapeworm infection in the UK between 1975–81, though this may be an underestimate since it is not a notifiable disease.[143] The adult beef tapeworm lives in the human intestine and its eggs are excreted, so eventually ending up in sewage sludge. Because the eggs are highly resistant they may survive long enough to be taken up by grazing cattle. Larvae then hatch and migrate from the intestine to the muscles where they form cysts – a condition known as bovine cysticercosis. Human consumption of the infested meat completes the cycle.

In the UK some 2 to 47 of every million slaughtered carcases contain sufficiently widespread infection that condemnation is necessary.[144] In most cases, though, the cause does not seem to be application of sludge to grazing land. Only seven per cent of the farms where *Taenia* infections had been reported in Scotland had also used sewage sludge.[145] Nonetheless, sewage sludge has been implicated. On one farm infection of 36 out of 40 carcases was linked to the application of sludge to pasture.[146] In most cases, farmers either used raw sewage or allowed a grazing period well below the recommended guideline.[147]

Elsewhere in the world there are occasional reports of illnesses arising from exposure to sewage effluent or sludge. An outbreak of gastroenteritis in southwest Madera, California, was traced to contamination of drinking water wells by pathogens escaping from a neighbouring farm irrigated with raw sewage.[148] Elsewhere, workers in Cincinatti, Chicago and Memphis engaged in the land application of sludge were found to have a higher level of gastroentestinal illness compared with those unexposed.[149] This was especially true of inexperienced workers. The role of wastewater irrigation in disease is discussed below (page 489).

There is also the possibility that bacteria may spread from sewage sludge. Bacteria have been found to travel in aerosol particles for distances ranging from 8 km to several hundred metres.[150] Much depends on the mode of application of the sludge. Injection into soil carries little risk but use of rain-guns is highly likely to produce aerosols containing bacteria. Temperature and humidity are also important factors, droplets surviving longer in cooler conditions.

Water-borne pollution

Crops and livestock may also be affected by contaminated water containing pathogenic organisms or toxic chemicals supplied in wastewater or extracted from streams, rivers and groundwater wells. The problems are likely to be most acute where irrigation is common and the sources are close to industrial or urban areas. (Irrigation is also a cause of salinity of agricultural land, but this topic is beyond the scope of this book.)

Pathogens in wastewater

In recent years there has been growing interest in wastewater irrigation, particularly in developing countries in arid and semi-arid regions that are faced with shortages of water for agriculture and for properly diluting sewage. Wastewater irrigation is now used in such localities to cultivate a wide range of crops (Table 9.18). It is a practice that presents a serious health hazard as well as, in some circumstances, also giving rise to nitrate contamination of groundwater, such as has occurred near Lima and Santiago (see Chapter 4).

Helminth and cholera transmission

Health problems from wastewater irrigation of foodcrops have been particularly severe in parts of what is now Israel.[151] Since 1935, infection of the general population by helminth worms, *Ascaris* and *Trichuris*, has varied according to the availability of vegetables grown in the irrigated Kidron (or Silwan), and later Refraim, Valleys and this, in turn, has been affected by political events. Before the partition of Jerusalem in 1948, infection rates were high (Table 9.19). These

Table 9.18 Selection of countries and cities using farms as a route for disposal of municipal wastewater

Site	Area of land receiving sewage (hectares)	Principal crops
Israel (countrywide)	10,000	Cotton citrus
USA (countrywide)	(3400 projects)	Various non-food crops
Mexico City, Mexico	42,000	Grain, fodder
Santiago, Chile	16,000	Vegetable and salad crops
Lima, Peru	(31 projects) Eventually 5000	Various non-food crops
India (countrywide)	12,000	Various non-food crops
Tunis, Tunisia	800	Grain, trees, forage
Kuwait City	9000	Alfalfa, fodder, some vegetables
Khartoum, Sudan	2800	Eucalyptus woodlots
Melbourne, Australia	10,000	Pastures

Source: Shuval et al., 1986, *op. cit.*

then fell dramatically in western Jerusalem between 1948–66, as the Kidron Valley was now in Jordan, and there were no commercial contacts between the two parts of the city. During this period there was a general improvement in socio-economic conditions in both parts of the city, including improved food hygiene and a supply of safe drinking water, but there was no reduction in helminth infection in eastern Jerusalem.

Table 9.19 Relationship between proportion of stool samples found positive for *Ascaris* in the population of western Jerusalem and supply of vegetables and salad crops irrigated with raw wastewater, 1935–82

Years	Supply of vegetables to western Jerusalem	Proportion of stool samples positive for Ascaris (%)
1935–47	Vegetables supplied	35%
1948	Partition: supply stopped	
1948–66	No supply of vegetables	1%
1968	War: unification of Jerusalem	
1968–70	Supply of vegetables resumed	12%
1975–82	No wastewater irrigation of vegetables or salad crops permitted	<1%

Source: Shuval et al., 1986, *op. cit.*

Following the 1967 war and the unification of the city, the supply of wastewater-irrigated vegetables resumed from both the Kidron and Refraim valleys. However as both were in the "administered territories" of Israel, where Ministry of Health regulations forbidding the use of wastewater on vegetables were not in force, the result was a steep rise in infections in the population of western Jerusalem. Salad crops were found to be heavily contaminated with helminths.

Simultaneous with the increase in helminth infection a cholera epidemic occured. The first cases were detected in August 1970, the disease appearing simultaneously in both parts of the city. The water supply could not be the source – all was chlorinated and came from deep wells. Moreover, in some cases, only the member of a family fell ill who had consumed vegetables. Cholera vibrios were then found in the soils and vegetables of the wastewater farms. All harvested crops were confiscated, and those still growing were destroyed in mid-September. The last clinical cases occurred some 12 days later. Following this outbreak the authorities put an end to wastewater irrigation of vegetables; since then helminth infections have fallen to less than one per cent again.

Typhoid fever and sewage irrigation

A further serious health hazard is typhoid. In the city of Santiago, Chile the annual incidence of typhoid is of the order of 150–200/100,000 population. Yet almost all homes are connected to a filtered, chlorinated drinking water supply, most milk and dairy products are pasteurized, and most houses have indoor sanitation. The city produces some 100 million cubic metres of sewage each year, which is mostly utilized for irrigation during the dry summer months of October to May.[152] About 4500 hectares are exclusively irrigated with these wastes, producing 20,000 tonnes of vegetables and salad crops for the city.

Several factors link typhoid incidence with this sewage irrigation. During the winter months the incidence of disease is at the same level as the rest of the country but then rises as irrigation begins in the late spring (Figure 9.9). The incidence of typhoid is also much higher than it is in comparable cities that do not practise wastewater irrigation (40–60/100,000). *Salmonella typhi*, the causative agent for typhoid fever, has been found in wastewater canals. In 1983 new regulations restricted the cultivation of certain types of salad crops, such as lettuce, and in early 1984 reported typhoid cases were down some 30 per cent.

Figure 9.9 Average seasonal variation of typhoid fever cases in Santiago and the rest of Chile, 1977–85

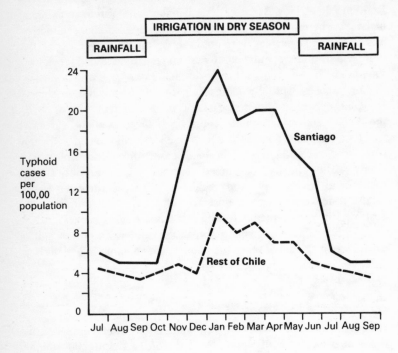

Source: Shuval et al., *op. cit.*

Organic chemicals

It is only in recent years that organic chemical compounds have been recognized as potentially significant pollutants of ground and surface water. The fastest growing hazard is the presence of chlorinated solvents in aquifers in the USA and UK, where altogether 175 different compounds have been found, frequently at concentrations one to two orders of magnitude higher than in surface water. Some of the most commonly detected compounds are listed in Table 9.20. In California recent surveys have found 540 wells containing solvents, some 30 per cent of which at levels exceeding state water quality standards; and in Nebraska 10 per cent of all the State's community water supplies contain some solvents.[153]

In the UK, concentrations of TriCE and TetraCE above WHO recommended values of 30 µg/l and 10 µg/l respectively have been

Table 9.20 Proportion of wells sampled in 18 US states by March 1980 containing six common organic compounds, and maximum concentrations detected

	Proportion of wells containing contaminants (%)					
	Tri-chloro-ethylene (TriCE)	Tetra-chloro-ethylene (TetraCE)	Carbon tetra-chloride	Vinyl chloride	1,1,1-tri-chloro ethane	1,2-di-chloro ethane
Alabama	10	4	0	1	10	3
Connecticut	2	nr	nr	nr	nr	nr
Delaware	79	nr	nr	nr	nr	73
Florida	33	20	50	16	15	15
Idaho	11	11	nr	nr	11	nr
Kentucky	0	0	5	0	0	0
Maine	0	0	0	0	18	0
Massachusetts	36	19	0	nr	21	3
New Hampshire	17	0	0	nr	0	nr
New Jersey	27	11	23	0	48	2
New York	13	15	5	nr	9	nr
North Carolina	18	5	0	34	2	7
Rhode Island	22	nr	0	nr	nr	nr
South Carolina	0	0	0	0	0	25
South Dakota	0	0	0	nr	nr	0
Tennessee	14	2	8	6	26	8
Virginia	100	nr	nr	nr	nr	nr
Washington	33	34	nr	0	66	0
Maximum concentration recorded (μ	27,300	1500	400	50	5440	250

nr = not recorded

Source: Conservation Foundation, *Groundwater Protection* (Washington DC: 1987).

found.[154] For example, concentrations of TriCE have reached 60–80 $\mu g/l$ and 200 $\mu g/l$ beneath an airbase and an engineering factory, while beneath an ex-aircraft manufacturing plant, the water content of TriCE peaked at 17,000 $\mu g/l$. In groundwater beneath the cities of Birmingham and Coventry, high values have been found in boreholes close to laundries and metal and engineering industry. As yet, however, such water is only for industrial use, and so does not affect agriculture. If used for irrigation much of the solvents could be expected to be lost by volatilization.

Little is yet known of the possible effects of these solvent chemicals on humans, livestock and plants. But mixed with these compounds, in both surface and groundwater, are many organic pesticides, herbicides and nematocides which can, of course, have a direct impact upon agriculture if applied in irrigation water (see Chapter 2, pages 37–44). In one incident in Britain, tomato plants grown in greenhouses were severely damaged through the presence of minute quantities of a herbicide, trichlorobenzoic acid (TBA). This had been discharged from a pesticide plant into a river from which the irrigation water for the tomatoes was drawn. Another example is damage to glasshouse crops from irrigation water contaminated with boron, derived from synthetic detergents.[155] Boron is essential to plants at very low concentrations, but it becomes toxic to fruit trees at only 0.3 ppm and to many other plants at 1 ppm.[156]

Discharges from industrial accidents represent the most potentially dangerous sources of pollution to agriculture. A recent case was the Sandoz fire in Basle in November 1986, during which some 30 tonnes of agro-chemicals and 150 kg of mercury were washed into the river Rhine, causing extensive and widespread damage to aquatic resources.[157] However because the accident occurred during winter there was no immediate impact upon agriculture.

Crops may be occasionally damaged by accidental release of toxic chemicals, resulting from the breaching of sewers or pipelines or through highway spillages. It has been estimated that 4 billion tonnes of hazardous substances, including toxic and corrosive chemicals, explosives, inflammables, hazardous wastes and radioactive wastes, are transported throughout the USA each year.[158] About half of the 500,000 daily shipments are made by road and, on average, there are more than 30 accidents each day resulting in spillage of materials. Most of these releases occur during handling and loading, and hence are not such a potential direct threat to agriculture. But when highway accidents do occur, hosing down of the roads after accidents often results in contamination of nearby fields.

Landfill leachate

An important source of contamination to groundwater, in addition to the industrial discharges discussed above, is the leached materials from landfill sites that have been used for waste disposal. These landfill sites are employed mainly for solid municipal wastes, though a relatively small quantity of hazardous industrial waste is disposed of in this way. In the USA, landfill is the route for 125 million tonnes of municipal wastes annually, compared with only three million tonnes of industrial waste.[159] An unspecified amount of industrial waste is disposed of to landfill on industrial premises.

Landfill sites are a potential risk for a number of reasons. Older sites were located often without consideration for potential leaching to groundwater – usually they are neither lined nor covered. Leaching is inevitable unless the site is completely sealed so that no rainwater enters. Of about 1250 sites examined by the US House Energy and Commerce Committee in 1985, nearly half showed signs of contamination to nearby groundwater. And in New York State alone, 82 per cent of all waste dumped is to facilities that leach or could leach – only 8 per cent of sites are well lined.[160]

At present little is often known about the contents of landfill sites or of the nature of the leachates. The original wastes have usually undergone considerable chemical and biological transformation. For the most part, this renders them harmless but the process may produce new chemical compounds of unknown effects. A further problem is that the groundwater in the vicinity of landfill sites typically remains free of contamination for a considerable period and it is only when the leachates reach the saturated zone that concentrations rise rapidly. Once again, most of the contamination is currently of significance to potable water quality, rather than having a direct impact upon agriculture.

Mine wastes in water

Effluents from mines and quarries may also contaminate surface and ground waters, even in some cases long after the mine has closed. The small disused lead and zinc mine of Cwm Ystwyth, in Wales, still annually discharges 35 tonnes of zinc in solution into a very small river, parts of which remain devoid of fish.[161] In addition to direct heavy metal contamination, problems are further created if mine wastes contain pyrites (iron sulphide) which, when it weathers, produces sulphuric acid. Water leaching through such wastes becomes highly acidic and potentially damaging for crop growth. It is usually associated with raised levels of lead, copper and zinc, and the acidity helps to further leach out these metals.

In many parts of the world mine tailings can also cause physical problems for agriculture. In the Philippines an estimated 140,000 tonnes is discharged daily into eight rivers, causing shallowing of river beds, overflowing of river banks, flooding and deposition of tailings in irrigation canals and paddy fields.[162]

Water borne pathogens

Finally, among these potential hazards, streams and rivers often receive the liquid effluent from sewage works sited along their banks, and this may be a source of pathogen risk for agriculture. A survey of streams and rivers in the UK showed them to be frequently contaminated with salmonella derived from sewage effluent. In one case this was linked to an outbreak of *Salmonella paratyphi* B in both humans and cattle.[163]

Summary

The complexity of effects of heavy metals on plants and animals, and of the interactions between them, makes it difficult to produce a general overview of the hazard they pose to agriculture. Most metals are essential, in trace quantities, for crops and livestock and adverse effects can occur either when they are deficient or in excess. High concentrations may arise naturally in soils, but contamination from mine workings or smelters are usually the most important sources. Lead uptake can be high in the vicinity of roads, as a result of the use of leaded petrol. Toxicities are rare to crops and largely result from high soil levels of copper and zinc.[164] There are several reasons for this damage. Uptake is often relatively small and seasonal, peaking in winter, and in many instances there is a threshold above which uptake is greatly reduced or ceases. Also many plants are able to develop tolerances to heavy metals.

Accumulations of metals also rarely reach levels likely to cause a hazard to livestock or humans. But there are significant exceptions. Acute lead poisoning may occur in livestock from eating contaminated forage but more important routes are the direct ingestion of soil and consumption of contaminated feedstuffs. Copper poisoning of sheep and cattle can be caused by pig slurry applied to pastures. But the most serious hazard to livestock comes from cadmium and selenium, resulting from grazing pastures overlying soils high in these metals. Livestock are also affected by synergistic interactions between a number of heavy metals. In particular, naturally high molybdenum levels in the soil can induce copper deficiency in cattle and sheep. Such soils occur in many countries, although in restricted localities.

Human beings can be affected by the lead contained in food crops, particularly winter vegetables, but the most serious hazard to humans, as for livestock, is cadmium. In the 1950s in Japan severe poisoning arose from feeding on rice containing 1 ppm Cd derived from industrially contaminated irrigation water. Cadmium levels are presently high in foods in a number of restricted locations in Japan, the USA and the UK and in some developing countries.

The second major source of land pollution is the application of sewage sludge. Despite the obvious potential hazards, in practice the damage caused is slight and there are few records of toxicity to crops or livestock. Heavy metal contamination is not as great a threat from this source as from the legacy of past mining and smelting activity, although long-term application of sludge can result in a heavy accumulation. Similarly there is little evidence of damage to crops and livestock from pesticides or other compounds contained in sludge. The threat from pathogens is probably greater. Salmonella and the beef tapeworm can be transmitted in this way but the number of cases of animal or human infection is small. There are, however, reports of higher incidence of gastrointestinal illnesses in workers applying sewage sludge to land. The most serious consequences of using domestic sewage appear to have occurred from the use of largely untreated effluent and waste water for irrigation, particularly for vegetables and salad crops. This has been implicated in outbreaks of typhoid in Chile and of cholera and helminth worms in Israel.

For the most part these are all long standing problems for which prevention and remedies are well known. A more recent concern has been the growing contamination by organic chemical compounds both of sewage sludge and of surface and groundwaters that may be used for irrigation. They include organic solvents and various pesticides. As yet, though, there is no evidence of damage to crops or livestock

References

1 Brady, N., *The Nature and Property of Soils* (New York: Macmillan, 1984).
2 Brady, N., 1984, *op.cit.*; Underwood, E.J., *Trace Elements in Human and Animal Nutrition*, 4th edn (New York: Academic Press, 1977); Underwood, E.J. "The incidence of trace element deficiency diseases", *Phil. Trans. R. Soc. Lond. B* **294** (1981) pp. 3–8.
3 Bradshaw, A.D. and Chadwick, M.J., *The Restoration of Land* (Oxford: Blackwell Scientific Publications, 1980).
4 Webb, J.S., Thornton, I., Howarth, R.J., Thompson, M. and Lowenstein, P.L., *The Wolfson Geochemical Atlas of England and Wales* (Oxford: Oxford University Press, 1980).
5 McNeal, J.M., "Regional-scale geochemical mapping in the United States", in: Thornton, I., (ed.), *Proceedings of the 1st International Symposium on Geochemistry and Health* (London: Science Reviews Ltd, 1986).
6 Piric, S. and Mashimovic, Z., "Methodology for geochemical mapping

in Yugoslavia", in: Thornton (ed.), 1986, *op. cit.*

7   Thornton, I. "Soil-plant-animal interactions in relation to the incidence of trace element disorders in grazing livestock", in: Suttle, N.F., Allen, W.M., Linklater, K.A. and Weiner, G. (eds), *Trace Elements in Animal Production and Veterinary Practice*, Occasional Publ. no.7 (London: British Society of Animal Production, 1983).

8   Borlase, W., quoted in Thornton, I., Abrahams, P.W., Culbard, E., Rother, J.A.P. and Olson, B.H., "The interaction between geochemical and pollutant metal sources in the environment: implications for the community", in: Thornton, I. and Howarth, R. (ed.), *Applied Geochemistry in the 1980s* (London: Graham and Trotman Ltd, 1986).

9   Matthews, H. and Thornton, I., "Seasonal and species variation in the content of cadmium and associated metals in pasture plants at Shipham", *Plant and Soil* 66 (1982) pp. 181–93.

10 Farey, J., *A General View of the Agriculture and Minerals of Derbyshire* vol. 2 (London: Board of Agriculture, 1817).

11 Farey, J., *A General View of the Agriculture and Minerals of Derbyshire* vol. 1 (London: Board of Agriculture, 1811).

12 Thornton, I., Abrahams, P.W., Culbard, E., Rother, J.A.P. and Olson, B.H., "The interaction between geochemical and pollutant metal sources in the environment: implications for the community", in: Thornton, I. and Howarth, R.J. (eds.), 1986, *op. cit.*

13 Hedgecock, G.G., "Injury by smelter smoke in southeastern Tennesse", *Wash. Acad. Sci. J.* 4 (1914) pp. 70–71; Thomas, M.D., "The effects of air pollution on plants & animals", in: Goodman, G.T., Edwards, R.W. and Lanbert, J.M. (eds.), *Ecology and The Industrial Society*, Special Symposium British Ecol. Soc. 5 (New York: John Wiley and Sons, 1965).

14 Harkins, W.D. and Swain, R.E., "The determination of arsenic and other solid constituents of smelter smoke, with a study of effects of high stacks and large condensing flues", *J. Am. Chem. Soc.* 29 (1907) pp. 970–98.

15 Haywood, J.K., "Injury to vegetation and animal life by smelter fumes", *J. Am. Chem. Soc.* 29 (1907) pp. 998–1009.

16 CDC, 1987. "Reduction of children's arsenic exposure following relocation – Mill Creek, Montana", *MMWR* 36 (1987) pp. 505–507.

17 Hutchinson, T.C., "The ecological consequences of acid discharges from industrial smelters", in: D'Itri, F. (ed.), *Acid Precipitation. Effects on Ecological Systems* (Michigan: Ann Arbor Science Publications, 1982).

18 David, P., "Arsenic and jobs trade-off", *Nature* 304 (1983) p. 200.

19 Thornton, I., "Geochemistry applied to agriculture" in: Thornton, I. (ed.), *Applied Environmental Geochemistry* (London: Academic Press, 1983).

20 Alloway, B.J. and Davies, B.E., "Heavy metal content of plants growing on soils contaminated by lead mining", *J Agric. Sci., Camb.* 76 (1971) pp. 321–3.

21 Matthews, and Thornton, 1982, *op. cit.*

22 Wainwright, S.J. and Woolhouse, H.W. "Physiological mechanisms of heavy metal tolerance in plants", in: Chadwick, M.J. and Goodman, G.T. (eds), *The Ecology of Resource Degradation and Renewal* (Oxford: Blackwell Scientific Publ., 1975); Bradshaw, M.D., "Populations of *Agrostis tenuis* resistant to lead and zinc poisoning", *Nature* 169 (1952) pp. 1098.

23 Wainwright and Woolhouse, 1975, *op. cit.*

24 Delas, J., "The toxicity of copper accumulating in soils", *Agrochimica* 7 (1963) p. 258; Webber, J., "Effects of toxic metals in sewage on crops", *Water Pollution Control* (1972) pp. 405–413.

25 Lewis, G., "Geochemistry and animal health", in: Thornton, I. and Howarth, R.J. (eds), *Applied Geochemistry in the 1980s* (London: Graham and Trotman, 1986).

26 Mills, C.F., Campbell, J.K., Bremner, I. and Quarterman, J., "The influence of dietary composition on the toxicity of cadmium, copper, zinc and lead to animals", in: *Inorganic Pollution and Agriculture*, MAFF Reference Book no.326 (London: HMSO, 1980).

27 Ng, A., and Patterson, C.C., "Natural concentrations of lead in ancient Arctic and Antarctic ice", *Geochem. Cosmochim. Acta* 45 (1981) pp. 2109–21; Murozumi, M., Chow, T.J. and Patterson, C., "Chemical concentrations of pollutant lead aerosols, terrestrial dusts and sea salts, in Greenland and Antarctic Snow Strata", *Geochem. Cosmochim. Acta* 33 (1969) pp. 1247–94.

28 RCEP, *Lead in the Environment*, Royal Commission on Environmental Pollution (London: HMSO, 1983).

29 Chamberlain, A.C., "Fallout of lead and uptake by crops", *Atmosph. Environ.* 17 (1983) pp. 693–706.

30 Davies, B.E., "Base metal mining and heavy metal contamination of agricultural land in England and Wales", in: *Inorganic Pollution and Agriculture*, MAFF Reference Book no. 326 (London: HMSO, 1980).

31 RCEP, 1983, *op. cit.*

32 Chamberlain, 1983, *op. cit.*; Davies, B.E. and Roberts, L.J., "Heavy metals in soils and radish in a mineralised limestone area of Wales, Gt Britain", *Sci. Total Environ.* 4 (1975) pp. 249–61; Davies, B.E., Conway, D. and Holt, S., "Lead pollution of London soils: a potential restriction on their use for growing vegetables", *J. Agric. Sci., Camb.* 93 (1979) pp. 749–52.

33 RCEP, 1983, *op. cit.*

34 Roberts, T.M., Gizyn, W. and Hutchinson, T.C., "Lead contamination of air, soil, vegetation and people in the vicinity of secondary lead smelters", in: Hemphill, D.D. (ed.), *Trace Substances and Environmental Health VIII* (Columbia: University of Missouri Press, 1974).

35 RCEP, 1983, *op. cit.*

36 Smith, W.H., "Lead contamination of the roadside ecosystem", *J. Air. Pollut. Control Assoc.* 26 (1976) pp. 753–66; MARC, *Biological*

Monitoring, Monitoring and Assessment Research Centre, and Global Environmental Monitoring System, MARC Report No. 32 (London: Kings College, 1986).

37 MARC, 1986, *op. cit.*; Thornton, I. and Abrahams, P., "Historical records of metal pollution in the environment", in: Nriagu, J.O. (ed.), *Changing Metal Cycles and Human Health* (Berlin, Dahlem Konferanzen: Springer Verlag, 1984).

38 Roberts et al., 1974, *op. cit.*

39 Chamberlain, 1983, *op. cit.*

40 Davis, R.D. and Beckett, P.H.T., "The use of young plants to detect metal accumulations in soils", *Water Pollution Control* 77 (1978) pp. 193–205, 206–210.

41 Rains, D.W., "Lead accumulation by wild oats (*Avena fatua*) in a contaminated area", *Nature* 233 (1971) pp. 210–211.

42 Thornton and Abrahams, 1984, *op. cit.*

43 Rains, 1971, *op. cit.*

44 RCEP, 1983, *op. cit.*; Thornton and Abrahams, 1984, *op. cit.*; Steward, W.L. and Allcroft, R., "Lameness and poor thriving in lambs on farms in old lead mining areas in the Pennines, Field investigations", *Vet. Rec.* 68 (1956) pp. 723–8; Harbourne, J.F. and Watkinson, J., "An unusual outbreak of lead poisoning in calves", *Vet. Rec.* 83 (1968) pp. 515–17; Clegg, F.G. and Rylands, J.M., "Osteoporosis and hydronephrosis of young lambs following the ingestion of lead", *J. Comp. Path.* 76 (1966) pp. 15–22.

45 Thornton, 1983, *op. cit.*

46 *Farmers Weekly* (London), Nov–Dec 1989, *passim.*

47 RCEP, 1983, *op. cit.*

48 RCEP, 1983, *op. cit.*

49 RCEP, 1983, *op. cit.*

50 RCEP, 1983, *op. cit.*; United Nations Environmental Program, *Environmental Data Report* (Oxford: Blackwell, 1988).

51 Nriagu, J.O. and Pacyna, J.M., "Quantitative assessment of worldwide contamination of air, water and soils by trace metals", *Nature* 333 (1988) pp. 134–9.

52 Nriagu and Pacyna, 1988, *op. cit.*

53 Unwin, R.J. "Copper in pig slurry: some effects and consequences of spreading on grassland", in: MAFF, 1980, *op. cit.*

54 MAFF, *Survey of Copper and Zinc in Food*, Food Surveillance Paper no. 5 (London: HMSO, 1981).

55 Wong, M.H. and Cheung, Y.H., "Heavy metal concentrations in caterpillars fed with waste-grown vegetables", *Agric. Wastes* 18 (1986) pp. 61–8.

56 Curry, J.P., Cotton, D.C.F., Bolger, T. and O'Brien, V., "Effects of landspread animal manures on the fauna of grassland", in: Gasser, J.K.R. (ed.), *Effluents from Livestock* (London: Appl. Science Publ., 1980).

57 Underwood, 1977, *op. cit.*

58 Underwood, 1977, *op. cit.*

59 MAFF, 1981, *op. cit.*

60 MAFF, 1981, *op. cit.*

61 Mills et al., 1980, *op. cit.*

62 Underwood, 1977, *op. cit.*

63 Gracey, J.F. and Todd, J.R., "Chronic copper poisoning in sheep following the use of copper sulphate as a molluscide", *Br. Vet. J.* **116** (1960) pp. 405–408; Shaper, F. and Lutje, F., "Copper poisoning in sheep and cattle after the control of fruit tree pests by copper sulphate solution", *Vet. Bull.* **1** (1931) pp. 172–73.

64 Underwood, 1977, *op. cit.*

65 WHO, *Trace Elements in Human Nutrition*, Technical Report Series No. 532 (Geneva: WHO, 1973).

66 MAFF, 1981, *op. cit.*

67 Matthews and Thornton, 1982. *op. cit.*; Thornton and Abraham, 1984, *op. cit.*

68 Thornton et al., 1986, *op. cit.*

69 Nriagu and Pacyna, 1988, *op. cit.*

70 Chumbley, C.G. and Unwin, R.J., "Cadmium and lead content of vegetable crops grown on land with a history of sewage sludge application", *Environ. Poll. Series B* **4** (1982) pp. 231–237.

71 Matthews and Thornton, 1982, *op. cit.*

72 Martin, M.H., Coughtrey, P.J., Shales, S.W. and Little, P., "Aspects of airborne cadmium contamination of soils and natural vegetation", in: MAFF, 1980, *op. cit.*

73 Page, A.L., El-Amanny, M.M. and Chang, A.L. "Cadmium in the environment and its entry into terrestial food chain crops", in: Foulkes, E.C. (ed.), *op. cit.*

74 Underwood, 1977, *op. cit.*

75 Matthews and Thornton, 1982, *op. cit.*

76 Nomiyama, K., "The chronic toxicity of cadmium: influence of environmental and other variables", in: Foulkes, E.C. (ed.), 1986, *op. cit.* Bernard, A. and Lauwerys, R. "Effects of cadmium exposure in humans", in: Foulkes, *op. cit.*; Reilly, C., *Metal Contamination of Food* (London: Applied Science Publ. Ltd, 1980).

77 Bernard et al, 1986, *op. cit.*; Foulkes, E.C., *Absorption of cadmium*, in: Foulkes, 1986, *op. cit.*

78 Suzuki, S., Djuangshi, N., Hyodo, K. and Soemarwoto, O., "Cadmium, copper and zinc in rice produced in Java", *Arch. Env. Contam. Toxicol.* **9** (1980) pp. 437–49; Asami, T., in: Nriagu, J.O. (ed.), *Changing Metal Cycles and Human Health* (Berlin: Springer, 1988).

79 Feeney, S., Peterson, R., Zenz, D.R. and Lue-Hing, C., *Natural survey of the metals cont. of seven vegetable species*, Dept. of Research and Development, Report no. 84–4 (Chicago, Illinois: Metropolitan Sanitary Dist. of Greater Chicago, 1984).

80 Bartop, D. and Strehlow, C.D., "Cadmium and health in Shipham", *The Lancet* ii (1982) pp. 1394–5; Thornton and Abraham, 1984, *op. cit.*

81 Foulkes, 1986, *op. cit.*

82 Anon, "Cadmium: Commission keeps close eye on health risks", *Europe Environ.*, **292** (1987) p. 4.

83 Nriagu, J.O., "A silent epidemic of environmental metal poisoning", *Environ. Poll.* **50** (1988) pp. 139–61.

84 Suzuki et al., 1980, *op. cit.*

85 Reilly, A. and Reilly, C., *Med. J. Zambia* **6** (1972) pp. 125–7.

86 Thoresby, P. and Thornton, I., in: Hemphill, J.J. (ed.), *Trace Substances in Environmental Health* (Colombia: Univ. of Missouri, 1979).

87 Porter, E.K. and Peterson, P.J., "Arsenic accumulation by plants on mine waste (UK)", *Sci. Total Environ.* **4** (1975) pp. 365–71.

88 Thomas, R., "Arsenic pollution arising from mining activities in south-west England", in: MAFF, 1980, *op. cit.* Lisk, D.J., "Trace metals in soils, plants and animals", *Adv. Agron.* **24** (1972) pp. 267–325.

89 Elsokkary, I.H., "Contamination of soils and plants by mercury as influenced by the proximity to industries in Alexandria, Egypt", *Sci. Total Environ.* **23** (1982) pp. 55–60.

90 Bull, K.R., Roberts, R.D., Inskip, M.J. and Goodman, G.T., "Mercury concentrations in soil, grass, earthworms and small mammals near an industrial emission source", *Environ. Pollut.* (Series A) **12** (1977) pp. 135–40; Huckerbee, J.W., Sanz Diaz, F., Jansen, S.A. and Solomon, J., "Distribution of mercury in vegetation at Almaden, Spain", *Environ. Pollut. (Series A)* **30** (1983) pp. 211–24.

91 WHO, *Evaluation of Certain Food Additives and the Contaminants: Mercury, Lead and Cadmium*, Technical Report Series 505 (Geneva: WHO, 1972).

92 Kubota, J., Allaway, W.H., Carter, D.L., Cary, E.E., "Selenium in crops in the United States in relation to selenium responsive diseases of animals", *J. Food Agric. Chem.* **15** (1967) pp. 448–53; Shamberger, R.J., Tytko, S.A. and Willis, C.E., "Antioxidants and cancer. Part VI. Selenium and age-adjusted human cancer mortality", *Arch. Environ. Health.* **31** (1976) pp. 231–5.

93 Lisk, 1972, *op. cit.*

94 Mitchel, R.L., "Cobalt and nickel in soils and plants", *Soil Sci.* **60** (1945) pp. 63–70; Hunter, J.G. and Vergaro, O., "Nickel toxicity in plants", *Ann. Appl. Biol.* **39** (1952) p. 279.

95 Thomas, 1980, *op. cit.*

96 Arora, S.P., "Livestock problems related to geochemistry in India including selenium toxicity and goiter", in: Thornton (ed.), *op. cit.*; Singh, M. and Kumar, P., "Se distribution in soils of bioclimatic zones of Haryana", *J. Ind. Soc. Soil Sci.* **24** (1956) pp. 62–7.

97 Walsh, T., Fleming, G.A., O'Connor, R. and Sweeney, A., "Selenium toxicity associated with an Irish soil series", *Nature* **168** (1951) p. 881.

98 NAS, *Water Quality Criteria* EPA. R3. 73.003. Marl. (Washington:

NAS, 1972).

99 Mikkelsen, R.L., Page, A.L. and Chang, A.C., "Geochemistry and health in the United States: a recent occurrence with selenium", in: Thornton (ed.), 1986, *op. cit.*

100 NAS, 1972, *op. cit.*

101 Mills et al., 1980, *op. cit.*

102 Mills et al., 1980, *op. cit.*

103 Lewis, 1986, *op. cit.*

104 Ferguson, W.S., Lewis, A.H. and Watson, S.J., "The teart pastures of Somerset. I. The cause and cost of teartness", *J. Agric. Sci. Camb.* **33** (1943) pp. 44–51.

105 Thornton, 1983, *op. cit.*; Alloway, B.J., "Copper and molybdenum in swayback pastures", *J. Agric. Sci. Camb.* **80** (1983) pp. 521–4.

106 Barshad, I., "Molybdenum content of pasture plants in relation to toxicity to cattle", *Soil Sci.* **66** (1948) pp. 187–95; Britton, J.W. and Goss, H., "Chronic molybdenum poisoning in cattle", *J. Amer. Vet. Med. Assoc.* **108** (1946) pp. 176–8.

107 Mills et al., 1980, *op. cit.*

108 Leech, A., Howarth, R.J., Thornton, I. and Lewis, "Incidence of bovine copper deficiency in England and the Welsh Borders", *Vet. Record* **111** (1982) pp. 203–204.

109 Arora, 1985, *op. cit.*

110 Lewis, 1986, *op. cit.*

111 WHO, *Selenium*, Environmental Health Criteria no. 58 (Geneva: WHO, 1987).

112 Bray, F., "Part II Agriculture", in: Needham, J., *Science and Civilisation in China, vol 6. Biology and Biological Technology* (Cambridge: Cambridge Univ. Press, 1984).

113 Shuval, H.I., Adin, A., Fattal, B., Ravitz, E. and Yekatiel, P., *Wastewater Irrigation in Developing Countries*, World Bank Technical Paper no. 51 (Washington: The World Bank, 1986).

114 Shuval et al., 1986, *op. cit.*

115 Fuller, G.W., *Broad Irrigation in Sewage Disposal* (New York: McGraw-Hill, 1912).

116 RCEP, 1985, *Managing Waste: The Duty of Care*, Royal Commission on Environmental Pollution, (London: HMSO, 1985); House of Commons, *The Effects of Pesticides on Human Health* vol. 1, House of Commons Select Committee on Agriculture (London: HMSO, 1985).

117 EPA, *Standards for the Disposal of Sewage Sludge*, 40 CFR. Parts 257 & 503, Part II (Washington D C: EPA, 1989). EPA, *Guidance for Writing Case-by-Case Permit Requirements to Municipal Sewage Sludge*, Office of Water Enforcement and Permits (Washington DC: EPA, 1990).

118 ENDS, "Sewage sludge incineration to make a comeback in Yorkshire", **154** (1987) pp. 7–8.

119 House of Lords, *Sewage Sludge in Agriculture* Report of House of Lords Select Committee on European Communities Session 1983–84, 1st

Report (London: HMSO, 1983).

120 EPA, *Environmental Regulations and Technology, Use and Disposal of Municipal Wastewater*, Office of Water (Washington DC: EPA, 1989); House of Lords, 1983, *op. cit.*

121 RCEP, *Agriculture and Pollution* 7th Report, Royal Commission on Environmental Pollution (London: HMSO, 1979).

122 EPA, 1989, *op. cit.*; House of Lords, 1983, *op. cit.*

123 EPA, 1989, *op. cit.*

124 Webber, J., "Metals in sewage sludge applied to land and their effects on crops", in: MAFF, 1980, *op. cit.*

125 Webber, 1980, *op. cit.*

126 Webber, 1980, *op. cit.*

127 Sanders, J.R., McGrath, S.P. and Adams, T. McM, "Zinc, copper and nickel concentrating in the grass grown on sewage sludge – contaminated soils of different pH", *J. Sci. Food Agric.* **37** (1986) pp. 961–8; Williams, J.H., "Effects of soil pH on the toxicity of zinc and nickel to vegetable crops", in: MAFF, 1980, *op. cit.*

128 Webber, 1980, *op. cit.*; Gaynor, J.D. and Halstead, R.L., "chemical and plant extractability of metals and plant growth on soils amended with sludge", *Can. J. Soil Sci.* **56** (1976) pp. 1–8.

129 Sabey, B.R. and Hart, W.E., "Lead application of sewage sludge. I. Effects on growth and chemical composition of plants", *J. Environ. Qual.* **4** (1975) pp. 252–6; Kirkham, M.B., "Trace elements in corn grown on a long-term sludge disposal site", *Environ. Sci. Tech.* **9** (1975) pp. 265–8; Linnman, L., Andersson, A., Nilson, K.O., Lind, B., Kjellstrom, T. and Friberg, L., "Cadmium uptake by wheat from sewage sludge used as a plant nutrient source", *Arch. Environ. Health* **27** (1973) pp. 45–7.

130 Delgarno, A.C. and Mills, C.F., "Retention by sheep of copper from aerobic digests of pig faecal slurry", *J. Agric. Sci. Camb.* **85** (1975) pp. 11–18.

131 Davis, R.D., Carlton-Smith, C.H., Stark, J.H. and Campbell, J.A., "Distribution of metals in grassland soils following surface applications of sewage sludge", *Environ. Poll. A.* **49** (1988) pp. 99–115; Thornton, 1983, *op. cit.*; McGrath, L.D., Poole, D.B.R., Fleming, G.A. and Sinnott, J., "Soil ingestion by grazing sheep", *Ir. J. Agric. Res.* **21** (1982) pp. 135–45.

132 RCEP, 1979, *op. cit.*

133 McGrath, S.P., Brookes, P.C. and Giller, K.E., "Effects of potentially toxic metals: soil derived from part applications of sewage sludge on nitrogen fixation by *Trifolium repens, Soil Biol.*" *Biochem.* **20** (1988) pp. 415–24; Giller, K.E., McGrath, S.P. and Hirsch, P.R., "Absence of nitrogen fixation in clover grown on soil subject to long-term contamination with heavy metals is due to survival of only ineffective rhizobium", *Soil. Biol. Biochem.* **21** (1989) pp. 841–8.

134 ENDS, "Organochlorine levels in sewage sludge", **114** (1984) p. 5.

135 ENDS, "Organic chemicals in sewage emerge on pollution agenda", **148**

(1987) p. 5–6.
136 Davies, R.D., Howell, K., Oake, R.J. and Wilcox, P., "Significance of organic contamination in sewage sludges and on agricultural land", paper presented to international conference on environmental contamination, Imperial College, London, July 10–13, 1984.
137 RCEP, 1979, *op. cit*; HL, 1983, *op. cit.*
138 HL, 1983, *op. cit.*
139 HL, 1983, *op. cit.*; Ottolenghi, A.O. and Hamparian, V.V., "Multiyear study of sludge application to farmland: prevalance of bacterial enteric pathogens and antibody status of farm families", *Appl. and environ. Microbiol.* **53** (1987) pp. 1118–24.
140 Ayanwale, L.F., Kaneene, J.M.B., Sherman, D.M. and Robinson, R.A., "Investigation of *Salmonella* infection in goats fed corn silage grown on land fertilised with sewage sludge", *Appl. and environ. Microbiol.* **40** (1980) pp. 285–6; Jack, E.L. and Hepper, P.T., "An Outbreak of *Salmonella typhimurium* infection in cattle associated with the spreading of slurry", *Vet. Rec.* **84** (1969) p. 196.
141 MAFF, 1983, in: HL, 1983, *op. cit.*
142 Grabow, W.O.K., "The virology of waste water treatment", *Water Res.* **2** (1968) pp. 675–701; Craun, G.F., "Microbiology – waterborne outbreaks", *J. Water Pollut. Control Fed.* **46** (1974) pp. 1384–95.
143 WRC, in: HL, 1983, *op. cit.*
144 Blamire, R.V., Goodhand, R.H. and Taylor, K.C., "A review of some animal diseases encountered at meat inspections in England and Wales. 1969–1978", *Vet. Rec.* **106** (1980) pp. 195–9.
145 HL, 1983, *op. cit.*
146 MacPherson, R., Mitchell, G.B.B. and McCance, C.B., letter, *Vet. Rec.*, 18 February (1978) pp. 156–7.
147 Pike, in: HL, 1983, *op. cit.*
148 Burge, W.D. and Marsh, P.B., "Infectious disease hazards of land-spreading sewage wastes", *J. Environ. Qual.* **7** (1978) pp. 1–9.
149 Shuval et al., 1986, *op. cit.*
150 Burge and Marsh, 1978, *op. cit.*; IEHO, in: HL, 1983, *op. cit.*
151 Shuval et al., 1986, *op. cit.*
152 Shuval et al., 1986, *op. cit.*; Schalscha, E.B., Vergara, I., Schirado, T. and Moraks, M., "Nitrate movement in a Chilean agricultural area irrigated with untreated sewage water", *J. Environ. Qual.* **8** (1979) pp. 27–30.
153 CF, 1987, *Groundwater Protection* (Washington DC: The Conservation Foundation, 1987).
154 ENDS, "Chlorinated solvents in groundwater: a problem awaiting official action", **141** (1986) pp. 13–5; ENDS, "Solvent leaks from metal industries contaminate Birmingham, Coventry aquifers", ENDS **157** (1988) pp. 6–7.
155 RCEP, 1979, *op. cit.*
156 Shainberg, I. and Oster, S.D., *Quality of Irrigation Water* (Bet Dagan, Israel: International Irrigation Information Centre, 1978).

157 HC, 1987, *op. cit.*
158 OTA, *Transportation of Hazardous Materials – State and Local Activities*, Office of Technology Assessment, US Congress (Washington DC: US Government Printing Office, 1986).
159 CF, 1987, *op. cit.*
160 *Ground Water Monitor*, "New York study says 82% of waste is dumped in landfills that leak", 10 June (1986) p. 92.
161 Bradshaw and Charwick, 1980, *op. cit.*
162 Briones, N.D., "Mining pollution: the case of the Baguio mining district, the Philippines", *Environ. Manage.* 11 (1987) pp. 335–44.
163 Harbourne, J.F., Randall, C.J., Luer, K.W. and Wallace, J.F., "*Salmonella paratyphi B* infection in dairy cows: Part I", *Vet. Rec.* 29 July (1972) pp. 112–4.

10   The Control of Pollution

Pollution diminishes the value of our resources and places burdensome costs on farmers and their families and on society as a whole. We can reduce these costs in several ways. We can act against the pollutants themselves, or to change the circumstances under which damaging effects occur, or against the underlying causes of the problem. We can stop pollution altogether, or we can encourage the adoption of alternative agricultural practices that are low polluting. Thus, control of pollution can be targeted against any or all of the components in the chain we described in the introduction to this book (see Figure 1.1). The actions taken are essentially technological, such as installing a treatment plant to remove nitrates from a domestic water supply or introducing a biological agent to control a pest that does away with the need to use pesticides. But whether they are adopted depends on the presence of knowledge, economic incentives and legal regulations. Farmers' practices and behaviour may be changed by the provision of advice and information, or by incentives in the form of prices, taxes, subsidies or by regulations that enforce change. In practice, effective control of pollution inevitably requires a mix of all three approaches and an integration of different disciplines and sectors.

In this chapter we first review the economic costs of pollution and the value to society and farmers of pollution control. We then discuss the advisory measures, economic incentives and legal regulations that have been, or could be, applied to control agricultural pollution. Lastly we describe examples of control and specific agricultural pollutants that illustrate a number of different approaches. In this and the next chapter we do not aim to provide detailed prescriptions for the control of agricultural pollution. That will require a separate book. Instead we confine ourselves to illustrating some of the key principles of control.

The cost of pollution

Pollution is essentially an economic problem. A pollutant is a contaminant of the environment that, in one way or another, causes us, our resources or our possessions harm. At their most toxic, pollutants kill or produce serious illness; less importantly they may give rise to nuisance or result in a loss of amenity. All of these represent costs, to the individuals who suffer and to society as a whole. There are costs, too, involved in monitoring pollution, in treating polluted effluents and in cleaning up after pollution accidents. However, these costs are not equally born, largely because pollution affects different individuals and groups in different ways. Pollution control is, thus, also a matter of equity and social justice.

Externalities

Sometimes farmers are directly harmed by their own polluting activities. They may fall ill from using pesticides or their water supply may be polluted by the fertilizers they apply to their land. On the highly intensive corn lands of western Nebraska, farmers introduce pesticides and fertilizers directly into the overhead irrigation systems and some leaches down through the soil to contaminate the farm wells which are the farmers' sources of drinking water. Indirectly, and over the long term, the various agricultural practices described in Chapter 7 that are contributing to global warming will have an adverse effect on agricultural production. Again farming households will suffer, not necessarily in this generation but certainly their descendants.

But most of the time those who suffer from pollution are not the polluters. Farmers are harmed by pollutants emitted from industry and, in turn, may harm people who drink water or eat food contaminated with pesticides. Often the costs are borne by the victims, those who directly suffer from the pollutant. But sometimes they are incurred by intermediary agencies or by the community as a whole. Part of the costs of pesticide pollution falls on the government and other agencies responsible for monitoring residues in food. In the case of fertilizer pollution the costs are mostly borne by the consumers of domestic water. As yet, there are few places in the world where there are restrictions on fertilizer use, so that domestic water agencies have to treat the water to remove the nitrate and then pass on the costs to the consumer, even though not all the consumers are at risk: methaemoglobinaemia, for instance, is only likely to occur in infants. Similarly, if damage to crops from ambient sulphur dioxide and nitrogen oxides is to be prevented by reducing emissions from power stations, then the costs will borne by the electricity consumers rather than, as at present, by the farmers.

To some extent, the costs imposed on society by farmers are offset by costs they have to incur. For instance, legal restrictions on the availability and use of pesticides may result in farmers having to use more expensive materials or to take greater care in their application. But as a general rule, the levels of pollutant emissions from agriculture are higher than would be the case if farmers had to bear all the social costs of their activities. In making decisions, farmers attempt to keep their costs to a minimum but since they largely do not perceive pollution as directly, or even indirectly, affecting their farms or their livelihoods, the costs of pollution fall outside their calculations and are thus ignored. In other words, the costs are external costs to the producer of the pollution. An external cost is defined as a cost that "exists when a production or consumption activity induces a direct loss of utility, or an increase in production cost, which does not enter the decision calculus of the controller of the activity."[1]

Polluters can ignore these external costs because there is no requirement or incentive that they match them with corresponding payments. The damage caused is not reflected in market prices and consequently those who suffer from pollution are not compensated.[2] It is a central concern of pollution economics to devise ways that induce or cause producers of pollution to internalize some or all of the external costs in their calculations so that a more equitable balance is struck.

Whose costs?

The private costs of an activity, such as applying a fertilizer, are those incurred by the farmer. To these may then be added the total of external costs that occur because of the activity, for example the extra costs to water consumers and the costs of ill health in infants. This results in the true inclusive social cost of the activity. The consequences are illustrated in the theoretical example in Figure 10.1. Line S represents a private supply curve of the fertilizer industry, and line D the demand for fertilizers from farmers. At price P the industry sells N amount of fertilizer – the supply is equal to the demand. But if external costs are added to produce a true social cost the price at any given quantity will increase. The new supply curve is then S' and the socially desirable outcome is now N^*, where the demand corresponds to the social, not private, costs.[3] The difference between N^* and N represents the excess of fertilizer used because the current market price, P, does not account for the external costs of fertilizer pollution.

Clearly an economic approach to pollution control assumes the costs can be measured, but this is not easy. Attempts have been made to get

Figure 10.1   The impact of the inclusion of social costs of fertilizer use on the supply and demand relationship

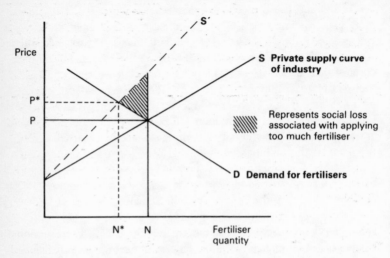

Source: Barbier, E.B., *Economics, Natural-Resource Scarcity and Development. Conventional and Alternative Views* (London: Earthscan Publications, 1989).

approximate figures for the costs of certain classes of pollutants. These are usually based on assigning monetary values to losses of crop yield or to human illnesses or death. Two examples are the costs of pesticide pollution in the USA and the costs of air pollution damage on crops.

Costs of pesticide pollution

Any attempt to put an overall cost on the effects of pesticides on human health and wildlife will necessarily be very crude. Pimentel and colleagues[4] have estimated the total cost of damage due to pesticides in the United States to be US$839 million annually (Table 10.1). The total, however, is based on several contentious assumptions. The $184 million loss because of human pesticide poisoning largely rests on the assumption that 0.5 per cent of all human cancers in the USA are caused by pesticides. As we have seen, there is as yet no clear evidence of cancers arising from pesticide use. The $135 million attributable to honeybee poisoning and reduced pollination is partly based on the known $4 million a year compensation payments for honeybee poisoning but primarily assumes a considerable loss of pollination, particularly in cotton. The pollination losses are estimated at $80 million of costs, despite the fact that not all cotton varieties produce

Table 10.1 Total estimated environmental and social costs for pesticides in the United States

Environmental factor	Total costs ($)
Human pesticide poisonings	184,000,000
Animal pesticide poisonings and contaminated livestock products	12,000,000
Reduced natural enemies and pesticide resistance	287,000,000
Honeybee poisonings and reduced pollination	135,000,000
Losses of crops and trees	70,000,000
Fishery and wildlife losses	11,000,000
Government pesticide pollution	140,000,000
Total	839,000,000

Source: Pimentel, D. et al., "Environmental and social costs of pesticides: a preliminary assessment", *OIKOS* 34 (1980) pp. 126–40.

enhanced yields after good pollination.[5] Finally, the fishery and wildlife losses are estimated partly on the known numbers of fish kills (from all sources), but largely on the costs of monitoring pesticide levels in wildlife. In summary, the known costs are a very small fraction of the total known plus guessed costs. At present these are the best figures available. The true costs may be much greater or much less.

Costs of air pollution damage

One reason why so much early research focused on the relationship between leaf injury to crops and loss of yield was to provide a basis for compensating farmers in the vicinity of large smelters for the damage they claimed they were experiencing (see Chapter 8). Linear relationships were found for wheat, cotton and soybeans grown in the USA and these were then used for computing compensation (Figure 10.2). For instance, in the Sulphur Springs Valley in Arizona about 1.5 per cent of the 8500 hectares of crops were visibly injured by SO_2 each year during the mid-1970s and farmers were compensated accordingly (Box 10.1).

However, as more recent experiments and field studies have shown, most reductions in yield probably occur without signs of visible injury (see Chapter 8). There are now several estimates of the costs of such yield losses. In the USA, the National Crop Loss Assessment Network, using estimates of damage caused by ozone, has suggested an annual average crop loss of at least 2–5 per cent, and perhaps even 5–10 per cent (Figure 10.3). These are substantial losses. A 25 per cent

Figure 10.2 Relationship of typical cotton leaf injury in the field to actual compensation for yield loss

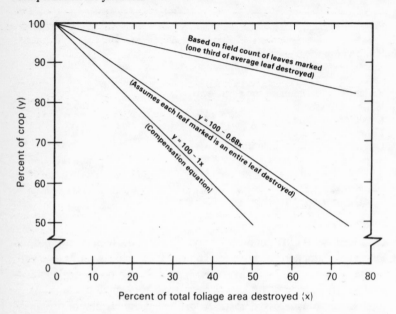

Source: Haase, E.F., Morgan, G.W. and Salem, J.A., *Field Surveys of SO₂ Injury to Crops and Assessment of Economic Damage*, report to 73rd Annual Meeting of the Air Pollution Control Association (1980) Montreal, Quebec.

reduction in ozone would benefit US society, both producers and consumers, by $1.6–$1.9 billion (at 1982 prices); but a 25 per cent increase would cost a further $1.9–$2.3 billion.[6] In all, current levels of ozone pollution are thought to cost the economy in excess of $3 billion in lost beans, maize, wheat and peanut crop productivity.[7] An estimate for the 11 European OECD countries, similarly based upon the impact of a single pollutant – this time SO_2 – put the loss to agriculture in those countries at $0.5 billion in 1981.[8]

These calculations, though, do not account for the effects of other pollutants, nor for the impact upon crop pests and diseases. In the Netherlands combinations of pollutants that exceed effect thresholds, namely ozone, sulphur dioxide and hydrogen fluoride, have been estimated to reduce total crop volume (a combination of price and production levels) by about 5 per cent annually, equivalent to 640 million guilders (US$320 million).[9] But these costs are not borne by producers, as yield reductions are compensated by higher prices. Reducing pollution to background levels would result in consumers

Box 10.1   Method for calculation of compensation for cotton, wheat and soybean growers in Arizona

---

A   Extensive research has demonstrated a linear relationship between a loss in crop yield and a loss in leaf area due to SO_2, where

$$y = a - bx$$

y = yield
a = intercept
b = slope (the percentage yield loss for each additional 1 per cent increase in total foliage destroyed)
x = foliage area destroyed (percentage of total production)

B   To assess economic damage the following equation is used to determine monetary value of the crop loss

$$y = 100 - bx$$

y = % of crop harvested
x = % of leaves marked by SO_2 of total leaves
b = assumed to be one (lower values found in experiments)

Thus if a farmer has had 5 per cent of his total leaves marked, he is assumed to have harvested 95 per cent of a crop and will be compensated for the balance. The settlement figure is a monetary value that is generally several times the actual amount of loss. This is because the x value includes all leaves marked, even those only slightly marked, and the b value is assumed to be one.

Source: Haase, E.F. et al., 1980, *op. cit.*

experiencing a net benefit equivalent to this cost of 640 million guilders. However, these calculations may be an underestimate as they assume additive effects of pollutants and do not include ammonia, nitrogen dioxide and the effects on pests and diseases. Mixtures of pollutants interact in a complex fashion with pests and diseases, mostly increasing, but sometimes also decreasing, their incidence and impact upon the crops. The precise economic costs of this synergy have yet to be quantified, but some preliminary estimates have been made for the losses due to increased aphid attack. The peak mean concentrations of SO_2 found in rural areas of the UK are sufficient to stimulate aphids to exceed the five per ear of grain threshold at which insecticide spraying is recommended, and this incurs a cost equivalent to some five per cent of the cereal crop value.[10]

Losses of yield may also be matched by losses in quality of produce.

Figure 10.3 Predicted yield losses for five crops in the USA using results from open-top chambers as a function of ozone concentration

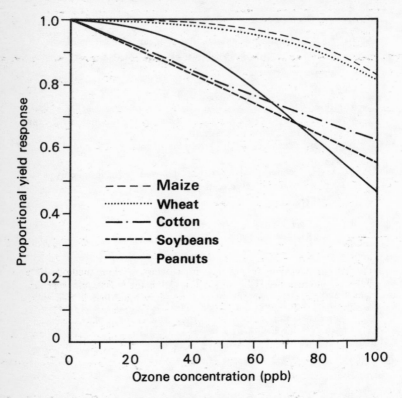

Source: Heck, W.W., "Assessment of crop losses from air pollutants in the United States", in: Mackenzie, J.J. and El-Ashry, M.T. (eds), *Air Pollution's Toll on Forests and Crops* (New Haven: Yale University Press, 1989).

In the 1960s, Californian grape farmers found grapes exposed to ozone tended to be sour.[11] Since then, small changes in the quality of several crops, such as soybean, alfalfa, potato, strawberry and tomato, in the form of protein, oil or vitamin content, have been found. However, these changes have usually been less significant than the yield losses suffered at the same dose of pollutant. Farmers also incur costs because they may have to switch to more pollution-tolerant cultivars. In the case of grasses and potatoes, this may involve a significant trade-off since the tolerant cultivars may yield less well in unpolluted conditions.

The economic costs to society of the gaseous pollutants produced

Box 10.2   Economic value

A number of different ways have been used to estimate the value of a particular resource that has been damaged or destroyed by pollution. Essentially there are three key components to value:

Total economic value = actual use value + option value
+ existence value

The actual use value is the benefit people derive from the resource – anglers fishing in a river, for example. The *option value*, which is more difficult to measure, is a measure of the potential benefit as opposed to the actual present value. It is an expression of peoples' preference for preservation of the environment in relation to their livelihood. Even more difficult is the *existence value*. This measures the value people place on the existence of a particular component of the environment, quite irrespective of whether they use it, or are likely to use it. For example a value can be placed on the existence of the golden eagle or peregrine falcon, simply because people feel such birds have a right to exist.

In effect, these definitions of value assume that it is possible to measure peoples' *willingness to pay* (WTP) for a particular environmental benefit or to prevent an environment loss, or their *willingness to accept* (WTA) compensation to put up with the loss. Various methods have been used to measure WTP and WTA. One is the *hedonic price approach*, which estimates the component of a property price that is due to an environmental factor. For example, it could be used to determine how the value of domestic housing is affected by proximity to an intensive livestock unit. Another approach is the *contingent valuation method* (CVM) in which people are asked how much they would be willing to pay (or accept) in relation to a particular environment resource. A study in Norway asked samples of people the WTP to prevent harm to freshwater fish by acid rain. The WTP was in the form of a special income tax – and the average "bid" was 800 Norwegian krone per capita. Given a population of 3.1 million this works out at a national economic value of 2.5 billion krone. Since the calculated user values total 1 billion krone this gives an implied existence value of about 1.5 billion krone.

Source: Pearce, D.W. and Turner, R.K., *Economics of Natural Resources and the Environment* (New York: Harvester Wheatsheaf, 1990); Strand, J., *Valuation of Freshwater Fish as a Public Good in Norway* (University of Oslo: Dept. of Economics, 1981).

by agriculture have not been quantified. But agriculture's 45 per cent contribution to methane emissions, 10–25 per cent to nitrous oxide and 90 per cent to ammonia, is clearly imposing significant present and future costs arising from acidification, depletion of the ozone layer and global warming. Estimating these costs is very difficult (Box 10.2). Easier to quantify are the costs of abatement. In the Netherlands, the recently formulated Acidification Abatement Plan has determined the abatement costs for controlling ammonia, nitrogen oxides, sulphur dioxide and volatile compounds emitted from industry, traffic and agriculture. By 1994 the control of ammonia emissions is expected annually to cost 730 million guilders (US $305 million) alone, out of a total cost of 1.48 billion guilders for all air pollution control.[12]

Advisory measures

Advisory measures have long formed the backbone of policies to control agricultural pollution. They rely on the voluntary actions of farmers, yet they are favoured by policy makers because they are cheap and give administrations freedom to manoeuvre and are adaptable – they can be changed easily as new knowledge or circumstances come to light. There are two important components of advisory measures – the information or message itself, and the means by which it is delivered to farmers.

Formulation and delivery of advice

Advice given to farmers on the control of agricultural contamination and pollution has largely been in the form of suggested compliance with good agricultural or farm practice. Examples include recommended rates of application of pesticides or specifications for slurry storage tanks, or for integrated plans designed to control all forms of pollution while sustaining yields – such as Water Catchment Plans. As this advice generally does not have the weight of economic incentives or legal sanctions, the likelihood of uptake depends upon the style and efficiency of the institution delivering the advice. Most governments have agricultural extension services and employ extension agents to take new technologies and knowledge out to farmers. These systems are further supplemented by advisory services run by non-governmental organizations and private commercial companies. The advice or technology can be delivered in person to a farm by an extension agent or it may be published in the media through the use of radio, television, the press or magazines.

Generally, extension systems work best when they are less concerned with transferring a technology in full from a research station to a farmer, and more involved in creating a constructive dialogue with farmers. Non or low-polluting technologies must fit each farmer's livelihood and farming system, and farmers and their households are inevitably the best judge of new practices. A partnership, in both problem-finding and problem-solving is essential if long-term solutions are to be found. Some of the most effective extension systems are those in which a message about, say, low-polluting agriculture is transferred in the context of farmer-led advice. In such farmer to farmer extension, extension workers act more as facilitators and moderators rather than as imposers of new technologies.[13] In the British agricultural revolution of the eighteenth and nineteenth centuries, there was no national agricultural ministry – all knowledge and advice on new rotation systems, new crops and new livestock breeds was transferred by farmers extending their advice to others through tours, open-days, publications and on-farm demonstration.[14] Today, rural people's knowledge is increasingly being sought by extension advisors to ensure better partnerships and greater success.[15]

Farming households, though, are not the only people who need targeting for advice. The consumer is an important element as is the demand for food produce. As we have seen in Chapter 3, the selection of fruit and vegetables in supermarkets by consumers allows for the rejection of cosmetically-imperfect produce. Educating consumers to understand that oranges that are rusty or scarred on the outside are tasty and wholesome could make a significant difference to the perceived need on the farm to apply extra pesticides in order to ensure that produce is graded at the highest, and therefore most profitable, level.

But advisory measures whether targeted against the farmer or consumer are rarely enough on their own. Extension workers are often specialists, rarely trained to appreciate the complete farm and livelihood system as experienced by the farmer. And extension systems may be poorly integrated with other government departments, resulting in the delivery of contradictory advice. Many focus on the contact, or progressive farmer, to the exclusion of those who may be the greatest contributors to contamination or pollution. Inevitably, too, whether the target be the farmer or consumer, there are powerful economic incentives working in the opposite direction. It is for these reasons that policy makers also turn to economic incentives and legal regulations.

Economic solutions and incentives

Economic approaches to pollution control are primarily designed to ensure the polluter bears the cost of the pollution damage and/or the costs incurred in controlling the pollution - the abatement costs. In other words, the costs are internalized, and hence become part of the normal (usually private) costs of agricultural food and non-food produce. This is the principle by which the polluter pays (Box 10.3). It implies that the free input to farming – the clean, unpolluted environment – is priced and treated as if it is similar to labour or capital costs. The effect of this internalization is threefold:[16]

1 The costs of production rise and so output of the polluting product or activity declines.
2 The polluter may pass on part of the increased cost of production to the consumer in the form of higher prices – the consumer pays too.
3 The polluter may switch to less polluting technologies in an effort to avoid the costs of adding on pollution control to existing technology.

Various economic instruments exist to achieve this internalization. They include free market mechanisms, taxes and charges, subsidies and grants, and transferrable permit and quotas.

Box 10.3 Definition of the Polluter-Pays Principle as accepted by all governments of the OECD in 1972

The principle to be used for allocating costs of pollution prevention and control measures to encourage rational use of scarce environmental resources and to avoid distortions in international trade and investment is the so-called "Polluter-Pays Principle". The Principle means that the polluter should bear the expenses of carrying out the above mentioned measures decided by public authorities to ensure that the environment is in an acceptable state. In other words, the costs of these measures should be reflected in the cost of goods and services which cause pollution in production and/or consumption.

Source: OECD, *Agricultural and Environmental Policies, Opportunities for Integration* (Paris: Organisation for Economic Co-operation and Development, 1989).

Market mechanisms

The first solution is to permit the free operation of markets, without any form of intervention, to solve all pollution problems. Polluters and those receiving the pollution could strike private bargains, with polluters paying compensation in order to be permitted to pollute. But markets are generally imperfect arenas for producing solutions that are both efficient and just.[17] First, it is sometimes difficult to ensure that those who are, or will be, affected are adequately represented in the bargaining process. Sufferers may be unaware they are suffering. Pesticide residues or heavy metals in food may be having a serious chronic effect on individuals without their knowledge. Lead contamination of food, for instance, may be affecting the intelligence of children. It is unlikely that the children will be aware of this and certainly will not be in a position to actively take part in the bargaining process. This problem of representation is even more apparent if the sufferers are from as yet unborn generations – who will be affected by such problems as global warming or loss of the ozone layer.

Assuming the sufferers are well represented, markets will still require, in order to be fair, adequate knowledge on the part of all those engaged in the bargaining process. Thus, unless both sides of the bargain have a good understanding of the impact of each successive marginal unit of pollution produced or abated, then it may be difficult to agree solutions that provide comparable benefits to both sides. Moreover such bargains are essentially political in nature, and information will tend to be misrepresented in the bargaining process. As we have seen in Chapter 1, individual and institutional perceptions of the benefits and costs of polluting activities often override more "objective" information. Polluters are likely to exaggerate the benefits of the activity, for example citing the increased production and vital role in food security of using fertilizers, while the receivers of the pollutants exaggerate their harmful impact suggesting, for instance, that nitrates are the primary cause of gastric cancers.

All bargains and negotiations also involve transaction costs – the costs incurred by both sides in arriving at the bargain. These include the costs of acquiring information, of hiring advisers and specialists, of lobbying and conducting publicity campaigns. As such costs escalate as more interested parties become involved and as the negotiations become more politicized, final bargains are determined more by those who can command the most resources than the merits of the case. Thus, large companies are often in a better position to carry the costs and so are more likely to win. However, in recent years professional lobbying by consumer groups has shown itself to be equally effective. In the case of alar (daminozide) treatment for apples, highly vocal lobbying in the USA, involving major public figures, resulted in a withdrawal of the product. Manufacturers then followed suit in the UK even though the government's Advisory Committee on Pesticides had stated there was no risk involved (see Chapter 3).

Taxes and charges

The alternative to free markets is some form of government intervention, such as the imposition of a tax or charge, that forces external costs to be internalized. Polluters can be taxed directly on their polluting activities, for instance on the basis of their actual emissions to the environment or, less directly, on their outputs or profits. Since taxes on emissions or on inputs are directly related to the polluting activity, they should encourage farmers to adopt less polluting technologies, for example to install slurry treatment units on the farm or to switch to use of organic manures. Much, of course, depends on the level of the tax. Set too low and it may be cheaper to pay the tax than install a new technology; set too high and the level of agricultural output may fall to the point at which farmers become bankrupt.

The use of taxes and charges to reduce agricultural pollution is becoming increasingly common in industrialized countries. Mostly, they have applied to the use of fertilizers or pesticides (Table 10.2). But

Table 10.2   Examples of uses of taxes and charges to control agricultural contamination and pollution

Fertilizer Taxes	
Austria	$0.49 kg/N; $0.14–0.29/kg K or P
Finland	$0.14 kg/P
Norway*	2% + $0.01/kg N; or + $0.05/kg P
Sweden	20% + $0.11/kg N; or + $0.22/kg P
USA: Iowa State	$0.00075/kg N
USA: Wisconsin State	$0.00020/kg N
Pesticide Taxes	
Denmark	17% on retail price
Norway	11% on retail price
Sweden	20% on retail price plus $5.3/ha/application
Finland	2.5% on retail price

* Fertilizer Taxes in Norway may increase to $0.23/kgN and $0.45 kg/P by the end of 1990

Source: OECD, *Agricultural and Environmental Policies* (Paris: OECD, 1989); Holden, P., *Pesticides and Groundwater Quality*, National Research Council (Washington DC: National Academy Press, 1986); D. Baldock and J. Hewett, *Economic Instruments for Reducing Agricultural Pollution* (London, Mimeo: Institute for European Environmental Policy, 1990).

rarely have they been imposed to produce a reduction in use of inputs: the levels are usually set too low to affect consumption. The principal objective has been to raise revenue for research or extension services – revenue which could, in theory, be used to pay compensation to those who suffer from the pollution. Most studies suggest the necessity for very high taxes if significant reductions in consumption are to be made.[18] In Germany, for example, a 200 per cent fertilizer tax would only reduce fertilizer use by 30 per cent, while reducing water pollution by 50 per cent. However, in Austria and Denmark there have been some reductions in consumption as a result of the taxes imposed.[19] A more effective tax has been the levy payment, which is currently being used in the Netherlands to penalize those farmers producing more livestock waste than their land can absorb.

In practice, it is virtually impossible to predict the appropriate tax, its consequences on input consumption, and hence the relative costs and benefits. A possible solution is to "iterate" the tax – set it at one level, observe what happens, and then alter it up or down accordingly.[20] But this introduces considerable uncertainties for both farmers and industry. A more important drawback to taxes is that farmers who use fertilizers or pesticides in a manner that does not contaminate or pollute the environment are penalized too. Thus while, in theory, taxes are a neat solution to pollution abatement, in practice they are rarely simple, fair or cost-free.

Subsidies and grants

An alternative to penalizing farmers is to encourage them to adopt alternative low- or non-polluting technologies through the provision of subsidies, grants, credit or low-interest loans. Currently subsidies of various kinds work in the opposite direction. Both the industrialized and developing countries adopt measures such as supporting farm prices or providing deficiency payments to farmers; subsidizing agricultural inputs such as fertilizers or pesticides; not charging for water used for irrigation; imposing tariffs or quotas on imports that would otherwise compete with home-grown produce; and giving direct income support to farmers.[21] These are powerful incentives that discriminate against alternative technologies.

Such technologies alter the character of the polluting activity so that either the pollutants or their impacts on people, wildlife or the environment are reduced. Farmers may adopt organic farming techniques or biological control, for example. Many such alternative technologies exist, and are briefly described in the next chapter, but switching from one process to another is rarely a costless means of abating pollution. Agricultural technologies that create pollution are, in effect, using a free input – the clean environment. Any alternative invariably involves the use of a substitute input, often in the form of energy, and this usually entails a higher cost.

The trade-off is illustrated by the example of organic farming. To produce the same level of output, farmers usually must invest more labour and other inputs to offset not using agrochemicals. Hand weeding is labour intensive, as is collecting and distributing manure. Even with a high level of labour yields may still remain lower than under agrochemical based agriculture. What makes organic farming profitable is that sufficient numbers of consumers prefer organic produce and will pay a sufficient premium to cover the increased costs of inputs and the loss of yield.

Sometimes, though, the costs of the alternative technologies can be very low. A classic example is the release of the Vedalia beetle in California against the cotton cushiony scale, a serious pest of citrus. The beetle was introduced from Australia in 1888 and produced a lasting control – for a total cost of $2000 (see Chapter 11). There is a growing range of applications of subsidies and grants that support particular alternative technologies (Table 10.3). Sometimes the grant

Table 10.3   Examples of subsidies and grants offered to farmers to use low- or non-polluting technologies

- Grants for construction of soil contour bunds in Australia
- Supply of trees at reduced prices in Turkey
- 30 per cent grant to upgrade slurry storage facilities to nine months storage capacity in Netherlands
- Grants to construct more efficient slurry storage facilities in Sweden and Denmark
- Low interest loans to farmers to use soil conservation techniques in Portugal
- Grants to improve wildlife habitats
- Grants to leave headlands and crop boundaries unsprayed in Germany

Source: OECD, *Agricultural and Environmental Policies* (Paris: OECD, 1989).

is designed to protect the environment as a whole, such as through the designation of environmentally sensitive areas and set-aside schemes. Farmers are paid to manage their farms in a manner consonant with the environment, such as not spraying meadows with pesticides, or leaving crop edges unsprayed or even, in set-aside schemes, not cropping the land at all.

Once again, though, subsidies have to be set at a level that will encourage adoption by a sufficient number of farmers to have the desired impact on environmental quality. An instance where hitherto this has not happened has been the Nitrate Sensitive Areas scheme in the UK (see below, page 540).

Transferable pollution permits and quotas

A problem with both tax and subsidy systems is that the levels are usually centrally determined and uniformly applied. They are typically insensitive to the mitigating and special circumstances of individual polluters. Farmers on particular soils or in certain climatic conditions may be able to use potential pollutants with less adverse effect than farmers in other environments and may thus be unfairly penalized by having to pay a uniform tax. In the UK, for example, fertilizer use in the eastern counties has a greater adverse effect on ground water quality than in other parts of the country because of the nature of the overlying rocks over aquifers. But, designing and administering a non-uniform system of taxes or charges demands detailed information and is normally costly.

One answer in this situation is the issuance of transferable permits. Such a system can be sensitive to local conditions and, moreover, rewards those polluters who are efficient in pollution control. It works through the local or regional pollution control authority determining the aggregate quantity of emissions to be permitted in its area of jurisdiction and issuing a limited number of permits that correspond to shares of this total.[22] Polluters are then permitted to buy and sell the permits in an open market; as a consequence their price should reflect the true social costs of pollution. Polluters facing high costs of abatement will tend to buy the permits, while those with low costs of abatement will make gains by selling the permits and reducing their pollution. In this way the abatement of pollution is concentrated among the low abatement cost polluters.[23] Permit trading under the Clean Air Acts in the USA has saved industry alone over $4 billion up to 1985.[24]

As yet there have been no cases of permit trading being used in agriculture. In theory, the system could be used to control fertilizer pollution. A water agency would set the total annual nitrogen burden for a particular watershed and from this compute the maximum nitrogen application per hectare. Each farm in the watershed would then receive a permit for so many tonnes of nitrogen based on its land area, but would be free to sell all or part of its share at whatever price the market would bear. The advantage to the water agency is that pollution would be kept to a desirable level with relatively small administrative costs – providing, of course, that policing to prevent non-permit use does not prove costly. The system also has the advantage that it would reward farmers who are efficient at producing high agricultural returns with low levels of fertilizer inputs.

This would work equally well for quotas for inputs. Farmers allocated a quota of units for pesticide and fertilizer use could then trade them with other farmers.

The legal control of pollution

Even taken together, advisory and economic measures are rarely sufficient to control pollution to levels that are both socially just and efficient. In theory, economic policies have a great deal of attraction; they appear simple and elegant, but if high levels of efficiency and justice are to be combined they have to be reinforced or replaced by a legal apparatus that is inevitably complex and cumbersome by comparison.

Laws to control pollution have a long history: in Britain the government of Edward I prohibited the use of coal in London in the thirteenth century because it was thought to be injurious to health; and during the Middle Ages local by-laws protecting watercourses were common.[25] Today, the legal control of pollution is provided for in two ways: individuals damaged or threatened by pollution can use private law to take polluters to court; and governments can use "public" law, which provides various mechanisms for the control of sources of pollution, together with support for enforcement agencies.

Private law

Private law is concerned with the rights of individuals and how they can obtain redress for damages they have suffered. In theory, it is a powerful deterrent, but in practice its usefulness is limited. In the UK the type of legal action appropriate to environmental pollution is the private nuisance action, concerned with the unlawful interference with a person's use or enjoyment of land, or some right over it, or in connection with it.[26] The victim, or plaintiff, must be a landowner or have some legal interest in land, and be able to prove that damage has occurred and can be traced to an identifiable source, the defendant. Should the interference not be considered sufficient to amount to a nuisance or the plaintiff has no interest in the land (for example a passer-by harmed by pesticide spray), legal action is still possible, but the plaintiff must be able to prove negligence on the part of the defendant. The victim or plaintiff goes to court and if the action is successful this results in either an award of damages against the polluter to compensate for past damage and/or the imposition of an injunction which restricts the polluter from a continuation of the practice that caused the nuisance.

There have been few examples of reported private actions relating to agricultural pollution, though fishing clubs have frequently been successful in settling claims for compensation where pollution incidents have killed fish stocks. But essential principles on civil liability and pesticides were recently established in New Zealand. A company growing roses for export sued a government department following the negligent spraying of 2,4,5-T on roadside weeds: the herbicide drift damaged the roses.[27] The New Zealand courts, applying common law principles which apply in Britain, found in favour of the plaintiff and awarded $667,000 plus special damages.

Nevertheless, the outcome of these private actions is often unsatisfactory. The damages awarded may not be a continuing incentive to the polluter to reduce pollution, since they can only be granted for past losses. They may redress past injustice but not prevent its recurrence. An injunction may produce, on the other hand, an unfair burden on polluters, causing them to incur abatement costs that exceed the value of the benefits to the victim. Theoretically partial injunctions offer a compromise but, in practice, they do not appear to be commonly used.

The major drawback to private law solutions is the considerable cost of litigation that often arises, particularly when cases involve a large number of pollutant victims. In Britain the "costs in the case" rule under which an unsuccesful plaintiff must pay the legal costs of the defendant is a particularly strong deterrent to litigation, coupled with a prohibition against lawyers undertaking cases on a contingency fee basis (that is, no win, no fees). The position of contingency fees is currently under review, but undertaking civil litigations remains a task of high financial risk for private citizens.[28] A major pollution case will involved costs of many thousands of pounds. The wider societal costs are also difficult to handle, since private law is largely concerned with the conflicts between individuals or between individuals and companies. The judiciary usually finds it difficult to balance the interests of victims against the needs of the polluting industry. It may be argued, for instance, that a national need to produce food may override damage by agricultural pollutants to individuals.

Under private law in the United States it is also possible for groups of victims to undertake "class actions", in which an individual files a pollution action and others can then join the case. Although there have been no class actions against agricultural polluters, one recent case does illustrate the principles and costs. It followed the discovery of birth defects in children of Santa Clara Valley (also known as Silicon Valley), California, which appeared to coincide with the presence of industrial solvents in aquifers supplying drinking water.[29] In 1982 a group of 530 residents were represented in a case against a company allegedly causing the pollution, the drinking water supplier and the building constructors of the faulty storage tank that was the source of the pollution. The preparations made by the plaintiffs cost them more than $500,000 over 3 years, and by 1986 the prospect was for a court case that could last 4–6 more years and cost several million dollars. These prospects led to a settlement out of court, in which each of the 530 individuals received an undisclosed amount of money, but said to be substantially more than $15,000 each.

In general, private remedies are unlikely to be a satisfactory form of pollution control. Individuals may have neither the resources nor motivation to enforce their rights; moreover they cannot act in the common interest, such as when common-property resources are damaged – rivers, forests, grazing land, the atmosphere.[30] Legal control over pollution is thus dominated by "public" law, which provides mechanisms of control, standards that should not be exceeded and sanctions against those who do so, and designates official agencies charged with enforcement.

Public law: setting standards

The principal role of public law in pollution control is to establish maximum ceilings, or standards, for pollution. It is an approach which is consonant with economic measures since the objective, again, is to internalize external costs. This is done either by setting emissions standards for the discharge of a contaminant, or by establishing environmental quality standards or objectives which relate to the environment receiving the contaminant. Polluters who exceed standards are then subject to penalties.

Standards can be set at all stages of the process from producer or manufacturer of a product through to consumption.[31] At the first stage there are Process or Operating Standards, designed to protect workers involved in manufacturing or production. Examples of these are the maximum levels of the toxic gases, hydrogen sulphide and ammonia, permitted in livestock housing (see Chapter 6). Often they serve both to protect the workforce and to minimize emissions to the environment.

At the next stage are Product Standards, which aim to limit the levels of contaminants or pollutants in produce, for example pesticide residue levels in food.[32] Like operating standards, they tend to limit the potential for pollutant emissions during production or manufacturing.

More directly aimed at emissions are emission standards. Examples are the standards which set maximum emissions of gases from industry or from motor vehicles. However, they have rarely been applied to control agricultural pollution, chiefly because they can only be set when pollution originates from a point source. Diffuse pollution, such as nitrates leaching from fields to groundwater, or nitrous oxide gases emitted to the atmosphere, cannot be controlled by emissions standards. Discharge of livestock or silage effluents is the only likely candidate.

A further disadvantage of emission standards is that all polluters are treated equally. Those in an enviroment capable of assimilating and breaking down pollutants are treated in the same way as those in a vulnerable environment. An alternative is to use Environmental Quality Standards (EQS), for instance standards for pesticide concentrations in surface water from which drinking water is taken. EQS are more flexible than emissions standards, as they can be established according to the resilience and assimilative capacity of the environment likely to be contaminated. In more vulnerable environments, controls can be more stringent. They also apply to both diffuse and point sources. However, they have to be supported by regular monitoring of the environment to ensure compliance. In this case approaching or exceeding a standard is a signal that action should be taken.

Similar to EQS are Exposure Standards, which protect the assumed target of the pollution, human or otherwise, during exposure to a resource that contains the contaminants or pollutants. An example is the limits set for pesticide concentrations in drinking water itself (see Chapter 2). The main advantage of this approach is that monitoring is easier. Pesticide concentrations in drinking water plants are readily measured but because, at this stage, the pollutant has almost reached the "target"; it is in some ways a last line of defence.

Finally, Biological Standards set the levels of contaminants or pollutants occuring in the target organisms. An example is the standard for concentration of pesticide in human blood or milk (see Chapter 3). Their advantage is that they cover the combined effect of all the sources of the pollutant in question but, of course, the signal to act only arises after the target has been reached.

Different traditions in standard setting

The setting of standards, governed by legal statutes, has been the key to centralized pollution control policy in most industrialized countries. Typically, various pollution control authorities set different kinds of standards, resulting in a complex mix of approaches. None the less, it is possible to distinguish two very different traditions that have developed over the years, one adopted by the USA, the European Community and many developing countries, and the other peculiar to the UK.

The first approach relies on specifying standards for emissions or ambient concentrations of pollutants in the environment that apply to all polluters and all environments. Polluters are not permitted to emit substances in greater concentrations than the standards specify and are subject to prosecution if they do. Where the standards are in terms of ambient environmental levels for specific substances, such as air quality targets in the USA, the standards apply to a wide range of industries.

The second approach to standard setting, which has long been the preferred practice in the UK, is to specify individual standards according to the particular circumstances and conditions of each potential polluter. This tradition has relied largely upon the use of flexible consents for the control of pollution, characterized by the use of the "best practicable means" (BPM) principle. Under BPM, standards are set for individual polluters by enforcement officers who determine, in their judgement, what is the best that can be achieved given what is technically and managerially feasible for that particular polluter. This is essentially an empirical approach relying on informal negotiation between government inspectors and factory owners, farmers and other polluters to arrive at an agreed level of pollution emission that balances off the damage to the neighbourhood, and to society in general, against the costs of abatement in the light of currently available technology.[33]

Each of these two traditions has its proponents and critics. Although both reflect the principle that the "Polluter Pays", neither necessarily produces economically efficient or just solutions. If uniform standards are fixed, there is no allowance for differences in the circumstances of individual polluters, and hence the true abatement costs cannot be taken into account. Nevertheless, where information is, for the most part, not confidential, as in the USA, it does become possible to at least judge whether a particular standard results in overall net gains.

This is much more difficult where the approach to pollution control is flexible. In fact, there is little way of knowing whether a BPM is efficient or just. The criteria for BPM are not openly published nor is it easy for victims of pollution to determine whether the best practicable means are indeed being employed. Thus for many years,

British law used the term "wholesome water" as the legal expression for its water quality standard. By contrast the terms used in USA and EEC legislation have tended to be more precise, being expressed in permitted concentrations of specific compounds.[34] Misgivings about BPM have been expressed by the Royal Commission on Environmental Pollution: "at its best BPM connotes a rigorous analysis of the objectives and consequences of . . . pollution control. At its worst the term can be used as a catchword to conceal the absence of any such analysis."[35]

One of the potential advantages of setting standards, if they are tough, is that they can be "technology forcing", that is, they encourage investment into new technology to meet the new standards. This has been one of the strongest arguments for imposing a ban on straw burning in the UK. Such a ban was resisted for many years on the grounds that there were no satisfactory alternatives to straw burning. But since the announcement in 1989 that a ban would indeed be in place from 1992 there has been a considerable improvement in the range of available technologies. Hitherto, various techniques available for incorporating the straw in the soil, for treating it on farm or for its use in paper and board making, were allegedly uneconomic. But now a greater effort is being made to produce economic alternatives.

The standards approach, on the other hand, is vulnerable to criticism when it is based on permitted ambient levels of pollution, because of the burden of proof required for enforcement. It is difficult to determine, for example, how much has been contributed from multiple possible polluters to ambient concentrations of a pollutant in groundwater. This is particularly relevant for contamination by nitrates and pesticides and is the reason why the UK government has had to establish Nitrate Sensitive Areas (NSA) and is considering Groundwater Protection Zones (GPZ), in which the principle is to protect a resource by restricting the practice of all farmers within a deemed area through regulation or payment (see below, page 540).

Which approach is "best" is largely a matter for empirical and political judgement. Some argue that the flexible approach is more likely to get the co-operation of polluters, while others maintain the standards approach incurs greater costs, particularly for enforcement. To some extent the present systems of control are reflections of the patterns of relationships which have evolved between individuals, industry and government in different societies. But these systems are now being seriously challenged by moves to create more uniform approaches to pollution control that transcend national boundaries.

For various reasons the traditional British approaches no longer dominate pollution legislation. Developments over the past five years, including the privatization of the water industry and heightened public interest in more open administration, have encouraged the development of a more formalized approach leading to a rapid increase in explicit legal standards. Above all, the UK's involvement and gradual acceptance of EEC-based approaches is leading to a rapid transformation of the existing legal and administrative culture.

Conflicts in standard setting

Both between and within these two legal and administrative traditions there are inevitably conflicts over emphasis and interpretation. Most arise because of a discrepancy between the goal central bodies have determined and what the implementing agencies, from their experience, believe is practical.

The UK, as a member state of the European Economic Community, is now subject to an increasing number of environmental Directives developed by the European Commission and agreed by the Council of Ministers, of which the UK is one member out of twelve. Since these Directives are based upon the use of standards in the form of emission limit values, they have conflicted, inevitably, with traditional UK approaches to pollution control. One example was the conflict that occurred over nitrates in drinking water. The EC Directive relating to the Quality of Water intended for Human Consumption set a maximum admissible concentration of 50 mg nitrate/litre, which came into effect in July 1985. This was half the earlier limit in the UK. The Directive, though, permitted member states to approve derogations from this limit in circumstances where there was no health hazard or in emergency situations.[36] The UK Department of the Environment took advantage of this by approving 52 derogations affecting a population of nearly one million people. The derogations permitted supply of water provided the nitrate concentration did not exceed 80 mg/l measured as a 3 monthly average and 100 mg/l as a maximum value. Action to reduce nitrate levels was only taken in seven water supplies that averaged more than 80 mg/l. The UK government has, however, now accepted that the Directive must be complied with and, from 1993 to 1995, supplies must not exceed the maximum of 50 mg/l.

In the USA conflicts largely arise over differing perceptions and priorities between Federal and State pollution control agencies. National standards are set by the Environmental Protection Agency (EPA), but then state legislatures have the opportunity either to loosen or tighten them. Loosening of standards, for instance, can occur under the Federal Insecticide, Fungicide and Rodenticide Act, 1947 (FIFRA). This act permits States to grant emergency registrations of pesticides in order to deal with unforeseen pest outbreaks or to meet special local needs. A particular product may then be applied at a higher rate than Federal legislation permits. To begin with the EPA could overrule the issuing of these emergency exemptions, but then in 1978 a Congressional amendment curtailed this right. As a consequence there are many exemptions each year, with the states of California, Texas and Washington together accounting for about one third.[37]

But tightening of standards is also possible, such as in Wisconsin's all-inclusive action to protect groundwater against agricultural chemicals.[38] In 1984 the Governor signed into law a groundwater protection bill, requiring each state regulatory agency to identify substances that had already been detected in groundwater or were likely to reach there in the future. The standards were then established on a two-tiered basis: enforcement standards based on Federal standards established by EPA; and preventative action limits (PALs), set at 10, 20 or 50 per cent of the enforcement standards, depending upon the relative potential harm to health of the substances concerned. The PALs are intended to trigger remedial actions that prevent the level of each compound reaching the level of the enforcement standards, at which point prohibition of the activity causing the emission is required. The act relies on a statewide monitoring scheme to detect contamination levels exceeding the PALs. Revenues to meet the expenses of the scheme are raised from annual license surcharges on pesticide manufacturers and formulators, and a $0.20 tax per tonne of fertilizer applied, to be paid by the applicators.

Mixed and integrated approaches to pollution control

So far we have discussed the individual measures available for the control of agricultural pollution – advisory measures, economic instruments and legal regulations. But, in practice, as no single solution is likely to suffice, pollution control inevitably involves a mixture of approaches. Policy-makers choose the appropriate mix and make changes whenever new pollutants arise, knowledge about old pollutants changes or new goals for environmental quality are set. A frequently advocated approach is to set standards on the best available environmental and social damage criteria and then use some combination of charges, transferable permits and advice or exhortation to achieve them.[39] This allows for a degree of progressive learning, making adjustments in the various controlling mechanisms as information becomes available on the damage caused by different levels of pollution and on the responses of the polluters to being controlled. Despite not being very tidy, such a mixture is more likely to lead to a solution that combines efficiency with justice.

But, in addition to the desirability of a flexible response is the need for administrative integration. There are often serious differences in approach between agencies responsible for pollution control in different environmental media, namely in air, land and water. This may lead to pollution problems being simply shifted from one medium to another. For instance, an agency that restricts or prohibits the disposal of livestock slurry to watercourses may, in effect, be encouraging greater pollution of the land.

The establishment of the Environmental Protection Agency in the USA in 1970 was an attempt to promote a more integrated approach to pollution control, but within the agency the media oriented approach has remained dominant.[40] This is also true of those states that have created mini-EPAs but some have attempted to set up bodies with a strong integrative function. Illinois, for example, has a Pollution Control Board (IPCB) which incorporates various air and water pollution boards scattered among various state agencies. The IPCB hears cases and makes rules for all media.[41]

In the UK provision for integrated pollution control has only been recently established with the creation of a new unified pollution inspectorate, known as Her Majesty's Inspectorate of Pollution (HMIP). Previously, there was no statutory basis on which control authorities could consider cross-media implications and pollution problems tended to be viewed in isolation. The creation of HMPI has also stimulated a search for methodologies for efficiently arriving at integrated control solutions. Out of this has emerged the concept of Best Practicable Environmental Option (BPEO) which implicitly accepts the notion of weighing the benefits and costs of all potential solutions to a problem, in all media (Box 10.4). A procedure for achieving this has been developed by the Royal Commission on Environmental Pollution although to date there have been no examples of its implementation (Table 10.4).

Integrated pollution control as a basis of regulation has now received statutory recognition in the UK Environmental Protection Act 1990, and will be applied to selected classes of industry. However, the implementation of these new controls will present a major challenge to regulators and industry over the next decade. There are many examples of agriculturally generated pollution, particularly livestock and other wastes, where an integrated approach is crucial, but it remains to be seen whether this will be achieved.

Box 10.4 The definition of a Best Practicable Environmental Option

A BPEO is the outcome of a systematic consultative and decision-making procedure which emphazises the protection of the environment across land, air and water. The BPEO procedure establishes, for a given set of objectives, the option that provides the most benefit or least damage to the environment as a whole, at acceptable cost, in the long term as well as in the short term . . . . It is a procedure that would lead, if properly implemented, to reductions in environmental pollution and to improvements in the quality of the environment as a whole. Because the procedure should be open, the interpretation of "practicable" would be subject to scrutiny and the risk of lax environment practices would be reduced.

Source: RCEP, *Best Practicable Environmental Option*, Royal Commission on Environmental Pollution, 12th Report (London: HMSO, 1988).

The control of pesticides

In the rest of this chapter we describe a number of examples of approaches to agricultural pollution control from the UK and the USA and the developing countries, to illustrate how different systems work. Although all employ a mixture of advice, incentives and legislation, it is still not clear which is the most efficient or just mix.

We deal first with the control of pesticide contamination and pollution. In this case, the first, and often primary, line of control is licensing and registration. Exhaustive testing is required of all new products and they are then registered for use on specified crops or livestock, provided they are applied according to certain conditions. At the application stage, however, advisory measures are preferred. Reliance is placed on the promotion of good agricultural practice, and, in some cases, economic incentives to reduce use. However, toward the end of the food production process, the level of regulation increases again, as maximum residue standards are set to protect the consumers.

Registration and licensing

Though the first legislation for pesticides was the United States Insecticide Act of 1910, which prohibited the manufacturing, selling or transporting of mislabelled or adulterated chemical substances, the first provisions for compulsory registration were made under the Federal Insecticide, Fungicide and Rodenticide Act of 1947 (FIFRA). Registration of pesticides was administered by the USDA

Table 10.4   Summary of steps in selecting a Best Practicable Environmental Option

---

Step 1: Define the objective
State the objective of the project or proposal at the outset, in terms which do not prejudge the means by which that objective is to be achieved.

Step 2: Generate options
Identify all feasible options for achieving the objective: the aim is to find those which are both practicable and environmentally acceptable.

Step 3: Evaluate the options
Analyse these options, particularly to expose advantages and disadvantages for the environment. Use quantitative methods when these are appropriate. Qualitative evaluation will also be needed.

Step 4: Summarize and present the evaluation
Present the results of the evaluation concisely and objectively, and in a format which can highlight the advantages and disadvantages of each option. Do not combine the results of different measurements and forecasts if this would obscure information which is important to the decision.

Step 5: Select the preferred option
Select the BPEO from the feasible options. The choice will depend on the weight given to the environmental impacts and associated risks, and to the costs involved. Decision-makers should be able to demonstrate that the preferred option does not involve unacceptable consequences for the environment.

Step 6: Review the preferred option
Scrutinize closely the proposed detailed design and the operating procedures to ensure that no pollution risks or hazards have been overlooked. It is good practice to have the scrutiny done by individuals who are independent of the original team.

Step 7: Implement and monitor
Monitor the achieved performance against the desired targets especially those for environmental quality. Do this to establish whether the assumptions in the design are correct and to provide feedback for future development of proposals and designs.

Throughout steps 1 to 7: Maintain an audit trail
Record the basis for any choices or decisions through all of these stages, that is, the assumptions used, details of evaluation procedures, the reliability and origins of the date, the affiliations of those involved in the analytical work and a record of those taking the decisions.

Note: The boundaries between each of the steps will not always be clear-cut: some may proceed in parallel or may need to be repeated.

Source: Owens, S., "The unified pollution Inspectorate and best practicable environmental option in the United Kingdom", in: Haigh, N. and Irwin, F. (eds), *Integrated Pollution Control in Europe and North America* (Washington DC: The Conservation Foundation, 1990).

and manufacturers and distributors were required to seek approval for their products. The authorities were also able to restrict the uses of a particular product, and require that certain compounds only be applied by well-trained and certified operators.

About this time the UK government acted in response to the deaths of seven operators using DNOC in 1947 with the introduction of the Agriculture (Poisonous Substances) Act in 1952 to promote safe working practices and protect workers from the more acutely toxic pesticides.

But then the two countries took quite different courses of action until the mid-1980s. In the USA, further legislation made registration procedures more comprehensive, while in the UK controls were based on a voluntary approach. In 1972 the US FIFRA was amended to establish a more comprehensive registration procedure. New products are now subjected to stricter standards before they can be marketed than existing products with which they would compete. In effect this means that new pesticides are generally safer and more benign. At the same time already approved products have to pass through special re-registration, because of new inadequacy (of today) of the older techniques of safety analysis. Inevitably the new review process has entailed lengthy delays.[42] Since the special reviews began in 1975 the EPA had completed 40 analyses of the most hazardous pesticides by September 1987, resulting in five cases where all agricultural uses were cancelled, 34 cases with some new restrictions applied, and one where no action was taken. In principle each review should take 300 days; in practice they take between two and seven years to complete. At this rate the 600 active ingredients registered for use in the USA will not be reviewed until well into the next century and the Office of Technology Assessment has predicted that the whole process will not be completed until 2015.[43] This means that new compounds, safer than the existing products they might replace, have been denied registration, so leaving potentially hazardous products on the market.[44]

In the UK, registration by contract has been through a non-statutory Pesticides Safety Precautions Scheme, in which manufacturers, distributors and importers undertook not to introduce new pesticides or new uses of pesticides until safety clearance had been granted by government departments. In return, industry was guaranteed complete confidentiality regarding all the safety data it submitted. Safety clearance was based, most latterly, on advice from the Advisory Committee on Pesticides (ACP) which included representatives of government departments and independent scientists, although none from commercial agriculture, agrochemical or allied industries, or the trade unions. The scheme has had one advantage of being flexible and adaptable, permitting rapid responses to events and new knowledge and providing an opportunity for policy to be developed in an anticipatory way.[45] However the scheme was replaced in the mid-1980s, by a new statutory approach under the Food and Environment Protection Act (FEPA). This Act provides powers to control many aspects of sales, supply, use, distribution and marketing pesticides; to set residue limits; and to provide information to the public. It takes the form of enabling legislation, in which requirements are not set in detail but are established by Ministers through secondary legislation (Table 10.5). A third tier

Table 10.5 Regulations introduced in the UK following the 1985 Food and Environment Protection Act

---

1986 Control of Pesticides Regulations (COPR)
These prohibit the sale, supply, use, and so on, of any pesticide unless it has been approved; and require that conditions for approval and consent be met.

1986 Reporting of Injuries, Diseases and Dangerous Occurrencies Regulations (RIDDOR)
These are intended to reduce the level of under-reporting of serious acute incidents by requiring an immediate report of an incident by an employer and a written report within seven days.

1988 Pesticides (Maximum Residues Levels in Food) Regulations
These set maximum levels for certain active ingredients and define powers to seize and dispose of food contaminated in excess of the maximum levels.

1989 Control of Substances Hazardous to Health (COSHH) Regulations
These were established to encourage farmers and spraymen to make full assessment of the risks they run from using hazardous substances. They should consider safer alternatives to using hazardous pesticides, technical measures to reduce exposure, and the use of full protective clothing.

---

of control is provided by Codes of Practice, such as those relating to storage, use and supply. In effect this means that the UK approach is now moving close to that of the USA, although it still retains a degree of administrative discretion which should enable it to continue to respond quickly to changing knowledge and events.

Export restrictions

In the 1950s and 1960s there was considerable dumping in the developing countries of pesticides that had been banned or restricted in the industrialized countries. More recently, though, some governments have introduced rules to regulate such exports.[46] In the

USA, a notification scheme was set up under a 1978 amendment to FIFRA, which requires that exporters must first inform foreign buyers of the known dangers of a product and notify whether the use of the pesticide has been registered or cancelled in the USA. The importer must then acknowledge to EPA receipt of this information, whereupon EPA informs the State Department, which in turn informs the foreign government. Should it wish, the government can then request further information from EPA. However, there are no provisions for enforcement, and the notification procedure is only necessary for the first shipment of a given product in a given year.

The UK on the other hand, does not as yet have any statutory controls over exports of chemical products on the grounds that UK legislation does not presume to extend out of the UK. The European Community also has no requirements for importing countries to be supplied with information, even though companies within the EC currently export some 65 per cent of the world trade in pesticides. Hitherto, all EC directives currently containing provisions for controlling hazardous chemicals have explicitly excluded any substances for export. However, in the late 1980s, a draft regulation on the export of banned and severely restricted chemicals was considered which would explicitly recognize the responsibility of the exporter.[47] The aim would be to prevent the export of such products unless full information had been provided to the importing country. Whether the EC will adopt such legislation is uncertain, but such a system of "prior informed consent" remains a potentially important method of supplementing developing countries' own control measures.

Controlling residues in food

There have also been differences over the control of pesticide residues and food. There is a similarity in the reliance, as a first line of control, on advisory measures at the stage of pesticide application, backed up by economic incentives or legislation. Farmers are encouraged to follow good agricultural practice and observe recommendations on the label, relating to harvest intervals – the period that should elapse between the final spraying and the harvesting of a crop.

The differences emerge in the approaches to monitoring and registrations. In the UK, a compound is cleared if the manufacturer or importer can show that residue levels will fall within acceptable limits if the label recommendations for application rates, frequency and timing of spraying, and harvest intervals are followed. This is backed up by a system of monitoring, carried out by the Working Party on Pesticide Residues, which was established in 1977, and reports to the Advisory Committee on Pesticides (ACP). The sampling, however, is neither random nor systematic but focuses "on the areas identified by intelligence or experience as representing the most likely areas where residues are present."[48] Periodic surveys are carried out, concentrating on particular classes of foodstuffs where a problem is suspected. In recent years the surveys have covered imported foodstuffs, post-harvest treatment during transit and storage, and analysis of specialist diets and infant foods.[49] The Royal Commission on Environmental Pollution has criticized this approach as inadequate and recommended random sampling.[50] But MAFF maintains that the wide safety margins incorporated into harvest intervals and recommended practices constitute sufficient consumer protection. They claim, moreover, that there is negligible risk to consumers even when residues approach presumptive Maximum Residue Levels (MRLs).[51] As we showed in Chapter 3, recent monitoring surveys have detected a generally low level of produce containing residues exceeding MRLs, with some exceptions, such as for thiram on lettuce. But the question is whether the proportion of sampled foodstuffs which exceed the MRLs constitute a satisfactory and safe level?

MAFF's conclusions from their surveys is that there is no widespread disregard for label recommendations. However, surveys of farmers aimed at analysing their attitudes to pest control and pesticide use, suggest that Good Agricultural Practice (GAP) is frequently not observed. Farmers interviewed in the early 1980s agreed that pesticides should under no circumstances be applied after the harvest interval, yet some 15 per cent still sprayed after the last approved application date had passed.[52] A further 37 per cent indicated that if clearance of DDT (commonly used on brassicas at the time and cheap compared with alternatives) were withdrawn, they would consider stockpiling for future use. MAFF had recommended substitution with a less persistent compound, but DDT remained common and was regularly added to other sprays.

In the USA, however, residues in food are subject to considerably more complex regulations. As in the UK, residue control policy depends on the prescription of label recommendations, but there is the added incentive to farmers that they may face prosecution should a food crop be deemed unmarketable. Before a pesticide compound can be registered for use on food crops it must be granted tolerances under the Food, Drug and Cosmetic (FDC) Act, 1954. The tolerances for residues on the raw commodities are set by the EPA under section 408 of the Act, which explicitly refers to the balance between the benefits that pesticides confer and the possible risks to public health, so that in granting registration EPA must conclude that food production benefits outweigh any risks. Residues in processed foods, however, are regulated under the considerably tougher section 409, which governs food additives in general. Residues must be proven safe, which is defined as a "reasonable certainty" that "no harm" to consumers will result when the pesticide is put to its intended use.[53] There is no possibility of weighing benefits against potential harm. This section also contains the Delaney Clause, which prohibits the approval of a food additive that has been found to induce cancer in humans or animals if those residues concentrate above the level permitted on raw food (see Chapter 3).

Tolerance levels are set by conducting trials that generate the highest residue levels under good agricultural practice, for example, using the maximum recommended application rates under conditions likely to prolong residues. The EPA then compares the quantity of residues to which humans might be exposed with the level it judges to be safe, based on available toxicological data. The conventional safety factor of 100 is applied, assuming that humans are ten times more sensitive than the most sensitive animal tested and some humans are ten times more sensitive than the least susceptible human. Section 408 tolerances are usually higher than the actual residues found at harvest; s.409 tolerances are set by taking the s.408 tolerance and then multiplying by the typical concentration factor following processing.

The strict application of s.409 and the Delaney Clause would seem theoretically to provide a very high degree of protection, but in practice there are difficulties.[54] The process of setting tolerance levels has become very complex, with different standards for old and new compounds and for raw and processed foods. One problem arises from early efforts of legislators to integrate the two sections. Congress exempted from s.409 regulations those residues present at levels no higher than the permitted levels under s.408, so that approval under s.408 will suffice for a given use so long as residues in any processed food do not exceed the levels that s.408 authorizes.[55] This process avoids the test of the Delaney Clause, so that cancer inducing pesticides may be permitted.

The number of tests required has also greatly increased. The amendments to FIFRA have meant tests are required before tolerances can be granted. As we have already pointed out, this has meant a lengthy delay in the re-registration of compounds, which, in turn, has created serious anomalies in standards for residues. For instance, EPA has denied the use of a "new" fungicide on hops because of the theoretical risk of one additional cancer per 100 million people;

however approval would have allowed it to replace an "old" product with a potential risk of one additional cancer per 10,000 people.[56] The National Research Council estimates that some 90 per cent of total dietary cancer risk is from pesticides first registered before 1978.

The EPA announced in 1988 that it intended to adopt a negligible risk approach, changing its interpretation of the Delaney Clause to permit the use of pesticides that would leave residues in processed food provided the cancer risk of a lifetime's exposure was less than one million.[57] The change would mean that old and new pesticides would be treated in the same way.

But like the more voluntary UK approach, the US approach has a number of drawbacks. In theory, it provides a legislative incentive to ensure farmers carry out GAP, but in practice it is almost impossible to trace a particular grower through the chain of storage, processing and distribution. A complicating factor is that perishable goods are often sold and consumed before the results of laboratory analyses are available. That GAP is not always adhered to is shown by the recent example of the extensive poisoning of people on the West Coast following consumption of water-melon illegally sprayed with aldicarb. In this case it was not possible to trace the grower (see Chapter 3). The US approach also requires extensive and more costly analytic resources, though residues are apparently not revealed any more regularly than those in the UK.[58] Residue levels in human fat and milk, for instance, are similar in both countries. Finally, the conflicting statutory arrangements and the excessive workload imposed on the EPA have led to a situation which is difficult to administer. The unanswered question remains: is this considerably more costly approach any more effective in protecting human health than the minimalist but considerably cheaper approach exemplified by the UK?

Pesticide control in the Third World

Most developing countries only began to think seriously about the need to control pesticides in the late 1960s and early 1970s and, today, there are still only a handful with both strong legislation and the means of enforcement (Table 10.6). Few, also, have the primary health care and occupational health systems necessary to detect and treat pesticide poisoning, or an efficient agricultural training and extension service that can ensure high standards of pesticide application.[59] Residues are often very high, but pollution monitoring and analytical calculations

Table 10.6 Components of pesticide regulation practices and enforcement measures in selected Asian countries in the 1980s

	INI	INO	MAL	PAK	PRC	PHL	RK	THA
Regulatory Scheme								
First introduction of legislation/registration	1968	1973	1974	1971	1982	1977	1957	1967
Average time required for registration (years)	0.5–3	2–3	2–3	2–3	0.3–1	0.5–1	2–5	0.5–1
Number of products registered								
active ingredients	127	264	140	148	130	158	214	153
formulations	n/a	406	326	314	300	328	338	214
Safety								
Products inspected for quality by regulatory authority	R	R	R	R	O	R	R	R
Enforcement of registration through inspection	O	O	O	O*	M	O	O	M
Training for:								
Dealers/Applicators	R	R	R	R	M	R	R	R
Farmers	O	O	O	O	M	O	R	O
Monitoring of residues:								
on food and horticultural crops	O	M	O	M	Zero	M	R	R
in environment	O	O	O	O	Zero	M	O	O

Key: O = Occasional
M = Minimal
R = Regular
* = At federal level only

INI – India
INO – Indonesia
MAL – Malaysia
PAK – Pakistan
PRC – People's Republic of China
PHL – Philippines
RK – Republic of Korea
THA – Thailand

Source: Asian Development Bank, *Handbook on the Use of Pesticides in the Asia–Pacific Region* (Manila: ADB, 1987).

and the lack of published data reduce the sense of urgency. Most of the recorded incidents of accidental acute pesticide poisoning have resulted from faulty application practices, inadequate storage facilities and contamination during transit (see Chapter 3). As a result regulations have tended to concentrate on these areas.[60]

Some compounds, such as the organochlorines and parathion, are commonly banned (Figure 10.4). In 1986 Indonesia took the step of banning 57 insecticides for use on rice, although this was principally to safeguard the natural predators of the brown planthopper, rather than on safety grounds. Pressure to adopt more rigorous safety policy also arises from the concern of industrialized countries over residues in imported foodstuffs from developing countries. Frequently the levels exceed the MRLs of the Codex Alimentarius Commission (CAC) (see Chapter 3). In many industrialized countries where statutory MRLs are set, imported foods are monitored and in some cases refused entry. In the USA the FDA carries out spot checks on one per cent of all shipments – between 1977 and 1979 some 40 shipments of foodstuffs were denied entry. The consequences of this action have led to countries such as Guatemala having to establish monitoring facilities to check food before it is exported.[61]

Groundwater protection

Our final example of comparative approaches focuses on the control of groundwater contamination by fertilizers and pesticides.

Nitrate sensitive areas scheme

At present, very few of the industrialized countries act to regulate the amounts of nitrate that enter ground or surface waters from agricultural activities. The favoured policy is to place maximum allowable tolerances on drinking water, obliging water treatment authorities to remove the nitrate before delivery to the consumer.

In 1989 the European Commission proposed a draft Directive aimed at imposing strict limits on the use of nitrogen fertilizers and natural manures. This would require member states to identify certain vulnerable zones where nitrogen applications would have to be reduced. The proposal, however, has been strongly opposed and is still under discussion. A UK House of Lords Committee, criticizing the proposal, concluded that reduction of nitrogen fertilizer applications would not be enough to get nitrate levels below the 50 mg/litre limit. They argued

Figure 10.4   Pesticides banned or restricted for agricultural uses in selected Asian countries (represents situation in 1987)

	INDIA	INDONESIA	MALAYSIA	PAKISTAN	PEOPLE'S REPUBLIC OF CHINA	PHILIPPINES	REPUBLIC OF KOREA	THAILAND
Aldrin/Dieldrin	Restricted	Restricted	Restricted	Restricted	Restricted	Restricted	Banned	Restricted
Aldicarb	Unrestricted	Restricted	Unrestricted	Unrestricted	Unrestricted	Restricted	Restricted	Restricted
Azinphos methyl/ethyl	Banned	Unrestricted	Unrestricted	Unrestricted	Banned	Unrestricted	Unrestricted	Unrestricted
Carbaryl	Unrestricted	Restricted	Unrestricted	Unrestricted	Unrestricted	Restricted	Unrestricted	Unrestricted
Chlordane	Restricted	Restricted	Restricted	Restricted	Restricted	Restricted	Restricted	Restricted
DBCP	Banned	Banned	Banned	Banned	Restricted	Banned	Banned	Banned
DDT	Unrestricted	Banned	Banned	Restricted	Banned	Banned	Banned	Banned
2,4 – D	Unrestricted	Unrestricted	Unrestricted	Unrestricted	Unrestricted	Unrestricted	Unrestricted	Unrestricted
2,4,5 – T	Banned	Banned	Unrestricted	Unrestricted	Unrestricted	Banned	Unrestricted	Unrestricted
Endrin	Banned	Banned	Banned	Banned	Banned	Banned	Banned	Banned
Ethylene dibromide	Unrestricted	Banned	Unrestricted	Unrestricted	Unrestricted	Restricted	Unrestricted	Banned
Heptachor	Restricted	Restricted	Restricted	Restricted	Restricted	Restricted	Banned	Restricted
Lindane (γ HCH)	Unrestricted	Unrestricted	Unrestricted	Unrestricted	Unrestricted	Unrestricted	Unrestricted	Restricted
Mephosfolan	Banned	Unrestricted	Unrestricted	Unrestricted	Unrestricted	Unrestricted	Unrestricted	Unrestricted
Monocrotophos	Unrestricted	Restricted	Unrestricted	Unrestricted	Restricted	Unrestricted	Unrestricted	Unrestricted
Other Organochlorines	Unrestricted	Restricted	Restricted	Restricted	Restricted	Restricted	Restricted	Restricted
Paraquat	Unrestricted	Restricted	Unrestricted	Unrestricted	Unrestricted	Restricted	Unrestricted	Unrestricted
Parathion	Banned	Banned	Banned	Banned	Restricted	Banned	Restricted	Unrestricted
Camphechlor (Toxaphene)	Banned	Banned	Unrestricted	Unrestricted	Unrestricted	Banned	Banned	Banned

■ Banned ; complete prohibition of use

◪ Restricted ; certain specific registered uses authorised

□ Unrestricted

Source: Asian Development Bank, *Handbook on the Use of Pesticides in the Asia-Pacific Region* (Manila, 1987).

that major changes in land use would be necessary, including a shift away from crops such as oilseed rape and vegetables, and switching from intensive arable to permanent grass and forestland. This would reduce national arable production by a third, or about £1.3 billion, compared with a cost of £200 million to treat contaminated water by blending and denitrification.

In the meantime, the UK government has introduced a pilot Nitrate Sensitive Areas Scheme under the Water Act 1989. On the advice of the newly established National Rivers Authority, MAFF has designated ten Nitrate Sensitive Areas (NSAs) totalling 15,000 hectares, where nitrate levels in drinking water exceed, or are at risk of exceeding, the 50 mg/litre limit.[62] These represent ten per cent of the total area that is nitrate sensitive on these criteria. Under the scheme farmers in the NSAs will be compensated at a rate of £55–95/ha for complying with a comprehensive range of practices aimed at cutting down nitrate levels in groundwater (Box 10.5). Farmers may receive up to £380/ha for conversion to arable grassland. The scheme, however, is initially voluntary and by mid-1990 the uptake by farmers in the designated areas had been poor. Farmers on only just over half the land area in the ten NSAs had applied to join the scheme, although this did constitute 65 per cent of farmers.[63]

By contrast a more rigorous approach has been adopted in Germany. More than 9000 groundwater protection zones have been established on 2 million hectares of farmland.[64] In these zones water authorities own the land in a 20 metre radius around all boreholes, wells or points of water extraction, and these areas are permanently grassed with no fertilizer or pesticide applications permitted. Beyond this zone farmers must apply fertilizers to such a level that after harvest 45 kg of soil nitrogen per hectare is not exceeded. Below this level the farmer receives compensation of some 310 marks/ha; between 45–90 kg/ha and there is no compensation; more than 90 kg/ha and the farmer is fined.

In the USA the tradition has not been to protect groundwater by regulations. Although the Safe Drinking Water Act Amendments of 1986 require that each state submit a programme to EPA describing how they will prevent contamination of groundwater, these only require the "implementation of control measures".[65] In almost all cases these measures are advisory only. State jurisdictions are said to be proceeding cautiously in developing land-use regulations because of the traditional distrust of planning measures for private property and the fear of legal challenges.[66] However, in Florida, two counties enacted wellfield protection legislation in 1984 and 1988, which regulates land-use close

Box 10.5 Pilot Nitrate Sensitive Areas Scheme in the UK – conditions for basic rate payment scheme

Inorganic fertilizer use
- Do not exceed economic optimum N fertilizer amounts for each year including full allowance for organic manures used
- Apply less than the economic optimum amount of N fertilizer for yield on the following crops as shown:
  Winter wheat 25 kg/ha N below optimum
  Winter barley 25 kg/ha N below optimum
  Winter oilseed rape 50 kg/ha N below optimum
- Do not apply inorganic N fertilizer in autumn or winter
- Applications should not be made between 1 Sept and the following 1 Feb to grass fields
- Applications should not be made between 15 Aug and the following 15 Feb to field not in grass
- Do not apply extra total N fertilizer to bread-making wheat varieties more than specified above
- Do not apply individual applications of more than 120 kg/ha of inorganic N fertilizer

Crop cover
- Drill autumn-sown cereals by 15 Oct if previous crop is harvested by that date
- If the previous crop is removed before 15 Oct and the next crop will not be sown before the next 1 Jan, sow a cover crop
- Where required, approved cover crop should be established as soon after harvest of previous crop. Do not apply inorganic N fertilizer for the cover crop
- The cover crop should not be removed by cultivation, herbicide or grazing before 1 Feb on sandy soils or 1 Dec on other soils, unless next crop is sown within four weeks of removal

Organic manure
- Organic manure should be limited to an annual application of 175 kg/ha total N
- No slurry, poultry manure or liquid sewage sludge to be applied between 1 Sept and 1 Nov to grass fields and between 1 July and 1 Nov to fields not in grass
- Manure stored in the NSA must not be a substantial point of source of nitrate leaching

Ploughing up grassland
- Where slurry, poultry manure or liquid sewage sludge have been applied to grass between 1 July and 1 Sept in any year, the field may not be cultivated or the grass killed off within four weeks of application

continued

Box 10.5   Continued

Ploughing up grassland – Continued
- Where grass is cultivated or reseeded the following crop must be sown as soon as soil conditions allow and in any event no later than 1 Oct in the same year. Grass may not be cultivated between 1 Oct and 1 Feb in the following year

Irrigation
- Where irrigation is practised, show evidence that a scheduling system is used which best uses water and avoids excessive applications

General
- Do not convert grass to arable unless the grass can be shown to be a ley in arable rotation
- Do not increase application of organic manures to the NSA land on the farm by more than 25 per cent of current application unless the manure is produced within the NSA
- Do not remove hedgerows or woodland unless replaced by an equivalent area
- Keep records of applications or organic and inorganic nitrogen fertilizer in terms of quantity, timing and areas of application

Pig/poultry plan
- An individually agreed manure plan will be required for the unit. This will show that the unit has appropriate storage, handling, transport and land to meet the following criteria
- Organic manure should be limited to an annual application of 175 kg/ha total N when applied to NSA land
- No slurry or poultry manure to be applied between 1 Sept and 1 Nov to grass fields and between 1 July and 1 Nov to fields not in grass
- Alternatively the manure may be disposed of in an approved way other than to NSA land. Manure applied to vulnerable land outside the NSA must meet the NSA criteria
- Manure stored in the NSA must not be a substantial point source of nitrate leaching

---

Source: Ministry of Agriculture, Fisheries and Food, London.

to wells. But a subsequent proposal to create a statewide programme to protect wellheads was thrown out by a Florida appellate court.[67]

Pesticide contamination

The finding in 1979 of traces of the insecticide aldicarb in water collected by EPA from beneath Suffolk County on Long Island, New York was quite unexpected[68] (see Chapter 2). It had been predicted that modern pesticides would degrade or volatilize before reaching groundwater. As a result, neither manufacturers nor regulatory bodies had appropriate baseline data on leaching properties, on the extent of potential contamination or possible health consequences.[69] Moreover, there existed no formal or informal regulatory mechanisms that could be enacted.

An immediate response was to extend the investigation through other parts of the USA. This soon revealed that a substantial proportion of wells were contaminated (see Chapter 2). Different agencies in various parts of the country set their own standards. A "no adverse effect" of 7 μg/l was set by the Suffolk County Department of Health Services (Box 10.6). However other agencies established Health Advisory Levels (HAL); which varied from 10–30 ug/l by Offices in EPA and 21–100 ug/l in the case of the Union Carbide Corporation.[70] (See Chapter 2.)

Application rates in Suffolk County, where the contamination was first detected, were reduced but this proved ineffective and the product was withdrawn in early 1980. All well owners with residues at greater than 7 μg/l were advised not to use their water. Proposed solutions to the problem included provision of bottled water, extending clean water supplies to affected households, capping contaminated wells, drilling

Box 10.6 Example of process of setting standards: the pesticide aldicarb in drinking water in the USA

The National Academy of Science recommended safe or no-adverse-effect level in drinking water for human consumption is seven parts per billion of aldicarb.

The assumptions made to calculate this level are as follows:

1 That the no-adverse-effect dose (based on animal and human studies) is 0.1 mg/kg body weight/day
2 That using an uncertainty factor of 100 reduces the acceptable daily intake to 0.001 mg/kg/day
3 That the average adult weighs 70 kg
4 That the average adult drinks two litres of water daily
5 That the aldicarb intake from water represents only 20 per cent of the total aldicarb intake

Thus the recommended level is:

(0.001 mg/kg/day × 70 kg × 0.2)/(2 litres/day)

= 0.007 mg/l = 7 μg/l
= 7 ppb

Source: Zaki, M.H., Moran, D. and Harris, D., "Pesticides in groundwater: the aldicarb story in Suffolk County, New York", *Am. J. Publ. Health* **72**, (1982) pp. 1391–5.

new wells and installing activated carbon filters in each household. The last action was deemed the most effective, and Union Carbide agreed to provide filtration systems free of charge. The company also funded the extensive monitoring programme and provided laboratory facilities.

Following these events, nationwide monitoring of groundwater began, but the costs are proving to be very high. It costs between $53 and $139 (at 1986 prices) to test a sample from a well for a single pesticide compound, though it is just $10–25 to test for nitrates. Nielson and Lee[71] using computer models to predict the regions of potential groundwater contamination by pesticides and nitrates, calculate the costs of testing the 10.9 million private wells systems in these areas to be $900–1400 million; and for the public systems, fewer in number but serving 29 million people, to be $14 million. These estimates are based on only two pesticide analyses and a 33 per cent resampling rate. Some states are also likely to incur much greater costs than others, in particular, Wisconsin, Michigan, Ohio, Pennsylvania, New York, Maine, Florida and California.

To date, protection of groundwater against pesticide contamination has lacked appropriate practices, laws or procedures. The responses, as in the aldicarb situation, have been largely *ad hoc*. EPA has set few maximum contaminant levels (MCLs) and this has led to states setting MCLs, HALs and guidelines that are inconsistent. There is also, as yet, no central policy on costs and distribution of costs – the cost effectiveness of different remedial actions is highly site specific and is often borne by different institutions at different locations. According to NRC[72], state and industrial officials have consistently argued for Federal leadership, so that all interested parties know at least where they stand. In 1984 the EPA did request data on the potential for groundwater contamination of 84 pesticides and 50 other active ingredients, with the ultimate aim of reassessing registration standards. But because the re-registration process in EPA is significantly behind schedule, these new assessments are not likely to be made rapidly.

In Britain, as in the USA, the extent of pesticide contamination of groundwater was unexpected, though the introduction of highly water soluble herbicides in the 1970s prompted a programme of monitoring of groundwater.[73] This revealed the presence of several pesticides (see Chapter 2). So far the government maintains that concentrations being detected routinely are lower, in almost all cases by several orders of magnitude, than those likely to cause adverse health effects[74]

Again the difficulty over predicting levels that will cause no adverse health effects has led to discrepancies in the setting of guidelines.

Numerous groundwater supplies, particularly in East Anglian chalk, exceed the EC Maximum Admissible Concentrations of 0.1 μg/l for any individual pesticide and 0.5 μg/l for total pesticides as given in Directive 80/778, issued in 1985.[75] But there is considerable disagreement over the guidelines. The authorities have themselves set only a small number of guidelines, primarily for organochlorines, but for most other products they use a mix of the guidelines developed by WHO and the US EPA, both of which allow much higher concentrations for most compounds than the EC (Table 10.7). As in the USA, there is a lack of coherent policy on guidelines for health or on monitoring arrangements.

Table 10.7   Selection of guidelines and maximum contaminant levels set by various authorities for pesticides in drinking water (μg/l)

	World Health Organization	European Communities	Department of the Environment (UK)	Environmental Protection Agency (USA)
Herbicides				
Atrazine	2	0.1	30	150
Simazine	17	0.1	30	1500
Alachlor	0.3	0.1		
Propanil	170	0.1		
MCPA	0.5	0.1	10	
Trifluralin	170	0.1		
2,4-D	100	0.1	100	100
Paraquat	0.3	0.1	0.3	60
Molinate	7	0.1		
Isoproturon	0.4	0.1		
Insecticides				
Aldicarb		0.1	7	10–30
Dimethoate	7	0.1	7	
Endrin		0.1		0.2
gamma HCH (Lindane)		0.1		4

Source: Lawrence, A.R. and Foster, S.S.D., *The pollution threat from agricultural pesticides and industrialised solvents: a comparative review in relation to British aquifer* (Wallingford, Oxon: British Geological Survey, 1987); Holden, P.W., *Pesticides and Groundwater Quality* (Washington DC: National Academy Press, 1986).

In both the USA and the UK many questions remain unanswered. For instance, little is known of the extent and rates of leaching of pesticides. A recent study of hydrogeological conditions in the UK suggests that once groundwater has been contaminated it will be difficult to determine the extent of pollution and expensive to clean up aquifers effectively. This is particularly true of fissure-flow aquifers, where pollutants can be transported long distances very rapidly[76] (see Chapters 2 and 4). More information is also required on the toxicological significance of pesticide residues in groundwater. Finally, there is a need to uncover the best policy and institutional responses, and the most appropriate adjustments to agricultural practice. In the USA these questions have to be posed against a growing public concern that may lead to the imposition of statewide or national bans, on the grounds of political expediency, even where contamination is controllable.

Global pollution control

To conclude this chapter we offer a few comments on the control policies for the wider international pollution problems where agriculture is both a polluter and an actual or potential victim. Currently, these are major topics of discussion and in this book there is only space to refer to the key areas of agreement and controversy.

We presently face three major global pollution threats – acid rain, depletion of the ozone layer and global warming. Although, to some extent, these are interconnected they pose two different kinds of control problem.[77]

Acid rain

Acid rain is an example of transboundary pollution. The pollutants are produced in one or more countries and affect their neighbours: acid rain precursors are generated in the northeast of the USA and the highly industrialized countries of western and central Europe, and much of the acid rain falls in Canada and Scandinavia, respectively.

The basis for control is essentially one of bargaining toward a negotiated agreement.[78] To some extent recipient countries can mitigate the effects. For instance, acidification of lakes and rivers can be ameliorated by liming, although this is likely to cause damages of another kind. In essence, though, acid rain control involves one or more countries incurring clean-up expenses for the benefit of other countries. Inevitably this is not easy to achieve. In 1983 Norway proposed a "30 per cent Club" under which countries would reduce their SO_2 emissions by 30 per cent by 1993, but it was strongly opposed by several significant polluters.

That progress has occurred is due to two factors. First, there is a growing recognition of self-interest. The USA, the UK and Germany are now recognizing that acid rain is falling on their countries and that significant damage is occurring. Second, various supernational bodies have been bringing increasing pressure to bear on the significant polluters. The basis for this was the 1983 Convention on Long Range Transboundary Air Pollution drawn up by the UN Economic Commission for Europe, but real action did not occur until the European Commission's 1988 directive on emissions from large combustion plants was agreed. Under this the UK, for instance, is required to reduce SO_2 and NO_x by 20 per cent and 15 per cent of 1980 levels by 1993, and 40 per cent and 30 per cent by 1998. cent by 1998.

Because the contribution of ammonia to the acid rain problem is only just being recognized it is not yet the subject of any agreement.

Depletion of the ozone layer and global warming

The other two major global problems are significantly different in that all countries are contributers to the problem and all are potential sufferers, even though there are considerable differences in relative contribution and impacts. This makes the position of arriving at agreements a great deal more complex.

Attempts to prevent the depletion of the ozone layer have largely concentrated on controlling the emissions of carbon fluorocarbons (CFCs). Some individual countries have taken unilateral action. The USA banned the use of CFCs in aerosols in 1978. But the significant step was the banning by all the major CFC-manufacturing countries agreed in the Montreal Protocol on Substances that Deplete the Ozone Layer in 1987. The agreement is for consumption to be frozen by mid-1990 and reduced by 50 per cent by the turn of the century. Part of the reason for the readiness with which the industrialized countries have signed the Protocol is the universal recognition of the threat that depletion of the ozone layer poses and a belief that substitute substances for CFCs can be produced. Significantly, however, India and China only indicated they would sign the Protocol in mid-1990. They are growing users of CFCs, particularly for refrigeration, and have infant CFC industries. They claim that any substitutes are likely to be developed by multinational companies and will prove a great deal more expensive than the presently used CFCs. Their agreement to sign the Protocol depends on compensation for these increased costs.

So far, no moves have been made against other pollutants implicated in ozone depletion, such as methane and nitrous oxide.

By far the most difficult problem to tackle is global warming. This is partly because there is still controversy over whether significant global warming is occurring and, if so, whether it is due to human activity. But even if this becomes widely accepted there remain formidable difficulties to agreeing on or enforcing control over the most significant pollutants.

One proposal is for a universal carbon tax that could raise the cost of using fossil fuels, so encouraging either less use of fossil fuel, such as coal, oil or petrol, or substitution by some less-polluting alternative, such as the harnessing of wind or tidal power to generate electricity. But there are serious equity difficulties associated with such proposals. Some countries would suffer more than others. Progress towards agreement depends on overcoming the major divide that exists between the industrialized and developing countries. The former perceive the threat more clearly and are urging a worldwide response, but the latter see it as trivial – a problem created by the industrialized countries and for them to solve. In principle, alternative technologies exist for reducing carbon dioxide and other emissions but their implementation in both the industrialized and developing countries will not be without major economic, social and political cost.

References

1 Burrows, P., *The Economic Threory of Pollution Control* (Oxford: Martin Robertson, 1979).

2 Baumol, W.J. and Oates, W.E., *The Theory of Environmental Policy*, 2nd edn (Cambridge: Cambridge Univ. Press, 1988); Barbier, E.B., *Economics, Natural Resource Scarcity and Development. Conventional and Alternative Views* (London: Earthscan Publ. Ltd, 1989); Burrows, 1979, *op. cit.*; Norton, G.A., *Resource Economics* (London: Edward Arnold, 1984); Pearce, D.W. and Turner, R.K., *Economics of Natural Resources and the Environment* (New York: Harvester Wheatsheaf, 1990).

3 Barbier, 1989, *op. cit.*

4 Pimentel, D., Andow, D., Dyson-Hudson, R., Gallahan, D., Jacobson, S., Irish, M., Kroop, S., Moss, A., Schreiner, I., Shepard, M., Thompson, T. and Vinzart, B., "Environmental and social costs of pesticides: a preliminary assessment", *OIKOS* 34 (1980) pp. 126–40.

5 McGregor, S.E., Rhyne, C., Worley, S., Jr. and Todd, F.E., "The role of honeybees in cotton pollination", *Agron. J.* 47 (1985) pp. 23–5.

6 Adams, R.M., Hamilton, S.A. and McCarl, B.A., *The Economic Effects of Ozone on Agriculture*, US EPA, Environmental Research Laboratory (Oregon: Corvallis, 1984).

7   Heck, W.W., "Assessment of crop losses from air pollutants in the United States", in: MacKenzie, J.J. and El-Ashry, M.T. (eds), *Air Pollution's Toll on Forests and Crops* (New Haven: Yale Univ. Press, 1989).

8   OECD, *The Costs and Benefits of Sulphur Control* (Paris: OECD, 1981).

9   van der Eerden, L.J., Tonneijck, A.E.G. and Wijnards, J.H.M., "Crop loss due to air pollution in the Netherlands", *Environ. Pollut.* 53 (1988) pp. 365–76.

10   ENDS, "Sulphur dioxide may trigger aphid outbreaks, extra pesticide spraying", ENDS 151 (1987) pp. 5–6.

11   Skarby, L., "Changes in the nutritional quality of crops", in: Koziol, M.J. and Whatley, F.R. (eds), *Gaseous Air Pollutants and Plant Metabolism* (London: Butterworths, 1984).

12   Ministry of Housing, Physical Planning and Environment, *The Netherlands Acidification Abatement Plan* (Netherlands: The Hague, 1989).

13   Bunch, R., *Low Input Soil Restoration in Honduras: The Contarranas as Farmer-to-Farmer Extension Programme*, Gatekeeper Series SA23, Sustainable Agricultural Programme (London: IIED, 1990); Rhoades, R. and Booth, R., "Farmer-back-to-Farmer: a model for generating acceptable agricultural technology", *Agric. Admin.* 11 (1982) pp. 127–37; Chambers, R., Pacey, A. and Thrupp, L.A., *Farmer First* (London: Intermediate Technology Publications, 1989); Jintrawet, A., Smutkupt, S., Wongsamun, C., Katawetin, R. and Kerdsuk, V., *Extension Activities for Peanuts after Rice in Ban Sum Jan, Northeast Thailand: A case study in Farmer-to-Farmer Extension Methodology* (Thailand: Khon Kaen University, 1985).

14   Pretty, J.N., "Farmers' extension practice and technology adaptation: agricultural revolution in 17–19th century Britain", *Agriculture and Human Values* (in press, 1991).

15   Howell, J. (ed.), *Training and Visit Extension in Practice* Agricultural Administration Unit Occasional Paper 8 (London: Overseas Development Institute, 1988); Kiara, J.K., Seggeros, M., Pretty, J.N. and McCracken, J.A., *Rapid Catchment Analysis: An application of rapid rural appraisal to the catchment approach of the soil and water conservation branch, Ministry of Agriculture* (London: Kenya and IIED, 1990); Pretty, J.N., *Rapid Catchment Analysis for Extension Agents: Notes on the 1990 Kericho training workshop the Minsitry of Agriculture, Kenya* (London: IIED, 1990); Chambers et al., 1989, *op. cit.*

16   Pearce, D., *The Polluter Pays Principle*, Gatekeeper Series no. LEEC 89–03 (London: IIED, 1989).

17   Burrows, 1979, *op. cit.*; Pearce and Turner, 1990, *op. cit.*

18   OECD, *Agricultural and Environmental Policies* (Paris: OECD, 1989).

19   OECD, 1989, *op. cit.*

20   Pearce, 1989, *op. cit.*

21   OECD, 1989, *op. cit.*; Barbier, 1989, *op. cit.*

22   Barbier, 1989, *op. cit.*; Brady, G.L. and Morrison, R.E., "Emissions trading: an overview of the EPA policy statement", *Intern. J. Environ.*

Studies **23** (1984) pp. 19–40.

23 Pearce, 1989, *op. cit.*

24 Hahn, R. and Hester, G., "The Market for bads" Regulation 3–4 (1987).

25 Pretty, J.N., "Sustainable agriculture in the middle ages: the English manor", *Agric. Hist. Rev.* **38** (1990) pp. 1–19.

26 Rogers, W.V.H. (ed.), *Winfield and Jolowicz on Tort* (London: Sweet and Maxwell, 13th edn, 1989).

27 Macrory, R., "In: Court" ENDS **168** (1989) pp. 17.

28 Macrory, R., Imperial College, London, personal communication, 10 October 1990.

29 Timberlake, L., *Only One Earth* (London: BBC Publications, 1987).

30 Macrory, R., "The legal control of pullution", in: Harrison, R. (ed.), *Pollution Cause, Effects and Controls*, 2nd edn (Nottingham: Royal Society of Chemistry, 1990).

31 Haigh, N., *EEC Environmental Policy and Britain*, 2nd edn (London: Longmans, 1988); Holdgate, M.W., *A Perspective of Environmental Pollution* (Cambridge: Cambridge University Press, 1979).

32 CAC, *Codex Maximum Limits to Pesticide Residues*, Codex Alimentarius vol. XIII (Rome: CAC FAO and WHO, 1986).

33 Holdgate, M.W., "Environmental policies in Britain and mainland Europe", in: Macrory, R.B. (ed.), *Britain, Europe and the Environment* (London: Imperial College, Centre for Environmental Technology, 1983).

34 Macrory, R., "Science, legislation and the courts", in: Conway, G.R. (ed.), *The Assessment of Environmental Problems* (London: Imperial College, 1986).

35 RCEP, *Air Pollution Control: an Integrated Approach*, Royal Commission on Environmental Pollution (London: HMSO, 1976).

36 Department of the Environment, reported in ENDS, "Setting water quality standards: science or expediency", **149** (1987) pp. 17–18.

37 Wasserstrom, R.F. and Wiles, R., *Field Duty: US Farmworker and Pesticide Safety* (Washington DC: World Resources Inst., 1985).

38 Holden, P.W., *Pesticides and Groundwater Quality* (Washington DC: National Academy Press, 1986).

39 Barbier, 1989, *op. cit.*; Pearce and Turner, 1990, *op. cit.*

40 Davies, T., "The United States: experiment and fragmentation", in: Haigh, N. and Irwin, F. (eds), *Integrated Pollution Control in Europe and North America* (Washington and London: Conservation Foundation and IEEP, 1990).

41 Rabe, B., "Overcoming fragmentation in Canadian environmental management", in: Haigh and Irwin (eds), 1990, *op. cit.*

42 NRC, *Alternative Agriculture* (Washington DC: National Research Council, 1989).

43 HC, *The Effects of Pesticides on Human Health* vol. 1, House of Commons Select Committee on Agriculture (London: HMSO, 1987).

44 NRC, 1989, *op. cit.*

45 Gilbert, D.G.R., *Pesticide Safety Policy and Control Arrangements in Britain*, PhD Thesis (London: Imperial College, 1987).

46 Bottrell, D.G., "Government influence on pesticide use in developing countries", *Insect Sci. Applic.* 5 (1984) pp. 151–5; Bull, D., *A Growing Problem. Pesticides and the Third World Poor* (Oxford: Oxfam, 1982).

47 Pallemaerts, M., *Export notification* EER 1(2) (1987) pp. 25–37.

48 MAFF, *Report of the Working Party on Pesticide Residues (1982–1985)*, Food Surveillance Paper no. 16 (London: HMSO, 1986).

49 MAFF, *Report of the Working Party on Pesticide Residues: 1985–1988*, Food Surveillance Paper no. 25 (London: HMSO, 1989); MAFF, 1986, *op. cit.*

50 RCEP, *Agriculture and Pollution*, Royal Commission on Environmental Pollution, 7th Report (London: HMSO, 1979).

51 Gilbert, 1987, *op. cit.*

52 Tait, E.J., Pest control decision making on brassica crops, *Adv. Appl. Biol.* 8 (1988) pp. 121–88.

53 NRC, *Regulating Pesticides in Food, The Delaney Paradox* (Washington DC: National Research Council, 1987).

54 NRC, 1987, *op. cit.*

55 NRC, 1987, *op. cit.*

56 NRC, 1987, *op. cit.*

57 Norman, C., "EPA sets new policy on pesticide cancer risks", *Science* 242 (1988) pp. 360–7.

58 MAFF, 1986, *op. cit.*

59 Bull, 1982, *op. cit.*

60 Boardman, R., *Pesticides in World Agriculture, The Politics of International Regulation* (Basingstoke, Hants: Macmillan Press Ltd, 1986).

61 ICAITI, *An environmental and economic study of the consequences of pesticide use in Central American cotton production* (Guatemala City, Guatemala: Instituto Centroamericano de Investigación de Tecnología Industrial, 1977).

62 MAFF, *Nitrate Sensitive Areas Scheme*, a consultation document by Agriculture Depts. of England and Wales (London: MAFF, 1989).

63 ENDS, "Farmers put voluntary approach to curbs on nitrate leaching in peril", 187 (1990) pp. 6–7.

64 *Farmers Weekly* (London), "Water protection means tough fine for Germans", 23 March (1990) p. 54.

65 Tell, P.S., "Groundwater protection zones: United States and European experiences", *International Environment Reporter*, March (1990) pp. 123–132.

66 Tell, 1990, *op. cit.*

67 Tell, 1990, *op. cit.*

68 Zaki, M.H., Moran, D. and Harris, D., "Pesticides in groundwater: the aldicarb storm in Suffolk County, New York", *Am. J. Publ. Health* 72 (1982) pp. 1391–5; Warner, M.E., *An environmental risk index to evaluate pesticide programs in crop budgets* (Ithaca, New York: Dept. Agric. Econ., Cornell Univ., 1985).

69 Holden, 1986, *op. cit.*

70 Holden, 1986, *op. cit.*

71 Neilson, E.G. and Lee, L.K., *The Magnitude and Costs of Groundwater Contamination from Agricultural Chemicals*, Econ. Res. Serv. Agric. Econ. Report 576 (Washington: USDA, 1987).

72 Holden, 1986, *op. cit.*

73 HC, 1987, *op. cit.*

74 HC, 1987, *op. cit.*

75 Lawrence, A.R. and Foster, S.S.D., *The pollution threat in agricultural pesticides and industrial solvents: a comparative review in relation to British aquifers*, Hydrogeol. Rep. of Brit. Geol. Survey no. 87/2 (Wallingford, Oxfordshire: BGS, 1987).

76 Lawrence and Foster, 1987, *op. cit.*

77 Pearce and Turner, 1990, *op. cit.*

78 Pearce and Turner, 1990, *op. cit.*

11   Agriculture Without Pollution

An agricultural system that does not cause pollution, or at least contamination, of the environment, is an impossible goal. All productive processes, whether they be of industry or agriculture, involve transformation of inputs of one kind or another to useful outputs, and the conversion can never be 100 per cent efficient. There is always a waste that goes into the environment.

The very first agriculture, 10,000 years ago, was a source of contamination. Vegetation was burnt to clear the land for crops and the process of cultivation itself produced run-off of soil sediments. But serious pollution – contamination that adversely affects ourselves or what we value in the environment – only began with the accelerated intensification of agriculture and the use of modern chemical inputs that began in the middle years of this century.

In this final chapter we review possible approaches to agricultural production that can significantly reduce the inputs of potentially polluting compounds or can ensure they are used in such a way as to minimize their pollution effects. The realistic goal is a low-polluting agriculture.

Inevitably this review will be brief and superficial. To do justice to the topic of low-polluting agricultural technologies would require one or more books. The reader should consult the references cited here for further information.

Pest management without pollution

Agricultural pests and pathogens are important constraints to agricultural production. They are commonly attributed with destroying between 10 and 40 per cent of the world's gross agricultural production and, on occasion, the consequences can be devastating (see Chapter 2). It is this potential for damage that has driven the search for powerful synthetic pesticides and their widespread use. But pesticides are not a perfect answer to controlling pests and pathogens. In addition to the dangers to human health and to the environment outlined in Chapters 2 and 3, pesticides are often inefficient at controlling pests. There are four reasons for this:[1]

1 They can cause resurgences by also killing off the natural enemies of the target pests.
2 They produce upset pests, by killing off the natural enemies of species which hitherto were not pests.
3 Pests can become resistant to pesticides.[2]
4 At best, pesticides have to be repeatedly applied; they produce no lasting or stable control.

In "wild" conditions, in natural grasslands and woodlands, outbreaks of pests and pathogens are rare. Most pest species are naturally regulated by a variety of ecological processes, such as competition for food or predation and parasitism by natural enemies. Their numbers are, thus, more or less stable and the damage they cause is relatively insignificant. The question is: can we make use of any of these processes in the semi-artificial environments of agro-ecosystems?

Agro-ecosystems are, of course, different from natural ecosystems. They are deliberately designed to be highly productive. Fields are planted with monocultures of uniform varieties, are well watered and provided with high inputs of fertilizers. Not surprisingly, such systems provide ideal conditions for pest and pathogen attack, and frequently the scale and speed of the attack is such that resort to pesticides is the only means of avoiding serious crop loss. But this does not mean that they cannot be used more efficiently and with a minimal pollution impact.

There are five broad strategies of pest control that, alone or in combination, have the potential for reducing the risk of pollution. They are:

- the use of natural enemies of pests and pathogens
- breeding crop plants or livestock for resistance to pests or pathogens
- agricultural or other practices to change the habitat of the pest or pathogen
- interference with reproduction of pest populations
- the selective use of pesticides, with low toxicity and little environmental hazard.

In the following sections we briefly review these stragegies, discussing their advantages and disadvantages both in terms of efficiency and potential environmental pollution.

Using natural enemies

The natural enemies of pests include a great variety of organisms – parasitic wasps and flies, and predators such as ladybird beetles, spiders, hoverflies and assassin bugs, as well as larger animals such as lizards and birds. Pests are also attacked by a range of pathogens – bacteria, fungi and viruses. In natural conditions many such natural enemies may be present, commonly acting together to regulate pest numbers. But in agro-ecosystems it is often only one or two enemy species that are required to keep pests in check. Sometimes the level of control is variable or intermittent but, ideally, the pest population needs to be brought down to a desired level and maintained there, hopefully permanently.[3] This implies that the pest population is not eradicated and, indeed, is tolerated to an extent. Inevitably, there is some degree of trade-off between the sustainability of control and the size and stability of the pest population. By comparison with pesticide use, the pest population may be relatively larger and may fluctuate more, but control tends to be cheaper and more durable (Figure 11.1).

Use of natural enemies is usually referred to as biological control. The term sometimes implies any form of non-pesticidal control but it is less confusing if restricted to the use of natural enemies. It is also important to distinguish between what is called "classical biological control" which involves the release of new or exotic natural enemies, and "augmentation" which relies on improving the degree of existing control.

Classical biological control

This approach often works best where a pest has become introduced to a part of the world distant from its origin. Usually such introduced pests arrive without their normal natural enemies and hence are able to multiply unchecked. The annual invasion of Japan by the rice brown planthopper from China is one such example, although the invasions only lasts for a few months. Examples of other, more lasting invasions are the Asian scale insect *Aonidiella*, which appeared in 1986 as a threat to cultivated neem (*Azadirachta indica*) in Central Africa, and

Figure 11.1 Contrasting dynamics of pesticide and biological methods for the control of pests

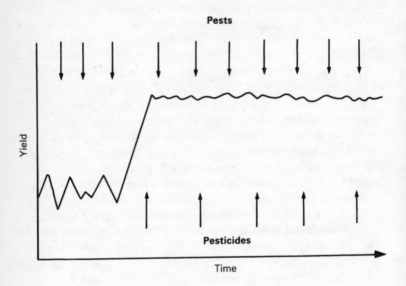

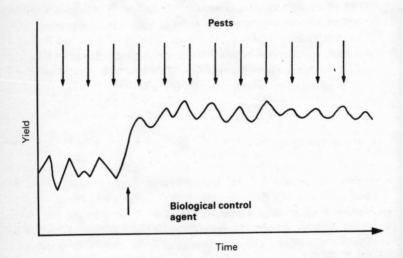

Source: Conway, G.R. and Barbier, E.B., *After the Green Revolution* (London: Earthscan Publications, 1990).

the *Heteropsylla* psyllid which has spread from Hawaii to Asia and is devastating *Leucaena* trees.[4]

In these situations it is theoretically possible to go to the original home of the pest, search out its natural enemies there and introduce them to the new locality, in the hope that they will restore the original level of control. Sometimes the results are spectacular. One of the earliest examples was the control of the cottony-cushion scale (*Icerya purchasi*) on citrus in California by the Vedalia beetle, introduced in 1888 from Australia where the scale had its origin.[5] The beetle was a voracious feeder on the scale and, very soon after its introduction, the citrus harvest tripled. The numbers of the scale have since remained insignificant, save for a brief period in the 1950s when DDT and malathion sprays killed off the predators. Another spectacular success was the control of the prickly pear, *Opuntia*, a cactus that was introduced into Australia as a garden plant from Mexico at the end of the last century. It soon spread to pasture land and by the 1920s some 25 million hectares were infested. But eventually *Cactoblastis cactorum*, the larvae of which tunnel inside and destroy the cactus, was discovered in Argentina and taken to Australia. Today the cactus only occurs as individual plants or in small patches.

The most recent success story has been the introduction of the parasitic wasp *Epidinocarsis lopezi* from South America to control the cassava mealybug (*Phenacoccus manihoti*) in Africa.[6] The mealybug first appeared in Congo and Zaire in the early 1970s, spreading rapidly through most of the African cassava belt and becoming a major pest (Figure 11.2). Widespread searches were conducted throughout South America, since this was the original home of cassava, and the wasp discovered there was released in Nigeria in 1981. By the end of 1984, it was found in 70 per cent of all fields in more than 200,000 km^2 in southwestern Nigeria. Now releases are being made in 16 other countries. A recent economic study has calculated that for every dollar spent on this programme, farmers have benefited by $150 – a spectacularly favourable cost-benefit ratio.[7]

However, there have also been failures. Indeed only 5 per cent of deliberate releases have achieved their aim.[8] Table 11.1 lists several important successes and failures. The problem is that still very little is known of the detailed population dynamics of pests and their natural enemies. In theory, it is possible to define the characteristics of the ideal natural enemy and seek it out. But in practice, the most effective approach has been to introduce several enemy species in the hope that one or another will work. If successful the pay-offs are considerable, but inevitably there are many failures.

Figure 11.2 Distribution of cassava mealybug (shaded) and *Epidinocarsis lopezi* (stripes) in Africa, showing the situation at the end of 1986

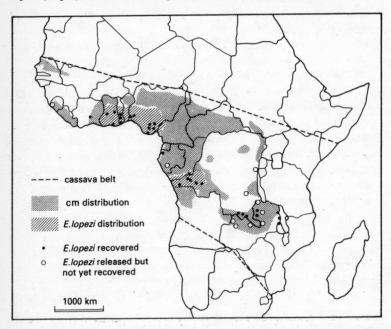

- - - - cassava belt

       cm distribution

       E.lopezi distribution

•   *E.lopezi* recovered

○   *E.lopezi* released but
       not yet recovered

1000 km

Source: Neuenschwander, P. and Herren, H.R., "Biological control of the cassava mealybug, *Penacoccus manihoti*, by the exotic parasitoid *Epidinocarsis lopezi* in Africa", *Phil. Trans. R. Soc. Lond. B* **318** (1988) pp. 319–333.

The target does not always have to be an introduced pest or weed. In Britain the fern bracken has long been a serious weed of marginal and hill land. It is carcinogenic to humans, acts as a reservoir for sheep ticks, and is poisonous to livestock. It currently occupies 3000–6700 km^2 and is spreading at a rate of 3 per cent per year. For these reasons Lawton and his colleagues have screened bracken communities throughout the world for natural control agents.[9] They identified several moths in temperate southern Africa and, following exhaustive tests, found that the larvae of one species, *Conservata cinisigna*, feeds exclusively on bracken. This currently represents the best option for biological control, but release into the wild is still some way off. If a licence is granted by the authorities, then field testing within cages will have to be conducted for several years.

Some of the most successful biological control programmes have been against pests of glasshouse crops, such as tomatoes, cucumbers and ornamentals. Pests become inadvertently introduced into

Table 11.1   Selected successes and failures of biological control agents

Successes

1 The ectoparasite *Aphytis holozanthus*, to control Florida red scale on citrus in Israel in 1956–7.
2 The parasitic chalcid wasp *Encarsia formosa* against whitefly under glass or plastic.
3 The predatory mite *Phytoseiulus persimilis*, against mites under glass or plastic.
4 The fungal mycoherbicide *Colletotrichum gloeosporioides*, against Northern joint vetch.
5 *Trichogramma* spp, an egg parasitoid of moth pests, now on 15 million ha worldwide.

Failures

1 Control of Bermuda cedar scales failed despite the introduction of over 50 species of natural enemies, mainly ladybird beetle predators, to cedar forests in Bermuda between 1946 and 1951.
2 Introduction of cane toads in Australia failed to control sugar cane beetles and the toads became pests.
3 Control of mosquito larvae by the nematode *Romanomermis culcivorax* failed due to handling, storage and shipping difficulties, host specificity and expense.
4 Control of *Heliothis* spp. by nuclear polyhedrosis virus failed because of poor forecasting of market needs, even though technically successful.

Sources: Jutsum, A.R., "Commercial application of biological control: status and prospects", *Phil. Trans. R. Soc. Lond.* B **318** (1988) pp. 357–73; Herzog, D.C. and Funderbank, J.E., "Ecological bases to habitat management and pest control", in: Kogan, M. (ed.), *Ecological Theory and Integrated Pest Control Management in Practice* (New York: John Wiley and Sons, 1986).

glasshouses and rapidly multiply in the controlled and favourable environment, often with devastating effects. However, the high degree of environmental control can also favour the planned release of natural enemies. This was first tried in Britain in the 1970s, not because of a concern over pesticide pollution but in response to the development of pesticide resistance among a number of glasshouse pests.[10] The first target was the two-spotted mite, a serious pest of cucumbers and tomatoes that first appeared in glasshouses in 1949. Releases were made of a South American predatory mite *Phytoseiulus*. It was soon found, however, that broad spectrum sprays killed the predatory mites and the biological control programme had to be rapidly extended. More selective pesticides were used but a second biological control agent, *Encarsia*, a predatory wasp, was then successfully released against the whitefly, one of the most important of the other pests. It is an example that illustrates the importance of establishing effective natural enemy control first and then developing other complementary control strategies. Today, some 60–70 per cent of the UK cucumber crop and 15–20 per cent of tomatoes are subject to biological control.

Releasing natural enemies is a pollution free-technology; nevertheless there is a risk that the released exotic may itself become an undesirable pest. This is particularly likely when insects are being introduced to control weeds since, in theory, they may turn from the weeds to crops. However, though shifts of weed control agents to other native plants have been recorded, none as yet has involved a serious threat to crop plants.[11] Today, elaborate screening of natural enemies is undertaken, in escape-proof conditions, to determine the range of possible hosts which they might attack when eventually released. An example is the stringent screening being undertaken of insects introduced to control bracken in the UK.

Augmenting natural enemies

Rather than introducing new species of natural enemies, those already present in an agro-ecosystem can be augmented by additional releases. To be effective, though, the releases usually have to be on a large scale. Rarely do they have more than a short-lived effect, because the constraints that apply to the existing natural enemy populations will eventually catch up with the new releases. But, sometimes, indigenous natural enemy populations are ineffective because in seasonal environments they take time to build up in sufficient numbers to bring about significant control before the damage is done. In this situation an augmented release can be effective. For instance, a single carefully timed released of the egg parasitoid *Trichogramma* early in the growing season gives as good control of moth pests on maize and sugar cane in China as weekly mass releases later in the season.[12]

Improving the natural enemy environment

In practice it is often more effective to understand the constraints under which natural enemy populations exist and attempt to remove, or at least minimize, them. One traditional technique on citrus trees has been to encourage populations of predatory ants. In China, bamboo bridges have long been placed between branches to facilitate movement of ants from tree to tree, and ant nests have been placed in orchards.

In particular, natural enemy populations can be encouraged by increasing the diversity of agro-ecosystems and their neighbouring environments, and by fostering crops and wild plants that favour natural enemies. For example mixes of cotton and alfalfa, alongside maize or soybeans increase the abundance of bollworm predators. The reason is that with a diversity of plants there is a greater range of insects available in both space and time, and this favours predators that are general feeders.[13] In the Philippines intercropping maize with peanuts controls maize stemborer, because the spiders which attack the stemborers need to feed, when they are young, on springtails and these live in the litter under the peanuts.[14]

Many natural enemies require food sources in the form of pollen or nectar, which can often be provided by wild vegetation near the crops. Often there are more natural enemies in fields bordered by weedy hedgerows. For example, perennial stinging nettle serves as a source of predators of aphids and psyllids. The predators increase in the spring, and their dispersal to crop fields can be encouraged by cutting nettle stands in June.[15] Sometimes, though, the management is more complex. An egg parasitoid *Anagrus* controls the economically important pest of grapes, the grape leafhopper, in California, but only in vineyards which are located within 5.5 km of streams and rivers. This is because the parasitoid has to overwinter on populations of another insect, the blackberry leafhopper, which is present on blackberry stands growing in river and stream bottoms. Control of the pest has not been successful when the distance has increased over 5.5 km.[16] Some examples of weeds that harbour natural enemies of pests are given in Table 11.2.

It is also possible to enhance natural enemies by cultivation practices. For example, strip cutting of alfalfa fields in North America produces two different aged hay growths, which allows a reservoir of natural enemies to survive and so maintain a close level of control.[17]

But experience suggests it is not enough to increase agro-ecosystem diversity and hope this will suffice. Indeed under certain conditions, predator numbers and activity are higher in monocrops than in more diverse cropping patterns. Successful manipulation depends either on luck or a good understanding of the system dynamics of the natural enemy and the pest.

Breeding for resistance

In response to attacks by insects and pathogens, wild plants and animals have evolved a great variety of defence machanisms. The wild forms of plants, as diverse as squashes, cabbages, potatoes, lima beans, mangoes and lettuce, contain bitter compounds (alkaloids, terpenoids,

Table 11.2 Examples of cropping systems in which weeds enhance the biological control of certain pests

Crop	Weeds	Pest regulated	Mechanism
Apple	Nasturtium	Aphids	Enhancement of hoverfly populations
Apple	Phacelia spp. and Bryngium spp.	San Jose scale and aphids	Increased abundance and activity of parasitic wasps
Apple	Natural weed complex	Tent caterpillar and codling moth	Increased abundance and activity of parasitic wasps
Brassicas	Amaranthus, Chenopodium, Xanthium	Green peach aphid	Increased abundance of predatory beetles
Cotton	Ragweed (Senecio)	Boll weevil	Alternative host for parasite Eurytoma
Maize	Giant ragweed	European corn borer	Alternative host for tachinid parasite
Peach	Ragweed	Oriental fruit moth	Alternative host for parasite Macrocentrus
Soybean	Sicklepod (Cassia)	Velvetbean caterpillar and southern green stinkbug	Increased abundance of predators
Sugar cane	Euphorbia	Sugar cane weevil	Provision of nectar and pollen for Lixophagus parasite
Sweet potato	Morning glory	Argus tortoise beetle	Alternative host for parasite Emersonella
Vineyards	Wild blackberry	Grape leafhopper	Alternative host for parasitic wasp, Anagrus

Source: Altieri, M.A. and Liebman, M., "Insect, weed and plant disease management in multiple cropping systems", in: Francis, C.A. (ed.), *Multiple Cropping Systems* (New York: Macmillan, 1986).

cynogenetic compounds and so on) that prevent them being eaten by herbivores. Other plants protect themselves by barriers of hairs, tough leaf or fruit surfaces or similar physical defences.[18]

During selection and breeding to produce high yielding crop varieties and livestock breeds, many of these defences are lost. This may be deliberate since bitter compounds reduce the palatability of plants to humans as well as wild animals. When breeders attempted, in the 1960s, to produce cotton varieties with low content of the terpenoid, gossypol, so that cotton seeds could be used for human food, the new varieties were found to be highly susceptible to insect attack.[19] But, often, the loss is inadvertent. The breeders' primary aim is increased yield and by focusing selection on the genes that govern yield characteristics, the genes that confer protection are not retained. High yielding, modern varieties of rice, for example, suffer higher proportionate yield losses, on average 20 per cent of yield (0.73 t/ha), compared to 13 per cent for traditional varieties (equivalent to 0.27 t/ha), although of course the yields of the former are in absolute terms larger.[20] A particularly dramatic illustration is the leguminous tree *Leucaena*, a highly favoured species for agroforestry. Varieties with very narrow genetic stock have been rapidly disseminated throughout Asia and it is now being devastated by a psyllid pest throughout the region.

One of the earliest ways of restoring or improving the resistance of a crop was by grafting the susceptible plant onto a related resistant variety or species. Over a hundred years ago an aphid, *Phylloxera*, was imported to Europe on American vines. The aphid feeds on the leaves of the American vines and does little harm, but on European vines it also attacks the roots, causing galls and eventual death to the whole plant. In 13 years some 1.5 million hectares of vines were destroyed in France. Much effort was wasted on insecticides, but immediate control was achieved when French vines were grafted onto American roots. The practice continues to the present day, and it remains a particularly useful approach to controlling pests and diseases of fruit trees in general.[21]

For the most part, though, improved resistance has been brought about by crossing and selection. Since the degree of pest or pathogen resistance in a plant population will vary from individual to individual it is possible, by careful screening, to identify those with exceptionally high resistance and use them as parents of new resistant lines. Alternatively, the resistance can be brought in from related varieties or species. The susceptible crop plant is crossed with the resistant relative to produce a new generation plant that combines the characters of both parents. The hybrid is then repeatedly back-crossed with the crop plant parent until finally a plant is obtained which is identical with this parent, except that it retains the resistance genes of the other.

The early success of the post-war Green Revolution in cereal cultivation was strongly centred upon breeding varieties resistant to key pests and diseases. During the 1940s wheat grown in Mexico was subject to destructive epidemics of wheat rust and the first task of the international wheat improvement programme was to breed for stem rust resistance. Some 700 native and imported wheat varieties were tested for resistance, and used in a breeding programme that attempted to combine resistance with high yield, early ripening and adaptation to local conditions. By 1949 four pioneer hybrids with high levels of resistance were available to farmers. By 1956 national average yields had risen from 650 to 1100 kg/ha.

More recently breeding for resistance to a pest of sorghum, the greenbug, has greatly reduced pesticide use in the USA.[22] In 1968, greenbugs caused $100 million loss to the sorghum crop, and farmers spent some $50 million in the following year to control the pest. By 1976, however, resistance to green bug was found, and the new hybrids were being grown on one and a half million hectares. A new biotype of the pest capable of attacking this hybrid emerged in 1980, but again researchers have been successful in finding another resistant variety.

Rice, too, has benefited from the incorporation of resistant genes drawn from a variety of Asian sources. The first so-called "miracle rices" produced at the International Rice Research Institute in the Philippines in the 1960s were very high yielding but had narrow genetic resistance. The breeders had selected for a limited number of desired characteristics – short straw, high tillering ratio, insensitivity to photoperiod and early maturity – but left new varieties prone to various insect pests, and to viral and bacterial diseases. Subsequently, however, protection has been built in, year by year, so that modern rice varieties are resistant to a wide range of pests and pathogens (Table 11.3).

However, as in the case of the sorghum greenbug, evolution also works to counter the breeder's selection. New species of pests and pathogens appear and, more important, new strains of existing pests and pathogens that overcome the hard-won resistance. In 1950 a hitherto rare strain of wheat rust exploded in the USA and Canada and, on reaching Mexico, overcame two of the varieties released a year earlier. Then two years later another of the new varieties succumbed. This pattern has continued to the present day, forcing plant breeders to keep pace with changing races and patterns of disease by continuously breeding new resistant wheat varieties. Another example is the brown planthopper, a serious pest of rice, of which at least three strains have appeared in recent years. Each new strain results in a major outbreak and the hurried distribution of new resistant rice varieties. But sometimes this is not enough. In Indonesia nearly half the lowland riceland was planted to a planthopper resistant variety, IR36, by 1980, but it then proved susceptible to tungro virus, carried by another pest,

Table 11.3 Disease and insect resistance of rice varieties from the International Rice Research Institute, Philippines

Variety	Blast	Bacterial blight	Grassy stunt	Tungro	BPH biotypes 1	2	3	Green leaf-hopper	Stem borer	Gall midge
IR5	MR	S	S	S	S	S	S	R	MS	S
IR8	S	S	S	S	S	S	S	R	S	S
IR20	MR	R	S	MR	S	S	S	R	MR	S
IR22	S	R	S	S	S	S	S	S	S	S
IR24	S	S	S	S	S	S	S	R	S	S
IR26	MR	R	MR	MR	R	S	R	R	MR	S
IR28	R	R	R	R	R	S	R	R	MR	S
IR29	R	R	R	R	R	S	R	R	MR	S
IR30	MS	R	R	MR	R	S	R	R	MR	S
IR32	MR	R	R	MR	R	S	R	R	MR	R
IR34	R	R	R	R	R	S	R	R	MR	S
IR36	R	R	R	R	R	R	S	R	MR	R
IR38	R	R	R	R	R	R	S	R	MR	R
IR40	R	R	R	R	R	R	S	R	MR	R
IR42	R	R	R	R	R	R	S	R	MR	R
IR44	R	R	S	R	R	R	S	R	MR	S
IR46	R	R	S	MR	R	S	R	MR	MR	S
IR48	R	R	R	R	R	R	S	R	MR	S
IR50	MS	R	R	R	R	R	S	R	MR	S
IR52	MR	R	R	R	R	R	S	R	MR	–
IR54	MR	R	R	R	R	R	S	R	MR	–
IR56	R	R	R	R	R	R	R	R	MR	–
IR58	R	R	R	R	R	R	S	R	MR	–
IR60	R	R	R	R	R	R	R	R	MR	–
IR62	MR	R	R	R	R	R	R	R	MS	–
IR64	MR	R	R	R	R	MR	R	R	MR	–
IR65	R	R	R	R	R	R	S	R	MS	–
IR66	MR	R	R	R	R	R	R	R	MR	–

R = resistant
MR = moderately resistant
MS = moderately susceptible
S = susceptible
BPH = brown planthopper

Source: Khush, G.S., "Multiple disease and insect resistance for increased yield stability in rice", in: *Progress in Irrigated Rice Research* (Los Baños, The Philippines: International Rice Research Institute, 1990).

the green leafhopper. Serious losses occured in 1981 and the problem was only solved by a crash programme to introduce further new resistant varieties.

Despite the often "treadmill" nature of breeding for resistance, it remains the most successful alternative to pesticides in controlling pests and pathogens. It also offers considerable promise for the exploitation of genetic engineering techniques. In theory, resistance genes can be inserted into high performing crop plants without any adverse effects on their other desirable characters. The engineered plants will reproduce normally, passing the anti-insect or anti-disease genes to their offspring. Field testing of genetically altered tomatoes and tobacco has pointed toward some success for these "pesticidal" plants, but as yet they have not been extended to farmers (see page 000 below).

Varietal mixes

The inherent variability in pest and pathogen resistance may also be harnessed by deliberately planting a diversity of genotypes in a field. One technique is to create multilines by mechanical mixing of seeds from similar lines of a crop variety. The lines are closely identical in most of their characteristics, but have different genes for resistance. In theory, when new strains of a disease appear only one or two of the lines will prove susceptible. Build-up of the disease is slow, an epidemic is prevented and most of the crop escapes damage. Two successful examples are an oat multiline against crown rust in the USA and a rice multiline against rice blast fungus in Asia.[23] An alternative is to sow a mixture of crop varieties. These are less similar than the lines in a multiline, although in practice they have to mature at the same date.

Environmental manipulation

In grasslands, woodlands and other natural ecosystems, insects and pathogens are kept at relatively low and stable levels, not only by natural enemies, but also by the action of a range of environmental factors that constrain population growth. Many of these factors are lost in the creation of agro-ecosystems and one general approach to pest control is to try and build these back in, without sacrificing yield. Several strategies are possible: most are based on increasing the environmental diversity, either in time or space, although one strategy, involving the removal of alternate hosts of pests, will reduce diversity.

Cultivation practices

The most straightforward approach is to use standard cultivation practices to disrupt the pest or pathogen population. Tillage, for example, is often effective against soil pests. Ploughing in autumn or spring greatly reduces overwintering populations of the bollworm while ploughing during the summer months, when the soil is very dry, reduces wireworm numbers. Timing of the planting of crops can also be effective, especially in reducing the rate of build-up of pests. For example, sorghum planted late in the USA escapes injury from sorghum midge populations which have increased during spring and summer on wild grass hosts. But if planted early, midges migrate to the sorghum fields as the crop begins to flower.[24] Synchrony of planting can also be important. Loevinsohn has shown that when rice is planted synchronously in the Philippines, there is less damage by insects at each stage of development of the crop.[25] But when rice planting is staggered, the continuous presence of plants at a favourable stage of growth for the pests encourages population increases.

Rotation

A more complicated approach is to rotate non-host crops with susceptible crops in sequence. While the non-host crop is growing, the pest or pathogen populations decline so that they are very low or even absent when the susceptible crop is grown again. The non-host crop provides a "break", disrupting the relationship between a pest or pathogen and its host. It is a practice that rarely has ecological or economic drawbacks, and many farmers regard rotation as an essential component of prudent management.

It has great antiquity as a means of pest control, dating back to at least Roman times. The classic example is the Norfolk four course rotation of eighteenth century Britain. This rotation was wheat, followed by turnips, then barley, and, finally, clover intercropped with ryegrass. The clover was usually undersown in the barley and hence was a relay crop. The turnips helped to clean the soil, allowing for efficient weeding and improved soil structure. They also provided a break between the two cereals and so helped to keep down cereal pests and weeds. The grass/clover crop also acted as break, helped to suppress weeds and the clover added to the nitrogen in the soil. Livestock could be fed on the turnips in the field and grazed on the grass/clover and their manure improved fertility. Manure could also be created by feeding turnips, straw and hay to livestock indoors in winter, and then returning it to the soil. The whole system was operated on four fields, out of phase in any one year, so that a diversity of crops was available at any one time. This allowed for close integration of crops and livestock and acted as an insurance against crop failure.

The remains of this rotation exist today in the UK in the practice of break cropping in cereals. It is particularly used against the disease "take all" (*Gaeumannomyces graminis* v. *tritici*), which remains alive in the stubble of wheat and barley, but dies away over a period of ten months. Since it does not attack rape, grass or beans, these are good break crops in sequences of cereals. The breaks are sufficient to keep the overall level of attack low. A similar effect is obtained in the USA by rotating soybean with either maize or grass. This reduces populations of white-fringed beetle that attacks the soybean. The beetles lay many eggs when feeding on soybean, and cause serious damage. But when they lay on maize or grass the larvae that hatch cannot gain enough food. The maize or grass is largely undamaged and the following soybean crop only lightly infested. Similarly, soybean loopers are rare if soybean is planted after rice or on cleared forest land, but there is a large infestation when soybean follows cotton or is located near cotton. The reason, in this case, is that looper adults feeding on cotton nectar mate more frequently, lay more eggs and live longer. Finally, one answer to the ubiquitous wireworm problem in the USA is a rotation of susceptible crops – clovers, vegetables or field crops – with alfalfa or pasture, which reduce wireworm populations.[26]

Mosaic crops and environments

Perhaps of greater potential than rotation is the building of spatial and structural diversity into agro-ecosystems and their environments.[27] Different crops can be grown row by row, or in alternate strips each consisting of several rows of the same crop, or they may be grown in a more complicated spatial pattern or, indeed, at random.[28] Perhaps the most complete and sophisticated of such cropping mosaics are to be found in the home or kitchen gardens of tropical countries. In Java, individual home-gardens, although less than a hectare in size, can contain upwards of 60 species, planted in a carefully designed fashion – tall trees such as coconuts above, bananas, citrus and other fruits in the middle layer and vegetables, root crops, and herbs of many kinds on the ground.[29] It is very rare for such a garden to suffer serious pest attack, partly as a result of the diversity and its associated factors, and partly because of the close attention paid to the garden by the householder and his or her family.

There are various factors in crop mosaics that help constrain pest and pathogen attack. For instance a host plant may be protected from insect pests by the physical presence of other plants that may provide a camouflage or a physical barrier. Mixtures of cabbage and tomato reduce colonization by the diamond-back moth, while mixtures of maize, beans and squash have the same effect on the chrysomelid beetles. The odours of some plants can also disrupt the searching behaviour of pests. Grass borders repel leafhoppers from beans, and the chemical stimuli from shallots prevents carrot fly from finding carrots.

Alternatively one crop in the mosaic may act as a trap or decoy – the so-called "fly-paper effect". Strips of alfalfa interspersed in cotton fields in California attract and trap *Lygus* bugs. There is a loss of alfalfa yield but this represents less than the cost of alternative control methods for the cotton. Similarly crucifers interplanted with beans, grass, clover or spinach reduce damage from cabbage maggot and cabbage aphid. There is less egg-laying on the crucifers and the pests are subject to increased predation.[30] Interplanting can also be combined with selective use of pesticides, applying them at the appropriate time but solely to the trap crop.

Mixtures of crops may cause changes in shade and the microclimate which are adverse to pests and pathogens. Coffee under shade is less affected by woolly aphid. Shade is particularly important in suppressing weeds: light interception by maize/mung bean, maize/peanut and maize/sweet potato mixtures is greater than for monocultures[31], and in all these examples the canopy closes earlier and suppresses weed growth. Nevertheless, there are significant exceptions and, in other situations, shade may have the opposite effect. Increased shade and relative humidity, for instance favours angular leaf spot and wilt on common beans.[32]

Weeds in a crop increase diversity. In Brussels sprout fields, the presence of weeds reduces damage by aphids, and pests tend to be attracted to weed-free fields.[33] Similarly, weed-free fields of beans in Mexico harbour greater numbers of Mexican bean beetle than weedy fields. However, there are often serious trade-offs involved since the weeds may cause as much, or more, damage than the pests.

In all these cases, though, it is difficult to be prescriptive without a full understanding of the cropping system and of the potential pests and pathogens. Some mixtures will control damaging populations, while others may lead to outbreaks. For example corn/cotton strip cropping in Peru helps control *Heliothis* on corn; but in Tanzania it produces an increase in incidence of the pest.[34] In India, larval populations of *Heliothis* were higher in sorghum/pigeon pea mixes than in sole pigeon pea plots, and losses were also greater in the mixtures. It is sometimes thought that mosaics are intended to mimic the diversity of natural ecosystems. More pragmatically, the aim of fostering variety is simply a means of ensuring that at least one or two controlling factors are present. Inevitably it is a rather hit or miss approach.

Management of wild vegetation

In some situations the presence of non-crop plants may be a cause of problems since rather than providing a solution to pest or pathogen problems they serve as active refuges. Weeds, for instance, can act as reservoirs for pests: the clover seed chalcid, a major pest of alfalfa seed in the USA, thrives on bur clover and volunteer alfalfa along roads and ditches, and destruction of these wild plants reduces damage in alfalfa fields. Destruction of stands of range shrubs and shinnery oak (*Quercus havardii*) in Texas also helps control cotton boll weevil, since the leaf litter from these shrubs and trees normally serves as an overwintering habit for the boll weevil.[35] In some situations, clean field borders and ditch banks can reduce populations of generalist herbivores. Japanese beetle is attracted to elder and smartweed which act as reservoirs for reinfestation of field crops. Weedy field borders and wind breaks also act as reservoirs for aphid vectors of viral diseases of apples, cowpea and tobacco.

Destruction of alternative hosts is also appropriate for the control of pests and diseases of livestock in some circumstances. In Africa pests such as tsetse fly and diseases such as rinderpest can be reduced by destroying wild ungulates. In the UK, destruction of badgers has been used to prevent the spread of the tuberculosis that attacks cattle.

But a serious drawback is that this approach requires continuous maintenance and vigilance to keep the wild hosts absent. For example, in Idaho when the various grass species that were hosts of beet leafhopper were eliminated and replaced by broadleafed annual crops there was a significant reduction in damage to beet. But as control became successful so less effort was given to keeping down the grass hosts, and the pest returned.[36]

As a control strategy destruction of wild hosts is non-polluting but, of course, it may have other serious environmental consequences. The vegetation that is eliminated may have other uses or may be of value to conservation. Similarly, the wild animal hosts of livestock pests and diseases may be valued for tourism or as an alternative source of meat.

Disruption of reproduction

Certain pest populations can also be controlled by disrupting their reproduction. Synthetic chemicals that mimic pheromones – hormones released by females to attract males – will greatly reduce the chances of insects mating, while the release of larger numbers of pre-sterilized males will ensure that most matings are sterile.

If applied on a large scale, slow-release formulations of synthetic pheromones that confuse males are very effective in disrupting mating in a variety of pests. Successful control has occurred of the pink bollworm (*Pectinophora*) on cotton in Egypt, Pakistan and the USA, and on grape leafroller, oriental fruit moth on peaches, tomato pinkworm and some pests of stored products.[37] In Egypt pheromone formulations are sold at the same price as conventional insecticides and two to three aerial applications are an adequate alternative to four or five sprays of conventional pesticide. Predators are more numerous in pheromone-treated than in insecticide-treated fields, and also more bees survive, leading to bumper crops of honey.[38] In the USA the pink bollworm disruptant is applied to up to 40,000 ha annually, holding infestations down to one per cent or less with a single application and insecticide applications have been reduced by nearly 90 per cent.[39] All these situations, however, require intervention on a large-scale involving co-operation among a large number of individual farmers to ensure success. So far it has only been an effective technique on large enterprises or as part of government or co-operative run schemes.

The alternative approach, to release sterile males, requires an even larger scale of operation. Massive rearing facilities are needed to raise large numbers of pests that are then sterilized by irradiation and released in the field in sufficient a quantity to swamp the natural population. The first pest eradicated by this technique was the screwworm, *Cochliomya hominivorae*, a serious pest of cattle in the southwestern United States.[40] The adult fly lays its eggs in the skin of the animals, and when the larvae hatch they feed on the flesh, causing large wounds. However, it was known that the adult female fly only mated once, and a massive operation to rear screwworms was begun in 1957. From early 1958 over 50 million sterile flies were released each week, eventually eradicating the pest over large areas within a year. Although there have been other successes, the technique is only likely to succeed where the pest populations are relatively small and isolated.

Using pesticides

The final strategy is to use pesticides that do not lead to pollution, and ideally do not interfere with natural enemy control, nor result in the pests or pathogens evolving resistance. Needless to say, this is not easy. In general, the most polluting pesticides, the organochlorines for example, also have had the worst record for destroying natural enemies and for eliciting resistance. Many of the newer compounds are more selective, less damaging to natural enemies and less persistent in the environment. Increasingly stringent laws and regulations in the industrialized countries have forced manufacturers to engage in exhaustive safety and environmental testing. In addition to conducting laboratory testing, the chemical industry is now assessing the behaviour and effects of compounds on whole ecosystems.[41]

One consequence of this greater regulation is the development, in recent years, of a number of compounds that are highly targeted in their effect. Examples are the chemicals that act as mimics of juvenile hormones in insects. These hormones are involved in the transition from one life cycle stage of an insect to another. The mimicking compounds arrest development and hence kill the insect, but their particular advantage is that they often only work on a single pest species. New herbicides that act as inhibitors of photosynthesis or mimic growth hormones may also be selective. Most of these carry little or no environmental hazard, as far as is presently known. But the nature of evolution is such that resistance is a recurring problem, requiring a continuous search for new compounds.

Natural plant products

Compounds based on the chemicals in plants that kill or repel pests are, in theory, an alternative solution to the problem of finding non-polluting pesticides. Derris, nicotine and pyrethrum, for example, have long been used in agriculture. But some are toxic to humans and are very broad spectrum in their action, killing natural enemies as well as pests.

The most promising of natural plant compounds are the antifeedants, that render plants unattractive and unpalatable to pests.[42] Derivatives of the following plants are all strong repellents to herbivorous insects: neem (*Azadirachta indica*), chinaberry (*Melia*), *Warburgia*, custard apple (*Annona* spp.), fenugreek (*Trigonella*), turmeric (*Curcuma longa*) and *Ajuga* spp. They are, generally, pest specific and, hence, harmless to non-target organisms.

Of these neem is probably the most widely grown, occurring in large areas of Asia and Africa. Almost every part of the tree is bitter, although the seed kernel possesses the maximum deterrent value. The derivatives are known to repel insects and to cause pronounced behavioural and physiological effects.[43] It is also safe for humans. The seed is most commonly formulated in an oil or cake: in parts of India neem cake has been applied to the rice since at least the 1930s. But there is a disadvantage, since neem degrades fairly rapidly in sunlight, and as a consequence the most successful applications have been in the control of stored grain, rather than field pests.

Microbial pesticides

Equally promising, in terms of selectivity and lack of potential for pollution, are pesticides based on micro-organisms – bacteria and viruses, in particular. The greatest successes so far have been preparations of *Bacillus thuringiensis* (*B.t.*). The bacillus produces a toxic crystalline compound, which dissolves when ingested by insects producing toxic proteins, that paralyse the gut and mouthparts. Strains of *B.t.* are particularly toxic to moths, flies and beetles. They have been used against moth pests for some 25 years, but are now being increasingly applied against other forms of pest in environmentally sensitive areas and where pesticide resistance is a problem.

The crystal toxins of *B.t.* are produced by a single gene, which has now been cloned and inserted through genetic engineering techniques into non-pathogenic bacteria that colonize plant roots, and also directly into crop plants such as tobacco and tomato. The potential for engineering plants to contain their own defensive compounds in this fashion is considerable. But as yet restrictions on genetically engineered micro-organisms have not permitted extensive field trials.[44]

A successful example of the use of viruses has been the release of live coconut rhinoceros beetles infected with a baculovirus in islands of the South Pacific. Rates of spread of the virus have reached 3 km per month, and beetle populations have declined at some locations by 60–80 per cent within 18 months of release.[45]

Some strains of bacteria are also effective at controlling crop diseases caused by other bacteria or fungi.[46] One strain of *Agrobacterium* produces an antibiotic substance that controls the crown gall tumours of orchard trees and ornamental plants.[47] Bacterial diseases successfully controlled in this way include stem rot of carnation and brown blotch of mushrooms and other fruits, while among the fungal diseases that have been controlled are silverleaf of plum and other fruits, root rot of pines and dry bubble of mushroom. Some nematode pests have also been controlled by various pathogenic bacteria, but they are expensive to produce on a large scale.[48]

The safe use of pesticides

The alternative to seeking safer compounds is to rely on more efficient and careful application of existing pesticides. In the short run this is probably the most effective way of reducing pollution. Most damage today arises not so much because of the intrinsic characteristics of the pesticide compounds but because of the way they are used. This was not so true when the organochlorine compounds were the dominant class of compounds being used. But in recent years, stringent testing of compounds before release has reduced the likelihood of products highly toxic to either ourselves or wildlife becoming generally available. In Chapters 2 and 3 we alluded to safe and effective ways in which today's pesticides should be applied. Operators can be protected by appropriate clothing and by using well designed application machinery. Such precautions and the following of codes on good agricultural practice will also greatly reduce the likelihood of pesticides affecting the nearby public. Accidental poisonings, which are the prime category of poisoning, can be prevented by distinctive bottling and labelling with clear warnings. Food consumers can be protected by adherence to minimum intervals between spraying and harvesting.

More generally, environmental contamination can be greatly reduced by better targeting of pesticides, using application methods that ensure only the crop is treated, and by keeping pesticide application to a minimum. The latter implies careful monitoring of the crop, critical timing and the abandonment of spraying by the calendar. Against the brown planthopper on rice, such monitoring can maintain yields yet reduce the cost of pest control by over half.[49] In the industrialized countries there are now sophisticated computer models and monitoring systems to help the farmer decide when and where to spray.[50]

The problem, of course, with all these "better" methods of pesticide use is that they tend to be costly, particularly in terms of equipment, skills and human labour. Safety, in particular, requires strict legislation, and an effective enforcement agency, while economic incentives are needed to keep use to a mimimum.

Integrated pest management

In simplest terms, Integrated Pest Management (IPM) is the integrated use of some or all these pest control strategies in a way that not only reduces pest populations to satisfactory levels but is sustainable and non-polluting. It is by no means a new approach. It was applied first, in 1954, to the control of alfalfa pests in California, making use of alternative strip cropping and selective pesticide use.[51] And also in the 1950s, co-operative cotton growers in the Canete Valley of Peru developed IPM in the face of massive breakdown of control due to excessive use of pesticides.[52] Similarly, such excesses led to IPM on oil palms and cocoa in Malaysia in the early 1960s – mostly involving environmental manipulation and selective pesticide use.[53]

More recent examples of IPM in practice are given in Box 11.1 with a brief indication of the extent of their success. In recent years IPM has become widely adopted in the USA. On many crops IPM is employed on more than 15 per cent of total acreage; for some, such as apple, citrus and tomato, it is now the preferred approach (Table 11.4).

IPM as currently practised, however, is not necessarily non-polluting. Often the primary factor has been heavy costs of conventional control, pest resurgences or pesticide resistance rather than a concern for environmental safety. Increasingly, IPM is taking this into account, but inevitably IPM is a more complex process than, say, relying on regular calendar spraying. It requires a level of analytical skill and certain basic training, although this should not be overstated. As the large scale IPM for rice programmes are demonstrating in the Philippines and Indonesia, ordinary farmers are capable of rapidly acquiring the principles and approaches.[54] Perhaps more important constraints are the costs involved and the lack of institutional support. Strong economic incentives are required for IPM and require support and advice from extension staff or advisors from private consulting companies.

Nutrient conservation

While pests, at least in theory, can be controlled without using pesticides it is virtually impossible to maintain crop production without adding nutrients. When crops are harvested, nutrients are invariably removed and, hence, have to be replaced. There are a variety of sources: the mobilization of existing nutrients in the soil and parent rocks; the fixing of nitrogen from the atmosphere, or the

Box 11.1   Examples of integrated pest management programmes

Rice in Orissa, India (Brader, 1979)

Pests: gall midge, brown planthopper, stemborers

1 Establish thresholds below which spraying uneconomic
2 Develop forecast system based on rainfall patterns
3 Monitor pest densities in fields
4 Plant early-maturing, short-duration varieties; avoid times of high pest density
5 Select varieties resistant to the pests
6 Plough in crop residues after harvest, thus preventing carry-over of pests
7 No application of pesticides when predators abundant

Result: insecticide applications cut in half; increase in use of modern varieties

Rice in Kwangtung, China (Brader, 1979)

Pests: weeds, leafhoppers, planthoppers, leafrollers, stemborers

1 Insect forecasting and monitoring in national network
2 Herd ducks through fields to eat pests
3 Flood rice fields to drown stemborer larvae
4 Catch flying insects at night in light-traps
5 Plant resistant varieties
6 Rear and release parasites of leafroller eggs
7 Conserve frogs to prey on pests
8 Apply *Bacillus thuringiensis*

Result: pesticide costs reduced by 30 per cent; but more labour required for rearing predators, maintaining traps and monitoring

Cotton in Texas, USA (Dover, 1985)

Pests: boll weevil, pink bollworm, tobacco budworm

1 Establish uniform planting period and short duration varieties, so that emergence of bollworm moths occurs when there is no cotton fruit on which to lay eggs
2 Fine uncooperative farmers
3 Irrigate desert areas prior to planting
4 Apply insecticides only in areas where high boll weevil populations are expected
5 Selectively apply organophosphates during harvest to kill adult boll weevils before they emigrate to overwintering sites in wood and field margins
6 Defoliate mature crop so all cotton bolls open together
7 Use mechanical strippers for harvest, which kill larvae
8 Shred stalks and plough under remnants immediately after harvest, thus denying pests food during winter

Result: dramatic increase in area of cotton harvested; decrease in production costs; increase in yields

Box 11.1 Continued

Apple in Nova Scotia, Canada (Corbet, 1974; Flint and van den Bosch, 1981)

Pests: codling moth, European red mite, winter moth, apple maggot

1 Conserve natural enemies by using selective pesticides
2 Carefully time applications
3 Monitor and spray only when absolutely necessary
4 Introduce the parasite *Cyzenis* to control winter moth, although only successful where orchards near forests
5 Remove wild hosts and dispose of infested drop-fruit to control maggots
6 Use sticky traps
7 Selective use of pheromones and attractants

Result: ninety per cent of apple growers have been using this programme continuously since the 1950s

Alfalfa in California, USA (Flint and van den Bosch, 1981)

Pests: alfalfa caterpiller, spotted alfalfa aphid

1 Monitoring of numbers of healthy caterpillars by skilled entomologists: if unhealthy probably parasitized by wasp or dying from viral disease
2 Timely spraying in caterpillar numbers above economic threshold
3 Three species of wasp parasites imported from the Near East and Europe to control the aphid
4 Introduce strip harvesting to provide refuges for lady beetle natural enemies
5 Timely irrigation to enhance activity of virulent fungal diseases of the aphid
6 Establish monitoring of predators, to prevent spraying when abundant
7 Use selective aphicide demeton
8 Introduce resistant varieties of alfalfa

Result: rapid reduction in losses; pests now rarely seriously injurious

Tobacco in Canada (Corbet, 1974)

Pests: hornworm, cutworm

1 Control hornworm by using *B.t.*
2 Use viruses to control cutworms
3 Plant trap plants of tobacco among the rye cover crop, on which larvae develop and overwinter
4 Spray trap plants with virus

Result: scientifically successful, but uneconomic

Cotton in Central America (ICAITI, 1977)

Pests: boll weevil, leaf-eaters, sap-suckers, shoot-pruners, bollworm, whitefly

continued

Box 11.1   Continued

> **Cotton in Central America – Continued**
>
> 1 Leave small cotton islands of old stock standing after May to concentrate boll weevil remaining from previous season
> 2 Plant trap crops at field margins early where weevils known to invade
> 3 Selectively spray islands and trap crops when required
> 4 Establish uniform planting date
> 5 Add nitrogen fertilizer not before 60 days old, unless signs of deficiency, to reduce attraction to leaf-eaters and sap-suckers
> 6 *Trichogramma* predators released when leaf-damage greater than 50 per cent
> 7 Selective use of pesticides, including methyl parathion, monocroptofos, chlordimeform, metamidophos
> 8 Defoliate when 50 per cent of bolls open
> 9 Harvest promptly to avoid whitefly problems
>
> *Results*: yields still same, but relative profits up threefold; number of pesticide treatments fell; control costs and total variable costs also fell

Source: Brader, L., "Integrating pest control in the developing world", *Ann. Rev. Entomol.* 24 (1979) pp. 225–54; Dover, M.J., *A Better Mousetrap. Improving Pest Management for Agriculture* (Washington DC: World Resources Institute, 1985); Corbet, P.S., "Habitat manipulation in the control of insects in Canada", in: *Proc. Tall Timber Conf. Ecol. Animal Control Habitat Manage.* 5 (1974) pp. 147–71; Flint, M.L. and van den Bosch, R., *Introduction to Integrated Pest Management* (New York: Plenum Press, 1981); Instituto Centroamericano de Investigación y Tecnología Industrial, *An environmental and economic investigation of the consequences of pesticide use in Central American cotton production* (Guatemala City: ICAITI, 1977).

Table 11.4   The extent of IPM use on 12 major crops in the USA, 1986

Crop	Area under IPM (thousands of hectares)	Proportion of total area under IPM (%)
Alfalfa	515	4.7
Apple	121	65.0
Citrus	283	70.0
Cotton	1962	48.2
Maize	6073	19.5
Peanut	280	43.8
Potato	79	16.1
Rice	379	38.9
Sorghum	1606	25.8
Soybean	3602	14.4
Tomato	126	82.5
Wheat	4327	14.8

Source: NRC, *Alternative Agriculture* (Washington, DC: National Academy Press, 1989)

supply of organic or inorganic fertilizer. If, in total, all these new inputs are converted to useful crop yield, then no contamination of the environment will result. However, as we saw in Chapter 4, the efficiency of uptake is never 100 per cent. Depending on the conditions, between 20 per cent and 70 per cent of nitrogen is lost to the air or, through leaching and run-off, to surface and ground waters.

In the receiving environment the origin of the nutrient contamination is indistinguishable. It makes little difference to the eventual pollution whether the nitrate derives from inorganic fertilizers, organic manures, natural soil nitrogen or nitrogen fixation. Restricting fertilizer application may have little effect if other sources are still resulting in contamination. As we saw in Chapter 4, heavy applications of organic manure and livestock wastes or, indeed, the ploughing up of grassland can result in serious nitrate losses. Reducing contamination is thus primarily a task for overall nutrient conservation. The goal is to maximize uptake of nutrients, while minimizing the transformation processes that lead to losses to air, water and the soil system. Some of the factors involved, such as climate and soil properties, have to be taken as given, but the kind of nutrients that are applied and the nature of the cropping and cultivation practices are amenable to management.

Improved fertilizer application

Probably the most effective means of reducing current levels of contamination, at least in the short term, is to modify the way in which inorganic fertilizers are applied. As with pesticides, the timing and amounts of application and the nature of the compound applied are all important.

Timing and amount

At the very beginning of their growth, crop plants take up only a few ions of nitrogen each day, rising to 3–5 kg/ha per day of nitrogen and phosphorus at the peak growing period. The application of fertilizer, ideally, should closely match these needs but often farmers, for reasons of cost, will apply fertilizer only once. Inevitably, fertilizer is applied in excess of need and contamination of the environment results. For example most Asian rice farmers apply fertilizer directly into floodwater one to three weeks after transplanting the rice and this results in extensive losses to the atmosphere.[55] However, the practice of split application at carefully timed intervals is becoming more common in a number of crops. In temperate regions, nitrogen is split into two applications on wheat when the soil reserves are low, a quarter of a recommended dose of 160 kg/ha being applied during early tillering (in February) and the remainder at early stem extension (in April–May).[56] For rice farmers in Asia the current recommendation is for three split doses of nitrogen, the first just before transplanting, the second at maximum tillering and the last just before panicle initiation.[57]

The soil type and the source of nitrogen other than the fertilizer is also an important factor. As we saw in Chapter 4 up to a third of the crop uptake may come from soil nitrogen. If these reserves are known then it should be possible to make fertilizer recommendations tailored for the specific requirements of each field and each crop. In the UK fairly precise recommendations are based on cropping practice and, in particular, on knowledge of the crop previously grown on the land[58] (Table 11.5). Cereals are assumed fully to deplete reserves,

Table 11.5 Estimation of soil reserves based upon the previously grown crop

Low reserves	Medium reserves	High reserves
Cereals, including maize	Beans, peas	Any crop with frequent FYM or slurry
Leys (1–2 yr), cut	Potatoes	Long leys (high N)
Leys (1–2 yr) grazed, low N	Oilseed rape	Permanent pasture, average quality
Permanent pasture, poor quality	Leys (1–2 yr), grazed	Permanent pasture (high N)
Forage crops, removed	Long leys (low N)	
Sugar beet, tops removed	Forage crops, grazed	
Vegetables (less than 200 kg N/ha)	Sugar beet, tops ploughed in	
	Vegetables (more than 200 kg N/ha)	

Note: low N – less than 250 kg N/ha/yr
high N – more than 250 kg N/ha/yr
FYM – farmyard manure

Source: MAFF/ADAS, *Fertilizer Recommendations* Ref. 209, 5th edn (London: HMSO, 1988).

for instance, whereas permanent pasture leaves high reserves for the next crop. Further factors taken into account are the soil type and the nature of the winter rainfall; whether crop residues are removed or ploughed in and, finally, whether there have been applications of farmyard manure or slurry. Analysis of all these factors permits the soil to be categorized into one of three types, with high, medium or low nitrogen reserves. This avoids the need for soil analysis of nitrogen, although it is still required for phosphorus and potassium, since their reserves cannot be estimated from previous crops. The outcome is a set of recommendations for nitrogen fertilizer application rates dependent on both reserves and soil type (Table 11.6). For instance, winter wheat

Table 11.6   Recommended annual applications of nitrogen fertilizer in kg/ha to various crops for soil type and soil nitrogen reserves

Crop	Soil type	Low	Medium	High
			Reserves	
Winter wheat (less than 7 t/ha)	Sandy or shallow over chalk or limestone	175	150	75
	Deep silty	150	50	0
	Clay	150	75	0
	Organic	50	0	0
Winter wheat (more than 9 t/ha)	Sandy or shallow over chalk	275	250	175
	Deep silty	250	150	50
	Clay	250	175	50
Winter barley	Sandy or shallow over chalk	160	125	75
	Other mineral soils	160	100	40
	Organic	50	0	0
Spring barley	Sandy	125	100	50
	Shallow over chalk	150	125	50
	Other mineral soils	150	100	40
	Organic	40	0	0
Oats, rye	Sandy or shallow over chalk	125	100	50
	Other mineral soils	100	60	30
	Organic	40	0	0
Winter oilseed rape	Mineral soils	250	225	200
	Organic	100	50	0
Peas, beans	All soils	0	0	0

Source: MAFF/ADAS, 1988, *op. cit.*

which is likely to yield less than 7 t/ha when grown on sandy soil with low reserves, should receive 175 kg/ha of nitrogen fertilizer. But if the reserves are high and the soil a clay then no fertilizer needs be applied. These recommendations are, in turn, modified by climatic considerations. Thus if the winter has been dry then farmers are recommended to reduce their spring applications by 25 kg/ha, since reduced leaching will have left greater quantities of mineral nitrogen in the root zone.

The recommendations for grassland similarly depend on a limited range of factors (Table 11.7). Most important are the summer rainfall, the available water capacity of the soil and the altitude, all of which contribute to a classification in terms of grass growth. Vigorous, or very good, growth is more likely to absorb all the applied nitrogen than poor growth. High rainfall between April and September and good water capacity of the soil (organic, humic or deep loamy soils) define a very good growth class, whereas low rainfall and poor water capacity (sands, gravels and stony soils) define a poor growth class. The grass growth is placed one category lower if the grassland is at an altitude of greater than 300 metres.

Table 11.7 Recommendations for optimal annual nitrogen applications to grasslands for each grass growth class

Growth class	Fertilizer application (kg/ha)	Potential yield (t/ha)
Poor	300	8.4
Fair	330	9.5
Average	370	10.5
Good	410	11.6
Very good	450	12.7

Source: MAFF/ADAS, 1988, *op. cit.*

Farmers also must consider whether the grassland contains clover or is to be grazed by livestock. High applications of nitrogen depress clover growth which, in any case, as a nitrogen fixer returns nitrogen to the soil. Livestock return nitrogenous material to the surface of the grass and, in consequence, applications to grazing land should not exceed 300 kg/ha.

A survey of fertilizer practice for the UK indicates that average applications of nitrogen fertilizer to cereals and oilseed rape do not greatly exceed the recommendations when soil is low in nitrogen reserves[59] (Table 11.8). If the reserves happen to be high, though, and applications continue at the average rate, there may be large quantities of nitrogen not utilized in the soil, which then become available for leaching. On grasslands, in contrast, overall average applications are only 125 kg/ha, well below recommended levels. It remains to be seen whether increasing applications, up to 400 kg/ha that are likely in the future, can be made without significantly increasing contamination.

Table 11.8 Average annual application of nitrogen fertilizer to crops in the UK, 1983

Crop	Fertilizer (kg/ha)
Winter wheat	182
Winter barley	150
Spring barley	107
Oilseed rape	274
All tillage	*154*
Short leys (1 yr)	113
Longer leys (2–7 yrs)	182
Permanent grassland	96
All grassland	*125*

Source: ADAS/RES/FMA, *Survey of fertilizer practice, fertilizer use on farm crops in England and Wales*, Agricultural Development and Advisory Service, Rothamsted Experimental Station, Fertilizer Manufacturers' Association (London: HMSO, 1983).

These recommendations are all aimed an increasing the efficiency of uptake in specific situations. There are, however, a number of general recommendations for fertilizer application which, if observed, would have a major effect on current leaching losses in temperate climates. In particular, because the heaviest losses occur during the heavy rains of autumn and winter when the soil is bare, fertilizer application in the autumn should be avoided unless it is likely to be quickly taken up by a growing crop. Application to frozen soils is also highly undesirable. If winter crops are grown they should be sown as early as possible or, alternatively, a catch crop should be sown in the autumn before a spring crop the following year. In the UK there has been a dramatic increase in the proportion of cereals sown in the autumn since the 1970s. Virtually all of the wheat and over 60 per cent of the barley is autumn sown.[60] There is some indication that this is beginning to result in lower leaching losses. Similarly, over the same period there has been a shift in applying fertilizers from the autumn to the periods of most active growth and nitrogen uptake – mid-February to mid-May for cereals and March to August for grassland.[61] Nevertheless, it is clear from experimental evidence that considerable reductions in fertilizer application will be required before leaching is down to acceptable levels (Figure 11.3). In the drier parts of eastern England, leaching rates have to be below 20 kg N/ha if recharge groundwater levels are to be below 50 mg nitrate/litre. This implies a reduction of leaching rates of some 50 per cent and hence a 40–100 per cent reduction in fertilizer application.[62]

Figure 11.3 Experiment effects of nitrogen fertilizer reduction on leaching from winter wheat. Each line represents a different experiment

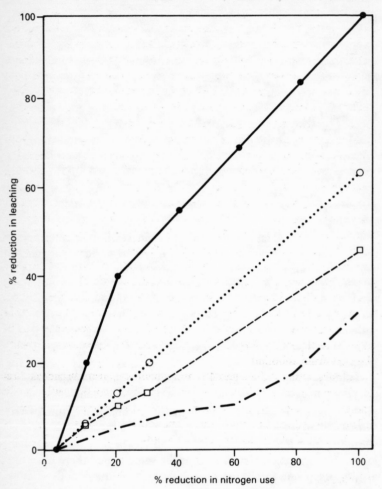

Source: Chilton, P.J. and Foster, S.S.D., *Control of Groundwater Nitrate Pollution in Britain by Land-use Change*, NATO workshop (mimeo, 1990).

Modified fertilizers

Nutrient uptake and absorption can also be improved by using slow-release products or by incorporating, with the fertilizer, certain compounds that inhibit bacterial conversion of one nitrogen compound to another.

A controlled release is best achieved by coating fertilizers with a compound such as sulphur. Use of sulphur-coated urea (SCU) on rice lowers the concentration of nitrogen in both the soil and water at any given time, thus reducing ammonia losses and providing the crop with adequate nutrition throughout the growing season.[63] SCU also reduces the need for split applications and helps to fulfil sulphur requirements of the crop. Costs are more than for ordinary urea, but economic returns are potentially of the order of US$6–7 for every dollar spent.[64] SCU is not appropriate for countries such as the UK, because of the small quantities of urea applied.

More commonly used are nitrification inhibitors. An important cause of nutrient loss is the conversion, in the soil, of one nitrogen compound to another by bacterial nitrification. For example, ammonium nitrogen may be converted in this way to nitrate which is then available for leaching. One answer is to incorporate compounds, such as dicyandiamide, that will inhibit bacterial action, into ammonium nitrate fertilizer. This technique has been employed for some time in the USA and has proved successful in maintaining the nitrogen as immobile ammonium and, hence, in controlling leaching and gaseous losses. However until recently, it has had the drawback of only being available in liquid form. Nitrification inhibitors have also been shown to improve rice yields, although in high temperatures they are more subject to breakdown. Like SCU, these products increase the cost of conventional fertilizers by 10–20 per cent and this is discouraging many farmers from adoption.

Inhibitors that reduce gaseous ammonia losses from broadcast urea applications to rice paddies have also been developed, but with variable results. One such urease inhibitor is phenyl phosphorodiamidate. It delays and reduces the build up of ammonium in the water, but it is not clear yet whether it also increases yields.

Placement

Appropriate placement is as critical as the timing and the amount of fertilizer applied. In the case of rice a recommended strategy is to incorporate the fertilizer deep in the soil prior to planting. To aid such deep placement fertilizers are formulated as urea briquettes, urea marbles or urea supergranules (USG). This can produce substantial increases in yield compared with broadcasting on standing water, even if applications are split.[65] But, in yield terms it is low-yield rice areas rather than high-yield areas that are the main beneficiaries. In Taiwan, USG increases rice yields by 20 per cent in the marginal area, but has no impact in the already high yielding zone.

The problem with deep placement for rice is that it is more costly than broadcast application. Labour is required for hand placement, and placement machines are still only at the development stage. None the less, economic analysis has shown a return to the farmer of US\$4–7 for every dollar spent on labour for USG application.[66] More generally, if fertilizer application is combined with seed drilling then it may not be more costly. One system that utilizes appropriate placement is the ridge tillage commonly used in the USA (see Figure 11.4 below). Fertilizers are drilled into the ridges to ensure they are placed beside the seed.

Environmental manipulation

As in pest control, environmental manipulation is a powerful tool for nutrient conservation. Crop types and tillage practices are important, as are carefully designed interventions that help to conserve soil and water.

Crop types

As we saw in Chapter 4, crops vary in the efficiency with which they take up nutrients (Table 4.7 and Figure 4.3). And this is true also of crop varieties within crop species. Breeding for efficiency of nitrogen use is thus a potentially productive approach. For instance, the very widely cultivated rice variety IR36 has been superceded by a later variety, IR42, that uses nitrogen more efficiently. There is also some evidence to suggest that long-duration rice varieties depend less upon supplementary inorganic nitrogen than short-season varieties.[67]

Conservation tillage

The way in which the soil is tilled can have a significant influence on how well soil nutrients are retained and hence affects nutrient conservation. In conventional tillage, the topsoil is inverted and mixed by means of a mouldboard plough or disc, or a handtool such as a hoe.[68] This serves to incorporate most of the crop residues or stubble and the nutrients they contain. However, it results in a lag period from the time the seed is sown to when there is sufficient vegetative cover to prevent soil erosion by wind or water. An alternative approach is to use no, or greatly reduced, tillage in which the soil surface is disturbed

Table 11.9 Comparison between conventional and conservation tillage practices

	Conventional	*Conservation*
Ploughing	Mouldboard (soil turned over)	Reduced tillage: chisel ploughing (crop stubble mixed into soil, leaving ground partially protected) or no-till: no ploughing
Soil properties	Soil temperatures fluctuate more readily, thus favourable in early spring, unfavourable in hot summers	Soil cooler in late spring – slows early season growth Soil cooler and moister in summer under residues
	Soil less likely to be compacted	Compaction of soil more likely – reduces plant growth
Pest control	Destroys perennial weeds, disrupts life cycle of pests and predators	Residues on surface can be favourable habitat to pests and overwintering diseases; perennial weeds not destroyed
Energy	Larger and more powerful tractors required	No till: no tractor Reduced: large tractors but use less energy
Nutrient cycling	Nutrients released in bursts	Slower and more even rate of nutrient release
Water run-off (taking soil, nutrients and herbicides)	All high when soil bare	All reduced very substantially

Source: NRC, 1989, *op. cit.*

as little as possible. Significant quantities of residue then remain on the soil surface, so helping to reduce run-off, sediment loss and loss of nutrients. The seed is directly drilled through the layer of residues. In no-till farming soil preparation and planting are done in one operation; in reduced till there is limited preparation with disc or chisel plough.

One advantage is the reduced need for mechanical power or human labour. But there are some important trade-offs, among which are the need for higher inputs of herbicides (Table 11.9). Conventional ploughing serves to control weeds and in its absence weed problems can become very serious. The reduction in surface run-off may also not be an absolute benefit since the nutrients may simply be lost through leaching to groundwater, while lack of incorporation of applied fertilizer in no-till or reduced till situations may generate increased atmospheric loss. Lack of tillage may also result in soil compaction.[69] Nevertheless in the UK an experiment showed significant reductions in the leaching losses under a field directly drilled with winter wheat compared with one subject to conventional ploughing (Figure 11.4). There is also a benefit in terms of reduced pesticide run-off.[70] Herbicides such as atrazine and simazine are lower by up to 50 per cent in the run-off from untilled compared with conventionally tilled watersheds.

Conservation tillage systems are widely promoted in the USA by the Soil Conservation Service. Between 1980 and 1987 the area devoted to conservation tillage grew from 16 million to some 40 million hectares, the latter being equivalent to about 38 per cent of all harvested land in the USA.[71] The main focus is on reduced tillage with chisel ploughing, using crop residues to provide a mulch cover. In practice this reduces soil erosion by up to 50 per cent. Other conservation tillage practices - no-tillage, strip tillage and ridge tillage systems – are more effective, reducing erosion by 75 per cent or more, but are less widely adopted.[72]

Figure 11.4   Profiles from the unsaturated zone of the chalk in Berkshire, UK, beneath experimental winter wheat sites subject to ploughing or direct drilling

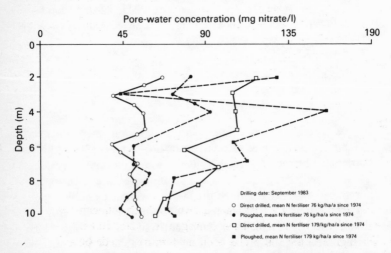

Source: Foster, S.S.D., Bridge, L.R., Geake, A.K., Lawrence, A.R. and Parker, J.M., *The Groundwater Nitrate Problem*, Hydrogeological Report 86/2 (Wallingford, Oxon: British Geological Survey, 1986).

Ridge tillage, in particular, also reduces weed problems (Figure 11.5). In this system only the tops of the ridges are tilled for planting

Figure 11.5   Ridge tillage system from Iowa

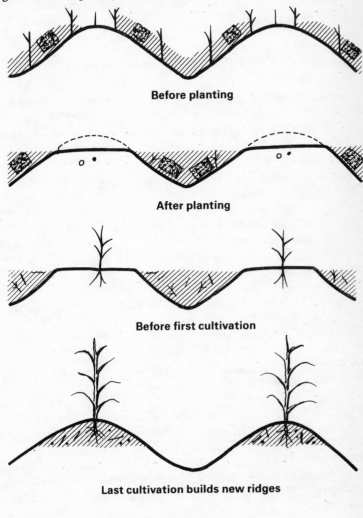

Before planting

After planting

Before first cultivation

Last cultivation builds new ridges

Old stubble	Residue	Seed	
Cover crop	Manure	Band fertilizer	

Source: National Research Council, *Alternative Agriculture* (Washington DC: National Academy Press, 1989), using information from the farm of Dick Thompson.

in the spring. The residues are removed and a seedbed created. Soil on the ridges is generally warmer and this improves crop germination, while fewer weed seeds are disturbed. Weeds that do emerge later tend to be between the ridges and can be controlled by subsequent cultivation. Erosion is slowed because soil and residues between the ridges are not disturbed.[73]

Soil and water catchment structures

A somewhat cruder approach to conserving soil nutrients is to resort to a wide range of physical structures of varying scale that can be used to contain soil and, therefore, their nutrients.[74] Most of these are designed to check the surface flow of water, and thus perform the dual role of water harvesting and retention. If successful they can minimize the need for fertilizer application although, of course, in some situations they may simply substitute groundwater nutrient loss for surface water loss.

The simplest approach is to throw up earth banks, 1.5 to 2 m wide, across the slope and 10–20 m apart to act as a barrier to run-off. They are suitable on slopes of 1°–7° and are frequently used on tropical small holdings in conjunction with contour planting (see page 597 below). Sometimes the earth bunds are reinforced with vegetation such as crop stalks or planted with trees to create greater stability, and because such vegetative bunds are partly permeable, crops planted in front of the bund also benefit from water run-off. They are not quickly damaged by run-off, and thus maintenance costs are low. Simple walls may also be constructed along the bunds, as in various parts of Africa, and these are quickly strengthened by natural processes.[75] After the first heavy rains, fine soil, branches and leaves began to fill in the walls making them even more impermeable. In some situations, instead of being built on the contour, walls are constructed across gullies, so retaining soil eroded from above and creating an enriched environment for crops.[76] More elaborate are various forms of terrace (Table 11.10; Figure 11.6). Diversion terraces are appropriate for slopes up to 7° and retention terraces for slopes up to 4.5°. Bench terraces are effective up to 30° but not on thin soils where the parent rock is close to the surface. Construction costs for bench terraces are usually high, however. In the Citanduy watershed of Java it was found that 500–700 days work per hectare were required to construct bench terraces.[77] Moreover where the soils are shallow, yields may fall in the first few years following construction as the subsoil is exposed.

Different structures are often combined to form an overall soil and

Table 11.10   Types of terraces

Diversion terraces	Used to intercept overland flow on a hillside and channel it across slope to a suitable outlet, e.g. grass waterway or soakaway to tile drain; built at slight downslope grade from contour
Mangum type	Formed by taking soil from both sides of embankment
Nichols types	Formed by taking soil from upslope side of embankment only
Broad-based type	Bank and channel occupy width of 15 m
Narrow-based type	Bank and channel occupy width of 3–4 m
Retention terraces	Level terraces; used where water must be conserved by storage on the hillside
Bench terraces	Alternating series of shelves and risers used to cultivate steep slopes. Riser often faced with stones or concrete. Various modifications to permit inward-sloping shelves for greater water storage or protection on very steep slopes, or to allow cultivation of tree crops and market-garden crops

Source: Morgan, R.P.C., *Soil Erosion and Conservation* (Harlow: Longman, 1986).

water conservation system for a watershed or district. In Kenya farmers chose from water retention ditches, reinforced ridges or *fanya juus* (in which the soil is thrown uphill), *fanya chini* (in which the soil is thrown downhill), bench terraces and infiltration pits, balancing the various costs and benefits associated with each (Table 11.11). The principal constraints usually relate to available labour and money.

Contour planting and grass strips

Rather than construct physical structures, an alternative is to plant crops along contours. This practice is now common in many parts of the USA as part of Best Management Plans, conservation tillage or the Conservation Reserve Program.[78] As water flows across the surface so it meets with rows of crops growing perpendicular to the flow, which slows it down and improves infiltration.

In strip cropping the main row crop is grown along the contour in 15–45 m wide strips alternating with strips of protective crop, such as grass or a legume (Figure 11.7). It is appropriate for well drained soils of 3°–8.5° slope.[79] If the protective strips are of grass they can be effective at filtering out particulate matter and nutrients from surface flow of water. Experiments in Indonesia have demonstrated that contour grass strips not only reduce loss of soil but help in

Figure 11.6 Various forms of terrace

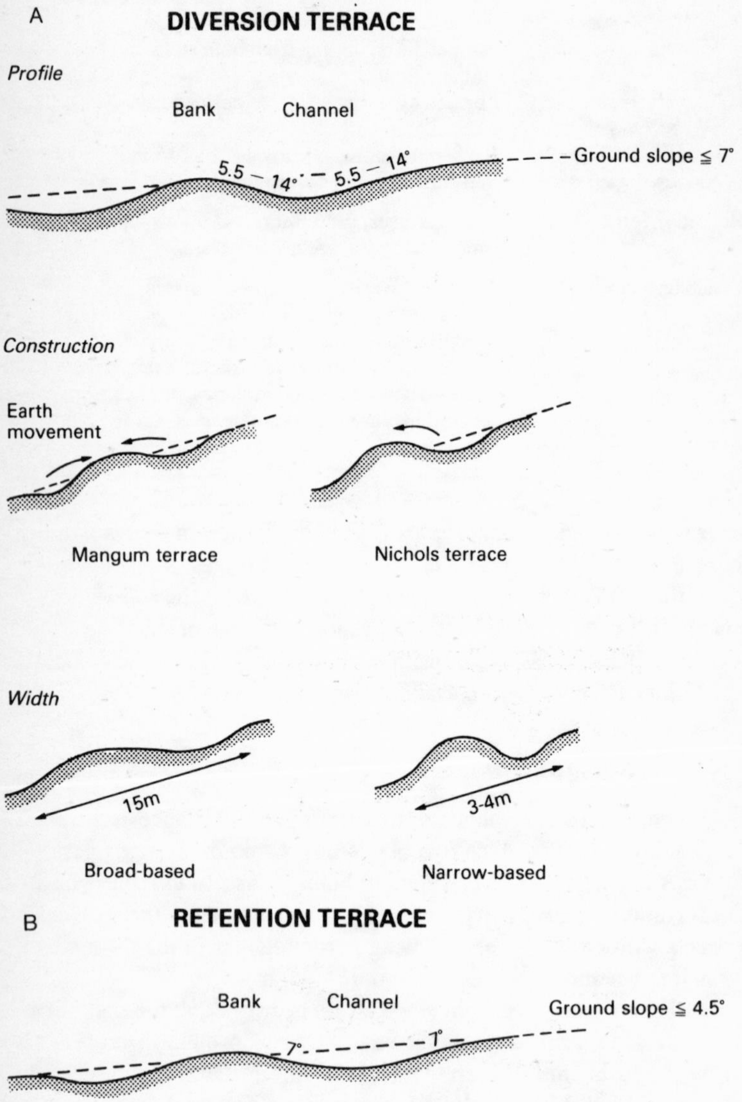

A   **DIVERSION TERRACE**

Profile

Bank   Channel

5.5 – 14° – 5.5 – 14°   – – – – Ground slope ≦ 7°

Construction

Earth
movement

Mangum terrace   Nichols terrace

Width

15m

3–4m

Broad-based   Narrow-based

B   **RETENTION TERRACE**

Bank   Channel   Ground slope ≦ 4.5°

7°   – – – – – – 7° –

C   **BENCH TERRACE**

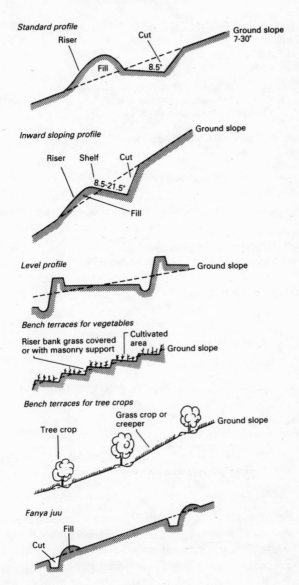

Source: Morgan, R.P.C., *Soil Erosion and Conservation* (Harlow: Longman, 1986).

Table 11.11   Favourable and unfavourable features of soil and water conservation strategies given by two farming families in Mbari-ya-Hiti, Murang'a District, Kenya

---

Retention ditches
Protects crops and structures below
Holds much water
Has two lines of napier grass
Forms a bench easily

But: Ends can break and water rush down farm
Uses up large proportion of farm
Requires much labour to construct

Fanya juu (soil thrown up-hill)
Reduces the slope
Prevents run-off down slope
Napier grass grown on topside
Does not use up much of farm

But: It is laborious work throwing the soil uphill when slope is steep

Bench terraces
No loss of nutrients when apply manures/fertilizers
When short and tilted back there will be no run-off and much infiltration
No waste of land

But: Very laborious to construct

Infiltration pits
Slow down flow
Increase infiltration

But: Risk that children will fall down holes

Fanya chini (soil thrown down-hill)
Easy to dig

But: Increases the slope
Wastes space on farm

Source: Kiara, J.K., Seggeros, M., Pretty, J.N. and McCracken, J.A., *Rapid Catchment Analysis* (Nairobi, Kenya: Soil and Water Conservation Branch, Ministry of Agriculture, 1990).

the process of establishing terraces.[80] Strips of either Bahia grass (*Paspalum notatum*) or signal grass (*Brachiaria decumbens*) 0.5–1 metre in width, alternated with strips of annual crops 3–5 m in width, were shown to reduce erosion by 20-fold compared with controls. Moreover at the end of a four year period, natural terraces up to 60 cm high had formed. One disadvantage is that the grass strips occupy arable land which could otherwise be used for crops. This can be overcome if the grasses are a source of livestock feed.

Alternatives to perennial grass strips include the use of woody shrubs and trees, which not only protect the soil, but can provide fodder, fuelwood and timber.[81] It has long been the practice in the countries of the Mediterranean to plant rows of trees such as olives with bands of cereals or vines in between. Most recently in tropical countries there has been a considerable interest in "alley cropping", in which trees of various kinds are planted in contour rows with, usually, subsistence crops in between. Often the trees are fast-growing legumes, which additionally fix nitrogen into the soil (see page 601 below). On flat lands such hedgerows, or lines of trees such as poplars, may also be valuable in reducing wind-induced erosion and so conserve nutrients.

Figure 11.7   Contour strip-cropping

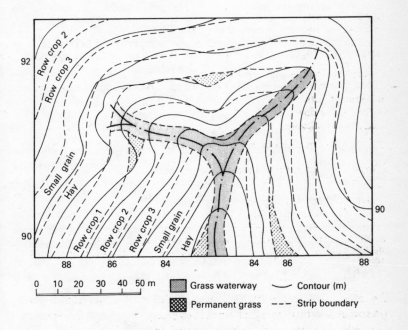

Source: Troeh, F.R., Hobbs, J.A. and Donahue, R.L., *Soil and Water Conservation for Productivity and Environmental Protection* (Englewood Cliffs, NJ: Prentice-Hall Inc., 1980).

Mulching and cover crops

Soil, water and nutrient conservation is also furthered by the use of mulches or cover crops. Mulching involves spreading organic or inorganic material on the soil surface to provide a physical cover which helps create a micro-environment in the topsoil that is largely independent of the weather. It protects the soil from erosion, desiccation and excessive heating, thus promoting optimal conditions for the decomposition and mineralization of organic matter. Various experiments have shown that the rate of soil loss decreases exponentially with the percentage of area covered by the mulch.[82]

The cheapest and easiest method is to use crop residues (see below), which may come from previous crops, from nearby perennials, such as in alley cropping, or be brought from wild areas, such as reeds from swamps.[83] No-till and reduced tillage systems both result in good cover with residues, re-inforcing the conservation value of an undisturbed soil. A particularly complex system has been developed by Brazilian Indians: heaps of sticks, branches and leaves are allowed to rot, and then mixed with soil from termite mounds, including living termites, and the final mulch is then applied to the soil.[84] But equally as useful as organic materials are non-degradable mulches like plastic film. Black plastic, for example, excludes light and thus prevents weed growth. Other types of non-crop mulches include newspaper, cardboard, sawdust, woodchips, leafmould and forest bark.

Cover crops consist of vegetation that is deliberately established after or intercropped with a main crop, not with a view to harvest but to serve various conserving functions. In the USA cover crops are mostly winter annuals also grown as green manures (see page 604 below). Typical crops are rye, oats, hairy vetch, sweet clover and lucerne in the northern states and Austrian winter peas, crimson clover, crotalaria and lespedeza in the south.[85] Legume cover crops are also common under perennial tree crops in the tropical climates, for example rubber or oil palm, where they primarily serve to control weeds but also probably conserve soil and water. Cover crops may take up residual soil nutrients that would otherwise be lost, but if they are legumes they may well increase the pool of nutrients, so increasing losses unless fertilizer applications are reduced.

Agroforestry

Alley cropping is but one form of agroforestry which is being promoted in both tropical and temperate climates as a form of ecologically sound agriculture.[86] Trees are typically grown in densely-planted rows, with alleys up to 4 metres wide containing annual crops. Fast-growing leguminous species, such as *Leucaena leucocephala* and *Gliricidia sepium*, are commonly used. They additionally fix nitrogen into the soil (see below) and are a source of surface mulch. Another example of agro-forestry is the home-garden whose benefits in terms of pest control have already been mentioned (see page 570). In home-gardens and other agroforestry systems erosion is reduced primarily because of the litter layer that derives from the trees rather than the tree cover.[87]

Alternatives to inorganic fertilizers

As an alternative to inorganic fertilizers, farmers can supply nutrients to crops indirectly by encouraging the growth of certain micro-organisms or directly in the form of plant or animal manures. Often these sources are cheaper and more efficient than inorganic compounds, but they may well be as contaminating of the environment as inorganic fertilizers. Nitrates, for example, are liable to leaching whether they have an inorganic or organic origin (See Chapter 4).

Soil micro-organisms

Micro-organisms are responsible for making nutrients available to plants in both natural ecosystems and agro-ecosystems (see Figure 4.4).[88] For example, bacteria that live in the root zones (rhizospheres) of plants fix nitrogen, and confer a number of other benefits.[89] Some strains are capable of fixing up to 40 kg N/ha/year and, in theory, can be cultivated and established in crop plant rhizospheres. However to date, this has not proved practicable.

Mycorrhizal fungi are important in improving the uptake by plants of nutrients from the soil. The filaments of the fungi invade the roots of certain plants, but in such a way that benefits often accrue to both the plants and the fungi. In effect they extend the root system of the plant, adding up to 80 cm of "root" for every centimetre of root infected by the fungus. This increases the area of soil from which nutrients and water can be absorbed by the plant; in return the plants provide the fungus with carbon compounds.

Vesicular–arbuscular (VA) are the commonest mycorrhizae asso-ciated with plants; many plants cannot grow without them.[90] They are particularly important in increasing the utilization of phosphate present in the soil and can enhance the uptake of trace elements, such as zinc and copper.[91] There is, also, some evidence to suggest that plants with mycorrhiza may be better equipped to withstand stress conditions, such as occur during transplanting or periods of drought. VA mycorrhiza are found in most crop species, except brassicas and sugar beet. Crops that especially benefit are those with thick, fleshy roots and few short root hairs, such as onions, citrus and grapevine.[92] In the tropics, pineapple, coffee, tea, cocoa, oil palm, papaya, rubber and cassava all have dense VA populations. The impact can be highly significant, especially in phosphate deficient soils, although there is little improvement in nitrogen uptake.

Blue-green algae

More successful interventions have been based on blue-green algae which are important sources of nitrogen fixation in certain circumstances. The most widely exploited alga is *Anabaena azollae*, which lives in cavities in the leaves of a genus of a small fern, *Azolla*, that grows on the water of rice fields in both tropical and temperate regions. It quickly covers the water surface in the ricefield, but does not interfere with the normal cultivation of the rice crop. However, the nitrogen accumulated is only available to the rice crop after *Azolla* has decomposed and thus exploitation consists of incorporating the ferns into the soil while wet (see green manuring below) or removing them for drying and then re-applying them to the ricefields.

Very high nitrogen production is possible following *Azolla* inoculation in rice fields.[93] Over the whole year, *Azolla* can fix more than 400 kg N/ha, a rate better than most tropical and subtropical legumes. Experiments in the Philippines have shown that after 100 days a total of 57 tonnes of *Azolla* (freshweight) can be harvested yielding more than 120 kg/ha of nitrogen.[94] The impact upon yields can be significant, especially in marginal conditions where labour and soil phosphorus are limiting (Table 11.12). In India, wheat crops following rice with *Azolla* have also been shown to produce improved yields.[95] But one drawback is that current *Azolla* strains are known to be intolerant of temperatures above 31°C.

There are also other forms of blue-green algae that are not associated with *Azolla*. These may be inoculated onto rice plants and, in the absence of inorganic fertilizers, can fix 25–30 kg N per hectare per cropping season.[96] In India, they can become permanently established in fields if inoculation is conducted repeatedly for 3–4 cropping seasons.

Table 11.12 Improvements in rice grain yield following inoculation with *Azolla*

Azolla	Labour (for puddling)	Phosphorus	Yield (kg/ha)	Proportional increase (%)
–	–	–	1480	100
Present	–	–	1850	125
–	Present	Present	2250	100
Present	Present	Present	2530	112

Source: Watanabe, I., Espinas, C.R., Berja, N.S. and Alimango, B.U., *Utilisation of the Azolla – Anabaena complex as a nitrogen fertilizer for rice*, IRRI Research Paper Series no. 11 (Los Baños, The Philippines: IRRI, 1977).

Symbiotic bacteria and legumes

In general, symbiotic bacteria associated with leguminous plants can be more effectively exploited than free-living bacteria. They belong to the genus *Rhizobium* and are present in specialized nodules that develop on the roots of the legumes. As with blue-green algae, the amounts of nitrogen they fix can be considerable, but they have the advantage of being potentially present in a wide range of agro-ecosystems. In a well-nodulated and managed stand of legumes, fixation can be of the order of 100–200 kg N/ha/year (Table 11.13).

Table 11.13 Amounts of nitrogen fixed by various leguminous crops

Species	N fixed (kg N/ha/year)
Alfalfa	80–220
Alfalfa – orchard grass	15–135
Birdsfoot trefoil	50–112
Chickpea	23–84
Clarke clover	21
Common bean	2–215
Crimson clover	64
Fava bean	177–250
Field peas	173–195
Hairy vetch	111
Ladino clover	163–187
Lentil	167–188
Red clover	68–113
Soybean	22–182
Sub clover	58–182
Sweet clover	5
White clover	127

Source: NRC, 1989, *op. cit.*

The impact of legumes grown either with or before a cereal crop has been long recognized. In the Americas the interplanting of maize and beans, often the seed of both crops being placed in the same planting hole, is a practice of great antiquity, probably dating to soon after agriculture began in the valleys of Mexico. In such situations, with soils of low inherent fertility, the cultivation of cereals and legumes crops together can improve both total yields and stability of production.[97] Experiments have shown that in maize and cowpea mixtures, some 30 per cent of the nitrogen taken up from the maize was of atmospheric origin, that is, was obtained from the legume.[98] In the USA, using legume crops in rotation with cereals can reduce and sometimes eliminate the need for nitrogen fertilizers. Subterranean clover and vetches have been used to increase rice yields, fixing up to 110 kg/ha under ideal conditions.[99] The vetches are aerial broadcast in the fields as they are drained.

Breeding is now being carried out specifically to produce high nitrogen fixing legumes for crop rotations. One recent product is the alfalfa, Nitro, which is grown in a two year rotation with maize.[100] The alfalfa is grown for a year and after its final cut in August is left to grow further until killed by frost. In this final phase it contributes about 100 kg N/ha for the subsequent maize crop.

In the tropics particularly useful legumes for inter-cropping with cereals are cowpea and lablab, the former because it is adapted to acid, infertile soils, and the latter because it is drought tolerant, produces good fodder and can regrow well after clipping. Here, legumes contribute not only through nitrogen fixation, but also because the green matter can be used as a mulch or green manure. For example, after a rice harvest, lablab can be allowed to continue growing through the dry season to produce a significant quantity of fresh biomass containing utilizable nitrogen.

Bushes and trees with nitrogen-fixing capacity – mostly confined to the tropics and subtropics (Box 11.2) – have been shown to have beneficial effects on plants growing with or after them. But how much of this is a result of the fixed nitrogen is not known: significant quantities can be supplied in the leaf litter or from intentional pruning, but trees can also improve the microclimate by acting as windbreaks, by improving the water-holding capacity of the soil, and by acting as shade trees for livestock – so focusing the deposition of manure.[101] Nonetheless, several trees and shrubs can fix quite significant amounts of nitrogen, typically in the range of 40–200 kg N/ha/year (Table 11.14). Much of the data is for pure stands, but it is plausible that trees and shrubs could be identified that would be capable of fixing 50–100 kg N/ha when mixed with other crops.

Box 11.2   Ten species of N-fixing tree that are beneficial for soil improvement

Acacia albida: high levels of soil organic matter and nitrogen beneath trees; unfertilized millet and groundnut yields up to 100 per cent higher under trees; Africa.

Acacia tortilis: sylvopastoral tree; benefits pastures and soils (like other Acacias); dense roots near surface; Africa.

Calliandra calothyrus: abundant litter with rapid decay; deep rooting with nutrient uptake; multipurpose tree; Java.

Casuarina equisetifolia: dense root mat stabilizes soil surface, especially good for sand-dune stabilization.

Erythrina poeppigiana: used in combination with coffee and cacao; prunings used as mulch; Latin America.

Gliricidia sepium: potential for hedgerow intercropping.

Inga jinicuil: nutrient recycling in litter; used in combination with coffee and cacao.

Leucaena leucocephala: high biomass production; high levels of N in leaves; high root biomass.

Prosopis cineraria: benefits pastures and crops in semi-arid to dry areas; improvement of waterholding capacity of soil, organic matter and physical conditions.

Sesbania sesban: hedgerow intercropping; other species tolerant of waterlogging.

Source: Young, A., *Agroforestry for Soil Conservation* (Wallingford: CAB International, 1989).

A problem with this kind of nitrogen fixation however, is its high variability. Nitrogen fixation by soybeans, for instance, can vary from 0–300 kg/ha depending on management practices, soil characteristics and water availability.[102] One factor is the amount of nitrate already in the soil since this can inhibit N-fixation. Soybeans on nitrate rich soil may only fix 40 per cent of their requirement, taking the rest from the nitrate in the soil and hence depleting rather than augmenting soil N.[103] Legume-derived nitrate may also contribute to leaching losses. This is particularly true when legumes are ploughed in. The nitrate concentration below the root zone of ploughed-in alfalfa may be twice that of irrigated or non-irrigated maize.[104] But even without ploughing, nitrate losses may be high. In one experiment, continuous soybean yielding 45 bushels/acre produced nearly two thirds the nitrate in the draining water of heavily fertilized corn yielding at 165 bushels/acre.[105]

Table 11.14 Comparison of nitrogen fixation by trees and shrubs and the amount of nitrogen from litter fall and prunings

Species	N fixation (kg N/ha/year)	Litter fall and prunings (kg N/ha/year)
Acacia albida	20	
Acacia mearnsii	200	
Casuarina equisetifolia	60–110	
Coriaria arborea	190	
Erythrina poeppigiana	60	
Gliricidia sepium	13	
Inga jinicuil	35–50	
Leucaena leucocephala	100–500	
Leucaena (in alley cropping)	75–120	
Prosopis glandulosa	25–30	
Prosopis tamarugo	200	
Leucaena leucocephala (alley cropping)		200
Gliricidia sepium (alley cropping)		100
Inga-Erythrina – coffee (tree only)		86
(trees and coffee)		172
Inga-Erythrina – Coffee (tree only)		175
(trees and coffee)		320

Source: Young, A., *Agroforestry from Soil Conservation* (Wallingford: CAB International, 1989).

Green manures

Apart from exploiting micro-organisms of various kinds, nutrients can also be supplied through organic manures of plant or animal origin. One approach is to incorporate vegetation as a "green manure". This may increase nutrient levels, as well as improving the physical properties of the soil. It has been practised for a long time; the Romans grew lupins – a nitrogen fixing legume - and ploughed them in before sowing cereals.

The organic matter may be a legume crop or the fern *Azolla*, ploughed directly into the soil, or may originate from nearby wild vegetation, for example the trimmings of shrubs or trees. Temperate examples include the incorporation of red clover following an earlier harvest for feed in late spring or summer. On the Spray Brothers farm (see Box 11.6) in Ohio, the red clover is disked into the ground in October and twice more in the following spring before maize is planted. This incorporation supplies about 60 per cent of nitrogen requirement of the maize. Other practices elsewhere include the growth of fava beans between rows of grapevines and purple vetches in a rotation with rice.[106] The combination of cover crops and green manures in the USA was described earlier (see page 598).

In tropical and sub-tropical countries quick-growing legumes are popular green manures. In Rwanda the shrub *Tephrosia vogelii* grows to a height of 3 metres in 10 months and produces 14 tonnes/ha of above-ground biomass which, when worked into the soil, can increase subsequent cereal yields by as much as fivefold.[107] In Northeast Thailand, short duration legumes can be grown following the first rainfall peak, which is insufficient for rice transplanting. Cowpeas, grown for 45–60 days before the rice, increase the rice yield by 5–20 per cent compared with fallowing.[108] The benefits are such that the use of inorganic manures is greatly reduced or even eliminated. In Rwanda green manuring, together with animal manures, produced better maize yields than using inorganic fertilizer (Table 11.15). It is claimed that incorporation of *Azolla* as a green manure in Brazil has allowed for a 30–50 per cent reduction in the use of N-fertilizers.[109]

However, incorporation of green manures is often demanding of labour. The timing of incorporation is also critical, since a sufficient period has to elapse for the green manure to decompose. For example, when legumes are grown before rice at least one month must elapse for decomposition before the rice is transplanted.[110] One reason for the success of combinations of leguminous trees, such as *Leucaena*, *Gliricidia*, *Flemingia* and *Cassia*, with maize is that nitrogen release from their prunings is well-synchronized with nitrogen uptake by the maize if the prunings are applied when the maize germinates.[111]

Table 11.15 Comparison of maize yields under different fertilizer regimes, Nyabisindu, Rwanda

Fertilizer (per ha)	Maize yield (kg/ha)
None	580
15t animal manure	1250
Green manure (*Tephrosia*)	2830
10t animal manure + green manure	3310
Inorganic NPK (120:100:10)	3040

Source: Kotschi, J., Waters-Bayer, A., Adelhelm, R. and Hoesle, U., *Ecofarming in Agricultural Development* (Eschborn: GTZ, 1988).

Livestock manures

Livestock manures have been the traditional key to maintaining agricultural productivity since agriculture began, at least in the Old World. Like plant manures they contribute not only to replenishing nutrients but also to improving soil structure. Their integral role in traditional rotational cropping systems such as the Norfolk 4-course rotation has already been described (page 569). In the industrialized countries today, their theoretical potential for supplying nutrients is considerable. In the USA about 110 million tonnes (dry weight) were produced by livestock and poultry in 1976 and this could have supplied some 15 per cent of the total nitrogen on all farms in that year. However, the geographic separation of livestock and crops has greatly reduced the use of manures in this way. In particular using wastes from intensive livestock units, as we saw in Chapter 7, may create rather than solve pollution problems.

Nevertheless, in developing countries animal manure remains an important source of fertility for arable cropping. In Africa migrating pastoralists and their livestock are frequently welcomed by farmers during the dry season. The livestock are kept in pens overnight on the crop fields and in some areas farmers are even willing to pay herdsmen for this overnight coralling.[112] They are important, too, in cash cropping. In the Chiang Mai Valley of Thailand, high value crops such as tobacco, garlic and vegetables all receive animal manures, typically 12–15 t/ha, along with inorganic fertilizers.[113]

The nutrient value of manures largely depends on how they are handled, stored and applied. Losses of nitrogen tend to be highest when liquid systems of storage are used (Table 11.16) and when the manure is broadcast without incorporation (Table 11.17). Total nitrogen content of manure derived from animal bedding varies

Table 11.16 Nitrogen losses in manure affected by handling and storage

Method	Nitrogen loss (%)
Solid systems	
Daily scrape and haul	15–35
Manure pack	20–40
Open lot	40–60
Deep pit (poultry)	15–35
Liquid systems	
Anaerobic deep pit	15–30
Above-ground storage	15–30
Earthen storage pit	20–40
Lagoon	70–80

Source: NRC, 1989, *op. cit.*

Table 11.17 Nitrogen losses in manure affected by application method

Method of application	Type of manure	Nitrogen loss* (%)
Broadcast without incorporation	Solid	15–30
	Liquid	10–25
Broadcast with incorporation	Solid	1–5
	Liquid	1–5
Injection or knifing	Liquid	0–2

* This does not include losses from storage

Source: NRC, 1989, *op. cit.*

from 3.6 kg/tonne for swine, to 4–9.5 kg for dairy and beef cattle respectively, to 9 kg for turkeys.[114] The greatest benefits would seem to arise from using cattle manures that are broadcast and incorporated in the soil. This will also reduce nutrient loss due to run-off, but as we saw in Chapter 4 leaching losses from manure can be significant.

Composting

Composting is a technique of similar long-standing that combines the use of animal manures, green material and household wastes. The materials are heaped in such a fashion that anaerobic decomposition occurs. Harmful substances and toxic products of metabolism are broken down, while pathogens and the seeds and roots of weeds are destroyed by the heat – up to 70°C at the centre – generated within the compost heap.

Composting is particularly valuable in the tropics since organic matter stores nutrients and protects them against leaching. Farmers in Tanzania make compost from stall litter which includes crop residues, leafy tree branches and old roofing grass; in Rwanda farmers mix household wastes, crop residues, weeds, dried leaves and twigs of trees.[115] Wood ash is also commonly used, being carried from burnt bushland to compost heaps. Composting, though, is demanding of labour, both in the building of the heaps and in spreading the compost on the fields. This is why in industrialized countries it is mostly confined to domestic gardens. And even in the tropics the amount of land that can be treated is usually small and its use is usually restricted to home or kitchen gardens. Another disadvantage is that there are often competing uses for the materials, for fuel or fodder, for instance.

Integrated nutrient conservation

These various methods and techniques represent a wide range of possible interventions that will reduce losses of nitrogen or act, at the least, as alternatives to inorganic fertilizers. As in the case of pest management, they can be integrated in such a way as to produce finely-tuned strategies, specific to the conditions of individual farmers and the capacity of particular environments to absorb contamination and pollution.

Farm Conservation Plans, developed in parts of the USA, are examples of such integrated nutrient conservation strategies.[116] Box 11.3 describes the elements of one such plan developed in Maryland. It

Box 11.3   Sample farm conservation plan for a single crop and livestock farm in Maryland, USA

A. Before Conservation Plan

  1 Maize planted every year, using mouldboard ploughing and disking across the slope.
  2 Crop residues removed in autumn when maize taken for silage, and fields remained bare all winter.
  3 Cattle allowed to drink from stream, had trampled streambanks, causing erosion.
  4 Annual soil losses 40–50 t/ha from cropland and 25–30 t/ha from pasture.

B. Conservation Plan: objective to increase productivity and correct water quality problems

  1 No-till farming, with direct planting into residues; save much time since fertilizers and pesticides applied at time of planting.
  2 Contour planting.
  3 Adoption of crop rotations.
  4 Grass waterways established where run-off greatest.
  5 Tile drains built to remove excess subsurface water.
  6 Improvement of pastures by liming and fertilizers.
  7 Cattle rotated across pasture by use of fences.
  8 Watering trough used to water cattle.
  9 Pond constructed between crop and pasture land for sediment control, water supply and recreation. A fence constructed 12 m away from pond to keep cattle out and protect water supply.
  10 Waste management system created for cattle wastes, so that wastes could be stored for up to 180 days.
  11 Sustainable woodland management plan developed.

Source: MDA, *Farm Conservation Plans: For Soil Conservation and Water Quality* (Maryland Department of Agriculture, 1989).

is designed to help farmers improve the efficiency of nutrient use while minimizing pollution. The plan represents a considerable improvement on previous practice but, it should be noted, it does not close off all routes to pollution. For instance if ponds are constructed to trap nutrients in run off, the nitrogen will not end up in the surface waters but instead may be lost to the atmosphere. Water pollution is reduced but at the expense of greater global contamination.

Waste management

As we pointed out in Chapter 6, the problems of pollution from agricultural waste have largely arisen as farming has become more specialized and sectoral in nature. Animal and crop husbandry have become separated geographically with the result that animal wastes can no longer be recycled for crop production and have to be disposed of in some manner. In addition to these wastes are the effluents from silage production and the agro-industrial wastes and crop residues characteristic of intensive crop production. All contain compounds of potential value to farmers or to society at large, and an important goal of waste management is to realize as much of this potential as possible and in a manner that is profitable. However, in practice, attention is often diverted to either reducing the production of wastes or to finding means of ameliorating their impact upon the environment.

Silage wastes

The potential for reducing wastes from intensive farming systems is unfortunately very small. In the case of silage production, the most effective approach is to reduce the moisture content by wilting the crop in the field after harvest and before ensiling. If weather conditions are favourable, wilting should last for at least 24 hours, although even three to four hours can be beneficial. Transport of a wilted crop is also easier and the subsequent fermentation is improved. Nevertheless, as we have seen in Chapter 6, this is often not done either because of adverse weather or because of the extra costs associated with moving machinery twice to a field.

Applying wastes to land

There seems even less likelihood of limiting the amounts of waste produced by livestock; for most farmers the problem is primarily that of finding the optimal means of disposal. One solution is to spread wastes on farm land, taking advantage of natural processes to render them harmless and, hopefully, reaping a benefit from any nutrients they contain. But this may increase nitrate run-off to watercourses, nitrate leaching to underground water and gaseous contamination of the atmosphere.

The hazards can be minimized by carefully regulating when and how much is applied. For example, leaching can be reduced by only applying manures to grassland after the beginning of the growing season, that is, from the spring onwards in temperate regions. Bright sunny days with fresh winds are often common at this time and there is the added benefit of rapid dispersion of unwanted odours but, of course, ammonia is more readily volatilized. The main constraint on timing is the availability of labour. In temperate countries the spring is a busy time of year and there are strong incentives to apply wastes during the autumn and winter. Leaching is high at this time and the benefits are questionable since the nitrogen may well have disappeared by the following spring.[117]

The most serious problems stem from applying wastes in too great a quantity and at too brief an interval. Too much waste leads to excessive build-up of nutrients and waterlogging of the soil and this increases the risk of damage to soil structure. Too short a time interval does not allow sufficient time to elapse for soil micro-organisms to break down the wastes, and for plants to take up the nutrients. On grassland in temperate regions, this interval should be no less than three weeks and the total quantity limited to not more than 50 m^3/ha for slurry and 25 m^3 for silage effluent.[118] Animals should not be allowed to graze on the land for six weeks after application.[119] To reduce the contamination of watercourses, slurry and manure are best applied to the land during dry weather, but safe application rates may be difficult to establish in regions susceptible to frequent and unpredictable summer thunderstorms.[120]

Ideally, the nutrients applied in the wastes should match the needs of the crop, but the ratios of N, P and K excreted by animals are generally different from the ratios that crops require (Table 11.18). Even when the amount of manure applied per hectare gives the correct application of one nutrient, further additions of inorganic fertilizer may be required to reach an optimum balance. Because of this imbalance, supplying the full requirement of nitrogen can also lead to an undesirable high level of potassium in the soil and this can depress magnesium uptake by plants. In certain situations it will lead to the condition known as hypomagnesaemia, or grass staggers, in

Table 11.18 Approximate quantities of nutrients available in animal wastes and annual maximum requirements of some crops

	N^*	P	K
Nutrients in wastes (kg/individual/year)			
Dairy cow	22	15	65
Pig	6	3	4
Hens (per 10 birds)	4	2	2
Maximum nutrient requirements (kg/ha/year)			
Grass for conservation	500	200	375
Grazed grass	500	60	150
Cereals	225	80	120
Potatoes	220	350	350

* Availability of nitrogen is variable according to storage, and method and time of application

Source: MAFF, *Advice on Avoiding Pollution from Manures and other Slurry Wastes*, Farm Management Booklet 2200 (Alnwick: MAFF Public., 1983a).

lactating cattle and sheep, in which disruption of metabolism quickly leads to the development of a stiff, stilted walk, nervous twitching, frequent urination, convulsions and then death.[121]

Methods of application

Liquid wastes are most commonly spread by spraying from the back of tractor-drawn tankers. This method is less polluting than the use of rain-gun irrigation systems and high trajectory slurry spreaders which create aerosols of airborne particles that can drift over considerable distances. Similar aerosols, produced by trickle filter systems in sewage treatment plants, often contain coliform bacteria and have been shown to travel up to a kilometre downwind of the plants.[122] The distance is likely to be much higher from the more intensive and high trajectory systems. The hazard can be reduced by using low level irrigation or slurry dribble bars, or completely removed by the use of injection equipment, in which the slurry is directly inserted into the soil by a moving tractor.

Recently, direct injection systems have been designed that make use of "umbilical systems", in which the heavy tanker is kept off the field, but is connected to the injection unit by a flexible hose.[123] The benefit is that the system can be used when crops are growing. Injection has the additional benefit of reducing odours and losses of ammonia.[124] But ammonia is readily converted to nitrate and thus, although injection may reduce surface water and atmospheric contamination, the effect may simply be to increase groundwater contamination. The final drawback is that injection systems are more costly than conventional tanker spreading.

Off-farm disposal

In many situations wastes cannot be applied on the farm where they are generated and because wastes are bulky, off-site disposal, for example in a landfill, incurs heavy transport costs. But manures can be traded, exchanged, or simply given away if there is a degree of subsidy. In the Netherlands manure banks (*Mestbanks*) were established in the early 1970s to promote the transfer of wastes from those farms with a surplus to those with a shortage.[125] The term "bank" is something of a misnomer: in practice each bank is simply an official whose function is to mediate between farmers. The bank does not handle the manure, but it does subsidize transport costs provided the distance is greater than 10 km. For the producer of the slurry there is no payment other than the benefit of having the wastes removed.

Physical management of wastes

As important as the means of disposal is the handling of the waste, since most of the severe pollution incidents result from design faults or accidental spills.

Housing design and storage

Design of housing for livestock and of the facilities for storing wastes can have a considerable influence upon the total amount of waste material produced. Because livestock wastes have such a high polluting potential, dilution does not significantly reduce the impact on the receiving streams and rivers. Thus not only the collected water, but all the water that passes through livestock housing, barnyards or feedlots has to be considered as a potential conduit for pollution and needs to be collected and appropriately managed.

For instance, run-off from surrounding land can be intercepted by a drain or ditch installed as close as possible to the livestock area. These diversions should have the capacity to carry peak run-off associated with rare and extreme storms.[126] Run-off from all roofs sloping towards barnyards needs also to be intercepted, either by gutters, trenches or appropriate shaping and grading of the land. Silos can be roofed to exclude rain or, if this is not possible, the silage can be covered by plastic sheeting.[127] Livestock confinement areas, too, can be covered with roofing, but inevitably this is expensive.

Within feedlots it may be necessary to design fairly complicated water management systems. Siting is important, with preference for well drained positions, located at the top of slopes, but not on long or steep slopes or overlooking flood plains. It may also be advisable to drain springs and wet areas and rechannel existing streams. Drinking areas in the feedlot need to be maintained so they do not leak, while paved areas should be regularly scraped to reduce the mixing with rainwater.[128]

As important as water management are the systems used for waste storage, in particular ensuring that sufficient capacity is installed. On mixed livestock and arable farms the capacity needs to be sufficient to allow storage throughout periods when it is undesirable to apply wastes to the arable land, that is in autumn and winter in temperate climates. Commonly, facilities are too small so that wastes have to be spread during the winter, even when the land is frozen or snow-covered.[129] In the latter situation the pollution is then delayed until the spring thaw.

Contamination of watercourses is prevented by making storage facilities water-tight. Atmospheric losses of ammonia can be reduced by keeping temperatures low during storage; nitrogen losses from manures in barns are minimal at 5°C, but can rise to 60 per cent at 25°C.[130] However, the biggest losses occur during loading when wastes are exposed to the atmosphere. Thus push-ramp systems, in which manures are scraped into the storage area directly from alleys in the barns, can lose large amounts of nitrogen. Bottom-loaded systems, relying on gravity to lead the manures through underground pipes, lose 5–10 times less.[131]

Silos and collection tanks

Because of its acidity, silage effluent is very corrosive to both concrete and metal structures, and thus special care has to be taken over construction and maintenance. In particular, effluent has to be prevented from seeping beneath the silo floor and there should be a provision for collecting effluent outside the clamp in case it seeps through the collecting walls. In Chapter 6 we described the large quantities of effluent produced each day by silage; grass ensiled at 20 per cent dry matter will discharge a peak yield of 25 litres per tonne each day.[132] Thus for a 1000 tonne silo a tank of 25 m³ is required, with an effluent channel of commensurate size. The tank needs to be leak-proof, with sides higher than the surrounding ground level.

Catchment structures

A second line of defence against pollution is to construct a variety of ponds, basins or barrier ditches that will intercept effluent escaping from feedlots and waste storage areas. Settling basins are often constructed in feedlots to reduce the flow velocity so that solids are retained in the lot. An alternative is a barrier ditch system, comprising a set of serial ditches carefully constructed to impede flow and prevent scum and settled solids from passing into the next compartment. But to be efficient the ditches must remain watertight and they require regular desludging.[133] In general, simple ponds and ditches can only reduce the potential pollution by a limited amount before the effluent is discharged to the main watercourses. They are no substitute for proper treatment.

Biological treatment of waste

Physical methods of containing and treating wastes are inevitably costly; by contrast biological treatment can be cheaper and may yield a benefit in terms of a usable product. Various forms of vegetation will take up wastes or they may be fed to animals. There is also considerable potential for converting wastes by bacterial action into a useful product, such as biogas.

Water hyacinth

One plant commonly exploited in waste treatment is the water hyacinth (*Eichhornia crassipes*) which grows on the surface of tropical ponds and lakes. It has the remarkable ability to grow rapidly in polluted conditions, yielding up to 500 kg of dry matter per hectare daily. In anaerobically digested liquor it can remove more than 80 per cent of the BOD, ammoniacal nitrogen, oil and grease as well as the coliform bacteria. Once harvested it can be used for compost, mulch or animal feeds or may be converted into methane through anaerobic digestion. In particular it has been used to treat agro-industrial wastes.[134] Lagoon systems growing water hyacinth have been developed in Malaysia for the rubber and oil palm agro-industries. There the experience is that the system is cheap, practical and adaptable to specific conditions.

However, the treated effluent still contains fairly high levels of solids, nitrogen and BOD, and so may yet cause pollution when discharged to watercourses.

Small farmers in the tropics have also made effective use of water hyacinth. In parts of Malaysian Borneo farmers rear pigs in slatted stalls built over ponds in which water hyacinth is growing. The hyacinth grows on the pig effluent and is, in turn, fed to the pigs. The ponds also usually yield a harvest of fish.

Grass buffer strips

Unfortunately no comparable plant exists for biological treatment in temperate regions, but vegetation can be used to filter wastes in such climates, although only where the pollution levels are relatively mild. For instance, a 30–35 metre wide mixed strip of the grasses *Phalaris arundinacea* and *Festuca arundinacea* has been shown to be efficient at filtering rainfall run-off from a dairy wastes site.[135] Concentrations of N, P and BOD all decline markedly over the 30 metre distance compared with the values at the point of emission (Table 11.19). Grass

Table 11.19   Effect of grass buffer strips on content of dairy parlour effluent

	Distance from source (metres)	Nitrate (mg/l)	Phosphate (mg/l)	BOD (mg/l)
Surface water	0	260	179	3900
	30	118	89	1000
Ground water	0	58	179	3500
	35	43	0.2	6

Source: Jones, J.H., Olsen, F.J., Patterson, J.J. and Rushing, K.A., "The pollution potential of rainfall run-off from a dairy liquid waste disposal site", *Agric. Wastes* **10** (1984) pp. 177–86.

strips of up to 15 metres width have been shown in North Carolina to be effective in providing an environment in which nitrates contained in surface run-off can be denitrified and emitted to the atmosphere as nitrogen gas, so preventing contamination of nearby rivers.[136]

Artificial wetlands

The principle of vegetation being used as a filter and absorber of wastes has been taken a step further by several towns in the USA, notably in the Tennessee Valley and in rural Pennsylvania, which have constructed artificial wetlands to treat municipal sewage wastes.[137] The sewage is first aerated in ponds, and then passed to a cattail and reed marsh, where the contaminants are metabolized, absorbed or just settle in the sediments. In the next open-water pond algae feed on remaining nutrients; and in the final stage the liquid is passed across a meadow of grasses to trap the algae and remaining nutrients.

Construction costs are thought to be between 10–50 per cent of conventional treatment plants, though the biggest drawback is their large requirement for land – a system for a community of 10,000 people producing 4.5 million litres daily would require 18 hectares of land. Although these have not yet been used to treat agricultural wastes, the Tennessee Valley Authority is building several wetlands to determine design requirements for treating feedlot wastes.

Wastes as animal feed

It has long been the practice, indeed since agriculture began, to feed crop residues to animals. The same principle can be applied to silage effluents. Pigs can be fed effluent, containing an average 7 per cent nutritive dry matter, up to a maximum of 6 litres daily.[138] In countries such as Indonesia it has also been customary to raise freshwater fish in ponds fed with livestock wastes.[139] But the practice of large-scale feeding of animals with animal wastes is more recent.

Today poultry manures can be successfully recycled as supplementary feed for chicks by first drying in drum-driers and then separating out the coarse solid.[140] Dried poultry manures have also been successfully incorporated into feedstuffs of laying hens with no loss of performance. It is particularly profitable in countries with an expanding poultry business that depend upon imported feed, such as Kuwait which has virtually no arable agriculture.[141] Pig manure can also be recycled in the same way, but the much higher water content imposes greater difficulties. A further problem is that pig wastes are often high in zinc and copper.

A further danger concerns the transfer of certain animal diseases through feedstuffs to other animals, and possibly to humans too. In recent years, livestock in industrialized countries have been increasingly fed protein-enriched feed derived in part from the remains of slaughtered animals. This practice, though, can lead to the transfer of two diseases of the brain of livestock, namely sheep scrapie and bovine spongiform encephalopathy. It is not yet certain whether these can be transferred to humans from infected carcasses.

Animal feed can also be produced by growing single-cell algae in shallow highly aerated ponds containing livestock effluent. The harvested algae contain up to 50 per cent crude protein which can be fed to poultry and pigs.[142] Most recently, systems have been developed that use a combination of worms and yeast to digest slurry.[143] The slurry is converted to compost, and the worms and yeast are periodically removed and ground up for high-protein, especially for turkey and mink production.

Producing biogas

Livestock and crop wastes not only have nutritive value, they are a potential source of energy. This is best realized by subjecting them to anaerobic digestion – fermentation in the absence of oxygen – in which bacteria convert the wastes into methane. The methane can then be used as a cooking gas, or to provide heating for an intensive livestock unit or, on a larger scale, as a source of industrial energy. The process has many advantages, apart from the production of the methane. The effluent that is left behind has few pathogens and a greatly decreased odour. The reduction in solids also makes it cheap and easy to handle; heavier application rates to land are possible without scorching vegetation and cattle can graze fields sooner after application.[144] The value of digester effluent as fertilizer or compost may indeed be greater than that of the methane.

However, while the concept is technically feasible, it is often very costly either in equipment or labour. The equipment necessary to produce usable quantities of methane on a large scale is not simple and requires considerable investment. Nevertheless, some large-scale operations are running in the southwest of the USA.[145] Moreover simple biogas plants have also been used in Asia, particularly in India and China, with some success. These small plants are designed on the basis of 1–2 m^3 of digester volume to treat the waste of a single pig, while each m^3 of tank volume produces about 0.15 m^3 gas daily for small units, and up to 2 m^3 for larger ones.[146]

Digester gas contains about 60 per cent methane, most of the remainder being CO_2. The gas is bulky and if possible needs to be used immediately in a boiler, space heater or stationary engine. It is most economic where there is a continuous need for gas, for example in a dairy with a demand for hot water year-round. However, a swine unit with a fluctuating demand for heat and for electricity would require a complex system using a generator as a heat and electrical source.[147]

The use of straw

Finally there is the special problem posed by the treatment of bulky crop residues, in particular straw. One answer is to burn the straw but this creates considerable nuisance and pollution (see Chapter 7). The alternatives are incorporation into the soil *in situ*, or baling for a variety of subsequent uses, on or off the farm. Incorporation is not yet a common practice in the UK: only 250–500,000 tonnes are incorporated annually, which is some 22–24 per cent of total production.[148] This is partly because it is believed that cereal yields are reduced. The high carbon:nitrogen ratio of straw means that soil bacteria and fungi break down the straw, so nitrogen is very rapidly used up and is not available for germinating seedlings. However, some of these problems appear to be avoided if the straw is thoroughly chopped before incorporation.[149] Experiments on wheat at Rothamsted Experimental Station have demonstrated that yield reductions are only of the order of 3 per cent and, more important, straw incorporation could have the crucial effect of reducing nitrate pollution to groundwater.[150] In the experiments some 60 per cent of applied N was lost by leaching in the absence of straw, but this decreased to 47 per cent when straw was incorporated.

Besides incorporation, straw has a wide variety of uses. Most commonly it is used for animal bedding, as it readily absorbs dung and urine. Baled straw can be used as a fuel in boilers for the heating of glasshouses and animal houses, and for crop drying. It can also be fed to animals, although to increase digestibility it usually requires treating with alkalis to break down lignins and celluloses. It can be used for bedding plants, though care has to be taken with possible herbicide residues in the straw. The mushroom industry is the largest off-farm market for straw in the UK, taking some 5 per cent of total production, where it is used to make mushroom compost. Finally, it is a raw product in the paper industry for making strawboards and strawboxes. Transport costs are high, although this can be partly overcome by compressing the straw into briquettes. Either the demand for straw has to come from close by the farm or farmers have to invest in appropriate storage space and a baler (Table 11.20).[151] Recently, in the UK, industry has announced plans for a straw pulping mill to make paper in East Anglia, which could take as much as 750,000 tonnes annually.[152]

Table 11.20   Overall costs of straw procurement

	Range (£/tonne)	Typical cost (£/tonne)
Cost of not burning	0–12	5
Baling and handling	7–14	9
Storage	3–6	5
Transport 40 km round trip	4–6	5
300 km round trip	6–16	9
Total (for 40 km trip)	14–38	23

Source: Larkin, S.B.C., "Straw availability and procurement", in: MAFF, *Straw Disposal and Utilisation. A Review of Knowledge* (London: MAFF, 1984); Martindale, L.P., "Straw as fuel", in: MAFF, 1984, *ibid.*

Reducing global pollution

Agriculture is a significant contributor to global air pollution but, as yet, little thought or research attention has been given to the topic of reducing agriculture's contribution.[153]

There is, theoretically, scope for reducing methane emissions. Microbiologists and dairy nutritionists have long been interested in reducing methanogenesis – the bacterial production of methane in dairy cattle – since it represents a net loss of energy from the animal and reduces efficiency. But the complexity of the food chain and the critical role of the bacteria in digestion have made the task difficult. Methanogenic bacteria from the rumen have been shown to be inhibited by antibiotics such as monensin, but this only lasts a short while, the bacteria evolving resistance to the antibiotic.[154] In the long run, however, finding an appropriate methanogenesis inhibiting substance to add to feed could both improve efficiency and reduce pollutant emissions. There are also possible benefits in changing the nature of cattle feed. High quality feed containing a high proportion of starch to cellulose lowers methane emissions and grain fed cattle emit less methane per pound of meat produced than do range cattle with a high cellulose diet.[155] But, of course, shifting to more intensive livestock rearing will only increase emissions from livestock waste.

The other main agricultural source of methane – the tropical rice paddies – might be amenable to a similar approach, although it seems likely that entirely different inhibitors may be required because of the different chemical processes at work. Producing new varieties of rice that leave less stubble in the fields may reduce methane production and

Ehrlich speculates that the cultivation of fish in rice paddies might be beneficial.[156]

So far, few researchers have investigated means of reducing the losses of nitrogen as nitrous oxide or ammonia, particularly in the tropics and subtropics. Gaseous losses from the use of inorganic fertilizers are reducible by the use of nitrification inhibitors, although this is still a new technique and its overall effectiveness is unknown (see page 587). Manures can be treated with certain chemicals to convert ammonia to non-volatile compounds, such as using paraformaldehyde to produce amines, but this will only be cost-effective when there are large quantities of manure in one place. Reducing the ventilation rate inside buildings also reduces ammonia loss, but if there is too little ventilation, the animals' health suffers.

Research may eventually come up with other options: strains of bacteria that absorb gases as they leave plants or capture gases from the soil as they pass by crops; or rice varieties that inhibit methane production in the root zone. But such developments lie some way in the future.

Finally, there is a need to reduce the amounts of biomass burnt, either during swidden cultivation or in clearing for new agricultural lands. The alternative to swidden cultivation is to invest in the development of more permanent and productive agroforestry systems such as we have described earlier (pages 570 and 598). There is good evidence that these can provide livelihoods as good as those of swiddening without the need for burning. In savanna agriculture the alternative is not so clear. For the long term the answer may lie in upgrading grasses using species that do not require burning to stimulate new productive growth. The clearing of new lands is even harder still to stop. In most of the developing countries most potentially cultivable land is already being exploited. The major land clearances, today, occur in the Amazon basin of South America, in parts of central Africa, and in Indonesia and Malaysia. Although these are, in part, a function of population pressure, they are more directly a result of unbridled investment by larger entrepreneurs seeking the timber wealth and the opportunities for large-scale agriculture. Consequently the answer lies primarily in the realm of national policies.

Integrated farming

We have so far talked about solutions in terms of individual problems – pesticides, nutrients, wastes and so on. In practice farmers, whether in the developed or developing countries, will adopt measures piecemeal to solve problems as they arise and as the economic conditions permit, or in response to legal pressures. However, it is possible to bring together many of these control strategies in an integrated fashion to produce farms that, by careful co-ordination and control, obtain the maximum benefit with the least pollution. The assumption here is that measures to reduce pesticides, conserve nutrients or recycle wastes do not merely complement one another but have a multiplicative effect, producing a whole that is, in some sense, greater then the sum of the parts.

In the industrialized countries integrated approaches are termed "organic farming" or alternative agriculture (Box 11.4). They have

Box 11.4   Definition of alternative agriculture

Alternative agriculture is any system of food or fibre production that systematically pursues the following goals:

- More thorough incorporation of natural processes such as nutrient cycles, nitrogen fixation, and pest–predator relationships into the agricultural production process;
- Reduction in the use of off-farm inputs with the greatest potential to harm the environment or the health of farmers and consumers;
- Greater productive use of the biological and genetic potential of plant and animal species;
- Improvement of the match between cropping patterns and the productive potential and physical limitations of agricultural lands to ensure long-term sustainability of current production levels; and
- Profitable and efficient production with emphasis on improved farm management and conservation of soil, water, energy and biological resources.

Source: NRC, *Alternative Agriculture* (Washington DC: National Research Council, 1989).

arisen for a variety of reasons. One factor has been growing concern over agrochemical residues in foodstuffs which has stimulated a consumer deamand for organically grown foods, where the farmer guarantees that no agrochemicals have been used. Another factor has been the growing costs of pest, disease and weed control and the frequent ineffectiveness of pesticides. Thirdly, and particularly in the USA, alternative agriculture has been developed as a way of countering growing soil erosion. Box 11.5 briefly describes six integrated farms from the USA and Europe.

Highly integrated farms are more common in developing countries and this reflects high labour availability (Box 11.6). They also require

Box 11.5   Integrated or alternative agriculture farms in Europe and the USA

Rushall Farm, Salisbury Plain, UK (Wookey, 1987)

Crops: 650 hectare mixed farm with winter wheat, oats, and ryegrass and red clover leys. Rotation is over eight years: three years ley – winter wheat – winter wheat, undersown with ryegrass and red clover – ley – winter wheat, undersown with oats – oats.

Livestock: cattle winter housed, manures replaced on land.

Weed control: tall varieties of wheat to choke weeds, e.g. Maris Wigeon; wheat contains grass, speedwell, red nottle at levels not affecting yield. Weed strike practised: after preparation, land left for 10–14 days before drilling, so weeds germinate and then are destroyed by drilling and harrowing. Fallows control perennial weeds.

Soil fertility: livestock manures, imported sewage sludge and clover. No inorganic fertilizers used as farm entirely organic.

Eichwaldof (Oak Forest Farm), Darmstadt, FRG (Gips, 1984)

Crops: 75 hectares of oats, barley, spinach, potatoes, winter wheat, grass/clover ley and carrots. Carrots contract-grown for juice and baby food industry, yield 75 tonnes/ha. Sorghum grown for silage.

Livestock: 250 pig fattening operation, 42 dairy cattle herd. Some 90 per cent of feed produced on farm.

Weed control: home-weeder for pre-emergent weeds in carrots; long rotation of oats – barley – spinach (May harvest) – millet – potatoes or carrots – winter wheat or winter barley – two years of grass clover ley with lucerne.

Insect control: choice of windy fields for carrots to discourage carrot fly; rotations; selective use of pyrethrum.

Soil fertility management: white lupin as green manure, livestock manures and composts applied.

Spray Brothers Farm, Mount Vernon, Ohio (NRC, 1989)

Crops: 290 hectares cropland, of which 14 per cent to wheat and oats, 14 per cent to maize and 45 per cent pasture and leys. Oats, soybeans and adzuki beans are sold to speciality health food distributer. Some 60 per cent of the maize is fed to the dairy herd of 32 cows and beef herd of 40–50 cattle.

Weed control: no herbicide applied for last 15 years; use rotations, two spring diskings and late planting of corn to uproot weeds, hand weeding in beans, plus rotary-hoeing of maize and soybeans at emergence.

Insect and nematode control: no problems apparent.

Soil fertility management: livestock manures; use of maize soybeans – small grain – red clover hay rotation; red clover green manures.

Yields: yields of maize, soybeans, wheat and oats all exceed the county average by between 5–40 per cent.

Box 11.5   Continued

BreDahl Farm, Southwest Iowa, USA (NRC, 1989)
Crops: 65 hectare farm of which approximately 25 per cent to maize, 20–25 per cent soybean, 13 per cent alfalfa and 30 per cent oats for seed. Turnips are double cropped following oats and sheep forage.

Livestock: 300–500 ewes and lambs, 30–50 cattle, 10–20 sows. Cattle and sheep glean fenced maize fields, turnip tops and grazed and turnip roots eaten in winter. Animals consume crop residues.

Weed control: ridge tillage, controlled burning and rotary hoeing (both pre-emergence and weekly for four weeks). Disk cultivation if weeds become a problem. Spot spraying of glyphosate or paraquat to control thistle and morning glory.

Insects and nematodes: no problems reported.

Soil fertility management: typical rotation of maize – soybeans – maize – oats/turnips – alfalfa. Small quantities of inorganic fertilizer applied to first year maize, and larger quantity after soybeans. Livestock manure applied to oats.

Performance: yields about average, but cost reduced by use of on-farm resources (forage, nitrogen fixation).

Sabot Hill Farm, Richmond, Virginia, USA (NRC, 1989)
Crops: 1430 hectares of which 42 per cent is to forest, 35 per cent to permanent pasture, 14 per cent to various hay mixtures and 9 per cent to maize and soybeans. Hay is produced for both cattle feed on farm and as a cash crop. Mixtures of alfalfa/orchard grass, orchard grass alone, and fescue/Johnsongrass/legumes/millet are grown.

Livestock: 500 beef cattle. Animal births are timed for Sept–mid-Nov to coincide with available labour. Improved pastures and rotational practices allow animals to graze year round with little supplemental feeding.

Weed control: rotation of maize – hay – soybeans sometimes double or triple cropped; interseeds Johnsongrass with legumes and harvest until grass depleted. Savings on not having to control Johnsongrass with herbicide is some $20,000 annually.

Insects and nematodes: no problem reported.

Animal disease control: conjunctivitis and lumpjaw are major problems. All cattle receive injections for bovine diseases. Calves are not fed antibiotics.

Soil fertility management: erosion substantially reduced through no-tillage planting, strip cropping. Rotations of legumes reduce need for inorganic fertilizer, which is applied to maize alone.

Kutztown Farm, eastern Pennsylvania, USA (NRC, 1989)
Crops: 123 hectares mixed crop and livestock farm, of which 30 per cent is to barley, oats, rye and wheat, 45 per cent to maize (for grain and silage) and

Box 11.5 Continued

Kutztown Farm, eastern Pennsylvania, USA – Continued
soybeans, and the remainder to alfalfa and red clover. Variety of crops
results in relatively even distribution of labour needs throughout the year.

Livestock: 250–290 beef cattle, 50–250 pigs. All the grain, hay and silage
needed is produced on the farm.

Weed control: crop rotations and multiple cultivations of row crops used.
Uncomposted imported chicken manure suspected source of weed seeds.
Herbicides applied to approximately 45 per cent of land.

Insects and nematodes: pest build-up avoided through rotations.

Soil fertility management: variable rotations of maize, soybean, small grain
and hay. Manure at 12 tonnes/ha applied twice per five year rotation.
Source of manure: both on and off-farm. Very small quantities of starter
fertilizer applied to maize.

Yields and performance: crop yields exceed county averages for soybeans,
hay, wheat and maize grain; but lower for maize silage and rye. Expenditure
on fertilizers and chemicals substantially below county averages.

Source: Wookey, B., *Rushall – The Story of an Organic Farm* (Oxford: Blackwells, 1987);
Gips, T., "European sustainable agriculture", *Manna* 1 (1984) pp. 1-2, 5–6; NRC, 1989,
op. cit.

considerable skill in design and close and careful management. But
very tight interconnectedness poses a hazard, since the collapse of one
element – say failure of a biogas digester, or a disease among one group
of livestock – can endanger the whole enterprise.

Economic and social constraints

In this chapter we have described the components of an agriculture
which is environmentally benign, with pollution and waste at a
minimum. In many ways this is a distant ideal. As we have seen,
there are many difficulties in the way of its implementation. First,
there are no broad-spectrum answers. What works in one set of
environmental, climatic or social conditions will not work in another.
In particular, solutions applicable to the industrialized countries are
likely to be inappropriate in the developing countries and vice versa.
Solutions have to be found for each situation, based on sound and
widely applicable principles, but without preconceptions regarding
technology or the nature of inducements or regulations.

Box 11.6 Integrated or alternative agriculture farms in the Philippines, China, Thailand and Kenya

The Maya Farm in Philippines
The farm covers 36 ha of land and houses 25,000 pigs, 70 head of cattle and 10,000 ducks. Ten biogas plants receiving animal manure and other wastes produce about 2000 m^3 of biogas and 4 tonnes of feed daily. The residue from the digester is conditioned in lagoons, some of the settled sludge used as a fertilizer and some as pig and duck feedstuff, while scum on the surface of the lagoon is eaten by ducks. Excess energy from the biogas plants is used in meat processing plants.

Xinbu Brigade, Leliu People's Commune, Guandong Province, China
This farm cultivates mulberry bushes around fish ponds and feeds leaves to silk worms, heated by biogas. Silkworm droppings are fed to fish (25%) and to biogas digesters (75%). Sugarcane is grown and processed with residual leaves being fed to carp and sun-dried baggasse used for cooking. Fish pond sludge and biogas residue is supplemented with chemicals and used to fertilize sugarcane, bananas, mulberry and Napier grass. Fish ponds support a polyculture of fish at an average of 4450 kg/ha/year. Napier grass is grown as an energy crop and fed to biogas digesters and pigs. The pigs consume mainly water hyacinth, imported grass and kitchen waste and their manure, along with regurgitated Napier grass and banana waste, are fed to family and communal biogas digesters.

Ecological Farm, Kunming, Yunnan, China
The farm, near Kunming in Yunnan, is about 100 hectares in size and employs over 700 people. It is a dairy farm which also grows corn. The corn is fed to the cattle and together with the milk is the basis for a number of small processing plants on the farm for milk powder, egg rolls, ovaltine, commercial and medicinal starch. The wastes from the starch processing are acid but those from the milk processing are alkaline. The wastes are thus combined to produce a neutral mixture before being applied to the land. Other farms go further and attempt to integrate a very large number of both animal and crop enterprises using biogas digesters as the central processor.

Small-scale farm in Thailand
This farm covers only about 0.4 ha. It comprises up to 30 pigs housed in pens overhanging a 1.25 m deep 0.2 ha fish pond and a 0.2 ha vegetable garden. Above the pig pens are enclosures for 60 laying hens. The chicken waste provides supplemental pig feed and the pig waste fertilizes both the fish pond and the garden. About 5000 Tilapia are reared in the pond, which also supports ducks. Maize, beans and other vegetables are grown in the garden. Periodically, the garden and pond areas are interchanged to utilise the high nutrient pond sludge as plant fertilizer.

Mrs Njeri's Farm in Murang'a District, Kenya
Coffee is the principal cash crop, and maize the main staple, but a significant proportion of the farm is set aside for Napier grass, bananas,

Box 11.6   Continued

Mrs Njeri's Farm in Murang'a District, Kenya – Continued
and fruit trees like avocado, mango and citrus and also a number of minor crops. Trees grow in abundance among the crops and on the field boundaries. Near the living quarters at the top of the silage there is a rudimentary zero-grazing unit for two cattle.

The farm is very well conserved with retention ditches and *fanya juus*; sacks, stones, trash and live plants to prevent gully erosion; bench terraces for coffee and infiltration pits.

The cattle eat Napier grass grown on the retention ditches and *fanya juus*, and paspalum grass grown on the terrace risers. Both grasses also serve to stabilize the soils. The animals also consume maize stalks and stover, banana leaves and stalks, tree leaves and during the times of shortage wild plants such as *maegoya*, plus sweet potato vines, cassava leaves and tubers. Plants such as *Euphorbia* and *Grevillea* are used as bedding for the cattle and for adding bulk to the manures.

Source: Pescod, M.B., "Agricultural wastes in urban areas", in: Chan, M.W.H. et al. (eds), *Pollution in the Urban Environment* (Amsterdam: Elsevier, 1985); Kiara, J.K., Segerros, M., Pretty, J.N. and McCracken, J.A., *Rapid Catchment Analysis: An Application of Rapid Rural Appraisal to the Catchment Approach of the Soil and Water Conservation Branch, Ministry of Agriculture, Kenya* (Nairobi, Kenya: MOA, 1990).

It is also clear from this chapter that solutions to pollution problems are, for the most part, not hampered by the lack of a technology. Alternatives to pesticides exist for a wide variety of situations, efficient methods of applying and conserving nutrients are available, as are technologies for containing or utilizing wastes. The technologies, however, are of little use without the inducement or the will to use them. Two issues have to be better understood and acted upon. First is the nature of the perceptions of farmers – of their environment and of the impact on the environment of the agricultural practices they follow. Second is the very real trade-offs involved in switching from high- to low-polluting practices.

We have already referred in Chapter 2 to the common perceptions held by farmers of the nature of pests, their damage and the efficacy of pesticides. We have argued that these are, in large part, responsible for the heavy use of pesticides. Present efforts to curb nitrate pollution of watercourses are revealing a similar set of perceptions. In the USA a number of "best management practices" have been developed in order to restrict the contamination of water from agricultural non-point sources. The technical aspects of the recommended practices suggest that they should be effective, but surveys of farmers' attitudes from many parts of the USA have indicated why adoption of these practices has been poor.[157] In general, farmers do not see themselves as responsible for water pollution. For instance, in the Great Lakes states the majority of farmers believe that no relationship exists between water quality and the use of fertilizers, manures and pesticides.[158] Similarly in Nebraska, farmers are unwilling to use corrective measures because of the lack of demonstrable links between pollution and specific farm sources.[159] Although they agree that water quality could be improved by using the recommended rates of fertilizer applications, they are entirely opposed to any reductions in fertilizer use. Part of the problem is a lack of good information. Farmers believe they receive insufficient information from extension and advisory services about the causes of pollution. It would seem that increased environmental education coupled with specific pollution control recommendations that avoid the expected consequence of lower yields could be effective in changing perceptions.

But here, as in all the other situations we have discussed, there are crucial trade-offs to be assessed and resolved. Pesticides are often reliable and efficient, at least in the short term. Alternatives may produce less stable control and require higher labour or management costs. This is also true of alternatives to inorganic fertilizers. Environmental manipulation requires skill and investment and often entails a loss of productive arable land. For instance, encouraging and replacing hedgerows to increase habitats for the natural enemies of pests inevitably results in less land for cultivation. Most of the problems of waste production arise from the intensification of agriculture in response to perceived or actual economies of scale. As we have seen, a switch to a more integrated agriculture may be too expensive in terms of labour and other costs. Solutions are often more acceptable in developing countries, partly because of greater biological potential for alternatives to agrochemicals or treatment of wastes, and partly because of the ready availability of cheap labour.

Much can be achieved by legislation and regulation, at least in the industrialized countries, but there also have to be complementary economic incentives or the penalties have to be very rigorously enforced. Even where farmers appreciate that a pollution problem exists, it is often only the wealthier who can afford to take corrective measures notwithstanding the existence of regulatory pressures. Those with high levels of debt are unlikely to undertake the perceived added burden of a greater investment of time and money, and will take only token measures.[160] Another problem to be overcome is the short time horizon of many farmers. As much as 50 per cent of US cropland is rented, and some studies suggest that tenants will consider yields and production costs foremost, despite possible long-term trade-offs with declining environmental quality.[161]

In the developing countries such incentives are even more important. It is difficult to implement legislation and for many, if not the majority of, farmers their survival depends on what they produce. They will be reluctant to adopt new practices unless they clearly see the benefits that they will reap. Reduction in the use of pesticides in order to lower food residues or in the use of nitrogen fertilizers to minimize the risk of methaemoglobinaemia or gastric cancer will only occur if farmers themselves receive an immediate economic return.

The final challenge is ensuring that a low-polluting agriculture is sustainable. This has several dimensions. Economic incentives need to be long-lasting and laws and regulations to become institutionalized. However, the fundamental task is to design agricultural systems that are not only less polluting but are intrinsically more efficient and productive, utilizing the natural biological processes and resources available to us in new ways that create bigger harvests without the attendant, unwelcome problems we have described in this book.

References

1 Conway, G.R., "Better methods of pest control", in: Murdoch, W.W. (ed.), *Environment, Resources, Pollution and Society* (Stanford: Sinauer Assoc. Inc., 1971a).

2 Conway, G.R. (ed.), *Pesticide Resistance and World Food Production* (London: Imperial College Centre for Environmental Technology, 1982); NRC, *Pesticide Resistance Strategies and Tactics for Management*, National Research Council (Washington DC: National Academy Press, 1984).

3 Waage, J.K. and Greathead, D.J., "Biological control: challenges and opportunities", *Phil. Trans. R. Soc. Lond. B* 318 (1988) pp. 111–28.

4 Waage and Greathead, 1988, *op. cit.*

5 Conway, 1971a, *op. cit.*

6 Neuenschwander, P. and Herren, H.R., "Biological control of the cassava mealybug, *Phenacoccus manihoti*, by the exotic parasitoid *Epidinocarsis lopezi* in Africa", *Phil. Trans. R. Soc. Lond. B* 318 (1988) pp. 319–33.

7 *Washington Post*, "Africa pest-control program saves lives, lifts productivity", June 20 (1988) Al, A20.

8 Jutsum, A.R., "Commercial application of biological control: status and prospects", *Phil. Trans. R. Soc. Lond. B* 318 (1988) pp. 357–71.

9 Lawton, J.H., "Biological control of bracken in Britain: constraints and opportunities", *Phil. Trans. R. Soc. Lond. B* 318 (1988) pp. 335–54; Heads, P. and Lawton, J.H., "Beat back bracken biologically", *New Scientist* 111 (1986) pp. 40–43.

10 Payne, C.C., "Pathogens for the control of insects: where next?" *Phil. Trans. R. Soc. Lond. B* 318 (1988) pp. 225–46.

11 Turner, C.E., "Conflicting interests and biological control weeds", in: Delfosse, E.S. (ed.), *Proc. VI Int. Symp. on Biological Control of Weeds, Vancouver Canada* (Ottawa: Agriculture Canada, 1985).

12 Waage and Greathead, 1988, *op. cit.*

13 Altieri, M.A. and Liebman, M., "Insect, weed and plant disease management in multiple cropping systems", in: Francis, C.A. (ed.), *Multiple Cropping Systems* (New York: Macmillan, 1986).

14 Conway, 1971a, *op. cit.*

15 Herzog, D.C. and Funderbank, J.E., "Ecological bases for habitat management and pest control", in: Kogan, M. (ed.), *Ecological Theory and Integrated Pest Management Practice* (New York: John Wiley and Sons, 1986).

16 Herzog and Funderbank, 1986, *op. cit.*

17 Herzog and Funderbank, 1986, *op. cit.*

18 Stoll, G., *Natural Crop Protection*, 2nd edn (Langen, Germany: Agrecol. Josef Margraf, 1987); Saxena, R.C., "Antifeedants in tropical pest management", *Insect Sci. Applic.* 8 (1987) 731–6.

19 Conway, 1971a, *op. cit.*

20 Litsinger, J.A., Canapi, B.L., Bandong, J.P., Dela Cruz, C.M. and G., Apostol, R.F., Pantua, P.C., Lumaban, M.D., Alviola, A.L., Raymundo, F., Libertario, E.M., Loevinsohn, M.E. and Joshi, R.C., "Rice crop loss from insect pests in wetland and dryland environments of Asia with emphasis on the Philippines", *Insect Sci. Applic.* 8 (1987) pp. 677–92.

21 Conway, 1971a, *op. cit.*

22 NRC, 1989, *Alternative Agriculture* (Washington DC: National Academy Press, 1989).

23 Mumford, J.D. and Baliddawa, C.W., "Factors affecting insect pest occurrence in various cropping systems", *Insect. Sci. Applic.* 4 (1983) pp. 59–64.

24 Herzog and Funderbank, 1986, *op. cit.*

25 Loevinsohn, M.E., *The Ecology and Control of Rice Pests in Relation to Intensity and Synchrony of Cultivation*, PhD Thesis (London: Centre for Environmental Technology, Imperial College, 1984).

26 Herzog and Funderbank, 1986, *op. cit.*

27 Altieri and Liebman, 1986, *op. cit.*; Herzog and Funderbank, 1986, *op. cit.*

28 Francis, C.E., *Multiple Cropping Systems* (New York: Macmillan, 1986).

29 Soemarwoto, O. and Conway, G.R., (in press) *The Javanese Home-Garden*

30 Coaker, T.H., "Insect pests management in *Brassica* crops by intercropping", *I.O.B.C.W.P.R.S. Bull.* 3 (1980) pp. 117–25.

31 Altieri and Liebman, 1986, *op. cit.*

32 Altieri and Liebman, 1986, *op. cit.*

33 Herzog and Funderbank, 1986, *op. cit.*

34 Altieri and Liebman, 1986, *op. cit.*

35 Slosser, J.E., Fewin, R.J., Price, F.R., Meinke, L.J. and Bryson, J.R., "Potential of shelterbelt management for boll weevil (*Coleoptera curculionidae*) control in the Texas rolling plains", *J. Econ. Entomol.* 77 (1984) pp. 377–85; Slosser, J.E., Jacoby, P.W. and Price, J.R., "Management of sand shinnery oak for control of the boll weevil (*Coleoptera: Curculionidae*) in the Texas rolling plains", *J. Econ. Entomol.* 78 (1985) pp. 383–9.

36 Herzog and Funderbank, 1986, *op. cit.*

37 Campion, D., Hall, D.R. and Prevett, P.F., "Use of pheromones in crop and stored products pest management: control and monitoring", *Insect Sci. Applic.* 8 (1987) pp. 737–41; NRC, 1989, *op. cit.*

38 Campion, D.G. and Hosny, M.M., "Biological, cultural and selective methods for control of cotton pests in Egypt", *Insect Sci. Applic.* 8 (1987) pp. 803–805.

39 NRC, 1989, *op. cit.*

40 Knipling E.F., "The eradication of the screw-worm fly", *Sci. Amer.* 203 (1960) pp. 54–61; Conway, 1971a, *op. cit.*

41 Crossland, N.O., "Laboratory to experiment", *Proc. V. Int. Congress of Toxicol.*, Brighton, July 1989 (1989) pp. 184–92.

42 Saxena, R.C., "Antifeedants in tropical pest management", *Insect Sci. Applic.* 8 (1987) pp. 731–6; Bernays, E.A., "Antifeedants in crop pest management", in: Whitehead, D.L. and Bowers, W.S. (eds), *Natural Products for Innovative Pest Management* (Oxford: Pergamon Press, 1983).

43 Saxena, 1987, *op. cit.*

44 Payne, 1988, *op. cit.*

45 Bedford, G.O., "Biology, ecology and control of palm rhinoceros beetles", *Ann. Rev. Entomol.* 25 (1980) pp. 309–39; Young, E.C., "The epizootiology of two pathogens of the coconut palm rhinoceros beetle", *J. Invert. Pathol.* 24 (1974) pp. 82–92.

46 Greathead, D.J. and Waage, J.K., *Opportunities for Biological Control of Agricultural Pests in Developing Countries*, World Bank Tech Paper 11 (Washington DC: The World Bank, 1983).

47 NRC, 1989, *op. cit.*

48 NRC, 1989, *op. cit.*

49 Kenmore, P., Litsinger, J.A., Bandong, J.P., Santiago, A.C. and Salac, M.M., "Philippine rice farmers and insecticides: thirty years of growing dependency and new options for change", in: Tait, E.J. and Napompeth, B. (eds), *Management of Pests and Pesticides: Farmers' Perceptions and Practices* (London: West View Press, 1987).

50 Conway, G.R., *Pest and Pathogen Control: Strategic Tactical and Policy Models* (Chichester: J. Wiley and Sons, 1984).

51 Conway, 1971a, *op. cit.*

52 Smith, R.F. and van den Bosch, R., "Integrated control", in: Kilgore, W.W. and Doutt, R.C. (eds), *Pest Control – Biological, Physical, and*

Selected Chemical Methods (New York: Academic Press, 1967).

53 Conway, G.R., "Ecological aspects of pest control in Malaysia", in: Farvar, T.G. and Milton, J. (eds), *The Careless Technology: The Ecology of International Development* (Doubleday Natural History Press, 1971b).

54 Kenmore et al., 1987, *op. cit.*

55 Craswell, E.T. and De Datta, S.K., *Recent Developments in Research on Nitrogen Fertilizers for Rice*, IRRI Research Paper Series 49 (Los Banos: IRRI, 1980).

56 MAFF/ADAS, 1988, *Fertiliser Recommendations*, 5th edn, Ref. Book 209 (London: HMSO, 1988).

57 De Datta, S.K., "Improving nitrogen fertilizer efficiency in lowland rice in tropical Asia", *Fert. Res.* 9 (1986) pp. 171–86.

58 MAFF/ADAS, 1988, *op. cit.*

59 ADAS/RES/FMA, 1983, *Survey of Fertilizer Practice*, ADAS, Rothamsted Expt. Station and Fertilizer Manufacturer's Association (London: HMSO, 1983).

60 Department of the Environment, *The Nitrate Issue* (London: HMSO, 1988).

61 House of Lords, *Nitrate in Water*, Select Committee on the European Communities, Session 1988–1989, 16th Report, HL Paper 73 (London: HMSO, 1989); DOE, 1988, *op. cit.*

62 Chilton, P.J. and Foster, S.S.D., *Control of Groundwater Nitrate in Britain by Land-use Change*, Proc. NATO Workshop (mimeo, 1990).

63 Mikkelson, D.S., De Datta, S.K. and Obcemea, W.N., "Ammonia volatilisation losses from flooded rice soils", *Soil Sci. Soc. Am. J.* 42 (1978) pp. 725–30.

64 De Datta, 1986, *op. cit.*

65 De Datta, 1986, *op. cit.*

66 Craswell and De Datta, 1980, *op. cit.*

67 De Datta, 1986, *op. cit.*

68 Morgan, R.P.C., *Soil Erosion and Conservation* (Harlow: Longman, 1986).

69 NRC, 1989, *op. cit.*

70 Glenn, S. and Angle, J.S., "Atrazine and simazine to run-off from conventional and no-till watersheds", *Agric. Ecosyst. Environ.* (1987) pp. 273–80.

71 NRC, 1989, *op. cit.*

72 NRC, 1989, *op. cit.*

73 NRC, 1989, *op. cit.*

74 Morgan, 1986, *op. cit.*

75 Heermans, J.G., "The Guesselbodi experiment: bushland management in Niger", in: Conroy, C. and Litvinoff, M. (eds), *The Greening of Aid* (London: Earthscan Publications Ltd, 1988); Harrison, P., *The Greening of Africa* (London: Paladin, 1987).

76 ERCS/IIED, *Wollo: A closer look at rural life*, Ethiopian Red Cross Society (London: Addis Ababa and Internat. Inst. for Environ. and Devt,

1988); Chambers, R., *Microenvironments Unobserved*, Gatekeeper Series SA 22, (London: Sustainable Agriculture Programme, International Institute for Environment and Development, 1990).

77 Abujamin, S. et al., *Contour Grass Strips as a Low-Cost Conservation Practice*, Ext. Bull. no. 225 (Taiwan: Food and Fertilizer Technol. Center, 1985).

78 NRC, 1989, *op. cit.*

79 Morgan, 1986, *op. cit.*

80 Abujamin et al., 1985, *op. cit.*

81 Kotschi, J., Waters-Bayer, A., Adelhelm, R. and Hoesle, U., *Ecofarming in Agricultural Development* (Eschborn: GTZ, 1989).

82 Laflen, J.M. and Colvin, T.S., "Effect of crop residues on soil loss from continuous row cropping", *Trans. Am. Soc. Agric. Engin.* **24** (1981) pp. 605–09; Lall, R., "Soil management and erosion control", in: Greenland, D.J. and Lal, R. (eds), *Soil Conservation and Management in the Humid Tropics* (Chichester: John Wiley and Sons, 1977); Morgan, 1986, *op. cit.*

83 Kotschi et al., 1989, *op. cit.*

84 Posey, D.A., "Indigenous management of tropical forest ecosystems: the case of the Kayapo Indians of the Brazilian Amazon", *Agroforestry Syst.* **3** (1985) pp. 139–58.

85 Morgan, 1986, *op. cit.*

86 Lundgren, B. and Nair, P.K.R., "Agroforestry for soil conservation", in: El-Swaify, S.A., Moldenhauer, W.C. and Lo, A. (eds), *Soil Erosion and Conservation* (Arkery, Iowa: Soil Conservation Society of America, 1985).

87 Soemarwoto and Conway (in press), *op. cit.*; Young, A., *Agroforestry for Soil Conservation* (Wallingford: CAB International, 1989).

88 Hendrix, P.F., Parmelee, R.W., Crossley, D.A. Jr, Coleman, D.C., Odum, E.P. and Groffmann, P.M., "Detritus food webs in conventional and no-tillage agroecosystems", *BioScience* **36** (1986) pp. 374–80.

89 Gaskins, M.H., Albrecht, S.L. and Hubbell, D.H., "Rhizosphere bacteria and their use to increase plant productivity: a review", *Agric. Ecosyst. Environ.* **12** (1985) pp. 99–116.

90 Gerdeman, J.W., "Vesicular-arbuscular mycorrhizae", in: Torrey, J.G. and Clarkson, D.T. (eds), *The Development and Function of Roots* (London: Academic Press, 1976).

91 Hayman, D.S., "Mycorrhiza and crop production", *Nature* **287** (1980) pp. 487–88.

92 Hayman, 1980, *op. cit.*

93 Watanabe I., Espinas, C.R., Berja, N.S. and Alimango, B.U., *Utilisation of the Azolla-Anabaena Complex as a Nitrogen Fertilizer for Rice*, IRRI Research Paper Series no. 11 (Los Banos: IRRI, 1977); Kolhe, S.S. and Mitra, B.N., "Effects of Azolla as an organic source of nitrogen in rice-wheat cropping system", *J. Agron. Crop. Sci.* **159** (1987) pp. 212–15.

94 Watanabe et al., 1977, *op. cit.*

95 Kolhe and Mitra, 1987, *op. cit.*

96 Agarwal, A., "Blue-green algae to fertilize Indian rice paddies", *Nature* 279 (1979) p. 181.

97 Agarwal, P.K. and Garrity, D.P., *Intercropping of Legumes to Contribute Nitrogen in Low-input Upland Rice-based Cropping Systems*, Int. Symp. Nutrient Manage. for Food Crop Prod. in Tropical Farming Systems (Malang, Indonesia: 1987).

98 Agarwal and Garrity, 1987, *op. cit.*

99 Dabney, S.M., Breitenbeck, G.A., Hoff, B.J. and Milam, M.R., "Management of subterranean clover as a source of nitrogen for a subsquent rice crop", in: Power, J.F. (ed.), *The Role of Legumes in Conservation Tillage Systems* (Arkeny, Iowa: Soil Conserv. Soc. America, 1987); Williams, W.A. and Dawson, J.H., "Vetch is an economical source of nitrogen in rice", *Calif. Agric.* 34 (1986) pp. 15–16.

100 Barnes, D.G., Heichel, G. and Sheaffer, C., "Nitro alfalfa may foster new cropping system", *News*, 20 Nov (St. Paul: Minnesota Extension Service, 1986).

101 Young, A., *Agroforestry for Soil Conservation* (Wallingford: CAB International, 1989).

102 NRC, 1989, *op. cit.*

103 Heichel, G.H., "Legumes as a source of nitrogen in conservation tillage systems", in: Power, J.F. (ed.), 1987, *op. cit.*

104 NRC, 1989, *op. cit.*

105 NRC, 1989, *op. cit.*

106 NRC, 1989, *op. cit.*

107 Kotshi et al., 1989, *op. cit.*

108 Craig, I.A., *Pre-rice-crop green manuring: a technology for soil improvement under rainfed conditions in Northeast Thailand*, Northeast Rainfed Agricultural Development Project, NEROA (Thailand: Tha Phra, Khon Kaen, Thailand: NERAD, 1987).

109 Kopke, U., *The Development of Cropping Systems Under Varied Ecological Conditions* (Eschborn: GTZ, 1984).

110 Craig, 1987, *op. cit.*

111 Yamoah, C.F., Agboola, A.A. and Wilson, G.F., "Nutrient contribution and maize performance in alley cropping systems" *Agroforestry Syst.* 4 (1986) pp. 247–54.

112 Bayer, W. and Waters-Bayer, A., *Crop Livestock Interactions for Sustainable Agriculture*, Gatekeeper Series SA13 Sustainable Agriculture Programme (London: IIED, 1989).

113 Rerkasem, M.K. and Rerkasem, M.B., *Organic Manures in Intensive Cropping Systems*, Multiple Cropping Project (Thailand: Faculty of Agric., Chiang Mai University, 1984).

114 Sutton, A.L., Nelson, D.W. and Jones, D.D., *Utilisation of animal manure as fertilizer*, Extension Bulletin AG-FO-2613 (St. Paul: University of Minnesota, 1985).

115 Kotschi et al., 1989, *op. cit.*

116 MDA, *Farm Conservation Plans: for Soil Conservation and Water Quality* (Maryland Dept of Agriculture, 1985).

117 MAFF, *Advice on Avoiding Pollution from Manures and other Slurry Wastes*, Farm Management Booklet 2200 (Alnwick: MAFF Publ., 1983a).

118 MAFF, 1983a, *op. cit.*; MAFF, *Farm Waste Management: Silage Effluent*, Farm Management Booklet 2429 (Alnwick: MAFF Publ., 1983b).

119 RCEP, *Agriculture and Pollution*, 7th Report, Royal Commission on Environmental Pollution (London: HMSO, 1979).

120 Patni, N.K., Toxopeus, R., Tennant, A.D. and Hore, F.R., "Bacterial quality of tile drainage water from manured and fertilized cropland", *Water Res.* 18 (1984) pp. 127–32.

121 West, G., *Black's Veterinary Dictionary*, 16th edn (London: A and C Black, 1988).

122 Katzenelson, E., Buium, I. and Shuval, H.I., "Risk of communicable disease infection associated with wastewater irrigation in agricultural settlements", *Science* 194 (1976) pp. 944–6.

123 *Farmers Weekly* (London), "Sludge. A sureshot soil salve", 25 October (1987) p. 27–8,

124 Kruse, M., ApSimon, H.M. and Bell, J.N.B., *An emissions inventory for ammonia arising from agriculture in Great Britain* (London: Imperial College, 1986).

125 RCEP, 1979, *op. cit.*

126 Ibbitson, L.C., Zaik, F.L. and Crowe, R.K., "Managing run off from dairy barn yards in New York", in: *Livestock Waste: A Renewable Resource* (American Society Agricultural Engineers, 1980).

127 MAFF, 1983b, *op. cit.*

128 MDA, 1985, *op. cit.*

129 Klausner, S.D., Zwerman, P., and Ellis, D.F., "Nitrogen and phosphorus losses from winter disposal of dairy manure", *J. Environ. Qual.* 5 (1976) pp. 47–9.

130 Muck, R.E. and Richards, B.K., "Losses of manurial nitrogen in free-stall barns", *Agric. Wastes* 7 (1983) pp. 65–79.

131 Muck, R.E., Guest, R.W. and Richards, B.K., "Effect of manure storage design on nitrogen conservation", *Agric. Wastes* 10 (1984) pp. 205–20.

132 MAFF, 1983b, *op. cit.*

133 MAFF, *Farm Waste Management Barrier Ditches*, Booklet 2199 (Alnwick: MAFF Public., 1982).

134 John, C.K., "Treatment of agro-industrial wastes using water hyacinth", *Wat. Sci. Tech.* 17 (1985) pp. 781-90.

135 Jones, J.H., Olsen, F.J., Paterson, J.J. and Rushing, K.A., "The pollution potential of rainfall run-off from a dairy liquid waste disposal site", *Agric. Wastes* 10 (1984) pp 177–86.

136 Jones *et. al.*, 1984, *op. cit.*

137 *New York Times*, "Small towns build artificial wetlands to treat sewage", 29 Nov (1988) p. 26.

138 MAFF, 1983b, *op. cit.*

139 Soemarwoto and Conway (in press), *op. cit.*

140 Wong, M.H., "Agricultural wastes and freshwater supply in Hong Kong", *Prog. Wat. Tech.* 11 (1979) pp. 121–32; Pescod, M.B., "Agricultural wastes in urban areas, in: Chan, M.W.U., Hoare, R.W.M., Holmer, P.R., Land, R.J.S. and Rood, S.B. (eds), *Pollution in the Urban Environment* (Amsterdam: Elsevier, 1985).

141 Ilian, M.A. and Salmon, A.J., "Feeding processed hatchery wastes to poultry", *Agric. Wastes* 15 (1986) pp. 179–86.

142 Garrett, M.K., Weatherup, S.T.C. and Allen, M.D.B., "Algal culture in the liquid phase of animal slurry – effect of light and temperature upon growth and phosphorus removal", *Environ. Pollut.* 15 (1978) pp. 141–54; Pescod, 1985, *op. cit.*

143 *The Independent*, "Worms turn slurry to cash", 5 Jan (1988).

144 Etheridge, S.P., Stafford, D.A., Hughes, D.A. and Leroff, U.E.A., "The production of fertilizer from anaerobic digestes used to treat agricultural residues" in: *Alternative Sources of Energy for Agriculture*, FFTC Series no. 28 (1985).

145 Fontenot, J.P. and Ross, I.J., "Animal waste utilisation", in: *Livestock Waste: A Renewable Resource* (ASAE, 1980).

146 Pescod, 1985, *op. cit.*

147 Smith, R.J., "Practicality of methane production from livestock: state of the art", in: *Livestock Waste: A Renewable Resource* (ASAE, 1980).

148 Larkin, S.B.C., "Straw availability and procurement", in: MAFF, *Straw Disposal and Utilization, A Review of Knowledge* (1984).

149 Butterworth, B., *The Straw Manual* (London and New York: E. and F. N. Spon, 1985).

150 Powlson, D.S., Jenkinson, D.S., Pruden, G. and Johnston, A.E., "The effect of straw incorporation on the uptake of nitrogen on winter wheat", *J. of Sci. Food Agric.* 36 (1985) pp. 26–30.

151 Larkin, 1984, *op. cit.*

152 NSCA, *The National Society for Clean Air Survey of Straw Stubble Burning* (NSCA: Brighton, 1989).

153 Ehrlich, A., "Agricultural contributions to global warming", in: Leggett, J. (ed.), *Global Warming. The Greenpeace Report* (Oxford: Oxford University Press, 1990).

154 Chen, M. and Wolin, M.J., "Effect of monensin and lasalocid-sodium on the growth of methanogeric and rumen sacharolytic bacteria", *Appl. Environ. Microbiol.* 38 (1979).

155 Ehrlich, 1990, *op. cit.*; Blaxter, K.L. and Clapperton, J.L., "Prediction of the amount of methane produced by ruminants", *Br. J. Nutrition* 19 (1965) pp. 511–22.

156 Ehrlich, 1990, *op. cit.*

157 Christensen, L.A. and Norris, P.E., "Soil conservation and water quality improvement: what farmers think", *J. Soil Water Conserv.* Jan–Feb (1983) pp. 115–20.

158 Powers, E.C. and Jarecki, E.A., *Survey of United States Great Lakes Basin Farmers regarding Water Pollution from Agricultural Activities*, IJC/PLUARG– 79/08 (Washington DC: EPA, 1977).

159 Hoover, H. and Oscar, R., *Farmer Participation in the Hall County ACP Special Water Quality Project, Nebraska* (Washington DC: Econ. Res. Service, US Dept. of Agriculture, 1982).

160 Kerns, W.R. and Kramer, R.A., "Farmers' attitudes toward non-point pollution control and participation in cost-share programs", *Water Resources Bull.* 21 (1985) pp. 207–215.

161 Christensen and Norris, 1983, *op. cit.*

Index